Hotels in Europe

*Right: Hotel Cannero, Cannero
Riviera, Lago Maggiore, Italy*

Published by RAC Publishing, RAC House,
PO Box 100, South Croydon CR2 6XW.
© RAC Motoring Services Limited 1996

ISBN 0 86211-366 0 (paperback)
ISBN 0 86211-376 8 (hardback)

A CIP catalogue record for this book is available from the British Library.

Written and compiled for RAC Publishing by Millrace Books

Editorial Office
PO Box 8
Harleston
Norfolk IP20 0EZ
Tel: 01986 788 808
Fax: 01986 788 195

Managing Editor:	Lawrie Hammond
Design:	Douglas Whitworth
Editorial:	Aardvark Editorial; Zibba George; Sandrine Thierry; Stephanie Wren
Display Advertising Sales:	West One Publishing Ltd Portland House 4 Great Portland Street London W1N 4AA Tel: 0171 580 6886
Cartography:	RAC Publishing.
Printed and bound in Spain by:	Grafo SA, Bilbao

CONTENTS

The French Ardennes

is a green and pleasant land too, waiting to be found . . . go and look for it.

. . . see what we mean

Freephone 0800 960064

. . . for more clues.

INTRODUCTION

Welcome to *RAC Hotels in Europe*, fully revised for 1997. Once again we have details of more than 1200 hotels, from Norway, to Portugal to Greece, and ranging from big, luxury hotels with every facility imaginable to small, family-run establishments.

More and more people are choosing the independent travel alternative for visiting Europe. Getting across the Channel has never been easier, with lots of choice offered by the Tunnel, by ferries and hovercraft, at increasingly competitive prices. Combined with an excellent European road network as well as attractive fly-drive and motorail packages, this makes for virtually unlimited destinations for the imaginative independent motorist (see Getting There on page 9). Whatever your destination, the *RAC Hotels in Europe* guide will help you find lodging and food to suit your purse, often in a spectacular location.

How the guide is organised

The guide is arranged alphabetically, first by *country*, then by town within the country. Find the appropriate country by turning to the Contents list on page 3 Within the guide, each country has its own colour indicator on every page edge to make using the directory just a little bit easier still.

Within each country, hotels are grouped under the name of their *city, town, resort or nearest centre*. Where one town has several hotels, these are listed in alphabetical order (ignoring the word 'Hotel'). Should you have trouble locating a particular town, consult the index at the back of the book, where you may find a small town has been grouped under a larger one.

Hotel entries

Opening times may vary at short notice, especially if there are local religious or other events, or during the low season. Where hotels are marked 'facilities for the disabled', this is in the opinion of the hotel management. Entries also include restaurant information where appropriate (for travellers in French speaking countries there is a glossary of menu terms at the back of the guide). Please pay particular attention to details of when restaurants are closed, especially in low season, LS; HS = high season. Where the hotel has made

Map locations

These refer to the series of maps near the end of the book. The hotel may not be in the town itself, but nearby. Refer to the hotel entry in the hotel directory for the full address and precise location.

special arrangements for its guests to participate at discounted rates in local activities, this is indicated so: ●, within the Activities section.

Prices: these are the hotel management's prediction for mid-season 1997 prices in local currency, unless otherwise stated. Depending on the time of your visit there may be a variation in price, and local taxes may be applied in addition. Prices are given for single and double rooms (includes two people), and usually include en suite facilities but no food. Separate sample prices are provided for a range of set menus, and for breakfast (Bk). Unlike hotels in the UK, continental hotels do not usually include breakfast in the room price.

Telephoning: some hotels now allow guests to use international telephone charge cards, where the cost of a call to the UK can be automatically charged to the home telephone bill. Many, however, do not. If you want to use an international charge card you may have to use a public phone in the hotel foyer (indicated ☎) rather than the phone in your room.

The following symbols and abbreviations appear within the directory, and these are also given on the front flap of the guide for ease of use:

5D	map location	TARIFF	guide prices in French francs for a typical single or double room, usually with en suite facilities
★	star rating of country or region		
☎	public telephone on site	HS	high season
♿	some facilities for disabled people	LS	low season
km	kilometres (1 km is 0.62 miles)	Bk	breakfast
m	metres (1 metre is about 1 yard)	CC	credit cards
		●	special activities arranged by hotel

Booking ahead

This is obviously a good idea at all times, but for high season breaks it is essential. Each hotel entry includes a full address and telephone number, and the majority also include a fax number. When telephoning a hotel from UK replace the first '0' or '9' with the international dialling code. eg to telephone the Hotel Reindl's in Garmisch, tel: 08821 58025, you should dial 0049 8821 58025. But to telephone from another part of Germany, then of course you would dial 08821 58025.

From 18 October 1996 most French telephone numbers gained an extra two digits. All Paris numbers already started with '01' followed by eight digits and did not change. Numbers in the rest of France gained either '02', '03', '04' or '05' in front of the normal eight digits depending on the geographical position, ie north east regions gained '03'.

As the numbers shown throughout the book are the numbers to dial *from that country,* to dial a French hotel from the UK you must suppress the first '0'.

Where a hotel entry gives *'English spoken',* this usually indicates that some members of staff speak enough English to understand basic requests such as booking a room, or being asked for the bill. Enquiring about or booking accommodation by fax is an excellent alternative as it overcomes many language difficulties as well as proving a written record of what has been agreed.

Discount for guide users

Some hotels offer a discount to RAC customers, and this is indicated in individual entries by the blue square. This of course means that you will need to show your guide when you check in. Future further discounts may be possible where we can show hoteliers that RAC guide users are good customers, so we would of course encourage you to show your guide whenever you book into an RAC listed hotel.

Valuable feedback

Year by year we are able to improve the scope and quality of the guide, helped by readers' feedback. Whether your experience is particularly good or particularly bad, we would be delighted to hear from you, using the Report Form at the back of the guide. Alternatively you may stay in an hotel not listed in the guide and which you feel worthy of inclusion. Again, we would be delighted to hear from you, using the Recommendation Form also at the back of the book.

Bon Voyage!

Whether you are planning a long week-end or a grand European tour, we hope the *RAC Hotels in Europe* guide will prove a reliable, easy-to use companion. Have a great time!

Star ratings

The star rating for each hotel is derived from the national star-rating system of its country. This is generally organised by the country's own tourist board, and you can usually rely on the number of stars as an indicator of quality. However there may not be a direct comparison between star ratings in different countries. Also, some private châteaux do not subscribe to any star scheme.

FERRY PORTS AND ROUTES

GETTING THERE

Getting across the English Channel is no longer the big deal it once was. For the short Dover–Calais crossing the Tunnel is increasingly popular, combining maximum speed and minimum fuss. But the Tunnel has prompted significant price-cutting from the ferry companies, and their high-standard ferries, offering restaurant facilities not found in many a high street, mean that the sea-crossing is still the preferred choice of many who consider the shipboard experience an enjoyable part of their holiday.

For more westerly destinations, more and more travellers are choosing to do more of their driving on this side of the water, making crossings like Plymouth–Roscoff increasingly busy. Others choose the overnight ferry option. For with good cabin facilities this can be a pleasant and economic alternative to the expense of the short crossing plus overnight accommodation in France. Or why not let the *Train Grand Vitesse* high speed trains take the strain out of the long haul south, to deliver you, your family *and* your car, daisy-fresh in, say, Avignon? Finally, the fly-drive option: by allowing you to fly out and *start* your holiday from a distant town, this can represent the best value in the long run, where time and/or driving stamina are in short supply. The fly-drive alternative opens up countless new possibilities for the British motorist with limited time at his or her disposal.

Talking of new possibilities for holiday destinations, the map on page 10 includes a number of ferry lines to the mythical, underpopulated countries of Scandinavia. If 'getting away from it all' is your priority, this could be for you... Scandinavian summer days are fine, warm, very clear and *very long!*

If you do decide to drive long distances, remember it can be a good idea to make your journey a part of the holiday. Far too often we opt to clock up the maximum number of kilometres on a motorway when we might do better to take a more leisurely route, allowing for a coffee stop in a pretty market square, or a picnic pause where the view compels a photo stop.

Whatever your chosen mode of *Getting there*, may we wish you *Bon voyage!*

Belgium
Ramsgate-Oostende 4 hr *Sally Ferries (Ostend line)* – 6 per day.
Also Jetfoil (Passengers only) 100 mins *Sally Ferries* – 2-6 daily
Hull-Zeebrugge 14 hr *North Sea Ferries* – 1 per day
Dover-Zeebrugge *P & O Stena Line* – (contact ferry company for details)

Denmark
Harwich-Esbjerg 19½-20 hr *Scandinavian Seaways* – up
to 3 per week
Newcastle-upon-Tyne-Esbjerg 19½- 20 hr *Scandinavian Seaways*
– every 5 days

France
Dover-Calais 1½ hr *P & O Stena Line* (catamaran and ferry) – up to
22 per day
1½ hr *Sea France* (contact ferry company for details)
Dover-Calais 35-50 min *Hoverspeed* Hovercraft/Seacat – up to 14 per day
Folkestone-Boulogne 55mins *Hoverspeed* Seacat – up to 6 per day
Newhaven-Dieppe (catamaran and ferry) 2-3½ hr *P & O Stena Line* – up
to 4 per day each
Plymouth-Roscoff 6 hr *Brittany Ferries* – up to 3 per day (summer),
up to 3 per week (winter)
Poole-Cherbourg 4¼ hr *Brittany Ferries* 2 per day
Poole-St Malo 8 hr *Brittany Ferries* (May-Sept) – 4 per week
Portsmouth-Caen 6 hr *Brittany Ferries* – up to 3 per day
Portsmouth-Cherbourg (day) 5 hr, (night) 7-8¼ hr
P & O European Ferries – up to 4 per day
Portsmouth-Le Havre (day) 5½ hr, (night) 7½-8 hr
P & O European Ferries – up to 3 per day
Portsmouth-St Malo 9 hr *Brittany Ferries*
– 1 per day (up to 2 per week in winter)
Ramsgate-Dunkerque 2½ hr *Sally Ferries* – 5 per day (service will
cease Spring 1997)
Southampton-Cherbourg 5-9 hr *Stena Line* – up to 2 per day

Germany
Harwich-Hamburg 23 hr *Scandinavian Seaways* – 3-4 per week
Newcastle-upon-Tyne-Hamburg 23½ hr *Scandinavian Seaways*
– every 4 days
Oslo-Kiel 19 hr *Color Line* – daily

Netherlands
Harwich-Hoek van Holland (day) 6½ hr, (night) 10 hr *Stena Line*
– 2 per day
Hull-Rotterdam (Europoort) 14 hr *North Sea Ferries* – 1 per day
Newcastle-Amsterdam *Scandinavian Seaways* 15-17½ hr – up to
4 per week
Sheerness-Vlissingen (day) 7½ hr (night) 9½ hr *Eurolink Ferries*
– 2 per day (route under review in 1997)

Norway

Hirtshals-Oslo $8^{1}/_{4}$ hr *Color Line* – daily (summer)
Kiel-Oslo 19 hr *Color Line* – daily
Hirtshals-Kristiansand $4^{1}/_{4}$ hr (day) $6^{1}/_{2}$ hr (night) *Color Line* – 3-4 per day
Newcastle upon Tyne-Bergen $19^{1}/_{4}$-$25^{1}/_{2}$ hr *Color Line*
– 3 per week (summer) 2 per week (winter)
Newcastle upon Tyne-Stavanger 17-$27^{1}/_{2}$ hr *Color Line* – 3 per week (summer)
2 per week (winter)
Newcastle upon Tyne-Haugesund $19^{3}/_{4}$-$25^{3}/_{4}$ hr *Color Line* – up to 2 per week

Spain

Plymouth-Santander (from mid March) 23-24 hr *Brittany Ferries* – up to 2 per week
Portsmouth-Santander (winter only) 30-31 hr *Brittany Ferries* – 1 per week
Portsmouth-Bilbao 30-35 hr *P & O European Ferries* – 2 per week

Sweden

Harwich-Göteborg 23 hr *Scandinavian Seaways* – up to 3 per week
Newcastle-upon-Tyne-Göteborg 23-24 hr *Scandinavian Seaways* – 1 per week

FERRY COMPANIES

Brittany Ferries
Millbay Docks, Plymouth PL1 3EW

☎ (01752) 221321
The Britanny Centre,
Wharf Road,
Portsmouth PO2 8RU
☎ (01705) 827701
Caen ☎ 02 31 96 88 80
Cherbourg ☎ 02 33 43 43 68
Cork ☎ (021) 277801
Roscoff ☎ 02 98 29 28 28
Santander ☎ 22 00 00
St Malo ☎ 02 99 40 64 41

Color Line
International Ferry Terminal,
Royal Quays, North Shields
NE29 6EE
☎ (0191)-296 1313

Eurolink Ferries
The Ferry Terminal,
Sheerness Dock, Sheerness
ME12 1AX
☎ (01795) 581000

Hoverspeed Ltd
International Hoverport,
Western Dock, Dover, Kent
CT17 9TG ☎ (01304) 240241
Boulogne ☎ 03 21 30 27 26
Calais ☎ 03 21 46 14 14

North Sea Ferries
King George Dock, Hedon
Road, Hull HU9 5QA
☎ (01482) 77177

P & O European Ferries
Channel House, Channel
View Road, Dover CT17 9TJ
☎ (01304) 203388
Calais ☎ 03 21 46 04 40
Cairnryan ☎ (01581) 200276
Le Havre ☎ 02 35 19 78 50
Cherbourg ☎ 02 33 88 65 70
Felixstowe ☎ (01394) 604040
Portsmouth ☎ (01705) 827677
Larne ☎ (01574) 274321
Bilbao ☎ (94) 423 4477

Sea France
106 East Camber Bdg, East
Docks, Dover CT16 1JA
☎ (01304) 212696

Sally Ferries
Sally Line Ltd, Argyle Centre,
York Street, Ramsgate, Kent
CT11 9DS
☎ (01843) 595522
☎ (0181)-858 1127
Dunkerque ☎ 03 28 21 43 44
Oostende ☎ 59 55 99 54

Scandinavian Seaways
Scandinavia House,
Parkeston Quay, Harwich,
Essex CO12 4QG
☎ (01255) 240240
Esbjerg ☎ 75 12 48 00
Göteborg ☎ (031) 65 06 00
Hamburg ☎ (040) 3 89 03 71

Stena Line
Charter House, Ashford,
Kent
☎ (01233) 647047
Calais ☎ 03 21 46 80 00
Cherbourg ☎ 02 33 20 43 38
Dieppe ☎ 02 35 06 39 00
Hoek van Holland
☎ 47 82 351

Escape

At the RAC we can release you from
the worries of motoring

But did you know that we can also
give you invaluable peace of mind
when you go on holiday,

Or arrange your hotel bookings,

Or even organise your entire
holiday, all over the phone?

RAC Travel Insurance   0800 550 055

RAC Hotel Reservations   0345 056 042

RAC Holiday Reservations   0161 480 4810

Call us

ANDORRA

An autonomous principality for 1,100 years, the 179 square miles of Andorra constitute the largest of the small states of Europe (Monaco, San Marino and Liechtenstein). It lies high in the Pyrenees between France and Spain on one of the main routes through the Pyrenees, and this perhaps accounts for it being a popular stopping-off place, with the added attraction of duty-free status. Andorra has no currency of its own but maximises its tourist income by accepting and using both French francs and Spanish pesetas.

The chief town of Andorra La Vella is extremely busy, but quieter villages are not far away. Les Escaldes is a year-round resort with sulphur springs and a hydroelectric station. Andorra offers excellent skiing in winter and, in summer, the same resorts make wonderful bases for hill-walking with chair-lifts to help those willing to compromise. The valley-and-peak landscape has dramatic summits rising to 2500 m. Only a small fraction of Andorra's land is arable; fields of cereals and potatoes in the sheltered lower valleys, a few vineyards, and everywhere, little corners of land growing tobacco. In summer, sheep graze the higher pastures which they share with small groups of wild horses.

Emergency numbers

Police 17

Fire Brigade and Ambulance 18

Warning information

Green card compulsory

ANDORRA LA VELLA   9D

Hotel Panorama ★★★★
Ctra de l'Obac, Andorra la Vella.
Tel 861861, Fax 861742. English spoken.
Open all year. 177 bedrooms (all en suite).
Indoor swimming pool, tennis, garage,
parking. ✆ &

Set on a hillside, this is one of the country's leading hotels. Ideal for private banquets and conferences.

■ RESTAURANT: Modern restaurant with fantastic views over the valley.
■ ACTIVITIES: Integral health/spa club. Rafting, horse-riding, trekking and excursions; aquatic park nearby.
■ TARIFF: Single 7,900–10,750, Double 8,400–12,600, Bk 1,300, Set menu 2,000–3,100 (Amex, Euro/Access, Visa).
■ DISCOUNT: 10%

ARINSAL   9D

Hotel St Gothard ★★★★
Ctra d'Arinsal, Erts, Arinsal.
Tel 836005, Fax 837051. English spoken.
Open all year. 170 bedrooms (all en suite).

Andorra

Outdoor swimming pool, tennis, garage, parking. &

At 1400 m, the hotel is surrounded by mountains and has a splendid setting in the Arinsal valley.

■ RESTAURANT: Several restaurants with a choice of traditional or international cuisine.
■ ACTIVITIES: Newly built spa and sauna; children's playground, mountain bikes, tennis, basket ball and crazy golf.
■ TARIFF: (1996) Single 5,400–6,250, Double 7,500–9,200, Set menu 2,100 (Amex, Euro/Access, Visa).

CANILLO   9D

Hotel Bonavida ★★★ Plaça Major, Canillo.
Tel 851300, Fax 851722.
Open 04/12 to 12/10. 43 bedrooms
(all en suite). Garage. &

A quiet, comfortable hotel with bar, lounge, terrace and garden. All rooms have balcony and overlook the mountains.

■ RESTAURANT: Closed May & June.
■ ACTIVITIES: Sauna, solarium, mountain-biking, walking tours; sports complex with swimming and gymnasium within easy reach. ● Special 6- or 7-day half-board ski packages.
■ TARIFF: Single 5,700–8,750, Double 7,500–11,500, Set menu 2,400 (Amex, Euro/Access, Visa).
■ DISCOUNT: 5%

ENCAMP   9D

Hotel Coray ★★★
Ctra de los Caballers 38, Encamp.
Tel 831513, Fax 831806. English spoken.
Open 01/12 to 15/11. 85 bedrooms
(all en suite). Garage, restaurant. &

Quiet and comfortable, a modern hotel with private garden and garage. Only a short distance from the France to Spain motorway and 4 km from town centre.

■ ACTIVITIES: Hotel will arrange entry to thermal bathing centre.
■ TARIFF: (1996) Single 3,200–5,000, Double 5,500–6,000, Set menu 1,000–1,250 (Euro/Access, Visa).

LES ESCALDES   9D

Hotel Comtes d'Urgell ★★★
29 Avda de les Escoles, Les Escaldes.
Tel 820621, Fax 820465. English spoken.
Open all year. 200 bedrooms (all en suite).
Garage, restaurant.

Modern, fully equipped hotel. From behind the church of Les Escaldes, take first turn on left and hotel is 100 m.

■ TARIFF: Single 5,225, Double 7,750, Set menu 2,350 (Amex, Euro/Access, Visa).

Hotel Delfos ★★★★
Avda del Fener 17, Les Escaldes.
Tel 824642, Fax 861642. English spoken.
Open all year. 200 bedrooms (all en suite).
Garage, parking, restaurant.

Located in the commercial centre, this modern hotel has very good facilities and is ideal for conferences.

■ TARIFF: Single 5,650–8,700, Double 9,500–10,400 (Amex, Euro/Access, Visa).
■ DISCOUNT: 10%

SOLDEU   9D

Hotel Del Tarter ★★★
Ctra General, El Tarter, Soldeu.
Tel 51165, Fax 51474. English spoken.

Open 01/12 to 15/10. 37 bedrooms
(all en suite). Garage, parking.

Most attractive chalet-style hotel built of stone, completely renovated and family run. Comfortable rooms, most with balcony. 50 m from the ski lifts and close to sports centre. On the main road, 3 km from Soldeu.

■ RESTAURANT: Wood panelled and cosy, offering French cuisine.
■ ACTIVITIES: Horse-riding, mountain bikes, trekking and trout fishing in summer; skiing in winter.
■ TARIFF: Single 5,000–6,000, Double 6,600–8,260, Bk 850, Set menu 2,000–2,500 (Amex, Euro/Access, Visa).

AUSTRIA

Typical Austrian landscape near Obernberg

Two-thirds of this landlocked country of richly varied topography is accounted for by the eastern Alps which march in from the south-west across the borders of Switzerland, Italy and former Yugoslavia.

Historic Innsbruck, its old town ringed round with snow-capped peaks, is an obvious centre for exploring the high Alps, but with countless smaller alternatives, each Tyrolean village seemingly prettier than the last. The toll road up to the Rattenbach glacier is worth every *Schilling...* as is the Gaislachkopf cable-car ride, rising to over 3000 m... while from Obergurgl, the highest parish in Europe, the Hohe Mute chair-lift affords views over 21 glaciers.

Salzburg is one of Europe's most beautiful cities, as well as enjoying a great musical reputation as the birthplace of Mozart – the Salzburg Festival is in August.

Vienna, Austria's capital in the north east, stands at the foot of the Vienna Woods on the River Danube and has a rich musical and theatrical inheritance; this, combined with fine museums and parks, makes the home of the Vienna Boys' Choir and the world-famous Opera House a great tourist magnet. Linger if you can, in one of the many historic coffee houses; take a 'Donaubus' boat trip on the Danube; or for wonderful views over the city, choose between St Stephen's Cathedral and the giant fairground wheel in Prater Park.

Emergency numbers

Police 133

Fire Brigade 122

Ambulance 144

These numbers are used with a local prefix

Warning information

First aid kit compulsory

Warning triangle must be carried

Blood alcohol legal limit 80 mg

ALPBACH 19C
Romantik Hotel Böglerhof ★★★★
6236 Alpbach.
Tel 05336 5227, Fax 05336 5227402.
English spoken.

Open 20/05 to 31/10 & 20/12 to 30/04.
48 bedrooms (all en suite). Indoor swimming
pool, tennis, garage, parking. ☎ ♿
*A charming combination of ancient and
modern. Warm, relaxing atmosphere,
beautifully decorated, excellent facilities.*

■ RESTAURANT: Choice of two cosy restaurants
offering fine food with Austrian specialities.
■ ACTIVITIES: Apart from taking advantage of all
the hotel's own facilities which also include
sauna and solarium, it is ideally located for
winter sports and walking/exploring the
spectacular countryside.
■ TARIFF: Single 850–1600, Double 1300–2500,
Set menu 250–380 (Euro/Access, Visa).
■ DISCOUNT: 10% except Christmas.

BERWANG 19C
Hotel Blitz ★★★ 6622 Berwang.
Tel 05674 8272, Fax 05674 827225.
English spoken.
Open all year. 24 bedrooms (all en suite).
Garage, parking. ☎ ♿
*Comfortable hotel with modern facilities. Also
incorporates the Chalet Traudel.*

■ RESTAURANT: Closed Nov. Traditional cuisine
with Italian specialities.
■ ACTIVITIES: Sauna at hotel; nearby is a
swimming pool (free for hotel guests) and sled-
dog racing school.
■ TARIFF: Single 250–475, Double 720–1620,
Set menu 80–165 (Amex, Euro/Access, Visa).
■ DISCOUNT: 8% LS.

BEZAU 19C
Ferienhotel Gasthof Gams 6870 Bezau.
Tel 05514 2220, Fax 05514 222024.
English spoken.
Open 19/12 to 01/11. 38 bedrooms
(all en suite). Outdoor swimming pool, tennis,
parking.
*Converted 17th-century coaching inn,
renovated in local style. On the edge of the
town with fine views, hotel is family run with
friendly atmosphere and modern-day
comforts. Bezau is the main town of the
Bregenzerwald, 30 km from Bregenz, capital
of the Vorarlberg.*

■ RESTAURANT: Very good local cuisine.
■ ACTIVITIES: Jacuzzi, sauna, Turkish bath, gym;
guided hiking tours from the hotel, free shuttle
to nearby ski slopes.
■ TARIFF: (1996) Single 680–1050,
Double 1060–1660, Set menu 220–460
(No credit cards).

BRAND 19C
Hotel Scesaplana ★★★★
Vorarlberg, 6708 Brand.
Tel 05559 221, Fax 05559 445.
English spoken.

Open all year. 72 bedrooms (all en suite).
Indoor swimming pool, outdoor swimming
pool, tennis, golf on site, parking.
*Comfortable, chalet-style hotel in beautiful
countryside. Leave the autobahn at Bludenz
and take Brandnertal exit.*

■ ACTIVITIES: Tennis, whirlpool, steambath,
solarium, sauna at hotel; superb location for
sightseeing and taking advantage of the
numerous sporting activities nearby.
● Reduced green fees.
■ TARIFF: (1996) Single 1300,
Double 1060–2820 (Amex, Euro/Access, Visa).

Austria

DURNSTEIN 19B

Hotel Schloss Dürnstein ★★★★★
Wachau Gorge, 3601 Dürnstein.
Tel 02711 212, Fax 02711 351. English spoken.
Open 25/03 to 05/11. 37 bedrooms
(all en suite). Indoor swimming pool, outdoor
swimming pool, golf 15 km, garage, parking. &
A Baroque castle is the setting for this
luxurious hotel which offers every convenience
and comfort in stunning surroundings.

■ RESTAURANT: Excellent cuisine and fine wines.
Beautiful terrace overlooking the Danube
where meals can be taken in fine weather.
■ ACTIVITIES: Very good sports/relaxation
facilities as well as bicycles at hotel. Lots of good
walks, hunting, fishing and water-skiing nearby.
■ TARIFF: Single 1550–1750, Double 1950–3600,
Set menu 300–380 (Amex, Euro/Access, Visa).
■ DISCOUNT: 5%

FUSCHL-AM-SEE 19B

Ebner's Waldhof-Silence Hotel ★★★★
Seepromenade, 5330 Fuschl-am-See.
Tel 06226 264, Fax 06226 644. English spoken.

Open 10/04 to 31/10 & 16/12 to 10/03.
70 bedrooms (all en suite). Indoor swimming
pool, outdoor swimming pool, tennis,
golf 4 km, parking. (&
Very pretty chalet-style hotel in extensive
grounds, right on the lake. Very comfortable and
beautifully kept. The hotel offers a complete
holiday package, not just a place to stay.

■ RESTAURANT: Three restaurants serving a
complete range of meals, all good. In summer,
dine on the terrace or enjoy a picnic in the hills.
■ ACTIVITIES: Inside: pools, sauna, massage etc.
Outside: walking, biking, tennis and lots of
golf. Boating, fishing. Trips to Salzburg.
■ TARIFF: (1996) Single 850–1050,
Double 1480–2340, Set menu 180–410
(No credit cards).

GARGELLEN 19C

Hotel Madrisa ★★★★ Vorarlberg, 6787 Gargellen.
Tel 0557 6331, Fax 0557 633182. English spoken.

Open 16/12 to 17/04 & 22/06 to 25/09.
65 bedrooms (55 en suite). Indoor swimming
pool, tennis, parking.
Near the church in Gargellen centre.
Traditional ski-hotel on the slopes. Close to
Madrisa drag-lift and Schafberg chair-lift.

■ RESTAURANT: Closed Tues. International
cuisine with local specialities.
■ ACTIVITIES: Hiking with mountain guide, rock
climbing, skiing, football, mountain-biking,
dancing; Schubert and Bregenz festivals.
■ TARIFF: (1996) Single 640–1490,
Double 1120–2740 (Amex, Euro/Access, Visa).

GMUNDEN 19B

Parkhotel Am See ★★★★
Schiffslände 17, 4810 Gmunden.
Tel 07612 4230, Fax 07612 423066. English spoken.
Open 23/05 to 21/09. 48 bedrooms (all en
suite). Tennis, golf 8 km, garage, parking.
Beautiful, quiet situation on the lakeside
where you can swim from bathing piers! Five
minutes' walk to town centre.

■ RESTAURANT: Bistro style, overlooking the lake
or shady terrace. Large buffet breakfasts;
national and international à la carte menu.
■ ACTIVITIES: Windsurfing, sailing, water-skiing
from hotel. ● Daily/weekly reduction on green
fees at nearby golf course for hotel guests.
■ TARIFF: Single 800–980, Double 1200–1560
(Euro/Access, Visa).
■ DISCOUNT: 10% B&B basis.

GRAZ 19D

Hotel Daniel ★★★★ Europaplatz 1, 8021 Graz.
Tel 0316 911080, Fax 0316 911085.
English spoken.
Open 10/01 to 23/12. 100 bedrooms

Austria

(all en suite). Garage, parking. &

Modern hotel in the heart of the new commercial centre. Near station and motorway; air terminal in the hotel.

■ RESTAURANT: International and Styrian cuisine.
■ ACTIVITIES: Sightseeing tours and excursions organised by hotel.
■ TARIFF: (1996) Single 1080–1580, Double 1640–2090, Set menu 200 (Amex, Euro/Access, Visa).

The Weitzer ★★★★ Grieskai 12-14, 8011 Graz. Tel 0316 9030, Fax 0316 90388. English spoken. Open all year. 200 bedrooms (all en suite). Golf 15 km, garage, parking. &

A traditional town centre hotel. On the banks of the Mur with a marvellous view of the old city.

■ RESTAURANT: International and Styrian cuisine.
■ ACTIVITIES: Hotel can organise sightseeing tours and excursions in Styria.
■ TARIFF: (1996) Single 1290–1690, Double 1860–2890, Set menu 200 (Amex, Euro/Access, Visa).

INNSBRUCK   19C

Gasthof Traube Isserwirt ★★★ 6072 Lans. Tel 0512 377261, Fax 0512 37726129. English spoken. Open 10/11 to 18/10. 24 bedrooms (all en suite). Golf 1 km, garage, parking. (

A warm welcome in this Tyrolean hotel overlooking Innsbruck with superb mountain scenery. From München/Kufstein motorway, take Innsbruck-Ost exit to Olympic Stadium, then left via Aldrans-Lans.

■ RESTAURANT: Well-known restaurant. International and Tyrolean cuisine.
■ ACTIVITIES: Close to tennis courts, ski slopes, bobsleigh track and lake; walking, paragliding, horse-drawn carriage rides, ice-skating, cross-country skiing, sledging, visit to Innsbruck (theatre, museum, castle).
■ TARIFF: Single 390–560, Double 780–920, Set menu 150–240 (Amex, Euro/Access, Visa).
■ DISCOUNT: 10%

KITZBÜHEL   19C

Hotel Zur Tenne ★★★★ 6370 Kitzbühel. Tel 05356 4444, Fax 05356 480356. English spoken. Open all year. 51 bedrooms (all en suite). Golf 1 km, parking.

Tyrolean-style apartments with open fireplace and balcony (some also with jacuzzi and steam-bath). At the very centre of Kitzbühel,

close to cable cars, ski lifts and the spa. Access to hotel is through the pedestrian area.

■ RESTAURANT: Typical Tyrolean cuisine.
■ ACTIVITIES: In summer: mountaineering, swimming in the Schwarzsee lake, tennis, squash, horse-riding, fishing, hang-gliding; twice-weekly open-air concert, Tyrolean folk evening; in winter: skiing, cross-country skiing, ice-skating, sledging, curling.
■ TARIFF: (1996) Single 950–1400, Double 1500–2300, Set menu 290 (Amex, Euro/Access, Visa).
■ DISCOUNT: 10%

KUFSTEIN   19A

Hotel Alpenrose Best Western ★★★★ Weissachstr 47, 6330 Kufstein. Tel 05372 62122, Fax 05372 621227. English spoken. Open all year. 21 bedrooms (all en suite). Tennis, golf 20 km, garage, parking. &

Elegant, warm and welcoming. Superb situation with some breathtaking views of the surrounding countryside.

■ RESTAURANT: Enjoys a good reputation for its fine Austrian cuisine. Game and fish dishes are specialities.
■ ACTIVITIES: The surrounding lakes and mountains provide an almost limitless choice of activities in both summer and winter. Visit the famous Riedel glass factory and showrooms nearby.
■ TARIFF: Single 590–850, Double 1080–1380, Set menu 270–360 (Amex, Euro/Access, Visa).
■ DISCOUNT: 8%

Alphotel Kufsteinerhof ★★★ Franz Josefs Platz 1, 6330 Kufstein. Tel 05372 71030, Fax 05372 71031. English spoken. Open all year. 42 bedrooms (all en suite). Garage.

Comfortable hotel in town centre. Some rooms have a balcony.

■ ACTIVITIES: Cycling, walking, cross-country skiing.
■ TARIFF: Single 580, Double 960 (Amex, Euro/Access, Visa).
■ DISCOUNT: 10% for stays over 2 days.

LANDECK   19C

Hotel Schrofenstein ★★★★ 6500 Landeck, Tyrol. Tel 05442 62395, Fax 05442 6495455. English spoken. Open 15/12 to 20/10. 100 bedrooms (54 en suite). Parking.

Family-run hotel in the centre of town;

summer centre for sightseeing tours.
■ RESTAURANT: Closed 01/11 to 15/12.
Specialises in very good Austrian cuisine.
■ ACTIVITIES: Hiking, rafting, paragliding; ski
trips to St Anton and Ischgl in winter (20 km).
■ TARIFF: (1996) Single 500–600,
Double 800–1200 (Amex, Euro/Access, Visa).

MILLSTATT   19D

Hotel Die Forelle ★★★★ Carinthia, 9872 Millstatt.
Tel 04766 20500, Fax 04766 205011. English spoken.
Open 01/05 to 31/10. 68 bedrooms (all en suite).
Outdoor swimming pool, golf 15 km, parking.
*Situated beside the lake with super views and
very good, modern facilities.*
■ RESTAURANT: Panoramic setting; good food
with fresh fish specialities.
■ ACTIVITIES: Water sports.
■ TARIFF: (1996) Single 700–850,
Double 1300–2300 (No credit cards).

MONDSEE   19B

Hotel Leitnerbräu ★★★★
Steinerbachstrasse 6, 5310 Mondsee.
Tel 06232 6500, Fax 06232 650022. English spoken.
Open 01/12 to 31/10. 31 bedrooms
(all en suite). Golf 1 km, garage, parking. ❧ ₺
*Cosy and comfortable, hotel is situated in the
centre of town and opposite the church made
famous in 'The Sound of Music'.*
■ RESTAURANT: Closed Wed. Austrian and
international specialities.
■ ACTIVITIES: ● Bicycles and fitness room with
sauna and steam bath free to hotel guests.
■ TARIFF: Single 700–880, Double 1150–1550,
Set menu 120–200 (Amex, Euro/Access, Visa).

MÖSERN   19C

Hotel Lärchenhof ★★★★
6100 Mösern bei Seefeld.
Tel 05212 4767, Fax 05212 47684. English spoken.

Open 15/05 to 31/10 & 15/12 to 01/04.
16 bedrooms (all en suite). Golf 4 km, garage. ₺
*Luxury hotel in its own grounds, offering
large, beautifully decorated rooms. Set high in
the mountains with wonderful views and truly
the perfect place to relax.*
■ ACTIVITIES: Putting green, sauna, solarium,
steam bath at hotel. ● 15% green fee reduction
at Seefeld Golf Club and 50% reduction at
Seefeld Golf Academy.
■ TARIFF: Single 370, Double 700–740 (Visa).

PERTISAU-AM-ACHENSEE   19C

Strandhotel Entner ★★★★
6213 Pertisau-am-Achensee.
Tel 05243 5259, Fax 05243 5985113. English spoken.
Open 18/12 to 31/03 & 04/05 to 31/10.
80 bedrooms (all en suite). Indoor swimming
pool, outdoor swimming pool, golf 1 km,
parking. ₺
*Very comfortable, family-run hotel. On the
lakeside, not far from the centre of town. A
welcome drink is offered to hotel guests on
arrival.*
■ RESTAURANT: Restaurant has a rustic
atmosphere and offers Tyrolean specialities
with fondue and raclette evenings in winter.
Live music, Tyrolean evenings and
après-ski parties.
■ ACTIVITIES: Tobogganing and skiing close by;
candlelit evening walks in winter.
■ TARIFF: Single 800–1200, Double 1300–2100,
Set menu 100–190 (Amex, Euro/Access, Visa).

ST WOLFGANG   19B

Hotel Tirol ★★★
Robert Stolzstrasse 111, 5360 St Wolfgang.
Tel 06138 23250, Fax 06138 25099.
English spoken.
Open 01/04 to 31/10. 13 bedrooms
(all en suite). Outdoor swimming pool,
golf 10 km, garage, parking.
*A charming lakeside hotel, offering the
personal touch. Suites and apartments
available with traditional farmhouse
furniture. From the village, it's the first hotel at
the end of the lake promenade.*
■ RESTAURANT: Fish and Austrian specialities can
be enjoyed in the cosy restaurant with terrace
overlooking the lake.
■ ACTIVITIES: Water sports and mountain-bike
hire on the doorstep; tennis, mini-golf and
horse-riding nearby.
■ TARIFF: (1996) Single 560–850, Double 1000–
1900, Set menu 180–280 (Amex, Visa).

Austria

Austria

SALZBURG 19A

Hotel Bristol ★★★★★
Marktplatz 4, 5020 Salzburg.
Tel 0662 873557, Fax 0662 8735576. English spoken.
Open 20/03 to 02/01. 65 bedrooms
(all en suite). Golf 20 km, garage, parking. &

Dating from 1890, classic and gracious, the privately owned Bristol is one of Austria's leading hotels. Occupying an enviable position in the old town, close to the business area, theatres and famous Mirabell Gardens, hotel accommodation was renovated in 1996 and offers every comfort with fine furnishings. Super view over the old town and the Hohensalzburg fortress.

■ RESTAURANT: Closed Sun except festivals. Elegant and comfortable; regional dishes with Italian and 'new-Austrian' specialities.
■ ACTIVITIES: Polo nearby. Skiing in winter, walking/hiking in summer. Special packages available for autumn, Advent, Christmas and New Year.
■ TARIFF: Single 1500–3200, Double 2300–5200, Set menu 350–700 (Amex, Euro/Access, Visa).
■ DISCOUNT: 10% stays of 2 nights or more.

SCHRUNS 19C

Hotel Krone ★★★
Ausserlitzstrasse 2, 6780 Schruns.
Tel 05556 72255, Fax 05556 74879. English spoken.
Open 20/12 to 18/04 & 01/06 to 15/10.
9 bedrooms (all en suite). Golf 1 km, parking.

Traditional, stylish hotel in pretty surroundings. 4 minutes' walk from village centre.

■ RESTAURANT: Closed Thur. Elegantly furnished wood-panelled dining room. Regional specialities.
■ ACTIVITIES: Summer and winter mountain sports close by.
■ TARIFF: Single 360–480, Double 700–940, Set menu 170–250 (No credit cards).

VELDEN-AM-WÖRTHERSEE 19D

Hotel Europa ★★★★ Wrannpark 3,
9220 Velden-am-Wörthersee.
Tel 04274 2770, Fax 04274 51120. English spoken.
Open 10/05 to 20/10. 82 bedrooms
(all en suite). Indoor swimming pool, outdoor swimming pool, tennis, golf 10 km, parking.

On the banks of the Wörthersee and set in its own grounds, the hotel is perfectly situated for all water sports. Three 18-hole golf courses within a few minutes' drive. From Salzburg to Villach (220 km) then from Villach 15 km on highway to Velden. (Prices quoted are for half-board.)

■ RESTAURANT: Closed 20/10 to 10/05.
■ ACTIVITIES: Sauna, solarium, whirlpool, fitness room, massage and cosmetic salon at the hotel; water sports, sailing and windsurfing school nearby. ● Golf packages available.
■ TARIFF: (1996) Single 1050–1650, Double 1980–3160 (Amex, Euro/Access, Visa).

VILLACH 19D

Kurhotel Warmbaderhof ★★★★★
Warmbad Villach, 9500 Villach.
Tel 04242 30010, Fax 04242 3001309.
English spoken.
Open all year. 125 bedrooms (all en suite).
Indoor swimming pool, outdoor swimming pool, tennis, golf 17 km, parking. ✆

Quietly situated and surrounded by a park, this health, sport and spa hotel combines elegance with a warm and friendly atmosphere. From A10/A2 motorways, take Warmbad Villach exit.

■ RESTAURANT: Austrian and international creative cuisine.
■ ACTIVITIES: Entertainment and excursions programme; casino in Velden.
■ TARIFF: Single 1050–1580, Double 1560–3600, Set menu 145–890 (Visa).

WEISSENBACH 19B

Hotel Post ★★★★ Ischlerstrasse 1,
4854 Weissenbach-am-Attersee.
Tel 07663 8141, Fax 07663 814145. English spoken.
Open 15/05 to 30/09. 37 bedrooms
(all en suite). Outdoor swimming pool, tennis, golf 20 km, garage, parking.

Situated on the lake shore at the foothills of the Höllengebirges. Very comfortable rooms and apartments with full or half-board terms available.

■ RESTAURANT: Closed 30/09 to 15/05. Fish and regional specialities.
■ ACTIVITIES: Own beach, health/fitness room; cycling, fishing and boat trips can be arranged from hotel.
■ TARIFF: (1996) Single 610–1160, Double 1220–1650, Set menu 140 (Amex, Euro/Access, Visa).
■ DISCOUNT: 5%

WELS 19B

Hotel Greif ★★★★
Kaiser Joseph Platz 50/51, 4600 Wels.
Tel 07242 45361, Fax 07242 44629.
English spoken.
Open all year. 61 bedrooms (all en suite).
Golf 10 km, garage, parking. ✆

Renovated in 1992 and conveniently situated in the historical town centre, hotel offers every modern comfort as well as being the only one in Wels to offer free parking facilities.

■ RESTAURANT: Restaurant is open throughout the day and offers a good selection of food including steaks and vegetarian dishes.
■ ACTIVITIES: In-house theatre; bikes for hire; swimming, fitness centre, tennis and squash close by.
■ TARIFF: Single 990, Double 1390, Set menu 150–210 (Amex, Euro/Access, Visa).
■ DISCOUNT: 20%

WIEN (VIENNA)   19B

Hotel Atlanta ★★★★
Währingerstrasse 33, 1090 Wien.
Tel 01 405 1239, Fax 01 405 5375. English spoken.
Open all year. 57 bedrooms (all en suite).
Golf 15 km, garage.

A completely renovated 19th-century hotel with every modern facility. Centrally situated in the 9th district, between Volksoper and Votivkirche and close to Freudhouse, the Palais of Liechtenstein and the clinic. Good public transport.

■ RESTAURANT: Closed Sun & Mon. Austrian and international cuisine.
■ ACTIVITIES: Sightseeing pick-up service; the hotel will reserve tickets for opera, musicals, concerts, boat trips and trips to Budapest, Prague and Salzburg.
■ TARIFF: (1996) Single 820–980, Double 950–1600, Set menu 80–250 (Amex, Euro/Access, Visa).
■ DISCOUNT: 8% cash payments only.

Hotel Austria ★★★ Wolfengasse 3, am Fleischmarkt 20, 1011 Wien.

Tel 0222 51523, Fax 0222 51523506. English spoken. Open all year. 46 bedrooms (42 en suite). Garage. ☏

A comfortable B&B hotel with good facilities, typical Viennese flair and friendly service. Quiet situation in the old city.

■ TARIFF: Single 610–1150, Double 880–1680 (Amex, Euro/Access, Visa).
■ DISCOUNT: 8%

Hotel Kaiserhof ★★★★
Frankenberggasse, 1040 Wien.
Tel 0222 5051701, Fax 0222 5058875. English spoken.
Open all year. 85 bedrooms (all en suite). Garage.

Centrally located in the cultural area of Wien, very comfortable hotel with good facilities.

■ ACTIVITIES: Sightseeing tours and visits to concerts can be booked by hotel; Spanish horse-riding school nearby.
■ TARIFF: Single 950–1400, Double 1100–2300 (Amex, Euro/Access, Visa).
■ DISCOUNT: 10%

ZELL-AM-SEE   19C

Hotel Berner ★★★★ Nikolaus Gassner Promenade 1, 5700 Zell-am-See.
Tel 06542 2557, Fax 06542 25577. English spoken.

Open 13/05 to 14/10 & 17/12 to 31/03. 35 bedrooms (all en suite). Outdoor swimming pool, golf 4 km, garage, parking.

Quietly situated, comfortable, family-run hotel with beautiful views. Centrally located 150 m from the tourist office.

■ RESTAURANT: Good restaurant, proud of its buffet specialities and vegetarian dishes.
■ ACTIVITIES: Health/relaxation area; excursions and guided walks arranged. ● 20% reduction on green fees.
■ TARIFF: (1996) Single 750–950, Double 1000–1400, Set menu 200 (Amex, Visa).
■ DISCOUNT: 10% stay of over 2 nights.

Austria

BELGIUM

The canals of Bruges

Belgium consists of two quite distinct parts, geographically and culturally.

Flemish-speaking Flanders in the north is mostly very low-lying, protected from the North Sea by man-made sea defences and sand dunes. Its best known towns are Bruges, a city of canals whose medieval heart is best seen by boat, Ghent, centre of the famous Flemish wool trade in the 13th and 14th centuries and Antwerp, centre of the world diamond trade – as well as birthplace of Rubens and Van Dyck.

Southern Belgium is called Wallonia and here the main language is French.

Every parent will agree that the one thing that can make – or break – a holiday, is the contented – or otherwise – child. The Belgians have accordingly set about enhancing the chances of family harmony by providing a very generous scattering of theme parks...Aqualibi and Walibi near Brussels, Bobbejaanland near Antwerp, and Bellewaerde near Ypres, to name a few.

Compared with Flanders, Wallonia is mountainous, rising to some 694 m near the German border!

Centre-stage between Flanders and Wallonia, Brussels is home to the European Commission. The *Grand-Place*, lined with fine guild houses, and decorated by a daily flower market, is considered by many to be one of Europe's finest squares. Ample museums, cafés to dally in, everywhere little parks, and plenty of places to buy the excellent chocolates for which Belgium is so famous.

Emergency numbers

Police 101

Fire Brigade & Ambulance 100

Warning information

Warning triangle must be carried

Blood alcohol legal limit 50 mg

ANTWERPEN (ANTWERP)   7A

Hotel Firean ★★★★
Karel Oomsstraat 6, 2018 Antwerpen.
Tel 032 370260, Fax 032 381168. English spoken.
Open 01/01 to 31/07 & 21/08 to 31/12.
15 bedrooms (all en suite). Golf 8 km, garage.

*Elegant and very comfortable period residence
in typical art deco style near the city centre
and old Antwerpen. Good access to ports and
airport. Peaceful location.*

■ TARIFF: (1996) Single 4500–7600,
Double 4950–7600 (Amex, Euro/Access, Visa).

Hotel Ibis Antwerpen Centrum ★★★
Meistraat 39, 2000 Antwerpen.
Tel 032 318830, Fax 032 342921. English spoken.
Open all year. 150 bedrooms (all en suite).
Golf 10 km. &

*Modern, comfortable hotel in city centre, near
old town and close to famous Vogelenmarkt and
Rubens' house. Business facilities. Buffet breakfast.*

■ ACTIVITIES: Visit weekend market.
■ TARIFF: (1996) Single 2990, Double 3450
(Amex, Euro/Access, Visa).

BOUILLON   7D

Hotel Le Feuillantin ★★★★
23 rue de la Ville, 6830 Bouillon.
Tel 061 466293, Fax 061 468074. English spoken.

Open 11/02 to 09/01. 11 bedrooms
(all en suite). Garage, parking. ℓ

*Overlooking Bouillon and the castle, hotel is
quietly situated with an exceptional panoramic
view. Comfortably furnished with small
lounges and open fireplaces. Off the E411.*

■ RESTAURANT: Excellent cuisine. Game in season.
■ TARIFF: (1996) Single 1650, Double 2500,
Set menu 980–1650 (Amex, Euro/Access, Visa).

Hotel Panorama
rue au-dessus de la Ville 25, 6830 Bouillon.
Tel 061 466138, Fax 061 468122. English spoken.

Open 15/03 to 30/10. 40 bedrooms
(all en suite). Garage, parking.

*Situated above the town, with superb views of the
château, town and river. Panoramic terrace.*

■ RESTAURANT: Carefully prepared cuisine.
■ TARIFF: Single 850–1250, Double 1750–2100
(Amex, Euro/Access, Visa).
■ DISCOUNT: 10% except holiday weekends.

Hotel Poste ★★★
place St-Arnauld 1, 6830 Bouillon.
Tel 061 466506, Fax 061 467202. English spoken.

Open all year. 76 bedrooms (66 en suite).
Garage, parking. ℓ &

*Well-established hotel, dating from the early
1700s and with a rich history. Centrally
located, it has a terrace and stands on the
banks of the River Semois.*

■ RESTAURANT: Choice of three restaurants,
offering a variety of menus. The main, gourmet
restaurant overlooks the river.
■ ACTIVITIES: Mountain-biking, kayaking on the
River Semois, walking (over 100 way-marked
countryside paths).
■ TARIFF: Single 975–1725, Double 1650–3100,
Set menu 495–1495 (Amex, Euro/Access, Visa).
■ DISCOUNT: 10%

Belgium

BRUGGE (BRUGES) 7A

Hotel Adornes ★★★ St-Annarei 26, 8000 Brugge.
Tel 050 341336, Fax 050 342085.
English spoken.
Open 12/02 to 31/12. 20 bedrooms
(all en suite). Golf 8 km, garage, parking. ℓ

*Small hotel, full of character where you are
assured of genuine, old-fashioned hospitality.
Excellent buffet breakfast. In the city centre
overlooking canals. Enter Brugge through
Dampoort, follow the canal and hotel is on left.*

■ ACTIVITIES: Free use of bicycles.
■ TARIFF: Single 2600–3400, Double 2800–3600
(Amex, Euro/Access, Visa).

Hotel Albert I ★★★
Koning Albert I Laan 2-4, 8000 Brugge.
Tel 050 340930, Fax 050 338418.
English spoken.

Open 01/02 to 25/12. 15 bedrooms
(all en suite). Golf 6 km, garage.

*A charming, family-run hotel ideally situated
for sightseeing and offering an excellent buffet
breakfast. From the E40, take exit 8 and drive
towards St-Michiels and 'Centrum 't Zand'.*

■ TARIFF: (1996) Single 2000–2400,
Double 2400–2800 (Amex, Euro/Access, Visa).

Hotel Aragon ★★★★
Naaldenstraat 24, 8000 Brugge.
Tel 050 333533, Fax 050 342805.
English spoken.
Open 01/02 to 31/12. 18 bedrooms
(all en suite). Golf 6 km, garage.

*Once a stately mansion, now a family-run
hotel occupying a quiet position in the city
centre. Take the ring road 30 to Ezelpoort.
Turn into Ezelstraat, keep left at St Jakob's
church and then go first left into
Naaldenstraat.*

■ ACTIVITIES: City sightseeing. ● Special packages
for golf, cycling and Flanders discovery tours.

■ TARIFF: (1996) Single 2250–3500,
Double 2950–3950 (Euro/Access, Visa).
■ DISCOUNT: 10% except weekends and bank
holidays.

Hotel Asiris ★★
Lange Raam Straat 9, 8000 Brugge.
Tel 050 341724, Fax 050 347458. English spoken.

Open all year. 11 bedrooms (all en suite).
Parking. ℓ

*A patrician house situated in a quiet quarter of
the city, in the shadow of a 15th-century
church. Comfortable, well-equipped rooms,
fine buffet breakfast and just 5 minutes' walk
along the canals to centre. Good promotional
offers available from hotel on request.*

■ ACTIVITIES: Exploring Brugge.
■ TARIFF: Single 1700–1900, Double 2000–2300
(Amex, Euro/Access, Visa).
■ DISCOUNT: 12% 1 or 2 nights.

Hotel Best Western Acacia ★★★★
Korte Zilverstraat 3a, 8000 Brugge.
Tel 050 344411, Fax 050 338817.
English spoken.
Open all year. 36 bedrooms (all en suite).
Indoor swimming pool, golf 7 km, garage. ℓ

*Small, comfortable hotel just 50 m from the
marketplace in the old city. Good facilities and
a warm welcome.*

■ ACTIVITIES: Excursions and sightseeing tours
arranged on request. ● Free sauna, solarium
and fitness facilities at hotel.
■ TARIFF: (1996) Single 3400–4900,
Double 3900–5900 (Amex, Euro/Access, Visa).

Hotel Bryghia ★★★★
Oosterlingenplein 4, 8000 Brugge.
Tel 050 338059, Fax 050 341430.
English spoken.
Open 01/01 to 05/01 & 26/02 to 31/12.
18 bedrooms (all en suite). Golf 10 km, garage.

A handsomely restored 15th-century hotel in the heart of Brugge with good view of the canal. Family run and an ideal base for exploring this medieval city.

■ TARIFF: (1996) Single 2950–3500,
Double 3950–5200 (Amex, Euro/Access, Visa).
■ ACTIVITIES: Bookings made for sightseeing tours and excursions.
■ TARIFF: (1996) Single 2950–3250,
Double 3500–4500 (Amex, Euro/Access, Visa).

Hotel Févery ★★★
Collaert Mansionstraat 3, 8000 Brugge.
Tel 050 331269, Fax 050 331791.
English spoken.

Open 01/01 to 15/01 & 27/01 to 31/12.
11 bedrooms (all en suite). Garage, parking.

Small B&B hotel, quietly situated near St Giles church. Friendly and welcoming, hotel was renovated in 1996 and offers guests free transport from the station.

■ ACTIVITIES: ● Free boat trip included for stays of 3 days or more. Reduction for Flanders Fields tour; reduction on bicycle hire nearby.
■ TARIFF: Single 1650–1800, Double 2150–2400 (Amex, Euro/Access, Visa).
■ DISCOUNT: 5%

Hotel Jacobs ★★★ Baliestraat 1, 8000 Brugge.
Tel 050 339831, Fax 050 335694.
English spoken.
Open 04/02 to 31/12. 26 bedrooms
(24 en suite). Golf 6 km, garage.

Highly recommended. Typical Brugge-style hotel occupying a quiet position close to the market square; ample street parking close by.

Hotel has good facilities and is very well run by the friendly, helpful staff.

■ ACTIVITIES: Sightseeing and exploring; bicycles for hire.
■ TARIFF: Single 1450–2050, Double 1650–2450 (Amex, Euro/Access, Visa).

Hotel Maraboe ★★★
Hoefijzerlaan 9, 8000 Brugge.
Tel 050 33 81 55, Fax 050 33 29 28. English spoken.

Open all year. 9 bedrooms (all en suite).
Golf 9 km, garage.

Small hotel with an ideal location in this lovely city. Very comfortable, lots of ambience, warm and welcoming. Chargeable parking. (Internet address: http://luc2.unicall.be:80/maraboe/)

■ RESTAURANT: Closed Sun & Mon HS, weekdays LS. Pretty dining room where you can enjoy fine, creative cuisine prepared by the owner.
■ ACTIVITIES: Exploring the city and canals, visiting museums and art galleries. Hotel can arrange discounts.
■ TARIFF: Single 2000–2100,
Double 2500–2950, Set menu 1150–1950 (Amex, Euro/Access, Visa).
■ DISCOUNT: 5% not valid with CC payments.

Belgium

Flanders Hotel ★★★★
Langestraat 38, 8000 Brugge.
Tel 050 338889, Fax 050 339345. English spoken.
Open 01/01 to 05/01 & 30/01 to 31/12.
16 bedrooms (all en suite). Indoor swimming
pool, golf 10 km, garage. ☎ ♿

*Small city centre hotel, which takes pride in
offering personal service. 5 minutes' walk from
the market square, canals and museums.
Good variety of restaurants and bars close by.
Exit ring road N30 at Kruisport. Turn left into
Langestraat.*

Mirabel Hotel ★★★
J Wauterstraat 61, 8200 Brugge.
Tel 050 380988, Fax 050 382310. English spoken.

Open all year. 48 bedrooms (all en suite).
Golf 10 km, parking. ♿

*Modern hotel on the outskirts, close to the A17
and E40 motorways but still within walking
distance of the old city centre. Excellent
restaurants nearby, including 'Le Boulevard'
which works closely with hotel.*

■ TARIFF: (1996) Single 2050–2300,
Double 2600–2900 (Amex, Euro/Access, Visa).
■ DISCOUNT: 10%

Hotel Navarra ★★★★
41 St-Jacobsstraat, 8000 Brugge.
Tel 050 340561, Fax 050 336790. English spoken.
Open all year. 88 bedrooms (all en suite).
Indoor swimming pool, golf 12 km.

*Located in the city centre a few minutes from
the central market square. From Brugge
station, go towards Ezelpoort (via Kon
Albertlaan, Hoefijzerlaan, Gulden Vlieslaan).
Turn into the Ezelstraat, continue along and
the hotel is on the right-hand side. (Charge for
parking.)*

■ ACTIVITIES: Arrangements made for city tours.
■ TARIFF: Single 3450–3950, Double 4350–4950
(Amex, Euro/Access, Visa).

Hotel de L'Orangerie ★★★★
Kartuizerinnenstraat 10, 8000 Brugge.
Tel 050 341649, Fax 050 333016. English spoken.
Open 01/01 to 25/01 & 15/02 to 31/12.
19 bedrooms (all en suite). Golf 20 km, garage. ☎

*Extremely comfortable, aesthetically pleasing
hotel set in a beautifully landscaped garden
and next to the most picturesque canal in
Brugge. In the heart of the city, close to superb
restaurants, famous museums and shops.
Chargeable garage/parking nearby.*

■ ACTIVITIES: Private guided tours, excursions by
minibus, boat trips, horse-drawn carriage rides;
restaurant reservations; indoor pool, sauna,
solarium, jacuzzi. Bike hire available nearby.
■ TARIFF: Single 5950–7950, Double 6950–8950
(Amex, Euro/Access, Visa).

Hotel de Pauw ★★
St-Gilliskerkhof 8, 8000 Brugge.
Tel 050 337118, Fax 050 345140. English spoken.

Open all year. 8 bedrooms (6 en suite). Garage.

*Charming, peaceful hotel with a family
atmosphere. A fine breakfast can be enjoyed in
the pretty breakfast room. 7 minutes from the
town square.*

■ ACTIVITIES: Lots to do and see nearby. Hotel
offers a free tour of the city for stays of 3 days
or more.
■ TARIFF: Single 1700, Double 2300 (Amex,
Euro/Access, Visa).

Hotel Portinari ★★★★
't Zand 15, 8000 Brugge.
Tel 050 341034, Fax 050 344180. English spoken.
Open all year. 40 bedrooms (all en suite).
Golf 6 km, garage. &
Comfortable hotel with pavement café on tree-lined square. Convenient for all city amenities.
■ TARIFF: (1996) Single 3000–4000,
Double 3500–4500 (Amex, Euro/Access, Visa).

Hotel Prinsenhof ★★★★
Ontvangersstraat 9, 8000 Brugge.
Tel 050 342690, Fax 050 342321. English spoken.
Open all year. 16 bedrooms (all en suite).
Golf 5 km, garage, parking. &
An elegant, family-run 'Silence' hotel, centrally positioned and very comfortable with some fine antiques. Buffet breakfast.
■ TARIFF: Single 3000–3400, Double 3900–6700 (Amex, Euro/Access, Visa).

Sofitel Brugge ★★★★
Boeveriestraat, 8000 Brugge.
Tel 050 340971, Fax 050 344053. English spoken.
Open all year. 155 bedrooms (all en suite).
Indoor swimming pool, golf 18 km, parking.
The hotel is built behind the walls of a 17th-century monastery, in the centre of town on the 't Zand Square. Very comfortable, with up-to-date facilities including sauna and extra-large beds. (Charge made for parking from 28/03/97.)
■ RESTAURANT: Regional and international dishes can be enjoyed in the cosy and attractive 'Ter Boeverie'.
■ TARIFF: Single 4000–6200,
Double 4500–6700, Set menu 950–1600 (Amex, Euro/Access, Visa).

Hotel Ter Duinen ★★★
Langerei 52, 8000 Brugge.
Tel 050 330437, Fax 050 344216. English spoken.

Open 01/02 to 31/12. 20 bedrooms
(all en suite). Golf 10 km, garage, parking.
An excellent hotel beside a very beautiful canal. 10 of the bedrooms are air conditioned; lavish buffet breakfasts! Choice of free parking right in front of the hotel or private garage for only 250 BF/night. Follow 'Dampoort' signs from ring road.
■ TARIFF: (1996) Single 2300–3500,
Double 2800–3950 (Amex, Euro/Access, Visa).

Hotel de Tuilerieen ★★★★
Dyver 7, 8000 Brugge.
Tel 050 343691, Fax 050 340400.
English spoken.
Open 01/01 to 15/12. 26 bedrooms
(all en suite). Indoor swimming pool, golf 6 km, garage. &
Former 15th-century mansion, now a luxurious hotel. Stands beside a picturesque canal in the enchanting atmosphere of the old city.
■ ACTIVITIES: Guided tours, bikes for hire, minibus and boat excursions, horse-drawn carriage rides. Restaurant bookings can be made by hotel.
■ TARIFF: (1996) Single 6950–7950, Double 8950–11,950 (Amex, Euro/Access, Visa).

Hotel Wilgenhof ★★★
Polderstraat 151, Sint Kruis, 8310 Brugge.
Tel 050 362744, Fax 050 362821.
English spoken.

Open all year. 6 bedrooms (all en suite). Golf, garage, parking.
Small country hotel on the banks of the canal, 2 km north of Brugge.
■ TARIFF: (1996) Single 2500–3600,
Double 3000–4100 (Amex, Euro/Access, Visa).

Belgium

BRUXELLES (BRUSSELS) 7A

Hotel Arenberg ★★★★
rue d'Assaut 15, 1000 Brussels.
Tel 511 07 70, Fax 514 19 76. English spoken.

Open all year. 155 bedrooms (all en suite).
Garage. ☏

Modern hotel with a family atmosphere in town centre near the Grand'Place and 200 m from the central station.

■ RESTAURANT: Cosy restaurant.
■ TARIFF: Single 3900–6000,
Double 4600–7000, Set menu 450–1000
(Amex, Euro/Access, Visa).
■ DISCOUNT: 20% on luxury rooms only.

Hotel Astoria ★★★★
103 rue Royale, 1000 Bruxelles.
Tel 02 2176290, Fax 02 2171150. English spoken.
Open all year. 122 bedrooms (all en suite).
Garage. ☏

Belle Epoque-style hotel dating from the early 1900s.

■ RESTAURANT: Closed 15/07 to 15/08. Excellent
French cuisine with fish specialities.
■ TARIFF: (1996) Single 5400–6500,
Double 7500–8300, Set menu 1550 (Amex,
Euro/Access, Visa).

Hotel Ibis Brussels Centre Ste-Catherine
★★★ 2 rue Joseph Plateau, 1000 Bruxelles.
Tel 02 5137620, Fax 02 5142214. English spoken.
Open all year. 235 bedrooms (all en suite).
Golf 15 km, garage, parking. ☏ ♿

Modern hotel in centre of city, just 400 m from the Grand'Place. Buffet breakfast. Public parking in front of the the the hotel.

■ TARIFF: (1996) Single 2950–3550,
Double 2950–3800 (Amex, Euro/Access, Visa).

Hotel Royal Windsor ★★★★
5 rue Duquesnoy, 1000 Bruxelles.
Tel 02 5055555, Fax 02 5055500. English spoken.
Open all year. 275 bedrooms (all en suite).
Parking.

Ideally located in the historic heart of the city, only minutes from the medieval grandeur of La Grand'Place and the central railway station air terminal, with its direct link to Bruxelles airport.

■ RESTAURANT: Good choice of regional and
international cuisine.
■ ACTIVITIES: ● Special offer weekends, plus July
and August, includes VIP welcome, de luxe
accommodation, champagne breakfast and
access to Griffin's nightclub and the fitness
centre.
■ TARIFF: (1996) Single 9750–12,450,
Double 10,250–12,450, Bk 700 (Amex,
Euro/Access, Visa).

BURG REULAND 7D

Hotel Motel du Val de l'Our Boswg 150,
4790 Burg Reuland.
Tel 080 329009, Fax 080 329700.
English spoken.

Open all year. 16 bedrooms. Outdoor
swimming pool, tennis, parking. ☏

Super position close to the German and Luxembourg borders and within easy reach of France. Very comfortable hotel in picturesque surroundings.

■ RESTAURANT: Gourmet cuisine with French and
fish specialities.
■ ACTIVITIES: Sauna, keep-fit, table tennis at
hotel; bikes available, fishing, canoeing and
hunting.
■ TARIFF: (1996) Single 1800–2450,
Double 2250–2850, Set menu 850–1295
(No credit cards).

DE HAAN 7A

Auberge des Rois/Beach Hotel ★★★★
Zeedyk, 8420 De Haan aan Zee.
Tel 059 233018, Fax 059 236078. English spoken.

Open 05/03 to 25/10 & 20/12 to 05/01.
30 bedrooms (all en suite). Golf on site, garage,
parking. ☏

*Only 10 km from Oostende, a modern hotel,
warm and inviting, with an excellent location
on the beach in De Haan. Complimentary
bottle of champagne for 5-day stay or more.*

SEE ADVERTISEMENT.

■ RESTAURANT: Closed Tues. Very good food and
fine wines can be enjoyed in the pretty dining
room, which overlooks the sea.
■ ACTIVITIES: Lots to do and see nearby
including golf almost on the doorstep.
■ TARIFF: (1996) Single 3000–4200,
Double 3025–5600, Set menu 1400–1850
(Euro/Access, Visa).

DINANT 7D

Hotel du Moulin de Lisogne ★★★
60 rue de la Lisonette, Lisogne, 5500 Dinant.
Tel 082 226380, Fax 082 222147. English spoken.
Open 15/02 to 15/12. 10 bedrooms (all en
suite). Tennis, golf 15 km, garage, parking. ☏ ё

*Charming stone-built hotel/restaurant built
over a 17th-century watermill. Very comfortable,
warm and inviting. Lisogne is 3 km north-east
of Dinant in quiet, peaceful countryside.*

■ RESTAURANT: Closed Sun eve & Mon. Beautiful
restaurant with an excellent reputation. Classic
French cuisine and specialities using only the
best of fresh, natural ingredients.
■ ACTIVITIES: Trout fishing, hunting and good
forest walks nearby; 20 minutes' drive from the
caves at Han.
■ TARIFF: (1996) Double 2800–3500,
Set menu 1250–1900 (Amex, Euro/Access, Visa).
■ DISCOUNT: 10% weekdays only.

EUPEN 7B

Hotel Rathaus ★★★
Rathausplatz 13, 4700 Eupen.
Tel 087 742812, Fax 087 744664. English spoken.
Open 01/01 to 24/12 & 26/12 to 31/12.
18 bedrooms (all en suite). Golf 10 km,
parking. ё

*Family-owned hotel in centre of town, opposite
town hall and near the Hertogenwald and
Hautes Fagnes; ideal for walking. Renovated
accommodation; buffet breakfast. Good
Italian restaurant nearby.*

■ ACTIVITIES: Mini-golf, swimming pool nearby,
lots of festivities in the town. Don't forget the
carnival in February!
■ TARIFF: (1996) Single 2250, Double 2850
(Amex, Euro/Access, Visa).

FLORENVILLE 7D

Auberge de la Vallée ★★★★ 7 rue du Fond
des Naux, 6821 Lacuisine-sur-Semois.
Tel 061 311140, Fax 061 312661. English spoken.
Open 15/02 to 02/01. 10 bedrooms
(all en suite). Outdoor swimming pool,
golf 15 km, parking. ☏

Belgium

Belgium

Country hotel set in parkland. 2 km north of Florenville.

■ RESTAURANT: Closed Sun eve & Mon LS. Excellent cuisine and international wine cellar. Meals can be taken outside in fine weather.
■ ACTIVITIES: Heated pool with spa bath therapy, mountain bikes and kayacks available at hotel; tennis, cross-country skiing, horse-riding and walking in the forest all nearby.
■ TARIFF: Single 2000–2200, Double 2000–2300, Bk 300, Set menu 950–1700 (Amex, Euro/Access, Visa).
■ DISCOUNT: 25% stays over 4 days.

FRANCORCHAMPS 7B

Hotel Moderne ★★★
rte de Spa 129, 4970 Francorchamps.
Tel 087 275026, Fax 087 275527. English spoken.
Open all year. 14 bedrooms (all en suite).
Golf 8 km, garage, parking. ℂ
In the very heart of the village. Some rooms have a flowered terrace. Francorchamps is between Spa and Malmédy on N621.

■ RESTAURANT: Closed Wed LS. Specialities: game (in season) and fois gras frais.
■ ACTIVITIES: Mountain and valley walks; ski-run and Mont des Brumes circuit nearby.
■ TARIFF: (1996) Single 1700–1850, Double 2500–2850, Bk 60, Set menu 800–1500 (Amex, Euro/Access, Visa).

Hotel Le Roannay ★★★★
rue de Spa 155, 4970 Francorchamps.
Tel 087 275311, Fax 087 275547. English spoken.
Open all year. 20 bedrooms (all en suite).
Outdoor swimming pool, golf 8 km, garage, parking. ⅚
Very comfortable hotel set in lovely countryside with large, park-like gardens. 1 km from famous Francorchamps car and motorbike circuit.

■ RESTAURANT: Closed Tues. Comfortable, air-conditioned dining room. Renowned for its wine cellar and excellent cuisine which is prepared by the owner.
■ ACTIVITIES: Private heliport, sauna; flying lessons at Spa-Francorchamps; walking and mountain-biking with guide available.
■ TARIFF: (1996) Single 2500–3500, Double 3500–4800, Bk 400, Set menu 1490–2350 (Amex, Euro/Access, Visa).

GENT 7A

Hotel Cours St Georges ★★★
Botermarkt 2, 9000 Gent.
Tel 092 242424, Fax 092 242640. English spoken.

Open all year. 28 bedrooms (all en suite). Garage.
Built in 1228, and rich in history, this hotel is considered to be the oldest in Europe. Beautifully furnished and decorated with all modern comforts. Terrace within the historic courtyard. In centre of town, opposite town hall.

■ RESTAURANT: Closed Sun eve. Specialises in classic and regional cuisine, based on market-fresh produce. Try home-smoked salmon, lobster soup with Armagnac, waterzooi, anguilles au vert or lapin à la Flamande in the splendid, old, galleried dining room. Brunch can be had on Sundays except July and August and candlelit dinners are held every Friday.
■ ACTIVITIES: Well placed for the wealth of sightseeing opportunities Gent has to offer.
■ TARIFF: (1996) Single 2600–4400, Double 3500–5500, Set menu 920 (Amex, Euro/Access, Visa).

Sofitel Gent-Belfort ★★★★ 9000 Gent.
Tel 09 2333331, Fax 09 2331102. English spoken.
Open all year. 127 bedrooms (all en suite).
Golf 10 km, garage. ℂ ⅚
Hotel is in the heart of the historic centre of Gent, opposite the Belfort. Very comfortable, well-appointed accommodation and a warm, friendly atmosphere.

■ RESTAURANT: A fine choice of regional and international gourmet dishes can be enjoyed in 'Brasserie Van Artevelde'. Elegant, convivial atmosphere and realistic prices.
■ ACTIVITIES: Well placed for exploring Gent and the surrounding area.
■ TARIFF: (1996) Double 4750–6950, Bk 625, Set menu 450–1150 (Amex, Euro/Access, Visa).
■ DISCOUNT: 10%

HAMOIS-EN-CONDROZ   7D

Château de Pickeim ★★★★ 136 rte Ciney-Liège, 5360 Hamois-en-Condroz.
Tel 083 611274, Fax 083 611351.

Open 01/02 to 31/12. 20 bedrooms (all en suite). Golf 8 km, parking. ℄ ⅖
Pretty château set in 7 hectares of parkland, 8 km north-east of Ciney.

■ RESTAURANT: Closed Tues. French and game specialities using fresh local produce include côte de chevreuil aux champignons des bois and truite en eau de source aux écrevisses.
■ ACTIVITIES: Way-marked woodland walks, châteaux visits.
■ TARIFF: (1996) Single 1250–1500, Double 1250–1750, Bk 200, Set menu 775–1575 (Amex, Euro/Access, Visa).

HASSELT   7B

Hotel Ibis ★★★
Thonissenlaan 52, 3500 Hasselt.
Tel 011 231111/12, Fax 011 243323. English spoken.

Open all year. 59 bedrooms (all en suite). Golf 4 km, parking. ℄ ⅖
Close to the cultural and commercial centre of town, only two minutes' walk from the station.
■ TARIFF: (1996) Single 2300, Double 2950 (Amex, Euro/Access, Visa).
■ DISCOUNT: 10%

IEPER (YPRES)   7A

Hostellerie Kemmelberg ★★★★
Berg 4, 8956 Heuvelland-Kemmel.
Tel 057 444145, Fax 057 444089. English spoken.
Open 16/03 to 14/01. 16 bedrooms (all en suite). Tennis, golf 10 km, parking.
Luxury, small hotel with panoramic views. South-west of Ieper.
■ RESTAURANT: Closed Sun eve & Mon. Offers excellent cuisine.
■ TARIFF: (1996) Single 1875–2500, Double 2750–4000 (Amex, Euro/Access, Visa).

KNOKKE-HEIST   7A

Hotel Memlinc Palace ★★★★ Albert Plein 23, Knokke Zoute, 8300 Knokke-Heist.
Tel 050 601134, Fax 050 615743. English spoken.
Open all year. 66 bedrooms (all en suite). Tennis, golf 2 km, parking. ⅖
From Knokke take the road towards Het Zoute. Hotel is close to the casino, the shopping area and opposite the main beach of Zoute. Very comfortable accommodation.
■ RESTAURANT: French cuisine with seafood specialities. Lunchtime dance on Sundays.
■ ACTIVITIES: Hotel organises tours of the city by

Belgium

Belgium

horse-drawn carriage and boat trips on the canals. Free entrance to the casino. Visit the nearby nature park and butterfly gardens.
■ TARIFF: Single 2800–3300, Double 3900–4800, Set menu 795–995 (Amex, Euro/Access, Visa).
■ DISCOUNT: 5% except July and August.

LEUVEN 7B

Hotel New Damshire ★★★ Pater Damiaan Plein, Schapenstraat 1, 3000 Leuven.
Tel 016 232115, Fax 016 233208. English spoken.
Open 02/01 to 24/12. 22 bedrooms (all en suite). Golf 20 km, parking. ☎

Centrally located in Damiaan square and only 15 minutes from the airport. Easy to reach via Naamsepoort, Naamsestraat and St Antoniusberg.
■ TARIFF: (1996) Single 2700–3400, Double 3100–4400 (Amex, Euro/Access, Visa).
■ DISCOUNT: 8%

LIEGE 7B

Post Hotel SA ★★★★
160 rue Hurbise, 4040 Herstal.
Tel 042 646400, Fax 042 480690. English spoken.
Open all year. 93 bedrooms (all en suite).
Outdoor swimming pool, golf 5 km, garage, parking. ♿

North of Liège, modern hotel set in parkland. Excellent facilities.
■ RESTAURANT: 'La Diligence' has a good reputation and offers panoramic views over the Meuse valley. Classic French cuisine with regional specialities. Special diet meals on request.
■ ACTIVITIES: Sightseeing in and around Liège; visit to Spa-Francorchamps and Zolder racing circuits (half-hour drive away). Children's playground in the park.
■ TARIFF: Single 2700–4300, Double 3600–5700, Set menu 800–1200 (Amex, Euro/Access, Visa).

NAMUR 7B

Château de Namur ★★★
1 av de l'Ermitage, 5000 Namur.
Tel 081 742630, Fax 081 742392. English spoken.

Open 28/12 to 24/12. 30 bedrooms (all en suite). Tennis, golf 15 km, parking. ♿
Charming 19th-century château with splendid views. 10 minutes from town centre and station. (The hotel is closed from 01/12/96 to 28/02/97 for renovation.)
■ RESTAURANT: Gastronomic restaurant with French cuisine. Seafood specialities, including lobster and trout.

■ TARIFF: (1996) Single 3450–4950, Double 3950–4950, Bk 400, Set menu 895–1595 (Amex, Euro/Access, Visa).

New Hotel de Lives ★★★

Chaussée de Liège 1178, 5101 Lives-sur-Meuse. Tel 081 58 05 13, Fax 081 58 15 77. English spoken.

Open all year. 10 bedrooms (all en suite). Parking. ℃ ♿

19th-century hotel with a warm, homely atmosphere. Stylishly updated and offering the same conveniences and service as a first-class hotel. Situated beside the River Meuse, facing the rocks of Marche-Les-Dames.

■ RESTAURANT: Comfortable, pretty dining room specialising in Belgian cuisine. All dishes are freshly prepared and guests wishing to dine are asked to book in advance.

■ ACTIVITIES: Lots to do and see nearby including touring and sightseeing, visiting museums, the beautiful gardens at the Château d'Annevoie and the Goyet caves.

■ TARIFF: Single 2200–3700, Double 2800–4300, Set menu 450 (Amex, Euro/Access, Visa).

■ DISCOUNT: 15%

Novotel Namur ★★★

1149 chausée du Dinant, 5100 Namur. Tel 081 460811, Fax 081 461990. English spoken. Open all year. 110 bedrooms (all en suite). Indoor swimming pool, outdoor swimming pool, golf 3 km, garage, parking. ℃ ♿

Motorway E411 Bruxelles to Luxembourg, exit 14, then head towards Dinant. The hotel is 7 km from town centre, on the bank of the River Meuse.

■ RESTAURANT: French cuisine.

■ ACTIVITIES: Sauna, solarium, billiards, darts, table tennis, biking. Sightseeing tours of Namur and Dinant.

■ TARIFF: (1996) Single 3200, Double 3700, Bk 425 (Amex, Euro/Access, Visa).

OOSTENDE (OSTEND)　　　　7A

Hotel Acces ★★★★

Van Iseghemlaan 21-25, 8400 Oostende. Tel 059 804082, Fax 059 808839. English spoken.

Open all year. 63 bedrooms (all en suite). Golf 8 km, restaurant. ℃ ♿

Modern, city centre hotel, 50 m from the sea and 250 m from casino.

■ ACTIVITIES: Sauna and solarium free for hotel residents.

■ TARIFF: Single 2350–3050, Double 2600–3300, Set menu 700–1400 (Amex, Euro/Access, Visa).

■ DISCOUNT: 10%

Hotel Ostend ★★★

Londenstraat 6, 8400 Oostende. Tel 059 704625, Fax 059 804622. English spoken.

Open all year. 160 bedrooms (all en suite). Golf 8 km, restaurant.

50 m from the sea, a family hotel offering free accommodation for children under 12 and 50% discount for children between 12 and 16 (accommodation and meals).

Belgium

■ ACTIVITIES: Sauna, solarium and fitness centre free for hotel residents.
■ TARIFF: Single 1900–2700, Double 2100–2900, Set menu 500–1100 (Amex, Euro/Access, Visa).
■ DISCOUNT: 10%

Hotel Ambassadeur ★★★★
Wapenplein 8A, 8400 Oostende.
Tel 059 700941, Fax 059 801878. English spoken.
Open all year. 24 bedrooms (all en suite).
Golf 5 km, garage, parking, restaurant. ☎ ♿

Comfortable town centre hotel in Oostende's shopping area. Close to the casino and beach.
■ TARIFF: Single 2000–2400, Double 2800–3600, Set menu 400 (Amex, Euro/Access, Visa).

Hotel Pacific ★★★
Hofstraat 11, 8400 Oostende.
Tel 059 701507, Fax 059 803566. English spoken.

Open all year. 56 bedrooms (all en suite).
Golf 6 km, garage, restaurant.

Family-run hotel in the centre of Ostend. Rooms with sea view. Close to the railway station and 150 m from the beach. Restaurant is for hotel guests only.
■ ACTIVITIES: Fitness room, sauna and solarium, piano bar.
■ TARIFF: (1996) Single 1500–2200, Double 2400–3500, Set menu 600 (Amex, Euro/Access, Visa).
■ DISCOUNT: 10%

Hotel du Parc ★★★
Marie-Joseplein 3, 8400 Oostende.
Tel 059 701680, Fax 059 800879. English spoken.

Open 01/02 to 31/12. 45 bedrooms (all en suite). Garage. ☎
Completely renovated first-class hotel overlooking a beautiful square. Ideally situated in the city centre, 50 m from the casino and sandy beaches.
■ ACTIVITIES: Hotel organises competitively priced excursions to Brugge, Sluis and Bruxelles in June, July and August; sauna, solarium.
■ TARIFF: Single 1600–1700, Double 2050–2700 (Amex, Euro/Access, Visa).
■ DISCOUNT: 10%

Hotel die Prince
41 Albert 1 Promenade, 8400 Oostende.
Tel 059 706507, Fax 059 807851. English spoken.
Open all year. 46 bedrooms (40 en suite).
Golf 5 km, garage.

Very comfortable hotel with all modern facilities. Excellent location right on the sea-front. 100 m from market, casino and harbour.
■ TARIFF: (1996) Single 1200–2200, Double 1800–3700 (Amex, Euro/Access, Visa).

Belgium

Hotel Prince Charles
Visserskaai 19, 8400 Oostende.
Tel 059 705066, Fax 059 807836. English spoken.

Open all year. 7 bedrooms (all en suite).
Tennis, golf 10 km. ☏

Small and traditional, hotel is beside the harbour, 100 m from the station and ferry terminal and 5 minutes from the town centre.

■ RESTAURANT: Dining room has a romantic air and specialises in fish and seafood.
■ ACTIVITIES: Hotel will organise boat trips and sea fishing.
■ TARIFF: (1996) Single 1700–1900, Double 2100–2500, Set menu 795–1790 (Euro/Access, Visa).
■ DISCOUNT: 5%

Hotel Strand ★★★
Visserskaai 1, 8400 Oostende.
Tel 059 703383, Fax 059 803678. English spoken.
Open 31/01 to 01/12. 21 bedrooms (all en suite). Parking.

Opposite station and ferry/jet-foil terminals.

■ RESTAURANT: Closed Dec & Jan. One of Oostende's few hotels with an à la carte restaurant.
■ TARIFF: (1996) Single 2750–3300, Double 3300–4000, Set menu 775–995 (Amex, Euro/Access, Visa).

Tulip Inn Bero Oostende ★★★
Hofstraat 1A, 8400 Oostende.
Tel 059 702335, Fax 059 702591. English spoken.
Open all year. 73 bedrooms (all en suite).
Indoor swimming pool, tennis, golf 4 km, garage, parking, restaurant. ☏

Modern hotel with good facilities. Garage for 30 cars. Follow road to railway station,

continue along quayside to monument and turn left. Signposted.

■ ACTIVITIES: Sauna and solarium at hotel.
■ TARIFF: (1996) Single 2200–3200, Double 2800–3800, Set menu 500 (Amex, Euro/Access, Visa).
■ DISCOUNT: 5%

LA ROCHE-EN-ARDENNE 7D

Hotel Claire Fontaine ★★★★
rte de Hotton, 6980 La Roche-en-Ardenne.
Tel 084 412470, Fax 084 412111. English spoken.

Open all year. 25 bedrooms (all en suite).
Golf 20 km, parking, restaurant.

Traditional hotel set in parkland. Near the River Ourthe, just to the north of La Roche-en-Ardenne.

■ TARIFF: Single 2200–3000, Double 3000–4000, Set menu 890–2100 (Amex, Euro/Access, Visa).

Hostellerie Linchet ★★★★
11 route de Houffalize, 6980 La Roche-en-Ardenne.
Tel 084 411327, Fax 084 412410. English spoken.
Open all year. 11 bedrooms (all en suite).
Golf 25 km, garage, parking.

Very comfortable hotel, renovated in 1991. 1.5 km from town centre, surrounded by woods and overlooking the river and hills. Large, airy rooms, all with a view. Within an hour and a half of Luxembourg, Germany and France.

■ RESTAURANT: Closed 24/02 to 22/03 & 15/06 to 15/07. Beautiful dining room with super views. Specialites include seafood and wild game from the surrounding forests.
■ ACTIVITIES: Guided tours, mountain bikes and canoes on request.
■ TARIFF: (1996) Single 2500, Double 2500–4200, Set menu 1000–2000 (Amex, Euro/Access, Visa).
■ DISCOUNT: 5% for minimum stay of 2 nights.

Belgium

ROCHEFORT · 7D

Hotel Le Ry d'Ave ★★★★
Sourd d'Ave 5, 5435 Ave et Auffe.
Tel 084 388220, Fax 084 389550.
English spoken.

Open 01/02 to 30/06 & 08/07 to 03/01.
12 bedrooms (all en suite). Outdoor swimming pool, golf 10 km, parking. ℂ ♿

Small and comfortable, hotel has good facilities and is set in a quiet, peaceful location at the gateway to the Ardenne. Ave et Auffe is just south of Rochefort on the N94.

■ RESTAURANT: Closed Tues eve/Wed LS; Wed Jul & Aug. Specialities include gratin de homard en lasagne, homard rôti au four, braisé de ris de veau au pleurotes et tagliatelles.
■ ACTIVITIES: Tennis, mini-golf and horse-riding nearby. Excellent choice of excursions organised by the hotel.
■ TARIFF: (1996) Single 1550, Double 2150–2660, Bk 360, Set menu 780–1850 (Amex, Euro/Access, Visa).
■ DISCOUNT: 5% cash payments only.

ST-HUBERT · 7D

Hotel de l'Abbaye ★★★
place du Marche, 6900 St-Hubert.
Tel 061 611023, Fax 061 613422.
English spoken.
Open 01/01 to 08/09 & 23/09 to 31/12.
20 bedrooms (14 en suite). Garage, parking.

Follow signs to the town centre.

■ RESTAURANT: Rustic setting; Ardenne specialities include 12 ways of serving trout, local game (in season), young wild boar (all year).
■ ACTIVITIES: Walking in the forest, gliding, horse-riding, tennis.
■ TARIFF: (1996) Single 610–1495, Double 970–1825, Set menu 330–990 (Amex, Euro/Access, Visa).

ST-VITH · 7D

Hotel Pip-Margraff ★★★
Hauptstrasse 7, 4780 St-Vith, Oostkantons.
Tel 080 228663, Fax 080 228761.
English spoken.
Open all year. 23 bedrooms (all en suite).
Golf 25 km, parking.

Very comfortable, modern hotel with nice garden. 12 minutes from Francorchamps on the motorway. A welcoming apéritif is offered on arrival.

■ RESTAURANT: Closed Mon. French cuisine. Specialities: venison and seafood.
■ ACTIVITIES: Sauna, solarium, whirlpool and Turkish bath at hotel. Perfectly situated for cross-country skiing, hiking and mountain-biking.
■ TARIFF: (1996) Single 1975–2500, Double 2800–3500, Set menu 950–1450 (Amex, Euro/Access, Visa).

WATERLOO · 7A

Grand Hotel ★★★★
chaussée de Tervuren 198, 1410 Waterloo.
Tel 023 521815, Fax 023 521888.
English spoken.
Open all year. 79 bedrooms (all en suite).
Golf 10 km. ℂ ♿

Comfortable hotel 20 km from Bruxelles.

■ RESTAURANT: Closed Sat & Sun lunch. Brasserie restaurant 'La Sucrerie' occupies a superbly restored sugar refinery dating from 1836.
■ ACTIVITIES: Nearby walks in the Forêt de Soignes, sightseeing tours, fitness centre close by. ● Special discounts on green fees.
■ TARIFF: (1996) Single 4400–6950, Double 4400–7600, Set menu 495–1695 (Amex, Euro/Access, Visa).

Hotel La Joli-Bois ★★★
rue Ste-Anne 59, 1410 Waterloo.
Tel 023 531818, Fax 023 530516.
English spoken.
Open 09/01 to 23/12. 14 bedrooms (all en suite). Golf 5 km, parking.

Small 'Silence' hotel. Comfortable, pretty rooms in relaxing pastel colours. Good restaurants nearby.

■ ACTIVITIES: Excellent location for exploring historic Waterloo and surrounding countryside; horse-riding, swimming and tennis nearby.
■ TARIFF: (1996) Single 2800–3400, Double 3200–3800 (Amex, Euro/Access, Visa).
■ DISCOUNT: 10%

Belgium

CZECH REPUBLIC & SLOVAKIA

Since the Velvet Revolution of 1989 the Czech Republic & Slovakia have become very popular with British holidaymakers, intrigued by mighty castles, grand cathedrals, but especially by some of Europe's most spectacular landscapes.

Prague, the capital of the Czech Republic, is often called the most beautiful capital in Europe. The view from Charles Bridge up towards the castle and St Vitus' cathedral is particularly fine. Behind, in the old town, are the famous astronomical clock and the Powder Tower, both dating from the 15th century.

Bohemia is well known for its spas and the most famous of these is Karlovy Vary. It is also well known for its beer, and Pilsener have been brewing lager here since the Middle Ages in the town of Plzen – home, too, to the Skoda. The northern Bohemian region around Hrensko is noted for its amazing sandstone landscape rising above the River Elbe, making the area popular with walkers. Places to visit include Pravcická braná, the largest natural bridge in Europe, the smaller Malá Pravcická braná and the Kamenice gorge.

Moravia, part of the Czech Republic since 1918, has Brno as its capital. A fortified town in the Middle Ages, Brno retains the Spilberk fortress – an Austrian political prison until 1857 – the cathedral of St Peter and St Paul and, a rather different sort of tourist attraction, the mummified bodies of

the Capuchin tombs. About 30 km north of Brno is the area of huge limestone caves known as Moravsky Dras. Several of the caves are open to the public, though the Machyoca Abyss can be viewed from the surface. Alternatively, descend to the bottom of this 138-m hole and continue underground by boat along the Punkva river.

Slovakia, now an independent country since the division of Czechoslovakia, is a land of mountains rising towards the High Tatras on the Polish border. This too is a wonderful area for walking, with the added bonus of chair-lifts and cable-cars to help the faint-hearted to the high tops. A cable-car goes up Lomnicky st't which, at 2632 m, is the second highest peak in Slovakia. Or, to enjoy the landscape from a different angle, try rafting on the River Dunajec, from Cerveny Klastor on the Polish border.

On the drive east through Slovakia try to visit some spectacular castles, among them Oravsky Zamek and, perhaps most impressive of all, Spissky Hrad. Finally, in the villages around the Ukrainian border, watch out for storks nesting on specially built platforms high on the roof tops.

Emergency numbers

Police 158

Fire Brigade 150

Ambulance 155

Warning information

First aid kit compulsory

Warning triangle must be carried

Blood Alcohol Legal Limit 0 mg

* Please note: the limit shown above is correct ie any alcohol in the blood is illegal.

Pragues's Charles Bridge is said to be the strongest in the world because it was built with mortar made from eggs. All of Bohemia had to contribute eggs for this task but not everyone understood exactly what the eggs where going to be used for. So some, it is said, sent them hard boiled to make sure that they got to Prague intact.

HRADEC KRALOVE 22C

Alessandria Hotel ★★★
Slezské Predmesti, SNP 733 Hradec Kralove.
Tel 49 41521, Fax 49 42874. English spoken.
Open all year. 105 bedrooms (all en suite).
Parking. (&

*Quietly situated, the hotel has excellent
facilities including terrace and garden.*

■ RESTAURANT: Two restaurants offering
international cuisine with regional specialities.
■ ACTIVITIES: Nightclub, hairdresser, beauty
salon, massage and solarium. Hotel is happy to
assist with reservations/arrangements for the
excellent choice of sightseeing tours and
organised entertainment events.
■ TARIFF: Single 400–982, Double 500–1470,
Bk 100, Set menu 170 (Amex, Euro/Access, Visa).

KARLOVY VARY 22C

Grandhotel Pupp ★★★★★ Mirove namesti 2,
36091 Karlovy Vary, Czech Republic.
Tel 017 209111, Fax 017 3224032. English spoken.
Open all year. 263 bedrooms (all en suite).
Outdoor swimming pool, golf 5 km, parking.

*One of the oldest in Europe, this excellent hotel
enjoys a superb setting. Centrally located in the
verdant valley of the River Tepla, just 5 minutes
from Sprudel hot springs and within half an
hour of the business centre and airport.
Spacious and elegant with friendly service and
modern-day comforts.*

■ RESTAURANT: A choice of excellent restaurants
as well as beer cellar and café.
■ ACTIVITIES: Hotel has casino and health and
fitness centre; offers the chance of sightseeing
trips, social and entertainment events. A good
range of sporting activities nearby.
■ TARIFF: (1996) Single 2550,
Double 3250–7650, Bk 200,
Set menu 270–1000 (Amex, Euro/Access, Visa).

OSTRAVA 22D

Hotel Imperial ★★★★ Tyrsova u 6,
70138 Ostrava, Czech Republic.
Tel 069 236621, Fax 069 6112065. English spoken.
Open all year. 140 bedrooms (all en suite).
Indoor swimming pool, tennis, golf 15 km,
garage, restaurant. (&

*In the centre of the main city of northern
Moravia and only 18 km from the Polish
border.*

■ ACTIVITIES: Trip to Beskydy mountains; visit
the open-air museum.
■ TARIFF: (1996) Single 2200, Double 3400,
Set menu 300–500 (Amex, Visa).

PIESTANY 22C

Hotel Magnolia ★★★
Nalepkova 1, 92101 Piestany, Slovakia.
Tel 083 826251, Fax 083 821149. English spoken.
Open all year. 122 bedrooms (all en suite).
Outdoor swimming pool. (

*In the town centre, on the banks of the River
Váh and Lake Sinava.*

■ RESTAURANT: International cuisine.
■ ACTIVITIES: Casino and fitness room at hotel;
swimming pools with thermal water in town;
advice given on sightseeing tours.
■ TARIFF: (1996) Single 1250, Double 1640,
Bk 100, Set menu 200–300 (Amex,
Euro/Access, Visa).

PRAHA (PRAGUE) 22C

Club Hotel Praha ★★★★
25243 Pruhonice 400, Czech Republic.
Tel 02 677 50868, Fax 02 677 50064.
English spoken.

Open all year. 100 bedrooms (all en suite).
Indoor swimming pool, tennis, golf on site,
parking. (&

*Modern, friendly hotel complex with emphasis
on its sports and dining facilities. Located in a
green belt, 15 km from the centre of Praha
with direct access from exit 6 on the D1 (Wien
to Praha highway).*

■ RESTAURANT: Choose from a fast food
restaurant with national dishes, Mexican food
in the 'Tequilla' or the elegant and more
exclusive 'Club' restaurant. Each restaurant has
a summer terrace.
■ ACTIVITIES: Excellent sporting/fitness facilities
free to hotel guests. Hotel operates a
complimentary shuttle-bus service to Praha,
ideal for shopping and sightseeing trips.
■ TARIFF: Single 2200–3000, Double 2750–3750,
Set menu 200–350 (Amex, Euro/Access, Visa).
■ DISCOUNT: 10%

Hotel Forum ★★★★ Kongresova ulice 1,
14069 Praha 4, Czech Republic.
Tel 02 611 91111, Fax 02 420 684. English spoken.

Open all year. 531 bedrooms (all en suite).
Indoor swimming pool, garage. 📞 ♿

*24-storey, ultra-modern hotel offering every
comfort and facility for both holiday and
business visits alike. Includes multi-purpose
area suitable for conferences, symposia and
banquets. Close to the 11th-century royal castle
'Vysehrad', 2 metro stops from the centre and
just 30 minutes' drive from the airport.*

■ RESTAURANT: Enjoy gourmet cuisine in the
'Harmonie' restaurant, table d'hôte in the 'Ceska'
or lighter meals and snacks in the 'Café Praha'.
■ ACTIVITIES: 'Fitness Forum International' is an
excellent sports/fitness centre at the hotel
which includes a squash hall and sauna;
hairdressing and cosmetic facilities; 'Beer and
Bowling Pub' has 4-lane bowling alley; live
music from 6pm in the 'Lobby Bar' which is
open 24 hrs. Arrangements made for tours,
theatre and opera tickets.
■ TARIFF: (1996) Single 4040–6220,
Double 4590–7060 (Amex, Euro/Access, Visa).

Palace Hotel ★★★★★
Panska 12, 11000 Praha 1, Czech Republic.
Tel 02 240 93111, Fax 02 242 21240. English spoken.
Open all year. 125 bedrooms (all en suite).
Golf 12 km, garage, parking. ♿

*Centrally located hotel offering luxury in art-
nouveau surroundings.*

■ RESTAURANT: Choice of either the award-

winning 'Club' or the 'Café' restaurants.
■ TARIFF: (1996) Single 7540, Double 8900,
Set menu 200–3000 (Amex, Euro/Access, Visa).

Pariz Hotel ★★★★ U Obecniho domu 1,
11000 Praha 1, Czech Republic.
Tel 02 242 22151, Fax 02 242 25475. English spoken.
Open all year. 100 bedrooms (all en suite).
Golf 15 km, garage. 📞

(Prices in US$.)

■ RESTAURANT: Restaurant 'Sarah Bernhardt'
and 'Café de Paris'.
■ TARIFF: (1996) Single 210–220,
Double 250–340 (Amex, Euro/Access, Visa).

Rogner Hotel Don Giovanni ★★★★
Vinohradska 157A, 13061 Praha 3, Czech Republic.
Tel 02 670 31111, Fax 02 670 36704.
English spoken.
Open all year. 400 bedrooms (all en suite).
Golf 10 km, garage, parking. 📞 ♿

*Opened in 1995, this modern, luxury hotel has
a guarded underground car park and is close
to Wenzel Square and the museum. 8 minutes
to centre via metro, which is beside the hotel. 9
conference rooms for up to 200 people.*

■ RESTAURANT: Buffet breakfast/meals plus
national and international à la carte specialities.
■ ACTIVITIES: Special musical events on
Wednesdays, Fridays and Saturdays. Fitness
club with sauna, steam bath, solarium, exercise
room and massage facilities; tennis nearby.
■ TARIFF: Single 4275, Double 5400,
Set menu 300 (Amex, Euro/Access, Visa).
■ DISCOUNT: 5% on request and subject to
availability.

Czech Republic & Slovakia

DENMARK

The grand entrance arch to the Trivoli Gardens, Copenhagen

Arriving at Esbjerg on the Danish west coast, resist the temptation to head straight for Billund and *Legoland*. Denmark is a country of green landscapes and pleasant towns, distributed through her many islands, all ringed around with countless miles of sandy beaches. Mainland Jutland is itself only joined to Germany by a narrow neck of land.

The capital, Copenhagen, though two islands on from Esbjerg, is only one ferry crossing away, the arm of sea between Jutland and Fyn (Denmark's second largest island) being crossed by bridge. Fyn, with more than its fair share of handsome manor houses and gardens, deserves its reputation as the Garden of Denmark and its main town of Odense, birthplace of Hans Christian Andersen, draws many visitors.

Andersen is also remembered in Copenhagen harbour by his Little Mermaid statue. To get the best out of a visit to Copenhagen you should abandon your car and invest in a Copenhagen Card for free entry to over fifty places of interest plus free travel on public transport around the city.

The Viking past is frequently recalled in Denmark: Ladby on Fyn has a ship burial site while Aarhus in Jutland has a museum in the basement of a bank! Ribe, on Jutland's west coast and said to be the country's oldest town, was a Viking trading centre that remained important throughout the Middle Ages: well-preserved houses and a 14th-century church tower to climb for a rewarding view over the surrounding countryside.

Emergency numbers

Police, Fire Brigade and Ambulance 112

Warning information

Warning triangle must be carried

Blood alcohol legal limit 80 mg

ÅLBORG 12A

Hotel Scandic Ålborg
Hadsundvej 200, 9220 Ålborg.
Tel 98 15 45 00, Fax 98 15 55 88. English spoken.

Open all year. 101 bedrooms (all en suite).
Golf 5 km, parking. ℓ ᠕

*Totally renovated in 1996, a comfortable,
modern hotel in large, unspoilt grounds. Off
E45 highway, 10 km from airport, 6 km from
town centre.*

■ RESTAURANT: High standard of French-inspired
cuisine.
■ ACTIVITIES: On-site sports/fitness room with
solarium. ● Up to 20% discount on all golf
courses in the area.
■ TARIFF: Single 595–845, Double 595–945,
Set menu 98–195 (Amex, Euro/Access, Visa).

Hotel Scheelsminde ★★★★
Scheelsmindevej 35, 9000 Ålborg.
Tel 98 18 32 33, Fax 98 18 33 34. English spoken.
Open all year. 74 bedrooms (all en suite).
Indoor swimming pool, golf 8 km, parking. ℓ ᠕

*Dating from the early 1800s, Scheelsminde
was formerly one of Denmark's most beautiful
manor houses. It has been carefully and
tastefully transformed to provide a relaxing
atmosphere with all modern comforts. Set in a
large park, 3 km from the town centre. (Special
rate of DKK 795 for family room incl breakfast
from 15 June to 15 Aug.)*

■ RESTAURANT: Lovely dining room with
stunning panoramic views of the park.
International à la carte cuisine.
■ ACTIVITIES: Billiards, outdoor chess; tennis
2 km. ● 'Oasis' activity centre offers pool,
sauna, solarium, jacuzzi and fitness facilities,
plus light snacks, beverages, beer and wine
free of charge.
■ TARIFF: Single 780–980, Double 980–1280,
Set menu 115 (Amex, Euro/Access, Visa).
■ DISCOUNT: 15% with current membership card.

ÅRHUS 12A

Ansgar Hotel
Banegårdsplads 14, Box 34, 8100 Århus.
Tel 86 12 41 22, Fax 86 20 29 04. English spoken.
Open all year. 170 bedrooms (157 en suite).
Golf 5 km, parking. ℓ

*Modern hotel in the heart of Århus, close to
town hall and the famous concert hall.*

■ RESTAURANT: Offers a wide range of national
and international dishes.
■ TARIFF: (1996) Single 455–590,
Double 585–680 (Euro/Access, Visa).

ESBJERG 12C

Hotel Hermitage ★★★ Soevej 2, 6700 Esbjerg.
Tel 75 13 55 00, Fax 75 13 56 77. English spoken.
Open 01/02 to 20/12. 100 bedrooms
(all en suite). Golf 6 km, parking. ℓ ᠕

*Set in a deer park, this modern, very
comfortable hotel has excellent facilities and is
only minutes from the sea, harbour, town
centre and airport.*

■ RESTAURANT: Very pretty with nice views over
the park. Danish cuisine with seafood specialities.
■ ACTIVITIES: Fitness centre at hotel; visit
Legoland, museums, Sealarium and nearby
coast and marshland. ● Special arrangements
made for green fees at nearby golf course.
■ TARIFF: (1996) Single 570, Double 760,
Set menu 95 (Amex, Euro/Access, Visa).

HADERSLEV 12C

Hotel Norden ★★★★
Storegade 55, 6100 Haderslev.
Tel 74 52 40 30, Fax 74 52 40 25. English spoken.
Open 02/01 to 20/12. 68 bedrooms
(all en suite). Indoor swimming pool,
golf 2 km, parking. ℓ ᠕

*Modern hotel, purpose built to offer every
comfort and facility whether for holidays or
conferences. Excellent location near the old
part of town and beside 'Haderslev Pond'.
Special 2, 3 or 5-day mini-holidays available
on request. Leave E45 at exit 68, take route 47
into the town and hotel is on the right, about
400 m after crossing the bridge.*

■ RESTAURANT: Super views of lake, park and
cathedral. Good Danish cuisine and specialities.
■ ACTIVITIES: At hotel, fitness centre, nightclub;
canoeing and sailing on the lake; paddle
steamer trip on fjord; sightseeing. ● Reduced
green fees at Haderslev golf course.
■ TARIFF: (1996) Single 645, Double 845,
Set menu 145 (Amex, Euro/Access, Visa).

Denmark

KØBENHAVN (COPENHAGEN) 12D

71 Nyhavn Hotel ★★★★
Nyhavn 71, 1051 København.
Tel 33 11 85 85, Fax 33 93 15 85. English spoken.

Open all year. 82 bedrooms (all en suite).
Golf 15 km, parking. ☏

Originally an old warehouse, the hotel has rustic, historic charm. Most of the rooms have spectacular views over the water and all have modern facilities including international television/Filmnet.

■ RESTAURANT: Closed Sun, Jul & 24/12 to 01/01. The restaurant 'Pakhuskaelderens' is well regarded by locals and guests alike and the healthy Danish and French dishes are served by friendly, professional staff.
■ TARIFF: Single 995–1310, Double 1350–1560, Set menu 160–282 (Amex, Euro/Access, Visa).
■ DISCOUNT: 20% except during fairs/conventions.

Hotel Ascot Studiestraede 57, 1554 København V.
Tel 33 12 60 00, Fax 33 14 60 40. English spoken.

Open all year. 145 bedrooms (all en suite).
Golf 10 km, parking. ☏

A former bathhouse, built in classical design with many details having been retained. The hotel is ideally located in central København, next to the Tivoli Gardens and close to the airport link. Accommodation ranges from full suites to studios, some of which have kitchen facilities.

■ ACTIVITIES: Fitness centre, English pub.
■ TARIFF: (1996) Single 790–890, Double 890–1290 (Amex, Euro/Access, Visa).

Hotel Komfort ★★★
Longangstaede 27, 1000 København.
Tel 33 12 65 70, Fax 33 15 28 99. English spoken.
Open 01/01 to 21/12. 201 bedrooms
(all en suite). Garage. ☏

Modern hotel centrally located, just a few steps from the main shopping street, the Tivoli Gardens and town hall square. English-style pub.

■ RESTAURANT: 'Hattehylden' offers traditional Danish cuisine.
■ TARIFF: Single 625–900, Double 875–1200 (Amex, Euro/Access, Visa).

Hotel Mercur ★★★
Vester Farimagsgade, 1000 København.
Tel 33 12 57 11, Fax 33 12 57 17. English spoken.
Open all year. 109 bedrooms (all en suite).
Tennis, golf 10 km. ☏

Elegant and comfortable, hotel is in the heart of København just a few minutes' walk from the air terminal, central railway station, Tivoli Gardens and pedestrian shopping street 'Stroget'.

■ RESTAURANT: Well-known Danish/French restaurant 'Mirabelle' offers a traditional Scandinavian buffet breakfast as well as lunch and dinner.
■ TARIFF: Single 795, Double 955 (Amex, Euro/Access, Visa).
■ DISCOUNT: 15%

Hotel Palace ★★★★
Raadhuspladsen, 1550 København.
Tel 33 14 40 50, Fax 33 14 52 79. English spoken.
Open all year. 162 bedrooms (all en suite).
Golf 7 km. ☎ &

Close to the main shopping street, the hotel overlooks the town hall square and the Tivoli Gardens. 5 minutes from the railway station.
■ RESTAURANT: 'Brasserie on The Square' overlooks the town hall square and offers an excellent carvery buffet and large Danish buffet at lunchtime.
■ ACTIVITIES: City tour by bus.
■ TARIFF: Single 975–1525, Double 1175–1825 (Amex, Euro/Access, Visa).

Hotel Richmond ★★★
Vester Farimagsgade, 1780 København.
Tel 33 12 33 66, Fax 33 12 97 17.

Open all year. 127 bedrooms (all en suite).
Golf 10 km, parking. ☎

Elegant hotel situated in the heart of København and only a few minutes' walk from the air terminal, central railway station, Tivoli Gardens and pedestrian shopping street 'Stroget'.
■ TARIFF: Single 795, Double 955 (Amex, Euro/Access, Visa).
■ DISCOUNT: 15%

KOLDING   12C

Hotel Saxildhus
Banegaardspladsen, 6000 Kolding.
Tel 75 52 12 00, Fax 75 53 53 10. English spoken.
Open all year. 95 bedrooms (all en suite).
Golf 2 km. ☎

Charming old hotel dating from 1905, located in the centre of Kolding by the railway station.
■ RESTAURANT: Cosy cellar restaurant with international cuisine and fish and ostrich specialities; Mexican and buffet restaurants; English pub.
■ ACTIVITIES: New solarium/health and beauty centre at hotel; discount for hotel guests at nearby Slotssøbad Aqua-Park.
■ TARIFF: (1996) Single 345–645, Double 445–745 (Amex, Euro/Access, Visa).
■ DISCOUNT: 20%

NAESTVED   12D

Menstrup Kro
Menstrup Bygade 29, 4700 Menstrup.
Tel 53 74 30 03, Fax 53 74 33 63. English spoken.
Open all year. 80 bedrooms (all en suite).
Indoor swimming pool, tennis, golf 15 km, parking, restaurant. ☎ &

Recently renovated, 200-year-old countryside resort hotel. Conveniently situated for both sightseeing and sporting activities. A one-hour drive from København, between Naestved and Skaelskor.
■ TARIFF: (1996) Single 498–588, Double 688–788, Set menu 90–158 (Amex, Euro/Access, Visa).
■ DISCOUNT: 10%

NYBORG   12D

Hotel Hesselet ★★★★★
Christianslundsvej 119, 5800 Nyborg.
Tel 65 31 30 29, Fax 65 31 29 58. English spoken.

Open 05/01 to 15/12. 46 bedrooms (all en suite). Indoor swimming pool, tennis, golf 3 km, parking. ☎

Nestled amidst beautiful woods right on the sandy shore of Funen, just 5 minutes north of the historic town of Nyborg with a fine view across the Great Belt. 3 minutes from the

Denmark

motorway E20 exit 45. Contact the hotel for English brochure.

■ RESTAURANT: Elegant gourmet restaurant with magnificent views over the sea and the new Great Belt Suspension Bridge. Nouvelle cuisine (seasonal) with fresh fish and seafood.
■ ACTIVITIES: Hunting, off-shore fishing (groups of 12 or more), sandy beach with jetty; natural paths along the beach and in the woods for walking or biking (bikes available at hotel).
■ TARIFF: Single 890–990, Double 1310–1450, Set menu 275–525 (Amex, Euro/Access, Visa).

ODENSE   12D

Blommenslyst Kro
Middelfartvej 420, 5491 Blommenslyst.
Tel 65 96 70 12, Fax 65 96 79 37. English spoken.
Open 02/01 to 22/12. 52 bedrooms
(all en suite). Tennis, golf 2 km, parking. ℓ
Renowned hotel set in peaceful, park-like gardens. 8 km from the centre of Odense and its many attractions. Leave the motorway at exit 53 and drive towards Blommenslyst on the 161.

■ RESTAURANT: Closed 22/12 to 02/01. Well known for its good food and cosy atmosphere.
■ TARIFF: Single 450–560, Double 655–710, Set menu 95–198 (Amex, Euro/Access, Visa).
■ DISCOUNT: 10%

Hotel Scandic
Hvidkaervej 25, 5250 Odense.
Tel 66 17 66 66, Fax 66 17 25 53.
English spoken.
Open all year. 100 bedrooms (all en suite).
Golf 2 km, parking, restaurant. ℓ ♿
■ ACTIVITIES: Swimming pool nearby.
■ TARIFF: (1996) Single 695–845,
Double 695–945 (Amex, Euro/Access, Visa).

SORØ   12D

Sorø Storkro ★★★★ Abildvej 100, 4180 Sorø.
Tel 53 63 56 00, Fax 53 63 56 06. English spoken.

Open 02/01 to 20/12. 94 bedrooms
(all en suite). Indoor swimming pool,
golf 2 km, parking. ℓ ♿
Ultra-modern, thatched hotel in a lovely location overlooking Lake Pedersborg. Every comfort and excellent amenities. Take exit 37 from E20.

■ RESTAURANT: Most attractive dining room with some lovely lake views. Specialises in top quality Danish cuisine.
■ ACTIVITIES: Pool complex with very good facilities including children's pool and jacuzzi; recreation room, library and nightclub. Fishing and canoeing at nearby lakes; touring and visiting the Great Belt Suspension Bridge.
● Special arrangements made for green fees at Sorø Golf Club.
■ TARIFF: Single 725, Double 925, Set menu 150 (Amex, Euro/Access, Visa).
■ DISCOUNT: 15%

SVENDBORG   12D

Hotel Tre Roser Faborgvej 90, 5700 Svendborg.
Tel 62 21 64 26, Fax 62 21 15 26. English spoken.

Open all year. 70 bedrooms (all en suite).
Outdoor swimming pool, golf 2 km, parking. ℓ ♿
Modern, comfortable hotel approx 2 km from the idyllic port of Svendborg and 5 km from the nearest beach. Attractive gardens. Apartments for up to 4 persons also available.

■ RESTAURANT: Pretty dining room with good food.
■ ACTIVITIES: Billiards, table tennis, sauna, solarium.
■ TARIFF: Single 405, Double 515, Bk 55, Set menu 105 (Amex, Euro/Access, Visa).

FRANCE

Canal du Midi, Sète

Whether beach, mountain or river holiday, wine drinking tour or gourmet binge, France has it all.

The longest beach in Europe stretches 250 km along the Atlantic Coast, from the mouth of the Gironde in the north to Biarritz, close to the Spanish border, in the south. The highest cable car station in Europe looks out over Mont Blanc in the French Alps, while the mountains of the Massif Central, formed by volcanic action, offer curiosities like hot springs at Chaudes-Aigues.

The great rivers of France, used until the last century as the main arteries of trade, today introduce visitors to the great châteaux of the Loire, the troglodyte cave dwellings of the Dordogne, or the wild and wonderful canoeing on the Ardèche.

In Provence, in the south – so called because it was once a province of the Roman empire – there are buildings in Arles, Orange and Nîmes still standing 1500 years after Barbarian invaders brought five centuries of Roman rule to an end.

But if Northern France is your choice for a mini-break… after Paris, discover historic Arras, or Rouen, where the old town is much as it was 500 years ago. Or walk the limestone tunnels beneath the Champagne city of Rheims.

Emergency numbers

Police 17

Fire Brigade 18

Ambulance Use number shown in call box or phone police

Warning information

Carrying a warning triangle recommended

Blood Alcohol Legal Limit 50 mg

ABBEVILLE Somme 2B

Hôtel de France ★★
19 place du Pilori, 80100 Abbeville.
Tel 03 22 24 00 42, Fax 03 22 24 26 15.
English spoken.

Open all year. 69 bedrooms (all en suite).
Golf 3 km, garage, parking. ☎ ♿

Situated near a pretty park with flowers and a stream. Hotel is peaceful and relaxing whilst being only 2 minutes from the pedestrian area in the heart of the city. Comfortable accommodation; suite with jacuzzi available. Abbeville is 15 km from the sea, halfway between Calais and Paris (N1).

■ RESTAURANT: Restaurant specialises in regional and roasted dishes. Terrace rôtisserie with a view over the square. Children's menu available.
■ ACTIVITIES: Ideal base for sightseeing. ● Day trips by bike free of charge for RAC members on advanced bookings, discounts on green fees.
■ TARIFF: Single 199–290, Double 254–340, Bk 40, Set menu 69–100 (Amex, Euro/Access, Visa).
■ DISCOUNT: 10% excluding suites.

Hôtel Jean de Bruges ★★★
18 place de l'Eglise, 80135 St-Riquier.
Tel 03 22 28 30 30, Fax 03 22 28 00 69.
English spoken.

Open 01/01 to 15/12 & 01/03 to 31/12.
8 bedrooms (all en suite). Golf 6 km, garage. ☎ ♿

17th-century white stone mansion, completely renovated in the original style. Cosy atmosphere, peaceful and very good service. 8 km north-east of Abbeville on the D941 towards Arras. On the market place of this small medieval town.

■ ACTIVITIES: Hunting, fishing; bicycles available at hotel.
■ TARIFF: Single 400–500, Double 500–600, Bk 50 (Euro/Access, Visa).

AGDE Hérault 5C

Hôtel Azur ★★ 18 av Illes d'Amérique,
Le Cap d'Agde, 34305 Agde.
Tel 04 67 26 98 22, Fax 04 67 26 48 14.
English spoken.

Open all year. 34 bedrooms (all en suite). Outdoor swimming pool, golf on site, garage, parking. ♿

Hotel is at Cap d'Agde just 400 m from Plage Richelieu, 50 m from the marina and 100 m from the golf course. Restaurant 50 m from hotel. Special group discounts. English satellite television in all rooms. Free private parking.

■ ACTIVITIES: Sauna and games room at hotel; 100 m from Aqualand.
■ TARIFF: Single 200–350, Double 250–400, Bk 32 (Amex, Euro/Access, Visa).
■ DISCOUNT: 10% Oct to Apr, min stay 4 days.

Hôtel La Tamarissière ★★★
lieu-dit La Tamarissière, 34300 Agde.
Tel 04 67 94 20 87, Fax 04 67 21 38 40.
English spoken.
Open 15/03 to 31/12. 27 bedrooms (all en suite).
Outdoor swimming pool, golf 8 km, parking.

Overlooking the Hérault estuary and tiny fishing port. Pretty bedrooms with balconies; pretty garden.

■ RESTAURANT: Closed Sun eve & Mon.

Renowned for its excellent cuisine including tempting Languedoc dishes. Dining room has panoramic view of river; meals can be taken on shady terrace in fine weather.

- TARIFF: (1996) Single 400–620, Double 440–620, Bk 65, Set menu 149–350 (Amex, Euro/Access, Visa).

AIGUES-MORTES   Gard   5D

Hôtel des Croisades ★★
2 rue du Port, 30220 Aigues-Mortes.
Tel 04 66 53 67 85, Fax 04 66 53 72 95.
Open 16/02 to 14/11 & 16/12 to 14/01.
14 bedrooms (all en suite). Golf 6 km, garage, parking. &

The hotel overlooks the fortified town and the port of Aigues-Mortes.

- ACTIVITIES: Tennis, horse-riding and water sports nearby.
- TARIFF: (1996) Single 240–260, Double 240–320, Bk 31 (Euro/Access, Visa).

AIX-EN-PROVENCE   Bches-du-Rhône   5D

Domaine de Châteauneuf ★★★★
au Logis de Nans, 83860 Nans-les-Pins.
Tel 04 94 78 90 06, Fax 04 94 78 63 30.
English spoken.
Open 01/03 to 30/11. 30 bedrooms (all en suite). Outdoor swimming pool, tennis, golf on site, parking.

19th-century country house set on a golf course with its own helipad. A8/E80 motorway exit St-Maximin, N560, D80 south.

- RESTAURANT: Closed Mon LS. Charming restaurant offering specialities of bouillabaisse en gelée au safran, pigeonneau rôti et son jus aux épices douces and truffes glacées avec sauce au miel.
- ACTIVITIES: ● Special half-board golf package available on request.
- TARIFF: (1996) Single 580–675, Double 620–1200, Bk 75, Set menu 170–380 (Amex, Euro/Access, Visa).

Hôtel Mas d'Entremont ★★★★
Montée d'Avignon, 13090 Aix-en-Provence.
Tel 04 42 17 42 42, Fax 04 42 21 15 83.
English spoken.
Open 15/03 to 01/11. 18 bedrooms (17 en suite). Outdoor swimming pool, tennis, golf 10 km, parking. &

Set in lovely parkland, comfortable, air-conditioned hotel with lots of antiques. 4 km north of Aix on the N7 towards Avignon.

- RESTAURANT: Closed Sun eve & Mon lunch.
- TARIFF: (1996) Single 550–630,

Double 640–840, Bk 70, Set menu 200–230 (Euro/Access, Visa).

Hôtel Le Pigonnet ★★★★
5 av Pigonnet, 13090 Aix-en-Provence.
Tel 04 42 59 02 90, Fax 04 42 59 47 77.
English spoken.
Open 01/01 to 30/12. 52 bedrooms (all en suite). Outdoor swimming pool, golf 8 km, parking.

Beautiful old hotel once beloved of Cézanne. Family run, with sun terrace, gardens and fountains, close to centre of Aix but in a peaceful location.

- RESTAURANT: Closed Sat & Sun lunch. Attractive décor, gourmet and local dishes. Meals served on a shady terrace in summer.
- ACTIVITIES: Jogging track, tennis and horse-riding nearby.
- TARIFF: Single 500–850, Double 700–1500, Bk 65, Set menu 250–320 (Amex, Euro/Access, Visa).
- DISCOUNT: 10% by prior reservation & not Jul.

Grand Hôtel Roi René ★★★★
24 bd du Roi René, 13100 Aix-en-Provence.
Tel 04 42 37 61 00, Fax 04 42 37 61 11.
English spoken.

Open all year. 134 bedrooms (all en suite). Outdoor swimming pool, garage. ✆ &

Recently built in Provençal style, hotel is ideally situated in the heart of the city, close to the Mazarin area with its 17th-century buildings and monuments. Very comfortable accommodation; warm, friendly atmosphere and pretty tropical gardens.

- RESTAURANT: Attractive restaurant with terrace where meals can be taken in summer. Has a good reputation for its fine traditional and Provençal cuisine.
- ACTIVITIES: Organised tours of the town available through Tourist Office.
- TARIFF: (1996) Single 590, Double 730–880, Bk 70, Set menu 165 (Amex, Euro/Access, Visa).

AIX-LES-BAINS Savoie   6A

Résidence Hôtel Les Loges du Park ★★★
rue Jean-Louis Victor Bias, BP 525,
73105 Aix-les-Bains Cedex.
Tel 04 79 35 74 74, Fax 04 79 35 74 00.
English spoken.

Open all year. 71 bedrooms (all en suite).
Indoor swimming pool, golf 2 km, garage,
parking. ☎ &

*Set in parkland, accommodation consists of
modern, light and airy apartments and
studios, each with its own terrace and
accommodating from 2 to 4 persons. Excellent
service and facilities.*

■ RESTAURANT: Integrated with the Park Hotel du
Casino. Special arrangements made for half or
full board with the 'Brasserie du Parc'.
■ ACTIVITIES: Golf, boating, cycling, water
sports; winter sports.
■ TARIFF: Single 215–325, Double 369–545,
Bk 61, Set menu 118 (Amex,
Euro/Access, Visa).

Park Hôtel ★★★★ av Charles de Gaulle, BP
525, 73105 Aix-les-Bains.
Tel 04 79 34 19 19, Fax 04 79 88 11 49.
English spoken.

Open all year. 102 bedrooms (all en suite).
Indoor swimming pool, golf 2 km, garage,
parking. ☎ &

*Situated in large leisure complex on the shore of
Lake Bourget. Excellent facilities. Apartments
and suites are also available. At crossroads of
Lyons, Genève and Turin motorways.*

■ RESTAURANT: Gourmet restaurant 'La Symphonie'
and café-restaurant 'Brasserie du Parc'. Fine
cuisine in modern, elegant surroundings.
■ ACTIVITIES: Golf, tennis, horse-riding, sailing,
water-skiing, boating, walking, skiing, snow
trekking.
■ TARIFF: Single 520–710, Double 620–810, Bk 68,
Set menu 78–120 (Amex, Euro/Access, Visa).
■ DISCOUNT: 15%

ALBERT Somme   2B

Hôtel Le Royal Picardie ★★★
av du Général Leclerc, 80300 Albert.
Tel 03 22 75 37 00, Fax 03 22 75 60 19.
English spoken.

Open all year. 23 bedrooms (all en suite).
Tennis, golf 15 km, parking. ☎ &

*Purpose built to offer every comfort in
stunning, contemporary surroundings.*

■ RESTAURANT: Closed Sun eve. A choice of
extremely pretty, light and airy dining rooms.
Gastronomic cuisine, invitingly presented.
■ TARIFF: (1996) Single 260, Double 290, Bk 35,
Set menu 78–240 (Amex, Euro/Access, Visa).

ALBI Tarn   5C

Hôtel Mercure Albi Bastides ★★★
41 rue Porta, 81000 Albi.
Tel 05 63 47 66 66, Fax 05 63 46 18 40.
English spoken.
Open all year. 56 bedrooms (all en suite).
Golf 2 km, parking. &

Former mill on the River Tarn, facing the cathedral. Completely renovated in 1994, the hotel has every modern comfort including rooms with river views and air conditioning. Follow 'Moulins Albigeois' signs.

■ RESTAURANT: Closed Sun lunch & Sat. Regional specialities. Meals are served on the terrace in summer.

■ ACTIVITIES: ● The hotel offers one free entry to the Toulouse Lautrec Museum.

■ TARIFF: Single 350–460, Double 350–530, Bk 55, Set menu 100–130 (Amex, Euro/Access, Visa).

ALENCON Orne 2C

Hôtel Dauphin ★★
rte Alençon, 53370 St-Pierre-des-Nids.
Tel 02 43 03 52 12, Fax 02 43 03 55 49.
English spoken.

Open all year. 9 bedrooms (7 en suite).
Golf 20 km, parking.

Highly recommended small inn in a pretty village. St-Pierre-des-Nids is on D121, 12 km from Alençon.

■ RESTAURANT: Excellent cuisine using local produce. Seafood specialities.
■ TARIFF: Single 155–215, Double 245–275, Bk 35, Set menu 95–265 (Euro/Access, Visa).

ALTKIRCH Haut-Rhin 3D

Hôtel La Terrasse ★★
44-46 rue du 3ème Zouave, 68130 Altkirch.
Tel 03 89 40 98 02, Fax 03 89 08 82 92.
English spoken.
Open 01/03 to 31/10. 19 bedrooms (4 en suite, 9 bath/shower only). Golf 15 km, garage, parking. ㅎ

Delightful overnight accommodation in quiet country area outside town, close to St-Morand hospital. Ideal for touring; 30 km from Basle.

■ TARIFF: Single 140–230, Double 140–250,

Bk 25 (Amex, Euro/Access, Visa).
■ DISCOUNT: 20%

AMBOISE Indre/Loire 2C

Hôtel Le Choiseul ★★★★
36 quai Ch Guinot, 37400 Amboise.
Tel 02 47 30 45 45, Fax 02 47 30 46 10.
English spoken.
Open 20/01 to 25/11. 32 bedrooms (all en suite). Outdoor swimming pool, golf 20 km, garage, parking. ㅌ ㅎ

A charming 18th-century house set in a valley between hills and the River Loire. The rooms and apartments are elegantly decorated and extremely comfortable. Lovely gardens. On D751.

■ RESTAURANT: Very pretty dining room with panoramic views of the river and gardens. Has earned a good reputation for its regional specialities and fine Touraine wines.
■ ACTIVITIES: Boating, fishing, horse-riding, tennis, archery and pleasure trips by plane, balloon or helicopter are possible nearby. Lots of châteaux and museums to visit.
■ TARIFF: Double 600–1650, Bk 85, Set menu 250–440 (Amex, Euro/Access, Visa).
■ DISCOUNT: 8%

AMELIE-LES-BAINS Pyrénées Orient 5C

Hôtel Castel Emeraude ★★
route de la Corniche, Petit Provence, 66110 Amélie-les-Bains.
Tel 04 68 39 02 83, Fax 04 68 39 03 09.
English spoken.
Open 01/02 to 30/11. 59 bedrooms (all en suite). Golf 1 km, parking. ㅎ

In a verdant riverbank setting with panoramic views. Excellent opportunity to discover the Vallespir area. On D115 just south of Céret.

■ RESTAURANT: Fine cuisine and vintage wines.
■ TARIFF: Double 230–360, Bk 40, Set menu 90–290 (Amex, Euro/Access, Visa).
■ DISCOUNT: 10% minimum 3-night stay.

AMIENS Somme 2B

Novotel ★★★ route de Roye, 80440 Boves.
Tel 03 22 46 22 22, Fax 03 22 53 94 75.
English spoken.
Open all year. 94 bedrooms (all en suite).
Outdoor swimming pool, golf 10 km, parking, restaurant. ㅎ

Quiet, modern hotel with a garden area. On D934 with easy access from city centre. Follow Longueau or 'Paris A1 par Autoroute' signs.

■ TARIFF: (1996) Single 410–430, Double 450–470, Bk 51 (Amex, Euro/Access, Visa).

France

ANCY-LE-FRANC Yonne   3C

Hostellerie du Centre ★★
34 Grande rue, 89160 Ancy-le-Franc.
Tel 03 86 75 15 11, Fax 03 86 75 14 13.
English spoken.
Open all year. 22 bedrooms (all en suite).
Indoor swimming pool, outdoor swimming
pool, golf 8 km, garage, parking. ℓ ₰
*Friendly and pleasant, hotel stands the château
square. Good base from which to tour the region.*
■ RESTAURANT: The proprietor is also the chef
and offers an imaginative Bourguignonne menu.
■ ACTIVITIES: Visits to the château and vineyards;
walking in the Morvan mountains.
■ TARIFF: (1996) Single 195, Double 250–300,
Bk 40, Set menu 78–260 (Amex,
Euro/Access, Visa).

ANGERS Maine/Loire   2C

Hôtel du Mail ★★
8 rue des Ursules, 49100 Angers.
Tel 02 41 88 56 22, Fax 02 41 86 91 20.
English spoken.

Open all year. 28 bedrooms (25 en suite, 3 bath/
shower only). Indoor swimming pool, outdoor
swimming pool, tennis, golf 6 km, parking.
*Pretty 17th-century hotel quietly situated in
heart of the city, offering warm atmosphere
and quality service. Easy access from A11 (exit
Angers-Centre) and TGV.*
■ TARIFF: (1996) Single 150–240, Double 180–
295, Bk 31 (Amex, Euro/Access, Visa).

Hôtel Le Progrès ★★
26 rue Denis Papin, 49100 Angers.
Tel 02 41 88 10 14, Fax 02 41 87 82 93.
English spoken.
Open all year. 40 bedrooms (all en suite).
Golf 5 km, garage, parking. ℓ
*Recently renovated town centre hotel, close to
railway station and within walking distance of*

*the château. Well placed for a night out in one
of the many restaurants.*
■ TARIFF: Single 200–270, Double 250–320,
Bk 39 (Amex, Euro/Access, Visa).
■ DISCOUNT: 10%

ANGOULEME Charente   4B

Hôtel Orée des Bois ★★
Maison Neuve, 16410 Angoulême.
Tel 05 45 24 94 38, Fax 05 45 24 97 51.
English spoken.
Open all year. 7 bedrooms (all en suite).
Outdoor swimming pool, golf 8 km, garage,
parking. ℓ ₰
*In a tranquil setting of forest and countryside,
with rooms overlooking the flower garden.
15 km from Angoulême on the D25.*
■ RESTAURANT: Closed Sun eve & Mon LS.
Restaurant has a good reputation for its fine
cuisine, using only fresh, local produce.
Specialities include home-made foie gras and
seafood dishes.
■ ACTIVITIES: Cellar visits; 3-day 'discovery' stay
which includes cookery lessons. ● Free
mountain bikes available from hotel.
■ TARIFF: Single 200–250, Double 250–280,
Bk 40, Set menu 95–250 (Euro/Access, Visa).
■ DISCOUNT: 5%

ANNECY Haute-Savoie   6A

Hôtel d'Alery ★★ 5 av d'Aléry, 74000 Annecy.
Tel 04 50 45 24 75, Fax 04 50 51 26 90.
English spoken.
Open all year. 22 bedrooms (all en suite).
Golf 8 km, garage, parking. ℓ
*Quiet hotel close to the old town and just 5
minutes' walk from the lake. Soundproofed
rooms decorated in typical Savoyard style.*
■ ACTIVITIES: Hiking and sightseeing.
■ TARIFF: Single 190–295, Double 240–370,
Bk 38 (Amex, Euro/Access, Visa).
■ DISCOUNT: 8%

Hôtel Arcalod ★★ Doussard, 74210 Bout-du-Lac.
Tel 04 50 44 30 22, Fax 04 50 44 85 03.
English spoken.
Open 15/02 to 15/10. 33 bedrooms
(all en suite). Outdoor swimming pool,
golf 3 km, garage, parking. ℓ ₰
*Family-run hotel in unspoilt countryside, 1 km
from Lake Annecy. Doussard is on N508
between Annecy and Albertville.*
■ RESTAURANT: Closed 15/02 to 15/04. Regional
specialities: terrine de canard, filet de féra,
parfait chartreux.

■ ACTIVITIES: Very good sporting activities nearby as well as helicopter trips, mountain-hiking, hang-gliding and archery. ● Free mountain bikes for RAC members.
■ TARIFF: (1996) Single 250–350, Double 250–450, Bk 45, Set menu 90–150 (Amex, Euro/Access, Visa).
■ DISCOUNT: 10% LS.

Hôtel Faisan Doré ★★★
34 av Albigny, 74000 Annecy.
Tel 04 50 23 02 46, Fax 04 50 23 11 10.
English spoken.

Open 25/01 to 12/12. 40 bedrooms (all en suite). Golf 15 km, garage, parking.

1 km from the old town of Annecy and 100 m from the lake, casino and beach. From the centre of Annecy follow directions to the 'Impérial' and Thônes.

■ RESTAURANT: Closed Sun eve LS. Traditional restaurant offering specialities of fresh lake fish and Savoyard dishes.
■ ACTIVITIES: Water sports on the doorstep in summer, winter sports within easy reach. Coach tours depart from the hotel in summer.
■ TARIFF: (1996) Single 300–400, Double 350–500, Bk 45, Set menu 140–200 (Euro/Access, Visa).

ANTIBES Alpes-Marit   6D
Manoir Castel Garoupe Axa ★★★
959 bd de la Garoupe, 06600 Cap d'Antibes.
Tel 04 93 61 36 51, Fax 04 93 67 74 88.
English spoken.

Open 15/03 to 04/11. 27 bedrooms (all en suite). Outdoor swimming pool, tennis, golf 5 km, parking.

Comfortable hotel with a range of accommodation to suite all tastes. Situated in the centre of Cap d'Antibes with terraces and very pretty gardens. Take N98 11 km from Cannes toward Antibes. The hotel is on the boulevard de la Garoupe which follows the coastline.

■ RESTAURANT: Closed Closed until 8 May 1997.
■ ACTIVITIES: Ideal location for touring the surrounding area; all water sports nearby.
■ TARIFF: Single 500–710, Double 650–800 (Amex, Euro/Access, Visa).

APT Vaucluse   5D
Auberge du Lubéron ★★★
17 quai Léon Sagy, 84400 Apt.
Tel 04 90 74 12 50, Fax 04 90 04 79 49.
English spoken.
Open 19/01 to 01/07 & 08/07 to 01/01.
15 bedrooms (all en suite). Garage, parking. ℂ

Quiet hotel near town centre, with lovely views over Apt and the River Calavon. In the Lubéron Regional Park and 50 km from Avignon.

■ RESTAURANT: Closed Mon lunch. Fine food, based on fresh, quality products. Meals can be enjoyed on the pretty terrace overlooking the town and river.
■ ACTIVITIES: ● 6 days (5 nights) half-board organised tour 'Discovering Lubéron' includes visits to châteaux, museums, vineyards and many other beautiful sites in Provence/1700 FF per person.
■ TARIFF: (1996) Single 235–390, Double 235–490, Bk 45, Set menu 130–340 (Amex, Euro/Access, Visa).

France

ARGELES-SUR-MER Pyrénées Orient 5C

Hôtel La Belle Demeure ★★★
chemin du Roua, 66700 Argelès-sur-Mer.
Tel 04 68 95 85 85, Fax 04 68 95 83 50.
English spoken.

Open 01/03 to 30/11. 10 bedrooms
(all en suite). Outdoor swimming pool,
golf 7 km, parking. ℄ ♿

*A tastefully restored 17th-century mill nestling
between mountains and sea in the luxuriant
wine country of the Languedoc-Roussillon. The
air-conditioned rooms have lovely views over
the mountains, the vineyards or the garden.
2 km from the sea. From the centre of Argelès,
go towards the railway station.*

■ RESTAURANT: Typical Catalan cuisine served in
the rustic dining room. Grills and meals can be
taken beside the pool in summer.
■ ACTIVITIES: Table tennis, mountain-biking.
■ TARIFF: Double 390–530, Bk 40-75,
Set menu 140–240 (Amex, Euro/Access, Visa).
■ DISCOUNT: 10%

ARGENTAN Orne 2C

Hôtel Faisan Doré ★★
Fontenai-sur-Orne, 61200 Argentan.
Tel 02 33 67 18 11, Fax 02 33 35 82 15.
English spoken.
Open 01/01 to 15/02 & 01/03 to 31/12.
15 bedrooms (all en suite). Golf 10 km, parking. ℄

*A pretty, half-timbered inn with landscaped
gardens, on the road to Flers.*

■ RESTAURANT: Closed Sun eve. 'Norman Inn'
offers regional specialities including marbré de
foie gras aux pommes and boeuf ficelle et sa
crème de camembert.
■ ACTIVITIES: Children's playground and
billiards; tennis and horse-riding nearby.
■ TARIFF: (1996) Single 265–300,
Double 315–350, Bk 40, Set menu 95–290
(Amex, Euro/Access, Visa).
■ DISCOUNT: 10%

Hôtel Renaissance ★★
20 av 2e-Division-Blindée, 61200 Argentan.
Tel 02 33 36 14 20, Fax 02 33 36 65 50.
English spoken.
Open all year. 11 bedrooms (all en suite).
Golf 15 km, garage, parking. ℄

In the town centre.

■ RESTAURANT: Closed Sun eve. Traditional
cuisine. Dining room overlooks a flower-filled
garden.
■ TARIFF: (1996) Double 227–345, Bk 33,
Set menu 82–238 (Euro/Access, Visa).

ARGENTAT Corrèze 5A

Hôtel Lac ★★ 19430 Camps.
Tel 05 55 28 51 83, Fax 05 55 28 53 71.
English spoken.

Open all year. 11 bedrooms (10 en suite).
Tennis, parking. ♿

*Modern, good value Logis hotel; nearby chalets
also available. From Argentat, south on the
D120, then right on the D41 to Camps, about
20 km from Argentat.*

■ RESTAURANT: Closed Sun eve & Mon LS.
■ ACTIVITIES: Hiking, fishing.
■ TARIFF: Single 210, Double 230, Bk 28,
Set menu 70–210 (Euro/Access, Visa).
■ DISCOUNT: 5% Jul & Aug; 10% in LS.

ARGENTON-SUR-CREUSE Indre 4B

Manoir de Boisvillers ★★
11 rue Moulin de Bord,
36200 Argenton-sur-Creuse.
Tel 02 54 24 13 88, Fax 02 54 24 27 83.
English spoken.
Open 09/01 to 03/12. 14 bedrooms
(13 en suite, 1 bath/shower only). Outdoor
swimming pool, golf 20 km, garage, parking.

*In the heart of Argenton, an 18th-century
manor situated on the river in an area steeped*

France

*in Roman history. Very quiet and charming.
Fully equipped, personalised rooms.*
- TARIFF: (1996) Single 200–280, Double 240–
380, Bk 40 (Amex, Euro/Access, Visa).
- DISCOUNT: 8% LS only.

Château de Bouesse 36200 Bouesse.
Tel 02 54 25 12 20, Fax 02 54 25 12 30.
English spoken.

Open 15/03 to 15/11. 11 bedrooms
(all en suite). Golf 25 km, parking.

*Medieval château three hours south of Paris on
the N20 and a few minutes east of Argenton-
sur-Creuse on the D927. Formerly the fortress
home of one of Joan of Arc's top generals, the
castle is being painstakingly restored by an
English couple.*
- RESTAURANT: Closed Mon & Tue LS. Attractive
dining room with 17th-century panelling. Home-
made foie gras and fresh salmon delicacies.
- ACTIVITIES: Cycle and hiking trails right on the
doorstep.
- TARIFF: (1996) Double 350–480, Bk 55,
Set menu 160–190 (Amex, Euro/Access, Visa).

ARLES Bouches-du-Rhône   5D

Hôtel d'Arlatan ★★★
26 rue Sauvage, 13200 Arles.

Tel 04 90 93 56 66, Fax 04 90 49 68 45.
English spoken.
Open all year. 40 bedrooms (all en suite).
Golf 15 km, garage.

*15th-century mansion with Roman relics,
courtyard and garden. On the east bank of the
Rhône. Leave N113 at Nouveau-Pont.*
- TARIFF: (1996) Single 465–560, Double 465–
695, Bk 60 (Amex, Euro/Access, Visa).

Hôtel Calendal ★★
22 place Pomme, 13200 Arles.
Tel 04 90 96 11 89, Fax 04 90 96 05 84.
English spoken.
Open all year. 27 bedrooms (all en suite).
Parking. &

*Charming hotel with garden shaded by century-
old trees. Rooms are tastefully decorated in
Provençal style. Between 'les Arènes' (the bull-
ring) and 'le Théâtre Antique'.*
- RESTAURANT: Lights meals served in the garden
or in the dining room with fireplace.
- ACTIVITIES: 4x4 tour of the Camargue; organised
excursions can be booked by the hotel.
- TARIFF: Single 250–380, Double 250–460,
Bk 36 (Amex, Euro/Access, Visa).
- DISCOUNT: 20% LS only.

Auberge La Fenière ★★★
RN 453/BP 15, 13280 Raphèle-lès-Arles.
Tel 04 90 98 47 44, Fax 04 90 98 48 39.
English spoken.
Open all year. 25 bedrooms (all en suite).
Golf 15 km, garage, parking. &

*Overlooking the grasslands of La Crau, ideally
located for sightseeing trips. From Arles centre,
go towards Raphèle for 5 km on the N453.*
- RESTAURANT: Closed 10/11 to 20/12. Offers
refined, traditional cuisine.
- TARIFF: (1996) Single 307–363,
Double 363–640, Bk 47, Set menu 170–250
(Amex, Euro/Access, Visa).
- DISCOUNT: 5%

ARMENTIERES Nord   2B

Hôtel Albert 1er ★★
28 rue Robert Schuman, 59280 Armentières.
Tel 03 20 77 31 02, Fax 03 20 77 05 16.
English spoken.
Open all year. 21 bedrooms (all en suite).
Garage, parking.

*Small hotel in a quiet street near the town
centre and station.*
- TARIFF: (1996) Single 165–250,
Double 185–270, Bk 30 (Euro/Access, Visa).
- DISCOUNT: 10%

France

ARRAS Pas-de-Calais   2B

Hôtel Les 3 Luppars ★★
49 Grand'Place, 62000 Arras.
Tel 03 21 07 41 41, Fax 03 21 24 24 80.
English spoken.

Open all year. 42 bedrooms (all en suite).
Golf 2 km, parking. ☎ ♿
*Sympathetically restored and tastefully
decorated 15th-century house. In the centre of
Arras, famous for its history and fine arts.
From Lille, south on the D925 to Lens, then
N17 south to Arras.*

■ ACTIVITIES: Sauna at hotel; guided tours, visits
to museums and nearby abbeys.
■ DISCOUNT: 10%

ARROMANCHES-LES-BAINS Calvados 2A

Hôtel Victoria ★★
24 chemin de l'Eglise, 14117 Tracy-sur-Mer.
Tel 02 31 22 35 37, Fax 02 31 21 41 66.
English spoken.

Open 01/04 to 30/09. 14 bedrooms
(all en suite). Golf 7 km, parking. ☎ ♿
Renovated 19th-century manor house. Set in

*parkland with lovely gardens, 2 km from
Arromanches, towards Bayeux. Breakfast is
offered to RAC members when paying full
room rate (not public holidays); restaurant
specialising in fish and seafood nearby.*

■ ACTIVITIES: Children's playground; 5 minutes
from beach; tennis and D-Day museum nearby.
■ TARIFF: (1996) Single 260–350,
Double 280–490, Bk 40 (Euro/Access, Visa).

AURILLAC Cantal   5A

Auberge de la Tomette ★★ 15220 Vitrac.
Tel 04 71 64 70 94, Fax 04 71 64 77 11.
English spoken.
Open 01/04 to 31/12. 21 bedrooms (all en suite).
Outdoor swimming pool, golf 14 km. ♿
*A charming, friendly hotel in lovely
countryside. 25 km south of Aurillac, Vitrac is
a small village amongst the hills. From Aurillac
N122 south then left on to D66 to Vitrac.*

■ RESTAURANT: Traditional and regional cuisine.
■ ACTIVITIES: Cycling, canoeing and walking.
■ TARIFF: Single 230–280, Double 230–310, Bk 40,
Set menu 70–185 (Amex, Euro/Access, Visa).

AUXERRE Yonne   2D

Hôtel Soleil d'Or ★★
3 N77, 89230 Montigny-la-Resle.
Tel 03 86 41 81 21, Fax 03 86 41 86 88.
English spoken.
Open all year. 16 bedrooms (all en suite).
Indoor swimming pool, tennis, parking. ♿
*On the N77, next to the church in the middle of
the village.*

■ RESTAURANT: Elegant, bright dining room with
lots of flowers and a fountain. Specialities are
fresh foie gras with exotic fruits, gently fried in
a caramel sauce; filet of sea bream in crayfish
sauce; suckling pig with honey and seasonal
game dishes.
■ TARIFF: (1996) Single 195–265,
Double 195–295, Bk 35, Set menu 95–320
(Amex, Euro/Access, Visa).
■ DISCOUNT: 5%

AVIGNON Vaucluse   5D

Hôtel Cloître St-Louis ★★★★
20 rue Portail Boquier, 84000 Avignon.
Tel 04 90 27 55 55, Fax 04 90 82 24 01.
English spoken.
Open all year. 80 bedrooms (all en suite).
Outdoor swimming pool, parking. ☎ ♿
*An oasis of tranquillity, ideally located in the
heart of Avignon.*

■ RESTAURANT: Closed Sat & Sun. Traditional and regional cuisine including croustillant de saumon à l'oseille and crème brûlée à l'orange et sa tuile.
■ ACTIVITIES: Visit the Palais des Papes, the Avignon bridge and the Lubéron.
■ TARIFF: (1996) Double 450–820, Bk 65, Set menu 99–180 (Amex, Euro/Access, Visa).

Hôtel La Ferme ★★ chemin des Bois, Ile de la Barthelasse, 84000 Avignon.
Tel 04 90 82 57 53, Fax 04 90 27 15 47.
Open 01/03 to 31/10. 20 bedrooms (all en suite). Outdoor swimming pool, parking. &

Situated on an island on the Rhône. Take the road to Pont-Daladier (towards Villeneuve), turn right on to D228 and hotel is 5 km.

■ RESTAURANT: Closed Sat lunch.
■ TARIFF: (1996) Single 320–350, Double 350–430, Bk 48 (Amex, Euro/Access, Visa).

AVRANCHES Manche   1D

Hôtel Les Abricantes ★★ 37 bd du Luxembourg, 50300 Avranches.
Tel 02 33 58 66 64, Fax 02 33 58 40 11.
English spoken.
Open 10/01 to 20/12. 29 bedrooms (all en suite). Parking. &

In the centre of Avranche with superb views of Mont-St-Michel, which is 20 km away on the opposite side of the bay.

■ RESTAURANT: Closed 27/12 to 08/01. Traditional cuisine with seafood specialities.
■ ACTIVITIES: Horse-riding in the bay of Mont-St-Michel.
■ TARIFF: (1996) Single 260–290, Double 270–350, Bk 35, Set menu 66–96 (Euro/Access, Visa).

BAGNERES-DE-LUCHON Hte-Garonne 4D

Hôtel Panoramic ★★
6 av Carnot, 31110 Luchon.
Tel 05 61 79 30 90, Fax 05 61 79 32 84.
English spoken.
Open all year. 30 bedrooms (26 en suite).
Golf 1 km, parking, restaurant.

Hotel is opposite the church in the centre of this famous spa town. Traditional and comfortable with super views. On D125 near Spanish border.

■ ACTIVITIES: All summer and winter sporting activities nearby; a host of cultural and sightseeing opportunities.
■ TARIFF: (1996) Single 160–310, Double 190–380, Bk 38, Set menu 78–180 (Euro/Access, Visa).

BAGNOLES-DE-L'ORNE Orne   2C

Hôtel Beaumont ★★ 26 bd Le Meunier de Raillère, 61140 Bagnoles-de-l'Orne.
Tel 02 33 37 91 77, Fax 02 33 38 90 61.
English spoken.

Open 01/03 to 30/11. 38 bedrooms (37 en suite). Golf 1 km, parking.

Comfortable Logis de France hotel dating from the turn of the century. Set behind the church in peaceful surroundings but only 5 minutes' walk from the town centre. Bar and tea room.

■ RESTAURANT: Closed Sun eve & Mon/Mar & Nov. Air-conditioned verandah opening onto the garden. Typical French and gourmet cuisine. Specialities include magret de canard fumé en salade, coquilles St-Jacques et gambas à la provençale, duo de cailles farcies, tartare de saumon et crème de citron and grenadins de veau aux langoustines.
■ ACTIVITIES: Swimming pool, tennis, casino, horse-riding and mountain-biking nearby; walks in the forest and by the lake.
■ TARIFF: (1996) Single 200–305, Double 255–390, Bk 34, Set menu 95–260 (Amex, Euro/Access, Visa).
■ DISCOUNT: 20%

Hôtel Lutetia-Reine Astrid ★★★
bd Paul Chalvet, 61140 Bagnoles-de-l'Orne.
Tel 02 33 37 94 77, Fax 02 33 30 09 87.
English spoken.
Open 01/04 to 15/10. 33 bedrooms
(30 en suite). Golf 2 km, parking.

Situated in the heart of the Andaine forest, the hotel has a large sun terrace, flower garden and lovely grounds. The comfortable rooms have an individual, personal touch.

■ RESTAURANT: High quality cuisine using fresh local produce.
■ ACTIVITIES: Tennis, swimming pool, archery, mountain-biking, horse-riding and casino nearby.
■ TARIFF: Double 295–450, Bk 50, Set menu 120–340 (Amex, Euro/Access, Visa).
■ DISCOUNT: 10%

BAR-SUR-AUBE Aube   3C

Hôtel Moulin du Landion ★★★
Bar-sur-Aube, 10200 Dolancourt.
Tel 03 25 27 92 17, Fax 03 25 27 94 44.
English spoken.
Open 01/02 to 30/11. 16 bedrooms
(all en suite). Outdoor swimming pool, golf 20 km, parking.

Set in magnificent landscape, the hotel, mill and river are just over 2 hours from Paris, in this small, peaceful village.

■ RESTAURANT: Local dishes based on seasonally available produce. Restaurant has view of the turning mill wheel.
■ ACTIVITIES: Fun and recreation park in the village. Tennis, horse-riding and water sports within easy reach. Wine tasting; Brienne Military College and Napoleonic museum 18 km, Charles de Gaulle museum 42 km.
■ TARIFF: Single 320–350, Double 375–435, Bk 44, Set menu 99–320 (Amex, Euro/Access, Visa).
■ DISCOUNT: 15% 01/10 to 01/05.

LA BAULE Loire-Atlan   1D

Hôtel Welcome ★★
7 av des Impairs, 44504 La Baule.
Tel 02 40 60 30 25. English spoken.
Open 01/04 to 05/11. 18 bedrooms
(all en suite). Golf 5 km.

Well-appointed hotel with pleasant atmosphere. 30 m from the sea, between the casino and shopping centre.

■ TARIFF: Single 340–390, Double 340–400, Bk 37 (Amex, Euro/Access, Visa).
■ DISCOUNT: 20% LS.

BAYEUX Calvados   1B

Hôtel Churchill ★★★
14 rue St-Jean, 14404 Bayeux.
Tel 02 31 21 31 80, Fax 02 31 21 41 66.
English spoken.

Open 01/03 to 15/11. 32 bedrooms
(all en suite). Golf 7 km, parking. ☎ ♿

Highly recommended, hotel is in a quiet street in the centre of Bayeux, near the tapestry museum and cathedral. Complimentary breakfasts on presentation of this guide when paying full room rate (excluding public holidays).

■ RESTAURANT: Specialities: blanc de St-Pierre Orly sauce tartare, escalopes de saumon à la fondue de poireaux, émincé de veau sauce au curry.
■ ACTIVITIES: Visit the famous tapestry, Normandy landing beaches, Battle of Normandy museum and English World War II cemetery.
■ TARIFF: (1996) Single 260–350, Double 280–490, Bk 42, Set menu 90–200 (Amex, Euro/Access, Visa).

Hôtel Reine Mathilde ★★
23 rue Larcher, 14400 Bayeux.
Tel 02 31 92 08 13, Fax 02 31 92 09 93.
English spoken.
Open 01/02 to 15/12. 16 bedrooms
(all en suite). Golf 8 km, parking.

In the town centre, close to the post office and 150 m from the cathedral, the hotel is very quiet with comfortable, individually-decorated rooms. Take the N13 towards 'Bayeux centre-ville'.

■ RESTAURANT: Closed 15/11 to 15/03. Brasserie-style restaurant. Specialities: jambon au cidre, steak flambé au calvados, tarte normande.

■ ACTIVITIES: Visit the famous tapestry, the lace museum and many surrounding châteaux.

■ TARIFF: (1996) Single 230–255, Double 270–295, Bk 35, Set menu 46–97 (Euro/Access, Visa).

■ DISCOUNT: 15% 01/11 to 31/03 only.

BEAUGENCY Loiret   2D

Hôtel La Tonnellerie ★★★★
12 rue des Eaux-Bleues, Tavers,
45190 Beaugency.
Tel 02 38 44 68 15, Fax 02 38 44 10 01.
English spoken.

Open 01/03 to 02/01. 20 bedrooms (all en suite). Outdoor swimming pool, golf 9 km, parking. ☎

In the Châteaux de la Loire region. Discreet charm of an old manor in a quiet location. 3 km east of Beaugency (towards Blois).

■ RESTAURANT: One 'winter garden' dining room, another with antique furniture. Meals also served on the terrace in fine weather. Nouvelle and classic cuisine based on fresh, local produce.

■ ACTIVITIES: Lovely walks; tennis 5 minutes' walk; convenient for touring major Loire châteaux and surrounded by 7 beautiful golf courses.

■ TARIFF: Single 300–450, Double 350–840, Bk 65, Set menu 135–240 (Amex, Euro/Access, Visa).

■ DISCOUNT: 10%

BEAUJEU Rhône   5B

Hôtel Anne de Beaujeu ★★
28 rue de la République, 69430 Beaujeu.
Tel 04 74 04 87 58, Fax 04 74 69 22 13.
English spoken.
Open 20/01 to 31/07 & 13/08 to 22/12.
7 bedrooms (all en suite). Parking. ☎

An old house in an old village surrounded by beautiful countryside. 13 km from the Paris-Lyon motorway. Exit Belleville, then west on the D37 to Beaujeu.

■ RESTAURANT: Closed Sun eve & Mon. Comfortable and intimate dining room. Specialities include lotte, escargots, filet de boeuf and crème brûlée.

■ ACTIVITIES: Mountain-biking, micro-light, horse-riding, hiking.

■ TARIFF: Double 290–365, Bk 37, Set menu 115–350 (Euro/Access, Visa).

Hôtel Mont-Brouilly ★★
69430 Quincie-en-Beaujolais.
Tel 04 74 04 33 73, Fax 04 74 69 00 72.
English spoken.

Open 01/03 to 01/02. 29 bedrooms (all en suite). Outdoor swimming pool, golf 25 km, garage, parking. ☎

In the heart of the Beaujolais region. West of Belleville and A6 on the D37, towards Beaujeu. Hotel is 1 km from the village of Cercié.

■ RESTAURANT: Air-conditioned restaurant. Specialities include coq au vin, grenouilles en persillade, escargots de Bourgogne, filet de carpe and tournedos au Brouilly.

■ ACTIVITIES: Cycling, boules, good walks, wine tasting; mountain bikes available.

■ TARIFF: Single 220–300, Double 270–320, Bk 35, Set menu 90–250 (Amex, Euro/Access, Visa).

France

BEAUNE Côte-d'Or 3C

Hôtel Belle Epoque ★★★
15 Fg Bretonnière, 21200 Beaune.
Tel 03 80 24 66 15, Fax 03 80 24 17 49.
English spoken.
Open all year. 16 bedrooms (all en suite).
Golf 5 km, garage.

*Local-style, medieval house, now modernised.
On the N74 going from the town centre towards
Autun, close to the famous Hospices de Beaune.*
■ TARIFF: (1996) Double 370–700, Bk 45
(Amex, Visa).

Hôtel du Château de Challanges ★★★
rue des Templiers, 21200 Beaune.
Tel 03 80 26 32 62, Fax 03 80 26 32 52.
English spoken.

Open 01/04 to 30/11. 14 bedrooms
(all en suite). Golf 2 km, garage, parking. ☎

*A small château set in a large park, close to the
historic town of Beaune. From Beaune exit off
A6, follow signs towards Dole-Seurre then turn
right into rte de Challanges.*

■ ACTIVITIES: Jogging and mountain-biking
within the hotel grounds. Arrangements made
for golf, tennis, horse-riding, balloon flights
and wine tasting.
■ TARIFF: Single 530–800, Double 530–950,
Bk 60 (Amex, Euro/Access, Visa).

Hôtel Climat de France ★★ av Charles de
Gaulle, Parc Hôtelier, 21200 Beaune.
Tel 03 80 22 74 10, Fax 03 80 22 40 45.
English spoken.
Open all year. 50 bedrooms (all en suite).
Golf 2 km, parking. ♿

*A modern hotel with good facilities including
several family rooms and a wine bar. Friendly,
efficient service. 500 m from A6 exit towards
Beaune, and 500 m from town centre.*

■ RESTAURANT: Modern restaurant offering an
hors d'oeuvre buffet, regional specialities and a
special menu for children. Extensive list of

Burgundy wines at reasonable prices.
■ ACTIVITIES: Cycles for hire, sauna and
playground at hotel; hotel will arrange tours of
Beaune, the Hospices de Beaune and vineyards
on request. English-speaking guides available.
■ TARIFF: Double 305–340, Bk 37,
Set menu 60–120 (Amex, Euro/Access, Visa).
■ DISCOUNT: 10%

BELLEVILLE Rhône 5B

Hôtel Le Villon ★★
Le Bourg, 69910 Villié-Morgon.
Tel 04 74 69 16 16, Fax 04 74 69 16 81.
English spoken.
Open 20/01 to 20/12. 45 bedrooms
(all en suite). Outdoor swimming pool, tennis,
golf 20 km, parking. ☎ ♿

*Comfortable and friendly with a lovely position
amongst vineyards. From A6 take Belleville
exit, go north on N6 for 6 km and then follow
signs to Villié-Morgon.*

■ RESTAURANT: Closed Sun eve & Mon LS. Good
range of menus. Regional specialities include
andouillette, coq au vin roulade de volaille
farcie, cassolette d'escargots and filet de carpe
au Morgon.
■ ACTIVITIES: Mountain-biking, microlighting,
hiking and wine tasting.
■ TARIFF: Single 290, Double 320, Bk 37,
Set menu 115–279 (Euro/Access, Visa).

BENODET Finistère 1C

Hôtel Armoric ★★★
3 rue Penfoul, 29950 Bénodet.
Tel 02 98 57 04 03, Fax 02 98 57 21 28. English spoken.
Open all year. 30 bedrooms (all en suite).
Outdoor swimming pool, tennis, golf 3 km,
garage, parking. ☎

*A charming family hotel close to beaches and
marina. Bar, terrace, tranquil, very pretty
flower-filled garden. From Quimper go to
Fouesnant and then Bénodet.*

France

■ RESTAURANT: Hotel offers half board 01/07 to 31/08. 3-course menu 125F, children 65F.
■ ACTIVITIES: A variety of sports nearby including water sports, fishing and horse-riding. Museums and other places of cultural interest within easy reach.
■ TARIFF: Single 200–450, Double 250–750, Bk 45, Set menu 125–170 (Amex, Euro/Access, Visa).
■ DISCOUNT: 20% except 02/07 to 15/09.

BERCK-SUR-MER Pas-de-Calais 2B

Hôtel Banque ★★
2 rue Rothschild, 62600 Berck-sur-Mer.
Tel 03 21 09 01 09, Fax 03 21 09 72 80.
English spoken.
Open all year. 14 bedrooms (all en suite).
Golf 18 km.

Recently refurbished, the hotel is situated in the centre of the town and 300 m from the beach.

■ RESTAURANT: Modern dining room. Fish and foie gras specialities.
■ ACTIVITIES: Sand-yachting, swimming pool and tennis nearby.
■ TARIFF: (1996) Single 140–160, Double 160–255, Bk 25, Set menu 98–135 (Amex, Euro/Access, Visa).
■ DISCOUNT: 5%

BESANCON Doubs 3D

Hôtel de Paris ★★
33 rue des Granges, 25000 Besançon.
Tel 03 81 81 36 56, Fax 03 81 61 94 90.
English spoken.
Open all year. 59 bedrooms (42 en suite, 17 bath/shower only). Golf 10 km, parking. &

In the heart of the town, the hotel offers quiet rooms overlooking the courtyard and gardens. Free private parking.

■ TARIFF: (1996) Single 185–265, Double 240–320, Bk 37 (Amex, Euro/Access, Visa).
■ DISCOUNT: 10%

BEZIERS Hérault 5C

Château de Cabrerolles ★★★
34290 Espondeilhan.
Tel 04 67 39 21 79, Fax 04 67 39 21 05. English spoken.
Open all year. 15 bedrooms (all en suite).
Outdoor swimming pool, golf 10 km, parking.

Former 19th-century residence, now a quiet, comfortable hotel set amongst vineyards. 20 km from the sea and 10 km from Pézenas, the town associated with Molière. 10 km from Béziers taking D909 north towards Roujan.

■ RESTAURANT: Closed Mon. Meals are served in front of a wood fire in winter and on outdoor terraces in summer. Specialities include gigot d'agneau à la crème d'ail.
■ ACTIVITIES: Visits to local cellars and wine tasting.
■ TARIFF: (1996) Double 320–590, Bk 45, Set menu 145 (Amex, Euro/Access, Visa).

BIARRITZ Pyrénées-Atlan 4C

Hôtel Miramar ★★★★
av Impératrice, 64200 Biarritz.
Tel 05 59 41 30 00, Fax 05 59 24 77 20.
English spoken.

Open all year. 126 bedrooms (all en suite).
Outdoor swimming pool, golf on site, garage, parking. &

Hotel of great comfort and character. Facing the sea, with its own private beach and just 3 km from the airport.

■ RESTAURANT: Restaurant has an excellent reputation for its gourmet cuisine. Local and seafood specialities are prepared under the supervision of chef Patrice Demangel.
■ ACTIVITIES: Gym, beauty centre, thalassotherapy centre with sea-water treatment at hotel; water sports and many other activities and excursion possibilities nearby. ● Preferential rates for golf on nearby course (500 m).
■ TARIFF: (1996) Single 725–2370, Double 930–2635, Bk 100, Set menu 280–290 (No credit cards).

Hôtel Palais ★★★★
1 av Impératrice, 64200 Biarritz.
Tel 05 59 41 64 00, Fax 05 59 41 67 99.
English spoken.

Open all year. 155 bedrooms (all en suite).
Outdoor swimming pool, golf 1 km, parking. &
Formerly an imperial palace, the hotel is in the heart of the city and overlooks the fine beaches of Biarritz. Fully renovated with a worldwide reputation for luxury.

■ RESTAURANT: Enjoy lunch around the pool and dinner in either 'La Rotonde' overlooking the sea or in the award-winning 'Le Grand Siècle'. Specialities: rougets en filets poêlés, chipirons à l'encre.
■ ACTIVITIES: Good sports facilities and sea-water cure centres nearby.
■ TARIFF: Single 1150–2000, Double 1450–2750, Bk 120, Set menu 280 (Amex, Euro/Access, Visa).
■ DISCOUNT: 10% except Aug.

BIDARRAY Pyrénées-Atlan   4C

Hôtel Noblia ★★ 64780 Bidarray.
Tel 05 59 37 70 89.
Open 15/01 to 15/12. 23 bedrooms
(15 en suite). Parking. &
On the outskirts of town coming from Bayonne, hotel stands beside the river and has mountain views. 30 km from the sea.

■ RESTAURANT: Specialities: anguille persillade, pipérade, omelette aux cèpes.
■ TARIFF: (1996) Double 140–220, Bk 25, Set menu 55–120 (Amex, Visa).

BISCARROSSE Landes   4C

Hôtel Atlantide ★★
place Marsan, 40600 Biscarrosse.
Tel 05 58 78 08 86, Fax 05 58 78 75 98.
English spoken.
Open all year. 33 bedrooms (all en suite).
Golf 5 km, parking. &

Modern and comfortable, hotel is in a quiet town centre position near beaches and lakes.
■ ACTIVITIES: Cycling, tennis and sailing nearby; cultural guided tours available within the area.
■ TARIFF: (1996) Single 190–320, Double 245–360, Bk 38 (Amex, Euro/Access, Visa).

LE BLANC Indre   4B

Domaine de l'Etape ★★★
route de Bélâbre, 36300 Le Blanc.
Tel 02 54 37 18 02, Fax 02 54 37 75 59.
English spoken.

Open all year. 35 bedrooms (all en suite).
Golf 6 km, parking. &
Delightful 19th-century building in 152-hectare park, with 18-hectare boating and fishing lake. From Le Blanc, head south-east on D10 for 6 km towards Bélâbre.

■ RESTAURANT: Meals can be served on the large terrace in fine weather. Chef's specialities include salade de homard à l'émulsion d'olives et de corail, escalope de sandre au vinaigre de cidre et tête de veau avec beignets de cervelles et oignons frits.
■ ACTIVITIES: Boating, horse-riding and fishing at hotel; flying, gliding and parachuting nearby.
■ TARIFF: (1996) Single 210–400, Double 210–440, Bk 48, Set menu 125–300 (Amex, Euro/Access, Visa).

BLOIS Loir-et-Cher   2D

Hôtel La Caillère ★★ 36 route des Montils, 41120 Candé-sur-Beuvron.
Tel 02 54 44 03 08, Fax 02 54 44 00 95.
English spoken.
Open 01/03 to 01/01. 14 bedrooms
(all en suite). Golf 8 km, parking. &

La Caillère combines modern amenities with old architecture. On the left bank of the Loire, 10 minutes' drive from Blois towards Tours on the N751.

■ RESTAURANT: Closed Wed. Jacky Guindon, chef and owner, has a highly original cuisine. He combines traditional ingredients with the best produce from local markets.

■ ACTIVITIES: In the heart of châteaux country, close to four of the most famous. Horse-riding and bike hire nearby.
■ TARIFF: (1996) Single 300, Double 320–360, Bk 50, Set menu 88–278 (Amex, Euro/Access, Visa).
■ DISCOUNT: 5%

BORDEAUX Gironde   4B

Hôtel Clémenceau ★★
4 cours G Clémenceau, 33000 Bordeaux.
Tel 05 56 52 98 98, Fax 05 56 81 24 91.
English spoken.
Open all year. 45 bedrooms (all en suite).
Garage.

Large 18th-century house right in the city centre. All modern facilities.

■ ACTIVITIES: ● Wine tasting can be arranged at a restaurant associated with the hotel at a reduced price for RAC members.
■ TARIFF: Single 150–220, Double 190–220, Bk 25 (Amex, Euro/Access, Visa).

LA BOUILLE Seine Marit   2A

Hôtel Bellevue ★★
13 quai Hector-Malot, 76530 La Bouille.
Tel 02 35 18 05 05, Fax 02 35 18 00 92.
English spoken.
Open all year. 20 bedrooms (all en suite).
Golf 15 km, garage, parking.

Pleasing, traditional hotel in a quiet position opposite the River Seine. From Rouen, drive south-west on A13 for 15 km. Exit for Maison Brulée, turn right after 500 m to the village and the river.

■ RESTAURANT: Closed 20/12 to 27/12. Gourmet cuisine with seafood specialities.
■ ACTIVITIES: Trips on the River Seine.

■ TARIFF: (1996) Single 190–350, Double 230–350, Bk 35, Set menu 105–225 (Euro/Access, Visa).
■ DISCOUNT: 10% except weekends.

BOULOGNE-SUR-MER Pas-de-Calais   2B

Hôtel Cléry Château d'Hesdin ★★★
62360 Hesdin-l'Abbé.
Tel 03 21 83 19 83, Fax 03 21 87 52 59.
English spoken.

Open 30/01 to 13/12. 21 bedrooms (all en suite). Tennis, golf 9 km, parking.

Elegant hotel with lovely grounds. Completely renovated and redecorated in 1996.

■ RESTAURANT: Closed Sat & Sun lunch. Fresh and light traditional cuisine.
■ TARIFF: Double 290–630, Bk 50, Set menu 115–155 (Amex, Euro/Access, Visa).
■ DISCOUNT: 5% except May to Sept.

France

France

Hôtel Metropole ★★★
51 rue Thiers, 62200 Boulogne-sur-Mer.
Tel 03 21 31 54 30, Fax 03 21 30 45 72.
English spoken.

Open 05/01 to 20/12. 25 bedrooms
(all en suite). Golf 6 km, garage.
*Town centre hotel with well-decorated
accommodation and luxury bathrooms.
Pleasant lounge and pretty garden.*
■ TARIFF: (1996) Single 335–380, Double 380–
430, Bk 42 (Amex, Euro/Access, Visa).

BOURG-ST-MAURICE Savoie   6A

Hôtel L'Autantic ★★★
rte d'Hauteville, 73700 Bourg-St-Maurice.
Tel 04 79 07 01 70, Fax 04 79 05 51 55.
English spoken.
Open all year. 23 bedrooms (all en suite).
Golf 18 km, garage, parking. ✆ ⅙
*A modern stone and pine chalet-style hotel set
back from the road at the edge of town. Offers
very comfortable accommodation and
excellent facilities.*
■ ACTIVITIES: Sauna at hotel; mountain sports,
canoeing and rafting nearby.
■ TARIFF: (1996) Single 260, Double 260–440,
Bk 40 (Amex, Euro/Access, Visa).

BOURGES Cher   2D

Hôtel d'Angleterre ★★★
1 place des Quatre Piliers, 18000 Bourges.
Tel 02 48 24 68 51, Fax 02 48 65 21 41.
English spoken.
Open all year. 31 bedrooms (all en suite).
Golf 2 km, garage.
*Quiet and comfortable, the hotel has been fully
renovated and is not far from the cathedral in
the old town.*
■ RESTAURANT: Closed 15/12 to 15/01. Louis XVI-
style 'Le Windsor' restaurant offers Berry cuisine.
■ ACTIVITIES: Spring music festival.

■ TARIFF: (1996) Single 395, Double 450, Bk 40,
Set menu 94–146 (Amex, Euro/Access, Visa).

BOURGOIN-JALLIEU Isère   5B

Hôtel Otelinn ★★
13 rue du Creuzat, 38080 L'Isle d'Abeau.
Tel 04 74 27 13 55, Fax 04 74 27 22 21.
English spoken.
Open all year. 45 bedrooms (all en suite).
Golf 3 km, parking. ⅙
*Modern hotel, convenient for both the airport
and the autoroute. From A43, take exit to L'Isle
d'Abeau-Est and follow signs to L'Isle d'Abeau
village. 5 km west of Bourgoin.*
■ RESTAURANT: Closed Sun.
■ TARIFF: (1996) Single 269, Double 299, Bk 36,
Set menu 82–155 (Amex, Euro/Access, Visa).
■ DISCOUNT: 10%

BREIL-SUR-ROYA Alpes-Marit   6C

Hôtel Castel du Roy ★★
route de Tende, 06540 Breil-sur-Roya.
Tel 04 93 04 43 66, Fax 04 93 04 91 83.
English spoken.
Open 01/03 to 31/10. 19 bedrooms
(all en suite). Outdoor swimming pool,
golf 20 km, parking. ⅙
*Set in 2 ha of parkland near the Vallée des
Merveilles, the hotel has a lovely position beside
the River Roya.*
■ RESTAURANT: Closed Tues LS.
■ ACTIVITIES: Mountain-bike hire; fishing, skiing,
horse-riding nearby.
■ TARIFF: Single 250–300, Double 310–410, Bk 40,
Set menu 110–210 (Amex, Euro/Access, Visa).
■ DISCOUNT: 5% LS.

BRELIDY Côtes-du-Nord   1C

Château de Brélidy ★★★ 22140 Brélidy.
Tel 02 96 95 69 38, Fax 02 96 95 18 03.
English spoken.

Open 05/04 to 02/11. 10 bedrooms
(all en suite). Golf 25 km, parking. ＆

*Beautiful 16th-century château standing in 10
hectares of parkland, with woods and river.
Rooms furnished in keeping with period. From
Guingamp take the D767 towards Bégard and
Lannion. In Bégard take the D15 to Pontrieux.*

■ RESTAURANT: Dining room with granite
fireplace, beamed ceiling, tapestries and period
furniture. Specialities include nage de
coquillages au safran and compote de pommes
au jus de gingembre.
■ ACTIVITIES: Jacuzzi at hotel. Fishing, walking
and mountain biking within the grounds.
■ TARIFF: Single 380–430, Double 420–755, Bk 50,
Set menu 140–180 (Amex, Euro/Access, Visa).
■ DISCOUNT: 5% except July & Aug.

LA BRESSE Vosges   3D

Résidence des Vallées ★★★
31 rue P Claudel, 88250 La Bresse.
Tel 03 29 25 41 39, Fax 03 29 25 64 38.
English spoken.

Open all year. 54 bedrooms (all en suite). Indoor
swimming pool, tennis, garage, parking. ＆
*A modern hotel with relaxing, family
atmosphere. In the heart of the Hautes Vosges,
12 km from Gérardmer.*

■ RESTAURANT: Quality cuisine in light, bright
and very restful surroundings. Raclette
evenings a speciality.
■ ACTIVITIES: Fitness room, sauna, squash, table
tennis and mountain-biking; skiing nearby.
■ TARIFF: Single 310–335, Double 370–390, Bk 40,
Set menu 88–230 (Amex, Euro/Access, Visa).

BREST Finistère   1C

Hôtel de la Paix ★★★ 32 rue Algésiras, 29200 Brest.
Tel 02 98 80 12 97, Fax 02 98 43 30 95.
English spoken.
Open all year. 25 bedrooms (all en suite).
Golf 15 km, parking. ☎

*Located in the heart of Brest, a few steps away
from the St-Louis covered market, near the post
office, town hall, conference centre and
famous rue de Siam. Take autoroute N12
towards the coast to Brest.*

■ TARIFF: (1996) Single 245–275, Double 270–
300, Bk 30 (Amex, Euro/Access, Visa).
■ DISCOUNT: 10%

BRIANCON Hautes-Alpes   6A

Hôtel Paris ★★
41 av Général de Gaulle, 05100 Briançon.
Tel 04 92 20 15 30, Fax 04 92 20 30 82.
English spoken.
Open all year. 22 bedrooms (all en suite).
Golf 14 km, garage, parking. ☎ ＆

*Near the town centre and railway station. On
the N94 close to the Italian border.*

■ RESTAURANT: Specialises in classic and regional
traditional cuisine.
■ ACTIVITIES: 300 m from sports centre and ski-lifts.
■ TARIFF: (1996) Single 175–250, Double 190–
265, Bk 30, Set menu 49–130 (Amex, Visa).
■ DISCOUNT: 5%

BRICQUEBEC Manche   1B

Hôtel Vieux Château ★★★
4 cours du Château, 50260 Bricquebec.
Tel 02 33 52 24 49, Fax 02 33 52 62 71.
English spoken.

Open all year. 25 bedrooms (24 en suite, 1 bath/
shower only). Tennis, golf 15 km, garage,
parking. ＆
*Hotel is built within a 12th-century medieval
castle, surrounded by its ramparts. Take the
D900 from Cherbourg.*

■ RESTAURANT: In the former Knights' Hall.
■ TARIFF: (1996) Single 160–300,
Double 180–390, Bk 40, Set menu 80–170
(Amex, Euro/Access, Visa).
■ DISCOUNT: 20% from Oct to May only.

France

BRIONNE Eure 2A

Hôtel Soleil d'Or ★★
27550 La Riviere-Thibouville.
Tel 02 32 45 00 08, Fax 02 32 46 89 68.
English spoken.
Open all year. 10 bedrooms (all en suite).
Golf 15 km, parking. ✆ ♿

5 km south of Brionne towards Beaumont-le-Roger, on the right.

■ RESTAURANT: Closed Wed & Sun eve.
Gastronomic cuisine with regional specialities.
Extensive wine and Calvados list.
■ ACTIVITIES: Mountain bikes for hire; hiking;
lake and river fishing.
■ TARIFF: (1996) Single 200–250,
Double 250–300, Bk 35, Set menu 95–208
(Amex, Euro/Access, Visa).

LE BUGUE Dordogne 4B

Manoir de Bellerive ★★★ route de Siorac,
24480 Le Buisson-de-Cadouin.
Tel 05 53 27 16 19, Fax 05 53 22 09 05.
English spoken.
Open 01/04 to 15/11. 16 bedrooms
(all en suite). Outdoor swimming pool, tennis,
golf 10 km, garage, parking. ♿

*Small Relais du Silence château in a 3-hectare
park on the edge of the Dordogne. Peaceful
setting near Lascaux and Les Eyzies.*

■ RESTAURANT: Closed Wed eve for non-residents. Specialities: seafood, foie gras poêlé
aux fruits and seasonal dishes using fresh
produce.
■ ACTIVITIES: Good sports facilities plus
sauna/Turkish bath at hotel; canoeing, cycling
and horse-riding nearby. In the centre of the
Périgord Noir touring and rambling area.
■ TARIFF: (1996) Single 430–590,
Double 450–830, Bk 68, Set menu 120–220
(Amex, Euro/Access, Visa).
■ DISCOUNT: 5%

BUSSANG Vosges 3D

Hôtel des Sources ★★ 88540 Bussang.
Tel 03 29 61 51 94, Fax 03 29 61 60 61.
English spoken.
Open all year. 11 bedrooms
(all bath/shower only). Parking.

*On the banks of the Moselle, in a quiet
environment near the forest. Between Epinal
and Mulhouse towards the source of the Moselle.*

■ RESTAURANT: Gourmet cuisine, extensive wine
list, welcoming family atmosphere.
■ ACTIVITIES: For lovers of nature, skiing in
winter, walking all year round.

■ TARIFF: (1996) Single 270–290, Double 290–335, Bk 34, Set menu 100–280 (Euro/Access, Visa).
■ DISCOUNT: 10% on stays of minimum 3 nights.

Hôtel du Tremplin ★★
8 rue du 3ème RTA, 88540 Bussang.
Tel 03 29 61 50 30, Fax 03 29 61 50 89.
English spoken.
Open 04/12 to 04/11. 19 bedrooms
(13 en suite). Garage, parking.

*Small, family-run hotel in the centre of
Bussang which is in the heart of the Hautes-Vosges, the source of the Moselle river.*

■ RESTAURANT: Closed Sun eve & Mon. Award
winning with a character dining room offering
Lorraine and Alsace specialities.
■ ACTIVITIES: Winter skiing centre. Good sports
facilities nearby.
■ TARIFF: Single 150–260, Double 150–300, Bk 35,
Set menu 75–300 (Amex, Euro/Access, Visa).
■ DISCOUNT: 10%

BUZANCAIS Indre 4B

Hôtel Le Croissant ★★
53 rue Grande, 36500 Buzançais.
Tel 02 54 84 00 49, Fax 02 54 84 20 60.
English spoken.
Open all year. 14 bedrooms (all en suite).
Golf 10 km, parking. ✆

Small, modern hotel in the town centre.

■ RESTAURANT: Closed Fri eve, Sat lunch & Feb.
Gourmet restaurant. Meals are served on the
garden terrace in summer.
■ ACTIVITIES: Zoological park and swimming
pool nearby; walking, cycling.
■ TARIFF: Single 225–245, Double 245–265,
Bk 32, Set menu 82–230 (Euro/Access, Visa).

CABOURG Calvados   2A

Hôtel du Golf ★★
av Hippodrome, 14390 Cabourg.
Tel 02 31 24 12 34, Fax 02 31 24 18 51.
English spoken.
Open 28/02 to 05/01. 40 bedrooms
(all en suite). Outdoor swimming pool, golf on
site, parking. ℓ ₲

*Modern hotel quietly situated 2 km from the
centre of Cabourg. Follow signs to 'Golf public'.*

■ RESTAURANT: Closed Sun eve & Mon lunch
(Sep & June), Mon & Thur lunch (Jul & Aug).
Good simple cuisine using local produce.
Specialities include poularde à la Normande
and plateau de fuits de mer.
■ ACTIVITIES: Tennis, horse-riding and beach
within easy reach. Good area for sightseeing.
■ TARIFF: (1996) Bk 42, Set menu 65–185
(Amex, Euro/Access, Visa).
■ DISCOUNT: 5%

CAEN Calvados   2A

Hôtel Climat de France ★★ av Montgomery,
quartier du Mémorial, 14000 Caen.
Tel 02 31 44 36 36, Fax 02 31 95 62 62.
English spoken.
Open all year. 72 bedrooms (all en suite).
Golf 7 km, parking. ₲

*Modern hotel with secure parking, near the
Mémorial museum in Caen. Travelling on the
north ring-road towards Cherbourg, take the
Mémorial or Creully exit and the hotel is 400 m
from Mémorial. Special prices available for
long stays.*

■ RESTAURANT: Good food with buffet-style hors
d'oeuvres and desserts.
■ TARIFF: Double 270–305, Bk 35,
Set menu 92–102 (Amex, Euro/Access, Visa).
■ DISCOUNT: 10%

CAHORS Lot   4D

Hôtel Terminus ★★★
5 av Charles de Freycinet, 46000 Cahors.
Tel 05 65 35 24 50, Fax 05 65 22 06 40.
English spoken.
Open all year. 22 bedrooms (all en suite).
Golf 20 km, garage, parking. ₲

*Elegant, traditional hotel offering comfortable
accommodation. Near town centre and
station.*

■ RESTAURANT: Closed Mon LS. Turn-of-the-
century décor. The restaurant 'Le Balandre'
serves quality dishes using local produce.
Specialities: oeuf Pierre Marre; filet d'agneau
fermier; panaché de fois gras de canard.

■ ACTIVITIES: Mountain-biking, hiking,
canoeing; visits to wine cellars and local
producers of foie gras and truffles.
■ TARIFF: (1996) Single 300–460,
Double 350–850, Bk 38, Set menu 150–320
(Amex, Euro/Access, Visa).

CALAIS Pas-de-Calais   2B

Hôtel Climat de France ★★
digue Gaston Berthe, 62100 Calais.
Tel 03 21 34 64 64, Fax 03 21 34 35 39.
English spoken.
Open all year. 44 bedrooms (all en suite).
Parking. ℓ ₲

*Modern hotel on the seafront with private
parking. Just a few minutes from the ferry and
the Channel Tunnel. From town centre take
road to 'La Plage'.*

■ RESTAURANT: Closed Sun eve Oct to Mar.
Overlooks the seafront; mussels are a house
speciality.
■ ACTIVITIES: Many excursions and visits can be
organised for groups staying minimum 3
nights, including Calais, Boulogne, Brugges in
Belgium and Arques.
■ TARIFF: (1996) Double 250–304, Bk 35,
Set menu 90–130 (Amex, Euro/Access, Visa).
■ DISCOUNT: 8%

Hôtel du Golf ★★
digue Gaston Berthe, 62100 Calais.
Tel 03 21 96 88 99, Fax 03 21 34 75 48.
English spoken.
Open all year. 31 bedrooms (all en suite).
Parking. ₲

*Hotel overlooks the sea and is conveniently
situated within minutes of the ferry port,
Channel Tunnel and A26. From town centre
take road La Plage. Restaurants nearby; self-
catering facilities available for stays of a week
or more.*

■ TARIFF: (1996) Double 250–304, Bk 38,
Set menu 95–135 (Amex, Euro/Access, Visa).
■ DISCOUNT: 8%

Metropol Hôtel ★★★
45 quai du Rhin, 62100 Calais.
Tel 03 21 97 54 00, Fax 03 21 96 69 70.
English spoken.
Open 03/01 to 23/12. 40 bedrooms
(all en suite). Garage, parking. ₲

*A quiet hotel behind the railway station in the
town centre. 5 minutes from the ferry and
Channel Tunnel.*

■ TARIFF: (1996) Single 200–280, Double 300–380,
Bk 48 (Amex, Euro/Access, Visa).
■ DISCOUNT: 15%

France (side tab)

CANCALE Ille/Vilaine   1D

Hôtel l'Emeraude ★★
7 quai Thomas, 35260 Cancale.
Tel 02 99 89 61 76, Fax 02 99 89 88 21.
English spoken.
Open 15/12 to 15/11. 16 bedrooms
(15 en suite, 1 bath/shower only). Golf 20 km.

*Seafront hotel having a further building with
accommodation and wonderful views on top
of a nearby cliff. Hotel offers all modern
conveniences and overlooks the fishing/oyster
farming port.*

■ RESTAURANT: Closed 15/11 to 15/02 and Thur.
Overlooking the port, the restaurant has a
definite maritime feel to it and specialises in
fresh seafood dishes.

■ ACTIVITIES: Ideal base for touring, water
sports, fishing.

■ TARIFF: (1996) Double 285–480, Bk 42,
Set menu 95–300 (Amex, Euro/Access, Visa).

CANNES Alpes-Marit   6C

Hôtel Festival ★★★
3 rue Molière, 06400 Cannes.
Tel 04 93 68 33 00, Fax 04 93 68 33 85.
English spoken.
Open all year. 14 bedrooms (all en suite).
Golf 5 km, garage. ℄

*Contemporary-style hotel with air
conditioning. Room-service meals are
available. From motorway A8, take the Cannes
exit and the hotel is between La Croisette and
rue d'Antibes.*

■ ACTIVITIES: Sauna and jacuzzi; 100 m from the
beach. ● Special golf package in winter and
discounts on boat trips and at pay-beach in
summer.

■ TARIFF: (1996) Single 380–590, Double 480–
690, Bk 45 (Amex, Euro/Access, Visa).

■ DISCOUNT: 10% except during festivals,
congresses, etc.

Hôtel L'Horset-Savoy ★★★★
5 rue F Einessy, 06400 Cannes.
Tel 04 92 99 72 00, Fax 04 93 68 25 59.
English spoken.
Open all year. 106 bedrooms (all en suite).
Outdoor swimming pool, golf 15 km, garage. ℄ ♿

*Recently renovated hotel, at the centre of La
Croisette, just 25 m from the sea and close to
the shops. Wonderful view of the old town and
sea from the pool.*

■ RESTAURANT: Air-conditioned restaurant
offering excellent cuisine. Meals served on a
shady terrace overlooking the pool and town
when weather permits.

■ ACTIVITIES: Hotel can book excursions, boat
and car rental ● Reduced entry to Festival
Beach, special rates for helicopter and taxi
transfers for hotel guests.

■ TARIFF: Single 600–1275, Double 665–1430, Bk 98,
Set menu 105–150 (Amex, Euro/Access, Visa).

CARCASSONNE Aude   5C

Hôtel Donjon ★★★ 2 rue Comte Roger, Cité
Médiévale, 11000 Carcassonne.
Tel 04 68 71 08 80, Fax 04 68 25 06 60.
English spoken.
Open all year. 38 bedrooms (all en suite).
Golf 3 km, garage, parking.

*In the middle of the medieval city, the hotel
dates back to the Middle Ages but now provides
modern comforts, tranquillity and a warm
welcome. From the motorway A61, exit at
Carcassonne-Est towards Cité.*

■ RESTAURANT: Closed Sun eve from 1/11 to
31/03. Modern brasserie. Specialities: cassoulet
Languedocien, saumon fumé Danemark, foie
gras, confit, fruit flambé.

■ ACTIVITIES: Guided walk around the old town;
visits to wine co-operatives; tennis nearby.

■ TARIFF: (1996) Single 300–650,
Double 360–750, Bk 52, Set menu 69–125
(Amex, Euro/Access, Visa).

Hôtel des Remparts ★★ 3 place du Grand
Puits, Cité Médiévale, 11000 Carcassonne.
Tel 04 68 71 27 72, Fax 04 68 72 73 26.
English spoken.
Open all year. 18 bedrooms (all en suite).
Golf 2 km, parking. ♿

*The hotel is converted from an old house
within the walls of the medieval city of
Carcassonne. From A61 exit at Carcassonne-
Est and follow 'Cité Médiévale' signs.*

France

■ TARIFF: Single 300, Double 300–330, Bk 35 (Amex, Euro/Access, Visa).

CARNAC Morbihan 1C

Hôtel Armoric ★★★ 53 av de la Poste, 56340 Carnac.
Tel 02 97 52 13 47, Fax 02 97 52 98 66.
English spoken.
Open 05/04 to 12/11. 25 bedrooms (all en suite). Tennis, golf 6 km, parking.

Quiet, relaxing hotel in extensive grounds, set back from the beach opposite the salt-marshes. Access from D781 coastal road.

■ RESTAURANT: Closed Thur LS. Traditional cuisine with an emphasis on seafood.
■ ACTIVITIES: ● Hotel has arranged price reductions for a number of activities including sightseeing tours.
■ TARIFF: (1996) Single 280–300, Double 330–450, Bk 41, Set menu 70–160 (Amex, Euro/Access, Visa).
■ DISCOUNT: 10% except July & August.

CARPENTRAS Vaucluse 5D

Auberge La Fontaine
place de la Fontaine, 84210 Venasque.
Tel 04 90 66 02 96, Fax 04 90 66 13 14.
English spoken.

Open 15/12 to 15/11. 5 bedrooms (all en suite). Golf 8 km, parking.

Warm and cosy, the Auberge has been beautifully restored. Accommodation comprises spacious suites, each having a fully equipped kitchen/dining room, living room with fireplace and private terrace. Added to these are all the little extras that make life just that bit more enjoyable! South-east of Carpentras, on D4 (8 km).

■ RESTAURANT: Closed Wed. Gourmet restaurant with regional and classic cuisine as well as a bistro (which is closed on Mondays). Specialities include wild asparagus, herb-fed rabbit and fresh Mediterranean seafood.
■ ACTIVITIES: Mountain bikes available at the

hotel; good sports facilities nearby; festivals, theatre; cookery courses available.
■ TARIFF: (1996) Double 700, Bk 50, Set menu 80–200 (Euro/Access, Visa).
■ DISCOUNT: 8%

Hôtel Les Trois Colombes ★★★
148 av des Garrigues, 84210 St-Didier.
Tel 04 90 66 07 01, Fax 04 90 66 11 54.
English spoken.
Open 01/03 to 31/12. 30 bedrooms (all en suite). Outdoor swimming pool, tennis, golf 6 km, parking. &

Charming Provençal country residence with shady grounds covering 800 sq metres. From the A7 take the Avignon-Nord exit and go through Carpentras towards St-Didier, following signposts to the hotel.

■ RESTAURANT: Offers classic French cuisine with Provençal specialities.
■ ACTIVITIES: Hang-gliding, parachuting, flying school, horse-riding and mountain-biking nearby.
■ TARIFF: (1996) Single 300, Double 320–400, Bk 45, Set menu 105–190 (Amex, Euro/Access, Visa).

CASSIS Bouches-du-Rhône 5D

Hôtel La Plage du Bestouan ★★★
plage du Bestouan, 13260 Cassis.
Tel 04 42 01 05 70, Fax 04 42 01 34 82.
English spoken.

Open 15/03 to 15/10. 30 bedrooms (all en suite). Golf 10 km.

Seaside hotel with a panoramic terrace and super location right beside the beach. Cassis is a lively fishing port off the D559.

■ RESTAURANT: Traditional restuarant with gastronomic cuisine.
■ ACTIVITIES: Excellent facilities for sports, boating and fishing nearby. Good base for sightseeing and excursions.
■ TARIFF: (1996) Single 300–400, Double 400–600, Bk 45, Set menu 100–200 (Amex, Euro/Access, Visa).

France

CASTELJALOUX Lot/Garonne 4D

Château de Ruffiac ★★★
Ruffiac, 47700 Casteljaloux.
Tel 05 53 93 18 63, Fax 05 53 89 67 93.
English spoken.
Open 01/03 to 31/01. 20 bedrooms
(all en suite). Outdoor swimming pool,
golf 8 km, parking. &

*Vast 14th-century vicarage, next to church,
with views of both mountains and valleys.
Comfortable rooms with good facilities. From
Casteljaloux, north-west on D655 for 8 km.*

■ RESTAURANT: Closed Feb. Good regional cuisine;
excellent choice of local and regional wines.
■ ACTIVITIES: French billiards; water sports and
mountain-biking nearby.
■ TARIFF: (1996) Single 320–420, Double 380–480,
Bk 40, Set menu 150–290 (Euro/Access, Visa).

CASTERA-VERDUZAN Gers 4D

Hôtel Thermes ★★ 32410 Castéra-Verduzan.
Tel 05 62 68 13 07, Fax 05 62 68 10 49.
English spoken.
Open 01/02 to 01/01. 47 bedrooms
(37 en suite). Parking. &

*In the village centre of Castéra-Verduzan and
on the D930 north west of Auch.*

■ RESTAURANT: Closed Jan. Restaurant has 3
dining rooms offering good, regional cuisine.
Specialities include foie gras and cassoulet.
■ ACTIVITIES: Day trips, bathing lake 400 m from
hotel; evening entertainment.
■ TARIFF: (1996) Single 190–210, Double 245–260,
Bk 32, Set menu 68–190 (Amex, Euro/Access, Visa).
■ DISCOUNT: 3%

CAVAILLON Vaucluse 5D

Hôtel du Parc ★★
183 place François Tourel, 84300 Cavaillon.
Tel 04 90 71 57 78, Fax 04 90 76 10 35.
English spoken.
Open all year. 40 bedrooms (all en suite).
Garage, parking.

*At the foot of 'Colline St-Jaques', 300 m from
the town centre. Follow signs towards 'Arc
Romain' and hotel is opposite the arch.*

■ TARIFF: (1996) Single 150–250,
Double 230–300, Bk 36 (Euro/Access, Visa).

CHAGNY Côte-d'Or 3C

Château de la Crée ★★★★ Les Hauts de
Santenay, 21590 Santenay-en-Bourgogne.
Tel 03 80 20 62 66, Fax 03 80 20 66 50.
English spoken.

Open all year. 4 bedrooms (3 en suite,
1 bath/shower only). Tennis, golf on site,
garage, parking. &

*Surrounded by vineyards, an 18th-century
manor offering a warm atmosphere and
comfortable rooms with antique furnishings.
The hotel is open in January and February by
prior reservation only. Santenay is about 5 km
west of Chagny.*

■ ACTIVITIES: Putting green; swimming pool, horse-
riding, hiking, fishing, sailing, hot-air ballooning,
casino and spa centre within easy reach.
■ TARIFF: Single 480–650, Double 580–800
(Euro/Access, Visa).
■ DISCOUNT: 10% minimum 2-night stay.

CHALON-SUR-SAONE Saône/Loire 3C

Hôtel Relais du Montagny ★★ 71390 Buxy.
Tel 03 85 92 19 90, Fax 03 85 92 07 19.
English spoken.
Open all year. 30 bedrooms (all en suite).
Outdoor swimming pool, golf 15 km, garage,
parking. & &

*From the A6, take Chalon-Sud exit towards
Monceau on the E607/N80. After 200 m turn
left onto the D981 and carry on for 13 km. The
hotel is on the outskirts of the village.*

■ RESTAURANT: Closed Sun eve from Nov to Feb.
Regional and traditional cuisine served on
terrace in summer.
■ TARIFF: (1996) Single 270–335,
Double 300–395, Bk 40, Set menu 80–215
(Amex, Euro/Access, Visa).

CHALONS-EN-CHAMPAGNE Marne 3A

Hôtel aux Armes de Champagne ★★★
31 av du Luxembourg, 51460 L'Epine.
Tel 03 26 69 30 30, Fax 03 26 66 92 31.
English spoken.
Open 16/02 to 07/01. 37 bedrooms
(all en suite). Tennis, golf 5 km, garage,
parking.

*Traditional French hostelry, very tastefully
decorated and with good facilities. In the
shadow of the basilica of Notre Dame in pretty
L'Epine. 8 km from Châlons-sur-Marne on N3
to Metz/Verdun.*

■ RESTAURANT: Closed Sun eve & Mon, Nov to
Mar. The hotel organises special 'Arts de la
Table' evenings and wine-tasting dinners.
Gourmet cuisine with long wine list.
■ ACTIVITIES: Mini-golf.
■ TARIFF: (1996) Single 320–690,
Double 400–780, Bk 55, Set menu 210–490
(Amex, Euro/Access, Visa).

CHAMBORD Loir-et-Cher   2D

Château de Nanteuil ★★
Huisseau-sur-Cosson, 41350 Vineuil.
Tel 02 54 42 61 98, Fax 02 54 42 37 23.
English spoken.
Open 15/02 to 31/12. 9 bedrooms (7 en suite).
Golf 10 km, parking.

A wisteria-clad château standing in peaceful surroundings, it was bought by the present owner's English grandfather in 1921. Welcoming apéritif is offered.

■ RESTAURANT: Closed Mon & Tues lunch. Attractive 18th-century dining room with family portraits. Seafood specialities and children's menu.
■ ACTIVITIES: Sightseeing tours; hunting and horse-drawn carriage rides nearby.
■ TARIFF: (1996) Double 200–400, Bk 35, Set menu 90–210 (Euro/Access, Visa).

Château des Marais
27 rue de Chambord, 41500 Muides-sur-Loire.
Tel 02 54 87 05 42, Fax 02 54 87 05 43.
English spoken.
Open 15/05 to 15/09. 12 bedrooms (all en suite). Outdoor swimming pool, tennis, golf 10 km, parking. ✆

Comfortable, pretty rooms either in the château itself or in a small pavillion in the beautiful, 12-hectare park-like grounds (also home to the château's campsite). From Chambord, 6 km north on the route 'François 1er' to Muides and the river.

■ RESTAURANT: Closed 15/09 to 15/05. Regional specialities.
■ ACTIVITIES: Châteaux visits and wine tasting; canoeing, fishing, horse-riding and cycling nearby.
■ TARIFF: Double 280–350, Bk 35, Set menu 59–95 (Euro/Access, Visa).
■ DISCOUNT: 5%

CHAMONIX-MONT-BLANC Hte-Savoie 6A

Hôtel Albert 1er ★★★★ 119 impasse du
Montenvers, 74400 Chamonix-Mont-Blanc.
Tel 04 50 53 05 09, Fax 04 50 55 95 48.
English spoken.
Open 01/12 to 02/05 & 10/05 to 24/10.
32 bedrooms (all en suite). Outdoor swimming pool, golf 2 km, garage, parking. ♿

Beautiful hotel with a backdrop of mountains and only a stone's throw from the centre of town. Traditional Savoyard welcome. Just to the south of the N506.

■ RESTAURANT: Closed Wed lunch. Highly acclaimed restaurant with fine, inventive cuisine, regional specialities and an excellent cellar.

■ ACTIVITIES: Sauna, jacuzzi, massage, solarium, gym and practice golf at hotel; a variety of mountain and river activities with qualified instructors; scrambling.
■ TARIFF: (1996) Single 500–900, Double 590–1450, Bk 70, Set menu 190–470 (Amex, Euro/Access, Visa).
■ DISCOUNT: 10%

Hôtel Cairn ★★★ Praz-de-Chamonix,
74400 Chamonix-Mont-Blanc.
Tel 04 50 53 18 03, Fax 04 50 53 29 57.
English spoken.

Open 15/04 to 15/09. 14 bedrooms (all en suite). Golf on site, parking. ✆ ♿

Quiet, friendly hotel built in traditional Savoyard style only 5 minutes' drive from Chamonix town centre. Some rooms have a balcony and overlook Mont-Blanc. Terrace and large garden.

■ RESTAURANT: Typical regional specialities served by the fireplace or on the terrace.
■ ACTIVITIES: Children's entertainment, board games and library at hotel; fitness centre, hiking, cycling, tennis, rafting, paragliding and climbing nearby. The hotel can arrange fully inclusive sporting packages.
■ TARIFF: (1996) Double 320–420, Bk 38, Set menu 80 (Euro/Access, Visa).
■ DISCOUNT: 15%

France

France

Hôtel Frantour ★★
74400 Chamonix-Mont-Blanc.
Tel 04 50 53 07 56, Fax 04 50 53 54 79.
English spoken.

Open 01/12 to 31/10. 133 bedrooms
(all en suite). Golf 5 km, garage. &

*Large and comfortable in typical style, the hotel
is in the centre of Chamonix close to the station.*

■ RESTAURANT: Carefully prepared regional
cuisine in a Savoyard atmosphere; terrace with
view of Mont-Blanc.
■ ACTIVITIES: Sunbeds, sauna, jacuzzi, disco, bar-
club, nursery.
■ TARIFF: (1996) Single 379–472,
Double 486–578, Bk 35 (Amex, Visa).
■ DISCOUNT: 8%

Hôtel Grands Montets ★★★
340 chemin des Arbérons, Argentière,
74400 Chamonix-Mont-Blanc.
Tel 04 50 54 06 66, Fax 04 50 54 05 42.
English spoken.

Open 23/12 to 03/05 & 20/06 to 15/09.
40 bedrooms (all en suite). Golf 6 km, garage,
parking.

*Chalet-style hotel off the road and close to the
cable car. Each room has a balcony and lovely
views. 8 km from Chamonix-Mont-Blanc*

*towards Vallorcine and Switzerland. Follow
'Téléphérique de Lognan-Grands Montets'
signs.*

■ RESTAURANT: Traditional alpine cuisine.
Elegant dining room with panoramic view over
the valley of Chamonix and the Mont-Blanc
chain of mountains.
■ ACTIVITIES: Off-piste downhill and cross-
country skiing on the doorstep. In the
summertime: hiking, mountain-climbing and
mountain-biking.
■ TARIFF: Single 379–610, Double 450–654,
Set menu 98–135 (Euro/Access, Visa).
■ DISCOUNT: 5%

Hôtel Vallée Blanche ★★★ 36 rue du Lyret,
74400 Chamonix-Mont-Blanc.
Tel 04 50 53 04 50, Fax 04 50 55 97 85.
English spoken.

Open all year. 24 bedrooms (all en suite).
Golf 3 km, parking. &

*A charming hotel, cosy and comfortable with
hand-painted furniture. Piano bar and
riverside terrace. Five minutes' walk from the
cable cars and all facilities. From the
autoroute take the first Chamonix-Sud exit,
then follow signs to the town centre.*

■ RESTAURANT: Delicious regional and traditional
cuisine served in the pub-restaurant or on the
riverside terrace.
■ ACTIVITIES: Skiing, fishing, climbing, tennis,
para-gliding and mountain-biking nearby.
■ TARIFF: (1996) Single 366–505,
Double 412–522, Bk 38, Set menu 70–150
(Amex, Euro/Access, Visa).
■ DISCOUNT: 10% LS only.

CHAMPAGNOLE Jura   3C

Hôtel Ripotot ★★
54 rue Maréchal Foch, 39300 Champagnole.
Tel 03 84 52 15 45, Fax 03 84 52 09 11.
English spoken.

Open 01/04 to 30/11. 55 bedrooms (35 en suite). Tennis, golf 19 km, garage, parking. &

Owned by the fourth generation of the Ripotot family, hotel is set in large gardens with quiet, spacious accommodation. Motorway A36 to Poligny, then N5 to Champagnole.

■ RESTAURANT: 19th-century décor. Overlooks the garden and offers local specialities.
■ ACTIVITIES: Horse-riding, walking, swimming, golf and trout fishing nearby.
■ TARIFF: (1996) Single 160–270, Double 190–300, Bk 35, Set menu 70–220 (Amex, Euro/Access, Visa).
■ DISCOUNT: 5%

CHANTILLY Oise   2B

Hôtel Parc ★★★
36 av Maréchal Joffre, 60500 Chantilly.
Tel 03 44 58 20 00, Fax 03 44 57 31 10.
English spoken.

Open all year. 58 bedrooms (all en suite). Golf 3 km, garage. &

Located in the main avenue of Chantilly, close to the forest, château, racecourse and horse museum. Access via A1 Lille/Paris exit no 8. Several restaurants nearby as well as Indian restaurant in same building.

■ ACTIVITIES: English bar and disco at hotel; visit the horse museum and château.
■ TARIFF: Single 385, Double 440–520, Bk 48 (Amex, Euro/Access, Visa).
■ DISCOUNT: 10%

CHARTRES Eure-et-Loir   2D

Manoir des Prés du Roy ★★★ 28300 St-Prest.
Tel 02 37 22 27 27, Fax 02 37 22 24 92.
English spoken.
Open all year. 18 bedrooms (all en suite).
Tennis, golf 10 km, parking. ☎ &

A 15th-century manor set in a 10-hectare

park. From Chartres take the road to Maintenon, following signs for Vallée-de-l'Eure.

■ RESTAURANT: Closed Sun eve & Mon LS. Dining room has beamed ceiling and a fireplace. Meals also served in the park when weather permits.
■ ACTIVITIES: Billiards, walking, hot-air ballooning.
■ TARIFF: Single 350–580, Double 350–580, Bk 48, Set menu 140–250 (Amex, Euro/Access, Visa).
■ DISCOUNT: 10% LS.

CHATEAUBOURG Ille/Vilaine   1D

Hôtel Ar Milin ★★★ 35220 Châteaubourg.
Tel 02 99 00 30 91, Fax 02 99 00 37 56.
English spoken.
Open 02/01 to 23/12. 31 bedrooms (all en suite). Tennis, golf 15 km, parking.

An old mill house built of stone and huge beams. Cleverly restored to retain its original character and surrounded by the river and lovely, wooded parkland. Rooms are either in the mill house itself or in the park. The hotel is 1 km from the Châteaubourg exit off the E50 motorway between Rennes and Laval.

■ RESTAURANT: Closed Sun eve Nov to end Mar. Lovely beamed dining room with terrace opening onto the grounds. Specialities: feuilleté de coquillages St-Pierre aux coteaux du Layon, volailles fermières, poissons grillés ou en sauce.
■ ACTIVITIES: Lots to do for young and old including boating, fishing and watching the ducks, geese, lambs and rabbits that are kept in the grounds.
■ TARIFF: (1996) Single 325–640, Double 365–685, Bk 49, Set menu 99–196 (Amex, Euro/Access, Visa).

Hôtel Pen'Roc ★★★
La Peinière, 35220 St-Didier.
Tel 02 99 00 33 02, Fax 02 99 62 30 89.
English spoken.
Open all year. 33 bedrooms (all en suite).
Outdoor swimming pool, golf 15 km, garage, parking. &

An attractive, modern 'Silence' hotel built in local style and situated between Rennes and Paris in a quiet rural setting. Take motorway Paris to Rennes A81/N157 then exit Châteaubourg D857 and go 7.5 km to St-Didier (D33).

■ RESTAURANT: Closed Sun eve. Refined cuisine using local ingredients; the seafood is especially delicious.
■ ACTIVITIES: Sauna and fitness room.
■ TARIFF: Single 355–390, Double 400–450, Bk 48, Set menu 109–330 (Amex, Euro/Access, Visa).

France

CHATEAUDUN Eure-et-Loir   2D

Hôtel St-Michel ★★ 28 place du 18 Oct/5 rue
Péan, 28200 Châteaudun.
Tel 02 37 45 15 70, Fax 02 37 45 83 39.
English spoken.
Open all year. 19 bedrooms (15 en suite).
Golf 20 km, garage.

*An old coaching inn in the main square of the
town. Near the château, the caves and the
museum. From Paris, take motorway to Chartres
and then N10 south for 40 km to Châteaudun.*

■ ACTIVITIES: Sauna and solarium.
■ TARIFF: (1996) Single 150–250, Double 195–335,
Bk 33 (Amex, Euro/Access, Visa).
■ DISCOUNT: 5% LS.

CHATEAUROUX Indre   5A

Auberge Arc en Ciel ★★
La Forge-de-l'Ile, 36330 Châteauroux.
Tel 02 54 34 09 83, Fax 02 54 34 46 74.
English spoken.
Open all year. 24 bedrooms (18 en suite,
6 bath/shower only). Parking.

*Attractive setting beside the Indre river and
near an oak forest. Ten minutes from the town
centre on the D943 leading to Châtre.
Restaurant 20 m from hotel.*

■ ACTIVITIES: Châteaux visits.
■ TARIFF: (1996) Single 150–195,
Double 180–230, Bk 25 (Euro/Access, Visa).

CHATELAILLON-PLAGE Charente-Marit 4A

Hôtel de la Plage ★★
bd de la Mer, 17340 Châtelaillon-Plage.
Tel 05 46 56 26 02. English spoken.
Open 01/04 to 30/09. 10 bedrooms
(all en suite). Parking.

*Lounge and rooms overlooking the sea, Ile de Ré,
d'Oléron, d'Aix and Fort Boyard. An absolutely
safe, fine sandy beach in front of the hotel.*

■ ACTIVITIES: Swimming pool, tennis, sailing
school, fishing and clay-pigeon shooting nearby.
■ TARIFF: Double 220–260, Bk 30 (Visa).

CHATELGUYON Puy-de-Dôme   5A

Hôtel Bains ★★
12/14 av Baraduc, 63140 Châtelguyon.
Tel 04 73 86 07 97, Fax 04 73 86 11 56.
English spoken.
Open 25/04 to 01/10. 37 bedrooms
(30 en suite). Golf 5 km, parking.

*Town centre hotel with a pretty garden.
Châtelguyon is 15 km from Clermont-Ferrand,
just off the A71.*

■ RESTAURANT: Restaurant overlooks the garden.
Auvergne specialities: truite au lard, confit de
canard aux lentilles du Puy, chiffonade de salers,
coq au vin and bavette au bleu d'Auvergne.
■ ACTIVITIES: Sporting activities and volcanic
park nearby.
■ TARIFF: (1996) Single 200–280,
Double 200–315, Bk 36, Set menu 95–110
(Amex, Euro/Access, Visa).
■ DISCOUNT: 5% including restaurant.

Hôtel Mont Chalusset ★★★
rue Punett, 63140 Chatelguyon.
Tel 04 73 86 00 17, Fax 04 73 86 22 94.
English spoken.

Open 02/05 to 30/09. 45 bedrooms
(40 en suite). Golf 6 km, parking.

Quiet location in a magnificent verdant setting.

■ RESTAURANT: Gourmet cuisine and excellent
Bordeaux wine list. Specialities include filet de
truite bourguignone and coq en barbouille.
■ ACTIVITIES: Sauna, solarium, keep-fit room,
evening dancing; mountain-biking, horse-
riding, rafting, hiking and hot-air ballooning.
■ TARIFF: Double 290–350, Bk 46,
Set menu 100–230 (Amex, Euro/Access, Visa).
■ DISCOUNT: 5%

France

Hôtel Régence ★★
31 av Etats-Unis, 63140 Châtelguyon.
Tel 04 73 86 02 60, Fax 04 73 86 12 49.
English spoken.

Open 10/03 to 20/11. 27 bedrooms
(24 en suite). Golf 5 km, garage.

Traditional French hotel displaying 18th-century antique furniture. Châtelguyon is a thermal spa town and can be reached from the Riom-Est exit off A71 or D78 off N9. Special package available including room, dinner and breakfast. Details from hotel on request.

■ RESTAURANT: Regional and traditional dishes including coq au vin and salmon with oseille sauce; roast turkey with peaches and prunes and apple crumble are served once a week.
■ ACTIVITIES: Thermal centre, tennis, golf practice pitch, ballooning, hang-gliding and swimming pool nearby. Good area for astronomy as there is no light pollution and the stars are particularly bright.
■ TARIFF: (1996) Single 170–190, Double 195–200, Bk 38, Set menu 80–95 (Amex, Euro/Access, Visa).
■ DISCOUNT: 5%

CHATILLON-SUR-SEINE Côte-d'Or   3C

Hôtel de la Côte d'Or ★★★
rue Charles Ronot, 21400 Châtillon-sur-Seine.
Tel 03 80 91 13 29, Fax 03 80 91 29 15.
English spoken.
Open 01/03 to 31/12. 10 bedrooms
(all en suite). Golf 20 km, garage, parking.

Built in 1738, an old coaching house that still offers a warm welcome to weary travellers.

■ RESTAURANT: Closed from 15/12 to 31/01. Gourmet cuisine with Burgundian specialities. Meals served outside in summer.
■ TARIFF: Double 320–600, Bk 38, Set menu 95–185 (Amex, Euro/Access, Visa).

CHAUMONT Haute-Marne   3C

Hôtel Le Grand Val ★★ rte Langres,
52000 Chaumont.

Tel 03 25 03 90 35, Fax 03 25 32 11 80.
English spoken.
Open all year. 52 bedrooms (46 en suite).
Golf 18 km, garage, parking. &

Panoramic vista over the Marne Valley. The Grand Val is located at the southern exit of Chaumont on the road to Lausanne and the French Riviera, via Langres (N19).

■ RESTAURANT: Offers well-prepared meals and a carefully selected wine list.
■ TARIFF: (1996) Single 150–310, Double 175–320, Bk 27.50, Set menu 60–160 (Amex, Euro/Access, Visa).

CHENONCEAUX Indre/Loire   2C

Hôtel du Roy ★★
rue du Dr Bretonneau, 37150 Chenonceaux.
Tel 02 47 23 90 17, Fax 02 47 23 89 81.
English spoken.
Open 15/02 to 15/11. 37 bedrooms
(24 en suite). Tennis, golf 20 km, parking. &

Hotel with garden, in the village centre and close to château. From A10, exit at Amboise or Blois.

■ RESTAURANT: Gourmet restaurant with excellent meat, fish and game specialities.
■ TARIFF: Single 100–310, Double 140–310, Bk 30, Set menu 65–170 (Amex, Euro/Access, Visa).
■ DISCOUNT: 10%

CHERBOURG Manche   1B

Hôtel Louvre ★★
2 rue H Dunant, 50100 Cherbourg.
Tel 02 33 53 02 28, Fax 02 33 53 43 88.
English spoken.
Open 01/01 to 24/12. 42 bedrooms
(37 en suite). Golf 2 km, garage. &

A cheerful, friendly hotel close to town centre. Facilities include a lift and covered, secure garage. From the town centre, turn right after the bridge and then left after statue of Napoleon and traffic lights.

■ TARIFF: Single 235–330, Double 280–360, Bk 36 (Amex, Euro/Access, Visa).
■ DISCOUNT: 8%

France

CHINON Indre/Loire   2C

Hôtel Diderot ★★
4 rue Buffon, 37500 Chinon.
Tel 02 47 93 18 87, Fax 02 47 93 37 10.
English spoken.
Open 10/01 to 20/12. 28 bedrooms
(all en suite). Parking. &

*Highly recommended. A few yards from place
Jeanne d'Arc, this interesting 18th-century
building features half-timbered walls and an
especially fine staircase. Walled courtyard.
Family atmosphere.*
■ TARIFF: (1996) Single 250–320, Double 300–400,
Bk 40 (Amex, Euro/Access, Visa).
■ DISCOUNT: 20% Nov to Mar.

Hôtel de France ★★
47 place du Général de Gaulle, 37500 Chinon.
Tel 02 47 93 33 91, Fax 02 47 98 37 03.
English spoken.
Open 01/03 to 01/12. 30 bedrooms
(all en suite). Golf 15 km, garage, parking.

*Renovated 16th-century building combining
comfort with a respect for tradition. In the heart
of medieval Vieux-Chinon and the Loire Valley,
an ideal centre for exploring the 'Garden of
France'. View of the château and easy access.*
■ ACTIVITIES: Good area for cycling and walking.
■ TARIFF: (1996) Single 270–320, Double 270–
380, Bk 42 (Amex, Euro/Access, Visa).

CLERMONT-FERRAND Puy-de-Dôme   5A

Hôtel Lyon ★★★
16 place Jaude, 63000 Clermont-Ferrand.
Tel 04 73 93 32 55, Fax 04 73 93 54 33.
English spoken.
Open all year. 32 bedrooms (all en suite).
Golf 5 km, garage, parking.

*Situated in the old quarter of Clermont-
Ferrand, close to the cathedral.*
■ RESTAURANT: Lively brasserie/pub offering a
selection of salads and pizzas; good choice of
beers.
■ TARIFF: (1996) Single 280–310, Double 320–350,
Bk 35, Set menu 90 (Amex, Visa).
■ DISCOUNT: 15%

Novotel Clermont-Ferrand ★★★ Le Brezet,
32 rue G Besse, 63100 Clermont-Ferrand.
Tel 04 73 41 14 14, Fax 04 73 41 14 00.
English spoken.
Open all year. 96 bedrooms (all en suite).
Outdoor swimming pool, golf 6 km, parking. &

*The hotel is located near the A71 (Paris), A72
(Lyon) and A785 (Espagne) crossroads, 5 km
from the city centre and close to the Auvergne*

*volcanic peaks. Free pick-up from the airport
can be arranged.*
■ RESTAURANT: Air-conditioned restaurant.
French cuisine served on the terrace in
summer. Fish specialities.
■ ACTIVITIES: Exploring the volcanic parks.
■ TARIFF: Single 450, Double 490–530, Bk 53
(Amex, Euro/Access, Visa).
■ DISCOUNT: 10% except for weekends, Jul & Aug.

COGNAC Charente   4B

Hôtel Urbis ★★
24 rue Elisée Moushier, 16100 Cognac.
Tel 05 45 82 19 53, Fax 05 45 82 86 71.
English spoken.
Open all year. 40 bedrooms (39 en suite,
1 bath/shower only). Golf 5 km, parking. &

*Modern hotel with garden and private, locked
car park. Conveniently situated; very helpful staff.*
■ ACTIVITIES: Exploring the famous Cognac area;
boat hire on the Charente; visit to Norman city
of Saintes (25 km).
■ TARIFF: (1996) Single 270, Double 295, Bk 35
(Amex, Euro/Access, Visa).

COLMAR Haut-Rhin   3D

Hôtel Husseren-les-Châteaux ★★★
rue Schlossberg, 68420 Husseren-les-Châteaux.
Tel 03 89 49 22 93, Fax 03 89 49 24 84.
English spoken.

Open all year. 38 bedrooms (all en suite).
Indoor swimming pool, tennis, golf 22 km,
garage, parking. ✆ &

*Modern, interesting hotel with individually
decorated bedrooms on two levels. Views over
vineyards and the Rhine Valley. 6 km south of
Colmar on the N83.*
■ RESTAURANT: The well-appointed restaurant
and bar open out onto a terrace with
breathtaking views. Excellent cuisine.
■ ACTIVITIES: Well equipped children's

France

playroom, table tennis, sauna, solarium and fitness centre. Hotel organises once a week wine tastings.
■ TARIFF: Single 400–520, Double 510–620, Bk 55, Set menu 105–220 (Amex, Euro/Access, Visa).

Romantik Hôtel Le Maréchal ★★★★
4 place des 6 Montagnes Noires, Petite-Venise, 68000 Colmar.
Tel 03 89 41 60 32, Fax 03 89 24 59 40.
English spoken.
Open all year. 30 bedrooms (all en suite).
Golf 10 km. ✆

Beautiful, old, heavily-timbered building dating back to 1565, Le Maréchal is situated in the old quarter known as Little Venice. Elegantly furnished and with every comfort. Parking facilities nearby.

■ RESTAURANT: Dining rooms overlook the river. Excellent cuisine.
■ ACTIVITIES: Walking, cycling and exploring the wonderful countryside.
■ TARIFF: (1996) Single 450–550, Double 600–1500, Bk 75, Set menu 160–400 (Amex, Euro/Access, Visa).
■ DISCOUNT: 8%

Hôtel St-Martin ★★★
38 Grand'rue, 68000 Colmar.
Tel 03 89 24 11 51, Fax 03 89 23 47 78.
English spoken.

Open 01/03 to 31/12. 24 bedrooms (all en suite). Golf 10 km. ✆

Tastefully renovated, a former residence with quiet, intimate rooms, Louis XVI facade and Renaissance turret. In the historic heart of old Colmar, between the cathedral of St-Martin and the Old Customs House. Excellent restaurants close by.

■ ACTIVITIES: Reservations service for tours.
■ TARIFF: Single 290–450, Double 350–650, Bk 48 (Amex, Euro/Access, Visa).
■ DISCOUNT: 10%

COMBLOUX Haute-Savoie   6A

Hôtel Feug ★★★
route de Megève, 74920 Combloux.
Tel 04 50 93 00 50, Fax 04 50 21 21 44.
English spoken.
Open 20/12 to 20/09. 28 bedrooms (all en suite). Golf 2 km, garage, parking. ♿

Facing Mont-Blanc, chalet-style hotel offering every comfort and wonderful views.

■ RESTAURANT: Very pretty, panoramic restaurant with regional specialities including fondue, raclette, tartiflette and fresh fish dishes.
■ ACTIVITIES: Skiing, mountain sports, tennis and swimming pool close by.
■ TARIFF: Double 290–550, Bk 45, Set menu 105–195 (Amex, Euro/Access, Visa).

COMPIEGNE Oise   2B

Auberge à la Bonne Idée ★★★
St-Jean-aux-Bois, 60350 Compiègne.
Tel 03 44 42 84 09, Fax 03 44 42 80 45.
English spoken.
Open 01/01 to 15/01 & 15/02 to 31/12.
24 bedrooms (all en suite). Golf 8 km, parking. ✆ ♿

In the heart of the Forêt de Compiègne, hotel dates back to the 17th century. Located in the centre of St-Jean-aux-Bois on the D85, just 10 minutes' drive from the A1.

■ RESTAURANT: Gourmet restaurant with lots of atmosphere; meals served on a covered terrace when weather permits.
■ ACTIVITIES: Mountain bikes, horse-riding and archery nearby.
■ TARIFF: (1996) Double 280–480, Bk 55, Set menu 130–380 (Amex, Euro/Access, Visa).

Hôtel Relais Brunehaut
3 rue de l'Eglise, 60350 Chelles.
Tel 03 44 42 85 05, Fax 03 44 42 83 30.
Open 15/04 to 15/11. 6 bedrooms (all en suite).
Golf 15 km, parking. ♿

A former mill restored to working order. Situated in a pretty garden full of flowers in the heart of this picturesque village. 16 km from Compiègne.

■ RESTAURANT: Closed Mon & Tues. Ancient dining room with stained-glass windows, large chimney with open fireplace, beamed ceiling and stone walls.
■ TARIFF: (1996) Single 230–250, Double 260–300, Bk 36, Set menu 130–250 (Euro/Access, Visa).

France

COMPS-SUR-ARTUBY Var   6C

Grand Hôtel Bain ★★
83840 Comps-sur-Artuby.
Tel 04 94 76 90 06, Fax 04 94 76 92 24.
English spoken.
Open all year. 18 bedrooms (all en suite).
Tennis, golf 17 km, garage, parking.

*Located on the road between Draguignan and
Castellane, the hotel has been handed from
father to son since 1737. Currently being run
by Jean-Marie Bain, the 8th generation, with
his son Arnaud being the Chef de Cuisine.*

■ RESTAURANT: Authentic Var cuisine as well as
secret family recipes.
■ ACTIVITIES: Fishing, hang-gliding, paragliding,
mountain-biking, walking, bungee-jumping.
■ TARIFF: Single 240–260, Double 240–330,
Bk 35, Set menu 78–190 (Euro/Access, Visa).

CONCARNEAU Finistère   1C

Hôtel des Sables Blancs ★★ Plage des Sables
Blancs, BP 130, 29900 Concarneau.
Tel 02 98 98 01 39, Fax 02 98 50 65 88.
English spoken.

Open 01/04 to 30/10. 48 bedrooms
(43 en suite). Golf 5 km. ℄

*Set on the beach, this family-run hotel offers a
warm welcome. All rooms have sea views. 1 km
from Concarneau town.*

■ RESTAURANT: Restaurant and terrace have
panoramic sea views. Excellent cuisine with
seafood specialities.
■ ACTIVITIES: Fishing, boat trips, windsurfing
school; tennis 3 km. ● 10% discount (LS) at
nearby golf course.
■ TARIFF: (1996) Single 170–300, Double 190–350,
Bk 34, Set menu 85–195 (Amex, Euro/Access, Visa).
■ DISCOUNT: 10%

CORBEIL-ESSONNES Essonne   2D

Hôtel Mercure ★★★ rte de Milly,
91830 Le Coudray-Montceaux.

Tel 01 64 99 00 00, Fax 01 64 93 95 55.
English spoken.
Open all year. 125 bedrooms (all en suite).
Outdoor swimming pool, tennis, golf 5 km,
parking. ℄ ♿

*Modern and comfortable, surrounded by a
20-hectare wooded park. Excellent conference
facilities. 35 km south of Paris. Motorway A6
towards Lyon exit 11.*

■ RESTAURANT: Refined cuisine and excellent
wine cellar. Two dining rooms (one no-
smoking) overlooking the swimming pool and
park. Meals can be taken on the terrace by the
pool in fine weather.
■ ACTIVITIES: Indoor driving range, fitness room,
archery, rifle shooting, forest obstacle course;
mountain bikes available.
■ TARIFF: (1996) Double 595–615, Bk 59,
Set menu 95–125 (Amex, Euro/Access, Visa).
■ DISCOUNT: 8%

CORPS Isère   6A

Boustigue Hôtel ★★
rte La Salette, 38970 Corps.
Tel 04 76 30 01 03, Fax 04 76 30 04 04.
English spoken.
Open 01/05 to 20/10. 30 bedrooms
(28 en suite, 2 bath/shower only). Outdoor
swimming pool, tennis, golf 15 km, garage,
parking.

*Most attractive family-run hotel set in lovely
natural parkland. Offers relaxation, a warm
and cosy atmosphere and wonderful views.
From Corps take the route La Salette and hotel
is signposted along this road.*

■ RESTAURANT: Spacious, airy dining room
overlooking the gardens with specialities
including magret de canard au miel and civet
de porcelet.
■ ACTIVITIES: Indoor driving range at hotel;
hiking and exploring the beautiful countryside.
■ TARIFF: (1996) Single 237–292, Double 286–
345, Bk 38, Set menu 90–150 (Visa).

CORSE (CORSICA)

EVISA Corse-du-Sud   6D

Hôtel Scopa Rossa ★★ 20126 Evisa, Corse.
Tel 04 95 26 20 22, Fax 04 95 26 24 17.
Open 01/04 to 30/10. 25 bedrooms
(all en suite). Garage, parking. &

*In a peaceful setting just outside the village of
Evisa, a pleasant walk from the Spelunca Gorges
and with a playground for children. On D84.*

■ RESTAURANT: Offers home-cooked Corsican
food; breakfasts on the terrace.
■ ACTIVITIES: Mountain walks (organised for
groups); tennis and horse-riding nearby.
■ TARIFF: (1996) Single 200–250,
Double 220–350, Bk 35, Set menu 90–150
(Euro/Access, Visa).

ILE ROUSSE Haute-Corse   6D

Hôtel Cala di l'Oru ★★ 20220 Ile Rousse, Corse.
Tel 04 95 60 14 75, Fax 04 95 60 36 40.
English spoken.
Open all year. 24 bedrooms (all en suite).
Golf 10 km, parking.

*600 m from the beach with panoramic sea and
mountain views.*

■ ACTIVITIES: Sports facilities nearby.
■ TARIFF: Single 200–350, Double 250–450,
Bk 30 (Euro/Access, Visa).
■ DISCOUNT: 15%

PROPRIANO Corse-du-Sud   6D

Hôtel Roc e Mare ★★★
20110 Propriano, Corse.
Tel 04 95 76 04 85, Fax 04 95 76 17 55.
English spoken.
Open 01/05 to 15/10. 60 bedrooms
(all en suite). Parking.

*Located in the Gulf of Valinco, overlooking the
sea and 1 km from Propriano. The hotel has a
bar and lounge with panoramic views and a
private beach with snack bar.*

■ ACTIVITIES: Water sports from the private beach;
horse-riding, tennis and thermal spa nearby.
■ TARIFF: Single 350–480, Double 445–665,
Bk 50 (Amex, Euro/Access, Visa).
■ DISCOUNT: 10%

END OF CORSE (CORSICA) HOTELS

COURCHEVEL Savoie   6A

Hôtel Byblos des Neiges ★★★★
BP 98, 73122 Courchevel.

Tel 04 79 00 98 00, Fax 04 79 00 98 01.
English spoken.
Open 18/12 to 16/04. 77 bedrooms
(all en suite). Indoor swimming pool, garage,
parking. &

*At the foot of the largest expanse of ski slopes in
the world, in the heart of the alpine garden of
Courchevel, hotel is as luxurious as a palace
and as warm as a chalet. 15 minutes from the
centre of town. Prices quoted are for half
board.*

■ RESTAURANT: Excellent hot or cold buffets can
be enjoyed at 'La Clairière' with its pleasant
outdoor terrace, or try seafood specialities at
'L'Ecailler' in the evenings.
■ ACTIVITIES: Sauna, Turkish bath, hairdressing
and beauty salon at hotel; skiing on the doorstep.
■ TARIFF: (1996) Single 1650–1750,
Double 2160–3670, Bk 125, Set menu 330–370
(Amex, Euro/Access, Visa).

COUTANCES Manche   1B

Hôtel Cositel ★★
route de Coutainville, 50200 Coutances.
Tel 02 33 07 51 64, Fax 02 33 07 06 23.
English spoken.
Open all year. 55 bedrooms (all en suite).
Golf 10 km, garage, parking. (&

*Quiet hotel set amongst greenery and with lovely
views over the town. From Coutances, head
towards Coutainville and hotel is on the left.*

■ RESTAURANT: Closed 24 Dec eve. Comfortable
restaurant with regional cuisine and seafood
specialities.
■ ACTIVITIES: Tennis, swimming pool, horse-
riding and beach within easy reach. Good area
for sightseeing.
■ TARIFF: (1996) Single 275–330,
Double 305–360, Bk 40, Set menu 72–195
(Amex, Euro/Access, Visa).
■ DISCOUNT: 5%

France

LA CROIX-VALMER Var   6C

Thalotel Les Mas de la Magnanerie ★★★★
10 bd de la Mer, 83420 La Croix-Valmer.
Tel 04 94 79 56 15, Fax 04 94 79 73 73.
English spoken.

Open all year. 32 bedrooms (all en suite).
Indoor swimming pool, outdoor swimming
pool, parking. &

*On St-Tropez peninsula, only 400 m from the
beach, the hotel consists of apartments
surrounding a fountain, each with their own
jacuzzi. From the A8 take the D25 to St-
Maxime, N98 to Port Grimaud, then the D559
to La Croix-Valmer.*

■ ACTIVITIES: Hotel has its own private beach;
swimming pool is covered and heated in
winter. Water sports nearby.
■ TARIFF: Single 350–1110, Double 390–1150,
Bk 55 (Amex, Euro/Access, Visa).
■ DISCOUNT: 10%

DAX Landes   4C

Hôtel Splendid ★★★ cours Verdun, 40100 Dax.
Tel 05 58 56 70 70, Fax 05 58 74 76 33.
English spoken.
Open 03/03 to 24/11. 165 bedrooms
(all en suite). Outdoor swimming pool,
parking. ◖ &

*Purpose built in 1930, the hotel and gardens
are typical of the period. Comfortable
accommodation and good service.*

■ RESTAURANT: Art deco dining room with a
good choice of menus.
■ ACTIVITIES: Thermal centre and keep-fit at
hotel; mountain-biking, walking and hiking.
■ TARIFF: Single 340–400, Double 395–465, Bk 55,
Set menu 130–185 (Amex, Euro/Access, Visa).
■ DISCOUNT: 10%

DEAUVILLE Calvados   2A

Hôtel Helios ★★ 10 rue Fossorier, 14800 Deauville.

Tel 02 31 14 46 46, Fax 02 31 88 53 87.
English spoken.
Open all year. 44 bedrooms (all en suite).
Outdoor swimming pool, golf 3 km. &

*The hotel is right in the centre of Deauville in a
quiet area between the beach and the
racecourse, a few minutes' walk from the
casino, the C.I.D. (International Congress
Centre) and the sea-water therapy institute.*

■ ACTIVITIES: Tennis, sailing, horse-riding and
golf can be booked from the hotel. Details of
sightseeing tours and other activities available
on request.
■ TARIFF: (1996) Single 290–460, Double 390–
460, Bk 45 (Amex, Euro/Access, Visa).
■ DISCOUNT: 10%

Hôtel Marie-Anne ★★★
142 av République, 14800 Deauville.
Tel 02 31 88 35 32, Fax 02 31 81 46 31.
English spoken.
Open all year. 25 bedrooms (all en suite).
Golf 3 km, parking. ◖ &

*In the heart of Deauville, hotel is furnished
and equipped to a high standard and offers a
warm welcome and attentive service.*

■ ACTIVITIES: Within walking distance of all the
facilities Deauville has to offer, including the
racecourse and polo ground.
■ TARIFF: (1996) Double 250–500, Bk 50 (Amex,
Euro/Access, Visa).
■ DISCOUNT: 10% LS.

Hôtel Le Relais du Haras ★★★ 23 rue Louvel
et Brière, Touques, 14800 Deauville.
Tel 02 31 14 60 00, Fax 02 31 14 60 01.
English spoken.
Open all year. 8 bedrooms (all en suite).
Golf 2 km, parking. ◖

*In a medieval village close to Deauville, this
charming hotel overlooks the Meautry stud
farm, owned by the Rothschild family. Very*

*comfortable with individually decorated
rooms. Coming from Deauville, the hotel can
be found just as you enter Touques.*

■ RESTAURANT: Closed from 10/01 to 10/02.
Gastronomic restaurant offering light
traditional cuisine using only fresh local
produce. Specialities include pot-au-feu de
poisson and blanquette d'huîtres aux St-Jacques.
■ TARIFF: Single 300–600, Double 350–850,
Bk 50, Set menu 75–165 (Amex, Visa).
■ DISCOUNT: 10%

DIEPPE Seine Marit 2A

Hôtel de l'Europe ★★ 63 bd Verdun,
76200 Dieppe.
Tel 02 32 90 19 19, Fax 02 32 90 19 00.
English spoken.
Open all year. 60 bedrooms (all en suite).
Golf 4 km, parking. &

*With a super location facing the sea, hotel is
just a short walk from the pretty little harbour.
Modern, attractively decorated
accommodation with good facilities including
sound insulation and 2-way ventilation; all
rooms have a sea view. Several restaurants
within walking distance; business facilities.*

■ ACTIVITIES: Games room at hotel; tennis, horse-
riding, water sports and air club nearby. Visit
Cité de la Mer (50 m) and the Château-Musée,
displaying the finest ivory collection in Europe.
■ TARIFF: (1996) Single 300–320,
Double 320–340, Bk 35 (Euro/Access, Visa).

DIJON Côte-d'Or 3C

Hôtel Wilson ★★★ place Wilson, 21000 Dijon.
Tel 03 80 66 82 50, Fax 03 80 36 41 54.
English spoken.

Open 01/01 to 30/12. 27 bedrooms
(all en suite). Golf 10 km, garage. &

*A former coaching inn, this 17th-century hotel,
full of character, is situated south of Dijon just 5
minutes' walk from town centre towards airport.*

■ RESTAURANT: Closed Sun & Mon lunch. Truly
gastronomic cuisine is served in this highly
acclaimed restaurant.
■ ACTIVITIES: Visits to vineyards.
■ TARIFF: Single 345–480, Double 385–480,
Bk 55 (Euro/Access, Visa).

DINAN Côtes-du-Nord 1D

Hôtel de la Tour de l'Horloge ★★
5 rue Chaux, 22100 Dinan.
Tel 02 96 39 96 92, Fax 02 96 85 06 99.
English spoken.
Open all year. 12 bedrooms (all en suite).
Golf 10 km.

*Dating from the 18th century, hotel is cosy and
friendly with comfortable, up-to-date
accommodation. In the centre of Dinan, close
to the clock tower, old town and tourist office.*

■ ACTIVITIES: Swimming pool, tennis, horse-
riding, windsurfing, fishing, canoeing nearby.
■ TARIFF: Single 270–295, Double 295–335,
Bk 35 (Amex, Euro/Access, Visa).
■ DISCOUNT: 10% LS.

DINARD Ille-et-Vilaine 1D

Hôtel des Bains ★★★
20 rue du Poncel, 22770 Lancieux.
Tel 02 96 86 31 33, Fax 02 96 86 22 85.
English spoken.

Open all year. 14 bedrooms (all en suite).
Golf 3 km, parking. ℓ &

*Set 200 m from the main beach, this
refurbished hotel was once a family mansion.
An ideal starting point for excursions along the
Emerald Coast. On the D168 from Dinard.*

■ TARIFF: Single 320–500, Double 350–500,
Bk 35 (Amex, Euro/Access, Visa).
■ DISCOUNT: 15%

France

DONZENAC Corrèze 4B

Hôtel de la Maleyrie ★★ 19270 Sadroc.
Tel 05 55 84 50 67, Fax 05 55 84 20 63.
English spoken.
Open 25/03 to 01/11. 15 bedrooms
(12 en suite, 1 bath/shower only). Garage,
parking, restaurant.
*On the N20, 15 km north of Brive and 25 km
south of Uzerche.*
■ TARIFF: (1996) Double 110–230, Bk 28,
Set menu 65–160 (Euro/Access, Visa).

Hôtel Relais Bas Limousin ★★
Sadroc, 19270 Donzenac.
Tel 05 55 84 52 06, Fax 05 55 84 51 41.
English spoken.

Open all year. 22 bedrooms (all en suite).
Outdoor swimming pool, garage, parking.
*Quietly situated, a traditional Logis de France
hotel overlooking the Monts d'Auvergne and
Limousin. On N20 between Uzerche and Brive-
la-Gaillarde.*
■ RESTAURANT: Closed Sun eve LS. Home-made
dishes in attractive dining room overlooking
garden. Cèpes, girolles, saumon fumé, veau,
boeuf limousin, foie gras and confit are some
of the specialities on offer.
■ ACTIVITIES: Heated pool and children's
playground; horse-riding, rambling, fishing
and mountain-biking close by.
■ TARIFF: Double 210–350, Bk 33,
Set menu 82–250 (Euro/Access, Visa).

DUCEY Manche 1D

Auberge de la Selune ★★
2 rue St-Germain, 50220 Ducey.
Tel 02 33 48 53 62, Fax 02 33 48 90 30.
English spoken.
Open all year. 20 bedrooms (all en suite).
Parking. &

*Highly recommended (1996) as being
extremely comfortable and tremendous value
for money. Hotel is in a quiet, green setting by
the River Selune, famous for its salmon fishing.
South of Avranches and only 15 km from
Mont-St-Michel.*
■ RESTAURANT: Closed Mon LS. Completely
renovated in 1995, the pretty dining room
overlooks the gardens and offers a tempting
range of set menus.
■ ACTIVITIES: Salmon fishing, tennis nearby.
■ TARIFF: Double 270–290, Bk 40,
Set menu 78–200 (Euro/Access, Visa).

DUNKERQUE Nord 2B

Hôtel Climat de France ★★
59279 Loon-Plage.
Tel 03 28 27 32 88, Fax 03 28 21 36 11.
English spoken.
Open all year. 55 bedrooms (all en suite).
Parking. &

*Close to business centre, 12 km south-west of
Dunkerque on N1.*
■ RESTAURANT: Closed Sat lunch. All-you-can-eat
buffet and regional specialities.
■ TARIFF: Double 280, Bk 35, Set menu 85–145
(Amex, Euro/Access, Visa).
■ DISCOUNT: 10%

Europe'Hôtel ★★★
13 rue Leughenaer, 59140 Dunkerque.
Tel 03 28 66 29 07, Fax 03 28 63 67 87.
English spoken.
Open all year. 116 bedrooms (all en suite).
Golf 1 km, garage.

*In the heart of Dunkerque. Comfortable rooms;
piano bar.*
■ RESTAURANT: Choice of 2 restaurants: 'Le
Valentin' and 'Auberge La Ferme'.
■ TARIFF: Single 340, Double 390, Bk 46,
Set menu 90–220 (Amex, Euro/Access, Visa).
■ DISCOUNT: 10%

Green Hôtel ★★
route de Gravelines, 59279 Loon-Plage.
Tel 03 28 21 42 42, Fax 03 28 21 45 45.
English spoken.
Open all year. 64 bedrooms (all en suite).
Parking. &

*Modern and comfortable, hotel has fully
equipped rooms and is just two minutes from
the Sally Line terminal and ten minutes from
Dunkerque.*
■ RESTAURANT: Closed Sun & Mon eve. Light and
airy; offers a very good hors d'oeuvre buffet
and grill specialities.

■ TARIFF: Double 230, Bk 30, Set menu 35–75 (Amex, Euro/Access, Visa).
■ DISCOUNT: 10%

ENTRAIGUES Vaucluse   5D

Hôtel du Parc ★★
route de Carpentras, 84320 Entraigues.
Tel 04 90 83 62 43, Fax 04 90 83 29 11.
English spoken.
Open all year. 30 bedrooms (all en suite).
Outdoor swimming pool, parking,
restaurant. &

The hotel is situated in parkland. Leave the motorway at Avignon-Nord, towards Carpentras.

■ TARIFF: (1996) Single 200–250,
Double 250–300, Bk 36, Set menu 90–190
(Euro/Access, Visa).

EPERNAY Marne   3A

Château d'Etoges ★★★ 51270 Etoges.
Tel 03 26 59 30 08, Fax 03 26 59 35 57.
English spoken.
Open all year. 20 bedrooms (all en suite).
Golf 15 km, parking. &

Renovated 17th-century château surrounded by 12-hectare gardens in the heart of the Champagne region. Etoges is 20 km south of Epernay on D33.

■ RESTAURANT: Refined cuisine using fresh ingredients and fine selection of wines. Specialities include Saumon sauce champagne; pintade vigneronne.
■ ACTIVITIES: Hotel will make arrangements for visiting cellars and wine tasting.
■ TARIFF: Single 400, Double 550–700, Bk 70, Set menu 180–310 (Amex, Euro/Access, Visa).
■ DISCOUNT: 10%

ETRETAT Seine Marit   2A

Hôtel Dormy House ★★★
rte du Havre, 76790 Etretat.
Tel 02 35 27 07 88, Fax 02 35 29 86 19.
English spoken.
Open 15/02 to 03/01. 51 bedrooms
(all en suite). Golf on site, parking.

A typical old manor house, set on the cliff top in 4 ha of attractive parkland. Offers peace and quiet, wonderful views and comfortable accommodation. Bar and panoramic terrace. Walking distance from beach and town. On D940 from Le Havre.

■ RESTAURANT: Light and airy dining room with panoramic sea views. Gastronomic cuisine

with fish and seafood specialities including assiette de fruits de mer, moules de bouchot au cidre et Calvados and symphonie de la mer au beurre Dormy.
■ ACTIVITIES: Super base for touring and sightseeing; hotel will make reservations at local golf course.
■ TARIFF: Single 265–455, Double 260–650, Bk 50-65, Set menu 140–240 (Amex, Euro/Access, Visa).

EVIAN-LES-BAINS Haute-Savoie   6A

Hôtel Chez Tante Marie ★★
BP3, 74500 Bernex.
Tel 04 50 73 60 35, Fax 04 50 73 61 73.
English spoken.

Open 15/12 to 15/10. 27 bedrooms
(all en suite). Golf 12 km, parking.

Very cosy chalet hotel. Close to Lac Léman and 12 km from Evian, Bernex is a pretty alpine village in lovely surroundings. From Evian D21 to St-Paul and on to Bernex.

■ RESTAURANT: Charming restaurant and terrace with some wonderful views. Traditional and local specialities using fresh, local produce as well as home-cured charcuterie.
■ ACTIVITIES: Tennis, swimming, lake and mountain sports within easy reach.
■ TARIFF: Single 290–385, Double 320–385, Bk 47, Set menu 90–270 (Euro/Access, Visa).
■ DISCOUNT: 5%

France

France

Hôtel Ermitage ★★★★ Rive-Sud du Lac de Genève, 74500 Evian-les-Bains.
Tel 04 50 26 85 00, Fax 04 50 75 61 00.
English spoken.

Open 05/02 to 05/11. 91 bedrooms (all en suite). Indoor swimming pool, tennis, golf on site, parking. &

Set in a 16-hectare park overlooking the lake. Charming, fully restored country residence dating back to the turn of the century. Warm, relaxed atmosphere.

■ RESTAURANT: 3 inviting dining rooms offering cuisine based on local specialities and produce. Dishes include filet de féra du haut lac rôti au lard et aux cèpes and moelleux au chocolat pur Caraïbes aux griottes.
■ ACTIVITIES: The excellent facilities include own 18-hole Evian Masters golf course and tennis to jogging track and rifle shooting, horse-riding, sauna, steam bath, solarium, Turkish bath, children's club, concerts, shows, card and board game tournaments. Rafting, winter and water sports, paragliding and rock climbing nearby. ● Fitness and sports packages available at special rates.
■ TARIFF: Single 530–1750, Double 840–2870, Bk 90, Set menu 170–340 (Amex, Euro/Access, Visa).

EVREUX Eure   2A

Hôtel de France ★★
29 rue St-Thomas, 27000 Evreux.
Tel 02 32 39 09 25, Fax 02 32 38 38 56.
English spoken. Open all year. 16 bedrooms (all en suite). Golf 2 km, garage, parking.

An elegant, provincial building in a quiet location off the main street and offering traditional, high quality service.

■ RESTAURANT: Closed Sun eve & Mon. Superb restaurant overlooking the River Iton and gardens. Classic and contemporary cuisine.
■ ACTIVITIES: 4 golf courses within half an hour.
■ TARIFF: (1996) Single 245–340,

Double 265–340, Bk 34, Set menu 145–190 (Euro/Access, Visa).
■ DISCOUNT: 10%

LES EYZIES-DE-TAYAC Dordogne   4B

Hôtel Les Roches ★★
rte de Sarlat, 24620 Les Eyzies-de-Tayac.
Tel 05 53 06 96 59, Fax 05 53 06 95 54.
English spoken.

Open 15/04 to 30/10. 41 bedrooms (all en suite). Outdoor swimming pool, parking. &

Situated on the outskirts of the famous village of Les Eyzies-de-Tayac, in the heart of the Dordogne. Hotel has bar and garden.

■ ACTIVITIES: Canoeing, horse-riding and tennis nearby.
■ TARIFF: (1996) Double 280–350, Bk 38 (Euro/Access, Visa).

FECAMP Seine Marit   2A

Hôtel Poste ★★
4 av Gambetta, 76400 Fécamp.
Tel 02 35 29 55 11, Fax 02 35 27 48 74.
English spoken.
Open all year. 36 bedrooms (31 en suite, 5 bath/shower only). Golf 16 km, garage, parking.

Situated near the entrance to the port.

■ RESTAURANT: Closed 30/11 to 04/3 & Fri & Sun LS. Open for dinner only, restauraunt offers traditional cuisine with fish specialities including raie aux capres and filet de flétan au beurre blanc.
■ TARIFF: (1996) Single 145–270, Double 210–360, Bk 30, Set menu 79–240 (Euro/Access, Visa).

FERNEY-VOLTAIRE Ain   6A

Hôtel France ★★
1 rue Genève, 01210 Ferney-Voltaire.
Tel 04 50 40 63 87, Fax 04 50 40 47 27.
English spoken.

Open all year. 14 bedrooms (all en suite). Golf 5 km, garage, parking. ☎

Small and comfortable, the hotel is the closest French hotel to Genève, just 1 km from the airport, but very quiet. (Half board available from 385 FRF per night.)

■ RESTAURANT: Closed Sun & Mon lunch. Traditional French cuisine, excellent meat and fish dishes. Prepared by a former chef of the Ritz in Paris.
■ TARIFF: (1996) Single 290, Double 360, Bk 40, Set menu 115–225 (Amex, Euro/Access, Visa).
■ DISCOUNT: 10%

FONTAINEBLEAU Seine/Marne 2D

Hôtel de la Forêt ★★ 79 av Franklin Roosevelt, 77210 Fontainebleau-Avon. Tel 01 64 22 39 26, Fax 01 64 22 06 94. English spoken.
Open all year. 32 bedrooms (19 en suite). Outdoor swimming pool, golf on site, garage, parking. &

Just 2 minutes from Fontainebleau station, hotel is set in parkland with forest views. Discounts in LS.

■ RESTAURANT: Traditional French cuisine with a good choice of specialities.
■ TARIFF: (1996) Double 190–320, Bk 29.50, Set menu 75–92.50 (Euro/Access, Visa).

Hôtel Londres ★★★ place Général de Gaulle, 77300 Fontainebleau. Tel 01 64 22 20 21, Fax 01 60 72 39 16. English spoken.
Open 05/01 to 20/12. 12 bedrooms (all en suite). Golf 2 km, parking.

Family owned since 1850, hotel has an enviable position opposite the palace's main entrance. Comfortable rooms with antique furniture.

■ ACTIVITIES: Tennis, 'jeu de paume', water-skiing and health club nearby.
■ TARIFF: (1996) Double 250–800, Bk 50 (Amex, Euro/Access, Visa).

Hôtel Le Vieux Logis ★★★ 5 rue Sadi Carnot, Thomery, 77810 Fontainebleau. Tel 01 60 96 44 77, Fax 01 60 70 01 42. English spoken.
Open all year. 14 bedrooms (all en suite). Outdoor swimming pool, tennis, golf 7 km, parking.

Formerly a private mansion, hotel is situated in the heart of the small historic village of Thomery. Cosy, finely decorated accommodation. From the obelisk in Fontainebleau, take N5 to Sens and bear left at the 4th exit to Thomery.

■ RESTAURANT: Elegant, gourmet restaurant with relaxed atmosphere and flower-filled terrace.
■ ACTIVITIES: Forest walks; horse-riding nearby.
■ TARIFF: (1996) Double 400, Bk 50, Set menu 145–240 (Amex, Euro/Access, Visa).

FONTEVRAUD-L'ABBAYE Maine/Loire 2C

Hostellerie Prieuré St-Lazare
BP 14, 49590 Fontevraud-l'Abbaye. Tel 02 41 51 73 16, Fax 02 41 51 75 50. English spoken.

Open 15/03 to 02/01. 52 bedrooms (all en suite). Tennis, golf 4 km, parking. ☎ &

Comfortable relaxing hotel, situated on the site of the Royal Abbey of Fontevraud, finest and largest in the western Christian world. 16 km from Saumur on the D947.

■ RESTAURANT: Set in the cloister, offering refined, inventive cuisine. Specialities include croustillant de saumon and pommes de terre and pigeonneau braisé en cocotte au coulis de pêche.
■ ACTIVITIES: Medieval banquets, children's playroom. ● Free entry to the abbey.
■ TARIFF: (1996) Single 310–360, Double 290–460, Bk 50, Set menu 98–240 (Amex, Euro/Access, Visa).
■ DISCOUNT: 5%

FOUESNANT Finistère   1C

Hôtel Pointe Mousterlin ★★
Pointe de Mousterlin, 29170 Fouesnant.
Tel 02 98 56 04 12, Fax 02 98 56 61 02.
English spoken.
Open 15/04 to 30/09. 52 bedrooms
(all en suite). Tennis, golf 6 km, parking. &

*6 km from the village of Fouesnant, the hotel is
only 30 m from a long sandy beach.
Comfortable rooms, some of them inter-
connecting.*

■ RESTAURANT: Closed Sep to Apr. One rustic
restaurant, one modern. Traditional cuisine with
seafood specialities. Special menu for children.
■ ACTIVITIES: Health and fitness centre,
including sauna and jacuzzi; games room.
■ TARIFF: (1996) Single 262–290,
Double 290–425, Bk 38, Set menu 90–200
(Amex, Euro/Access, Visa).

GAVARNIE Htes-Pyrénées   4D

Hôtel Le Marbore ★★ 65120 Gavarnie.
Tel 05 62 92 40 40, Fax 05 62 92 40 30.
English spoken.

Open all year. 25 bedrooms (all en suite).
Outdoor swimming pool, golf 6 km, parking. &
*In the heart of the Pyrénées National Park, a
quiet, Logis de France hotel near the ski slopes.
Group discounts for parties of 6 or more.
Gavarnie is on the D921 south of Gedre.*

■ RESTAURANT: Decorated in Belle Epoque style
with house and regional specialities including
salade tiède aux langoustines, escalopes de
veau aux morilles fondue au magret de canard,
foie gras and patisseries.
■ ACTIVITIES: Sauna and keep-fit room at hotel;
horse-riding, fishing, mountain-biking, skiing.
Wonderful base for sightseeing (Lourdes only
50 km away) and nature lovers will be
delighted with the variety of flora and fauna.
■ TARIFF: Single 230, Double 270–295, Bk 32,
Set menu 100–185 (Amex, Euro/Access, Visa).

GEVREY-CHAMBERTIN Côte-d'Or   3C

Hôtel Arts et Terroirs ★★★
28 rte de Dijon, 21220 Gevrey-Chambertin.
Tel 03 80 34 30 76, Fax 03 80 34 11 79.
English spoken.

Open all year. 20 bedrooms (all en suite).
Golf 10 km, garage, parking.
*In the heart of a wine-producing area, very
comfortable hotel with fine antique furniture,
a wine bar and lovely gardens. South-west of
Dijon, off A31.*

■ ACTIVITIES: Exploring the region by bike;
wine tasting.
■ TARIFF: (1996) Single 250–430, Double 250–
480, Bk 45 (Amex, Euro/Access, Visa).
■ DISCOUNT: 10% except weekends.

GIEN Loiret   2D

Hôtel La Poularde ★★
13 quai de Nice, 45500 Gien.
Tel 02 38 67 36 05, Fax 02 38 38 18 78.
English spoken.
Open 15/01 to 31/12. 9 bedrooms (all en suite).
Tennis, golf 15 km, parking. ☎

*Small hotel with spacious rooms. Opposite the
River Loire and close to the Anne de Beaujeu
château.*

■ RESTAURANT: Traditional cuisine carefully
prepared by the chef Joël Danthu. Specialities
include poularde de Bresse aux girolles and
sandre au Chinon.
■ TARIFF: Single 240–260, Double 280–310, Bk 35,
Set menu 140–300 (Amex, Euro/Access, Visa).

Château de la Verrerie ★★★★ 18700 Oizon.
Tel 02 48 58 06 91, Fax 02 48 58 21 25.
English spoken.
Open 15/01 to 15/12. 12 bedrooms
(all en suite). Tennis, garage, parking.

*Comfort and tranquillity in this elegant,
Renaissance château which overlooks a lake in*

the middle of a forest. 32 km from Gien, going south on D940 to Aubigny-sur-Nère then D89. Follow signs to the château.

■ RESTAURANT: Closed Tues. The charming restaurant 'La Maison d'Hélène' is housed in a 17th-century cottage in the grounds. Specialities include fresh fish and game.
■ ACTIVITIES: Boating, fishing, bicycles and horse-riding (experienced riders only) at hotel; hot-air ballooning and horse-drawn carriage rides on request; possibility of game shooting in season.
■ TARIFF: (1996) Single 970–1360, Double 1000–1420, Set menu 95–195 (Amex, Euro/Access, Visa).
■ DISCOUNT: 15%

GIVET Ardennes   3A

Hôtel Val St-Hilaire ★★
7 quai des Fours, 08600 Givet.
Tel 03 24 42 38 50, Fax 03 24 42 07 36.
English spoken.

Open all year. 20 bedrooms (all en suite).
Golf 25 km, parking. ♿

Easy to find, it's the only hotel in Givet, near the Belgian border, on the waterfront alongside the River Meuse and bordered by a promenade. The hotel opened in 1990, is bright and cheerful and well situated in the heart of the cultural and artistic area of the town.

■ TARIFF: Single 290, Double 340, Bk 42 (Euro/Access, Visa).

LE GOLFE-JUAN Alpes-Marit   6D

Hôtel Beau Soleil ★★★
impasse Beau Soleil, 06220 Le Golfe-Juan.
Tel 04 93 63 63 63, Fax 04 93 63 02 89.
English spoken.
Open 26/03 to 15/10. 30 bedrooms (all en suite). Outdoor swimming pool, tennis, golf 10 km, garage, parking.

Completely renovated with all modern facilities including lift and underground car park. 500 m from the sea and 1 km from the centre of Golfe-Juan, towards Antibes.

■ RESTAURANT: Modern dining room overlooking the pool. Breakfast and dinner can be taken on the terrace in fine weather.
■ TARIFF: Single 300–485, Double 300–600, Bk 50, Set menu 89–125 (Euro/Access, Visa).

GRAMAT Lot   5A

Hôtel Le Relais des Gourmands ★★
av Gare, 46500 Gramat.
Tel 05 65 38 83 92, Fax 05 65 38 70 99.
English spoken.
Open all year. 16 bedrooms (all en suite).
Outdoor swimming pool, golf 20 km, parking.

A pleasant hotel complex, slightly off the beaten track. Light, comfortable rooms with some lovely views over the gardens and pool area. Gramat is on the A140.

■ RESTAURANT: Closed Sun eve & Mon lunch ex Jul/Aug. Refined, imaginative and regional cuisine complemented by some wonderful sauces and an excellent cellar. Meals can be taken outside on the terrace in summer.
■ ACTIVITIES: A host of things to see and do including hiking, mountain-biking, croquet, and table tennis.
■ TARIFF: (1996) Single 280–400, Double 280–440, Bk 40, Set menu 80–220 (Euro/Access, Visa).

GRANVILLE Manche   1B

Hôtel de la Gare ★★
1 place Cdt Godare, 50290 Bréhal.
Tel 02 33 61 61 11, Fax 02 33 61 18 02.
English spoken.
Open 01/02 to 19/12. 9 bedrooms (all en suite).
Golf 5 km, garage, parking. ☎

Small privately owned hotel near the sea. Bréhal is 10 km north of Granville on the D971.

■ RESTAURANT: Closed Sun eve & Mon LS. Professionally run restaurant with specialities including coquilles St-Jacques flambées, gratin de homard au whisky and magret de canard aux framboises.

■ ACTIVITIES: Tennis, horse-riding and pleasure flights are available nearby.

■ TARIFF: (1996) Single 160–280, Double 280–300, Bk 38, Set menu 77–180 (Amex, Euro/Access, Visa).

■ DISCOUNT: 5%

GRASSE Alpes-Marit 6D

Hôtel Relais Impérial ★★
06460 St-Vallier-de-Thiey.
Tel 04 93 42 60 07, Fax 04 93 42 66 21.
English spoken.
Open all year. 30 bedrooms (all en suite).
Tennis, golf 8 km, garage, parking. ℓ

Period hotel, completely refurbished and just 10 minutes from the centre of Grasse. Good atmosphere.

■ RESTAURANT: Rustic restaurant with a shady terrace. Regional and traditional cuisine with home-smoked salmon and foie gras.

■ ACTIVITIES: Good walks, rafting, canoeing, horse-riding and mountain-biking nearby.
● 10% discount on green fees.

■ TARIFF: (1996) Single 210–300, Double 230–450, Bk 35, Set menu 95–200 (Amex, Euro/Access, Visa).

■ DISCOUNT: 15%

LE GRAU-DU-ROI Gard 5D

Relais de l'Oustau Camarguen ★★★
3 rte Marines, Port-Camargue,
30240 Le Grau-du-Roi.
Tel 04 66 51 51 65, Fax 04 66 53 01 65.
English spoken.

Open 28/03 to 15/10. 39 bedrooms (all en suite). Outdoor swimming pool, golf 5 km, garage, parking. ♿

An old farmhouse which has been turned into a very comfortable hotel. From Port-Camargue follow signs to Plage-Sud.

■ RESTAURANT: Closed Mon lunch & Wed. Typical Camargue-style restaurant serving Provençal dishes: ballotine de lapin aux olives; papillote de raie au pistou; petits légumes farcis à la brandade; petite bourride de lotte.

■ ACTIVITIES: Water sports, fishing and water therapy centre nearby.

■ TARIFF: Double 380–520, Bk 50, Set menu 95–160 (Amex, Euro/Access, Visa).

■ DISCOUNT: 10% except Jul, Aug & Easter.

GRENOBLE Isère 6A

Hôtel Angleterre ★★★
5 pl V-Hugo, 38000 Grenoble.
Tel 04 76 87 37 21, Fax 04 76 50 94 10.
English spoken.
Open all year. 70 bedrooms (all en suite). ℓ

Comfortable hotel with all modern facilities. Near the gardens in a pedestrianised area of the city centre.

■ TARIFF: Single 380–580, Double 480–680, Bk 55 (Amex, Euro/Access, Visa).

Comfort Inn Primevère ★★
2 rue de l'Europe, 38640 Claix.
Tel 04 76 98 84 54, Fax 04 76 98 66 22.
English spoken.

Open all year. 45 bedrooms (all en suite). Outdoor swimming pool, golf 5 km, parking.

Small hotel with air-conditioned rooms and large terrace. 8 km south of Grenoble centre.

■ RESTAURANT: Enjoy the charming atmosphere while tasting the traditional, quality cooking featured in the various menus; à la carte gourmet food and specialities or the 'all you can eat' buffets; don't miss out on the wine selection!

■ ACTIVITIES: ● Special rates available for paragliding weekends.

■ TARIFF: (1996) Double 290, Bk 33, Set menu 82–190 (Amex, Euro/Access, Visa).

■ DISCOUNT: 10%

Château de la Commanderie ★★★

17 av Echirolles, 38320 Eybens.
Tel 04 76 25 34 58, Fax 04 76 24 07 31.
English spoken.

Open all year. 25 bedrooms (all en suite).
Outdoor swimming pool, golf 3 km, parking.

A comfortable 18th-century château set in parkland. From Grenoble, follow Rocade-Sud signs, then take exit 6 (Eybens/Bresson) and follow the signs.

■ RESTAURANT: Closed Sat & Sun. Refined, classic cuisine is served either in the elegant dining room or beneath the trees on the candlelit terrace.
■ ACTIVITIES: Good sports facilities including horse-riding and tennis close by and an international golf course at Bresson (5 minutes).
■ TARIFF: (1996) Single 412–670, Double 452–710, Bk 57, Set menu 153–255 (Amex, Euro/Access, Visa).

GREOUX-LES-BAINS Alpes/Hte-Prov 6C

Hôtel Villa Borghese ★★★

av des Thermes, 04800 Gréoux-les-Bains.
Tel 04 92 78 00 91, Fax 04 92 78 09 55.
English spoken.

Open 20/03 to 27/11. 67 bedrooms (all en suite). Outdoor swimming pool, tennis, golf 18 km, garage, parking.

Close to the Gorges du Verdon and facing the Thermal Park, a charming 'Silence' hotel with spacious accommodation and very pretty gardens.

■ RESTAURANT: Gourmet and creative cuisine with regional specialities.
■ ACTIVITIES: Health/beauty centre, bridge club; water sports nearby.
■ TARIFF: (1996) Single 360–670, Double 480–670, Bk 55, Set menu 160–250 (Amex, Euro/Access, Visa).
■ DISCOUNT: 10% except from 10/07 to 25/08.

GRIGNAN Drôme 5D

Manoir de la Roseraie ★★★

route de Valréas, 26230 Grignan.
Tel 04 75 46 58 15, Fax 04 75 46 91 55.
English spoken.

Open 14/02 to 05/11 & 14/11 to 04/01.
15 bedrooms (all en suite). Outdoor swimming pool, tennis, golf 8 km, garage, parking. ☎ ♿

De luxe 19th-century manor house in a 5-acre park, set at the foot of Madame de Sevigne's château.

■ RESTAURANT: Closed Mon LS. Enjoy the culinary delights of regional cooking together with the great wines of the Côte du Rhône. Specialities include foie gras maison, fish dishes and truffles in winter.
■ ACTIVITIES: Volley ball, table tennis and mountain-biking.
■ TARIFF: Single 700–1100, Double 700–1650, Bk 95, Set menu 185–240 (Amex, Euro/Access, Visa).
■ DISCOUNT: 10% except July & August.

France

HARDELOT Pas-de-Calais   2B

Hôtel du Parc-Intercontinental Resort
★★★ av Francois 1er, 62152 Hardelot.
Tel 03 21 33 22 11, Fax 03 21 33 29 71.
English spoken.
Open 01/02 to 18/12. 81 bedrooms
(all en suite). Outdoor swimming pool, tennis,
golf on site, parking. ✆ ♿

*The hotel lies in the heart of the Hardelot forest.
Close to the beach, it has two golf courses and
an equestrian centre. Rooms are of the highest
standard, most having a balcony or terrace
overlooking the forest. Between Boulogne and
Le Touquet.*

■ RESTAURANT: Hotel has a pretty dining room
offering local and seafood specialities. Both the
golf clubs also have a restaurant.
■ ACTIVITIES: Excellent sports and health
facilities at hotel and nearby. ● Special rates at
the two golf courses for hotel residents.
■ TARIFF: (1996) Single 415–515,
Double 520–620, Bk 50, Set menu 130 (Amex,
Euro/Access, Visa).

LE HAVRE Seine Marit   2A

Hôtel Mercure ★★★
chaussée d'Angoulême, 76600 Le Havre.
Tel 02 35 19 50 50, Fax 02 35 19 50 99.
English spoken.

Open all year. 96 bedrooms (all en suite).
Golf 15 km, garage, parking. ✆ ♿

*Recently renovated, air-conditioned hotel
facing the 'Bassin de Commerce'. Situated in
town centre within easy reach of railway
station, ferries, beach and shops. 6 km to
airport.*

■ RESTAURANT: Buffet breakfast. Traditional
cuisine in the 'Trois Mats' restaurant with fish
specialities; large choice of wines.
■ ACTIVITIES: ● 1 free entry to Dock Tonic
Sports Club.
■ TARIFF: Single 495–595, Double 545–595, Bk 55,
Set menu 129–159 (Amex, Euro/Access, Visa).

HYERES Var   6C

Hôtel Pins d'Argent ★★★ Port Saint-Pierre,
bd de la Marine, 83400 Hyères-Plage.
Tel 04 94 57 63 60, Fax 04 94 38 33 65.
English spoken.
Open all year. 20 bedrooms (all en suite).
Outdoor swimming pool, golf 15 km,
parking. ♿

*19th-century residence elegantly converted
into a hotel. Set in the middle of a pine wood
but only 800 metres from the beach. From
Hyères, follow directions to the airport.*

■ RESTAURANT: Closed 30/09-05/04 & Sun eve &
Mon LS. Very attractive, light and airy dining
room with seafood specialities. Meals served
beside the pool when weather permits.
■ TARIFF: (1996) Single 265–530,
Double 320–620, Bk 45, Set menu 110–180
(Amex, Euro/Access, Visa).

INGRANDES-SUR-LOIRE Maine/Loire   2C

Hôtel Le Lion d'Or ★★
26 rue du Pont, 49123 Ingrandes-sur-Loire.
Tel 02 41 39 20 08, Fax 02 41 39 21 03.
English spoken.

Open all year. 16 bedrooms (10 en suite,
6 bath/shower only). Garage, parking.

*Situated between Angers and Nantes, Le Lion
d'Or dates from 1660 and was the first hotel in
Ingrandes. Enjoy peace and relaxation in
renovated, modern rooms, close to the River Loire.*

■ RESTAURANT: Traditional French cuisine served
in a quiet dining room.

■ ACTIVITIES: Fishing, canoeing, cycling and tennis nearby.
■ TARIFF: (1996) Single 170–230, Double 170–270, Bk 26, Set menu 65–180 (Amex, Euro/Access, Visa).

L'ISLE-JOURDAIN Vienne 4B

Hôtel Val de Vienne ★★★
Port-de-Salle, 86150 Le Vigeant.
Tel 05 49 48 27 27, Fax 05 49 48 47 47.
English spoken.
Open all year. 20 bedrooms (all en suite).
Outdoor swimming pool, garage, parking. &

Beautifully situated on the banks of the River Vienne, each room has a private terrace overlooking the river. From L'Isle-Jourdain take D8 south towards Availles, turn left after 4 km to Port-de-Salles. Hotel well signposted on right.

■ RESTAURANT: Restaurant overlooking the River Vienne. Meals can be taken on the terrace in summer. Fine cuisine and good wine list.
■ ACTIVITIES: Mountain-bike hire, motor racing school, 4x4 track, microlighting, bungee-jumping. Also, fishing, hunting, and hiking.
■ TARIFF: (1996) Double 420–520, Bk 45, Set menu 90–250 (Euro/Access, Visa).

L'ISLE-SUR-LA-SORGUE Vaucluse 5D

Hôtel Mas des Grès ★★ route d'Apt,
84800 L'Isle-sur-la-Sorgue.
Tel 04 90 20 32 85, Fax 04 90 20 21 45.
English spoken.

Open 01/03 to 31/10 & 20/12 to 05/01.
14 bedrooms (all en suite). Outdoor swimming pool, golf 5 km, parking. &

Former farmhouse completely transformed into a charming inn. Family-run hotel offering a warm welcome and a relaxing atmosphere. Garden with century-old plane trees. From L'Isle-sur-Sorgue, drive 5 km on the N100 towards Apt and hotel is on the right.

■ RESTAURANT: Good Provençal cuisine using fresh market produce. Meals can be taken outside when weather permits.
■ ACTIVITIES: Kayaks and bikes available at hotel.
■ TARIFF: (1996) Double 430–550, Bk 55, Set menu 140 (Euro/Access, Visa).

JUAN-LES-PINS Alpes-Marit 6C

Beachôtel ★★★
av Alexandre III, 06160 Juan-les-Pins.
Tel 04 93 61 81 85, Fax 04 93 61 51 97.
English spoken.
Open all year. 43 bedrooms (all en suite).
Garage, parking. &

Modern hotel situated a few metres from the beach. West side of Juan.

■ RESTAURANT: Coffee shop/restaurant that offers a wide choice of grills and seasonal specialities.
■ TARIFF: Single 335–550, Double 410–650, Bk 45, Set menu 90–130 (Amex, Euro/Access, Visa).
■ DISCOUNT: 5%

KAYSERSBERG Haut-Rhin 3D

Hôtel Constantin ★★★
10 rue du Père Kohlmann, 68240 Kaysersberg.
Tel 03 89 47 19 90, Fax 03 89 47 37 82.
English spoken.

Open all year. 20 bedrooms (all en suite).
Golf 2 km, garage.

This 18th-century renovated wine grower's house is in the heart of the old city of Kayserberg near the Constantin fountain.

■ ACTIVITIES: Walking, cycling; good base for touring/sightseeing the Alsace.
■ TARIFF: (1996) Single 274–364, Double 408–458 (Euro/Access, Visa).

France

LALINDE Dordogne 4B

Hôtel Château ★★★ 24150 Lalinde.
Tel 05 53 61 01 82, Fax 05 53 24 74 60.
English spoken.
Open 15/02 to 01/01. 7 bedrooms (all en suite).
Outdoor swimming pool, golf 10 km, parking.

*Between the black and purple zones of the
Périgord, the Château is of 13th- and 18th-
century architecture and juts out over the River
Dordogne. Close to the town centre, but very
peaceful with a shaded terrace and pool area.*

■ RESTAURANT: Closed Mon lunch July & Aug.
Charming, typical of the region and overlooking
the river. Creative Périgord specialities, with
foie gras served in a variety of ways.
■ ACTIVITIES: Tennis nearby; good base for
touring and sightseeing.
■ TARIFF: Single 250–390, Double 390–850, Bk 60,
Set menu 160–220 (Amex, Euro/Access, Visa).
■ DISCOUNT: 15% for minimum 2-night stay with
meals taken in the restaurant.

LAMOTTE-BEUVRON Loir-et-Cher 2D

Motel des Bruyères ★★
Le Rabot, 41600 Lamotte-Beuvron.
Tel 02 54 88 05 70, Fax 02 54 88 98 21.
English spoken.
Open all year. 46 bedrooms (all en suite). Outdoor
swimming pool, tennis, golf 4 km, parking. ℂ

*On the N20, 30 km south of Orléans and 7 km
north of Lamotte-Beuvron.*

■ RESTAURANT: Rustic-style dining room.
Traditional cuisine with game in season.
■ ACTIVITIES: Indoor driving range, archery,
mountain bikes for hire, clay-pigeon shooting;
horse-riding nearby.
■ TARIFF: (1996) Double 215–333, Bk 28,
Set menu 89–197 (Euro/Access, Visa).

LANDIVISIAU Finistère 1C

Hôtel L'Enclos ★★
Lampaul Guimiliau, 29400 Landivisiau.
Tel 02 98 68 77 08, Fax 02 98 68 61 06.
English spoken.
Open all year. 36 bedrooms (all en suite).
Parking. ℂ ಸ

*Quiet hotel in country surroundings situated
in the heart of Brittany.*

■ RESTAURANT: Quiet, restful dining room.
Traditional cooking with seafood specialities.
■ ACTIVITIES: Rambling, trout and salmon
fishing; hiking, cycling circuit with mountain
bikes for hire.
■ TARIFF: Single 230, Double 268, Bk 32,
Set menu 68–200 (Amex, Euro/Access, Visa).

LANGEAIS Indre/Loire 2C

Hôtel Le Castel de Bray et Monts ★★★
Bréhémont, 37130 Langeais.
Tel 02 47 96 70 47, Fax 02 47 96 57 36.
English spoken.

Open 20/02 to 20/11. 12 bedrooms
(all en suite). Tennis, golf 10 km, parking. ಸ

*Unusual and rather eccentric 18th-century
manor house, with interesting rooms in the
main house but also in a converted chapel in
the grounds, which overlooks the vineyard.
From Langeais, cross the Loire and turn right
(west) along the southern bank for 3 km to
Bréhémont.*

■ RESTAURANT: Closed Wed 1/10 to 30/3.
Specialities include mousse de foie de Colvert
au Porto; mousse de brochet sauce écrevisse,
vol au vent aux escargots.
■ ACTIVITIES: Fishing and water sports close by.
● Cookery lessons with ex Ritz chef (Maxime
Rochereau) and Touraine visit.
■ TARIFF: (1996) Double 290–580, Bk 45,
Set menu 125–260 (Euro/Access, Visa).

Relais du Vieux Château d'Hommes ★★★★
Hommes, 37340 Savigné-sur-Lathan.
Tel 02 47 24 95 13, Fax 02 47 24 68 67.
English spoken.
Open all year. 5 bedrooms (all en suite). Indoor
swimming pool, outdoor swimming pool,
golf 10 km, garage, parking. ℂ ಸ

*In the heart of the Loire valley and its
vineyards, a 15th-century château with
comfortable rooms. North of Langeais on the
D57 to Hommes then right to Savigné.*

■ RESTAURANT: Specialities include aspèrges à la
crème, terrine de lapin and poulet à la Provençale.
■ ACTIVITIES: Walking; visits to Loire châteaux
and cellars.
■ TARIFF: (1996) Single 310–385, Double 485–
600, Set menu 150 (Euro/Access, Visa).
■ DISCOUNT: 15% from 01/09 to 01/06 only.

France

LANGRES Haute-Marne   3C

Auberge des Voiliers ★★
Lac de la Liez, 52200 Langres.
Tel 03 25 87 05 74, Fax 03 25 87 24 22.
English spoken.
Open 15/03 to 31/01. 8 bedrooms (all en suite).
Parking. ℄ ᕃ

*Small inn overlooking Lake Liez and offering a
warm welcome. Take the N19 towards Vesoul.
After 4 km turn right after the bridge and the
inn is 2 km ahead.*

■ RESTAURANT: Closed Sun eve & Mon from
01/10 to 01/05. Traditional regional cuisine
using local produce. Meals are served on the
terrace in fine weather and on a verandah
overlooking the lake at other times.
Specialities: milles-feuilles de grenouilles, filet
de brochet à l'ortie sauvage.
■ ACTIVITIES: Excellent sailing/boating facilities
nearby, including a national sailing school
800 m away. Opportunities for fishing, cycling
and lovely walks are also on the doorstep.
■ TARIFF: Double 220–300, Bk 35,
Set menu 78–200 (Euro/Access, Visa).
■ DISCOUNT: 5%

LANTOSQUE Alpes-Marit   6C

Hôtel Edward's et Chataigneraie ★★
06450 St-Martin-Vésubie.
Tel 04 93 03 21 22, Fax 04 93 03 33 99.
English spoken.
Open 10/06 to 29/09. 35 bedrooms (all en
suite). Outdoor swimming pool, parking.

*Quietly situated in this picturesque village, the
hotel is surrounded by a 1-hectare park. 15 km
north of Lantosque on the D2565.*

■ RESTAURANT: Open-air restaurant.
■ ACTIVITIES: Table tennis, mini-golf; tennis,
fishing, mountain-biking, horse-riding nearby.
Ideal base for mountain-hiking in the Parc National
du Mercantour and discovering its wildlife.
■ TARIFF: Single 310–420, Double 350–440,
Bk 20, Set menu 90 (Amex, Euro/Access, Visa).

LAON Aisne   2B

Hôtel Mercure ★★★
Golf de l'Ailette, 02860 Chamouille.
Tel 03 23 24 84 85, Fax 03 23 24 81 20.
English spoken.
Open 15/01 to 15/12. 60 bedrooms (all en suite).
Outdoor swimming pool, golf on site, parking. ᕃ

*Comfortable hotel in a peaceful, lakeside
setting with lovely views. From A26 south of
Laon, take Parc Nautique de l'Ailette exit and
follow signs to Chamouille and Golf de l'Ailette.*

■ RESTAURANT: Lake views. Excellent wine list at
very reasonable prices.
■ ACTIVITIES: Many leisure and sporting facilities
available including mountain-biking, water
sports and horse-riding. ● Special golf package:
room, breakfast and 1 green fee, 400 FF per
person on week days, 440 FF per person at
weekends.
■ TARIFF: (1996) Single 410–550,
Double 450–550, Bk 52, Set menu 110–160
(Amex, Euro/Access, Visa).

LE LAVANDOU Var   6C

Hôtel Tamaris ★★★
plage de St-Clair, 83980 Le Lavandou.
Tel 04 94 71 79 19, Fax 04 94 71 88 64.
English spoken.
Open 01/03 to 30/10. 41 bedrooms
(all en suite). Golf 5 km, parking. ᕃ

*Hotel is set on St-Clair beach, 2 km from Le
Lavandou. All the well-equipped rooms have
sea views.*

■ TARIFF: (1996) Single 350–450, Double 450–
500, Bk 35 (Amex, Euro/Access, Visa).

LEVENS Alpes-Marit   6C

Hôtel Malaussena ★★
9 place de la République, 06670 Levens.
Tel 04 93 79 70 06, Fax 04 93 79 85 89.
English spoken.
Open 15/12 to 31/10. 14 bedrooms
(10 en suite, 4 bath/shower only). Outdoor
swimming pool, tennis, parking. ᕃ

In the centre of Levens, 22 km north of Nice.

■ RESTAURANT: Closed eve except HS. Dining room
overlooks a garden. Regional cuisine with dishes
including ravioli, pissaladière, gigot and sole.
■ ACTIVITIES: Horse-riding, mountain walks.
■ TARIFF: (1996) Double 180–230, Bk 35,
Set menu 95–150 (Amex, Euro/Access, Visa).
■ DISCOUNT: 10%

France

LOCHES Indre/Loire   2C

Hôtel Château de Reignac
37310 Reignac-sur-Indre.
Tel 02 47 94 14 10, Fax 02 47 94 12 67.
English spoken.

Open all year. 10 bedrooms (8 en suite).
Golf 2 km, garage, parking.

Former property of Lafayette, this 15th-century château surrounded by a 7-hectare park has been converted in a luxury hotel. From Loches, drive 12 km north-west on the N143 towards Tours then turn right to Reignac-sur-Indre.

SEE ADVERTISEMENT

■ RESTAURANT: Traditional French cuisine and local specialities including gélines.
■ ACTIVITIES: Boules, billiards; health centre with qualified physiotherapist; sightseeing tours can be organized; tennis, fishing and football nearby.
■ TARIFF: (1996) Double 400–600, Set menu 100–150 (No credit cards).
■ DISCOUNT: 5%

LORIENT Morbihan   1C

Hôtel Astoria ★★ 3 rue Clisson, 56100 Lorient.
Tel 02 97 21 10 23, Fax 02 97 21 03 55.
English spoken.
Open all year. 34 bedrooms (all en suite).
Golf 5 km, garage, parking.

Close to the church in town centre, modern hotel with comfortable rooms.

■ ACTIVITIES: Diving and sailing club, swimming pool and horse-riding nearby.
■ TARIFF: Single 240–280, Double 270–325 (Amex, Euro/Access, Visa).

LOURDES Htes-Pyrénées   4D

Hôtel le Relais de Saux ★★★
Saux, 65100 Lourdes.
Tel 05 62 94 29 61, Fax 05 62 42 12 64.
English spoken.

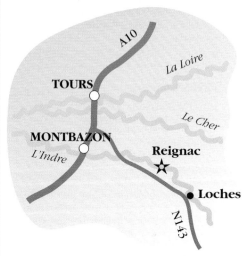

Open all year. 7 bedrooms (all en suite).
Golf 3 km, parking.
Situated between Tarbes and Lourdes in the beautiful Pyrénéan region with gardens. North-east of Lourdes on the N21 towards Tarbes.
■ RESTAURANT: Highly recommended restaurant. The chef buys only the best of local market-fresh produce.
■ TARIFF: (1996) Double 400–600, Bk 45, Set menu 140–310 (Amex, Euro/Access, Visa).

LUSIGNAN Vienne   4B

Hôtel Chapeau Rouge ★★
rue Nationale, 86600 Lusignan.
Tel 05 49 43 31 10, Fax 05 49 43 31 20.
English spoken.
Open 01/01 to 15/10 & 01/11 to 31/12.
8 bedrooms (all en suite). Golf 18 km, parking.
Pleasant, traditional hotel in the Vonne valley, home of the Mélusine fairy tales. Closed for two weeks school holidays in February and 2 weeks in October.
■ RESTAURANT: Closed Sun eve & Mon. Regional cuisine served in two country-style dining rooms with a superb feature fireplace.
■ ACTIVITIES: Fishing, swimming, tennis and nice walks nearby.
■ TARIFF: (1996) Single 220–240, Double 220–260, Bk 30, Set menu 90–200 (Euro/Access, Visa).

LUTZELBOURG Moselle   3B

Hôtel au Lion Bleu ★★
176 rue Koëberlé, 57820 Lutzelbourg.
Tel 03 87 25 31 88, Fax 03 87 25 42 98.
English spoken.
Open all year. 28 bedrooms (16 en suite).
Outdoor swimming pool, tennis, golf 2 km, garage, parking. ℂ ㄴ
Recommended. Traditional family-run hotel offering a warm welcome. Close to the canal and just 100 m from the pleasure boat quay.
■ RESTAURANT: Restaurant offers specialities of the region. Meals can be enjoyed on the shaded terraced when weather permits.
■ ACTIVITIES: Boating, fishing; touring and sightseeing.
■ TARIFF: (1996) Single 160–180, Double 195–320, Bk 30, Set menu 75–168 (Amex, Euro/Access, Visa).

LUXEUIL-LES-BAINS Haute-Saône   3D

Hôtel Beau Site ★★★ 18 rue Georges Moulimard, 70300 Luxeuil-les-Bains.

Tel 03 84 40 14 67, Fax 03 84 40 50 25.
Open all year. 33 bedrooms (all en suite).
Outdoor swimming pool, golf 10 km, garage, parking.
The hotel lies to the west of the town centre, follow signs to 'Les Thermes'. It is set in a large garden next to the thermal baths and close to the casino.
■ RESTAURANT: Closed Fri eve/Sat lunch 15/11-15/03. Seafood a. Seafood and foie gras maison specialities served in a rustic atmosphere, or on the terrace in summer.
■ ACTIVITIES: Cycling, walking in the forest, horse-riding. Thermal baths.
■ TARIFF: (1996) Single 220–265, Double 260–360, Bk 40, Set menu 90–200 (Euro/Access, Visa).
■ DISCOUNT: 5% including special offers.

LYON Rhône   5B

Château Perrache ★★★★ Grand Hôtel Mercure, 12 cours de Verdun-Rambaud, 69002 Lyon.
Tel 04 72 77 15 02, Fax 04 78 37 06 56.
English spoken.
Open all year. 121 bedrooms (all en suite).
Golf 10 km, garage. ℂ ㄴ
Traditional hotel built in 1906 and tastefully redecorated. Centrally located in Lyon.
■ RESTAURANT: Very comfortable dining room and fine cuisine based on high quality ingredients.
■ ACTIVITIES: Hotel can arrange water-taxi trips and dinner cruises.
■ TARIFF: Double 505–865, Bk 69, Set menu 120–250 (Amex, Euro/Access, Visa).
■ DISCOUNT: 10%

Hôtel Royal ★★★★
20 pl Bellecour, 69000 Lyon.
Tel 04 78 37 57 31, Fax 04 78 37 01 36.
English spoken.
Open all year. 80 bedrooms (all en suite).
Golf 20 km, garage.
In the heart of Lyon, between the Rhône and the Saône Rivers, the hotel overlooks a beautiful square and is close to the shops. From motorway, exit 'Centre ville-Bellecour'.
■ RESTAURANT: Closed Sat. The 'Petit Prince' restaurant is well known in Lyon for its fine food. Specialities include fish dumpling with langoustine sauce and lamb cutlets with thyme flower.
■ ACTIVITIES: Hotel will reserve theatre tickets and book excursions; car rental.
■ TARIFF: Single 630–950, Double 700–950, Bk 69, Set menu 98–142 (Amex, Euro/Access, Visa).
■ DISCOUNT: 10%

France

Hôtel La Tour Rose ★★★★
22 rue du Boeuf, 69005 Lyon.
Tel 04 78 37 25 90, Fax 04 78 42 26 02.
English spoken.

Open all year. 12 bedrooms (all en suite).
Garage. ☎ ♿

The hotel is a haven of comfort and conviviality, occupying three buildings dating from the 15th and 18th centuries. Its courtyards and gardens lead to the bar. Each room has been individually decorated and represents a different period in the history of Lyon's silk industry.

■ RESTAURANT: Closed Sun. The elegant dining room, with a glass roof, is in the 13th-century chapel. The chef Philippe Chavent, who is also the owner, adds a personal touch to every traditional recipe. In 'Le Comptoir du Boeuf' wine bar, which contains more than 30,000 bottles, a wine-tasting experience can be accompanied at any time of the day by simple but attractive dishes.
■ ACTIVITIES: Jazz concerts in the 'Jeu de Paume' bar every weekend ● During the cooking course, the chef sometimes reveals some of his secrets!
■ TARIFF: (1996) Single 950–1400, Double 1050–2800, Bk 95, Set menu 295–595 (Amex, Euro/Access, Visa).

MACON Saone-et-Loire   5B

Auberge La Sarrasine ★★★
Le Logis-Neuf, Confrançon, 01310 Polliat.
Tel 04 74 30 25 65, Fax 04 74 25 24 23.
English spoken.
Open 01/03 to 01/11. 11 bedrooms (all en suite). Outdoor swimming pool, golf 10 km, parking. ♿

From Mâcon cross the River Saône towards Bourg-en-Bresse. Continue for 18 km on the N79 to the village of Logis-Neuf and the hotel is beautifully situated just 1 km beyond.

■ RESTAURANT: Specialities include poulet de Bresse, grenouilles and pigeonneau rôti.
■ TARIFF: Single 350–490, Double 390–890, Bk 50, Set menu 100–290 (Amex, Euro/Access, Visa).
■ DISCOUNT: 5%

Hostellerie Sarrasine ★★★ 01750 Replonges.
Tel 03 85 31 02 41, Fax 03 85 31 11 74.
English spoken.

Open 01/02 to 04/01. 7 bedrooms (all en suite). Outdoor swimming pool, golf 2 km, parking. ♿

From Mâcon cross the River Saône towards Bourg-en-Bresse. Continue straight ahead on the N79 for 3 km to La Madeleine and this small, luxuriously decorated hotel is 500 m after the second set of traffic lights.

■ RESTAURANT: Regional specialities: poulet de Bresse, escargots de Bourgogne, filet de boeuf au Beaujolais.
■ TARIFF: Single 350–490, Double 390–790, Bk 55, Set menu 100–290 (Amex, Euro/Access, Visa).

MALAUCENE Vaucluse   5D

Résidence Arts et Vie Malaucène ★★★★
bd des Remparts, 84340 Malaucène.
Tel 04 90 12 62 00, Fax 04 90 12 62 99.
English spoken.
Open 01/01 to 02/11 & 21/12 to 31/12.

94 bedrooms (all en suite). Outdoor swimming pool, tennis, garage. ☎ ♿

A recently built residential complex, set in 5 ha at the foot of Mont Ventoux. Offers a choice of 2 to 4-room fully furnished and equipped apartments, as well as first-class facilities for seminars and conferences. Malaucène is just 200 m away, a beautiful village typical of the Vaucluse region, and offers a variety of restaurants and shops. (Prices quoted are per week based on a 2-room apartment suitable for up to 4 people. Special weekend rates available on request.)

SEE ADVERTISEMENT

■ ACTIVITIES: The excellent sports facilities, including an exceptional water sports complex (open June to September), are free to residents. Wonderful base for walking/hiking, sightseeing and taking advantage of all the cultural opportunities the region has to offer.
■ TARIFF: Double 1100–4200 (Amex, Euro/Access, Visa).

LE MANS Sarthe   2C

Hôtel Green 7 ★★
447 av G. Durand, 72100 Le Mans.
Tel 02 43 85 05 73, Fax 02 43 86 62 78.
English spoken.

Open all year. 50 bedrooms (all en suite). Golf 4 km, garage, parking. ☎ ♿

Modern hotel with red-bricked façade among oaks and chestnut trees.

■ RESTAURANT: Closed Fri & Sun eve. Gastronomic cuisine and light menu.
■ ACTIVITIES: Close to Mulsanne and Sargé golf courses, near the 24-hour race circuit, the go-karting circuit and the car museum.
■ TARIFF: (1996) Single 260, Double 260–315, Bk 34, Set menu 79.50–199 (Euro/Access, Visa).

MARLENHEIM Bas-Rhin   3D

Hostellerie du Cerf ★★★ 30 rue du Général de Gaulle, 67520 Marlenheim.
Tel 03 88 87 73 73, Fax 03 88 87 68 08.
English spoken.
Open all year. bedrooms. Golf 20 km.

A former staging post transformed in 1930 into a country inn. Elegant and comfortable rooms. In the centre of the pretty village surrounded by vineyards. From Strasbourg, go east on the motorway, then the N4 towards Saverne.

■ RESTAURANT: Closed Tues & Wed. Inventive cuisine taking the best of home-grown produce.
■ TARIFF: (1996) Single 300–450, Double 300–600, Bk 60, Set menu 295–500 (Amex, Euro/Access, Visa).

France

MARSEILLE Bouches-du-Rhône 5D

Hôtel Sofitel Vieux Port ★★★★
36 bd Ch Livon, 13007 Marseille.
Tel 04 91 15 59 00, Fax 04 91 15 59 50.
English spoken.

Open all year. 130 bedrooms (all en suite).
Outdoor swimming pool, golf 10 km, garage,
parking. ✆ ♿

*Hotel is situated by the old port, near the
Palace du Pharo. Very comfortable with a
wonderful view.*

■ RESTAURANT: Panoramic restaurant with
gourmet cuisine. Mediterranean specialities
based on seafood.
■ ACTIVITIES: All sports available in and around
Marseille.
■ TARIFF: Double 680–990, Bk 75,
Set menu 105–210 (Amex, Euro/Access, Visa).
■ DISCOUNT: 15%

MARTEL Lot 5A

Hôtel de la Bonne Famille ★
Sarrazac, 46600 Martel.
Tel 05 65 37 70 38, Fax 05 65 37 74 01.
English spoken.
Open all year. 24 bedrooms (6 en suite,
5 bath/shower only). Outdoor swimming pool,
tennis, parking.

*Small, comfortable and charming. The hotel has
been in the same family for three generations.*

■ RESTAURANT: Closed Fri eve & Sat HS. Good
food with local specialities can be enjoyed in
the pretty restaurant.

■ ACTIVITIES: Mountain-bike hire, table tennis,
boules, children's playground.
■ TARIFF: (1996) Double 145–230, Bk 35,
Set menu 75–150 (Euro/Access, Visa).

MAUSSANE-LES-ALPILLES 5D

Hôtel Val Baussenc ★★★ 122 av Vallée des
Baux, 13520 Maussane-les-Alpilles.
Tel 04 90 54 38 90, Fax 04 90 54 33 36.
English spoken.
Open 01/03 to 04/01. 21 bedrooms
(all en suite). Outdoor swimming pool,
golf 4 km, parking. ♿

*Attractive, spacious hotel offering a warm and
personal welcome. In Maussane, go towards
Mouries. The hotel is at the end of the village,
on the right-hand side.*

■ RESTAURANT: Closed Wed & Nov & Dec.
Regional cuisine offering Provençal specialities.
■ ACTIVITIES: ● Reduced green fees.
■ TARIFF: (1996) Single 490, Double 540–650, Bk 60,
Set menu 150–230 (Amex, Euro/Access, Visa).
■ DISCOUNT: 8% except Jul, Aug & public holidays.

MEGEVE Haute-Savoie 6A

Hôtel L'Igloo ★★★
au sommet du Mont d'Arbois, 74170 Megève.
Tel 04 50 93 05 84, Fax 04 50 21 02 74.
English spoken.
Open 15/06 to 15/09 & 15/12 to 20/04.
11 bedrooms (all en suite). Outdoor swimming
pool, golf 1 km, parking. ✆

*Only accessible by cable car (altitude 1850 m),
accommodation is in mountain-style chalets
with fantastic views towards Mt Blanc. Prices
quoted are for half board.*

■ RESTAURANT: Gourmet restaurant offering
Savoyard specialities, excellent food.
■ ACTIVITIES: Walking, winter skiing, sauna,
jaccuzi. Tennis courts 5 minutes.
■ TARIFF: Single 600–900, Double 1200–1800,
Set menu 150–250 (Euro/Access, Visa).
■ DISCOUNT: 10% half board.

MENDE Lozère 5C

Hôtel Pont Roupt ★★★
av 11 Novembre, 48000 Mende.
Tel 04 66 65 01 43, Fax 04 66 65 22 96.
English spoken.
Open 30/03 to 15/02. 27 bedrooms
(all en suite). Indoor swimming pool,
golf 25 km, garage, parking.

*In quiet quarter by the River Lot, 5 minutes from
town centre going towards the Tarn Gorges.*

■ RESTAURANT: Closed Sun eve and Mon.

Regional cuisine. Specialities: manouls de Lozère, coupetade, fromages de Lozère.
■ ACTIVITIES: Mountain-biking, walking, fitness facilities.
■ TARIFF: Single 260–330, Double 280–450, Bk 45, Set menu 95–190 (Euro/Access, Visa).
■ DISCOUNT: 10%

MENTON Alpes-Marit   6D

Hôtel Prince de Galles ★★★
4 av Général de Gaulle, BP 21, 06500 Menton.
Tel 04 93 28 21 21, Fax 04 93 35 92 91.
English spoken.
Open all year. 68 bedrooms (all en suite).
Golf 13 km, parking. &

Carefully restored, overlooking beach. Tropical garden with terrace. From Menton Casino follow promenade road towards Monaco for 2 km.

■ RESTAURANT: The restaurant 'Le Petit Prince' offering refined cuisine is situated in the garden.
■ ACTIVITIES: Within 300 m of the hotel: park with children's play area, heated pool, tennis courts. Trip bookings can be arranged at hotel.
■ TARIFF: Single 240–325, Double 310–540, Bk 42, Set menu 90–180 (Amex, Euro/Access, Visa).
■ DISCOUNT: 10% B&B only.

LES MENUIRES Savoie   6A

Hôtel L'Ours Blanc ★★★
Reberty 2000, 73440 Les Menuires.
Tel 04 79 00 61 66, Fax 04 79 00 63 67.
English spoken.

Open 15/12 to 01/05. 49 bedrooms (all en suite). Parking. (&

At an altitude of 2000 m, a chalet-style hotel in the skiing area of the 'Trois Vallées'. Take the D915 from Moutiers to the resort of Les Menuires, following the road to the left. The hotel is 1.5 km further along in Reberty 2000. (Prices based on half board.)

■ RESTAURANT: Breathtaking views of the mountains whilst enjoying gourmet cuisine prepared by Chef de Cuisine Pascal Casali.
■ ACTIVITIES: On the doorstep skiing! Fitness and games room, Turkish bath and solarium, cinema, billiards; outdoor swimming pool nearby.
■ TARIFF: (1996) Single 490–760, Double 720–940, Set menu 145–250 (Euro/Access, Visa).
■ DISCOUNT: 5%

MERIBEL-LES-ALLUES Savoie   6A

Hôtel Les Arolles ★★★
Méribel-Mottaret, 73550 Méribel-les-Allues.
Tel 04 79 00 40 40, Fax 04 79 00 45 50.
English spoken.

Open 21/12 to 04/05. 60 bedrooms (all en suite). Indoor swimming pool, garage, restaurant. (&

Situated on main ski run with a large south-facing terrace and excellent facilities. 4 km above Méribel; turn right over river on entering Méribel-Mottaret and go to top of resort.

■ ACTIVITIES: Gym, sauna and ski shop at hotel.
● Reduction on ski-lift passes at certain times during LS; 10% discount on ski hire.
■ TARIFF: Single 500–800, Double 800–1400, Set menu 120–180 (Euro/Access, Visa).

METZ Moselle   3B

Hôtel Cécil ★★ 14 rue Pasteur, 57000 Metz.
Tel 03 87 66 66 13, Fax 03 87 56 96 02.
English spoken.
Open all year. 39 bedrooms (36 en suite, 3 bath/shower only). Golf 8 km, garage.

This recently renovated hotel is quiet and comfortable. Near the station and A31 in the town centre.

■ ACTIVITIES: Organised tours depart from hotel for groups.
■ TARIFF: (1996) Double 220–280, Bk 30 (Amex, Euro/Access, Visa).
■ DISCOUNT: 10%

France

France

Hôtel du Théâtre ★★★ Port-St-Marcel,
1-3 rue du Pont-St-Marcel, 57000 Metz.
Tel 03 87 31 10 10, Fax 03 87 30 04 66.
English spoken.

Open all year. 36 bedrooms (all en suite).
Outdoor swimming pool, golf 3 km, garage,
parking. ❧ &

*In one of the oldest parts of Metz, this Châteaux
et Hôtels Independants hotel is part of a
redevelopment plan for the old port of St-
Marcel and so is right on the river. Rooms with
views of river or docks and waterside terraces.
Next to the cathedral.*

■ RESTAURANT: Restaurant dates back to 1649
and food is served by staff in regional costume.
Specialities: cochon de lait de Metz en gelée;
cuisses de grenouilles au gratin à la mode de
Boulay; matelote de brochet au vin de Contz.
Good selection of local wines.
■ ACTIVITIES: Health and fitness room (sauna,
solarium, spa) at hotel; tennis, water-skiing and
boat excursions (with lunch included), within
walking distance of hotel.
■ TARIFF: Single 395–550, Double 490–590, Bk 55,
Set menu 98–165 (Amex, Euro/Access, Visa).
■ DISCOUNT: 15% on presentation of this book.

MEURSAULT Côte-d'Or   3C

Hôtel Les Magnolias ★★★
8 rue P Joigneaux, 21190 Meursault.
Tel 03 80 21 23 23, Fax 03 80 21 29 10.
English spoken.
Open 01/03 to 01/12. 12 bedrooms
(all en suite). Golf 6 km, parking.

*In a small, quiet village surrounded by
vineyards. The bedrooms are individually
decorated with luxurious bathrooms.
Courtyard and garden. Exit from A6 at
Beaune and then N74, or A6 exit at Chalon-
sur-Saône then the N6 and N74. 6 km from
Beaune and 14 km from Chalon.*

■ TARIFF: (1996) Double 380–600, Bk 48
(Amex, Euro/Access, Visa).

MILLAU Aveyron   5C

Hôtel Cevenol ★★
115 rue du Rajol, 12100 Millau.
Tel 05 65 60 74 44, Fax 05 65 60 85 99.
Open 01/03 to 30/11. 42 bedrooms (all en
suite). Outdoor swimming pool, parking. &

*Highly recommended. 500 m from the town
centre going towards Montpellier-le-Vieux. A
modern hotel with a warm atmosphere and
lovely views from the terrace.*

■ RESTAURANT: Closed Sat & Sun lunch. Most
attractive dining room; specialities include
feuillete au Roquefort, magret de canard aux
baies de cassis, gigot d'agneau crème d'ail and
sabayon à la menthe chocolat chaud.
■ ACTIVITIES: Hotel will organise canoe hire for
Gorges du Tarn descent.
■ TARIFF: Single 280–308, Double 308–330,
Bk 37, Set menu 98–210 (Euro/Access, Visa).

MIREBEAU Côte-d'Or   3C

Auberge des Marronniers ★★
place Général Viard, 21310 Mirebeau-sur-Bèze.
Tel 03 80 36 71 05, Fax 03 80 36 75 92.
English spoken.
Open 08/01 to 20/12. 17 bedrooms
(16 en suite, 1 bath/shower only). Golf 20 km,
garage, parking. ❧ &

*A peaceful hotel on the river bank with
terraced flower gardens.*

■ RESTAURANT: Closed Sun eve. Overlooks the
gardens and river; meals served on the terrace
in summer.
■ ACTIVITIES: Tennis, swimming pool, canoeing
and kayaking nearby.
■ TARIFF: Single 160–200, Double 180–250,
Bk 25, Set menu 59–170 (Amex, Visa).

MISSILLAC Loire-Atlan   1D

Hôtel de la Bretesche ★★★ 44780 Missillac.
Tel 02 51 76 86 96, Fax 02 40 66 99 47.
English spoken.

Open 01/01 to 31/01 & 01/03 to 31/12.
29 bedrooms (all en suite). Outdoor swimming
pool, tennis, golf on site, parking. &

*On the bank of a beautiful lake and on the
edge of an 18-hole golf course, this 14th-century
château was completely renovated in 1996.
From Missillac, drive towards La Baule and the
hotel is 500 m from the village on the right.*

■ RESTAURANT: Closed lunch in Jul & Aug.
Gastronomic restaurant overlooking the
château de la Bretesche. Specialities include
soufflé de homard.
■ ACTIVITIES: Jogging trails around the lake and
in the forest. ● 20% discount on green fee.
■ TARIFF: Double 520–1200, Bk 60,
Set menu 150–250 (Amex, Euro/Access, Visa).

MONTE-CARLO   6D

Hôtel Mirabeau ★★★★ 1 av Princesse Grace,
98000 Monte-Carlo, Monaco.
Tel 04 92 16 65 65, Fax 04 93 50 84 85.
English spoken.
Open all year. 103 bedrooms (all en suite).
Outdoor swimming pool, garage.

*Located in the heart of Monte-Carlo, easily
accessible from both the Place du Casino and
the sea front. Beautifully appointed, spacious
rooms, most overlooking the swimming pool
and sea. Large terraces.*

■ RESTAURANT: Closed Aug. 'La Coupole' award-
winning restaurant; 'Café Mirabeau' and 'La
Terrasse de La Coupole' restaurants offer a full
range of dishes from gourmet to fixed price menus.
■ ACTIVITIES: Excursions and tickets to shows
arranged on request. ● Free access to all SBM
establishments and 50% reduction on tennis and
golf (Monte-Carlo Country Club and Golf Club).

■ TARIFF: Single 1100–2000, Double 1300–2400,
Bk 140, Set menu 300–430
(Amex, Euro/Access, Visa).
■ DISCOUNT: 10% Except during Monaco Grand
Prix.

Hôtel Vista Palace ★★★★ Grande Corniche,
06190 Roquebrune-Cap-Martin.
Tel 04 92 10 40 00, Fax 04 93 35 18 94.
English spoken.

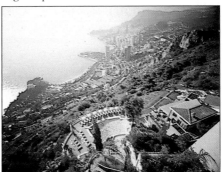

Open 15/03 to 30/11 & 20/12 to 06/01.
68 bedrooms (all en suite). Outdoor swimming
pool, golf 5 km, garage, parking. ℂ &

*De luxe hotel perched 350 m above the sea
overlooking Monte-Carlo and Cap Martin. 9-
acre landscaped Mediterranean gardens,
helicopter pad and boutique.*

■ RESTAURANT: Closed Sun eve & Mon. Gourmet
restaurant; restaurant for business meals,
functions and dances; summer restaurant
beside swimming pool.
■ ACTIVITIES: Workout centre with excellent
facilities including squash is free to guests.
Tennis nearby.
■ TARIFF: Single 1050–1300,
Double 1250–1600, Bk 100, Set menu 250–550
(Amex, Euro/Access, Visa).

MONT-LOUIS Pyrénées Orient ´   5C

Hôtel Corrieu ★★
La Lagonne, 66210 Mont-Louis.
Tel 04 68 04 22 04, Fax 04 68 04 16 63.
English spoken.
Open 21/12 to 28/03 & 02/06 to 28/09.
28 bedrooms (21 en suite). Tennis, golf 20 km,
parking.

*Situated in a pretty village at an altitude of
1700 m. Relaxing, family atmosphere; all the
rooms have panoramic views of the Pyrénées.
Lounge with fireplace. On the D118, 2 km
north of Mont-Louis.*

■ RESTAURANT: Carefully prepared dishes in a

France

panoramic setting. Local specialities include tourte jambon aux Banyuls, Capcir trout with almonds and Pyrénean lamb chops with herbs. ■ ACTIVITIES: In summer, discover the wildlife around the pretty lakes. ● Arrangements made for instruction and equipment hire for cross-country skiing.
■ TARIFF: Single 158–380, Double 178–380, Bk 40, Set menu 92–170 (Amex, Euro/Access, Visa).

LE MONT-ST-MICHEL Manche   1D

Hôtel de la Digue ★★★
50116 Le Mont-St-Michel.
Tel 02 33 60 14 02, Fax 02 33 60 37 59.
English spoken.
Open 01/04 to 15/11. 35 bedrooms (all en suite). Golf 20 km, parking.

2 km from Mont-St-Michel, which is illuminated at night, at the start of the famous dyke on the D976.

■ RESTAURANT: Panoramic views of Mont-St-Michel; seafood specialities.
■ ACTIVITIES: Horse-riding, tennis, water sports close by.
■ TARIFF: Single 320–380, Double 350–450, Bk 48, Set menu 85–220 (Amex, Euro/Access, Visa).

MONTBAZON Indre/Loire   2C

Château d'Artigny ★★★★ 37250 Montbazon.
Tel 04 47 26 24 24, Fax 04 47 65 92 79.
English spoken.

Open 10/01 to 30/11. 53 bedrooms (all en suite). Outdoor swimming pool, tennis, golf 17 km, garage, parking. &
Imposing château set in beautiful parkland. Excellent facilities and offering every comfort.
■ RESTAURANT: Gourmet cuisine with seafood and meat specialities.
■ ACTIVITIES: Excellent sports facilities as well as a fitness centre with jacuzzi and sauna. Balloon and helicopter pleasure flights depart from the

hotel. ● Special golf packages available.
■ TARIFF: (1996) Single 520–1670, Double 650–1670, Bk 90, Set menu 280–440 (Amex, Euro/Access, Visa).
■ DISCOUNT: 20% Nov to Mar.

MONTBELIARD Doubs   3D

Hôtel Bristol ★★ 2 rue Velotte, 25200 Montbéliard.
Tel 03 81 94 43 17, Fax 03 81 94 15 29.
English spoken.
Open 01/01 to 31/07 & 01/09 to 24/12.
43 bedrooms (40 en suite, 3 bath/shower only).
Golf 14 km, garage, parking.
Quiet, traditional hotel near the station and pedestrian area in the city centre.
■ TARIFF: Single 160–385, Double 180–410, Bk 33 (Amex, Euro/Access, Visa).
■ DISCOUNT: 10%

MONTLUCON Allier   5A

Hôtel Garden ★★
12 av Marx Dormoy, 03310 Neris-les-Bains.
Tel 04 70 03 21 16, Fax 04 70 03 10 67.
English spoken.
Open 22/01 to 31/12. 19 bedrooms (all en suite). Golf 4 km, garage, parking. ©
Pretty hotel 3 minutes from the centre of this spa town, in the Auvergne/Berry/Creuse triangle. 10 km from Montluçon, south on the A71.
■ RESTAURANT: Panoramic view over pretty parkland. Good choice of set or à la carte menus; meals served outside in fine weather.
■ ACTIVITIES: A variety of sports, plus tourist and historical sightseeing opportunities nearby.
● Free use of mountain bikes and nearby tennis court; guided walks on Wednesdays; discounts available for billards club, golf and horse-riding.
■ TARIFF: Double 240–295, Bk 32, Set menu 78–195 (Amex, Euro/Access, Visa).
■ DISCOUNT: 5%

MONTPELLIER Hérault   5C

Hôtel du Parc ★★
8 rue A Bège, 34000 Montpellier.
Tel 04 67 41 16 49, Fax 04 67 54 10 05.
English spoken.
Open all year. 19 bedrooms (all en suite).
Golf 4 km, parking. &
Former Languedocian residence built in the 18th century and now completely renovated. Located in the very heart of the city with garden and flowery breakfast terrace.

■ TARIFF: (1996) Single 200–350, Double 230–380, Bk 40 (Amex, Euro/Access, Visa).
■ DISCOUNT: 5%

MONTREUIL   Pas-de-Calais   2B

Auberge La Grenouillère ★★★ La Madelaine-sous-Montreuil, 62170 Montreuil-sur-Mer.
Tel 03 21 06 07 22, Fax 03 21 86 36 36.
English spoken.
Open 01/02 to 15/12. 4 bedrooms (all en suite).
Golf 15 km, parking. &

Picardy-style farmhouse set on the banks of the River Canche, at the foot of the ramparts of Montreuil-sur-Mer.

■ RESTAURANT: Closed Tues & Wed LS. Rustic atmosphere, good food with specialities such as cuisses de grenouilles and crêpes. Highly acclaimed.
■ TARIFF: (1996) Single 350, Double 350–500, Bk 45, Set menu 150–380 (Amex, Euro/Access, Visa).

Les Hauts de Montreuil ★★★ 21-23 rue Pierre Le Dent, 62170 Montreuil-sur-Mer.
Tel 03 21 81 95 92, Fax 03 21 86 28 83.
English spoken.
Open all year. 27 bedrooms (all en suite).
Golf 12 km, parking. &

This lovely old hotel is highly recommended and offers a warm welcome in delightful surroundings.

■ RESTAURANT: Closed from 06/01 to 30/01. Restaurant is surrounded by beautiful gardens and, dating from 1537, is one of the oldest in the town. Gastronomic cuisine, the freshly prepared dishes change with the seasons. Own cheese and wine cellars.
■ ACTIVITIES: Perfect base for exploring the region; within easy reach are Le Touquet, the Berck beaches, Bolougne-sur-Mer with its Nausicaa aquarium and Napoleonic souvenirs and the lovely fishing port of Etaples. Within walking distance, discover the ancient town of Montreuil itself.
■ TARIFF: (1996) Double 385–485, Bk 58, Set menu 145–235 (Amex, Euro/Access, Visa).
■ DISCOUNT: 10%

MONTRICHARD   Loir-et-Cher   2C

Hôtel de la Tête Noire ★★★
24 rue de Tours, BP3, 41401 Montrichard.
Tel 02 54 32 05 55, Fax 02 54 32 78 37.
English spoken.
Open 03/02 to 04/01. 36 bedrooms (30 en suite, 2 bath/shower only). Golf 17 km, parking.

A pretty hotel with comfortable rooms and a flower-filled terrace overlooking the river.

Montrichard is a small, friendly town on the River Cher, ideal for visiting nearby Loire Valley châteaux.

■ RESTAURANT: Closed 04/01 to 02/02. Omelette du Père Louis and poulet à la tourangelle are just two of the delicious dishes to choose from in the attractive dining room.
■ TARIFF: (1996) Single 200–285, Double 200–330, Bk 36, Set menu 96–260 (Euro/Access, Visa).

MORNAS   Vaucluse   5D

Hôtel Le Manoir ★★
av Jean Moulin, 84550 Mornas-en-Provence.
Tel 04 90 37 00 79, Fax 04 90 37 10 34.
English spoken.
Open 10/02 to 11/11 & 08/12 to 10/01.
25 bedrooms (all en suite). Golf 10 km, garage, parking.

An 18th-century manor house with stylish rooms and a beautiful terrace. Exit A7 at Bollene then go south on the N7 for 10 km or take exit from Orange and go north on N7.

■ RESTAURANT: Good, local cuisine in the elegant dining room or on the shaded terrace.
■ ACTIVITIES: Visit the medieval fortress in Mornas; close by are Orange, Vaison-la-Romaine and Côte du Rhône vineyards as well as facilities for horse-riding, tennis and swimming.
■ TARIFF: Single 250–305, Double 250–320, Bk 40, Set menu 100–185 (Amex, Euro/Access, Visa).
■ DISCOUNT: 10% on room only and on presentation of this book.

MORTAGNE-AU-PERCHE   Orne   2C

Hostellerie Genty-Home ★★
4 rue Notre Dame, 61400 Mortagne-au-Perche.
Tel 02 33 25 11 53, Fax 02 33 25 41 38.
English spoken.
Open all year. 11 bedrooms (all en suite).
Tennis, golf 15 km, parking. &

Situated in the centre of this picturesque town, near the church of Notre Dame. Small, elegant and comfortable. From Paris, take the N12 west towards Alençon.

■ RESTAURANT: Elegant Louis XV/XVI-style dining room. Restaurant enjoys a good reputation for its inventive menus and excellent cellar. Specialities include homard St-Jacques, filet de St-Pierre and boudin de Mortagne (Mortagne is the world capital of black pudding).
■ TARIFF: (1996) Single 210–285, Double 210–300, Bk 35, Set menu 55–169 (Amex, Euro/Access, Visa).
■ DISCOUNT: 10%

France

France

MORZINE Haute-Savoie   6A

Hôtel Soly ★★ Le Bourg,
Route de Télényon Avoriaz, 74110 Morzine.
Tel 04 50 79 09 45, Fax 04 50 74 71 82.
English spoken.
Open 15/12 to 20/04 & 15/06 to 15/09.
19 bedrooms (all en suite). Outdoor swimming
pool, golf 10 km, garage, parking. &

*A quiet, typical Savoyard chalet-hotel situated
100 m from the church. Good facilities and a
beautiful situation for both summer and
winter holidays. Half-board packages,
including ski-lifts are available.*

■ RESTAURANT: Savoyard specialities such as
fondue, raclette.
■ ACTIVITIES: Sauna, fitness centre.
■ TARIFF: Single 250, Double 320, Bk 39,
Set menu 95–140 (Amex, Euro/Access, Visa).
■ DISCOUNT: 5%

MOUGINS Alpes-Marit   6D

Hôtel Le Mas Candille ★★★★
bd Rebuffel, 06250 Mougins.
Tel 04 93 90 00 85, Fax 04 92 92 85 56.
English spoken.

Open 01/04 to 31/10. 23 bedrooms
(all en suite). Outdoor swimming pool, tennis,
golf 2 km, parking.

*Situated in the old village, five minutes' walk
from the centre, with beautiful views of the
surrounding hillside.*

■ RESTAURANT: Terrace restaurant with
panoramic view.
■ ACTIVITIES: 10 minutes from Cannes and
La Croisette.
■ TARIFF: (1996) Double 680–1150, Bk 85,
Set menu 185–250 (Amex, Euro/Access, Visa).
■ DISCOUNT: 8%

MULHOUSE Haut-Rhin   3D

Hôtel Bristol ★★★ 18 av de Colmar,
68100 Mulhouse.

Tel 03 89 42 12 31, Fax 03 89 42 50 57.
English spoken.
Open all year. 65 bedrooms (all en suite).
Golf 15 km, garage, parking. &

*From A36, situated in the centre of Mulhouse.
Colour TV, conference facilities, groups
welcome. Very comfortable and well furnished.*

■ ACTIVITIES: On the edge of the Vosges
mountains and the Black Forest.
■ TARIFF: (1996) Single 250–380, Double 280–450,
Bk 40 (Amex, Euro/Access, Visa).
■ DISCOUNT: 10%

Hôtel de Bâle ★★
19 passage Central, 68100 Mulhouse.
Tel 03 89 46 19 87, Fax 03 89 66 07 06.
English spoken.
Open all year. 32 bedrooms (22 en suite,
3 bath/shower only). Golf 8 km, parking.

*A well-kept, traditional hotel with garden and
offering a warm welcome. Leave motorway
A36 at Mulhouse-Centre. The hotel is in the
town centre opposite the Banque de France.*

■ ACTIVITIES: Good base for
sightseeing/organised tours, including 'route
du vin' and 'route des crêtes'.
■ TARIFF: (1996) Single 165–285,
Double 175–295, Bk 33 (Euro/Access, Visa).
■ DISCOUNT: 10% Except Jul & Aug.

Hôtel Inter Salvator ★★
29 passage Central, BP 1354, 68100 Mulhouse.
Tel 03 89 45 28 32, Fax 03 89 56 49 59.
English spoken.
Open all year. 54 bedrooms (all en suite).
Golf 15 km, garage.

*Quiet hotel offering a warm welcome, just after
the motorway exit to Mulhouse-Centre, turn
left at the tower and then go towards the station.*

■ ACTIVITIES: 2- and 5-day activity tours arranged
by hotel.
■ TARIFF: Single 260–280, Double 280–300,
Bk 35 (Amex, Euro/Access, Visa).
■ DISCOUNT: 10%

Hôtel du Musée ★★
3 rue del'Est, 68100 Mulhouse.
Tel 03 89 45 47 41, Fax 03 89 56 60 80.
English spoken.
Open 03/01 to 22/12. 44 bedrooms
(25 en suite, 3 bath/shower only). Golf 12 km,
garage, parking. ☎

*Traditional hotel with garden. Quiet and
comfortable, situated just in front of the museum,
close to town centre. Leave motorway at
Mulhouse-Centre exit and follow signs to station
and then 'Musée de l'Impression sur Etoffes'.*

■ ACTIVITIES: Fitness room at hotel. Cycling.
■ TARIFF: Single 155–280, Double 170–295,
Bk 34 (Amex, Euro/Access, Visa).
■ DISCOUNT: 10%

MUNSTER Haut-Rhin   3D

Hôtel Le Beau Site ★★
3 rue Principale, Hohrod, 68140 Munster.
Tel 03 89 77 31 55. English spoken.
Open 01/02 to 14/11. 14 bedrooms
(all en suite). Golf 15 km, garage, parking. ℓ

*In a quiet position on a hillside, the hotel has a
friendly atmosphere and all modern facilities.
Family rooms and apartment also available.
Large terrace with beautiful views. Follow
D417 from Colmar to Munster. After Munster,
turn right and the hotel is on the left.*

■ RESTAURANT: Local specialities in typical
Alsace setting. Possibility of half board with
set menu.
■ ACTIVITIES: In summer: mountain-bike trail,
tennis, horse-riding. In winter: cross-country
and down-hill skiing, tobogganing.
■ TARIFF: Single 155–170, Double 215–270,
Bk 30, Set menu 72–120 (Euro/Access, Visa).

NANCY Meurthe/Moselle   3D

Hôtel Mercure Nancy Centre Stanislas
★★★ 5 rue des Carmes, 54000 Nancy.
Tel 03 83 35 32 10, Fax 03 83 32 92 49.
English spoken.
Open all year. 80 bedrooms (all en suite).
Garage.

*Air-conditioned hotel near the historic town
centre, close to the station and 100 m from
Place Stanislas. Exit Nancy-Centre Ville and
follow signs to the station and place Stanislas.
Snacks are available at the hotel and there are
various restaurants nearby.*

■ TARIFF: Double 390–475, Bk 52 (Amex,
Euro/Access, Visa).
■ DISCOUNT: 5%

NANTES Loire-Atlan   1D

Hôtel Astoria ★★★
11 rue Richebourg, 44000 Nantes.
Tel 02 40 74 39 90, Fax 02 40 14 05 49.
English spoken.
Open all year. 45 bedrooms (42 en suite).
Garage. ৬

*In the centre of Nantes, near the cathedral,
Musée Beaux Arts and the railway station.
Quiet street close to public gardens.*

■ TARIFF: (1996) Single 290–320,
Double 290–350, Bk 38 (Euro/Access, Visa).

NANTUA Ain   6A

Hôtel de France ★★★
44 rue du Docteur Mercier, 01130 Nantua.
Tel 04 74 75 00 55, Fax 04 74 75 26 22.
English spoken.
Open 20/12 to 01/11. 17 bedrooms
(all en suite). Garage, parking.

*Old coaching inn offering a warm welcome.
Individually furnished bedrooms,
soundproofed and very comfortable. On A40
from Paris take exit 8, from Genève exit 9.*

■ RESTAURANT: Closed 01/11 to 20/12. Good
food, good wine list and excellent service.
Gratin de queues d'écrevisses, poulet aux
morilles à la crème and quenelle de brochet
maison are just three of the specialities.
■ ACTIVITIES: Water sports and mountain
pursuits nearby.
■ TARIFF: (1996) Single 215–280,
Double 300–405, Bk 33, Set menu 125–195
(Euro/Access, Visa).

NARBONNE Aude   5C

Novotel ★★★ quartier Plaisance,
route de Perpignan, 11100 Narbonne.
Tel 04 68 42 72 00, Fax 04 68 42 72 10.
English spoken.
Open all year. 96 bedrooms (all en suite).
Outdoor swimming pool, parking, restaurant. ℓ ৬

*Access from either the A9 or A61, exit Narbonne-
Sud. 5 km from town centre. Very comfortable,
with all the usual Novotel facilities.*

■ ACTIVITIES: Ideal base for visiting the Cathare
castles, Roman abbeys and the medieval city of
Carcassonne.
■ TARIFF: Single 410–450, Double 430–470, Bk 52,
Set menu 90–150 (Amex, Euro/Access, Visa).
■ DISCOUNT: 10%

France

Hôtel de la Clape ★★ rue des Flots Bleus, Narbonne Plage, 11100 Narbonne.
Tel 04 68 49 80 15, Fax 04 68 75 05 05.
English spoken.
Open 01/04 to 30/10. 15 bedrooms (6 en suite, 9 bath/shower only). Tennis, parking. ☎ ⅋

Exit Narbonne-Est from motorway and take D168 to this comfortable family hotel. Bar specialising only in non-alcoholic beverages.

■ TARIFF: (1996) Double 210–330, Bk 30 (Amex, Euro/Access, Visa).
■ DISCOUNT: 30% Apr & Oct; 15% May, Jun & Sep.

Hôtel Relais du Val d'Orbieu ★★★
11200 Ornaisons.
Tel 04 68 27 10 27, Fax 04 68 27 52 44.
English spoken.

Open all year. 20 bedrooms (all en suite). Outdoor swimming pool, tennis, golf 15 km, parking. ⅋

Within 15 minutes of the centre of Narbonne, in 2 acres of wooded garden. The hotel is an old mill which has been renovated and combines luxury and comfort together with charm. Take the A9 and exit Narbonne-Sud or the A61 and exit Lezignan-Corbières.

■ RESTAURANT: Closed lunch Nov to March. Renowned for its fine food.
■ ACTIVITIES: Solarium, indoor driving range, table tennis; visit to the vineyards and Corbières and Minervois wine tasting.
■ TARIFF: Single 390–590, Double 490–750, Bk 70, Set menu 175–295 (Amex, Euro/Access, Visa).
■ DISCOUNT: 8%

NEMOURS Seine/Marne   2D

Hôtel Les Roches ★★ av L. Pelletier, St-Pierre-lès-Nemours, 77140 Nemours.
Tel 01 64 28 01 43, Fax 01 64 28 04 27.
English spoken.
Open 01/01 to 31/01 & 01/03 to 31/12. .

15 bedrooms (13 en suite, 1 bath/shower only). Golf 10 km, garage, parking.

Former bistro converted into a comfortable hotel by present owners. 70 km from Paris and 12 km from Fontainebleau on N7.

■ RESTAURANT: Light and delicate traditional cuisine; regional value-for-money award.
■ ACTIVITIES: Water sports centre nearby.
■ TARIFF: (1996) Single 180–230, Double 230–270, Bk 35, Set menu 90–280 (Amex, Euro/Access, Visa).

NEUVILLE-AUX-BOIS Loiret   2D

L'Hostellerie ★★★ 48 place du Général Leclerc, 45170 Neuville-aux-Bois.
Tel 02 38 75 50 00, Fax 02 38 91 86 81.
English spoken.

Open all year. 34 bedrooms (all en suite). Golf 19 km, garage, parking. ☎ ⅋

Modern family hotel offering traditional hospitality and comfort. Situated in a typical village square, 20 km north of Orléans on D97 or from Paris, exit A10 at Artenay. Promotional weekend rates available on request.

■ RESTAURANT: Closed Sun eve from Oct to April. Has an excellent reputation for cuisine based on fresh, seasonal produce. Large selection of fine wines from the Loire Valley and Bordeaux area.
■ ACTIVITIES: Table tennis and keep fit at hotel; visit to Château de Chamerolles and the perfume museum (6 km). Ideal base for touring and sightseeing.
■ TARIFF: (1996) Single 340–600, Double 390–600, Bk 40, Set menu 85–180 (Amex, Euro/Access, Visa).
■ DISCOUNT: 10% standard rates only.

NEVERS Nièvre   2D

Hôtel de Diane ★★★ 38 rue du Midi, 58000 Nevers.
Tel 03 86 57 28 10, Fax 03 86 59 45 08.
English spoken.

Open 10/01 to 22/12. 30 bedrooms (all en suite). Golf 10 km, garage.

In the centre of town near the station and close to River Loire. From the station, take ave de Gaulle, in front of main gate, and then second right.

■ RESTAURANT: Closed Sun & Mon lunch.
■ TARIFF: Single 390–440, Double 450–590, Bk 40 (Amex, Euro/Access, Visa).

NICE Alpes-Marit   6D

Hôtel Agata ★★★ 46 bd Carnot, 06300 Nice.
Tel 04 93 55 97 13, Fax 04 93 55 67 38.
English spoken.
Open all year. 45 bedrooms (all en suite).
Garage, parking.

Set in a residential area close to the port of Nice. Soundproofed and air-conditioned rooms. Terraces with sea view.

■ ACTIVITIES: Beach 150 m from the hotel.
■ TARIFF: (1996) Single 400–480, Double 420–550 (Amex, Euro/Access, Visa).

Hôtel de Flore ★★★
2 rue Maccarani, 06000 Nice.
Tel 04 92 14 40 20, Fax 04 92 14 40 21.
English spoken.

Open all year. 63 bedrooms (all en suite).
Golf 10 km. ⚓ ♿

Recently renovated, the hotel is in the town centre, a few steps from the pedestrian streets and not far from the famous Promenade des Anglais and the beach. Its comfortable rooms provide charming, refined Provençal surroundings.

■ TARIFF: Single 370–550, Double 450–550, Bk 55 (Amex, Euro/Access, Visa).
■ DISCOUNT: 5%

Hôtel Harvey ★★ 18 av Suède, 06000 Nice.
Tel 04 93 88 73 73, Fax 04 93 82 53 55.
English spoken.
Open 01/02 to 31/10. 62 bedrooms (all en suite).

Modern hotel with a classical façade, right in the centre of Nice. Partly overlooking pedestrian area and 100 m from the beach and casino.

■ TARIFF: Single 260–370, Double 300–370, Bk 25 (Amex, Euro/Access, Visa).
■ DISCOUNT: 5% minimum 3-day stay.

Hôtel Windsor ★★★
11 rue Dalpozzo, 06000 Nice.
Tel 04 93 88 59 35, Fax 04 93 88 94 57.
English spoken.
Open all year. 60 bedrooms (all en suite).
Outdoor swimming pool, golf 10 km.

In the heart of Nice. From the Promenade des Anglais, close to Westminster Hotel, turn into Meyerbeer Street, take first right, then second left.

■ RESTAURANT: Closed Sun.
■ TARIFF: (1996) Single 350–525, Double 460–670, Bk 40 (Amex, Euro/Access, Visa).

NIMES Gard   5D

Hôtel Nimotel ★★ 30900 Nîmes.
Tel 04 66 38 13 84, Fax 04 66 38 14 06.
English spoken.
Open all year. 180 bedrooms (all en suite).
Outdoor swimming pool, golf 3 km, garage, parking. ⚓ ♿

2-star hotel with 3-star facilities. Attractive, well-equipped accommodation with air conditioning.

■ RESTAURANT: Attractive restaurant with a good choice of menus. Fish and couscous are specialities. Meals served outside on the terrace in summer.
■ ACTIVITIES: Ideal base for touring the Camargue and Cevennes and visiting the nearby beaches.
■ TARIFF: (1996) Single 245, Double 280, Bk 32, Set menu 83–125 (Amex, Euro/Access, Visa).

NIORT Deux-Sèvres   4B

Hôtel Les Ruralies ★★ 79230 Prahecq.
Tel 05 49 75 67 66, Fax 05 49 75 80 29.
English spoken.
Open all year. 51 bedrooms (50 en suite, 1 bath/shower only). Golf 8 km, parking. ♿

Hotel is in a quiet area, close to the Aquitaine A10 motorway between exits 22 and 23.

■ RESTAURANT: Regional and country cuisine in 'La Mijotière' restaurant; fast food in 'La Pergola' café.
■ TARIFF: Single 290–340, Double 340–390, Bk 35, Set menu 80–115 (Amex, Euro/Access, Visa).

France

NOIRMOUTIER-EN-L'ILE Vendée   1D

Hôtel Fleur de Sel ★★★
85330 Noirmoutier-en-l'Ile.
Tel 02 51 39 21 59, Fax 02 51 39 75 66.
English spoken.

Open 11/02 to 05/11. 35 bedrooms (all en suite). Outdoor swimming pool, tennis, parking. &

In a quiet island location between the port and beaches. Attractive flowered and exotic gardens. Approach island on D948.

■ RESTAURANT: Excellent restaurant overlooking gardens; seafood specialities.
■ ACTIVITIES: Indoor driving range, sauna, solarium, and bikes at hotel; windsurfing and sailing; many local places of interest to visit.
■ TARIFF: Single 325–475, Double 375–625, Bk 50, Set menu 120–168 (Amex, Euro/Access, Visa).
■ DISCOUNT: 10% 13/07 to 31/08.

OLORON-STE-MARIE Pyrénées-Atlan   4C

Hôtel Relais Aspois ★★ route du Col du Somport, Gurmençon, 64400 Oloron-Ste-Marie.
Tel 05 59 39 09 50, Fax 05 59 39 02 33.
Open all year. 25 bedrooms (20 en suite, 5 bath/shower only). Tennis, garage, parking.
☏

Chalet-style hotel with warm, comfortable accommodation and a family atmosphere. Gurmençon is 4 km south of Oloron on the N134.

■ RESTAURANT: Specialities from the Basque country: foie gras, magret de canard, confits, agneau des Pyrénées, fromage de montagne.
■ ACTIVITIES: Sightseeing tours including the wine and cheese routes; hotel organises a good range of activities including way-marked walks, trout fishing, mountain-biking and skiing.
■ TARIFF: (1996) Double 160–250, Bk 30, Set menu 70–150 (Amex, Euro/Access, Visa).

ORANGE Vaucluse   5D

Hôtel Mas de Bouvau
route de Cairanne, 84150 Violes.
Tel 04 90 70 94 08, Fax 04 90 70 95 99.
English spoken.

Open all year. 5 bedrooms (all en suite). Golf 5 km, parking. &

A highly recommended hotel set in the Mas Provençal, east of Orange. Take D975 north-east of Orange and after approx 13 km turn right on to D8. Hotel is 1 km ahead.

■ RESTAURANT: Closed Sun eve & Mon. Very comfortable. Has a good reputation for fine cuisine based on only the freshest of ingredients.
■ TARIFF: Single 300, Double 320–380, Bk 40, Set menu 130–265 (Amex, Euro/Access, Visa).
■ DISCOUNT: 10% on rooms only.

Hôtel Mas des Aigras chemin des Aigras, Russamp-Est, 84100 Orange.
Tel 04 90 34 81 01, Fax 04 90 34 05 66.
English spoken.
Open all year. 11 bedrooms (all en suite). Outdoor swimming pool, tennis, golf 4 km, parking.

In the middle of vineyards and orchards, a typically Provençal hotel in a garden setting. From Orange take the N7 north until you reach chemin des Aigras crossroads and then turn left.

■ TARIFF: Double 380–460, Bk 50 (Euro/Access, Visa).

ORBEY Haut-Rhin   3D

Hôtel de la Croix d'Or ★★
13 rue de l'Eglise, 68370 Orbey.
Tel 03 89 71 20 51, Fax 03 89 71 35 60.
English spoken.
Open 19/12 to 20/11. 19 bedrooms (16 en suite, 3 bath/shower only). Golf 10 km, parking.

A traditional, family-run hotel standing on a hillside just outside the village. Orbey, situated between the Vosges and Alsace, is 40 km from Gerardmer and 12 km from Kaysersberg, birthplace of Dr Albert Schweitzer, and is a perfect base for both summer and winter holidays.

■ RESTAURANT: Closed Mon & Wed lunch. Rustic-style restaurant serving regional specialities including gibier, truite au crèmant d'Alsace, saumon fumé à l'ancienne, coq au Pinot Noir and vacherin glacé 'Croix d'Or'.

■ ACTIVITIES: Sauna, mountain-biking and rambling; ski hire/lift passes available from hotel. ● Free wine tasting nearby for RAC guests taking breakfast and evening meal at the hotel.

■ TARIFF: (1996) Single 200–220, Double 250–290, Bk 45, Set menu 90–200 (Amex, Euro/Access, Visa).

■ DISCOUNT: 10% not May & Jul to Sep.

ORGEVAL Yvelines 2B

Hôtel Moulin d'Orgeval ★★★★
rue de l'Abbaye, 78630 Orgeval.
Tel 01 39 75 85 74, Fax 01 39 75 48 52.
English spoken.
Open all year. 14 bedrooms (all en suite).
Outdoor swimming pool, golf 3 km, parking.

Luxurious former abbey standing in beautiful grounds. From A13, exit at Poissy-Villennes. Turn right towards Orgeval, and look for signs.

■ RESTAURANT: Has facilities for the disabled and enjoys a very good reputation for fine cuisine.

■ TARIFF: (1996) Single 450–550, Double 600–720, Bk 60, Set menu 180–570 (Amex, Euro/Access, Visa).

■ DISCOUNT: 5%

ORLEANS Loiret 2D

Orléans Parc Hôtel ★★★ 55 rte d'Orléans, 45380 La Chapelle-St-Mesmin.
Tel 02 38 43 26 26, Fax 02 38 72 00 99.
English spoken.

Open all year. 32 bedrooms (all en suite). Garage, parking. ⅙

Quiet and comfortable 19th-century house in 8 acres, on the Loire. A71, exit Orléans-Centre. N152 to La Chapelle-St-Mesmin.

■ TARIFF: (1996) Single 300–320, Double 390–450, Bk 38 (Amex, Euro/Access, Visa).

OUISTREHAM Calvados 2A

Relais Mercure Côte de Nacre ★★
37 rue Dunes, 14150 Ouistreham.
Tel 02 31 96 20 20, Fax 02 31 97 10 10.
English spoken.
Open all year. 50 bedrooms (all en suite).
Golf 6 km, parking. ⅙

New hotel with all modern facilities. 500 m from the sandy beaches of the D-Day landings, opposite the car ferry terminal. 10 minutes from Caen, 30 km from Arromanches and Bayeux and 2 hours from Paris.

■ RESTAURANT: Has terrace overlooking the port. Traditional cuisine with fish specialities.

■ ACTIVITIES: Tennis, surfing, golf, therapy centre, casino and horse-riding within the area.

■ TARIFF: Single 225–280, Double 260–350, Bk 35, Set menu 50–140 (Amex, Euro/Access, Visa).

■ DISCOUNT: 10%

France

PARIS

PARIS I Paris   3B

Hôtel Britannique ★★★
20 av Victoria, 75001 Paris.
Tel 01 42 33 74 59, Fax 01 42 33 82 65.
English spoken.

Open all year. 40 bedrooms (all en suite).

*Located in a quiet avenue and a perfect base
for sightseeing. The hotel was renovated in
1993 and the comfortable, individualised
guest rooms have all modern facilities including
satellite television and Internet connection
(http://www.unimedia.Fr/britannique or
Email: britannique@unimedia.Fr).*

■ ACTIVITIES: Shopping; wine and chocolate tasting.
■ TARIFF: Single 646–752, Double 752–862,
Bk 50 (Amex, Euro/Access, Visa).
■ DISCOUNT: 10%

PARIS II Paris   3B

Hôtel Favart ★★★
5 rue Marivaux, 75002 Paris.
Tel 01 42 97 59 83, Fax 01 40 15 95 58.
English spoken.

Open all year. 37 bedrooms (all en suite). &

*Built in 1824, a quiet and comfortable hotel in
the central district of Paris where the most
important theatres and concert halls (the
Opera House, the Comédie Française, the
Opera Comique, the Folies Bergère) are found
as well as art galleries and antique dealers.*

■ TARIFF: (1996) Single 495–510,
Double 600–630 (Amex, Euro/Access, Visa).

PARIS III Paris   3B

Hôtel Pavillon de la Reine ★★★★
28 pl des Vosges, 75003 Paris.
Tel 01 42 77 96 40, Fax 01 42 77 63 06.
English spoken.

Open all year. 55 bedrooms (all en suite).
Garage, parking. ℂ

*In the historic Marais district, on the romantic
Place des Vosges, this air-conditioned hotel has
individually decorated rooms with antique
furniture, some overlooking flower-filled
courtyards.*

■ ACTIVITIES: Numerous museums around the
hotel: Picasso, Carnavalet..
■ TARIFF: Single 1600–1950, Double 1800–
2200, Bk 95 (Amex, Euro/Access, Visa).

PARIS VI Paris   3B

Holiday Inn Paris ★★★ St-Germain-des-Prés,
92 rue de Vaugirard, 75006 Paris.
Tel 01 42 22 00 56, Fax 01 42 22 05 39.
English spoken.
Open all year. 134 bedrooms (all en suite).
Garage. ℂ &

A super, friendly and well-run hotel in the

France

heart of the Left Bank. Modern, attractive and fully air conditioned, hotel has piano bar and own private underground garage. Good conference facilities.

■ RESTAURANT: Light and quick meals.
■ ACTIVITIES: Well placed for sightseeing, shopping and restaurants; fitness centre with squash, swimming pool and sauna next door.
■ TARIFF: (1996) Double 800–940, Bk 75 (Amex, Euro/Access, Visa).
■ DISCOUNT: 10%

Hôtel Relais Christine ★★★★
3 rue Christine, 75006 Paris.
Tel 01 43 26 89 38, Fax 01 43 26 89 38.
English spoken.

Open all year. 51 bedrooms (all en suite). Garage, parking. ☎

In the heart of St-Germain-des-Prés, on the left bank of the River Seine, this 16th-century hotel, formerly a cloister, offers a warm welcome. Air-conditioned rooms are individually decorated in warm-coloured fabrics and antique furniture.

■ TARIFF: Single 1630–1700, Double 1700–2550, Bk 95 (Amex, Euro/Access, Visa).

Hôtel Royal St-Germain ★★★
159 rue de Rennes, 75006 Paris.
Tel 01 44 39 26 26, Fax 01 45 49 09 23.
English spoken.

Open all year. 43 bedrooms (all en suite). ☎

Recently renovated and ideally situated between Montparnasse and St-Germain-des-Prés, close to the Latin Quarter and exhibition centre at Porte de Versailles.

■ ACTIVITIES: Hotel will arrange tours and sightseeing trips around Paris. Gymnasium, squash and swimming pool almost next door.
■ TARIFF: (1996) Single 450–600, Double 500–800, Bk 40 (Amex, Euro/Access, Visa).
■ DISCOUNT: 15%

Hôtel de Seine ★★★
52 rue de Seine, 75006 Paris.
Tel 01 46 34 22 80, Fax 01 46 34 04 74.
English spoken.
Open all year. 30 bedrooms (all en suite). ☎

At the corner of rue de Seine and rue Jacob, in the heart of St-Germain-des-Prés, the hotel offers comfortable rooms and family atmosphere.

■ TARIFF: (1996) Single 695, Double 980, Bk 45 (Euro/Access, Visa).

Hôtel Welcome ★★
66 rue de Seine, 75006 Paris.
Tel 01 46 34 24 80, Fax 01 40 46 81 59.
English spoken.
Open all year. 30 bedrooms (all en suite).

Small hotel ideally situated to explore the left bank of Paris and St-Germain-des-Prés.

■ TARIFF: Single 385, Double 495, Bk 40 (Euro/Access, Visa).

PARIS VII   3B

Hôtel Solférino ★★
91 rue de Lille, 75007 Paris.
Tel 01 47 05 85 54, Fax 01 45 55 51 16.
English spoken.

Open 03/01 to 21/12. 33 bedrooms (27 en suite, 6 bath/shower only). ☎

Close to the Tuileries, the Louvre, the Musée d'Orsay and St-Germain-des-Prés, the hotel is quiet and comfortable.

■ TARIFF: (1996) Single 265–455, Double 460–630, Bk 36 (Amex, Euro/Access, Visa).

France

PARIS VIII Paris 3B

L'Ouest-Hôtel ★★
3 rue de Rocher, 75008 Paris.
Tel 01 43 87 57 49, Fax 01 43 87 90 27.
English spoken.

Open all year. 53 bedrooms (all en suite).

Next to St-Lazare station, in the heart of the business centre, between Montmartre and the Champs-Elysées.

SEE ADVERTISEMENT

■ TARIFF: (1996) Single 360–480, Double 430–510, Bk 30 (Amex, Euro/Access, Visa).

PARIS IX Paris 3B

Hôtel du Pré ★★★
10 rue du P Sémard, 75009 Paris.
Tel 01 42 81 37 11, Fax 01 40 23 98 28.
English spoken.

Open all year. 145 bedrooms (all en suite). Parking.

Renovated throughout, central Paris location between the Opéra, Gare du Nord and Sacré Coeur. From Autoroute du Nord exit via Porte de la Chapelle to the Gare du Nord, then turn right down rue la Fayette to the hotel.

■ ACTIVITIES: Hotel will recommend and make reservaitons for restaurants, excursions and shows.
■ TARIFF: (1996) Single 425–445, Double 465–575, Bk 50 (Amex, Euro/Access, Visa).

Parrotel Paris Montholon ★★ 11 bis rue P Semard, 75009 Paris.
Tel 01 48 78 28 94, Fax 01 42 80 11 15.
English spoken.
Open all year. 46 bedrooms (all en suite). ☎

Comfortable hotel in the heart of Paris, near the Gare de l'Est and Gare du Nord. Buffet breakfast.

■ TARIFF: Single 300–400, Double 360–480 (Amex, Euro/Access, Visa).
■ DISCOUNT: 15%

PARIS XII Paris 3B

Nouvel Hôtel ★★ 9 rue d'Austerlitz, 75012 Paris.

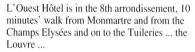

Tel 01 43 42 15 79, Fax 01 43 42 31 11.
English spoken.
Open all year. 24 bedrooms (all en suite). &

Ideally situated between Gare de Lyon and Gare d'Austerlitz. 10 minutes to Omnisport de Bercy and place de la Bastille. Three stops to Etoile and two stops to the Opéra on the métro. All rooms are comfortable, fully equipped and soundproofed.

■ TARIFF: (1996) Single 300–350, Double 380, Bk 25 (Euro/Access, Visa).
■ DISCOUNT: 10%

Hôtel Le Relais de Lyon ★★★
64 rue Crozatier, 75012 Paris.
Tel 01 43 44 22 50, Fax 01 43 41 55 12.
English spoken.

Open all year. 34 bedrooms (all en suite). Garage, parking.

Located in eastern central Paris, conveniently close to both the Bastille and the Gare de Lyon. Built in 1984, modern 5-storey building in a quiet location. Period furnishing; free garaging.

■ TARIFF: Single 356–386, Double 402–502, Bk 40 (Amex, Euro/Access, Visa).
■ DISCOUNT: 10% weekdays, 40% weekends.

PARIS XIII Paris   3B

Hôtel Arts ★★ 8 rue Coypel, 75013 Paris.
Tel 01 47 07 76 32, Fax 01 43 31 18 09.
English spoken.
Open all year. 37 bedrooms (all en suite).
Comfortable hotel in a quiet residential street. Close to the place d'Italie-Gobelins métro station.
■ TARIFF: (1996) Single 305–325, Double 350–420 (Amex, Euro/Access, Visa).

PARIS XIV Paris   3B

Hôtel Istria ★★
29 rue Campagne Première, 75014 Paris.
Tel 01 43 20 91 82, Fax 01 43 22 48 45.
English spoken.

Open all year. 26 bedrooms (all en suite).
Set in a very quiet street in artists' Montparnasse area, close to Luxembourg gardens. Fully equipped accommodation.
■ TARIFF: Single 470–530, Double 530–580, Bk 40 (Amex, Euro/Access, Visa).
■ DISCOUNT: 10% B&B.

Hôtel Mercure Paris Montparnasse ★★★
20 rue de la Gaîté, 75014 Paris.
Tel 01 43 35 28 28, Fax 01 43 27 98 64.
English spoken.
Open all year. 185 bedrooms (all en suite).
Garage. ✆ &

Modern hotel on the left bank, near Montparnasse TGV station and within walking distance of St-Germain-des-Prés, the Latin Quarter and Luxembourg Park. Access: Périphérique-Sud exit Pte Orléans towards Montparnasse.

■ RESTAURANT: Authentic bistro. Regional specialities plus a wide selection of daily dishes. Good wines at attractive prices.
■ ACTIVITIES: Hotel has an up-to-date information database on anything worth seeing or doing in Paris - all you have to do is ask!
■ TARIFF: (1996) Single 680–830, Double 800–860, Bk 68, Set menu 125–175 (Amex, Euro/Access, Visa).
■ DISCOUNT: 15% Jul & Aug only.

France

PARIS XV Paris   3B

Hôtel Arès ★★★
7 rue du Général de Larminat, 75015 Paris.
Tel 01 47 34 74 04, Fax 01 47 34 48 56.
English spoken.

Open all year. 43 bedrooms (all en suite).

Although close to the Eiffel Tower and the Champ de Mars, this Relais du Silence hotel boasts a very quiet city location. The bright, spacious rooms, some with balconies, are well furnished and have good facilities.

■ TARIFF: (1996) Single 530−560, Double 600−650, Bk 45 (Amex, Euro/Access, Visa).
■ DISCOUNT: 10% LS.

Hôtel Lecourbe ★★ 28 rue Lecourbe, 75015 Paris.
Tel 01 47 34 49 06, Fax 01 47 34 64 65.
English spoken.

Open all year. 47 bedrooms (all en suite).

Elegant, older hotel with an interesting history and charming, flower-filled private courtyard.

■ TARIFF: (1996) Single 400, Double 450, Bk 44 (Amex, Euro/Access, Visa).
■ DISCOUNT: 10%

Hôtel Lilas Blanc Grenelle ★★
5 rue de l'Avre, 75015 Paris.
Tel 01 45 75 30 07, Fax 01 45 78 66 65.
English spoken.

Open 01/01 to 31/07 & 24/08 to 31/12.
32 bedrooms (all en suite). Golf 18 km.

Located in the centre of the 15th district. Quiet and comfortable, its 32 personalised rooms, in harmony with the artist's palette, are equipped with the latest comforts. Visitor tax included in price.

■ ACTIVITIES: Swimming pool and tennis within 10 minutes of hotel; gymnasium 2 minutes.
■ TARIFF: (1996) Single 380−415, Double 405−455, Bk 35 (Amex, Euro/Access, Visa).
■ DISCOUNT: 5%

PARIS XVI Paris   3B

Demeure Hôtel Le Parc ★★★★
55-57 av Raymond Poincaré, 75116 Paris.
Tel 01 44 05 66 66, Fax 01 44 05 66 00.
English spoken.
Open all year. 120 bedrooms (all en suite). ☎ &

The hotel has been completely renovated and decorated in the English style and is situated between l'Etoile and the Trocadéro, in the heart of the 16th district.

■ RESTAURANT: Traditional cuisine in 'Le Relais du Parc' overlooking the interior garden or try Joël Robuchon restaurant next to the hotel, one of the best restaurants in the world.
■ TARIFF: (1996) Single 1990, Double 2300−2650, Bk 115 (Amex, Euro/Access, Visa).
■ DISCOUNT: 30% subject to availability.

Hôtel Hameau de Passy ★★
48 rue de Passy, 75016 Paris.
Tel 01 42 88 47 55, Fax 01 42 30 83 72.
English spoken.
Open all year. 32 bedrooms (all en suite). &

Recently renovated hotel with small garden and private garage nearby. In a residential area between Muette and Passy métro stations and close to the Eiffel Tower.

France

■ TARIFF: (1996) Single 450–520,
Double 500–590 (Amex, Euro/Access, Visa).
■ DISCOUNT: 10% June to Nov only.

Hôtel Pergolèse ★★★★
3 rue Pergolèse, 75116 Paris.
Tel 01 40 67 96 77, Fax 01 45 00 12 11.
English spoken.

Open all year. 40 bedrooms (all en suite).

Near Champs Elysées, between Arc de Triomphe and Palais de Congrès. Direct line to Louvre museum and business area La Défense. Decorated by the famous designer Rena Dumas.

■ TARIFF: Single 880–1180, Double 980–1580, Bk 65-90 (Amex, Euro/Access, Visa).
■ DISCOUNT: 20% except exhibition periods.

Hotel Saint James Paris ★★★★
43 av Bugeaud, 75116 Paris.
Tel 01 44 05 81 81, Fax 01 44 05 81 82.
English spoken.
Open all year. 48 bedrooms (all en suite).
Garage, parking. ✆

The only 'Château hotel' in Paris, this 19th-century hotel, completely renovated in 1987, was formerly the St James's club. Quiet and spacious bedrooms individually decorated in a

mixture of traditional and modern styles. The restaurant and the library-bar are reserved for residents and their guests only.

■ RESTAURANT: Closed weekend. French inventive cuisine with fish and seafood specialities. Meals served on the terrace in fine weather.
■ ACTIVITIES: Fitness room, sauna, jacuzzi at hotel. A few steps from the Champs Elysées and the Eiffel Tower.
■ TARIFF: Single 1600–2000,
Double 1850–1980, Bk 95, Set menu 350–900 (Amex, Euro/Access, Visa).

PARIS XVII Paris   3B

Hôtel Regent's Garden ★★★
6 rue Pierre Demours, 75017 Paris.
Tel 01 45 74 07 30, Fax 01 40 55 01 42.
English spoken.

Open all year. 39 bedrooms (all en suite).
Parking. ✆ ♿

Near the Etoile, this hotel built by Napoleon III, is furnished with antiques and offers breakfast in the gardens during summer months.

■ TARIFF: Single 620–810, Double 670–900, Bk 36 (Amex, Euro/Access, Visa).
■ DISCOUNT: 10%

PARIS WEST

LES ULIS Essonne   3B

Hôtel Mercure ★★★ 3 rue Rio Solado,
Courtaboeuf, 91952 Les Ulis.
Tel 01 69 07 63 96, Fax 01 69 07 92 00.
English spoken.
Open all year. 108 bedrooms (all en suite).
Outdoor swimming pool, tennis, golf 12 km,
parking, restaurant. ✆ ♿

*Modern hotel in a pleasant, shady park and
within easy access of Paris (20 km). Take
Ulis/Courtaboeuf exit coming from the west, or
coming from the south,
Ulis/Courtaboeuf/Versailles exit from A10.*

■ ACTIVITIES: Sports facilities at hotel; many
interesting châteaux to visit nearby.
■ TARIFF: Single 550, Double 600, Bk 60,
Set menu 90–140 (Amex, Euro/Access, Visa).
■ DISCOUNT: 15% Jul & Aug only.

MEUDON Yvelines   3B

Hôtel Holiday Inn ★★★
22 av de l'Europe, 78140 Vélizy-Villacoublay.
Tel 01 39 46 96 98, Fax 01 34 65 95 21.
English spoken.
Open all year. 182 bedrooms (all en suite).
Indoor swimming pool, golf 15 km, garage,
parking. ✆

*Comfortable and modern hotel opposite the
Vélizy Shopping Mall. Intimate bar 'La
Chinoiserie' with cosy atmosphere. Car rental
at hotel. Excellent conference facilities. 9 km
from Paris and 6 km from Versailles.*

■ RESTAURANT: Traditional restaurant 'L'Arc-en-
Ciel' offering refined French cuisine.
■ ACTIVITIES: Fitness equipment and solarium.
Sightseeing tours can be organised.
■ TARIFF: Double 840–1100, Bk 75,
Set menu 135–179 (Amex, Euro/Access, Visa).

ST-GERMAIN-EN-LAYE Yvelines   3B

Hôtel La Cazaudehore et La Forest ★★★★ 1
av Prés Kénnédy,
78100 St-Germain-en-Laye.
Tel 01 34 51 93 80, Fax 01 39 73 73 88.
English spoken.
Open all year. 30 bedrooms (all en suite).
Tennis, golf 1 km, parking.

*Stylish hotel located in the heart of the
St-Germain Forest. 1.5 km from the town
(towards Pontoise) and 20 km from Paris.*

■ RESTAURANT: Closed Mon. Refined cuisine in a
lovely setting. Meals are served in the garden in

fine weather. Specialities include foie gras and
gigot de lotte rôtie.
■ TARIFF: Single 770, Double 970, Bk 75,
Set menu 360 (Amex, Euro/Access, Visa).

VERSAILLES Yvelines   3B

Hôtel Aérotel ★★ 88 rue du Drocteur-Vaillant,
78210 St-Cyr-l'Ecole.
Tel 01 30 45 07 44, Fax 01 34 60 35 96.
English spoken.

Open all year. 26 bedrooms (all en suite).
Tennis, golf, parking.

*Cosy family-run hotel just behind the park of
the Château de Versailles and 30 minutes from
Paris. Relais du Silence hotel.*

■ RESTAURANT: Light meals using free-range and
fresh produce are prepared by the host.
■ ACTIVITIES: Swimming pool, tennis, horse-
riding, Thoiry zoo nearby. Magnificent
firework and waterfall show four times a year
at the château (not to be missed!). ● Hotel
organizes 'Paris by night' trips by mini-bus.
■ TARIFF: (1996) Single 285–325, Double 350–370,
Set menu 55–80 (Amex, Euro/Access, Visa).
■ DISCOUNT: 10%

PARIS NORTH-EAST

MARNE-LA-VALLEE Seine/Marne   3B

Hôtel Akena ★ ZI Souilly, 77410 Claye-Souilly.
Tel 01 60 26 89 89, Fax 01 60 26 86 64.
English spoken.
Open all year. 76 bedrooms (all en suite).
Golf 15 km, parking. ✆ ♿

*The hotel is in Claye-Souilly at the interchange
of the N3 and D212, linking Charles de Gaulle
airport to Marne-la-Vallée and Disneyland,
Paris (20 km). Airport 10 km.*

■ TARIFF: Double 149, Bk 24 (Amex,
Euro/Access, Visa).

Golf Hôtel ★★★
15 av du Golf, 77600 Bussy-St-Georges.
Tel 01 64 66 30 30, Fax 01 64 66 04 36.
English spoken.
Open all year. 94 bedrooms (all en suite).
Outdoor swimming pool, tennis, golf .05 km,
parking. ✆ ㄷ

*In a leafy and quiet setting only 8 km from
Disneyland, Paris. Good facilities. From
motorway A4 exit 12 then follow 'Bussy-St-
George-Centre/Golf'.*

■ RESTAURANT: The terrace of the restaurant 'Le
Clos St-Georges' overlooks the golf course.
■ ACTIVITIES: Table tennis, pool and volley ball
● Special discounts on green fees.
■ TARIFF: Single 460, Double 530, Bk 55,
Set menu 67–153 (Amex, Euro/Access, Visa).
■ DISCOUNT: 10%

Saphir Hôtel ★★★
Aire des Berchères, 77340 Pontault-Combault.
Tel 01 64 43 45 47, Fax 01 64 40 52 43.
English spoken.

Open all year. 180 bedrooms (all en suite).
Indoor swimming pool, tennis, golf 2 km,
garage, parking. ✆ ㄷ

*Hotel offers all the facilities and comforts of a
4-star establishment, including 20 suites. Set in
landscaped gardens, hotel is light and spacious
with excellent, friendly service. Between Paris
and Disneyland, Paris, leave A4 at Pontault-
Combault exit and go towards the town centre.*

■ RESTAURANT: Enjoy good food in the restaurant
'Le Jardin'.
■ ACTIVITIES: ● Excellent fitness/sports facilities
at hotel including heated pool complex, sauna,
UVA, jogging track and golf practice ground.
■ TARIFF: (1996) Single 400–485,
Double 400–530, Bk 52, Set menu 75–155
(Amex, Euro/Access, Visa).

PARIS SOUTH-EAST

CHARENTON Val-de-Marne   3B

Hôtel Atria Paris Charenton ★★★
5 place des Marseillais, 94227 Charenton.
Tel 01 46 76 60 60, Fax 01 49 77 68 00.
English spoken.

Open all year. 133 bedrooms (all en suite). ㄷ

*Situated close to the Bois de Vincennes. From
the Paris ring road (Périphérique) go to
Charenton-Centre. Métro station Liberté 20 m
away.*

■ RESTAURANT: Good à la carte choice as well as
the set menus.
■ ACTIVITIES: Fitness centre opposite the hotel.
■ TARIFF: Single 610, Double 660, Bk 60,
Set menu 98–128 (Amex, Euro/Access, Visa).

VINCENNES Val-de-Marne   3B

Hôtel Donjon Vincennes ★★
22 rue du Donjon, 94300 Vincennes.
Tel 01 43 28 19 17, Fax 01 49 57 02 04.
English spoken.
Open 01/01 to 26/07 & 26/08 to 31/12.
25 bedrooms (all en suite). Golf 5 km,
parking. ✆

*Quiet hotel just 100 m from the Château de
Vincennes. RER, Métro and bus station close by.*

■ ACTIVITIES: Tennis, swimming pool, jogging
nearby.
■ TARIFF: (1996) Single 270–320,
Double 280–360, Bk 30 (No credit cards).
■ DISCOUNT: 10% in spring only.

END OF PARIS HOTELS

PERIGUEUX Dordogne   4B

Hôtel Chandelles ★★★
Antonne-et-Trigonant, 24420 Périgueux.
Tel 05 53 06 05 10, Fax 05 53 06 07 33.
English spoken.
Open 01/02 to 01/01. 7 bedrooms (all en suite).
Outdoor swimming pool, tennis, golf 9 km,
parking.

*9 km from Périgueux on the way to Limoges,
an old farm building now converted into a
small hotel. Very good food.*

■ RESTAURANT: Closed Mon except Jul & Aug.
Classic and regional dishes based on market-
fresh produce.
■ ACTIVITIES: Visits to castles and prehistoric caves.
■ TARIFF: (1996) Single 200–350,
Double 280–350, Bk 40, Set menu 145–395
(Amex, Euro/Access, Visa).
■ DISCOUNT: 15%

LA PETITE-PIERRE Bas-Rhin   3B

Hôtel Vosges ★★ 67290 La Petite-Pierre.
Tel 03 88 70 45 05, Fax 03 88 70 41 13.
English spoken.
Open 01/01 to 15/11 & 16/12 to 31/12.
30 bedrooms (all en suite). Golf 30 km, garage,
parking. ☎ ♿

*Traditional hotel set in the forested region of
Alsace. 60 km north-west of Strasbourg on A4.
Turn off at Saverne and take D178 to village.*

■ RESTAURANT: Established in 1924, has
renowned kitchen. Specialities: foie gras frais
maison, truites au bleu, coq au Riesling and
gibiers.
■ ACTIVITIES: Good health/fitness facilities at hotel
including sauna, solarium and Turkish bath.
■ TARIFF: Single 290–370, Double 290–950,
Bk 50, Set menu 98–270 (Euro/Access, Visa).

PLOERMEL Morbihan   1D

Hôtel Le Cobh ★★★
10 rue des Forges, 56800 Ploërmel.
Tel 02 97 74 00 49, Fax 02 97 74 07 36.
English spoken.
Open all year. 13 bedrooms (all en suite).
Golf 2 km, garage, parking. ☎ ♿

*An old Breton house in the centre of Ploërmel,
near the magnificent church.*

■ RESTAURANT: Monsieur Cruaud, member of the
Académie Culinaire de France, offers a warm
welcome and specialises in traditional local
cuisine with excellent value set menus.
■ ACTIVITIES: Ideal base for touring Brittany;
sailing on nearby lake. ● Cookery lessons with
Monsieur Cruaud on request.

■ TARIFF: (1996) Single 200–300, Double 200–330,
Bk 40, Set menu 60–210 (Euro/Access, Visa).
■ DISCOUNT: 10%

POITIERS Vienne   4B

Hôtel Mondial ★★ 86240 Croutelle.
Tel 05 49 55 44 00, Fax 05 49 55 33 49.
English spoken.

Open 03/01 to 22/12. 40 bedrooms
(all en suite). Outdoor swimming pool,
golf 12 km, parking. ♿

*A motel-style hotel built around the swimming
pool. 10 minutes' drive from the centre of
Poitiers, take exit 30 from the N10 towards
Angoulême.*

■ TARIFF: Single 270–450, Double 305–450,
Bk 38 (Amex, Euro/Access, Visa).

POIX-DE-PICARDIE Somme   2B

Hôtel Le Cardinal ★★ place de la République,
80290 Poix-de-Picardie.
Tel 03 22 90 08 23, Fax 03 22 90 18 61.
English spoken.
Open all year. 35 bedrooms (all en suite). Parking.

*A 16th-century hotel situated in the centre of
the town. Completely refurbished. Ideally
situated on the way to Beauvais, Paris and the
south-west of France on the N29 Amiens/ Rouen.*

■ RESTAURANT: Warm atmosphere and traditional
French cuisine.
■ ACTIVITIES: Games room with snooker, pool
and French billiards.
■ TARIFF: (1996) Single 240, Double 270, Bk 32,
Set menu 85–160 (Amex, Euro/Access, Visa).
■ DISCOUNT: 10% RAC Members only.

POMPADOUR Corrèze   4B

Auberge de la Mandrie ★★ route de
Périgueux D7, 19230 Pompadour.
Tel 05 55 73 37 14, Fax 05 55 73 67 13.
English spoken.

Open all year. 22 bedrooms (all en suite).
Outdoor swimming pool, garage, parking. ℡ &

*5 km from Pompadour going towards Payzac
and Ségur-le-Château (D7). Comfortable rooms
in chalets opening out onto the countryside.*

■ RESTAURANT: Regional and traditional cuisine.
■ ACTIVITIES: Children's playground; tennis and
fishing nearby.
■ TARIFF: Single 210–235, Double 210–255,
Bk 35, Set menu 70–210 (Euro/Access, Visa).

PONT-AUDEMER Eure   2A

Hôtel Les Cloches de Corneville ★★★
rte de Rouen, 27500 Corneville-sur-Risle.
Tel 02 32 57 01 04, Fax 02 32 57 10 96.
English spoken.

Open 29/03 to 02/11 & 30/11 to 15/01.
13 bedrooms (12 en suite, 1 bath/shower only).
Parking.

*Comfortable, country inn, where you may visit
the bells of Corneville inside the property. On
the N175, on the Rouen side of Pont-Audemer
and just 4 km from A13.*

■ RESTAURANT: Closed Mon lunch. Speciality of
confit de lapin with garlic bread is served in
either the cosy, Norman-style restaurant or in
the terrace restaurant overlooking the river
valley.
■ ACTIVITIES: Good area for touring and
sightseeing including Normandy abbeys,
Deauville, Honfleur (30km) and Lisieux
basilica.
■ TARIFF: (1996) Single 260–380,
Double 260–420, Bk 40, Set menu 120–270
(Euro/Access, Visa).

Auberge du Cochon d'Or ★★
Place du Gnl de Gaulle, 27210 Beuzeville.
Tel 02 32 57 70 46, Fax 02 32 42 25 70.
English spoken.

Open 15/01 to 15/12. 20 bedrooms (18 en suite,
2 bath/shower only). Golf 12 km, parking.

*Charming family-run hotel with rooms
overlooking flower gardens. Half way between
Pont-Audemer and Pont-L'Evêque on the
N175, the hotel is in the centre of the village,
opposite the town hall.*

■ RESTAURANT: Closed Sun eve from Oct to Mar
& Mon. Good value for money restaurant.
Enjoy the traditional and personalised cuisine
in the elegant dining room. Specialities include
quenelles de volaille à la crème de camembert,
médaillon d'agneau et son jus, aile de raie au
chou, salade de coquillages aux herbes.
■ ACTIVITIES: Easy access for: Pont de
Normandie(10 minutes), Honfleur (14 km) and
Deauville (28 km).
■ TARIFF: Single 200–320, Double 200–335,
Bk 35, Set menu 81–240 (Euro/Access, Visa).

PONT-DU-GARD Gard   5D

Hôtel de la Castellas ★★★
Grand'rue, Collias, 30210 Pont-du-Gard.
Tel 04 66 22 88 88, Fax 04 66 22 84 28.
English spoken.
Open 06/03 to 06/01. 14 bedrooms
(all en suite). Outdoor swimming pool, tennis,
golf 7 km, parking.

*Delightful, mellow stone hotel in the old
Provence village of Collias. Charming little
garden/arbour. Equally charming, individually
decorated bedrooms and bathrooms.
Remoulins west to Pont-du-Gard and Collias.*

■ RESTAURANT: Cosy, light dining room. Cuisine
using local fresh produce.
■ ACTIVITIES: Canoeing, climbing, walking,
horse-riding; visits to Avignon, Arles, Nîmes
and the Camargue.
■ TARIFF: (1996) Single 395–580,
Double 430–620, Bk 50, Set menu 160–360
(Amex, Euro/Access, Visa).

France

PORNIC Loire-Atlan 1D

Hôtel Relais St-Gilles ★★
7 rue F de Mun, 44210 Pornic.
Tel 02 40 82 02 25. English spoken.
Open 01/04 to 10/10. 28 bedrooms
(23 en suite, 4 bath/shower only). Golf 1 km.

*A 19th-century posthouse, close to Pornic
castle. In a quiet location but not far from the
lively harbour, ancient burial ground and
health spa.*

■ RESTAURANT: Closed LS.
■ TARIFF: Double 230–360, Bk 35,
Set menu 100–120 (Euro/Access, Visa).

PORT-LA-NOUVELLE Aude 5C

Hôtel Méditerranée ★★★
BP 92, 11210 Port-la-Nouvelle.
Tel 04 68 48 03 08, Fax 04 68 48 53 81.
English spoken.

Open all year. 31 bedrooms (all en suite).
Garage, parking.

*A fine, modern building which is ideally
situated on the seafront, facing the beach. In
the centre of town.*

■ RESTAURANT: Restaurant overlooks sea and
beach. Specialities: poissons, bouillabaisse,
cassolette de baudroie, pareillade, coquillages,
fricassé de poulet aux langoustines sauce whisky.
■ ACTIVITIES: Tennis nearby, water sports, horse-
riding, walking tracks; boat trips, visit Ste-Lucie
island. ● Sea-fishing trips by catamaran: 2 half
days for 400FF inclusive.
■ TARIFF: Single 180–390, Double 200–490, Bk 35,
Set menu 60–190 (Amex, Euro/Access, Visa).
■ DISCOUNT: 10% on room LS only.

POUZAUGES Vendée 1D

Auberge de la Bruyère ★★
18 rue du Dr Barbanneau, 85700 Pouzauges.
Tel 02 51 91 93 46, Fax 02 51 57 08 18.
English spoken.

Open all year. 28 bedrooms (all en suite).
Indoor swimming pool, parking. ✆

*New hotel on a hillside with wonderful views of
countryside. From Nantes, take N137, turn off
to D960 bis at Chantonnay following signs for
Pouzauges and Bressuire. From the centre of
Pouzauges, drive towards La Pommeraie. The
hotel is 300 m beyond the church.*

■ RESTAURANT: Closed Sat & Sun eve Oct to May.
Enjoy panoramic views, seafood and regional
cuisine. In summer, eat on the lovely terrace
overlooking Pouzauges. There is also a
grill/crêperie near the swimming pool.
■ ACTIVITIES: Hiking.
■ TARIFF: (1996) Single 250–290,
Double 305–390, Bk 38, Set menu 80–175
(Amex, Euro/Access, Visa).

PRATS-DE-MOLLO-LA-PRESTE 5C

Hôtel Ribes ★★
66230 Prats-de-Mollo-la-Preste.
Tel 04 68 39 71 04, Fax 04 68 39 78 02.
English spoken.
Open 01/04 to 31/10. 24 bedrooms (3 en suite,
14 bath/shower only). Garage, parking. ✆

*Splendid views at an altitude of 1130 m.
10 minutes from Prats-de-Mollo-la-Preste
nature reserve. 15 minutes from medieval
village. Access: A9 Le Boulou, then D115 Prats-
de-Mollo, then D115A to La Preste.*

■ RESTAURANT: Closed 1/11 to 31/3. Panoramic
views over the River Tech valley. Good
reputation for its country cooking.
■ ACTIVITIES: Trout fishing, walking, excursions.
■ TARIFF: (1996) Single 160–285,
Double 160–325, Bk 32-41, Set menu 59–120
(Euro/Access, Visa).
■ DISCOUNT: 10% full & half-board basis only.

PUY-L'EVEQUE Lot 4D

Hostellerie de la Source Bleue ★★★
Moulin de Leygues, 46700 Touzac.
Tel 05 65 36 52 01, Fax 05 65 24 65 69.
English spoken.
Open 01/04 to 31/12. 12 bedrooms
(all en suite). Outdoor swimming pool,
golf 15 km, parking. ✆ &

*An 11th-century mill on the River Lot, in
beautiful surroundings including a lake set in
the middle of a giant bamboo forest. Rooms of
character and comfort.*

■ RESTAURANT: Closed Wed. Good food with
specialities of terrine maison de foie gras, pot
au feu de canard à l'ancienne and côtes
d'agneau à la crème de gingembre.

■ ACTIVITIES: Sauna; fishing and sailing.
■ TARIFF: (1996) Single 300, Double 300–450,
Bk 37, Set menu 105–220 (Amex,
Euro/Access, Visa).
■ DISCOUNT: 10% on presentation of valid RAC
membership card.

QUIMPER Finistère   1C

Hôtel Tour d'Auvergne ★★★
13 rue Réguaires, 29000 Quimper.
Tel 02 98 95 08 70, Fax 02 98 95 27 31.
English spoken.
Open all year. 41 bedrooms (38 en suite).
Golf 10 km, garage, parking.

*Traditional town centre hotel; free private car
park which is closed at night.*

■ RESTAURANT: Closed on Sundays from 10 Oct
to 30 Apr and for Saturday lunch from 01 Apr to
15 Jul. Overlooks a flower-filled patio.
■ ACTIVITIES: Horse-riding (8 km), tennis courts,
ice skating rink and swimming pool (4 km).
■ TARIFF: (1996) Single 295–450,
Double 325–550, Set menu 105–230
(Amex, Euro/Access, Visa).
■ DISCOUNT: 10% LS.

RANCOURT Somme   2B

Hôtel Le Prieuré ★★ N17, 80360 Rancourt.
Tel 03 22 85 04 43, Fax 03 22 85 06 69.
English spoken.
Open all year. 28 bedrooms (all en suite).
Tennis, garage, parking. ✆

*Beautiful, imposing hotel. Well placed in the
midst of this historic region. Found on the N17
midway between Bapaume and Péronne, just
a few minutes' drive from the Bapaume exit on
the motorway from Calais.*

■ RESTAURANT: Atmospheric brick and stone
interior. Specialities: pigeon aux queues de
boeuf et jus de volaille; ris de veau au beurre
de champagne.

■ ACTIVITIES: On war cemetery circuit, very
popular with British visitors.
■ TARIFF: (1996) Single 260, Double 260–290, Bk 28,
Set menu 65–240 (Amex, Euro/Access, Visa).
■ DISCOUNT: 5%

REIMS Marne   3A

Hôtel Best Western La Paix ★★★
9 rue Buirette, 51100 Reims.
Tel 03 26 40 04 08, Fax 03 26 47 75 04.
English spoken.
Open all year. 105 bedrooms (all en suite).
Outdoor swimming pool, golf 8 km, garage.

*Attractive, recently-built hotel in the centre of
Reims. Comfortable rooms with warm,
relaxing décor and air conditioning; pool
terrace and garden. Between railway station
and cathedral.*

■ RESTAURANT: The rustic-style 'Taverne de
Maitre Kanter' offers a wide range of dishes in
comfortable surroundings.
■ TARIFF: (1996) Single 390–550, Double 420–
620, Bk 52 (Amex, Euro/Access, Visa).

Hôtel Cheval Blanc ★★★★ 51400 Sept-Saulx.
Tel 03 26 03 90 27, Fax 03 26 03 97 09.
English spoken.
Open 23/02 to 31/01. 25 bedrooms (all en
suite). Tennis, golf 20 km, garage, parking.

*Relax and enjoy fine food in this hotel that has
been run by the same family for 150 years. A
river runs through the lovely grounds. From
Reims, N44 south then D37 to Sept-Saulx.*

■ RESTAURANT: Closed Feb. Restaurant overlooks
the garden. Specialities include rognons confits
aux raisins, bar en croute de sel, foie gras au ratafia.
■ ACTIVITIES: Wine tasting and visit to cellars
close to the hotel.
■ TARIFF: Single 350–800, Double 390–980,
Bk 50, Set menu 180–360 (Amex,
Euro/Access, Visa).
■ DISCOUNT: 5% on rooms only.

France

France

Hôtel Mercure ★★★
rte de Châlons-sur-Marne, 51100 Reims.
Tel 03 26 05 00 08, Fax 03 26 85 64 72.
English spoken.

Open all year. 103 bedrooms (all en suite).
Outdoor swimming pool, golf 10 km, parking. ☎ &

*5 minutes' drive from the town centre, the hotel
is quietly situated and has excellent facilities.
The bar 'Le Bulletier' offers a large choice of
champagne. A glass of champagne is offered to
each guest on presentation of this book. From
motorway A4 exit 26, then go towards Parc des
Expositions.*

■ RESTAURANT: Refined and inventive cuisine
served in the restaurant 'Les Vignobles' or by
the pool.
■ ACTIVITIES: Boat trips on the River Marne, visits
to champagne cellars, vineyards and the
cathedral at Reims.
■ TARIFF: (1996) Single 420–460,
Double 460–500, Bk 54, Set menu 94–115
(Amex, Euro/Access, Visa).
■ DISCOUNT: 10%

Hôtel Mercure Reims Cathédrale ★★★
31 bd P Doumer, 51100 Reims.
Tel 03 26 84 49 49, Fax 03 26 84 49 84.
English spoken.
Open all year. 124 bedrooms (all en suite).
Garage. ☎

*Take Reims-Cathédrale exit from A4
motorway. 5 minutes from town centre and
the cathedral.*

■ RESTAURANT: Closed Sat & Sun lunch.
Decorated in local style with regional cuisine.
Views over the River Marne.
■ ACTIVITIES: Exercise room at hotel; swimming
pool and go-karting nearby. Visits to all the
wonderful sights of Reims as well as a
champagne cellar.

■ TARIFF: Single 430–470, Double 470–510, Bk 54,
Set menu 90–120 (Amex, Euro/Access, Visa).

New Hôtel Europe ★★★
29 rue Buirette, 51100 Reims.
Tel 03 26 47 39 39, Fax 03 26 40 14 37.
English spoken.
Open all year. 54 bedrooms (all en suite).
Golf 12 km, garage. ☎ &

*Only 2 minutes from the A4 and A26, hotel is
situated in the town centre. Pleasant garden,
peaceful surroundings, comfortable rooms.*

■ TARIFF: Double 350–395, Bk 52 (Amex,
Euro/Access, Visa).
■ DISCOUNT: 10%

RENNES Ille/Vilaine   1D

Brit Hôtel ★★
6 av St-Vincent, St-Grégoire, 35760 Rennes.
Tel 02 99 68 76 76, Fax 02 99 68 83 01.
English spoken.
Open all year. 56 bedrooms (all en suite).
Golf 5 km, parking. ☎ &

*Modern hotel with well-appointed
accommodation, conference and banqueting
facilities. Special weekend rate of 210
FF/double room/night. On the Rennes/St-Malo
road.*

■ RESTAURANT: Closed 25 Dec. Attractive dining
room overlooking the terrace and gardens.
Gastronomic New Year's eve dinner.
■ TARIFF: (1996) Single 289–309, Double 309, Bk 40,
Set menu 85–180 (Amex, Euro/Access, Visa).

REVEL Haute-Garonne   5C

Château de Garrevaques 81700 Garrevaques.
Tel 05 63 75 04 54, Fax 05 63 70 26 44.
English spoken.
Open 01/03 to 01/12. 9 bedrooms (all en suite).
Outdoor swimming pool, tennis, golf 20 km,
garage, parking. ☎

*This turretted, 15th-century château was
refurbished in the 19th century and is now
modernised as an exclusive hotel, where you
are made to feel like privileged house guests by
the 15th generation to live in this family home.
Groups are welcome. From central Revel take
the D1 towards Montégut and turn right
opposite the police station on the D79 to
Garrevaques.*

■ RESTAURANT: Private table d'hôte by prior
reservation only; specialities include cassoulet,
truite and foie gras.
■ ACTIVITIES: Billiards lounge; visit to
reproduction furniture makers in Revel; duck

shoots in winter; hotel will arrange day tours, transport and guides on request.
■ TARIFF: (1996) Single 400–450, Double 600–700, Set menu 150–300 (Amex, Visa).
■ DISCOUNT: 10% minimum stay of 3 days.

RIBEAUVILLE Haut-Rhin   3D

Hôtel La Pepinière ★★★
rte de Ste-Marie-aux-Mines, 68150 Ribeauvillé.
Tel 03 89 73 64 14, Fax 03 89 73 88 78.
English spoken.

Open 29/03 to 15/11. 21 bedrooms (all en suite). Golf 18 km, garage, parking. &

A traditional, chalet-style hotel, in the middle of the forest. On the Ribeauvillé to Ste-Marie-aux-Mines road.

■ RESTAURANT: Closed Tues & Wed lunch. Panoramic views. Creative cuisine with specialities such as foie gras, saumon, choucroute and venison in season.
■ ACTIVITIES: Walks into the beautiful Vosges Forest.
■ TARIFF: Single 220–350, Double 360–450, Bk 48, Set menu 140–380 (Euro/Access, Visa).
■ DISCOUNT: 10% LS.

RIBERAC Dordogne   4B

Hôtel de France ★★
rue M Dufraisse, 24600 Ribérac.
Tel 05 53 90 00 61, Fax 05 53 91 06 05.
English spoken.
Open all year. 20 bedrooms (16 en suite, 3 bath/shower only). Parking.

An old post house converted into a comfortable, cosy hotel. In the centre of Ribérac near the place Général de Gaulle and in the heart of the Périgord region.

■ RESTAURANT: Good food in traditional dining room.
■ ACTIVITIES: Canoeing/kayaking (summer) and horse-riding nearby.

■ TARIFF: (1996) Single 160–200, Double 170–250, Bk 30, Set menu 70–165 (Euro/Access, Visa).
■ DISCOUNT: 2%

RIOM Puy-de-Dôme   5A

Hôtel Mikège ★★
40 place J B Laurent, 63200 Riom.
Tel 04 73 38 04 12, Fax 04 73 38 05 08.
English spoken.
Open all year. 15 bedrooms (all en suite). Golf 3 km, garage, parking.

Soundproofed hotel in the part-pedestrianised lower part of town. Riom has a rich heritage and is at the entrance to the National Volcanic Nature Park. Take the Riom exit from the A71.

■ ACTIVITIES: Hotel will be pleased to advise you on visits, activities, restaurants.
■ TARIFF: Single 190–220, Double 220–250, Bk 32 (Euro/Access, Visa).

ROCAMADOUR Lot   5A

Hôtel Pages ★★ route de Payrac, 46350 Calés.
Tel 05 65 37 95 87, Fax 05 65 37 91 57.
English spoken.

Open 03/02 to 15/10 & 28/10 to 03/01. 20 bedrooms (all en suite). Outdoor swimming pool, golf 18 km, parking.

Recently renovated, a quiet, relaxing hotel in the countryside, on the outskirts of Calés. D673, route de Payrac.

■ RESTAURANT: Closed 15 to 28 Oct & Jan. Traditional, rustic-style dining room. Regional specialities such as magret de canard aux baies de cassis and suprême de truite sauce crème romarin, noix de Saint-Jacques aux truffes.
■ ACTIVITIES: Hiking and mountain-biking; canoeing and tennis nearby.
■ TARIFF: (1996) Single 170–300, Double 180–450, Bk 30, Set menu 75–230 (Euro/Access, Visa).
■ DISCOUNT: 10%

LA ROCHE-SUR-YON Vendée 4A

Hôtel Marie Stuart ★★
86 rue Louis Blanc, 85000 La Roche-sur-Yon.
Tel 02 51 37 02 24, Fax 02 51 37 86 37.
English spoken.
Open all year. 14 bedrooms (all en suite).
Golf 4 km.

Friendly and comfortable, a town centre, family-run hotel dating from the 1800s, in the heart of picturesque Vendée.

■ RESTAURANT: Lots of ambiance and good food.
■ TARIFF: (1996) Single 239, Double 289, Bk 33, Set menu 79–210 (Amex, Euro/Access, Visa).

ROCHEFORT Charente-Marit 4A

Hôtel des Vermandois ★★
33 rue E. Combes, 17300 Rochefort.
Tel 05 46 99 62 75, Fax 05 46 99 62 83.
English spoken.
Open all year. 10 bedrooms (all en suite). ℄

Peaceful, 17th-century house in the town centre and close to Pierre Loti's house. Coming from La Rochelle on the D137, take the D733 and at the roundabout, take the 'Boulevard Pouzet'.

■ TARIFF: Double 210–300, Bk 30 (Euro/Access, Visa).
■ DISCOUNT: 10% from 01/11 to 01/03 only.

LA ROCHELLE Charente-Marit 4A

Hôtel du Commerce ★★
6 place de Verdun, 17000 La Rochelle.
Tel 05 46 41 08 22, Fax 05 46 41 74 85.
English spoken.
Open 30/01 to 31/12. 63 bedrooms (49 en suite). Golf 7 km.

Logis de France hotel in the centre of the old town, opposite cathedral and car park.

■ RESTAURANT: Closed Fri lunch & Sat 01/10 to 28/02.
■ TARIFF: Double 140–315, Bk 32, Set menu 75–102 (Amex, Euro/Access, Visa).

RODEZ Aveyron 5C

Hôtel Eldorado ★★
rte d'Espalion, 12740 Sébazac.
Tel 05 65 46 99 77, Fax 05 65 46 99 80.
English spoken.
Open all year. 22 bedrooms (all en suite).
Parking. ℄ ♿

A new hotel, 5 km north of Rodez on the D904 (off the D988) offering a warm welcome. Comfortable rooms.

■ RESTAURANT: Regional specialities.

■ ACTIVITIES: Sightseeing, guided tours.
■ TARIFF: (1996) Single 250, Double 280, Bk 35, Set menu 90–180 (Amex, Euro/Access, Visa).

ROLLEBOISE Yvelines 2B

Château de la Corniche ★★★
5 route de la Corniche, 78270 Rolleboise.
Tel 01 30 93 21 24, Fax 01 30 42 27 44.
English spoken.

Open 06/01 to 20/12. 38 bedrooms (all en suite). Outdoor swimming pool, tennis, golf 8 km, parking.

Standing on the banks high above the Seine, this château was the former home of King Leopold II. 58 km from Paris, 30 km from Versailles and 8 km from Giverny. Motorway A13, exit 13 coming from Paris or exit 15 from Rouen, or coming from Vernon, take the N15, hotel is on the right after Bonnières.

■ RESTAURANT: Closed Sun eve ex Easter & Whitsun. Panoramic restaurant overlooking the Seine. Renowned for its fine cuisine.
■ ACTIVITIES: Bikes for hire at hotel; water sports nearby; boat trips on the Seine. ● Visit to Giverny (8 km) with complimentary tickets for Monet's gardens.
■ TARIFF: (1996) Single 250–350, Double 350–750, Bk 60, Set menu 150–350 (Amex, Euro/Access, Visa).

ROUEN Seine Marit 2A

Hôtel Astrid ★★
121 rue Jeanne d'Arc, 76000 Rouen.
Tel 02 35 71 75 88, Fax 02 35 88 53 25.
English spoken.
Open all year. 40 bedrooms (all en suite).
Parking.

In the centre of the town opposite the station.

■ TARIFF: (1996) Single 280–320, Double 340–380 (Amex, Euro/Access, Visa).

Hôtel de Bordeaux ★★
9 place de la République, 76000 Rouen.
Tel 02 35 71 93 58, Fax 02 35 71 92 15.
English spoken.
Open all year. 48 bedrooms (all en suite).

In the centre of Rouen, between the River Seine and the cathedral. Good facilities in all rooms. Restaurants nearby.

■ TARIFF: Single 195–280, Double 225–330, Bk 30 (Amex, Euro/Access, Visa).
■ DISCOUNT: 15%

Hôtel Versan ★★ 3 rue Jean Lecanuet, 76000 Rouen.
Tel 02 35 07 77 07, Fax 02 35 70 04 67.
English spoken.
Open all year. 34 bedrooms (all en suite).
Garage. ⟨ 丂

Quiet hotel in the heart of the city, close to the Town Hall. Well-equipped rooms. From the town centre, go to the Hôtel de Ville and then turn left. The hotel is immediately on the left.

■ ACTIVITIES: All the monuments and museums of this city of art and history are within easy walking disance.
■ DISCOUNT: 10%

ROYAN Charente-Marit   4A

Hôtel Résidence de Rohan ★★★
Parc des Fées, route de St-Palais, 17640 Royan.
Tel 05 46 39 00 75, Fax 05 46 38 29 99.
English spoken.
Open 01/04 to 15/11. 41 bedrooms (all en suite). Outdoor swimming pool, tennis, golf 4 km, parking.

Old house opening on to the beach of Vaux-Nauzan, just at the end of the garden. From the centre of Royan go towards the beach at Pontaillac and St-Palais-sur-Mer (D25).

■ ACTIVITIES: Direct acces to the beach; horse-riding; ● 20% reduction on green fees.
■ TARIFF: (1996) Double 300–640, Bk 53 (Amex, Euro/Access, Visa).
■ DISCOUNT: 15% except Jul & Aug.

LES SABLES-D'OLONNE Vendée   1D

Hôtel Alize ★★ 78 av Alcide-Gabaret, 85100 Les Sables-D'Olonne.
Tel 02 51 32 44 90, Fax 02 51 21 49 59.
English spoken.
Open 15/02 to 20/12. 24 bedrooms (10 en suite, 11 bath/shower only). Golf 4 km, parking.

Modern hotel 5 minutes from the beach.

■ TARIFF: (1996) Single 170–230, Double 195–270, Bk 30 (Euro/Access, Visa).
■ DISCOUNT: 5%

SAIGNES Cantal   5A

Château de Trancis ★★★ 15210 Ydes.
Tel 04 71 40 60 40, Fax 04 71 40 62 13.
English spoken.

Open 01/04 to 30/09. 7 bedrooms (all en suite). Outdoor swimming pool, golf 20 km, parking.

Luxurious Italian Renaissance-style château, owned and run by Innes and Fiona Fennell. Situated in secluded parkland with terraces and lovely views. From the D922 going towards Mauriac, at Bort-les-Orgues take the D15 to Saignes.

■ RESTAURANT: Gastronomic delights are served by candlelight to guests of Château de Trancis.
■ TARIFF: (1996) Double 660–950, Set menu 280–300 (Amex, Euro/Access, Visa).
■ DISCOUNT: 5% except Jul & Aug.

ST-ALBAN-SUR-LIMAGNOL Lozère   5A

Hôtel Centre ★★
48120 St-Alban-sur-Limagnole.
Tel 04 66 31 50 04, Fax 04 66 31 50 76.
English spoken.
Open 01/02 to 31/12. 20 bedrooms (9 en suite). Outdoor swimming pool, tennis, golf 1 km, parking. ⟨ 丂

Quiet spot, 1000 m up in the Margeride mountains. Just off the main road between St-Flour and Mende. From the A9 exit 34.

■ RESTAURANT: Carefully prepared cuisine by the chef. Specialities: aligot, mushrooms, gardianne.
■ ACTIVITIES: Plenty of outdoor pursuits including walking, fishing, mushroom picking and winter skiing.
■ TARIFF: (1996) Single 100–300, Double 150–390, Bk 30, Set menu 60–150 (Amex, Euro/Access, Visa).

France

ST-AMAND-MONTROND Cher   5A

Auberge Moulin de Chameron
18210 Bannegon.
Tel 05 46 61 83 80, Fax 02 48 61 84 92.
English spoken.
Open 01/03 to 15/11. 13 bedrooms
(all en suite). Outdoor swimming pool,
parking.

*Former mill buildings were converted into a
hotel in 1972 and the mill equipment is still in
place as a small museum. The comfortable
rooms are in a separate building. Warm
welcome assured. Bannegon is a small village
between Nevers and St-Amand-Montrond.
From St-Amand drive east on D951 just past
the crossroads with the D953, turn left (north)
to Bannegon.*

■ RESTAURANT: The restaurant is in a former
water mill on the River Auron. In summer
meals are served outside.
■ TARIFF: Single 365–460, Double 365–680, Bk 49,
Set menu 150–285 (Amex, Euro/Access, Visa).

ST-AUBIN-SUR-MER Calvados   2A

Hôtel St-Aubin ★★ 14750 St-Aubin-sur-Mer.
Tel 02 31 97 30 39, Fax 02 31 97 41 56.
English spoken.
Open 01/02 to 31/12. 24 bedrooms
(all en suite). Tennis, golf 12 km, parking.

*Hotel overlooks the beach and offers
comfortable accommodation at realistic prices.*

■ RESTAURANT: Closed Sun eve & Mon Oct to
Apr. Gourmet cuisine.
■ ACTIVITIES: Horse-riding, casino and D-Day
beaches nearby.
■ TARIFF: (1996) Double 250–330, Bk 35,
Set menu 110–280 (Amex, Euro/Access, Visa).

ST-DIZIER Haute-Marne   3C

Hôtel Le Gambetta ★★★
62 rue Gambetta, 52100 St-Dizier.
Tel 03 25 56 52 10, Fax 03 25 56 39 47.
English spoken.
Open all year. 63 bedrooms (all en suite).
Golf 15 km, garage, parking. &
■ RESTAURANT: Closed Sun eve.
■ TARIFF: Single 210–340, Double 240–390,
Bk 35 (Amex, Euro/Access, Visa).

ST-EMILION Gironde   4B

Hôtel Aub de la Commanderie ★★
rue Cordeliers, 33330 St-Emilion.
Tel 05 57 24 70 19, Fax 05 57 74 44 53.
English spoken.

Open all year. 18 bedrooms (all en suite).
Parking. &

*Charming family hotel in the northern part of
the medieval town of St-Emilion. 30 km from
Bordeaux on the N89 to Libourne road. Then
take the D243 for 8 km.*
■ TARIFF: (1996) Double 250–450, Bk 38-48
(Euro/Access, Visa).

ST-ETIENNE Loire   5B

Hôtel Altea Parc de l'Europe ★★
rue de Wuppertal, 42100 St-Etienne.
Tel 04 77 42 81 81, Fax 04 77 42 81 89.
English spoken.
Open all year. 120 bedrooms (all en suite).
Golf 10 km, garage, parking. &

*Built in a contemporary and original style, the
hotel overlooks the alleys and the colourful
gardens of the 9-hectare park. Excellent
conference facilities. Motorway A47 and A72
towards St-Etienne Sud exit 'Le Rond Point'.*

■ RESTAURANT: Closed Sat & Sun lunch. Traditional
cuisine in the restaurant 'La Ribandière' and
cocktails in the American bar 'Le Diapason'.
■ TARIFF: (1996) Single 470, Double 530, Bk 50,
Set menu 110–180 (Amex, Euro/Access, Visa).

ST-FLOUR Cantal   5A

Hôtel Les Messageries ★★
23 av Charles de Gaulle, 15100 St-Flour.
Tel 04 71 60 11 36, Fax 04 71 60 46 79.
Open 05/02 to 21/01. 17 bedrooms (all en suite).
Outdoor swimming pool, garage, parking.

*Very quiet, yet only 5 minutes from town
centre. South of Clermont-Ferrand on A75, in
the 'ville basse' not far from the station.*

■ RESTAURANT: Closed Fri & Sat lunch Oct to
Easter except French school holidays. Regional
specialities.
■ ACTIVITIES: Sauna.
■ TARIFF: Single 200–395, Double 200–430,
Bk 50, Set menu 80–370 (Visa).
■ DISCOUNT: 10% except Jul & Aug.

ST-GIRONS Ariège   4D

Auberge des Deux Rivières ★
Pont de la Taule, 09140 Seix.
Tel 05 61 66 83 57, Fax 05 61 66 83 57.
English spoken.
Open 01/12 to 31/10. 11 bedrooms (5 en suite,
6 bath/shower only). Parking. &

*Quietly situated in a beautiful valley with a
terrace overlooking both the Salat and Alet
rivers. 21 km south of St-Girons.*

■ RESTAURANT: Rustic-style dining room.
■ ACTIVITIES: Walking, cycling, canoeing, skiing.
■ TARIFF: (1996) Double 130–190, Bk 25,
Set menu 75–145 (Euro/Access, Visa).

ST-JEAN-DE-LUZ Pyrénées-Atlan   4C

Hôtel Agur ★★
96 rue Gambetta, 64500 St-Jean-de-Luz.
Tel 05 59 51 91 11, Fax 05 59 51 91 21.
English spoken.
Open 15/03 to 15/11. 17 bedrooms
(all en suite). Golf 2 km, garage. ✆

*Modern hotel run by a Scottish family and
situated in town centre, 200 m from the beach.
Family rooms and self-catering studio flats
available. Leave A63 at St-Jean-de-Luz (nord)
and follow signs to Centre Ville and Plage
for 2 km.*

■ TARIFF: (1996) Single 245–325,
Double 285–345, Bk 35 (Amex,
Euro/Access, Visa).
■ DISCOUNT: 10% LS.

Le Grand Hôtel ★★★★
43 bd Thiers, 64500 St-Jean-de-Luz.
Tel 05 59 26 35 36, Fax 05 59 51 19 91.
English spoken.
Open 01/05 to 31/10. 48 bedrooms
(all en suite). Outdoor swimming pool,
golf 2 km, parking.

*The hotel enjoys a panoramic view over St-
Jean-de-Luz bay and the Basque mountains.
2 km from A63, in the centre of the town.*

■ RESTAURANT: Gourmet cuisine and healthy
buffet lunch.
■ ACTIVITIES: ● Golf packages.
■ TARIFF: Single 700–1400, Double 800–1500,
Bk 100, Set menu 170–220 (Amex,
Euro/Access, Visa).
■ DISCOUNT: 10% except Aug.

ST-JEAN-DE-MONTS Vendée   4A

Hôtel Robinson ★★
28 bd Général Leclerc, 85160 St-Jean-de-Monts.
Tel 02 51 59 20 20, Fax 02 51 58 88 03.
English spoken.
Open all year. 80 bedrooms (70 en suite,
10 bath/shower only). Indoor swimming pool,
golf 1 km, garage, parking. ♿

*Comfortable hotel with garden and terrace.
Close to town centre and 900 m from beach.
Half-board, full-board and weekend breaks
also available.*

■ RESTAURANT: Modern restaurant with a good
reputation for its refined regional cuisine.

■ ACTIVITIES: Fitness room at hotel; cycling and
windsurfing nearby.
■ TARIFF: Single 210–330, Double 210–350,
Bk 36, Set menu 73–230 (Amex,
Euro/Access, Visa).

ST-MALO Ille/Vilaine   1D

Hôtel Brocéliande ★★★
43 chaussée du Sillon, 35400 St-Malo.
Tel 02 99 20 62 62, Fax 02 99 40 42 47.
English spoken.

Open 15/12 to 16/11. 12 bedrooms
(all en suite). Golf 7 km, garage, parking.

*Facing the 'Emerald Coast', hotel is a warm,
refined family home. Situated between the old
town and the thermal sea baths, overlooking
the beach. Family apartment available; free
private parking. One free breakfast offered for
two people sharing a room on presentation of
this book.*

■ ACTIVITIES: Swimming pool, water sports,
horse-riding, tennis and cycling all available in
the vicinity.
■ TARIFF: Double 300–550, Bk 48 (Amex,
Euro/Access, Visa).

Hôtel La Rance ★★
15 quai Sebastopol, 35400 St-Malo.
Tel 02 99 81 78 63, Fax 02 99 81 44 80.
English spoken.
Open all year. 11 bedrooms (all en suite).
Golf 15 km, garage, parking.

*A delightful hotel overlooking the bay and only
5 minutes from the ferry terminal. Follow signs
for the Tower of Solidor (museum about Cape
Horn) and hotel is close by.*

■ ACTIVITIES: Bikes for rent. ● 20% reduction on
3-day green fee at certain courses.
■ TARIFF: Single 300–430, Double 300–500,
Bk 47 (Amex, Euro/Access, Visa).

France

ST-PAUL Alpes-Marit 6D

Hôtel Mas d'Artigny ★★★★
rte de la Colle, 06570 St-Paul.
Tel 04 93 32 84 54, Fax 04 93 32 95 36.
English spoken.

Open all year. 84 bedrooms (all en suite).
Indoor swimming pool, outdoor swimming
pool, tennis, golf 20 km, garage, parking. ✆ ♿

*On the heights of St-Paul-de-Vence, in 20 acres
of wooded parkland, the Mas d'Artigny
overlooks the Côte d'Azur. From Nice or
airport, take the motorway A8 or the coast
road to Cagnes-sur-Mer, then go towards
Grasse and turn right to Colle-sur-Loup and St-
Paul-de-Vence.*

■ RESTAURANT: Traditional and inventive dishes
can be served in the panoramic dining room or
on the terrace near the swimming pool.
Specialities: salade gourmande aux queues de
langoustines roties et caviar, suprême de loup
croustillant beurre aux amandes, canon
d'agneau roti à l'ail doux et basilic.
■ ACTIVITIES: Indoor games, pitch and putt,
jogging trails, obstacle course at hotel. Horse-
riding, fishing and most water sports nearby;
good choice of trips.
■ TARIFF: Single 525–1670, Double 640–1850,
Bk 100-140, Set menu 290–400 (Amex,
Euro/Access, Visa).

ST-PAUL-TROIS-CHATEAUX Drôme 5D

Hôtel L'Esplan ★★★ place Médiéval de
l'Esplan, 26130 St-Paul-Trois-Châteaux.
Tel 04 75 96 64 64, Fax 04 75 04 92 36.
English spoken.
Open 06/01 to 19/12. 36 bedrooms
(all en suite). Golf 4 km, garage, parking.

*Renovated building combining traditional
and contemporary achitecture/styles. The air-
conditioned bedrooms are very modern in
design. Garden and terraces. St-Paul is a*

*medieval town with easy access to motorway.
Going south on A7 take the Montelimar-Sud
exit, head towards Avignon and after 4 km
follow signs to St-Paul-Trois-Châteaux.*

■ RESTAURANT: Closed Sun eve from 15/10 to 15/04.
Lunch served on the terrace. Truffles in winter.
■ ACTIVITIES: Truffling, bowling, wine tasting.
Special weekends available including
accommodation, sightseeing, tours and
activities. Write to hotel for details.
■ TARIFF: (1996) Single 290–350,
Double 320–380, Bk 40, Set menu 98–198
(Amex, Euro/Access, Visa).

Auberge des Quatre-Saisons ★★★
26130 St-Restitut.
Tel 04 75 04 71 88, Fax 04 75 04 70 88.
English spoken.
Open 01/02 to 01/01. 10 bedrooms
(all en suite). Golf 25 km, parking.

*Lovely old building with comfortable antique-
furnished rooms. St-Restitut is a medieval
village lying just south-east of St-Paul and a
short distance from the main routes to the
south coast.*

■ RESTAURANT: Closed Sat lunch and Jan. Warm,
inviting dining room. Specialities: carré d'agneau
aux herbes de Provence, truffes du Tricastin.
■ ACTIVITIES: Horse-riding, swimming pool and
tennis nearby; Ardèche gorges and Grignan
château within easy reach.
■ TARIFF: (1996) Single 200–390,
Double 200–450, Bk 45, Set menu 130–215
(Amex, Euro/Access, Visa).
■ DISCOUNT: 10% on rooms only.

ST-QUAY-PORTRIEUX Côtes-du-Nord 1D

Hôtel Lucotel ★★ Parc Lannec,
rue des Fontaines, 22290 Lanvollon.
Tel 02 96 70 01 17, Fax 02 96 70 08 84.
English spoken.

Open all year. 20 bedrooms (all en suite).
Tennis, golf 5 km, garage, parking. ℂ ↻

*A comfortable, modern hotel just a short
distance from the sea.*

■ RESTAURANT: Seafood specialities: poêlée de
Saint-Jacques, raie aux poireaux.
■ ACTIVITIES: Crazy golf at the hotel.
■ TARIFF: (1996) Single 210–240,
Double 260–320, Bk 33, Set menu 75–220
(Amex, Euro/Access, Visa).
■ DISCOUNT: 10% 01/09 to 08/07.

ST-QUENTIN Aisne   2B

Hôtel Ibis ★★
14 pl Basilique, 02100 St-Quentin.
Tel 03 23 67 40 40, Fax 03 23 62 69 36.
English spoken.
Open all year. 49 bedrooms (all en suite).
Golf 5 km. ℂ ↻

*On a pretty square opposite the basilica and
close to the pedestrian streets.*

■ RESTAURANT: Closed Sun eve. Refined traditional
cuisine served in the air-conditioned restaurant
'Le Diamant' with musical background.
■ TARIFF: Single 300, Double 310, Bk 36,
Set menu 79–148 (Amex, Euro/Access, Visa).
■ DISCOUNT: 10%

Grand Hôtel et Restaurant President ★★★
6 rue Dachery, 02100 St-Quentin.
Tel 03 23 62 69 77, Fax 03 23 62 53 52.
English spoken.
Open all year. 24 bedrooms (all en suite).
Golf 5 km, parking. ↻

*Very comfortable hotel in the heart of St-
Quentin. Friendly staff; excellent facilities.*

■ RESTAURANT: Closed Sat lunch & Sun 28 Jul to
25 Aug & 22 to 29 Dec. Award winning; stylish
setting with a quiet, harmonious atmosphere.
Specialities include poêlée de langoustines et
Saint-Jacques au pistou; soissoulet d'agneau à
la Picarde and souffle à la chicorée.
■ ACTIVITIES: Many excursions available from
hotel; cookery lessons on request.
■ TARIFF: Single 420–500, Double 550–600, Bk 60,
Set menu 180–330 (Amex, Euro/Access, Visa).
■ DISCOUNT: 10%

ST-QUENTIN-EN-YVELINES Yvelines   2D

Novotel St-Quentin ★★★
1 av du Golf, 78114 Magny-les-Hameaux.
Tel 01 30 57 65 65, Fax 01 30 57 65 00.
English spoken.
Open all year. 130 bedrooms (all en suite).
Outdoor swimming pool, tennis, golf on site,
parking. ℂ ↻

*Built on a golf course, 12 km from Versailles
and 30 km from Paris. From N118 south-west
of Paris take Saclay exit then D36 to Magny-
les-Hameaux. From St-Quentin, go towards
Guyancourt and then Voisins-le-Bretonneux.*

■ RESTAURANT: Pleasant restaurant overlooking
the outdoor swimming pool and golf course.
■ ACTIVITIES: ● Gymnasium, table tennis, volley
ball, boules and mountain bikes free of charge
for hotel guests. Special weekend golf/leisure
packages.
■ TARIFF: (1996) Double 495–550, Bk 55,
Set menu 120–150 (Amex, Euro/Access, Visa).
■ DISCOUNT: 15%

ST-RAPHAEL Var   6D

Hôtel Sol e Mar ★★★
rte Corniche d'Or, 83700 St-Raphaël.
Tel 04 94 95 25 60, Fax 04 94 83 83 61.
English spoken.
Open 01/04 to 15/10. 47 bedrooms
(all en suite). Outdoor swimming pool,
golf 3 km, parking. ℂ ↻

*Adjacent to sea and beach, with exceptional
views. On N98, between St-Raphaël and Cannes.*

■ RESTAURANT: Panoramic restaurant. Locally
caught fish on the menu.
■ ACTIVITIES: Two sea-water pools. ● Special
prices for a wide range of activities including
golf, scuba diving and boat trips.
■ TARIFF: Double 400–690, Bk 50,
Set menu 145–210 (Amex, Euro/Access, Visa).

ST-REMY-DE-PROVENCE   5D

Hôtel Soleil ★★ 13 av Pasteur,
13210 St-Rémy-de-Provence.
Tel 04 90 92 00 63, Fax 04 90 92 61 07.
English spoken.
Open 10/03 to 15/11. 21 bedrooms
(all en suite). Outdoor swimming pool,
golf 12 km, garage, parking.

France

*Pleasant hotel with gardens and terrace. From
St-Rémy centre follow signs for Les Baux. After
the tourist office, turn left back on yourself into
av Pasteur. Hotel on right.*

■ ACTIVITIES: Mountain-bike hire; gliding lessons.
■ TARIFF: Single 290–325, Double 290–365,
Bk 35 (Amex, Euro/Access, Visa).

ST-SYMPHORIEN-LE-CHATEAU   2D

Château d'Esclimont ★★★★
28700 St-Symphorien-le-Château.
Tel 02 37 31 15 15, Fax 02 37 31 57 91.
English spoken.

Open all year. 53 bedrooms (all en suite).
Outdoor swimming pool, tennis, golf 17 km,
parking, restaurant.

*A superb 16th-century château with moat,
lake, landscaped gardens and 150 acres of
wooded parkland. From Paris, take A11 and
exit at Ablis, turn right on N10 after 6 km.*

■ ACTIVITIES: Fishing, boating, cycling at the
château; horse-riding, pleasure flights, hot-air
ballooning and golf can be arranged.
■ TARIFF: (1996) Single 740–1690,
Double 1160–2030, Set menu 320–495 (Amex,
Euro/Access, Visa).

ST-TROPEZ Var   6C

Hôtel Byblos ★★★★
av P Signac, 83991 St-Tropez.
Tel 04 94 56 68 00, Fax 04 94 56 68 01.
English spoken.
Open 01/03 to 31/10. 102 bedrooms
(all en suite). Outdoor swimming pool,
golf 9 km, garage, parking.

*Just a few steps away from the place des Lices,
in the shadow of the Citadel. Hotel has
excellent facilities including a beauty parlor.
Each fully-equipped room has its own personal
character, and some have a jacuzzi.*

■ RESTAURANT: Fresh, authentic Provençale
cuisine can be enjoyed in the restaurant 'Les
Arcades', which overlooks the swimming pool
or in 'Le Relais des Caves du Roy' the French
bistro open late at night.
■ ACTIVITIES: Turkish bath, sauna, gymnasium
and disco.
■ TARIFF: Single 700–2380, Double 1380–2380,
Bk 120 (Amex, Euro/Access, Visa).

ST-VAAST-LA-HOUGUE Manche   1B

Hôtel Demeure du Perron ★★
50630 Quettehou.
Tel 02 33 54 56 09, Fax 02 33 43 69 28.
English spoken.

Open all year. 15 bedrooms (all en suite).
Tennis, golf 8 km, parking. &

*Converted from four private houses and
standing in an acre of gardens with mature
trees and secure car park. All rooms are fully
equipped and comfortable. On the edge of
Quettehou, 2.5 km west of St-Vaast on the D1,
900 m from the sea and 3 minutes' drive from
St-Vaast harbour (boat to Tatihou).*

■ RESTAURANT: Closed Dec. Fish and seafood
specialities including lobster and hot oysters.
■ ACTIVITIES: Bar and games room at hotel;
sailing; tennis; visits to nearby Tatihou Island.
■ TARIFF: (1996) Double 230–290, Bk 37,
Set menu 82–125 (Amex, Euro/Access, Visa).

ST-VERAN Hautes-Alpes   6A

Hôtel Châteaurenard ★★ 05350 St-Véran.
Tel 04 92 45 85 43, Fax 04 92 45 84 20.
English spoken.
Open all year. 20 bedrooms (all en suite).
Parking. &

*At 2080 m, hotel overlooks historic St-Veran,
the highest commune in Europe, in the
Queyras regional nature park. The village is
famous for its traditional architecture,*

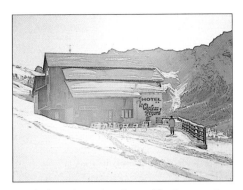

sundials and wood sculptors. The Queyras is famous for its climate (alpine/Mediterranean with over 300 days of sun a year). St-Veran is reached via Guillestre from Briançon, Gap or Turin. Half board also available.

■ RESTAURANT: Traditional French cooking taking full advantage of fresh, local produce.
■ ACTIVITIES: In winter: skiing, dog sleighs, snow-shoe walking. The rest of the year: mountaineering, alpine walking, mountain-biking, horse-riding, hang/paragliding (also on skis), white-water rafting, discovering the flora and fauna and excellent night stargazing (there is an observatory above St-Veran).
■ TARIFF: Single 275–365, Double 315–365, Bk 40, Set menu 99–116 (Euro/Access, Visa).
■ DISCOUNT: 5% LS only.

ST-VERAND Saône/Loire 5B

Auberge du St-Véran ★ 71570 St-Verand.
Tel 03 85 37 16 50, Fax 03 85 37 49 27.
English spoken.

Open all year. 11 bedrooms (all en suite).
Golf 15 km, parking.

Attractive, traditional auberge. Tranquil setting with large gardens and a river nearby. From A6, take Mâcon-Sud exit and follow

signs to Crêches-sur-Saône. Turn left at traffic lights and hotel is 4 km ahead.

■ RESTAURANT: Closed Mon, Tues lunch. Gastronomic regional cuisine. Candlelit dinner every Saturday.
■ TARIFF: (1996) Single 180–220, Double 200–250, Bk 35, Set menu 95–205 (Euro/Access, Visa).

STE-MAURE-DE-TOURAINE 2C

Hostellerie Hauts de Ste-Maure ★★★
2 av Charles de Gaulle,
37800 Ste-Maure-de-Touraine.
Tel 02 47 65 50 65, Fax 02 47 65 60 24.
English spoken.

Open 01/03 to 31/01. 19 bedrooms (all en suite). Outdoor swimming pool, tennis, golf 1 km, garage, parking. &

Recently renovated, a comfortable posthouse that has stood on the Paris to Madrid road (N10) for many centuries. Air-conditioned accommodation.

■ RESTAURANT: Closed Sun & Mon lunch LS. Tempting dishes are prepared by the proprietor's son. Specialities: potato shells with tarragon butter; braised pigeon; monkfish with ginger.
■ ACTIVITIES: Hotel has a vintage car collection. Good area for touring, sightseeing and visiting private châteaux and cellars. 20 minutes from Futurescope.
■ TARIFF: (1996) Double 300–420, Bk 50, Set menu 108–240 (Amex, Euro/Access, Visa).
■ DISCOUNT: 8%

STE-MAXIME Var 6C

Hôtel de la Poste ★★★
7 bd F Mistral, 83120 Ste-Maxime.
Tel 04 94 96 18 33, Fax 04 94 96 41 68.
English spoken.
Open 07/05 to 10/10. 24 bedrooms (all en suite).

France

Outdoor swimming pool, golf 2 km, parking.

The hotel is located in the middle of Ste-Maxime, opposite the Post Office. Only 100 m from a fine sandy beach and the port. Breakfast is served on a terrace overlooking the swimming pool and solarium, surrounded by a small garden.

■ TARIFF: (1996) Single 300–500, Double 330–610, Bk 45 (Amex, Euro/Access, Visa).

SAINTES Charente-Marit   4B

Hôtel au Terminus ★★
2 rue J Moulin, 17100 Saintes.
Tel 05 46 74 35 03, Fax 05 46 97 24 47.
English spoken.
Open 16/01 to 22/12. 28 bedrooms
(all en suite). Tennis, golf 4 km, garage.

Delightful, traditional 1920s building, recently modernised. Opposite the Gare SNCF, the hotel has little or no train noise and is run by an Irish/French couple who give a warm personal welcome.

■ ACTIVITIES: Wide range of historical and archeological sites to visit close by.
■ TARIFF: Single 200–295, Double 200–385, Bk 32 (Amex, Euro/Access, Visa).
■ DISCOUNT: 10%

SALBRIS Loir-et-Cher   2D

Domaine de Valaudran ★★★
av de Romorantin, 41300 Salbris.
Tel 02 54 97 20 00, Fax 02 54 97 12 22.
English spoken.

Open 03/03 to 03/01. 31 bedrooms
(all en suite). Outdoor swimming pool,
golf 25 km, parking. ☎ ♿

Charming hotel, situated in a park. From the N20, turn west towards Romorantin for 2 km. First roundabout after péage.

■ RESTAURANT: Gourmet restaurant. Specialities:

croustillant de pied de cochon, escalopes de foie gras aux lentilles, fine tarte aux poires confites.

■ ACTIVITIES: Horse-riding, tennis, clay-pigeon shooting, hunting, go-karting; helicopters and planes for hire nearby; visit to wine cellars.
■ TARIFF: (1996) Single 425–465, Double 595–900, Bk 70, Set menu 150–290 (Amex, Euro/Access, Visa).
■ DISCOUNT: 10%

SALERS Cantal   5A

Hostellerie de la Maronne ★★★
Le Theil, 15140 Salers.
Tel 04 71 69 20 33, Fax 04 71 69 28 22.
English spoken.
Open 03/04 to 05/11. 21 bedrooms
(all en suite). Outdoor swimming pool, tennis, golf 25 km, parking. ♿

A traditional Auvergne house dating from the 19th century. 4 km east of D922, on the D37.

■ RESTAURANT: Good restaurant with specialities of foie gras chaud au caramel de porto et choux vert étuvé, poitrine de pigeon rôti au vin and gâteau tiède aux marrons et chocolat.
■ ACTIVITIES: Sightseeing and rambling; fishing and horse-riding nearby.
■ TARIFF: Double 460–580, Bk 60, Set menu 150–250 (Amex, Euro/Access, Visa).

SALON-DE-PROVENCE B-du-Rhône   5D

Domaine de Roquerousse ★★
rte d'Avignon, 13300 Salon-de-Provence.
Tel 04 90 59 50 11, Fax 04 90 59 53 75.
English spoken.

Open all year. 30 bedrooms (all en suite). Outdoor swimming pool, tennis, golf 7 km, parking.

Peacefully set in 1000 acres in the heart of Provence, attractive, stone-built hotel with comfortable rooms and lovely gardens. 4 km from Salon, towards Avignon.

■ RESTAURANT: Closed 24/12 eve & 25/12. Country cuisine served on shady terrace or in 150-year-old dining room once used for breeding silkworms. Typical Provençal atmosphere.
■ ACTIVITIES: Gym, boules; mountain-biking, walking and hunting.
■ TARIFF: (1996) Single 240–430, Double 270–490, Bk 50, Set menu 78–175 (Amex, Euro/Access, Visa).

SARLAT-LA-CANEDA Dordogne 4B

Hôtel de Selves ★★★
93 av de Selves, 24200 Sarlat-la-Canéda.
Tel 05 53 31 50 00, Fax 05 53 31 23 52.
English spoken.
Open 10/02 to 09/01. 40 bedrooms (all en suite). Indoor swimming pool, outdoor swimming pool, golf 6 km, garage. &

200 m from the old town, a very comfortable, modern hotel with a lovely garden, satellite television, air conditioning and sauna.

■ ACTIVITIES: Tennis, horse-riding and canoeing nearby; ideal base for visiting Les Eyzies, Le Quercy and the châteaux of the Dordogne valley.
■ TARIFF: Single 380–500, Double 450–570, Bk 50 (Amex, Euro/Access, Visa).

SAUMUR Maine/Loire 2C

Hôtel Anne d'Anjou ★★★
32 quai Mayaud, 49400 Saumur.
Tel 02 41 67 30 30, Fax 02 41 67 51 00.
English spoken.
Open all year. 50 bedrooms (all en suite). Golf 15 km, garage, parking. &

Between the River Loire and the Château de Saumur, a classic 18th-century building overlooking the river. Extremely comfortable with some stunning features and a charming illuminated interior courtyard.

■ RESTAURANT: Imaginative menu using fresh local produce.
■ ACTIVITIES: Tennis nearby.
■ TARIFF: (1996) Single 270–640, Double 350–640, Bk 48 (Amex, Euro/Access, Visa).

SAUSSET-LES-PINS Bouches-du-Rhône 5D

Hôtel Paradou-Méditerranée ★★★ Le Port, 13960 Sausset-les-Pins.
Tel 04 42 44 76 76, Fax 04 42 44 78 48.
English spoken.
Open all year. 42 bedrooms (all en suite).
Outdoor swimming pool, parking. &

A modern hotel overlooking the sea in Sausset-les-Pins, just 15 km from Marseille airport, on the Côte Bleue with its pine trees and rocky bays. From the A55, take Carry-le-Rouet exit and follow the signs to Sausset-les-Pins.

■ RESTAURANT: Closed Sat. Provençale cuisine and fish specialities.
■ TARIFF: (1996) Single 380–450, Double 410–550, Bk 50, Set menu 155–250 (Amex, Euro/Access, Visa).

SCHIRMECK Bas-Rhin 3D

Château de Barembach ★★★
5 rue du Maréchal de Lattre, 67130 Schirmeck.
Tel 03 88 97 97 50, Fax 03 88 47 17 19.
English spoken.
Open all year. 15 bedrooms (all en suite).
Tennis, garage, parking. &

Small but elegant 19th-century château used as the owners' private home until 1983. Surrounded by mountains and forests, it has a terrace and pretty flower garden. General Patton made the château his headquarters in 1944. 40 km west of Strasbourg on A35/N392.

■ RESTAURANT: Excellent light cuisine, good choice of menus. Specialities include carpaccio of spice-marinated monkfish and salmon, fricassée of roast veal kidney with fresh mushrooms, butter-fried breast of guinea fowl and fillet of sole in Champagne.
■ ACTIVITIES: Horse-riding, fishing, skiing, cycling; sightseeing visits to museums and vineyards.
■ TARIFF: Single 385–665, Double 475–895, Bk 55, Set menu 145–398 (Amex, Euro/Access, Visa).
■ DISCOUNT: 10% 01/11 to 01/04.

SEDAN Ardennes 3A

Auberge du Port ★★
route de Remilly, 08140 Bazeilles.
Tel 03 24 27 13 89, Fax 03 24 29 35 58.
English spoken.
Open 15/01 to 15/08 & 01/09 to 20/12.
20 bedrooms (all en suite). Golf 20 km, garage, parking.

Quiet and comfortable, the hotel stands beside the River Meuse and is surrounded by gardens and open fields. East of Sedan, go through Bazeilles and hotel is 1 km beyond, on the D129 towards Remilly.

■ RESTAURANT: Closed Fri & Sun eve, Sat lunch. Pretty, contemporary-style dining room with panoramic views across the river. Gastronomic cuisine.
■ TARIFF: (1996) Single 260, Double 295, Bk 40, Set menu 138–230 (Amex, Euro/Access, Visa).
■ DISCOUNT: 8% restaurant only.

France

SENLIS Oise 2B

Auberge de Fontaine ★★
22 Grande rue, 60300 Fontaine-Chaalis.
Tel 03 44 54 20 22, Fax 03 44 60 25 38.
English spoken.
Open all year. 8 bedrooms (all en suite).
Golf 8 km, parking. &

In the centre of the village, a few kilometres from Senlis. N330 south-east of Senlis and then D126 to Fontaine-Châalis.

■ RESTAURANT: Closed Tues from Sep to Apr. Provençal specialities. Lunches on the terrace in summer and evening meals by the fireplace in winter.
■ ACTIVITIES: Trout fishing, visit of the Chaalis abbey and Jacquemart André Museum.
■ TARIFF: (1996) Single 245–275, Double 275–320, Bk 40, Set menu 135–190 (Euro/Access, Visa).

SIGNY-L'ABBAYE Ardennes 3A

Auberge de l'Abbaye ★★
2 place Briand, 08460 Signy-l'Abbaye.
Tel 03 24 52 81 27, Fax 03 24 53 71 72.
English spoken.

Open 01/03 to 31/12. 10 bedrooms (6 en suite, 2 bath/shower only). Golf 20 km, parking. ℂ

Former staging post surrounded by 5000 ha of superb, natural forest. Cosy, individually decorated and furnished rooms. (Hotel is closed Wed eve and Thurs.)

■ RESTAURANT: Closed Wed eve & Thu. Local specialities.
■ ACTIVITIES: Walking, horse-riding, mountain-biking.
■ TARIFF: (1996) Single 180–200, Double 300–350, Bk 30, Set menu 75–150 (Euro/Access, Visa).

SISTERON Alpes/Hte-Prov 6C

Grand Hôtel du Cours ★★★
place de l'Eglise, 04200 Sisteron.
Tel 04 92 61 04 51, Fax 04 92 61 41 73.
English spoken.

Open 01/03 to 30/11. 50 bedrooms (all en suite). Garage, parking. &

Situated in the middle of this historic town, hotel is beautifully presented and offers comfortable rooms with modern facilities. Bar and tea room. Sisteron, the Gateway to Provence, is on the A51.

■ RESTAURANT: Completely renovated in Provençal style, the restaurant faces the ancient ramparts and the citadel. Gigot d'agneau de pays à la crème d'ail is the speciality.
■ ACTIVITIES: A host of sporting activities nearby including the new swimming centre, only 5 minutes' walk away. Good area for cultural visits and sightseeing.
■ TARIFF: Single 230–330, Double 290–430, Bk 40, Set menu 80–150 (Amex, Euro/Access, Visa).

SOUILLAC Lot 4B

Auberge du Puits ★★
5 pl du Puits, 46200 Souillac.
Tel 05 65 37 80 32, Fax 05 65 37 07 16.
English spoken.
Open 01/01 to 01/11. 20 bedrooms (all en suite). Golf 5 km, parking. ℂ &

From Brive, N20 south to Souillac. In Souillac turn right after the Post Office and hotel is located in a lovely square.

■ RESTAURANT: Closed Sun eve & Mon LS. Local specialities.
■ TARIFF: Double 140–280, Bk 30, Set menu 78–250 (Euro/Access, Visa).

STRASBOURG Bas-Rhin 3D

Hôtel Europe ★★★ 38 rue Fosses des Tanneurs, 67000 Strasbourg.

Tel 03 88 32 17 88, Fax 03 88 75 65 45.
English spoken.
Open all year. 60 bedrooms (all en suite).
Golf 10 km, garage. &

Full of charm and character, 15th-century posthouse next to the pedestrian area of La Petite France. Houses a unique 1:50 scale model of Strasbourg Cathedral in the reception hall. Direct access from motorway, exit Place des Halles.

■ ACTIVITIES: ● Free bicycles.
■ TARIFF: Single 310–450, Double 370–590, Bk 46 (Amex, Euro/Access, Visa).

Hôtel des Rohan ★★★
17 rue du Maroquin, 67000 Strasbourg.
Tel 03 88 32 85 11, Fax 03 88 75 65 37.
English spoken.
Open all year. 36 bedrooms (all en suite).
Golf 15 km, garage.

Louis XV or rustic French-style rooms. From the ring road take place de l'Etoile exit and follow Centre-Ville and Parking-Gutenberg signs. The hotel is 80 m from the cathedral.

■ TARIFF: Single 360–600, Double 360–695, Bk 50 (Amex, Euro/Access, Visa).

TALLOIRES Haute-Savoie   6A

Hôtel Beau Site ★★★ 74290 Talloires.
Tel 04 50 60 71 04, Fax 04 50 60 79 22.
English spoken.
Open 07/05 to 06/10. 29 bedrooms (all en suite). Tennis, golf 3 km, parking.

Excellent location in a park, directly adjoining the east shores of Lake Annecy. Very quiet. Superb views of the lake and mountains. On D509A.

■ RESTAURANT: Gastronomic cuisine and panoramic views.
■ ACTIVITIES: Swimming, fishing and boating literally on the doorstep.
■ TARIFF: Single 300–340, Double 420, Set menu 170–280 (Amex, Euro/Access, Visa).

Hôtel Le Cottage Fernand Bise ★★★★
route du port, 74290 Talloires.
Tel 04 50 60 71 10, Fax 04 50 60 77 51.
English spoken.
Open 01/04 to 31/10. 35 bedrooms (all en suite). Outdoor swimming pool, golf 2 km, garage, parking. &

Completely renovated in 1996, the hotel faces Lake Annecy. Most of the rooms have a lake view and a balcony. Large flower garden.

■ RESTAURANT: Gourmet restaurant. Specialities: fresh fish from Lake Annecy specialities. In

summer, meals are served on the large terrace.
■ ACTIVITIES: Good sports facilities nearby.
● Accommodation plus golf package available and discount on green fees.
■ TARIFF: (1996) Double 500–1100, Bk 65, Set menu 180–270 (Amex, Euro/Access, Visa).

TENDE Alpes-Marit   6C

Hôtel Le Mirval ★★ 06430 La Brigue.
Tel 04 93 04 63 71, Fax 04 93 04 79 81.
English spoken.
Open 01/04 to 31/10. 18 bedrooms (all en suite). Parking. ✆

This turn-of-the-century hotel, located at the entrance of the medieval village, has been totally renovated. Comfortable and very quiet, the hotel has a family atmosphere. Terrace and garden with wonderful views. From Tende, 4 km south to St-Dalmas-de-Tende, then 2.5 km east to La Brigue.

■ RESTAURANT: Meals are taken in the veranda. Specialities include fresh pasta, cannelloni, lasagne, gambas au marsala, truites, canard au whisky.
■ ACTIVITIES: White-water rafting, mountain-biking, climbing, gliding, canoeing; hotel can organise 4x4 excursions.
■ TARIFF: Single 250–350, Double 260–350, Bk 35, Set menu 90–140 (Amex, Euro/Access, Visa).
■ DISCOUNT: 10%

THURY-HARCOURT Calvados   2A

Relais de la Poste ★★★
2 route de Caen, 14220 Thury-Harcourt.
Tel 02 31 79 72 12, Fax 02 31 39 53 55.
English spoken.
Open all year. 12 bedrooms (all en suite).
Indoor swimming pool, tennis, golf 7 km, garage, parking.

Typically French hotel with creepers covering the walls around shuttered windows. On the river and offering pleasant rooms and apartments. South from Caen on D562 to Thury-Harcourt.

■ RESTAURANT: Closed Sun eve & Mon. Specialities are: Seafood, especially shellfish. Large choice of wines.
■ ACTIVITIES: Sauna and solarium at hotel. Fishing, horse-riding, mountain-biking and canoeing nearby.
■ TARIFF: Single 300–420, Double 300–620, Bk 42, Set menu 135–400 (Amex, Euro/Access, Visa).
■ DISCOUNT: 10% LS.

France

TOULON Var 6C

Hôtel La Corniche ★★★
17 Littoral Frédérick Mistral, 83000 Toulon.
Tel 04 94 41 35 12, Fax 04 94 41 24 58.
English spoken.

Open all year. 22 bedrooms (all en suite).
Garage, parking. &

Simple stylish décor, recently renovated, each room now air conditioned. From Toulon, head for Le Mourillon and Les Plages, hotel overlooks the Port Saint-Louis.

■ RESTAURANT: The 'Bistro' and 'Oyster Bar' restaurants are renowned for their good food.
■ ACTIVITIES: ● Special rates for green fees.
■ TARIFF: (1996) Single 350–400, Double 350–550, Bk 50, Set menu 110–190 (Amex, Euro/Access, Visa).
■ DISCOUNT: 10%

TOULOUSE Haute-Garonne 4D

Hôtel des Beaux Arts ★★★★
1 place du Pont Neuf, 31000 Toulouse.
Tel 05 61 23 40 50, Fax 05 61 22 02 27.
English spoken.
Open all year. 20 bedrooms (all en suite).
Golf 8 km, garage. ✆

Completely renovated in 1995, a small, very comfortable hotel on the banks of the River Garonne. Close to 'place du Capitole' and the 'Brasserie des Beaux-Arts', in the heart of the historical district of Toulouse.

■ ACTIVITIES: Horse-riding, tennis, water sports and boating nearby. Good area for sightseeing.
■ TARIFF: Double 450–900, Bk 75 (Amex, Euro/Access, Visa).

LE TOUQUET Pas-de-Calais 2B

Grand Hôtel Park Plaza ★★★★ 4 bd de la
Canche, 62520 Le Touquet-Paris-Plage.
Tel 03 21 06 88 88, Fax 03 21 06 87 87.
English spoken.

Open all year. 135 bedrooms (all en suite).
Indoor swimming pool, golf 3 km, parking. ✆ &

Luxury hotel with tastefully furnished rooms and suites. Quietly situated on the River Canche, the hotel has everything to offer and is within a short walk of the town centre and beaches. Excellent conference and business facilities. 35 km south of Boulogne off N940.

■ RESTAURANT: Formal restaurant with a good choice of well-prepared dishes.
■ ACTIVITIES: Indoor heated pool complex with sauna and jacuzzi, fitness centre. Large choice of activities can be organised, ranging from sailing and golf to guided tours and pleasure flights.
■ TARIFF: (1996) Single 560–760, Double 760–960, Bk 65, Set menu 180–240 (Amex, Euro/Access, Visa).

Hôtel Manoir ★★★
62520 Le Touquet-Paris-Plage.
Tel 03 21 06 28 28, Fax 03 21 06 28 29.
English spoken.
Open 07/02 to 31/12. 42 bedrooms (all en suite). Outdoor swimming pool, tennis, golf on site, parking.

Facing its own golf course, the hotel offers the ideal holiday venue for those seeking luxury and seclusion. Coming from Boulogne-sur-Mer, turn left at the second set of traffic lights in Le Touquet. Hotel is on the right.

■ RESTAURANT: Closed 02 Jan to 06 Feb. Fine cuisine and excellent wine cellar.

■ ACTIVITIES: Arrangements for many activities can be made by the hotel ● Free green fees from 13/10 to 17/04, preferential rates at other times.
■ TARIFF: Single 535–705, Double 770–1110, Set menu 150–195 (Amex, Euro/Access, Visa).

TOURNUS Saône/Loire 5B

Hôtel Le Rempart ★★★
2 av Gambetta, 71700 Tournus.
Tel 03 85 51 10 56, Fax 03 85 51 77 22.
English spoken.
Open all year. 37 bedrooms (all en suite).
Golf 18 km, garage, parking. &

This highly recommended hotel, formerly a 15th-century guardhouse on the ramparts of the town wall, has been renovated to a high standard and is fully air conditioned. Take Tournus exit from A6/N6 and head towards town centre.

■ RESTAURANT: Specialities include poulet de Bresse, salade de queues de langoustines and filet de boeuf Charolais.
■ ACTIVITIES: Tennis and fitness centre nearby.
■ TARIFF: (1996) Single 340–690, Double 390–980, Bk 50, Set menu 162–410 (Amex, Euro/Access, Visa).

TOURS Indre/Loire 2C

Hôtel Le Royal Parine ★★★
65 av Grammont, 37000 Tours.
Tel 02 47 64 71 78, Fax 02 47 05 84 62.
English spoken.
Open all year. 50 bedrooms (all en suite).
Golf 12 km, garage, parking. &

Hotel is in the centre of Tours, in the heart of the Loire Valley. Suites are decorated in Louis XV and XVI style.

■ TARIFF: (1996) Single 295, Double 350, Bk 37 (Amex, Euro/Access, Visa).

TREMEUR Côtes-du-Nord 1D

Hôtel Les Dineux ★★★
Jugon-les-Lacs, 22250 Trémeur.
Tel 02 96 84 65 80, Fax 02 96 84 76 35.
English spoken.
Open all year. 15 bedrooms (all en suite).
Garage, parking. ✆ &

Built in 1989, the hotel is surrounded by its own park. 5 minutes from Jugon-les-Lacs, a small town full of character.

■ RESTAURANT: Meals are served in the garden in summer. Seafood specialities.
■ ACTIVITIES: Hiking, mountain-biking, fishing, water sports, horse-riding; organised tours.
■ TARIFF: (1996) Single 260, Double 320, Bk 35, Set menu 85–115 (Euro/Access, Visa).
■ DISCOUNT: 10%

TROUVILLE-SUR-MER Calvados 2A

Hôtel Mercure ★★★ 14360 Trouville-sur-Mer.
Tel 02 31 87 38 38, Fax 02 31 87 35 41.
English spoken.

Open all year. 80 bedrooms (all en suite).
Golf 6 km, parking. &

Town centre hotel close to beach and casino. From the A13, take 'Deauville-Trouville' exit.

■ RESTAURANT: Closed mid-Nov to mid-Dec. Terrace restaurant.
■ ACTIVITIES: Horse-riding, go-karting, tennis, fishing and casino nearby.
■ TARIFF: (1996) Single 360–595, Double 395–595, Bk 57, Set menu 100–150 (Amex, Euro/Access, Visa).
■ DISCOUNT: 10%

France

TROYES Aube   3C

Novotel Troyes Aéroport ★★★ 10600 Barberey.
Tel 03 25 71 74 74, Fax 03 25 71 74 50.
English spoken.
Open all year. 83 bedrooms (all en suite).
Outdoor swimming pool, golf 12 km, parking. &

*All the usual Novotel facilities surrounded by
pleasant, shady gardens. Free B&B for 2
children under 16 sharing parents' room.
Ideal for a stop-over, from A26 exit at junction
31, Troyes, Provins and then follow airport
signs; from A5 exit at junction 20, go towards
Troyes and then follow airport signs.*

■ RESTAURANT: Grill restaurant opens out on to
terrace beside the swimming pool. Local
specialities.
■ ACTIVITIES: Visit the St-Jean area of Troyes with
its 16th-century half-timbered houses. Gliding
and go-karting 2 km from hotel.
■ TARIFF: (1996) Single 410–420,
Double 440–460, Bk 52, Set menu 95 (Amex,
Euro/Access, Visa).
■ DISCOUNT: 15%

VAISON-LA-ROMAINE Vaucluse   5D

Le Logis du Château ★★ Les Hauts de Vaison,
84110 Vaison-la-Romaine.

Tel 04 90 36 09 98, Fax 04 90 36 10 95.
English spoken.
Open 01/04 to 31/10. 45 bedrooms
(all en suite). Outdoor swimming pool, tennis,
golf 25 km, parking. &

*Get away from it all. Panoramic views, silence
and tranquillity. Follow signs for 'Cité Médiévale'.*

■ RESTAURANT: Closed Wed & Sun lunch. Traditional
cuisine. Specialities: terrine Provençal au genièvre,
chausson d'escargots aux champignons, pieds et
paquets d'agneau Provençaux.
■ TARIFF: Single 235–350, Double 250–380,
Bk 40, Set menu 95–158 (Euro/Access, Visa).

VALENCIENNES Nord   2B

Auberge du Bon Fermier ★★★★
64-66 rue de Famars, 59300 Valenciennes.
Tel 03 27 46 68 25, Fax 03 27 33 75 01.
English spoken.
Open all year. 16 bedrooms (all en suite).
Tennis, golf 1 km, garage, parking. ℄
SEE ADVERTISEMENT.

*A truly extraordinary former 16th-century
posthouse. Restored to perfection inside and
out and now graded as an historic monument.
Open fires and brick floors abound; the*

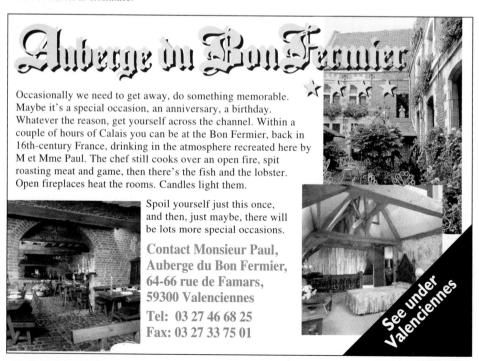

bedrooms are large, heavily beamed and luxuriously appointed. Centrally placed in the old town with private courtyard behind.

■ RESTAURANT: Exposed brick and beam. Regional cuisine cooked over wood fires. Specialities: spit-roasted game, lobster and fish.
■ ACTIVITIES: Sailing school, ice rink and pool nearby. Walking, local museum.
■ TARIFF: (1996) Single 400–600, Double 480–700, Bk 45, Set menu 120–200 (Amex, Euro/Access, Visa).

VALLON-PONT-D'ARC Ardèche   5D

Hôtel du Tourisme ★★
6 rue du Miarou, 07150 Vallon-Pont-d'Arc.
Tel 04 75 88 02 12, Fax 04 75 88 12 90.
English spoken.
Open 01/02 to 15/12. 29 bedrooms (all en suite). Golf 4 km, parking.
Family owned and run since 1937, hotel with friendly atmosphere in village centre but just 100 m from open countryside.

■ RESTAURANT: Closed Mon LS. Specialities include charcuteries maison, omelette aux truffles, civet de cailles and poulet aux écrevisses. Cosy dining room and large terrace with lovely views.
■ ACTIVITIES: Cycling, white-water rafting. Exhibition 'Grotte Chauvet-Pont d'Arc'.
■ TARIFF: (1996) Double 260–405, Bk 32, Set menu 85–165 (Euro/Access, Visa).

VALOGNES Manche   1B

Hôtel de l'Agriculture ★
16 rue Léopold Delisle, 50700 Valognes.
Tel 02 33 95 02 02, Fax 02 33 95 29 33.
English spoken.
Open 01/01 to 18/02 & 05/03 to 31/12.
30 bedrooms (15 en suite, 1 bath/shower only).
Outdoor swimming pool, golf 15 km, garage, parking.
A pretty, creeper-clad building with many fine

features inside. From the Valognes central square, head towards the station (Carteret road), turn second left.

■ RESTAURANT: Closed Mon & Sun eve in LS. Attractive stone-clad, beamed dining room. Specialities: homard grillé farci; soupe de poisson; ris de veau poêlé à la Normande.
■ ACTIVITIES: Sightseeing; sporting facilities within easy reach.
■ TARIFF: Single 100–280, Double 140–280, Bk 30, Set menu 70–180 (Euro/Access, Visa).
■ DISCOUNT: 10%

VALRAS-PLAGE Hérault   5C

Hôtel Albizzia ★★
12 bd du Chemin Creux, 34350 Valras-Plage.
Tel 04 67 37 48 48, Fax 04 67 37 58 10.
English spoken.
Open all year. 28 bedrooms (all en suite). Outdoor swimming pool, golf 20 km, parking. ₺
Recently built and located just 200 m from a fine, sandy beach. Via the A9 coming from Montpellier, take Béziers-Est exit. Coming from Narbonne, take Béziers-Oest exit.

■ ACTIVITIES: Tennis, water sports, fishing and horse-riding close by.
■ TARIFF: Single 230–400, Double 250–420, Bk 37 (Amex, Euro/Access, Visa).

VANNES Morbihan   1D

Hôtel France ★★
57 av Victor Hugo, 56000 Vannes.
Tel 02 97 47 27 57, Fax 02 97 42 59 17.
English spoken.
Open all year. 25 bedrooms (21 en suite, 4 bath/shower only). Golf 10 km, parking.
Charming hotel with garden terrace. Rooms with full facilities including some large family rooms. Near the railway station and the centre of this historical town.

■ TARIFF: (1996) Single 150–300, Double 160–320, Bk 35 (Euro/Access, Visa).

VARENNES-SUR-ALLIER Allier   5A

Auberge de l'Orisse ★★★
03150 Varennes-sur-Allier.
Tel 04 70 45 05 60, Fax 04 70 45 18 55.
English spoken.
Open all year. 23 bedrooms (all en suite). Outdoor swimming pool, tennis, golf 8 km, parking.
Small hotel with good restaurant. On N7 south of Moulins towards Laplisse.

■ TARIFF: (1996) Double 250–300, Bk 30, Set menu 75–200 (Amex, Euro/Access, Visa).

France

VENCE Alpes-Marit   6D

Hôtel Closerie des Genêts ★
4 impasse M Maurel, 06140 Vence.
Tel 04 93 58 33 25. English spoken.
Open all year. 10 bedrooms (all en suite).

Charming, family-run establishment with lovely garden. In town centre, 100 m from Tourist Office.

■ RESTAURANT: Closed Sun eve. Pretty restaurant overlooking the garden. Fresh, seasonal cuisine.
■ ACTIVITIES: Good location for walking and touring. Swimming pool 200 m.
■ TARIFF: Single 180–200, Double 220–280, Bk 25, Set menu 118–170 (Euro/Access, Visa).
■ DISCOUNT: 10% Apr to Oct.

VERNET-LES-BAINS Pyrénées Orient   5C

Hôtel Châtaigneraie ★
Sahorre, 66360 Vernet-les-Bains.
Tel 04 68 05 51 04.
Open 01/05 to 01/10. 10 bedrooms (8 en suite). Parking.

Hotel with peaceful gardens situated in an unspoilt mountain valley 3 km from Vernet-les-Bains on the D27. Take the N116 from Perpignan and turn on to the D116 to the village.

■ RESTAURANT: Traditional and regional cooking in pleasant surroundings.
■ ACTIVITIES: Good walking/hiking area; tennis and swimming pool 3 km. ● Jeep rides to nearby canyon at reduced rates.
■ TARIFF: Single 170–220, Double 175–263, Bk 30, Set menu 79–128 (Visa).

VERNEUIL-SUR-AVRE Eure   2C

Hostellerie Le Clos ★★★★ 98 rue de la Ferté Vidame, 27130 Verneuil-sur-Avre.
Tel 02 32 32 21 81, Fax 02 32 32 21 36.
English spoken.

Open 15/01 to 15/12. 5 bedrooms, 5 apartments, (all en suite). Tennis, golf 7 km, parking. ♿

Halfway between a country house and a mansion, hotel has all the charm of a Norman manor complete with terrace overlooking lovely gardens. Apartments with air-conditioned veranda (price range 900 FF to 1100 FF), lounge and jacuzzi are also available. On N12, 110 km west of Paris.

■ RESTAURANT: Closed Mon except holidays. Lovely dining room full of flowers, where everything is of the highest quality. Fine regional cuisine and excellent service.
■ ACTIVITIES: Bicycle treks with picnic provided; fitness room, sauna, whirlpool; tours/sightseeing arrangements made.
■ TARIFF: (1996) Single 600–800, Double 700–900, Bk 80, Set menu 180–330 (Amex, Euro/Access, Visa).

VERNON Eure   2B

Hôtel Climat de France ★★
17 rue de la Poste, 27950 St-Marcel.
Tel 02 32 21 25 00, Fax 02 32 21 25 00.
English spoken.
Open all year. 44 bedrooms (all en suite).
Golf 14 km, parking. ✆ ♿

Recently built hotel on the outskirts of Vernon; a short drive from Giverny with the world-famous Claude Monet museum and garden.

■ RESTAURANT: Good choice of menus with hors d'oeuvres and dessert buffet.
■ ACTIVITIES: Water-skiing, swimming and tennis nearby ; impressionist American museum in Giverny, Bizy castle in Vernon. ● Special rates for green fees for hotel guests.
■ TARIFF: (1996) Double 300, Bk 40, Set menu 95–130 (Amex, Euro/Access, Visa).
■ DISCOUNT: 10%

VERVINS Aisne   3A

Hôtel Tour du Roy ★★★
45 rue du Général Leclerc, 02140 Vervins.
Tel 03 23 98 00 11, Fax 03 23 98 00 72.
English spoken.
Open all year. 15 bedrooms (all en suite).
Tennis, golf 6 km, parking. ♿

A splendid manor house, steeped in history, overlooking the old city of Vervins. Interior features include hand-painted bathrooms and stained-glass windows. Rooms overlook terraces, park or landscaped square. On N2 in the centre of Vervins. A welcoming glass of champagne is offered on arrival.

■ RESTAURANT: Renowned, elegant restaurant

France

specialising in traditional, seafood and country cuisine.
■ ACTIVITIES: Canoeing, race course and Reims within easy reach. ● Green fee at nearby 18-hole golf course 150F/day.
■ TARIFF: (1996) Single 300–600, Double 350–800, Bk 70, Set menu 160–400 (Amex, Euro/Access, Visa).

VICHY Allier   5A

Hôtel Arverna ★★
12 rue Desbrest, 03200 Vichy.
Tel 04 70 31 31 19, Fax 04 70 97 86 43.
English spoken.
Open all year. 26 bedrooms (all en suite).
Golf 2 km, garage.

Comfortable hotel with private garden in centre of Vichy. Near health centre, casino and parks.
■ ACTIVITIES: Sightseeing tours around Vichy.
■ TARIFF: (1996) Single 170–250, Double 200–280, Bk 35 (Amex, Euro/Access, Visa).
■ DISCOUNT: 10%

VIEILLEVIE Cantal   5C

Hôtel Terrasse ★★ 15120 Vieillevie.
Tel 04 71 49 94 00, Fax 04 71 49 92 23.
English spoken.
Open 01/04 to 01/11. 32 bedrooms (27 en suite, 5 bath/shower only). Outdoor swimming pool, tennis, parking. ら

Charming hotel on the banks of the River Lot, in the heart of the countryside. The village of Vieillevie is 15 km from Conques.
■ RESTAURANT: Friendly and attractive; meals served on a shady terrace in good weather. Speciality: civet de lotte.
■ ACTIVITIES: Fishing, canoeing, rafting, climbing and mountain-biking nearby.
■ TARIFF: (1996) Double 150–260, Bk 35, Set menu 67–180 (Amex, Euro/Access, Visa).
■ DISCOUNT: 10%

VIERZON Cher   2D

Hôtel Arche ★★
Forum République, 18100 Vierzon.
Tel 02 48 71 93 10, Fax 02 48 71 83 63.
English spoken.

Open all year. 40 bedrooms (all en suite).
Golf 2 km, garage, parking. ら
Modern, quiet and comfortable, hotel is in the centre of Vierzon with panoramic view of Berry canal. Free closed parking.
■ RESTAURANT: Closed Sun. French regional cuisine; grill specialities.
■ TARIFF: (1996) Single 210–300, Double 235–350, Bk 35, Set menu 55–75 (Amex, Euro/Access, Visa).

VILLEDIEU-LES-POELES Manche   1B

Hôtel St-Pierre et St-Michel ★★ 12 place de la République, 50800 Villedieu-les-Poêles.
Tel 02 33 61 00 11, Fax 02 33 61 06 52.
English spoken.
Open all year. 23 bedrooms (21 en suite).
Garage, parking.

Charming hotel dating from 1850, located in the town centre. Between St-Lô and Avranches.
■ RESTAURANT: Closed 04/01 to 27/01. Good restaurant with wide acclaim.
■ ACTIVITIES: Lots of museums in town. Also within reach of Bayeaux and Mont-St-Michel. Good walking and biking; visit D-Day landing beaches.
■ TARIFF: (1996) Double 240–300, Bk 35, Set menu 95–215 (Euro/Access, Visa).
■ DISCOUNT: 8%

VILLEFRANCHE-DE-ROUERGUE   5C

Hôtel Relais de Farrou ★★★ au Farrou, 12200 Villefranche-de-Rouergue.
Tel 05 65 45 18 11, Fax 05 65 45 32 59.
English spoken.

France

Open all year. 26 bedrooms (all en suite).
Outdoor swimming pool, tennis, garage,
parking. ☎ &

*Modern comfort in a former coaching inn. Set
in the countryside 3 minutes from Villefranche-
de-Rouergue. South of Figéac on D922.*

■ RESTAURANT: Closed Sun eve & Mon LS.
Imaginative, creative cuisine. Specialities: les
escalopines de foie gras de canard poêlées au
muscat de Mireval; civet de homard au vieux
Banyuls; ris d'agneau aux morilles.
■ ACTIVITIES: Very good sports/health facilities at
hotel (Turkish bath, jacuzzi, mini-golf, table
tennis); arrangements made for canoeing,
pony-trekking and rides in horse-drawn carriage.
■ TARIFF: Single 270–385, Double 330–580,
Bk 44, Set menu 122–350 (Euro/Access, Visa).

VILLEFRANCHE-DU-PERIGORD   4D

Hôtel La Clé des Champs ★★
Fontenilles, 24550 Villefranche-du-Périgord.
Tel 05 53 29 95 94, Fax 05 53 28 42 96.
English spoken.

Open 01/04 to 31/10. 13 bedrooms
(all en suite). Outdoor swimming pool, tennis,
garage, parking. &

*Set in the heart of the woodlands of south
Dordogne, this former farmhouse provides
comfortable accommodation. From
Villefranche-du-Périgord, take the D660
towards Monpazier and the hotel is signposted.*

■ RESTAURANT: Regional specialities prepared
with fresh local produce: home-made foie gras,
breast of duck, goose.
■ ACTIVITIES: Table tennis, mountain-bike hire;
rambles in the countryside by foot or on
horseback can be arranged on request.
■ TARIFF: (1996) Bk 40, Set menu 98–200
(No credit cards).
■ DISCOUNT: 15% on presentation of this guide.

VILLEFRANCHE-SUR-MER   Alpes-Marit 6D

Hôtel Welcome ★★★ 1 quai Courbet,
06230 Villefranche-sur-Mer.
Tel 04 93 76 76 93, Fax 04 93 01 88 81.
English spoken.

Open 20/12 to 17/11. 32 bedrooms
(all en suite). Golf 15 km, garage. &

*Waterfront hotel in former 17th-century
convent and a favourite spot for the famous
(Jean Cocteau, Graham Sutherland and
Somerset Maughan used to stay here). Seafood
specialities and haute cuisine. On coast road
to the east of Nice. Breakfast is offered to RAC
Members.*

■ RESTAURANT: Closed Mon.
■ ACTIVITIES: Scuba-diving, water-skiing, boats
for hire, mini-excursions by train.
■ TARIFF: (1996) Single 400–820, Double 550–
890, Bk 40 (Amex, Euro/Access, Visa).
■ DISCOUNT: 5% except public holidays.

WIMEREUX   Pas-de-Calais   2B

Hôtel Centre ★★
78 rue Carnot, 62930 Wimereux.
Tel 03 21 32 41 08, Fax 03 21 33 82 48.
English spoken.
Open 15/01 to 15/12. 25 bedrooms
(all en suite). Golf 2 km, garage.

*From Boulogne-sur-Mer, follow the coast road
and Wimereux is 5 km to the north. The hotel
is in the main street.*

■ RESTAURANT: Closed Mon. 1920s décor.
Seafood specialities.
■ ACTIVITIES: Walking along the coast.
■ TARIFF: (1996) Single 225, Double 295, Bk 35,
Set menu 98–160 (Euro/Access, Visa).
■ DISCOUNT: 5%

GERMANY

The Black Forest at Todtnau-Fahl

Standing at the very heart of Europe, and sharing its borders with nine other countries, recently united Germany has traditionally been best known to the tourist for the Black Forest – or *Schwarzwald* – and the River Rhine.

The *Schwarzwald* lies close to the French and Swiss borders and is counted the most visited upland area of Europe. The Rhine runs from Basle in Switzerland north through Germany, then on into the Netherlands, to enter the North Sea at Rotterdam.

The Rhine's commercial traffic is as important as the *Rheindampfer* tourist cruisers with on-board orchestras, that steam daily up and down this important waterway. South of Koblenz, the river passes the famous *Loreleifelsen,* where legend has it the siren Lorelei lures ships on to the rock.

In the East, the Elbe flows from the Czech Republic through Dresden and Magdeburg (formerly in East Germany) on to the North Sea at the great port of Hamburg. Here, one of Germany's two stretches of coastline runs from the Netherlands in the west, north to the Danish border; while the second stretch of German coast borders the Baltic.

Munich is southern Germany's largest city, lying between the Danube and the Alps near the Austrian border. It is a city of 36 museums, abundant baroque and rococo architecture and a passion for beer.

Emergency numbers

Police 110

Fire Brigade 112

Ambulance 110 (115 in former East German states)

Warning information

Warning triangle must be carried

Blood alcohol legal limit 80 mg

Germany

AACHEN 16A

Quellenhof Aachen ★★★★
Monheimsalle 52, 56062 Aachen.
Tel 0241 91320, Fax 0241 9132555.
English spoken.
Open all year. 185 bedrooms (all en suite).
Indoor swimming pool, golf 8 km, garage. &

Spacious hotel in the Kongresscentrum, immediately next to the casino. An 8-minute walk from the city centre and old town. Excellent conference facilities.

■ RESTAURANT: Bistro restaurant offering international specialities.
■ ACTIVITIES: Spa bath therapy. Casino nearby. Lots of things to do and see in and around Aachen.
■ TARIFF: Single 195–295, Double 245–345, Bk 24, Set menu 48 (Amex, Euro/Access, Visa).

ALT-DUVENSTEDT 14B

Hotel Töpferhaus ★★★★
Am Bistensee, 24791 Alt Duvenstedt.
Tel 04338 333, Fax 04338 551. English spoken.

Open all year. 46 bedrooms (all en suite).
Outdoor swimming pool, tennis, golf 15 km, parking. ℓ

Charming country hotel, to the north of Hamburg and quietly situated on the banks of the lake. From the A7, take the Rendsburg/Eckernförde exit and after 2 km follow signs to hotel.

■ RESTAURANT: Comfortable dining room overlooking the Bistensee. Excellent cuisine.
■ ACTIVITIES: Tennis, cycling, fishing, hiking.
■ TARIFF: Single 125–195, Double 195–295, Set menu 45–98 (Amex, Euro/Access, Visa).

ALTÖTTING 17C

Flair Hotel Zum Bauernsepp ★★★
Kiefering 42, 8261 Tüssling.
Tel 08633 8940, Fax 08633 894200.
English spoken.

Open all year. 39 bedrooms (all en suite).
Tennis, golf 15 km, parking. ℓ

Modern hotel with romantic summer garden. Just 2 km south-west of Altötting, off the B299.

■ RESTAURANT: Fish specialities and traditional German cuisine. Family brunch on Sundays.
■ ACTIVITIES: Dance hall; river trips; hiking, cycling.
■ TARIFF: (1996) Single 85–92, Double 125–132, Set menu 25–85 (Amex, Euro/Access, Visa).

ALZEY 16A

Hotel Rheinhessen Treff ★★★
Industriestrasse 13, 55232 Alzey.
Tel 06731 4030, Fax 06731 403106.
English spoken.

Open all year. 143 bedrooms (all en suite).
Outdoor swimming pool, tennis, golf 5 km, parking.

Comfortable hotel with friendly atmosphere. From the motorway A61/A63, exit Alzey then follow 'Industriegebiet' signs.

■ RESTAURANT: Regional and international cuisine. Buffet on Sundays.
■ ACTIVITIES: Bowling alley, squash.
■ TARIFF: Single 80–135, Double 110–185 (Amex, Euro/Access, Visa).
■ DISCOUNT: 10%

ANDERNACH 16A

Rhein Hotel
Konrad Adenauer Allee 20, 5470 Andernach.
Tel 02632 42240, Fax 02632 494172.
English spoken.
Open 01/04 to 31/10. 25 bedrooms (all en suite). Parking. &

Friendly, family-run hotel overlooking the beautiful riverside promenade and gardens beside the Rhein. 2 minutes from the town centre. Comfortable, well-equipped rooms, some having balcony or terrace.

Germany

■ RESTAURANT: Enjoy good food in the light and pretty grill restaurant, 'Pfeffermühle'.
■ TARIFF: (1996) Single 60–65, Double 90–130 (Amex, Euro/Access, Visa).

ASCHAFFENBURG 16B

Hotel Zum Goldenen Ochsen ★★
Karlstrasse 16, 63739 Aschaffenburg.
Tel 06021 23132, Fax 06021 25785. English spoken.
Open all year. 39 bedrooms (all en suite).
Golf 18 km, parking. ☏

Fine historic hotel run by the same family since 1894. Centrally located in one of the most beautiful parts of Aschaffenburg with views over the Schloss gardens.

■ RESTAURANT: Closed Mon lunch. International and Bavarian dishes.
■ ACTIVITIES: Indoor and outdoor swimming pools 2 km; sightseeing and exploring the lovely surrounding area.
■ TARIFF: (1996) Single 92–99, Double 135–150, Set menu 19.90–26.90 (Amex, Euro/Access, Visa).

AUGSBURG 17C

Hotel Langer/Hennemann ★★★
Gogginger Str 39, 8900 Augsburg.
Tel 0821 578077, Fax 0821 592600. English spoken.

Open all year. 25 bedrooms (all en suite).
Golf 4 km, garage, parking. ☏

Friendly atmosphere and quiet rooms in this centrally located hotel. From all directions, follow signs for 'Kongress-Halle'.

■ RESTAURANT: Choice of two restaurants offering international cuisine.
■ ACTIVITIES: Bus and walking tours of the 2000-year-old town; discover the nearby Bavarian Alps and lakes.

■ TARIFF: Single 90–115, Double 120–158, Set menu 12.50–18 (Amex, Euro/Access, Visa).
■ DISCOUNT: 10%

Hotel Steigenberger Drei Mohren ★★★★
Maximilianstr 40, 86150 Augsburg.
Tel 0821 50360, Fax 0821 157864. English spoken.

Open all year. 107 bedrooms (all en suite).
Golf 20 km, garage, parking.

On the famous Maximilianstrasse, in the centre of the historic old town of Augsburg. Very comfortable hotel offering traditional service and almost every facility.

■ RESTAURANT: Choice of restaurants offering a wide range of excellent dining. Summer garden terrace.
■ TARIFF: (1996) Single 235–279, Double 280–350, Set menu 30–35 (Amex, Euro/Access, Visa).

BADEN-BADEN 16C

Queens Hotel ★★★★
Falkenstrasse 2, 76530 Baden-Baden.
Tel 07221 2190, Fax 07221 219519. English spoken.

Open all year. 121 bedrooms (all en suite). Indoor swimming pool, golf 3 km, garage, parking. &

Situated on the famous Lichtentaler Allee, the hotel is surrounded by beautiful parks and

Germany

Germany

trees. *The town centre and the Kurhaus, with its world-famous casino, are only minutes away.*

■ RESTAURANT: Local and international cuisine; cosy, relaxed atmosphere.
■ ACTIVITIES: Fitness centre; cycle hire.
■ TARIFF: (1996) Single 190–260, Double 230–330, Set menu 32–89 (Amex, Euro/Access, Visa).

BADENWEILER   16C

Hotel Römerbad ★★★★★
Schlosspl 1, 79410 Badenweiler.
Tel 07632 700, Fax 07632 70200. English spoken.

Open all year. 84 bedrooms (all en suite). Indoor swimming pool, outdoor swimming pool, tennis, golf 15 km, garage.
Situated at the edge of the Black Forest and close to the French and Swiss borders, this elegant hotel has been family owned and managed since 1825. Tastefully decorated, very comfortable rooms.

■ RESTAURANT: Very good restaurant.
■ ACTIVITIES: Excellent sports/health and beauty facilities.
■ TARIFF: Single 240–290, Double 360–420, Set menu 55–80 (Amex, Euro/Access, Visa).

BAD HERSFELD   16B

Romantik-Hotel Zum Stern ★★★
Lingg Platz 11, 36251 Bad Hersfeld.
Tel 06621 1890, Fax 06621 189260. English spoken.
Open all year. 53 bedrooms (all en suite). Indoor swimming pool, tennis, golf 25 km, garage, parking. &

Traditional hotel with friendly atmosphere. Originally part of an old monastery but now completely renovated. In the pedestrian area of Bad Hersfeld. Access: follow the blue signs 'Parkhaus Neumarkt' and go another 50 m to hotel car park.

■ RESTAURANT: Closed 01/01 to 22/01. High quality restaurant using fresh produce.
■ ACTIVITIES: 'Champagne', 'Fairytale', 'Keep-fit' and 'Romantic' weekend packages available. Special Christmas and New Year activities.
■ TARIFF: (1996) Single 115–139, Double 195–230, Set menu 39–69 (Amex, Euro/Access, Visa).

BAD KISSINGEN   16B

Steigenberger Kurhaushotel ★★★★★
Am Kurgarten 3, 97688 Bad Kissingen.
Tel 0971 80410, Fax 0971 8041597. English spoken.
Open all year. 100 bedrooms (all en suite). Indoor swimming pool, golf 5 km, garage.

In the town centre opposite the Kurpark, hotel has fully equipped rooms and direct access to the famous spa.

■ RESTAURANT: Two restaurants with local and first-class international cuisine. Menus include healthy, low fat dishes.
■ ACTIVITIES: Close to theatre and casino (hotel guests receive a free ticket). Spa and other health and beauty facilities. Sightseeing tours to local historic sites including Fulda, Würzburg and Meiningen organised by the hotel.
■ TARIFF: (1996) Single 160–235, Double 250–395, Set menu 25–85 (Amex, Euro/Access, Visa).

BAD SODEN-AM-TAUNUS   16B

Treff Parkhotel Bad Soden ★★★★
Konigsteiner Str 88, 6232 Bad Soden-am-Taunus.
Tel 06196 2000, Fax 06196 200153. English spoken.
Open all year. 130 bedrooms (all en suite). Parking. (&

First-class, modern hotel and convention centre with extensive facilities. Convenient suburban location. Fully equipped rooms with balcony; non-smokers rooms also available. 15 km from Frankfurt, 22 km from Rhein-Main airport.

■ RESTAURANT: Choice of 2 restaurants.
■ ACTIVITIES: Health club with whirlpool/sauna and jogging track at hotel; indoor/outdoor swimming pools, tennis, bowling, horse-riding and mini-golf nearby.
■ TARIFF: (1996) Single 215–315, Double 270–375 (Amex, Euro/Access, Visa).

BAMBERG   17A

Hotel Sankt Nepomuk ★★★★
Obere Mühlbrücke 9, 96049 Bamberg.
Tel 0951 98420, Fax 0951 9842100. English spoken.

Open all year. 47 bedrooms (all en suite). Garage. &

Beautifully restored and converted watermill. In a stunning location, right on the river and in the centre of this lovely old town which ranks among the finest architectural settings in Germany. Tastefully decorated; open fires.

■ RESTAURANT: Regional and international specialities.

■ ACTIVITIES: Bicycles for hire.

■ TARIFF: (1996) Single 130–150, Double 180–220, Set menu 30–100 (Euro/Access, Visa).

BAYREUTH   17A

Transmar Travel Hotel ★★★★
Bühlstrasse 12, 95463 Bayreuth-Bindlach.
Tel 09208 6860, Fax 09208 686100.
English spoken.
Open all year. 146 bedrooms (all en suite).
Golf 2 km, garage, parking. &

Located close to the A9 Berlin to München motorway. Exit Bayreuth-Nord towards the industrial area. Excellent conference facilities.

■ RESTAURANT: Hearty regional and international cuisine. Exceptional combination of first-class food at reasonable prices.

■ ACTIVITIES: Various visits and guided tours which include a beer museum, the Opera House, the Hermitage, Iwalewa House and porcelain and glass works. ● Reduction on green fees.

■ TARIFF: (1996) Single 115–185, Double 135–265, Set menu 13.80–57.80 (Amex, Euro/Access, Visa).

BAYRISCHZELL   17C

Hotel Postgasthof Rote Wand
Geitau 15, 8163 Bayrischzell.
Tel 08023 243, Fax 08023 656. English spoken.
Open 15/12 to 15/04 & 01/05 to 31/10.
30 bedrooms (all en suite). Golf 20 km, garage, parking. ℓ

Quiet, chalet-style hotel surrounded by mountains and away from the traffic. Family atmosphere.

■ RESTAURANT: Closed Tues. Home-made regional cuisine.

■ ACTIVITIES: Cross-country skiing in winter; swimming pool, tennis, mountaineering, cycling and sailing nearby.

■ TARIFF: (1996) Single 55–70, Double 110–140 (Amex, Euro/Access, Visa).

BEDERKESA   14B

Hotel Waldschlosschen Bösehof ★★★★
Hauptmann-Böse-Str 19, 27624 Bederkesa.
Tel 04745 9480, Fax 04745 948200. English spoken.

Open all year. 30 bedrooms (all en suite). Indoor swimming pool, golf 3 km, garage, parking.

Family-run hotel situated next to woodland. Access from A27 north of Bremerhaven, exit at Debstedt and follow signs to Bederkesa (12 km).

■ RESTAURANT: 'Wintergarten' and 'Böse's' restaurants are well regarded for their regional and international cuisine. Meals on the sun terrace in summer.

■ ACTIVITIES: Walking, cycling, sauna, swimming pool, ten-pin bowling, tennis and golf close at hand; excursions to North Sea area.

■ TARIFF: Single 75–95, Double 180–205, Set menu 45–85 (Amex, Euro/Access, Visa).

BEILNGRIES   17C

Hotel Gams ★★★
Hauptsrasse 16, 8432 Beilngries.
Tel 08461 256, Fax 08461 7475. English spoken.
Open all year. 62 bedrooms (all en suite).
Garage, parking, restaurant.

Attractive hotel in small town in the heart of Bavaria. From A9 Berlin to München, take exit for Denkendorf or Altmühltal. From A3 Nürnberg to Regensbserg, take exit for Neumarkt or Parsberg.

■ TARIFF: (1996) Single 95–125, Double 130–190, Set menu 18–38 (Amex, Euro/Access, Visa).

BERCHTESGADEN   17D

Hotel Geiger ★★★★
Stanggass, 83471 Berchtesgaden.
Tel 08652 9653, Fax 08652 965400.
English spoken.
Open 15/12 to 05/11. 50 bedrooms (all en suite). Indoor swimming pool, outdoor swimming pool, golf 3 km, garage, parking.

Set in its own large park, the hotel dates from the mid-1800s and has been owned by the family for 5 generations. Apart from a warm and genuine welcome, the hotel offers stunning views and very tasteful, carefully modernised accommodation.

■ RESTAURANT: Quiet and efficient with good cellar. Regional, national and international cuisine.

■ ACTIVITIES: Fitness, massage rooms and sauna at hotel; explore the mountainous national park, nearby salt mines and lakes; mountain-biking, ballooning, rafting and children's adventure camp.

■ TARIFF: (1996) Single 100–140, Double 200–300, Set menu 45–84 (Visa).

Germany

Germany

BERLIN 15D

Alsterhof Ringhotel Berlin ★★★★
Augsburger Str 5, 10789 Berlin.
Tel 030 212420, Fax 030 2183949.
English spoken.
Open all year. 200 bedrooms (all en suite).
Indoor swimming pool, garage.

Central downtown location but in a quiet, green setting. An elegant, first-class hotel two minutes' walk from Kurfürstendamm in this exciting city with a character all of its own.

■ RESTAURANT: Seasonal and regional dishes.
■ ACTIVITIES: Hotel will make arrangements for theatre tickets and sightseeing tours on request; excellent shopping.
■ TARIFF: Single 225–275, Double 290–390 (Amex, Euro/Access, Visa).

BERNKASTEL 16A

Hotel Landhaus Arnoth 54483 Kleinich.
Tel 06536 286/93990, Fax 06536 1217.
English spoken.

Open all year. 23 bedrooms (all en suite).
Golf 6 km, parking.
From the centre of Bernkastel, take the road to Longkamp. In Longkamp, follow the signs to Kleinich.

■ RESTAURANT: Closed Sun eve & Mon. Good choice of menus using fresh, market produce.
■ ACTIVITIES: Tennis, outdoor and indoor swimming pools, horse-riding, horse-drawn carriage rides, wine tasting and good walks all nearby.
■ TARIFF: (1996) Single 100–130, Double 140–160, Set menu 55–85 (Euro/Access).

BLANKENHEIM 16A

Hotel Schlossblick ★★★
Nonnenbacherweg 4-6, 53945 Blankenheim.
Tel 02449 95500, Fax 02449 955050. English spoken.

Open all year. 33 bedrooms (30 en suite).
Indoor swimming pool, garage, parking.

Well-known hotel in the Eifel mountains with international atmosphere. Good views. Leave the A1 from Köln at B51 Blankenheim exit; turn first right in the town centre and then immediately left into Nonnenbacherweg.

■ RESTAURANT: International and regional Eifel dishes.
■ ACTIVITIES: Taking advantage of over 400 km of mapped walks; rowing and mini-golf nearby; exploring the Mosel, Rhein and Ahr valleys; visit the famous Nürburgring race track, Trier, Aachen and Köln.
■ TARIFF: Single 70–80, Double 110–130, Set menu 20–35 (Amex, Euro/Access, Visa).
■ DISCOUNT: 5% except weekends in Aug.

BOCHUM 14C

Queens Hotel ★★★★
Kohlleppelsweg, 44791 Bochum.
Tel 0234 92590, Fax 0234 9259625.
English spoken.
Open all year. 108 bedrooms (all en suite).
Golf 6 km, parking. &

Holiday or business hotel quietly located close to developing commercial and cultural centre. From the A40 take exit for Bochum/Werne.

■ RESTAURANT: 'Starlight' restaurant offers German and French cuisine.
■ ACTIVITIES: Aquapark and theatre nearby.
■ TARIFF: (1996) Single 190–205, Double 237–247, Bk 23 (Amex, Euro/Access, Visa).

BONN 16A

Team Hotel President ★★★
Clemens August Str 32-36, 53115 Bonn.
Tel 0228 72500, Fax 0228 725072.
English spoken.
Open all year. 98 bedrooms (all en suite).
Garage.

Conveniently situated in the historic quarter of Poppelsdorf, with direct access to the federal expressway and just a short distance from the castle and botanical garden. Comfortable, soundproofed rooms with non-smoking accommodation available on request. Excellent public transport.

■ RESTAURANT: International and regional cuisine.
■ ACTIVITIES: Theatres, museums; visit Beethoven's birthplace.
■ TARIFF: Single 149–289, Double 179–349, Set menu 24–37 (Amex, Euro/Access, Visa).

BOPPARD 16A

Bellevue Rheinhotel ★★★★

Rheinallee 41-42, 56154 Boppard.
Tel 06742 1020, Fax 06742 102602. English spoken.

Open all year. 94 bedrooms (all en suite).
Indoor swimming pool, tennis, golf 12 km,
garage, parking.

*One of the Best Western group. Hotel is situated
on the banks of the Rhein and offers excellent
facilities. Central location in Boppard and well
signposted. From A61 take Boppard exit; B9
passes through the town. Details of special Easter
and Christmas packages on request from hotel.*

■ RESTAURANT: Closed Mon to Fri lunch.
'Pfeffermühle' restaurant offers French cuisine
using fresh produce. Speciality: pepper steak
cooked at your table. 'Bistro Bellevue' is open
for light buffet lunches and specialises in
dishes from different countries of the world,
with the menu changing monthly. Piano-café
with live music daily.

■ ACTIVITIES: At the hotel, sauna and steam bath,
children's playroom; arrangements can be
made for hiking, cycling, boat trips, wine
tasting and historic sightseeing tours.

■ TARIFF: Single 125–220, Double 180–320,
Set menu 35–95 (Amex, Euro/Access, Visa).

■ DISCOUNT: 10% LS.

Hotel am Ebertor ★★★

Heerstrasse B9, 56154 Boppard.
Tel 06742 2081, Fax 06742 82542. English spoken.
Open 01/03 to 31/12. 66 bedrooms (all en suite).
Tennis, golf 12 km, garage, parking. ♿

*Comfortable, well-located hotel with good
facilities. Leave the A61 at Boppard exit and
hotel is just off the main street (B9).*

■ RESTAURANT: Good continental cuisine.
Medieval grill room 'Kloster Kellar' and large

garden restaurant with river views.

■ ACTIVITIES: Boat trips on the Rhein, visit the
Thonet museum.

■ TARIFF: Single 97–117, Double 126–152
(Amex, Euro/Access, Visa).

■ DISCOUNT: 10% advance bookings only.

Hotel Günther ★★★

Rheinallee 40, 56154 Boppard.
Tel 06742 2335, Fax 06742 1557. English spoken.

Open 15/01 to 15/12. 19 bedrooms
(all en suite). Golf 12 km.

*Enjoy the friendly atmosphere of this attractive,
family-run hotel. Modern rooms with all
facilities including cable television. Ideally
located on the Rhein promenade with some
wonderful views. Take Boppard exit from A61,
drive into town to 'Rheinallee', turn right and
hotel is about 150 m.*

■ ACTIVITIES: Arrangements made by hotel for
bike hire, boat trips, scenic chair-lift ride and
wine tasting.

■ TARIFF: (1996) Single 59–120, Double 84–148
(Amex, Euro/Access, Visa).

Germany

Hotel Weinhaus Patt
Steinstrasse 30, 56154 Boppard.
Tel 06742 2366, Fax 06742 81280. English spoken.

Open all year. 17 bedrooms (all en suite). ☎
Quietly situated in the city centre, hotel has been run by the same family for three generations and offers a warm welcome.
■ ACTIVITIES: Ideal location for exploring the Rhein and Mosel valleys.
■ TARIFF: (1996) Single 35–65, Double 66–100 (No credit cards).

BRAUNLAGE   14D

Hotel Romantik Zur Tanne ★★★
Herzog-Wilhelmstrasse 8, 38700 Braunlage.
Tel 05520 93120, Fax 05520 3992. English spoken.
Open all year. 22 bedrooms (all en suite).
Golf 24 km, garage, parking.

In the historic centre of Braunlage, a wood-panelled building with window-boxes of red geraniums in summer. Large garden opposite.
■ RESTAURANT: Specialises in regional and 'neue deutsche' cuisine.
■ ACTIVITIES: A nostalgic steam engine train ride through the lovely Harz Mountains to the famous 'Brocken' - it must be seen to be believed!
■ TARIFF: (1996) Single 75–150, Double 100–225, Set menu 39–85 (Amex, Euro/Access, Visa).

CELLE   14D

Hotel Caroline Mathilde ★★★
Bremer Weg 37, 3100 Celle.
Tel 05141 320 23, Fax 05141 320 28. English spoken.
Open all year. 50 bedrooms (all en suite).
Indoor swimming pool, golf, parking.

In the green region of 'Old Herzogstadt Celle', just a few minutes from the town centre and 2 km from the railway station.
■ ACTIVITIES: Hiking, cycling, canoeing, boat trips, sightseeing.
■ TARIFF: Single 100–160, Double 150–250 (Amex, Euro/Access, Visa).
■ DISCOUNT: 10%

Hotel Schaper ★★★ Heese 6-7, 29225 Celle.
Tel 05141 94880, Fax 05141 948830. English spoken.
Open all year. 14 bedrooms (all en suite).
Golf 8 km, parking.

Modern, family-run hotel in quiet location close to city centre. Friendly and traditional. Special 3-night package including breakfast and two dinners 199DM per person for two people sharing a double room.
■ RESTAURANT: Closed 15/07 to 30/07. Has a good reputation for its regional and international dishes. Cosy atmosphere.
■ ACTIVITIES: Horse-drawn carriage rides, theatre.
■ TARIFF: (1996) Single 95–110, Double 130–160, Set menu 20.50–35 (Euro/Access, Visa).
■ DISCOUNT: 10%

Hotel Schifferkrug ★★★
Speicherstrasse 9, 29221 Celle.
Tel 05141 7015, Fax 05141 6350. English spoken.
Open all year. 12 bedrooms (all en suite).
Golf 6 km, parking.

Traditional hotel dating from the 17th century, formerly a lodging house for river boatmen. Lying between the town centre and the station, follow signs to Bahnhof/Kreishaus.
■ RESTAURANT: Closed Sun & Bank Hols. Renowned throughout the region for its excellent regional cuisine.
■ ACTIVITIES: Bike hire.
■ TARIFF: Single 75–95, Double 110–160, Set menu 22.50–38 (Euro/Access, Visa).
■ DISCOUNT: 10% RAC Members only.

COCHEM   16A

Hotel Zur Winneburg ★★★
Endertstrasse 141, 56812 Cochem.
Tel 02671 98730, Fax 02671 4523. English spoken.
Open all year. 12 bedrooms (all en suite).
Garage, parking.
■ RESTAURANT: Game and trout specialities.
■ ACTIVITIES: Squash, fitness training with

qualified instructor; cycling, hiking; boat trips, castle visits, wine tasting.
■ TARIFF: (1996) Single 60–90, Double 86–150, Set menu 18.50–38.00 (Amex, Euro/Access, Visa).

Hotel Wilhelmshöhe Auderath, 56766 Ulmen. Tel 02676 260, Fax 02676 1527. English spoken. Open all year. 13 bedrooms (all en suite). Garage, parking.

19 km from Cochem, the hotel offers a friendly welcome and warm atmosphere. Situated on the B259 in Auderath near Ulmen.

■ RESTAURANT: Closed Tues.
■ TARIFF: Single 50–55, Double 85–95 (No credit cards).

DAUN   16A

Hotel Kucher's Land ★★★ Karl Kaufmann Str 2, 54552 Darscheid/Vulkaneifel. Tel 06592 629, Fax 06592 3677. English spoken. Open 01/01 to 13/01 & 06/02 to 31/12. 14 bedrooms (all en suite). Tennis, golf 25 km, parking. ✆

Beautiful country house on the edge of a wood. Access from A48 Koblenz to Trier motorway, exit Nurbürgring/Ulmen.

■ RESTAURANT: Closed Mon & Tues lunch. One of the leading restaurants in the area, specialising in fish and game. Extensive wine list.
■ ACTIVITIES: Bikes for hire, sailing, swimming. Cross-country skiing in winter.
■ TARIFF: Single 65–80, Double 130–160, Set menu 43–124 (Amex, Euro/Access).

DONAUESCHINGEN   16D

Hotel Oschberghof ★★★★ Golfplatz 1, 7710 Baden-Wurttemberg. Tel 0771 840, Fax 0771 84600. English spoken. Open 20/01 to 26/12. 53 bedrooms (all en suite). Indoor swimming pool, golf on site, garage, parking. ✆

Set in lovely park-like grounds about 5 km east of Donaueschingen. Extremely comfortable with excellent facilities, the tranquil surroundings offering the perfect base to relax. Go straight over the junction of B33/B27 just east of Donaueschingen, turn first left and then right at 'Golfplatz' sign for hotel.

■ RESTAURANT: 2 restaurants offering a choice of international, local and national cuisine.
■ ACTIVITIES: Superb indoor thermal/fitness centre; own 18-hole golf course; tennis, archery, canoeing, rafting, ballooning, mountain-biking and horse-riding can be arranged by hotel.
■ TARIFF: Single 188–238, Double 276–296, Set menu 39–75 (Amex, Euro/Access, Visa).

DONAUWÖRTH   17C

Hotel Traube ★★★ Kapellstrasse 14, 86609 Donauwörth. Tel 0906 706440, Fax 09066 23390. English spoken. Open all year. 43 bedrooms (41 en suite, 2 bath/shower only). Outdoor swimming pool, tennis, golf 3 km, garage, parking. ✆ &

In the centre of Donauwörth, the hotel has the 'Café Mozart', a garden and wine and souvenir shops.

■ RESTAURANT: Regional specialities from Bavaria and Schwabia. Wine bar.
■ ACTIVITIES: Sauna at hotel. Bicycle track along the Danube; interesting places to visit nearby.
■ TARIFF: (1996) Single 85–120, Double 135–185, Set menu 26.90–38 (Amex, Euro/Access, Visa).

EISENACH   16B

Romantik Hotel Kaiserhof ★★★ Wartburgallee 2, 99817 Eisenach. Tel 03691 213513, Fax 03691 203653. English spoken.

Open all year. 64 bedrooms (all en suite). Tennis, parking.

One of the best known and oldest hotels of the region, the Kaiserhof is now fully restored but has retained its individual character. Special weekend prices for groups and individuals. Exit at Eisenach-Ost from the A4 motorway and follow the Zentrum and Wartburg signs.

■ RESTAURANT: Two original old restaurants, one

Germany

offering wine with meals, the other beer.
- ACTIVITIES: Organised programmes can be arranged for groups, such as 'In the Footsteps of Martin Luther'. Sights to see include Wartburg Castle, the houses of Luther and Bach and various churches and museums.
- TARIFF: (1996) Single 130–150, Double 170–220, Set menu 23–68 (Amex, Euro/Access, Visa).

EISENBERG 16A

Hotel Magnushof
Unterreuten 51, 87637 Eisenberg.
Tel 08363 91120, Fax 08363 911250.
English spoken.
Open all year. 12 bedrooms (all en suite).
Indoor swimming pool, parking.

Quiet situation. From the end of A7 go towards Seeg, then from Seeg towards Füssen. At Weizern Hopferau station turn right at hotel sign (about 1 km), towards Unterreuten. Hotel is approximately 15 minutes by car from Füssen.

- RESTAURANT: Restaurant is for residents of the hotel only.
- ACTIVITIES: Good summer and winter sporting activities nearby.
- TARIFF: (1996) Single 75–125, Double 180–250 (Euro/Access, Visa).

ERLANGEN 17A

Hotel Grille Bunsenstrasse 35, 91058 Erlangen.
Tel 09131 7630, Fax 09131 76310.
English spoken.
Open all year. 62 bedrooms (all en suite).
Garage, parking.

Warm hospitality and culinary pleasures make the stay a pleasant one. A3 Nürnberg-Würzburg, exit Tennenlohe. In Erlangen turn left at the third set of traffic lights.

- RESTAURANT: Closed Aug. International cuisine.
- TARIFF: (1996) Single 110–155, Double 192 (Amex, Euro/Access, Visa).

Hotel Transmar Motor ★★★
Wetterkreuzstrasse 7, 8520 Erlangen.
Tel 09131 6080, Fax 09131 608100.
English spoken.
Open all year. 126 bedrooms (all en suite).
Golf 6 km, parking.

Completely refurbished in 1996, the hotel has modern, well-equipped rooms. Conference facilities for 300. Close to A3 motorway, access via the Tennenlohe exit.

- RESTAURANT: Traditional décor; regional and international cuisine.
- TARIFF: (1996) Single 164–254, Double 194–294 (Amex, Euro/Access, Visa).

FRANKFURT-AM-MAIN 16B

Hotel Excelsior ★★★ Mannheimerstrasse 7-9, 60329 Frankfurt-am-Main.
Tel 069 256080, Fax 069 25608141.
English spoken.
Open all year. 184 bedrooms (all en suite).
Garage, restaurant. ✆

In the heart of Frankfurt and recently refurbished. Located opposite the main railway station with direct access to the subway and a 5-minute ride to the main shopping area.

- TARIFF: (1996) Single 135–172, Double 179–239, Set menu 25–35 (Amex, Euro/Access, Visa).

Hotel Kempinski Gravenbruch ★★★★★
63263 Neu-Isenburg.
Tel 06102 5050, Fax 06102 505900.
English spoken.
Open all year. 285 bedrooms (all en suite).
Indoor swimming pool, outdoor swimming pool, tennis, golf 7 km, garage, parking.

A first-class hotel facing its own lake and surrounded by park-like grounds. Excellent business facilities; beauty centre and hairdressing salon; close to the airport and city centre.

- RESTAURANT: 'Forsthaus' restaurant offers fine European cuisine whilst 'Forsthausschänke' specialises in typical German dishes.
- ACTIVITIES: Horse-riding, cycling, sightseeing; tours of the city, Rhein valley and Heidelberg.
- TARIFF: (1996) Single 250–470, Double 290–520, Bk 29, Set menu 46–120 (Amex, Euro/Access, Visa).

Le Meridien Parkhotel Frankfurt ★★★★★
Wiesenhüttenplatz 28/38, 60329 Frankfurt-am-Main.
Tel 069 26970, Fax 069 2697884.
English spoken.
Open all year. 299 bedrooms (all en suite).
Golf 12 km, garage, parking.

Built in 1905, the hotel combines traditional style and modern-day comfort. City centre location, but in the quiet and peaceful Wiesenhüttenpark. Casablanca bar with piano live entertainment. All rooms individually decorated and children under 16 stay free in their parents' room. From the A5, take Frankfurt-Süd exit and follow signs to the Hauptbahnhof.

Germany

■ RESTAURANT: Noted for its creative cuisine, with a wide variety of German and international specialities.
■ ACTIVITIES: Fitness facilities with sauna, solarium, steam bath and massage.
■ TARIFF: (1996) Single 298–488, Double 398–538, Bk 28 (Amex, Euro/Access, Visa).

Hotel Monopol ★★★★ Mannheimerstrasse 11-13, 60329 Frankfurt-am-Main.
Tel 069 227370, Fax 069 25608374.
English spoken.
Open all year. 95 bedrooms (all en suite).
Garage, restaurant. ☏

Recently refurbished, hotel is in the heart of the city opposite the main railway station. Direct access to the subway and just 5 minutes' ride to the main shopping area.
■ TARIFF: (1996) Single 159–278, Double 225–328, Set menu 25–35 (Amex, Euro/Access, Visa).

Motel Frankfurt ★★ Eschersheimer Landstrasse 204, 6000 Frankfurt-am-Main.
Tel 069 568011, Fax 069 568010.
English spoken.
Open all year. 58 bedrooms (all en suite).
Garage, parking. ♿

Close to the city but very quiet. Located 2 minutes' drive from the A66.
■ TARIFF: (1996) Single 113–133, Double 153–173 (Euro/Access, Visa).

Hotel Palmenhof ★★★ Bockenheimer Landstr 89-91, 60325 Frankfurt-am-Main.
Tel 069 7530060, Fax 069 75300666. English spoken.

Open 02/01 to 23/12. 46 bedrooms (all en suite). Garage, parking. ☏

An oasis of peace and comfort in this busy city! Tastefully decorated and furnished with a successful blend of antique and modern.
■ RESTAURANT: Closed 23/12 to 02/01. Good food and a welcoming atmosphere. Specialises in fish and regional German dishes using fresh,

local produce. Good wine list.
■ ACTIVITIES: Everything that Frankfurt has to offer. Golf course 30 km.
■ TARIFF: Single 110–295, Double 170–395, Set menu 45–48 (Amex, Euro/Access, Visa).
■ DISCOUNT: 8%

FREIBURG IM BREISGAU   16C

Hotel Rappen Münsterpl 13, 79098 Freiburg.
Tel 0761 31353, Fax 0761 382252.
English spoken.
Open all year. 20 bedrooms (13 en suite).
Golf 10 km.

Comfortable, cosy hotel in the pedestrian zone. Typical Black Forest hospitality.
■ RESTAURANT: Good food with regional specialities.
■ ACTIVITIES: Cycling.
■ TARIFF: Single 80–140, Double 110–195, Set menu 35 (Amex, Euro/Access, Visa).

FREUDENSTADT   16D

Hotel Adler ★★ Forstrasse 15-17, 72250 Freudenstadt.
Tel 07441 91520, Fax 07441 915252. English spoken.
Open all year. 13 bedrooms (10 en suite).
Golf 2 km, garage, parking.

Small, family-run hotel with sun terrace. In pedestrian zone between the famous market square (the largest in Germany) and railway station Stadtbahnhof (100 m).
■ RESTAURANT: Closed Wed. Local specialities; vegetarian and English dishes are also available.
■ ACTIVITIES: Good sports facilities nearby including bowling, horse-riding, tennis and cycling.
■ TARIFF: Single 59–75, Double 99–126, Set menu 21–40 (Amex, Euro/Access, Visa).

Hotel Langenwaldsee
Strassburger Str 99, 7290 Freudenstadt.
Tel 07441 88930, Fax 07441 88936. English spoken.
Open 19/12 to 01/11. 35 bedrooms (all en suite). Indoor swimming pool, outdoor swimming pool, golf 2 km, garage, parking. ☏

Typical Black Forest mansion. 2 km from Freudenstadt, on the banks of a small lake in the heart of the forest. Very quiet, with an intimate, cosy atmosphere.
■ RESTAURANT: Regional specialities.
■ ACTIVITIES: Tennis, squash, mini-golf, horse-riding and skiing nearby; organised trips to the most famous sightseeing points of the Black Forest.
■ TARIFF: (1996) Single 70–130, Double 130–250, Set menu 14.50–39.50 (Euro/Access, Visa).

Germany

FÜRTH 17A

Hotel Forsthaus ★★★★
Zum Vogelsang 20, 90768 Fürth.
Tel 0911 779880, Fax 0911 720885.
English spoken.
Open all year. 107 bedrooms (all en suite).
Indoor swimming pool, golf 10 km, garage,
parking.

*Luxurious hotel with elegantly furnished
rooms and suites and all modern facilities.
Motorway München-Nürnberg to intersection
Nürnberug-Süd.*

■ RESTAURANT: Furnished to a very high
standard; French and international specialities,
varied selection of wines.
■ ACTIVITIES: Sauna, whirlpool, fitness centre,
solarium, cycle hire, walking and jogging
paths; tennis nearby.
■ TARIFF: (1996) Single 190−210,
Double 270−800, Set menu 64 (Amex,
Euro/Access, Visa).

FÜSSEN 17C

Schlosshotel Lisl und Jägerhaus ★★★★
Neuschwansteinstr 1, 87643 Hohenschwangau.
Tel 08362 8870, Fax 08362 81107.
English spoken.

Schloßhotel Lisl und Jägerhaus

*Halfway between Neuschwanstein Castle and
Hohenschwangau Castle (500m), very
attractive hotel combining elegant traditional
décor with modern facilities and cuisine both
regional and international.*

Courtesy bus to Neuschwanstein Castle.

**Ortsteil Hohenschwangau
Neuschwansteinstrasse 1-3**

Tel: 08362 88 70
Fax: 08362 81 107

See under Füssen

Open 15/03 to 31/12. 47 bedrooms
(all en suite). Golf 20 km, garage, parking. ✆

*This attractive hotel, decorated in Ludwig II
style, has modern, fully equipped rooms.
Situated between the royal castles of
Neuschwanstein and Hohenschwangau. Leave
the München to Garmisch motorway at
Murnau, follow signs towards Füssen, then
Hohenschwangau and castles.*

SEE ADVERTISEMENT.

■ RESTAURANT: Traditional and international
cuisine.
■ ACTIVITIES: Visits to castles with hotel's own
bus transfers.
■ TARIFF: (1996) Single 170, Double 280, Bk 18,
Set menu 18−42 (Amex, Euro/Access, Visa).

GARMISCH-PARTENKIRCHEN 17C

Hotel Garmischer Hof Chamonixstrasse 10,
82467 Garmisch-Partenkirchen.
Tel 08821 51091, Fax 08821 51440.
English spoken.
Open all year. 43 bedrooms (all en suite).
Parking.

*Chalet-style hotel in centre of town. Quiet
rooms with lovely mountain views from
balcony. Pretty gardens. Close to railway
station and swimming pool.*

■ TARIFF: Single 80−115, Double 150−210
(Amex, Euro/Access, Visa).

Hotel Riessersee ★★
Riess 6, 8100 Garmisch-Partenkirchen.
Tel 08821 95440, Fax 08821 72589. English spoken.
Open 20/12 to 10/11. 5 bedrooms (all en suite).
Outdoor swimming pool, golf 4 km, garage,
parking. ✆

Chalet-style hotel lying right on the shore of the lake, 3 km from Garmisch.

■ RESTAURANT: Specialities include fish, game and pastries. Meals can be taken on the large terrace overlooking the lake.
■ ACTIVITIES: Sleigh rides, boat trips, skating.
■ TARIFF: (1996) Single 115–140, Double 150–200, Set menu 13.50–35.00 (Amex, Euro/Access, Visa).
■ DISCOUNT: 10%

Hotel Reindl's Partenkirchner Hof ★★★★★
Bahnhofstrasse 15, 82454 Garmisch-Partenkirchen.
Tel 08821 58025, Fax 08821 73401.
English spoken.
Open 15/12 to 15/11. 65 bedrooms (all en suite). Indoor swimming pool, golf 4 km, garage.

In the middle of the picturesque town but with quiet, beautifully furnished and equipped rooms, each having balcony or terrace and facing the Bavarian Alps. 23 luxury apartments also available.

■ RESTAURANT: Renowned gourmet restaurant 'Reindl's' offers typical Bavarian specialities.
SEE ADVERTISEMENT.

■ ACTIVITIES: Gym and sauna at hotel; excellent summer and winter sports facilities nearby.
● Special golf, tennis and hiking weeks arranged by hotel.
■ TARIFF: Single 120–160, Double 140–200, Bk 18, Set menu 46–55 (Amex, Euro/Access, Visa).
■ DISCOUNT: 10%

Germany

GLOTTERTAL 16C

Hotel Zum Adler Talstr 11, 79286 Glottertal.
Tel 07684 1081, Fax 07684 1083.
English spoken.
Open all year. 12 bedrooms (all en suite).
Parking.

*Located in a romantic valley in the southern
Black Forest (8 miles from Freiburg). Old,
typical Black Forest 'Gasthous' with a relaxing
atmosphere.*

■ RESTAURANT: Closed Tues. Renowned gourmet
restaurant offering local and seasonal
specialities, home-made wines and brandies.
■ ACTIVITIES: Sightseeing tours of the
surrounding towns and countryside.
■ TARIFF: (1996) Single 40–100, Double 70–160,
Set menu 18–40 (Amex, Euro/Access, Visa).

GRAFENAU 17D

Steigenberger Avance Sonnenhof ★★★★
Sonnenstr 12 (Postfach 12 64), 94481 Grafenau.
Tel 08552 4480, Fax 08552 4680.
English spoken.

Open all year. 193 bedrooms (all en suite).
Indoor swimming pool, outdoor swimming
pool, tennis, golf 20 km, garage, parking. ☏

*Splendid location overlooking Grafenau and
close to city centre. Very comfortable hotel with
excellent facilities.*

■ RESTAURANT: Local and regional cuisine.
■ ACTIVITIES: Full health farm facilities: indoor
pool, sauna, fitness centre, spa, massage,
solarium. Also bowling, mini-golf and tennis.
Good hiking country; winter sports within reach.
■ TARIFF: Single 114–148, Double 198–266,
Set menu 35–39 (Amex, Euro/Access, Visa).

HAMBURG 14B

Aussen Alster Hotel ★★★★
Schmilinskystr 11-13, 20099 Hamburg.
Tel 040 241557, Fax 040 2803231. English spoken.

Open all year. 27 bedrooms (all en suite).
Golf 1 km.

*Small, elegant and comfortable, hotel is in a
quiet, central location with a pretty patio.*

■ RESTAURANT: Closed Sun. Italian-style
restaurant with good food.
■ ACTIVITIES: ● Boats (2 minutes from the
boating area) and bikes available to hotel
guests free of charge.
■ TARIFF: (1996) Single 180–210,
Double 280–310, Set menu 49–69 (Amex,
Euro/Access, Visa).

Hotel Graf Moltke ★★★
Steindamm 1, 2000 Hamburg.
Tel 040 2801154, Fax 040 2802562.
English spoken.

Open all year. 97 bedrooms (89 en suite).

*Approaching the city by car, watch for signs to
Hauptbahnhof or Centrum. The hotel is
situated directly at the Hauptbahnhof, in the
city centre. Garage nearby.*

■ ACTIVITIES: Sightseeing tours.
■ TARIFF: (1996) Single 140, Double 180
(Amex, Euro/Access, Visa).
■ DISCOUNT: 20% on presentation of RAC
membership card.

Hotel Hamburg International ★★★
Hammer Landstrasse 200, 20537 Hamburg.
Tel 040 211401, Fax 040 211409.
English spoken.
Open all year. 112 bedrooms (all en suite).
Garage, restaurant.

*Modern, comfortable and conveniently
situated. Excellent buffet breakfast. Conference
facilities; public transport on the doorstep.*

■ TARIFF: (1996) Single 125–195,
Double 170–275 (Amex, Euro/Access, Visa).

Germany

Hotel St Raphael ★★★★
Adenauerallee 41, 20097 Hamburg.
Tel 040 248200, Fax 040 24820333. English spoken.

Open all year. 130 bedrooms (all en suite).
Golf 15 km. ☎

Modern hotel offering every comfort including some individually equipped designer rooms.

■ RESTAURANT: Enjoy the culinary delights on offer in the most attractive 'Le Jardin'. Special buffet Thursday and Friday; champagne brunch on Sundays.
■ ACTIVITIES: Fitness centre; hotel will be happy to arrange bookings for musicals and theatre, sightseeing tours and boat trips. Visit the nearby fish market, 'Reeperbahn' and Hagenbeck's zoo.
■ TARIFF: Single 190–250, Double 230–300, Set menu 30–60 (Amex, Euro/Access, Visa).

Hotel Stillhorn Jakobsberg 9,
21109 Hamburg.
Tel 040 750170, Fax 040 75017189. English spoken.
Open all year. 45 bedrooms (40 en suite).
Garage, parking. ☎ &

Ten minutes from the city centre and close to the motorway A1, exit Stillhorn.

■ RESTAURANT: Regional cuisine. Buffet breakfast.
■ TARIFF: (1996) Single 70–110, Double 100–140, Set menu 9.80–25 (Amex, Euro/Access, Visa).

HAMELN   14D

Hotel Zur Börse ★★★ Osterstrasse 41a,
Zufahrt Kopmanshof, 31785 Hameln.
Tel 05151 7080, Fax 05151 25485. English spoken.
Open 06/01 to 19/12. 34 bedrooms
(all en suite). Golf 15 km, garage.

Family owned for over 100 years, a renovated hotel offering all modern conveniences. In the town centre.

■ RESTAURANT: Good traditional German cooking in a rustic setting. Special diet meals prepared on request.
■ ACTIVITIES: 'Rat catchers' days – a guided tour of the town; excursions.
■ TARIFF: Single 75, Double 140, Set menu 20–30 (Amex, Euro/Access, Visa).

Hotel Zur Krone ★★★★
Osterstrasse 30, 31785 Hameln.
Tel 05151 9070, Fax 05151 907217. English spoken.

Open all year. 34 bedrooms (all en suite).
Golf 10 km, garage, restaurant.

In the centre of the historic part of town, this timbered house/hotel has old, interesting rooms together with modern-day comforts.

■ TARIFF: (1996) Single 120–240, Double 170–380, Bk 15, Set menu 19–49 (Amex, Euro/Access, Visa).

HANNOVER   14D

Holiday Inn Crowne Plaza ★★★★
Petzelstr 60, 30855 Langenhagen.
Tel 0511 77070, Fax 0511 737781. English spoken.
Open all year. 210 bedrooms (all en suite).
Indoor swimming pool, golf 10 km, parking. &

First-class business hotel with modern, comfortable rooms and all facilities including air conditioning and soundproofing. Free airport transfers. Special offers/group rates available year-round. From the A2 or A7 take the airport exit. Bus service to city centre.

■ RESTAURANT: The 'Brasserie' restaurant, which has an outside terrace, offers an international menu.
■ ACTIVITIES: Leisure complex with super swimming pool, sauna, solarium, massage and fitness equipment. Bike hire.
■ TARIFF: (1996) Double 195–495, Bk 20, Set menu 30–60 (Amex, Euro/Access, Visa).

Germany

HASSLOCH 16A

Silencehotel Sägmühle
Sägmühlweg 140, 67454 Hassloch.
Tel 06324 1031, Fax 06324 1034.
English spoken.

Open all year. 27 bedrooms (all en suite).
Golf 5 km, garage, parking.

A beautifully restored building, on the site of a 13th-century saw mill. Take the Hassloch-Ost exit from the A61/A65 motorways.

■ RESTAURANT: Closed 01/01 to 21/01. Rustic-style dining room offering new German cuisine. Attractive outdoor terrace/café.
■ ACTIVITIES: Cycling and walking; visits to deer park and theme park; wine tasting.
■ TARIFF: Single 85–115, Double 135–165, Set menu 29–75 (Amex, Euro/Access, Visa).

HEIDELBERG 16B

Der Europäische Hof, Hotel Europa
★★★★★ Friedrich-Ebert-Anlage 1,
69117 Heidelberg.
Tel 06221 5150, Fax 06221 515506.
English spoken.

Open all year. 135 bedrooms (all en suite).
Golf 20 km, garage.

Within walking distance of the castle, hotel has the atmosphere of a traditional European grand hotel. Managed by the owner, with exclusive service and international standards of efficiency. (Internet: http://www.europaei scherhof.com; E-mail: europa@cubus.de)

■ ACTIVITIES: Shopping arcade on the premises.
■ TARIFF: Single 359–389, Double 450–480, Bk 30 (Amex, Euro/Access, Visa).

Hotel Hirschgasse ★★★★★
Hirschgasse 3, 6900 Heidelberg.
Tel 6221 4540, Fax 6221 454 111.
English spoken.

Open all year. 20 bedrooms (all en suite).
Parking.

In a small valley opposite the Heidelberg castle, the hotel provides luxurious rooms in Laura Ashley style with antique furniture and excellent facilities. Terrace.

■ RESTAURANT: Choice of two award-winning restaurants offering high quality food. Inventive cuisine and extensive wine list.
■ ACTIVITIES: Jogging paths; very good base for walking and mountain-biking.
■ TARIFF: Single 295–350, Double 295–550, Bk 25, Set menu 65–125 (Amex, Euro/Access, Visa).
■ DISCOUNT: 10% except during trade fairs/conventions.

Holiday Inn Heidelberg-Walldorf ★★★★
Roter Str, 69190 Walldorf.
Tel 06227 360, Fax 06227 36504.
English spoken.
Open all year. 158 bedrooms (all en suite). Indoor swimming pool, outdoor swimming pool, tennis, golf 10 km, garage, parking.

Comfortable hotel with every modern facility and a choice of accommodation to suit all tastes. 15 km south of Heidelberg on the A5 or A6 exit at Walldorf/Wiesloch.

■ RESTAURANT: Enjoy international and traditional dishes in the 'Walldorf'.

■ ACTIVITIES: Excellent sports/fitness facilities at hotel; ideally situated for sightseeing and discovering the romantic town of Heidelberg with its famous castle; within easy reach of Frankfurt, Mannheim and Karlsruhe.

■ TARIFF: (1996) Single 154–284, Double 184–358, Set menu 35–45 (Amex, Euro/Access, Visa).

Hotel Neckar ★★

Bismarckstrasse 19, 69115 Heidelberg.
Tel 06221 10814, Fax 06221 23260.
English spoken.
Open all year. 35 bedrooms (all en suite).
Parking.

Modern hotel on the banks of the Neckar river and next to the Bismarck Gardens.

■ TARIFF: (1996) Single 130–190, Double 170–250 (Amex, Euro/Access, Visa).

HEITERSHEIM   16C

Landhotel Krone ★★★

Haupstr 7, 79423 Heitersheim.
Tel 07634 51070, Fax 07634 510766.
English spoken.
Open all year. 23 bedrooms (all en suite).
Golf 15 km, garage, parking.

Family-run hotel dating back to 1777. Warm, inviting interior with traditional furnishings; pretty terrace. About 20 km south of Freiburg.

■ RESTAURANT: Good food in pleasant surroundings.

■ TARIFF: (1996) Single 90–138, Double 130–200, Set menu 55–90 (Visa).

HINTERZARTEN   16C

Parkhotel Adler ★★★★★

Adlerplatz 3, 79856 Hinterzarten.
Tel 07652 1270, Fax 07652 127717. English spoken.

Open all year. 78 bedrooms (all en suite).
Indoor swimming pool, tennis, golf 18 km, garage, parking.

Beautiful hotel set in parkland in the Black Forest. Hinterzarten is 5 km west of Titisee-Neustadt, off B31.

■ RESTAURANT: Good, varied cuisine.

■ ACTIVITIES: Sauna and massage facilities, beauty salon, skittle alley, billiards, mountain bikes, swimming pool with whirlpool.

■ TARIFF: (1996) Single 165–285, Double 310–480, Set menu 32–68 (Amex, Euro/Access, Visa).

Hotel Reppert ★★★★

Adlerweg 21-23, 79856 Hinterzarten.
Tel 7652 12080, Fax 7652 120811. English spoken.

Open all year. 39 bedrooms (all en suite).
Indoor swimming pool, tennis, golf 15 km, garage, parking. ☏

Comfortable and welcoming, with its high gables, this attractive chalet-style hotel is typical of the region and has been family owned and run since it was built. Centrally situated with easy access to A5. Half-board available on stays of 3 days or over.

■ RESTAURANT: Restaurant has a good reputation and offers international, local and Black Forest specialities in a relaxed atmosphere. Light meals are available all day.

■ ACTIVITIES: Mountain-biking, guided tours, water sports and ballooning available nearby; guided walks from hotel with a ranger or member of hotel staff; evening entertainment at hotel; ● Free use of the excellent 'Fountain of Youth' spa complex.

■ TARIFF: Single 140–205, Double 190–320, Set menu 40–62 (Amex, Euro/Access, Visa).

■ DISCOUNT: 10% LS.

Germany

Hotel Sassenhof
Adlerweg 17, 7824 Hinterzarten.
Tel 07652 1515, Fax 07652 484. English spoken.
Open all year. 24 bedrooms (all en suite).
Indoor swimming pool, tennis, golf 10 km,
parking.

Charming chalet-style hotel, ideally situated right in the heart of Hinterzarten. Very comfortable, full of character and you are assured of a warm welcome. No restaurant, but hot and cold drinks are conveniently available on request all day long. Guests are encouraged to prepare their own meals which can be taken in their room. 4 apartments are also available.

■ ACTIVITIES: Sauna with power shower, solarium. ● Free bikes available at hotel.
■ TARIFF: Single 98–106, Double 168–188 (No credit cards).
■ DISCOUNT: 5%

INGOLSTADT   17C

Queens Hotel-Ambassador ★★★
Goëthestrasse 153, 85055 Ingolstadt.
Tel 08415 030, Fax 08415 037. English spoken.
Open all year. 119 bedrooms (all en suite).
Parking. &

Modern hotel located near the old town and easily accessible from A9. 500 m from the Danube.

■ RESTAURANT: International and regional cuisine.
■ ACTIVITIES: Sauna and solarium at hotel.
■ TARIFF: Single 130–195, Double 160–240, Bk 23, Set menu 35–85 (Amex, Euro/Access, Visa).

KAMP-BORNHOFEN   16A

Hotel Anker Rheinuferstrasse 46,
56341 Kamp-Bornhofen.
Tel 06773 215, Fax 06773 215. English spoken.
Open 01/04 to 31/10. 16 bedrooms
(all en suite). Outdoor swimming pool,
golf 7 km, garage, parking.

Family-run hotel in the centre of the town and on the banks of the Rhein.

■ RESTAURANT: Fresh fish specialities.
■ ACTIVITIES: Boat trips, tennis, fishing, hiking.
■ TARIFF: (1996) Single 49, Double 86–98, Set menu 20–45 (Euro/Access, Visa).

KARLSRUHE   16D

Hotel Eden ★★★
Bahnhofstrasse 15-19, 76137 Karlsruhe.
Tel 0721 18180, Fax 0721 1818222.
English spoken.

Open all year. 68 bedrooms (all en suite).
Golf 5 km, garage.

Family owned and managed, the hotel was recently renovated and is in a central but quiet location with a large, attractive garden. Close to railway station, Zoological Gardens, Congress and shopping area.

■ RESTAURANT: Local and international specialities as well as vegetarian dishes.
■ TARIFF: Single 140–150, Double 188–208, Set menu 35–45 (Amex, Euro/Access, Visa).

KASSEL   14D

Burghotel Trendelburg, 3526 Hessen.
Tel 05675 9090, Fax 05675 9362.
English spoken.
Open 15/01 to 31/12. 22 bedrooms
(all en suite). Parking.

13th-century castle standing high above the Diemel river and overlooking the forest of Reinhard. Rooms are individually decorated with period furniture. From Kassel, north on B7, then turn right on the B83 to Trendelburg.

■ RESTAURANT: Good cuisine using fresh local produce and original Trendelburg specialities.
■ TARIFF: Single 110–150, Double 190–230 (Euro/Access, Visa).

Schlosshotel Wilhelmshohe ★★★★
Am Schlosspark 2, 3500 Hessen.
Tel 0561 30880, Fax 0561 3088428.
English spoken.
Open all year. 106 bedrooms (all en suite).
Indoor swimming pool, golf 3 km. ✆ &

5 km from the city centre, in Europe's largest mountainous park and standing at the foot of 'Herkules', the famous landmark of Kassel.

■ RESTAURANT: Hessian and international cuisine.
■ ACTIVITIES: Whirlpool, sauna and solarium at hotel; casino, horse-riding, ice-skating, squash and tennis nearby; many places of interest to visit (Wilhelmshöhe Castle, Lion's fortress, the historic greenhouse). ● Special arrangements made for the Kurhessen Therme (leisure centre).
■ TARIFF: (1996) Single 175–195, Double 230–250, Bk 19, Set menu 25–55 (Amex, Visa).
■ DISCOUNT: 15%

KERPEN   16A

Hotel Park ★★ Kerpenerstrasse 183,
50170 Kerpen-Sindorf.
Tel 02273 570094, Fax 02273 54985.
English spoken.
Open all year. 25 bedrooms (all en suite).
Golf 10 km, garage, parking.

Germany

Small, modern hotel. Leave A4 (Aachen to Köln) at Kerpen exit. Turn left after 500 m.

■ RESTAURANT: Steakhouse and Balkan specialities.
■ TARIFF: Single 84–95, Double 110–145, Set menu 18–45 (Amex, Euro/Access, Visa).
■ DISCOUNT: 10%

KESTERT 16A

Hotel Goldener Stern
Rheinstrasse 38, 56348 Kestert.
Tel 06773 7102, Fax 06773 7104.
English spoken.
Open all year. 10 bedrooms (all en suite).
Parking.

Family run since 1779, the hotel stands on the banks of the Rhein with a truly wonderful view of the river. Completely renovated, it now provides comfortable accommodation with modern-day facilities. 8 km from Loreley, on the B42, 30 km south of Koblenz.

■ RESTAURANT: Closed Mon. Regional dishes with wild game specialities.
■ ACTIVITIES: Walking and hiking; ideal base for touring; indoor/outdoor swimming pools, thermal baths, tennis and golf within easy reach.
■ TARIFF: (1996) Single 45–65, Double 70–110, Set menu 14–50 (Amex, Euro/Access, Visa).

KIEL 14B

Avance Conti-Hansa ★★★★
Schlossgarten 7, 24103 Kiel.
Tel 0431 51150, Fax 0431 5115444.
English spoken.
Open all year. 166 bedrooms (all en suite).
Golf 10 km, garage, restaurant.

Modern and comfortable in downtown location. Opposite Oslo Kai and 5 minutes' drive from main station or Kiel to Hamburg motorway. Very good conference facilities.

■ ACTIVITIES: Hotel organises sailing trips, special regional and candlelit dinners at a nearby castle.
■ TARIFF: Single 235–295, Double 285–350, Set menu 45–85 (Amex, Euro/Access, Visa).

Parkhotel Kieler Kaufmann
Niemannsweg 102, 24105 Kiel.
Tel 0431 88110, Fax 0431 8811135.
English spoken.
Open all year. 47 bedrooms (all en suite).
Indoor swimming pool, golf 10 km, parking.

Most attractive hotel, quietly situated in its own park-like grounds. Ideally located just minutes from the city centre, main station and harbour.

■ RESTAURANT: Elegant but cosy, specialising in regional and international cuisine based on fresh produce. Good wine list.
■ TARIFF: (1996) Single 179–195, Double 220–300, Set menu 45–105 (Amex, Euro/Access, Visa).

KOBLENZ 16A

Cityhotel Metropol ★★★
Munzplatz/Altstadt, 56068 Koblenz.
Tel 0261 35060, Fax 0261 160366.
English spoken.

Open all year. 50 bedrooms (all en suite).
Golf 15 km, garage, parking.

Small, modern hotel in historic setting in old town.

■ RESTAURANT: Closed LS. Bistro with traditional German fare.
■ ACTIVITIES: 50 m to swimming pool and fitness centre. A perfect base for exploring the region.
■ TARIFF: Single 105–195, Double 165–295 (Amex, Euro/Access, Visa).

Hotel Hamm ★★★
St Josefstrasse 32, 56068 Koblenz.
Tel 0261 34546, Fax 0261 160972.
English spoken.
Open all year. 30 bedrooms (all en suite).
Garage, parking.

City hotel, near main railway station. 1 km from arrival/departure point of Rhein and Mosel steamers.

■ TARIFF: (1996) Single 65–105,
Double 130–160 (Amex, Euro/Access, Visa).

Hotel Kleiner Riesen ★★★ Jaiserin Augusta
Anlagen 18, 56068 Koblenz.
Tel 0261 32077, Fax 0261 160725.
English spoken.
Open all year. 50 bedrooms (all en suite).
Golf 15 km, garage, parking. ℭ

Hotel is on the banks of the Rhein in a pretty park. River steamers stop in front.

■ ACTIVITIES: Tennis nearby.
■ TARIFF: (1996) Single 100–180,
Double 180–220 (Amex, Euro/Access, Visa).

KÖLN (COLOGNE)   16A

Hotel Euro Garden Cologne ★★★★
Domstrasse 10-14, 50668 Köln.
Tel 0221 123051, Fax 0221 121041.
English spoken.
Open all year. 85 bedrooms (all en suite).
Garage.

Hotel occupies a central position and is just a few minutes' walk from the main railway station and cathedral. Modern, with a homely atmosphere, attractive ash wood furnishings and fully equipped rooms.

■ RESTAURANT: The 'Pergola' offers German and international dishes, regional specialities and a buffet breakfast.
■ ACTIVITIES: Attractions in Köln include the cathedral, museums and town centre; guided tours can be arranged.
■ TARIFF: Single 125–460, Double 165–545,
Bk 23 (Amex, Euro/Access, Visa).

Hotel Euro Plaza Cologne ★★★★
Breslauer, Platz 2, 50668 Köln.
Tel 0221 16510, Fax 0221 1651333.
English spoken.
Open all year. 116 bedrooms (all en suite).

Centrally located next to the main railway station and cathedral. Modern, elegant interior, following the classic art deco style. Rooms are fully equipped with mahogany furnishings.

■ RESTAURANT: German and international cuisine

as well as classic and regional specialities; breakfast buffet.

■ ACTIVITIES: Guided tours of all the tourist attractions in Köln.
■ TARIFF: Single 125–460, Double 165–545,
Bk 23 (Amex, Euro/Access, Visa).

Hotel Im Wasserturm ★★★★★
Kaygasse 2, 50676 Köln.
Tel 0221 20080, Fax 0221 2008888.
English spoken.
Open all year. 90 bedrooms (all en suite).
Golf 5 km, garage, parking.

This extraordinary, circular building was formerly an historic water tower erected in 1872 and was converted into a luxury hotel in 1990. Surrounded by a park yet in the city centre. 500 m to Neumarkt, 1.5 km to the cathedral, 3 km to the exhibition halls. From A3, take A4 to Aachen. Exit at Köln-Deutz, then to Severinsbrücke. Over bridge, left at first traffic lights, first right into Poststrasse. Second right (Grosser Griechenmarkt) and first right into Kaygasse.

■ RESTAURANT: On the 11th floor with a spectacular view over Cologne. International cuisine. In summer, meals are also served on the roof terrace.
■ ACTIVITIES: The hotel can organise trips and activities: visits to Brühl and Falkenlust castles, the cathedral, museums, theatres and opera, sightseeing tours with chauffeur.
■ TARIFF: Single 390–490, Double 490–2400,
Bk 29, Set menu 60–140 (Amex, Euro/Access, Visa).

Hotel Pullman Mondial ★★★★
Kurt-Hackenberg-Platz 1, 50667 Köln.
Tel 0221 20630, Fax 0221 2063522.
English spoken.
Open all year. 204 bedrooms (all en suite).
Garage. ℭ

In the centre of Köln, near the cathedral, the Rhein, the old town and the shopping area. Close to the main railway station.

■ RESTAURANT: In the 'Symphonie' restaurant, the menu changes several times a year in accordance with the seasons and special events organised by the hotel. Terrace for outside dining in summer.
■ ACTIVITIES: Lots to do and see nearby.
■ TARIFF: (1996) Single 241–374,
Double 272–374, Bk 23, Set menu 28–38 (Amex, Euro/Access, Visa).

Queens Hotel ★★★★
Dürener Str 287, 50935 Köln.
Tel 0221 46760, Fax 0221 433765. English spoken.

Open all year. 147 bedrooms (all en suite). Garage, parking. ✆ ♿

Surrounded by trees and beautifully tended parkland, right on the Stadtwaldweiher. Well placed for access, within minutes of the motorway junction Köln-West and Köln-City.

■ RESTAURANT: Enjoy the culinary delights of 'Im Stadtwald' which specialises in regional and international cuisine. Relaxing atmosphere with lovely views and adjoining terrace.
■ TARIFF: (1996) Single 168–447, Double 198–554, Set menu 42 (Amex, Euro/Access, Visa).

Hotel Spiegel ★★ Herman Lons Str 122, 51147 Köln-Porz.
Tel 02203 61046, Fax 02203 695653.
English spoken.
Open all year. 27 bedrooms (all en suite).
Tennis, golf 15 km, garage, parking.

Quietly positioned in the Porzer woods, 5 minutes from the A3 and 14 km south of Köln centre.

■ RESTAURANT: Closed Fri. Garden terrace with open fireplace. Seasonal specialities: asparagus, game, fish.
■ ACTIVITIES: Tennis and horse-riding nearby; walking.
■ TARIFF: Single 95–190, Double 150–280, Set menu 30–60 (Amex, Euro/Access).
■ DISCOUNT: 10% except during trade fairs.

Waldhotel Mangold
Am Milchbornbach 39-43,
51429 Bergisch Gladbach.
Tel 02204 95550, Fax 02204 955560.
English spoken.
Open all year. 21 bedrooms (all en suite).
Outdoor swimming pool, golf 1 km, parking.

Beautifully situated in leafy woodland with its own stream, the hotel is comfortable and spacious with high standards throughout.
Leave Köln on the A4 heading due west, go over the ring road intersection and take exit 19 for Bergisch Gladbach/Bensberg. From B55 towards Bensberg, turn left to Leverkusen, then right and then left again.

■ RESTAURANT: Closed Sun eve & Mon. National and regional menus with seasonal specialities.
■ ACTIVITIES: Within easy reach of the Köln-Messe and other sights in Köln. Good walking and biking.
■ TARIFF: (1996) Single 135–200, Double 200–300, Set menu 50–120 (Amex, Euro/Access, Visa).

KÖNIGSWINTER 16A

Hotel Siebengebirge ★★
Hauptstrasse 342, 53639 Königswinter.
Tel 02223 21359, Fax 02223 1803.
English spoken.

Open 01/02 to 15/12. 9 bedrooms (5 en suite, 2 bath/shower only). Garage.

Family hotel in the pedestrian area of town centre.

■ RESTAURANT: Closed Wed & Thur. International dishes with Rhineland specialities.
■ ACTIVITIES: ● 7-day stay at hotel includes one free trip by cog-railway to Drachenfels. 14-day stay includes one free boat trip and free ticket to the Seven Mountains museum.
■ TARIFF: (1996) Single 65–80, Double 100–150, Set menu 18–30 (Amex, Euro/Access, Visa).
■ DISCOUNT: 5%

Germany

KRONBERG 16B

Schlosshotel Kronberg ★★★★★ Hainstrasse 25, 61476 Kronberg.
Tel 06173 70101, Fax 06173 701267.
English spoken.

Open all year. 58 bedrooms (all en suite). Golf on site, parking. ℂ

Built for the Empress Frederick, daughter of Queen Victoria, Schlosshotel Kronberg still contains furnishings and works of art from her collection. A haven of peace and elegance, the hotel is set in magnificent parkland with its own 18-hole golf course, an Italian-style rose garden, banks of rhododendrons and majestic specimen trees from different parts of the world. North-west of Frankfurt on A5, take Eschborn exit at Nordwestkreuz, follow signs to Kronberg and then green signs to hotel.

■ RESTAURANT: Beautifully proportioned, English-style dining room with wood panelling and fine antiques. Exquisitely presented, impeccably served classic and inventive cuisine can be enjoyed together with fine wines, including some from the hotel's own vineyard.
■ ACTIVITIES: Gentle strolling through the grounds, jogging or a game of golf at the hotel; touring and sightseeing in Kronberg, Frankfurt and Wiesbaden.
■ TARIFF: Single 295–405, Double 420–800, Bk 30, Set menu 65–110 (Amex, Euro/Access, Visa).

LANDSHUT 17C

Romantik Hotel Fürstenhof ★★★
Stethaimerstrasse 3, 84034 Landshut.
Tel 0871 92550, Fax 0871 925544.
English spoken.
Open all year. 24 bedrooms (all en suite). Golf 10 km, garage, parking.

Most attractive art-nouveau villa near the

centre of Landshut. The beautifully decorated and furnished rooms offer peace and comfort in a particularly warm and friendly atmosphere.

■ RESTAURANT: Closed Sun. Enjoy fine food in a choice of two stylish restaurants; one cool and elegant, the other with a rustic, typically Bavarian atmosphere. Traditional and regional specialities. The 'Pavillion Bistro Café' offers home-made cakes and pies.
■ ACTIVITIES: Excellent base for sightseeing; visit St Martin's church with its unique, 131-metre-high brick-built steeple.
■ TARIFF: Single 135–180, Double 180–250, Set menu 56–110 (Amex, Euro/Access, Visa).

LEIPZIG 15C

Hotel Inter Continental Leipzig ★★★★★
Gerberstr 15, 04105 Leipzig.
Tel 0341 9880, Fax 0341 9881229.
English spoken.
Open all year. 447 bedrooms (all en suite). Indoor swimming pool. ℂ &

Set in the heart of the city, this is the tallest building in Leipzig. Comfortable, elegantly furnished accommodation. Excellent conference facilities.

■ RESTAURANT: Closed Sun (Yamato restaurant). Hotel has 2 excellent restaurants: the 'Brühl' offers gourmet food with international and Saxon specialities; 'Yamato' is the Japanese restaurant where you can enjoy sushi, sashimi and teppan-yaki.
■ ACTIVITIES: Sauna, solarium, fitness room; sightseeing tours.
■ TARIFF: (1996) Single 290–420, Double 320–460, Bk 29, Set menu 39–65 (Amex, Euro/Access, Visa).

LIMBURG-AN-DER-LAHN 16A

Hotel Zimmermann ★★★ Blumenroder Str 1, 65549 Limburg-an-der-Lahn.
Tel 06431 4611, Fax 06431 41314.
English spoken.
Open 05/01 to 20/12. 30 bedrooms (all en suite). Golf 15 km, garage.

An English-style hotel with a romantic atmosphere. Furnished with antiques, original paintings and Italian marble. Limburg is an historic old town with an 800-year-old cathedral. On the A3 between Frankfurt and Köln.

■ RESTAURANT: Closed Fri & Sun.
■ TARIFF: (1996) Single 135–205, Double 148–285 (Amex, Euro/Access, Visa).

LINDAU IM BODENSEE   16D

Hotel Bayerischer Hof ★★★★
Seepromenade, 88131 Lindau im Bodensee.
Tel 08382 9150, Fax 08382 915591.
English spoken.
Open 27/03 to 01/11. 104 bedrooms
(all en suite). Outdoor swimming pool,
golf 4 km, garage. ☏

*On the island's traffic-free promenade, with
magnificent south-facing view over the lake to
the Austrian and Swiss Alps. 450 m above sea
level and close to railway station, harbour and
landing stage.*

■ RESTAURANT: International cuisine with
regional and fresh lake fish specialities.
■ ACTIVITIES: Boat trips, beautiful walks and
good sports facilities nearby.
■ TARIFF: Single 150–250, Double 250–520,
Set menu 60–71 (Euro/Access, Visa).

LÜBECK   15A

Hotel Jensen ★★★ Am Holstentor, an der
Obertrave 4-5, 23552 Lübeck.
Tel 04517 1646, Fax 04517 3386.
English spoken.
Open all year. 42 bedrooms (all en suite).
Golf 20 km, garage, parking. ☏

*A family run hotel in the centre of Lübeck.
Historic building, totally renovated in 1995
with no expense spared. Extremely comfortable
and offering all modern amenities.*

■ RESTAURANT: Award-winning and offering
international and regional dishes with fish
specialities.
■ ACTIVITIES: Boat trips, sailing and sightseeing
tours.
■ TARIFF: (1996) Single 110–130,
Double 160–190, Set menu 21–50 (Amex,
Euro/Access, Visa).

Movenpick Hotel ★★★★
Beim Holstentor, 23554 Lübeck.
Tel 04511 5040, Fax 04511 504111.
English spoken.
Open all year. 197 bedrooms (all en suite).
Golf 20 km, garage. ♿

*Centrally located hotel, next to the famous
Holstentor and just 3 minutes' walk to the
railway station. Children up to 16 free if
sharing parents' room.*

■ RESTAURANT: German and international
cuisine.
■ TARIFF: Single 140–200, Double 170–240,
Bk 22, Set menu 26–72 (Amex,
Euro/Access, Visa).

LUDWIGSHAFEN   16B

Hotel Excelsior ★★★
Lorientallee 16, 6700 Ludwigshafen.
Tel 0621 59850, Fax 0621 5985500. English spoken.
Open all year. 160 bedrooms (all en suite).
Garage, parking. ♿

*Close to the station and the motorway.
Cocktail bar.*

■ RESTAURANT: Restaurant 'Kornkammer' is on
the 17th floor with panoramic views. Brasserie
offering French and international cuisine.
■ ACTIVITIES: Visit Heidelberg; wine tasting and
touring the German wine route.
■ TARIFF: (1996) Single 123–160,
Double 156–190, Set menu 35–78 (Amex,
Euro/Access, Visa).

LÜNEBURG   14B

Hotel Bremer Hof ★★
Lüner Str 12-13, 21335 Lüneburg.
Tel 04131 36070, Fax 04131 38304.
English spoken.
Open all year. 56 bedrooms (all en suite).
Golf 10 km. ☏

*Comfortable and interesting interior with lots
of exposed old brick and studwork. Follow the
red 'Hoteltouristikroute' signs in Lüneburg.*

■ RESTAURANT: Regional specialities.
■ TARIFF: (1996) Single 79–175, Double 133–
215, Set menu 25–50 (Amex, Euro/Access, Visa).

MARKTBREIT   16B

Hotel Löwen ★★ Marktstr 8, 97340 Marktbreit.
Tel 09332 3085, Fax 09332 9438. English spoken.
Open all year. 50 bedrooms (all en suite).
Golf 15 km, garage, parking, restaurant.

*Charming hotel dating from the 15th century,
located in the centre of town.*

■ TARIFF: Single 82–90, Double 122–130
(Amex, Euro/Access, Visa).

MEERSBURG   16D

Gasthof Zum Baren
Marktplatz 11, 88709 Meersburg.
Tel 07532 43220, Fax 07532 432244.
English spoken.
Open 01/03 to 30/11. 19 bedrooms
(all en suite). Garage.

Small hotel in the market square.

■ RESTAURANT: Closed Mon. Choice of two
restaurants offering fish from Lake Konstanz
and traditional German dishes.
■ TARIFF: Single 85, Double 120–170,
Set menu 25–35 (No credit cards).

Germany

MONSCHAU   16A

Hotel Haus Vecqueray
Kirchstr 5, 52156 Monschau.
Tel 02472 3179, Fax 02472 4320. English spoken.
Open all year. 11 bedrooms (all en suite).
Garage.

More a guest-house than hotel, family run with a warm atmosphere. The prettily decorated bedrooms have polished antiques and rugs on wooden floors and are reached via a spiral staircase. Fine views over the roofs of the picturesque town of Monschau.

■ ACTIVITIES: Hiking, walking, sightseeing, touring.
■ TARIFF: Single 55–65, Double 90–120 (Euro/Access, Visa).

MÜNCHEN (MUNICH)   17C

Hotel Bayerischer Hof ★★★★★
Promenadeplatz 2-6, 80333 München.
Tel 089 2120900, Fax 089 2120906.
English spoken.
Open all year. 428 bedrooms (all en suite).
Indoor swimming pool, garage. &

Traditional de luxe hotel, privately owned since 1897 by the Volkhardt family. Unique central location opposite the cathedral. Excellent facilities including shopping gallery with a variety of top-name boutiques.

■ RESTAURANT: Choice of restaurants: 'Garden' restaurant with winter garden and terrace offers international cuisine, the 'Palais Keller' regional cuisine and 'Trader Vic's' Polynesian dishes.
■ ACTIVITIES: Piano bar, nightclub, in-house theatre. Beauty centre, indoor pool/health and fitness complex.
■ TARIFF: Single 335–480, Double 440–520, Bk 31.50, Set menu 49.50–128 (Amex, Euro/Access, Visa).

Hotel G'haus Englischer Garten Munchen
40 Schwabing, Liebergesellstr 8, 8000 Bayern.
Tel 089 392034, Fax 089 391233.
English spoken.
Open all year. 26 bedrooms (20 en suite).
Garage, parking.

Converted 200-year-old watermill complete with ivy-clad walls and shutter-framed windows. Close to the English garden park and only 5 minutes' walk from bars, restaurants and shops.

■ ACTIVITIES: Walking, boating, tennis, cycling, cross-country skiing and sightseeing nearby.
■ TARIFF: Single 98–175, Double 130–195, Bk 6 (No credit cards).

Hotel Olymp ★★★★ Wielandstrasse 3,
85386 München-Eching.
Tel 089 327100, Fax 089 32710112.
English spoken.
Open all year. 92 bedrooms (all en suite).
Indoor swimming pool, golf 20 km, garage, parking. ☎ &

Modern hotel with a warm, Mediterranean atmosphere. Just one minute from the A9, take Eching exit 69, turn left at the first lights and right at the next.

■ RESTAURANT: 3 restaurants offering a choice of nouvelle Bavarian, Mediterranean and international specialities. Special themed evenings and barbecues organised.
■ ACTIVITIES: Well situated for sightseeing and touring the numerous attractions that München and the surrounding area have to offer.
■ TARIFF: Single 125–285, Double 145–398, Set menu 15–75 (Amex, Euro/Access, Visa).

Platzl Ringhotel ★★★★
Platzl 1, 8000 München 2.
Tel 089 237030, Fax 089 23703800.
English spoken.

Open all year. 167 bedrooms (all en suite).
Garage. ☎ &

Completely renovated within the last few years, hotel has an excellent location in the heart of the historic old town and offers first-class comfort and a warm Bavarian welcome.

■ RESTAURANT: Closed Sat lunch and Sun. A 17th-century vault is now the home of 'Pfistermühle', well known for its fine regional and international dishes. Culinary delights, prepared by a renowned chef, are also available in 'Platzl's Theaterie'.
■ ACTIVITIES: Fitness area plus the very popular 'Platzl's Theaterie' for shows and variety

entertainment at hotel. Shopping, sightseeing, touring the surrounding countryside and water sports are just a few of the hotel's suggestions for outside activities.

■ TARIFF: (1996) Single 220–285, Double 290–410, Set menu 43–70 (Amex, Euro/Access, Visa).

Queens Hotel ★★★★
Effnerstrasse 99, 81825 München.
Tel 089 927980, Fax 089 983813.
English spoken.
Open all year. 152 bedrooms (all en suite). Garage, parking.

15 minutes' drive from the city centre, and only 5 minutes from the Englischer Garten.

■ RESTAURANT: Regional and international cuisine.

■ ACTIVITIES: Sauna, steam bath, fitness room; cycling; explore the town.

■ TARIFF: (1996) Single 130–337, Double 180–414, Set menu 33–67 (Amex, Euro/Access, Visa).

Hotel Schrenkhof ★★★★ Leonhardsweg 6,
Unterhaching, 8025 München.
Tel 089 6100910, Fax 089 61009150.
English spoken.

Open all year. 25 bedrooms (all en suite). Golf on site, garage, parking.

The interior décor of this Bavarian hotel is extraordinary – full of decorated wood panelling to floors, walls and ceiling and rooms with beautiful painted furniture. Traditional values are also kept with the friendliness and warmth of the welcome. Unterhaching is just south of München, close to the A8/A99 interchange. 20 minutes' bus ride to the centre.

■ ACTIVITIES: Bike hire; golf and swimming pool nearby.

MÜNSTER   14C

Central-Hotel Münster ★★★
Aegidiistrasse 1, 4400 Münster.
Tel 0251 510150, Fax 0251 5101550.
English spoken.
Open all year. 25 bedrooms (all en suite). Golf 5 km, garage.

A private, small and comfortable hotel in this historic city.

■ TARIFF: (1996) Single 135–185, Double 185–225 (Amex, Euro/Access, Visa).

NECKARZIMMERN   16B

Hotel Burg-Castle Hornberg
Burg-Hornberg, 74865 Neckarzimmern.
Tel 06261 92460, Fax 06261 924644.
English spoken.

Open 01/03 to 15/12. 21 bedrooms (all en suite). Golf 7 km, parking.

A tastefully and warmly restored medieval castle, situated high above the Neckar river in the small village of Burg Hornberg. Just north of Neckarzimmern. Suites are also available.

■ RESTAURANT: Closed 15/12 to 28/02. Charming dining room with wonderful panoramic views. Specialities include fish, wild game and lamb dishes.

■ ACTIVITIES: Many things to do and see in the area: wine tasting, cycling, walking, boat trips on the Neckar river.

■ TARIFF: Single 130–180, Double 180–280, Set menu 50–98 (Euro/Access, Visa).

Germany

NEUSTADT-AN-DER-AISCH 16B

Hotel Romerhof ★★★ Richard Wagner Str 15,
91413 Neustadt-an-der-Aisch.
Tel 09161 3011, Fax 09161 2498. English spoken.
Open all year. 20 bedrooms (all en suite).
Golf 12 km, garage, parking.

*Comfortable, family-run hotel set in pretty
gardens. On B8, halfway between Würzburg and
Nürnberg, in a quiet situation at the edge of town.*

■ RESTAURANT: A most attractive restaurant with
large terrace. Tempting cuisine in a warm
atmosphere.
■ TARIFF: Single 60–75, Double 115–150,
Set menu 15–35 (Amex, Euro/Access, Visa).
■ DISCOUNT: 10%

NIERSTEIN 16B

Rheinhotel Mainzer Str 16,
55283 Nierstein-am-Rhein.
Tel 06133 97970, Fax 06133 979797. English spoken.

Open 10/01 to 15/12. 15 bedrooms
(all en suite). Golf 5 km, garage, parking.

*Faces the river with a terrace surrounded by
trees. Drive along the B9 between Mainz and
Worms to Nierstein or from the A63 take the
Cau Bickelheim exit.*

■ RESTAURANT: Good food, specialising in fish
dishes, with an excellent choice of fine and
rare wines.
■ ACTIVITIES: Cycling (hotel hires bikes), wine
tasting, Rhein river trips. Hotel will organise
travel to/from golf course.
■ TARIFF: Single 111–255, Double 122–344,
Bk 13, Set menu 18–100 (Amex,
Euro/Access, Visa).
■ DISCOUNT: 10%

NÖRTEN-HARDENBERG 14D

Romantik-Hotel Menzhausen ★★★★
Lange Str 12, 37170 Uslar.
Tel 05571 2051, Fax 05571 5820. English spoken.

Open all year. 40 bedrooms (all en suite).
Indoor swimming pool, garage, parking. &

*Picturesque family hotel, dating from 1565
when it served as an inn for travelling
merchants. Sympathetically restored, it now
provides very comfortable accommodation with
excellent facilities. Pretty gardens and terrace.
Uslar is on the 241, south-west of Hannover via
the A7, and to the west of Nörten-Hardenberg.*

■ RESTAURANT: Grill restaurant offering seasonal
menus including game from the local woods.
■ ACTIVITIES: Whirlpool and sauna. Horse-
drawn carriage rides, cycling, wine tasting.
■ TARIFF: (1996) Single 105–180,
Double 165–310, Set menu 28–65 (Amex,
Euro/Access, Visa).

NÜRNBERG 17A

Hotel Drei Linden ★★★
Äussere Sulzbacher Strasse 1, 90489 Nürnberg.
Tel 0911 533233, Fax 0911 554047. English spoken.
Open all year. 28 bedrooms (all en suite).
Garage, parking.

*A traditional hotel that has been run as a
family business since 1877. Warm, welcoming
atmosphere and modern comforts.
Conveniently situated directly on the B41, only
minutes from the Berlin-München motorway.*

■ RESTAURANT: Regional and international
cuisine with fresh fish, local and Swiss
specialities.
■ TARIFF: Single 120–150, Double 170–190,
Set menu 21–36 (Amex, Euro/Access, Visa).

Queens Hotel ★★★★
Münchener Str 283, 90471 Nürnberg.
Tel 0911 94650, Fax 0911 468865. English spoken.
Open all year. 141 bedrooms (all en suite).
Golf 2 km, parking.

*A modern hotel, located in a quiet park area
which is surrounded by small lakes.*

■ RESTAURANT: Closed 27/12 to 06/01.
International and regional cuisine.
■ ACTIVITIES: In-house fitness centre with sauna,
steam bath, solarium and gym. ● Free bicycles.
■ TARIFF: (1996) Single 198–246,
Double 246–312, Bk 24, Set menu 39–49
(Amex, Euro/Access, Visa).
■ DISCOUNT: 15% except during fairs.

OBERAMMERGAU 17C

Hotel Zur Rose Dedlerstr 9,
82487 Oberammergau.
Tel 08822 4706, Fax 08822 6753. English spoken.
Open 15/12 to 31/10. 24 bedrooms
(all en suite). Garage, parking.

Cosy Bavarian inn. Also has 13 apartments.
- RESTAURANT: Very good kitchen.
- TARIFF: Single 55–63, Double 100–105, Set menu 20–48 (Amex, Euro/Access, Visa).

OBERKIRCH 16C

Romantik Hotel Zur Obere Linde ★★★★
Hauptstrasse 25, 7602 Oberkirch.
Tel 07802 8020, Fax 07802 3030.
English spoken.
Open all year. 37 bedrooms (all en suite).
Tennis, garage, parking. ℂ ♿

Dating back to 1659, this traditional hotel has a fine reputation. Leave A5 at Appenweier exit for Oberkirch and hotel is in the centre of town.

- ACTIVITIES: Hiking, skiing in winter; sightseeing and exploring the surrounding towns and beautiful countryside.
- TARIFF: (1996) Single 130–195, Double 195–330 (Amex, Euro/Access, Visa).
- DISCOUNT: 10% subject to reservation 24 hrs in advance.

OBERSTDORF 16D

Hotel Haus Wiese
Stillachstr 4a, 8980 Oberstdorf.
Tel 08322 3030, Fax 08322 3135.
English spoken.
Open all year. 13 bedrooms (all en suite).
Indoor swimming pool, golf 4 km, parking.

Charming, family-run hotel that enjoys a good reputation. Wonderful situation with some stunning views. 3 apartments are also available. From Kempten take A7 towards Oberstdorf, then towards Klein-Walsertal and finally take B19 towards Fellhornbahn and you will be on Stillachstrasse.

- ACTIVITIES: Exploring the spectacular mountains and surrounding countryside.
- TARIFF: (1996) Single 100–105, Double 170–190 (No credit cards).

Hotel Wittelsbacher Hof ★★★★
Prinzenstr 24, 87561 Bayern.
Tel 08322 6050, Fax 08322 605300.
English spoken.
Open 10/05 to 31/10 & 18/12 to 06/04.
86 bedrooms (all en suite). Indoor swimming pool, outdoor swimming pool, golf 3 km, garage, parking. ℂ

Comfortable hotel quietly situated close to the marketplace. Many rooms have a balcony.

- RESTAURANT: Regional and international specialities.

- ACTIVITIES: In summer: hiking, cycling, tennis, mountaineering, fishing and ice-skating. In winter: skiing and cross-country skiing.
- TARIFF: Single 88–130, Double 156–230, Set menu 34–48 (Amex, Euro/Access, Visa).

OFFENBURG 16C

Hotel Sonne ★★
Haupstr 94, 77652 Offenburg.
Tel 0781 71039, Fax 0781 71033.
English spoken.
Open all year. 33 bedrooms (21 en suite).
Garage, restaurant.

In the pedestrian zone and centre of Offenburg, next to the baroque town hall. One of the oldest hotels in Germany and has been in the same family since 1858.

- ACTIVITIES: Visit Strasbourg, Baden-Baden and the Schwarzwald (Black Forest), which are all within easy reach.
- TARIFF: (1996) Single 70–100, Double 98–190, Set menu 26–95 (Amex, Euro/Access, Visa).

OLDENBURG 14B

Hotel Wieting ★★★
Damm 29, 26135 Oldenburg.
Tel 0441 924005, Fax 0441 9240222.
English spoken.

Open all year. 69 bedrooms (63 en suite).
Golf 10 km, garage, parking. ℂ ♿

Quiet family hotel with a warm and comfortable personal touch. 3 km from A28 and A29.

- RESTAURANT: The 'Aubergine' offers German and Greek specialities and a convivial atmosphere.
- ACTIVITIES: Well placed for sightseeing and just 5 minutes' walk to the old pedestrian zone.
- TARIFF: Single 80–130, Double 140–200 (Amex, Euro/Access, Visa).

Germany

OPPENHEIM 16B

Hotel Kurpfalz ★
Wormser Str 2, 6504 Oppenheim.
Tel 06133 94940, Fax 06133 949494.
English spoken.
Open all year. 16 bedrooms (all en suite). Indoor swimming pool, tennis, golf 2 km, garage.

The hotel is in the old part of the city, near the marketplace and St Katherin church.
Oppenheim lies between Mainz and Worms on the B9, exit Nierstein-Oppenheim.

■ RESTAURANT: Closed Sun & Mon. Regional specialities are served in the historic wine bar.
■ ACTIVITIES: Walking round Oppenheim and through the vineyards, cycling, wine tasting; visit the wine museum, guided tour of St Katherin's church.

OSNABRÜCK 14D

Hotel Hohenzollern ★★★★ Heinrich-Heine-Str 17, Postfach 24 04, 4500 Osnabrück.
Tel 05413 3170, Fax 05413 317351. English spoken.

Open all year. 98 bedrooms (all en suite). Indoor swimming pool, golf 12 km, parking. ☎

Modern hotel with a warm atmosphere. Suites also available. Situated near the station in Osnabrück. (Charge is made for parking.)

■ RESTAURANT: Renowned for its service and high quality, French and regional menus.
■ ACTIVITIES: Cultural and culinary programme. Archaeological excursion to Roman battlefield.
■ TARIFF: Single 125–175, Double 185–200, Set menu 39.50–65 (Amex, Euro/Access, Visa).

PEGNITZ 17A

Pflaums Posthotel ★★★★★
Nürnberger Str 12-16, 91257 Pegnitz.
Tel 09241 7250, Fax 09241 80404. English spoken.
Open all year. 50 bedrooms (all en suite).
Indoor swimming pool, tennis,

golf 12 km, garage, parking. &

Luxury Bavarian country inn, winner of Gold Key for Design award for 'the most exciting suites worldwide'. Set in quiet, beautiful countryside and run by the same family for 11 generations. Leave the Berlin to München motorway at Pegnitz. 4 km to the hotel.

■ RESTAURANT: Choose the gourmet 'Pflaumen-Garten', or rustic 'Stube'. Excellent French and local cuisine, fine wines.
■ ACTIVITIES: Health club; fly-fishing nearby; transport and arrangements made for the Wagner concerts at Bayreuth Festival. ● Own 27-hole golf course.
■ TARIFF: (1996) Single 195–350, Double 255–690, Bk 25, Set menu 115–175 (Amex, Euro/Access, Visa).

PFORZHEIM 16D

Queens Hotel Pforzheim/Niefern ★★★★
Pforzheimer Str 52, 75223 Niefern.
Tel 07233 70990, Fax 07233 5365. English spoken.
Open all year. 67 bedrooms (all en suite).
Golf 8 km, garage, parking.

In an ideal position on the edge of the Black Forest, between Karlsruhe and Stuttgart. Leave the A8 at the Pforzheim-Ost exit and turn right at the first lights towards Niefern.

■ RESTAURANT: Modern restaurant serving regional dishes.
■ TARIFF: (1996) Single 125–210, Double 165–250 (Amex, Euro/Access, Visa).

PFRONTEN 16D

Hotel Bavaria ★★★★
Kienbergstr 62, Pfronten Dorf, 87459 Pfronten.
Tel 08363 9020, Fax 08363 6815. English spoken.
Open 01/01 to 31/10 & 01/12 to 31/12.
40 bedrooms (all en suite). Indoor swimming pool, outdoor swimming pool, garage, parking. ☎ &

Close to the village of Pfronten, hotel is surrounded by woods and mountains. Take Nesselwang exit from motorway to Pfronten following signs to the Tirol. (Open dates shown are for 1996. Check with hotel in advance for 1997.)

■ RESTAURANT: Gourmet restaurant with regional specialities; hot and cold Bavarian buffet.
■ ACTIVITIES: Sauna, whirlpool and massage; hiking, cross-country skiing, skating, sledging; day trips, visit the royal castle, the Linderhof castle and the church.
■ TARIFF: (1996) Single 110–155, Double 220–390, Set menu 30 (Amex, Euro/Access).

POTSDAM 15C

Hotel Schloss Cecilienhof ★★★★
Neuer Garten, 14467 Potsdam.
Tel 0331 37050, Fax 0331 292498. English spoken.
Open all year. 43 bedrooms (all en suite).
Golf 15 km, parking.

Site of the signing of the Potsdam Agreement in 1945; the conference rooms are now commemorative and open to the public, whilst the remainder of the palace is used as a hotel. To the north of Potsdam, situated in beautiful surroundings within the English park 'Neuer Garten' and beside the lake Jungfernsee. 10 minutes to Potsdam and 'Sanssouci'.

■ RESTAURANT: Elegant restaurant with a beautiful terrace. Has a good reputation for its local and international cuisine.
■ ACTIVITIES: Hotel is a starting point for sightseeing tours; jogging path and swimming area beside the lake; sauna and massage.
■ TARIFF: Single 195–255, Double 290–470, Set menu 35–130 (Amex, Euro/Access, Visa).

PRIEN-AM-CHIEMSEE 17C

Hotel Bayerischer Hof ★★★
Bernauer Str 3, 83202 Prien-am-Chiemsee.
Tel 08051 6030, Fax 08501 62917. English spoken.
Open 01/12 to 30/10. 48 bedrooms (all en suite). Golf 3 km, garage, parking.

Good, medium-grade hotel in the centre of Prien and just five minutes' walk from the station. Well-appointed accommodation, all with private facilities and most with balcony.

■ RESTAURANT: Closed Mon. Attractively furnished dining room offering very good Bavarian and international cuisine. Fresh lake fish specialities.
■ ACTIVITIES: ● 20% discount at the Höslwang golf course.
■ TARIFF: Single 92–95, Double 158–165, Set menu 24–32 (Amex, Euro/Access, Visa).

RAMSAU-HINTERSEE 17C

See Hotel Gamsbock
Am See 75, 83486 Ramsau-Hintersee.
Tel 08657 98800, Fax 08657 748. English spoken.
Open 01/01 to 31/10 & 25/12 to 31/12.
17 bedrooms (12 en suite, 1 bath/shower only). Parking.

Pretty chalet-style hotel. Idyllic situation right on the lake, offering wonderful mountain views.

■ RESTAURANT: Overlooks the terrace and lake. Specialities include game and fish.
■ ACTIVITIES: Walking and boating in summer; fishing in the lake; winter sports.

■ TARIFF: (1996) Single 45–98, Double 39–99 (No credit cards).

REGEN 17D

Hotel Burggasthof Weissenstein
Weissenstein 32, 94209 Regen.
Tel 09921 2259, Fax 09921 8759.
Open 01/01 to 30/10 & 15/12 to 30/12.
15 bedrooms (all en suite). Golf 10 km, garage, parking. ✆

In lovely surroundings overlooking the valley. Chalet-style hotel with a warm and friendly family atmosphere. Super terrace.

■ RESTAURANT: Closed Tues & 01/11 to 15/12. Traditional dining room with good, regional cuisine and local specialities.
■ ACTIVITIES: Lots to do and see in both summer and winter. Wonderful base for walking, hiking and cross-country skiing. Tennis and sports/ fitness facilities close by.
■ TARIFF: Single 43–48, Double 80–96, Set menu 14–25 (No credit cards).
■ DISCOUNT: 10% stays of 10 days or more.

REGENSBURG 17C

Hotel Münchner Hof
Tandlergasse 9, 93047 Regensburg.
Tel 0941 58440, Fax 0941 561709. English spoken.
Open all year. 53 bedrooms (all en suite).
Golf 14 km. ♿

Hotel is in the heart of the city's pedestrian zone. You may load or unload your car at the door.

■ RESTAURANT: Traditional Bavarian décor and regional cuisine.
■ ACTIVITIES: Within easy walking distance of the multitude of places to visit in this 2000-year-old town.
■ TARIFF: Single 90–120, Double 135–170, Set menu 12–20 (Amex, Euro/Access, Visa).

RODACH 15A

Hotel Zur Alten Molkerei ★★★
Ernststr 6, 96476 Rodach/Bayern.
Tel 09564 8380, Fax 09564 838155. English spoken.
Open all year. 45 bedrooms (all en suite).
Indoor swimming pool, tennis, golf 20 km, garage, parking.

Quiet location near centre of the 1100-year-old village, only 5 minutes from thermal baths.

■ RESTAURANT: Regional Frankish and international cuisine.
■ ACTIVITIES: Sauna, massage, walking, hiking, cycling, table tennis, billiards and mini-golf.
■ TARIFF: (1996) Single 55–88, Double 88–140, Set menu 15–30 (Amex, Euro/Access, Visa).

Germany

ROTHENBURG-OB-DER-TAUBER 16B

Hotel Goldener Hirsch ★★★★
Untere Schmiedgasse 16/25,
91541 Rothenburg-ob-der-Tauber.
Tel 09861 7080, Fax 09861 708100.
English spoken.
Open all year. 72 bedrooms (60 en suite).
Golf 18 km, garage.

*A first-class hotel in this famous medieval
town. Quiet location in the downtown area,
overlooking the Tauber valley. Chargeable
parking nearby.*

■ RESTAURANT: 'The Blue Terrace' has wonderful
views over the river and town and is well
known for its high standard of cuisine.
■ TARIFF: Single 140–210, Double 180–295
(Amex, Euro/Access, Visa).

Hotel Kloster Stuble ★★
Heringsbronnengasse 5,
91541 Rothenburg-ob-der-Tauber.
Tel 09861 6774, Fax 09861 6474.
English spoken.

Open all year. 13 bedrooms (all en suite).
Golf 12 km, garage, parking. ☎

*Comfortable guest house in a beautiful, quiet
setting above the Tauber valley. Situated
behind the church only 200 m from the market
square. Open sun terrace.*

■ RESTAURANT: Closed Jan & Feb. Excellent
dining room specialising in regional cuisine,
based on fresh, seasonal produce.
■ TARIFF: Single 90, Double 120–160 (Visa).
■ DISCOUNT: 8%

RÜDESHEIM 16A

Hotel Café Post ★★★★ Rheinuferstrasse 2,
65382 Assmannshausen-am-Rhein.
Tel 06722 2326, Fax 06722 48249.
English spoken.
Open 01/03 to 15/11. 15 bedrooms
(10 en suite). Garage, parking.

*Right on the banks of the Rhein with a
wonderful view over the river and its castles.
On the B42 in Assmannshausen, near
Rüdesheim.*

■ RESTAURANT: Comfortable, with lovely views
and a good reputation for its food and wines.
■ ACTIVITIES: Hotel suggests a range of activities
from walking the beautiful countryside to river
trips, sightseeing tours, horse-riding, concerts
and wine tasting.
■ TARIFF: (1996) Single 90–100,
Double 110–180 (Amex, Euro/Access, Visa).

Hotel Jagdschloss Niederwald ★★★★
65385 Rüdesheim.
Tel 06722 1004, Fax 06722 47970.
English spoken.
Open 15/02 to 31/12. 52 bedrooms
(all en suite). Indoor swimming pool, tennis,
garage, parking.

*Historic building in a peaceful location.
Former hunting lodge of the Duke of Nassau.*

■ RESTAURANT: Has an excellent reputation for
its fine cuisine. Specialities include pâté de fois
gras, spring rolls with mangetout salad and
stuffed pike served on a bed of Riesling
cabbage.
■ TARIFF: (1996) Single 145–185,
Double 240–280 (Amex, Euro/Access, Visa).

Hotel Krone ★★★★★ Rheinuferstrasse 10,
65385 Assmannshausen-am-Rhein.
Tel 06722 4030, Fax 06722 3049.
English spoken.

Open all year. 65 bedrooms (all en suite). Outdoor swimming pool, golf 20 km, garage, parking.

Beautiful old castle on the banks of the Rhein. The rooms and suites are sumptuously furnished offering the highest standard of comfort and luxury. Located east of Rüdesheim on the B42. German 'Hotel of the Year' 1993.

■ RESTAURANT: Closed 01/01 to 15/02. Gourmet French/classic cuisine and excellent wines. Voted 'One of the best 100 restaurants'.
■ ACTIVITIES: Rhein river cruises, wine tasting, visits to castles and vineyards.
■ TARIFF: Single 150–280, Double 220–320, Bk 22, Set menu 48–135 (Amex, Euro/Access, Visa).

Hotel Rüdesheimer Hof ★★
Geisenheimerstr 1, 65385 Rüdesheim.
Tel 06722 2011, Fax 06722 48194.
English spoken.
Open 15/02 to 15/11. 42 bedrooms (all en suite). Golf 20 km, parking.

The hotel is located in the centre of town. All tourist and sightseeing attractions are within walking distance. On the main road as you approach the town centre.

■ RESTAURANT: Closed 15/11 to 15/02. Traditional restaurant 'Bauernstube' is cosy and inviting. A speciality is fillet of pork with mushrooms, bacon and fried potatoes. Meals can be taken outside on the pretty terrace when the weather is fine.
■ ACTIVITIES: Boat trips on the Rhein, wine tasting, cable car ride to the Germania monument; short walk to outdoor swimming pool and tennis courts. Rüdesheim's wine festival is held on varying dates in August each year.
■ TARIFF: Single 85–95, Double 120–160 (Amex, Euro/Access, Visa).
■ DISCOUNT: 5%

SAARBRÜCKEN   16A

Hotel Bliesbruck ★★★
Rubenheimer Str, 6657 Gersheim-Herbitzheim.
Tel 06843 1881, Fax 06843 8731.
English spoken.
Open all year. 29 bedrooms (all en suite).
Golf 3 km, garage, parking, restaurant.

Modern, chalet-style hotel with a very pretty garden. Peacefully set in the village of Herbitzheim, close to the French border. Take the Homburg/Einod exit from the motorway and go southwards for 13 km to Gersheim-Herbitzheim.

■ ACTIVITIES: Bikes for hire, walking, touring.
■ TARIFF: (1996) Single 65–95, Double 100–158, Set menu 20–47 (Euro/Access, Visa).

SAARLOUIS   16A

Hotel Ratskeller ★★★
Kleiner Markt 7, 6630 Saarlouis.
Tel 06831 2090, Fax 06831 48347.
English spoken.
Open all year. 29 bedrooms (all en suite).
Golf 7 km, garage, parking.

Furnished with antiques, hotel is in the centre of Saarlouis. Ideally situated for visiting Metz (50 km), Luxembourg (75 km) and Trier (50 km).

■ TARIFF: (1996) Single 89–130, Double 140–150 (Amex, Euro/Access, Visa).

ST-GOAR   16A

Hotel Landsknecht ★★★
An der Rheinuferstr, 56325 St-Goar.
Tel 06741 2011, Fax 06741 7499.
English spoken.

Open 01/03 to 01/12. 14 bedrooms (all en suite). Golf 15 km, garage, parking.

Stands by the river's edge, on a castle-strewn stretch of the Rhein and almost opposite the Loreley. Most of the very comfortable bedrooms have panoramic river views. 2 km north of St-Goar and one hour from Frankfurt airport.

■ RESTAURANT: Closed 01/12 to 28/02. Lovely views of the river. Special priced menus available at certain times of the year.
■ ACTIVITIES: Hiking, horse-riding, tennis, swimming pool nearby; wine tasting, visit the medieval castle, take a boat trip on the Rhein, visit the theatre.
■ TARIFF: (1996) Single 95–150, Double 115–360, Set menu 35–110 (Amex, Euro/Access, Visa).

Germany

Germany

Hotel Hauser

Heerstrasse 77, 56329 St-Goar-am-Rhein.
Tel 06741 333/7378, Fax 06741 1464.
English spoken.
Open 01/02 to 15/12. 16 bedrooms
(12 en suite). Outdoor swimming pool,
golf 10 km. ☎

*Newly renovated hotel with views over the
Rhein and hills beyond. Some rooms have a
balcony. On the west bank, south of Koblenz.
(Show this guide and room price will be DM98,
even with a balcony!)*

■ RESTAURANT: German and international
cuisine, fish specialities. Home-made
confectionery.
■ ACTIVITIES: Castle visit, rambling, boat trips,
wine tasting, trips to Mainz, Köln, Heidelberg
and Trier; fitness programme.
■ TARIFF: (1996) Single 42–95, Double 98–130,
Set menu 10.50–38 (Amex, Euro/Access, Visa).

ST-GOARSHAUSEN   16A

Hotel Erholung Nastaetter Str 15,
56346 St-Goarshausen.
Tel 06771 2684, Fax 06771 2502.
English spoken.
Open 15/03 to 15/11. 57 bedrooms
(all en suite). Golf 10 km, garage, parking. ☎ &

*Traditional hotel on banks of the Rhein by
Loreley Rock and opposite Rheinfeld Castle.
Wine bar. On the B42, south of Boppard exit
from A61.*

■ RESTAURANT: Closed 15/11 to 14/03. Fine
cuisine. Lavish buffet breakfast. Rhein
specialities include braised beef.
■ ACTIVITIES: Tennis nearby; boat trips on the
Rhein, wine tasting, wine festival in winter,
hiking.
■ TARIFF: (1996) Single 45–52, Double 90–100,
Set menu 10–33 (No credit cards).

SAULGAU   16D

Hotel Kleber-Post

Hauptstrasse 100, 88348 Saulgau.
Tel 07581 5010, Fax 07581 4437.
Open all year. 69 bedrooms (all en suite).
Golf 5 km. ☎ &

*New hotel in an historic building. Motorway
A8 exit Ulm, then take the B30 towards
Friedrichshafen exit Biberach/Saulgau.*

■ RESTAURANT: Award-winning restaurant
offering regional and international cuisine;
large choice of wines.
■ ACTIVITIES: Thermal baths, hiking trails, tennis,
cycling and climbing nearby. Good area for

sightseeing and touring; hotel will reserve
theatre tickets.
■ TARIFF: (1996) Single 88–170,
Double 130–270, Set menu 47
(Amex, Euro/Access, Visa).

SCHÖNWALD   16C

Hotel Zum Ochsen ★★★★

Ludwig-Uhland-Str 18, 7741 Schönwald.
Tel 07722 1045, Fax 07722 3018.
English spoken.
Open all year. 40 bedrooms (all en suite).
Indoor swimming pool, tennis, golf on site,
garage, parking. ☎

*Comfortable country house with winter
garden, surrounded by gardens and a golf
course. From A5 Frankfurt to Basel, take B33
to Triberg, then go towards Schönwald.*

■ RESTAURANT: Seasonal, regional and light
cuisine.
■ ACTIVITIES: Sauna, solarium, massage, fitness
centre, table tennis, badminton, bowls;
mountain-biking, fishing, sightseeing tours.
■ TARIFF: (1996) Single 102–132,
Double 178–218, Set menu 42–90 (Amex,
Euro/Access, Visa).

SCHWALENBERG   14D

Hotel Schwalenberger Malkasten ★★ Neue

Torstr 1-3, 32816 Schieder-Schwalenberg 2.
Tel 05284 5278, Fax 05284 5108.
Open 01/02 to 31/12. 45 bedrooms
(all en suite). Golf 12 km, garage, parking.

*Traditional hotel with exposed beams. From
the Hannover to Rinteln motorway, take Bad
Eilsen exit. Through Rinteln, Barntrup and
Blomberg to Schieder-Schwalenberg.*

■ RESTAURANT: Closed Jan.
■ ACTIVITIES: Sauna and solarium.
■ TARIFF: (1996) Single 65–70, Double 94–144,
Set menu 20–45 (Visa).

SIEGEN 16A

Hotel Johanneshöhe ★★★
Wallhausenstr 1, 57072 Siegen.
Tel 02713 10008, Fax 02713 15039. English spoken.
Open all year. 25 bedrooms (all en suite).
Golf 12 km, garage, parking.

*Situated about 2 km from the railway station
and town centre, hotel occupies a quiet
position with panoramic views of Siegen.*

■ RESTAURANT: Closed Sun eve. Very good food
with French and regional specialities.
■ TARIFF: (1996) Single 75–120,
Double 130–175, Set menu 20–28 (Amex,
Euro/Access, Visa).

STADTALLENDORF 16B

Parkhotel Schillerstrasse 1,
3570 Stadtallendorf.
Tel 06428 7080, Fax 06428 708259. English spoken.
Open all year. 50 bedrooms (all en suite).
Tennis, golf 15 km, garage, parking. ℄ ⅋

*Hotel stands in extensive grounds just five
minutes' walk from the town centre and only
15 km from the romantic university town of
Marburg. Stadtallendorf is known as the
'garden city'.*

■ RESTAURANT: Regional specialities and a good
selection of desserts. Beer garden.
■ ACTIVITIES: Sightseeing, touring, lovely walks.
■ TARIFF: (1996) Single 59–119, Double 85–168
(Amex, Euro/Access, Visa).

STOLBERG 16A

Romantik Hotel Altes Brauhaus Burgkeller
Steinweg 22, 52222 Stolberg.
Tel 02402 27272. English spoken.
Open all year. 5 bedrooms (all en suite). Indoor
swimming pool, tennis, golf 6 km, parking. ⅋

*Quietly situated in the old town. Luxurious
individually decorated rooms with every comfort.*

■ RESTAURANT: Closed Sat lunch. Light cuisine
using fresh local produce.
■ ACTIVITIES: Visit Maastricht in the Netherlands.
● Special gourmet weekend packages
including sightseeing tours.
■ TARIFF: (1996) Single 140, Double 200–240,
Set menu 12.50–35 (Amex, Euro/Access, Visa).

Parkhotel am Hammerberg ★★★
Hammerberg 11, 52222 Stolberg.
Tel 02402 12340, Fax 02402 123480. English spoken.
Open all year. 28 bedrooms (all en suite). Indoor
swimming pool, tennis, golf 6 km, parking. ⅋

*Modern, very quiet hotel, surrounded by
gardens and the forest. Some of the rooms have*

*a balcony. 50 km from Düsseldorf, Köln and
Maastricht. From the A44 motorway, take the
Aachen/Brand/Stolberg exit.*

■ RESTAURANT: Closed Sat lunch. Restaurant is
renowned in the region for good quality, light
cuisine using fresh market produce.
■ ACTIVITIES: Walking, cycling; good area for
sightseeing and touring including Aachen,
Stolberg's castle, Maastricht and Lüttich.
■ TARIFF: (1996) Single 98–140,
Double 175–260, Set menu 14.50–38.50
(Amex, Euro/Access, Visa).

TITISEE-NEUSTADT 16A

Romantik Hotel Adler Post Haupstrasse 16,
Ortsteil Neustadt, 7820 Titisee-Neustadt.
Tel 07651 5066, Fax 07651 3729. English spoken.
Open 01/01 to 19/03 & 07/04 to 31/12.
30 bedrooms (all en suite). Indoor swimming
pool, golf 25 km, garage, parking.

*Dating back to 1516 and once a mail staging
post, this very comfortable family-run hotel is
located 5 km east of Lake Titisee.*

■ RESTAURANT: Closed Tues lunch. German,
Black Forest and French specialities based on
fresh, seasonal produce, accompanied by fine
wines and draught beers.
■ ACTIVITIES: A wide choice of summer and
winter activities close by.
■ TARIFF: (1996) Single 93–128, Double 158–218,
Set menu 30–88 (Amex, Euro/Access, Visa).

TRABEN-TRARBACH 16A

Hotel Moseltor ★★★
Moselstrasse 1, 56841 Traben-Trarbach.
Tel 06541 6551, Fax 06541 4922. English spoken.
Open all year. 11 bedrooms (all en suite).
Golf 15 km, garage.

*On the right bank of the Mosel, a four-storey
building dating from 1838. The charming
combination of old and new creates a warm
mixture of comfort and convenience. Take
B53 from Trier or B49 from Koblenz. Special
wedding packages available.*

■ RESTAURANT: Closed Tues. Small restaurant (11
tables) serving light, regional cuisine prepared
by renowned chef Ruth Bauer.
■ ACTIVITIES: Gliding, water-skiing, wine tasting,
boat trips on the Mosel, international 'Belle
Epoque' meetings, visit mineral spring in Bad
Wildstein and Arur-Veda-Centre; ideal location
for exploring the Mosel valley.
■ TARIFF: Single 85–115, Double 125–185,
Set menu 53–110 (Amex, Euro/Access, Visa).
■ DISCOUNT: 10% Jan to May, minimum 4 nights.

Germany

TÜBINGEN 16D

Hotel am Bad ★★★
Europastrasse 2, 7400 Tübingen.
Tel 07071 73071, Fax 07071 75336.
English spoken.
Open 07/01 to 21/12. 35 bedrooms
(all en suite). Outdoor swimming pool, tennis,
golf 20 km, garage, parking, restaurant. &

*Quietly situated in very pretty, park-like
gardens. From Stuttgart-Singen autobahn take
Herrenberg exit.*

■ ACTIVITIES: Cycling and fishing.
■ TARIFF: (1996) Single 76–108, Double 134–
162, Set menu 15–20 (Amex, Euro/Access, Visa).
■ DISCOUNT: 5%

ÜBERLINGEN 16D

Bad Hotel Christophstrasse 2,
88662 Überlingen.
Tel 07551 8370, Fax 07551 67079.
English spoken.
Open all year. 68 bedrooms (all en suite).
Golf 5 km, garage, parking.

*Modernised hotel overlooking Lake Constance.
Good conference and children's facilities.
Discounts in LS.*

■ RESTAURANT: Local specialities; café on terrace
overlooking lake; bistro.
■ ACTIVITIES: Boat trips, hiking; explore the
historic town. ● Next door swimming pool free
of charge for hotel guests.
■ TARIFF: Single 90–170, Double 140–250,
Set menu 35–79 (Amex, Euro/Access, Visa).

Romantic Hotel Johanniter-Kreuz ★★★★
Johanninterweg 11, Andelshofen,
88662 Überlingen.
Tel 07551 61091, Fax 07551 67336.
English spoken.
Open all year. 26 bedrooms (all en suite).
Golf 1 km, garage, parking.

*300-year-old house in the small village of
Andelshofen. Comfortable accommodation,
family atmosphere and only 3 km from the
lake. Offers 7 nights for the price of 6.*

■ RESTAURANT: Closed Mon. Attractive restaurant
with an open fireplace. Fish and game
specialities.
■ ACTIVITIES: Fishing, tennis and horse-riding
close by. ● Boating week with a different trip
on the Bodensee each day; golfing week
offering 50% reduction on green fees, playing
at a different course each day.
■ TARIFF: (1996) Single 88–160,
Double 165–260, Set menu 45–88 (Amex,
Euro/Access, Visa).

ULM 16D

Hotel Gasthof Zum Ritter
Bertholdstr 8, Gogglingen, 89079 Ulm.
Tel 07305 7365/6025, Fax 07305 22935.
English spoken.
Open all year. 19 bedrooms (12 en suite,
7 bath/shower only). Garage, parking. ✆

*Very old building, recently refurbished. In the
centre of Gogglingen, 8 km from Ulm.*

■ RESTAURANT: Closed Wed. Regional and
international specialities.
■ ACTIVITIES: Ideal for cycling, hiking and fishing.
■ TARIFF: (1996) Single 40–55, Double 75–95,
Set menu 10 (No credit cards).

WALSRODE 14D

Hotel Heide-Kröpke ★★★★
Ostenholzer Moor, 29690 Essel.
Tel 05167 9790, Fax 05167 979291.
English spoken.

Open all year. 128 bedrooms (all en suite).
Indoor swimming pool, tennis, golf 15 km,
garage, parking. &

*Traditional, family-run hotel with a range of
accommodation to suit all needs. From
Hannover to Hamburg motorway take
Westenholz exit and go 8 km to Ostenholz,
then Ostenholzer Moor.*

■ RESTAURANT: Warm and inviting. Regional and
wild game specialities.
■ ACTIVITIES: Fitness room with sauna, whirlpool
and massage; tennis, bowling alley. Boating
and exploring the beautiful countryside.
■ TARIFF: (1996) Single 85–175,
Double 195–230, Set menu 35–85
(Euro/Access, Visa).
■ DISCOUNT: 10%

Germany

Parkhotel Luisenhöhe ★★★
Am Vogelpark Walsrode, 29664 Walsrode.
Tel 05161 2011, Fax 05161 2387.
English spoken.
Open 02/01 to 20/12. 47 bedrooms
(all en suite). Golf 8 km, garage, parking. ✆

*Modern hotel with comfortable, well-equipped
accommodation. Opposite 'Vogelpark
Walsrode', the world's largest bird sanctuary.*

■ RESTAURANT: Closed 26 Dec & 01 Jan.
Traditional Lower Saxony-style dining room
with regional and international cuisine.
■ ACTIVITIES: Visit to Vogelpark; tour the
wonderful surrounding countryside.
■ TARIFF: (1996) Single 140–200,
Double 170–300, Set menu 20 (Amex,
Euro/Access, Visa).

WARENDORF   14D

Hotel im Engel ★★★★
Brünebrede 37, 48231 Warendorf.
Tel 02581 93020, Fax 02581 62726.
English spoken.
Open all year. 22 bedrooms (all en suite).
Golf 5 km, garage, parking. ৬

*Family-run hotel, steeped in history. Elegantly
furnished in traditional style. B64 into
Warendorf, turn right into
Frackenhorsterstrasse, right into Ostwall, then
second left.*

■ RESTAURANT: Restaurant is well regarded for its
high quality cuisine.
■ ACTIVITIES: Visit the lovely old town; horse-
riding.
■ TARIFF: (1996) Single 95–115,
Double 145–175, Set menu 35–95 (Amex,
Euro/Access, Visa).
■ DISCOUNT: 10%

WERTHEIM   16B

Hotel Schwan 97877 Wertheim-am-Main.
Tel 09342 92330, Fax 09342 21182.
English spoken.
Open 24/01 to 22/12. 30 bedrooms
(all en suite). Golf 10 km, garage, parking.

*Small, traditional hotel, tastefully and
comfortably furnished. Lovely surrounding
countryside. Conference facilities.*

■ RESTAURANT: Very good traditional and
gourmet cuisine. Fish specialities.
■ ACTIVITIES: Cycle tracks and rambling paths;
discover the interesting old town.
■ TARIFF: (1996) Single 85–120,
Double 120–240, Set menu 20–29 (Amex,
Euro/Access, Visa).

WIESBADEN   16B
Hotel Schwarzer Bock ★★★★
Kranzplatz 12, 65183 Wiesbaden.
Tel 06111 550, Fax 06111 55111.
English spoken.
Open all year. 150 bedrooms (all en suite).
Indoor swimming pool, golf 8 km, garage,
parking. ৬

*A first-class business hotel, Germany's oldest,
completely renovated in 1996.*

■ RESTAURANT: Regional specialities.
■ ACTIVITIES: Sightseeing tours of the region.
■ TARIFF: Single 245–305, Double 295–355, Bk 25,
Set menu 45–130 (Amex, Euro/Access, Visa).

WINTERBERG   16B
Hotel Dorint U Ferienpark ★★★ Winterberg
7, Postwiese, 59955 Winterberg-Neuastenberg.
Tel 02981 8970, Fax 02981 897700.
English spoken.
Open all year. 140 bedrooms (all en suite).
Indoor swimming pool, tennis, golf 8 km,
garage, parking.

*Chalet-style hotel with self-catering apartments
also offered. On B480.*

■ RESTAURANT: International and regional
cuisine.
■ ACTIVITIES: Bowling, skittles, sauna/solarium,
children's playground; mountain bikes for hire;
mini-golf and horse-riding nearby. Well-known
area for winter sports. Evening entertainment.
■ TARIFF: (1996) Single 135–175,
Double 225–290, Set menu 37–62 (Amex,
Euro/Access, Visa).

Landhotel Grimmeblick ★★★★
Am Langen Acker 5, 59955 Winterberg.
Tel 02981 7070, Fax 02981 3552.
English spoken.
Open all year. 14 bedrooms (all en suite).
Outdoor swimming pool, golf 3 km, parking,
restaurant. ✆ ৬

*Traditional family hotel of character adorned
with musical instruments of all kinds. The
hotel lies in a valley surrounded by mountains
and is an ideal spot for exploring the region.
Free accommodation for under 10-year-olds.*

■ ACTIVITIES: Lots to do here for the active
including: parascending, diving, golf, horse
riding, sailing, surfing. ● Special organised
programme for children including: skiing,
bobsleighing, sailing and windsurfing
depending on the season.
■ TARIFF: Single 56–86, Double 110–164,
Set menu 25–45 (Amex, Euro/Access, Visa).
■ DISCOUNT: 10%

Germany (sidebar)

WUPPERTAL   16A

Hotel Rubin Paradestrasse 59,
42107 Wuppertal.
Tel 0202 450077, Fax 0202 456489.
Open all year. 16 bedrooms (all en suite).
Garage, parking.

Small and modern, hotel is in a central but quiet location.

■ TARIFF: (1996) Single 80–105,
Double 125–145 (No credit cards).

Hotel Zur Krone ★★★ Gemarker Ufer 19,
5600 Wuppertal.
Tel 0202 595020, Fax 0202 559769.
English spoken.
Open all year. 17 bedrooms (all en suite).
Golf 10 km, garage. ✆

Town centre hotel with friendly atmosphere. 2 km from A46 exit 38.

■ ACTIVITIES: Walking, cycling; swimming pool nearby.
■ TARIFF: (1996) Single 85–113,
Double 125–155 (Euro/Access, Visa).

WÜRZBURG   16B

Hotel Zur Stadt Mainz Semmelstr 39,
8700 Würzburg.
Tel 0931 53155, Fax 0931 58510.
English spoken.
Open 20/01 to 20/12. 15 bedrooms
(all en suite). Golf 6 km, garage.

Charming and welcoming, a traditional 15th-century inn with cosy atmosphere, rustic and antique furniture. Würzburg is an artistic, historic city with an 11th-century Romanesque cathedral.

■ RESTAURANT: Closed Sun & Mon eve.
Acclaimed restaurant specialising in fish dishes.
The imaginative menus, many from a 19th-century cookbook, include local eel in dill sauce, carp and pike. Don't miss the home-made apple strudel. Very good value for money.
■ ACTIVITIES: Wine tasting; sightseeing.
■ TARIFF: (1996) Single 130–150,
Double 180–200, Set menu 20–70 (Amex, Euro/Access, Visa).

Hotel Walfisch ★★★★ Am Pleidenturm 5,
97070 Würzburg.
Tel 0931 35200, Fax 0931 3520500.
English spoken.
Open all year. 40 bedrooms (all en suite).
Golf 2 km, garage.

A good family-run hotel on riverside in town. Pleasant atmosphere, friendly service, fine views of Marienburg fortress, vineyards and the river. Conference facilities.

■ RESTAURANT: Closed Sun eve. Very attractive with good food.
■ TARIFF: Single 160–180, Double 220–280 (Amex, Euro/Access, Visa).

Germany

GREECE

Shoreline at Mykonos town

Many British holidaymakers choose to fly to one of the Greek islands for their annual fix of Mediterranean sunshine, but exploring the mainland, from the Turkish border in the north-east to Cape Ta'naron at the foot of the Mani peninsula, is an exciting alternative.

Salonica, in the north, is the country's second largest city and to its east lies the part of Greece where you are least likely to find tourists in large numbers. You will meet more if you drive south towards Athens. The road follows the coast passing between the sea and Mount Olympus, Greece's highest mountain and the mythical home of the gods. Athens is crowded in summertime, but you may still feel a visit to the Acropolis is an essential part of your holiday.

West of Athens, the road crosses the Corinth canal on its way to the hand-shaped Peloponnese, the most southern region of the Greek mainland. Snatch a look as you cross the bridge, for this is the best view you will have of the amazing canal. Built between 1882 and 1893 it is only 23 m wide but cuts through rock which is sometimes as much as 80 m deep, Originally on the drawing board in the first century AD, this project took some 1800 years to come to fruition. In the Peloponnese, the two outstanding ancient sites are Mycenae, with its famous lion gate, and Olympia, home of the ancient games for over a thousand years.

Emergency numbers

For emergency numbers see the local directory

Warning information

Warning Triangle must be carried

Blood Alcohol Legal Limit 50 mg

Fire extinguisher essential

First aid kit compulsory

ATHINA (ATHENS) 24C

Hotel Amalia ★★★★
Amalias Avenue 10, 10557 Athina.
Tel 0132 37301, Fax 0132 38792.
English spoken.
Open all year. 98 bedrooms (all en suite).
Restaurant.

In front of the National Gardens in Syntagma Square.

■ ACTIVITIES: The hotel can book sightseeing tours and cruises.
■ TARIFF: (1996) Single 19,600, Double 27,400, Set menu 4,900 (Amex, Euro/Access, Visa).

Hotel Pan 11 Metropoleos Street, Syntagma Square, 10557 Athina.
Tel 0132 37817, Fax 0132 37819.
English spoken.
Open all year. 48 bedrooms (all en suite).
Golf 12 km, garage. ℄

Conveniently situated in the centre of town, fully air conditioned and offering 24-hour room service.

■ ACTIVITIES: Tennis and swimming pool 1.5 km.
● Hotel offers 10% discount on any organised excursion in Greece if booked with accommodation.
■ TARIFF: (1996) Single 8,500–12,000, Double 12,000–18,000 (Amex, Euro/Access, Visa).
■ DISCOUNT: 10%

Hotel Poseidon ★★★
Palio Faliro, 17562 Athina.
Tel 0198 22086, Fax 0198 29217.
English spoken.

Open all year. 90 bedrooms (all en suite).
Outdoor swimming pool, golf 3 km, parking. ℄

On the coast road, 8 km from Athina town centre and 3 km from the airport.

■ RESTAURANT: Choice of three restaurants, one of which is a traditional seafood taverna on the beach.

DELFI (DELPHI) 24A

Hotel Amalia ★★★★ 1
Apollonos St, 33054 Delfi.
Tel 0265 82101, Fax 0265 82290.
English spoken.
Open all year. 184 bedrooms (all en suite).
Outdoor swimming pool, parking, restaurant.

In picturesque countryside, the hotel overlooks the olive groves of Itea and the gulf of Korinthos.

■ ACTIVITIES: Exploring the ruins; skiing nearby in winter.
■ TARIFF: Single 23,300, Double 33,000, Set menu 4,900 (Amex, Euro/Access, Visa).

GLIFADA 24C

Hotel Astir Glifada Attica.
Tel 0189 46461/6, Fax 0189 45901.
English spoken.
Open all year. 128 bedrooms (all en suite).
Golf 5 km, parking. ໐
■ TARIFF: (1996) Double 13,000–24,000, Bk 2,500 (Amex, Euro/Access, Visa).

Hotel Emmantina Glifada Attica.
Tel 0898 0683, Fax 0894 8110. English spoken.

Open all year. 80 bedrooms (all en suite).
Outdoor swimming pool, golf 1.5 km, parking. ℄ ໐

Comfortable, modern hotel with good facilities including air conditioning and soundproofing. 150 m from the beach, 4 km from the airport and 15 km from Athina. (Internet: http://www.xr.com/greece)

Greece

■ RESTAURANT: International menus with Greek specialities.
■ ACTIVITIES: Lots to do and see nearby. Great base for sightseeing and tours.
■ TARIFF: (1996) Single 15,200–19,900, Double 19,900–24,900 (Amex, Euro/Access, Visa).
■ DISCOUNT: 20%

Hotel Palmyra Beach Glifada Attica.
Tel 0898 1183. English spoken.
Open 01/05 to 30/09. 58 bedrooms (all en suite). Outdoor swimming pool, golf 2 km, parking. ⟨ ⟨

Renovated and fully air conditioned, hotel offers all modern amenities. 100 m from the beach, 4 km from the airport and 15 km from Athina.

■ RESTAURANT: International menus with Greek specialities.
■ ACTIVITIES: Good base for sightseeing and touring; lots to do and see nearby.
■ TARIFF: (1996) Single 15,200–19,900, Double 19,900–24,900 (Amex, Euro/Access, Visa).
■ DISCOUNT: 20%

KALAMBAKA   24A

Hotel Amalia ★★★★ 42200 Kalambaka.
Tel 0432 72216, Fax 0432 72457.
English spoken.
Open all year. 175 bedrooms (all en suite).
Outdoor swimming pool, parking, restaurant. ⟨

On the road between Trikala and Kalambaka, the hotel offers wonderful views. Only 3 km from Meteora, where monasteries were built on top of impressive rocky formations.

■ TARIFF: Single 23,300, Double 33,000, Set menu 4,900 (Amex, Euro/Access, Visa).

KEFALLINIA (KEFALONIA)

ARGOSTOLI (ARGOSTOLION)   24C

Lara Hotel Lourdata, Kefalonia.
Tel 0671 31157, Fax 0671 31156.
English spoken.
Open 01/05 to 16/10. 40 bedrooms (all en suite). Tennis, parking. ⟨

Typical Kefalonian hotel surrounded by olive and lemon trees. In a very quiet location, Lourdata is 20 minutes' drive from Argostolion and 300 m from the beach. Driving towards Poros, turn off right at the Vlachata Avia petrol station.

■ ACTIVITIES: Lovely walks. ● 1 free lesson and 25% discount at the nearby horse-riding club.
■ TARIFF: (1996) Single 6,000–13,500, Double 8,000–15,800 (Euro/Access, Visa).

END OF KEFALLINIA (KEFALONIA) HOTELS

KOSTA   24C

Hotel Lido Kosta, Argolida.
Tel 0754 57393, Fax 0754 57364. English spoken.
Open 05/04 to 30/09. 40 bedrooms (all en suite). Parking. ⟨

Hotel is on the beach at Kosta, 5 km south of Porto Heli. Coming from Korinthos, take the new coast road to Epidavros and turn right to Porto Heli and Kosta after 3 km.

■ RESTAURANT: Greek and international cuisine. The restaurant is open in July and August only. Taverna nearby.
■ ACTIVITIES: Water sports; many places to visit.
■ TARIFF: (1996) Single 6,000–10,000, Double 10,000–14,000 (Amex, Euro/Access, Visa).

KRITI (CRETE)

AGIOS NIKOLAOS   24C

Hotel Ormos ★★★★
Agios Nikolaos Lassithi, Kriti.
Tel 0841 24094/28144, Fax 0841 25394.
English spoken.
Open all year. 47 bedrooms (all en suite).
Outdoor swimming pool, tennis, parking. ⟨

Set in large, pretty gardens beside the sea, hotel has a family atmosphere and offers comfortable accommodation, good service and some lovely sea views. 1 km north of Agios Nikolaos on the coast road towards Elounda.

■ RESTAURANT: Fresh fish, lobster and Greek specialities.

Greece

■ ACTIVITIES: Hotel organises boat and fishing trips, barbecue and poolside parties as well as competitive tennis matches; water sports and children's playground.
■ TARIFF: (1996) Single 3,500–19,000, Double 4,400–28,000, Bk 1,460, Set menu 2,640–3,950 (Amex, Euro/Access, Visa).

HANIA   24C

Hotel Samaria ★★★
69 Kidonias str, 73135 Hania, Kriti.
Tel 0821 71271/5, Fax 0821 71270.
English spoken.
Open all year. 62 bedrooms (all en suite).
Parking. ✆

Comfortable, air-conditioned hotel, renovated in 1992. All rooms have balcony and sound insulation. Roof garden with good views. Located in town centre, opposite central bus terminal. Conference facilities.

■ TARIFF: (1996) Single 12,000–18,600, Double 15,000–26,800 (Amex, Euro/Access, Visa).
■ DISCOUNT: 10% room only.

END OF KRITI (CRETE) HOTELS

LEMNOS

MYRINA   24A

Hotel Akti Myrina 81400 Myrina, Lemnos.
Tel 0254 22681, Fax 0254 22352.
English spoken.
Open 18/05 to 02/10. 125 bedrooms (all en suite).
Outdoor swimming pool, tennis, parking.

Beautiful self-contained Greek-style cottages with private gardens and beach. The excellent facilities also include poolside and piano bars. An ideal resort for peace and relaxation. (Rates quoted are for half-board.)

■ RESTAURANT: Three restaurants offering excellent cuisine. Beach buffet and bar.
■ ACTIVITIES: Water sports, volley ball, mini-golf, fitness centre. Excursions by boat and fully air-conditioned bus. Children's playground.
■ TARIFF: (1996) Single 44,000–56,000, Double 63,000–120,000 (Amex, Euro/Access, Visa).

END OF LEMNOS HOTELS

MYKONOS

MYKONOS   24C

Hotel Adonis PO Box 68,
84600 Mykonos, Mykonos Island.
Tel 0289 22434, Fax 0289 23449. English spoken.
Open 01/04 to 31/10. 31 bedrooms (all en suite). Garage, parking. ✆

A friendly town centre hotel with balconies overlooking the sea and only 5 minutes' walk to the beach.

■ ACTIVITIES: Horse-riding; excursions; car and bike rental.
■ TARIFF: Single 9,350–18,000, Double 12,250–22,500 (Amex, Euro/Access, Visa).
■ DISCOUNT: 10%

END OF MYKONOS HOTELS

NAFPLION   24C

Hotel Amalia ★★★★
Nea Tyrins, 21100 Nafplion.
Tel 0752 24401, Fax 0752 24400. English spoken.
Open all year. 175 bedrooms (all en suite).
Outdoor swimming pool, parking, restaurant.

Neo-classical-style hotel surrounded by beautiful gardens. Nea Tyrins is 2 km from Nafplion.

■ TARIFF: Single 23,300, Double 33,000, Set menu 4,900 (Amex, Euro/Access, Visa).

OLYMPIA   24C

Hotel Amalia ★★★★ 27065 Olympia.
Tel 0624 22190, Fax 0624 22444. English spoken.
Open all year. 147 bedrooms (all en suite).
Outdoor swimming pool, parking, restaurant.

Surrounded by green forests, hotel is close to the world-famous archaeological site.

■ TARIFF: Single 23,300, Double 33,000, Set menu 4,900 (Amex, Euro/Access, Visa).

PREVEZA   24A

Hotel Margarona ★★★ 48100 Preveza.
Tel 0682 24360, Fax 0682 24369. English spoken.
Open all year. 117 bedrooms (all en suite).
Outdoor swimming pool, tennis, parking, restaurant.

2 km from the town centre, near the mouth of the Amvrakikos Gulf on the Ionian Sea.

■ TARIFF: Single 14,600, Double 21,000, Set menu 3,900 (Amex, Euro/Access, Visa).

HUNGARY

Budapest, the capital of Hungary, is known as the 'Pearl of the Danube' and rightly so, for it is one of the great cities of Europe. It lies astride the river – with Buda rising to the west, overlooking Pest sprawled out below on the opposite bank. For a first impression, go to Castle Hill in Buda and look out from the decorative Fisherman's Bastion across the Danube to the bustling streets of Pest. Visit the richly decorated Mátyás church, the Royal Palace with its museums and the Gellért Turkish Baths, all in Buda; and, having crossed the river, try to see the neo-Gothic parliament building and the Opera House. If you are lucky enough to be here on 20 August, Hungary's Constitution Day, the Fisherman's Bastion is an ideal place from which to watch the grand fireworks display.

To the west, Lake Balaton, the largest area of fresh water in central Europe, is understandably the most popular tourist destination. For a comprehensive view, go to Csúcs Hill on the Tihany peninsula, which became Hungary's first National Park in 1952. From here, a car ferry crosses the lake. This may be of interest if you are heading south to Pécs, a delightful city lying beneath the vine-covered slopes of the Mecsek Hills. Its main square is dominated by a church converted from a redundant mosque, reminding the visitor of this region's years of Turkish occupation.

North of Budapest, the Danube turns at right angles between Szentendre and Esztergom. Known as the Danube Bend, this area is popular with Hungarian holidaymakers. At Szentendre, there is a village museum, whose ambitious aim is to show reconstructed villages from all over Hungary, and at Esztergom the main attraction is its huge domed basilica.

To try Hungary's most famous wines, you need to visit the hilly region south of the Slovakian border. Here, the principal wine-producing towns are Eger and Tokaj. Eger, which is also famous for its mosqueless minaret, produces Egri Bikavér, the strong red wine which we know as Bull's Blood. In Tokaj, the wine comes in varying degrees of sweetness, so you are advised to visit one of the many cellars in the town for a sampling session before deciding what to buy.

Finally, there is the great plain to the south with the Hortobágy National Park at its centre. This is described as a living heritage museum and is Hungary's answer to the Wild West. It is at its liveliest during the International Horse Show in July and the Bridge Fair, which is held to coincide with Hungary's Constitution Day in August.

If you are hoping to go to an evening class and pick up Hungarian in a week or two forget it. But don't worry the Hungarians are used to the fact that few foreigners can speak their complicated language. Try English, French and perhaps German before resorting to pointing at your question in a phrase book. Pointing is necessary for attempting to pronounce what you see on the printed page will be almost impossible. Try asking the way to Sártoraljaúhely after a glass or two of Bull's Blood!

Emergency numbers

Police 007, Fire Brigade 005, and Ambulance 004.

If phoning from Budapest, drop one of the 0s

Warning information

Warning triangle must be carried

Blood alcohol legal limit 0 mg

BAJA 23C

Sugovica Hotel ★★★ Petofi-sziget, 6500 Baja.
Tel 79 321 755, Fax 79 323 155. English spoken.
Open all year. 34 bedrooms (all en suite).
Outdoor swimming pool, tennis, parking. ℄

*Modern hotel with every facility. On a small
island on the Danube, but only 500 m from the
town centre. (Prices in DM.)*

■ RESTAURANT: Hungarian dishes with fish
specialities.
■ ACTIVITIES: Own bowling alley.
■ TARIFF: (1996) Single 90, Double 103 (Amex,
Euro/Access, Visa).

BALATONFÖLDVAR 23C

Pannonia Hotel Neptun ★★★
8623 Balatonföldvar.
Tel 84 340388, Fax 84 340212. English spoken.

Open 25/04 to 10/10. 210 bedrooms
(all en suite). Outdoor swimming pool, tennis,
parking, restaurant.

*Modern hotel set in a beautiful park on the
southern shore of Lake Balaton, 300 m from
the beach. 'Family friend' hotel with
reductions for children and baby-sitting
service. (Prices in DM.)*

■ ACTIVITIES: Children's playground/playroom,
sauna, volley ball, table tennis, bikes rental.
■ TARIFF: Single 60–100, Double 72–125
(Amex, Euro/Access, Visa).

BALATONLELLE 23C

Hotel Giuseppe ★★
Köztarsasag ut 36-38, 8638 Balatonlelle.
Tel 085 350 433, Fax 085 350 074.
English spoken.
Open all year. 90 bedrooms (all en suite).
Tennis, parking. ℄

*Medium-sized hotel in lovely location right beside
Lake Balaton, famous for its natural beauty.*

■ RESTAURANT: Friendly restaurant with
Hungarian specialities.
■ ACTIVITIES: Lots to do and see around the lake.
■ TARIFF: Single 30–60, Double 40–80
(Euro/Access, Visa).
■ DISCOUNT: 10%

BUDAPEST 23A

Buda Center Hotel ★★
Csalogany u 23, 1027 Budapest.
Tel 1 201 6333, Fax 1 201 7843. English spoken.
Open all year. 37 bedrooms (all en suite).
Parking. ℄

*Modern, comfortable hotel situated in the heart
of the city.*

■ RESTAURANT: Chinese restaurant or 'Buda
Centre' pub with Hungarian and international
specialities. Exotic dishes include crocodile,
kangaroo, ostrich and bison.
■ TARIFF: Single 5500–10,000,
Double 6500–12,000, Set menu 800–2500
(Amex, Euro/Access, Visa).

Budapest Hilton ★★★★★L
Hess Andras ter 1-3, 1014 Budapest.
Tel 1 214 3000, Fax 1 156 0285. English spoken.

Open all year. 322 bedrooms (all en suite).
Golf 18 km, garage, parking. ℄ ♿

*Exclusively designed hotel incorporating 20th-
century architecture and ingeniously built
around a 13th-century cloister and
monastery. The unique blending of the two
styles is both tranquil and harmonious. Fully
equipped rooms with individually controlled
air conditioning; state-of-the-art business
facilities; excellent service. (Prices in DM.)*

■ RESTAURANT: The international 'Dominican'
restaurant offers seafood and foie gras
specialities; Hungarian cuisine can be enjoyed
in 'Kalocsa' and buffet breakfast and popularly
priced dishes in the Corvina Coffee Shop.
■ ACTIVITIES: Hotel will arrange city tours,

Hungary

excursions to the Hungarian Puszta and Danube Bend, nightclub tour, horse shows and wine tasting.
■ TARIFF: Single 280–450, Double 365–555, Bk 29, Set menu 60–100 (Amex, Euro/Access, Visa).

Danubius Hotel Gellért ★★★★
Szt Gellért tér 1, 1111 Budapest.
Tel 1 185 2200, Fax 1 166 6631. English spoken.

Open all year. 233 bedrooms (232 en suite, 1 bath/shower only). Indoor swimming pool, outdoor swimming pool, golf 20 km, parking. ✆

Dating from 1918 and built in art-noveau style, hotel occupies a superb position at the foot of the Gellért Hill where the Szabadság (Freedom) bridge, with its mythical eagles, crosses the Danube. Corridors and an elevator lead directly to the spa baths from three floors of the hotel. (Prices in DM.)

■ RESTAURANT: The main, de luxe restaurant offers excellent service, international and Hungarian cuisine. Local dishes with daily specialities can be enjoyed in the brasserie and home-made pastries, confectionary and snacks in the café.
■ ACTIVITIES: Hotel can arrange sightseeing tour of Budapest with English-speaking guide, day tours to other towns, 'Budapest by night', boat trips on the Danube and horse-riding. ● Free admission to the spa for hotel guests (charge for any treatment given).
■ TARIFF: Single 185–245, Double 326–378, Set menu 20–45 (Amex, Euro/Access, Visa).
■ DISCOUNT: 15% advance bookings only.

Danubius Grand Hotel Margitsziget ★★★★
(formerly Ramada Grand Hotel),
Margitsziget, 1138 Budapest.
Tel 1 311 1000, Fax 1 153 2753. English spoken.

Open all year. 164 bedrooms (all en suite). Indoor swimming pool, tennis, golf 20 km, garage, parking. ✆ &

Built in 1873, restored in 1987 to traditional style and set in picturesque surroundings on Margaret Island. Luxuriously furnished rooms; three thermal springs offer balneo and physicotherapy. Special spa packages at reasonable prices are also available. (Prices in DM.)

■ RESTAURANT: Choose from a fine selection of national and international cuisine in the 'Széchenyi' terrace restaurant and 'Gösser' brasserie.
■ ACTIVITIES: The spa centre of the neighbouring hotel is connected via a heated underground corridor and offers thermal baths, fitness centre and pool complex with sauna, solarium and sun terrace; jogging. ● Free bicycle hire.
■ TARIFF: Single 220–260, Double 270–310, Set menu 25–60 (Amex, Euro/Access, Visa).

Kempinski Hotel Corvinus ★★★★★
Erzsébet tér 7-8, 1051 Budapest.
Tel 1 266 1000, Fax 1 266 2000. English spoken.
Open all year. 367 bedrooms (all en suite). Indoor swimming pool, golf 20 km, garage. &

A de luxe, city centre hotel opened in 1992. Offers up-to-date conference facilities. (Prices in DM.)

■ RESTAURANT: International cuisine or lighter dishes and snacks are on offer from the 'Corvinus' restaurant, the 'Bistro Jardin' or 'Pub V'.
■ ACTIVITIES: Kempinski gallery.
■ TARIFF: (1996) Single 350–430, Double 430–510, Bk 29, Set menu 30–120 (Amex, Euro/Access, Visa).

Hungary

Danubius Hotel Aquincum ★★★★★
Arpad fejedelem utja 94, 1036 Budapest.
Tel 1 2503360, Fax 1 2504672. English spoken.

Open all year. 312 bedrooms (all en suite).
Indoor swimming pool, golf 20 km, garage,
parking. ☎ &

*Overlooking the river, an imposing spa hotel,
very comfortable with excellent facilities.
(Prices in DM.)*

■ RESTAURANT: International and Hungarian
cuisine. Vegetarian and diet menus also available.
■ ACTIVITIES: Hotel offers diagnostic
examinations, balneo, hydrotherapy,
mechanotherapy and electrotherapy.
■ TARIFF: Single 250–290, Double 290–340,
Set menu 35 (Amex, Euro/Access, Visa).

Hotel Mercure Buda ★★★★
Kirsztina krt 41-43, 1013 Budapest.
Tel 1 156 6333, Fax 1 155 6964. English spoken.

Open all year. 395 bedrooms (all en suite).
Indoor swimming pool, garage, parking. ☎

*Large, modern and well-equipped hotel. Easy
access to the city centre. Located in the
business area near the junctions of the M1 and
M7, to the west of the city. (Prices in DM.)*

■ RESTAURANT: Choice of 3 restaurants offering
national and international cuisine.
■ ACTIVITIES: Nightclub and disco.
■ TARIFF: Single 170, Double 170–220,

Set menu 25–40 (Amex, Euro/Access, Visa).
■ DISCOUNT: 10%

Normafa Hotel ★★★
Eötvös ut 52-54, 1121 Budapest.
Tel 1 156 3444, Fax 1 175 9583. English spoken.
Open all year. 70 bedrooms (all en suite).
Outdoor swimming pool, tennis, golf 10 km,
parking. ☎

*On the highest point of the Buda hills in a
picturesque oak forest. Only 15 minutes from
the town centre. (Prices in DM.)*

■ RESTAURANT: 'C'est la Vie' offers international
and Hungarian cuisine while the 'Normafa Grill'
and the 'Garden Restaurant' serve local dishes.
■ ACTIVITIES: Fitness centre, sauna, solarium and
massage at hotel; walking.
■ TARIFF: (1996) Single 60–116, Double 80–158,
Bk 8, Set menu 10–18 (Amex,
Euro/Access, Visa).

Danubius Thermal Hotel Margitsziget
★★★★ Margitsziget, 1138 Budapest.
Tel 1 311 1000, Fax 1 153 2753. English spoken.

Open all year. 206 bedrooms (all en suite).
Indoor swimming pool, tennis, golf 20 km,
garage, parking. ☎ &

*Located in the picturesque surroundings of
Margaret Island, in the capital's most beautiful
park, yet in the heart of the city. The therapy
section utilises the thermal springs and offers
balneo/physiotherapy. (Prices in DM.)*

■ RESTAURANT: Hungarian and international
gourmet delights as well as entertainment can
be enjoyed in the restaurant; dietetic menus are
also available. For something lighter, visit one
of the bars or coffee/pastry shop.
■ ACTIVITIES: Hotel's spa centre offers thermal
baths, fitness centre, pool complex with sauna,
solarium and sun terrace; tennis and jogging
track nearby. ● Free use of bicycles.
■ TARIFF: Single 220–260, Double 270–310,
Set menu 25–60 (Amex, Euro/Access, Visa).

Novotel Budapest Centrum ★★★★
Alkotas u 63-67, 1123 Budapest.
Tel 1 869 588, Fax 1 665 636. English spoken.

Open all year. 324 bedrooms (all en suite).
Indoor swimming pool, parking. ☏

Surrounded by picturesque parkland full of chestnut trees, the hotel is just a few minutes from the city centre and within easy reach of Lake Balaton and Vienna. Accommodation and breakfast are free for 2 children under the age of 16 sharing their parents' room. (Prices in DM.)

■ RESTAURANT: Three restaurants with terrace: the 'Karolina' specialises in Hungarian and international cuisine, the 'Bowling Brasserie' has beer specialities and the 'Piccolino Pizzeria' offers Italian food.
■ ACTIVITIES: 4 automatic bowling alleys; sauna, solarium and beauty salon; jogging in the park.
■ TARIFF: (1996) Single 150, Double 150–220, Set menu 23–35 (Amex, Euro/Access, Visa).

Panorama Hotel ★★★
Rege u 21, 1121 Budapest.
Tel 1 750 522, Fax 39 30 743. English spoken.
Open all year. 88 bedrooms (all en suite).
Outdoor swimming pool, parking.

Situated in the green belt in quiet surroundings. Fully equipped bungalows surrounded by giant fir trees are also available. The hotel is easily accessible by the cog railway. (Prices in DM.)

■ RESTAURANT: Typical home-made Hungarian cuisine; garden parties with barbecues; good selection of wines.
■ ACTIVITIES: Sauna, solarium; folk dancing show.
■ TARIFF: (1996) Single 65–115, Double 100–150, Set menu 12–23 (Amex, Euro/Access, Visa).
■ DISCOUNT: 10%

Danubius Thermal Hotel Helia ★★★★
Karpat u 62-64, 1133 Budapest.
Tel 1 270 3277, Fax 1 270 2262. English spoken.
Open all year. 262 bedrooms (all en suite).
Indoor swimming pool, tennis, golf 20 km. ♿

Centrally located on the banks of the River Danube, opposite Margaret Island. Fully equipped accommodation (including 4 suites with private sauna/bar), most with wonderful views of the river and Buda Hills. (Prices in DM.)

■ RESTAURANT: Enjoy live music, international cuisine and a wide range of delicious Hungarian pastries in the restaurant. Lighter meals can be taken in the 'Neptunas' café or poolside bar.
■ ACTIVITIES: First-class health and sports facilities. An ultra-modern unit offers diagnostic and therapeutic treatment by highly qualified, multi-lingual physicians.
■ TARIFF: Single 200–280, Double 240–320, Set menu 25 (Amex, Euro/Access, Visa).
■ DISCOUNT: 10%

Hotel Victoria ★★★★
Bem rakpart 11, 1011 Budapest.
Tel 1 201 8644, Fax 1 201 5816. English spoken.

Open all year. 27 bedrooms (all en suite).
Garage, parking.

Small, private, air-conditioned hotel, in the centre of Budapest with beautiful views of the Danube.

■ TARIFF: Single 12,600–16,650, Double 13,500–17,550 (Amex, Euro/Access, Visa).
■ DISCOUNT: 10%

Hungary

BÜK   23A

Danubius Thermal & Sport Hotel Bük
★★★★ 9740 Bük-Fürdd.
Tel 94 358 500, Fax 94 358 620. English spoken.

Open all year. 200 bedrooms (all en suite).
Indoor swimming pool, outdoor swimming
pool, tennis, golf on site, parking. &

*Modern and extremely comfortable, hotel offers
fully equipped accommodation including
rooms for non-smokers and the disabled. 25 km
from the Austrian border, Bük is one of the most
important spa's in Hungary. (Prices in DM.)*

■ RESTAURANT: Hungarian, international and
special diet menus in main restaurant; brasserie
with bowling alley.
■ ACTIVITIES: As well as a golf course, hotel has
superb sports/fitness facilities with indoor/
outdoor swimming pools, cycling, volley ball,
basket ball, indoor tennis courts and mini-golf.
■ TARIFF: Single 135–157, Double 190–226,
Set menu 14 (Amex, Euro/Access, Visa).

ESZTERGOM   23A

Oktav Hotel ★★
Wesselényi u 35-39, 2509 Esztergom.
Tel 33 311 755, Fax 33 313 640. English spoken.
Open all year. 55 bedrooms (all en suite).
Parking. ℂ

*Small hotel in the Danube Bend, right on the
border of Slovakia and 40 km from Budapest.*

■ RESTAURANT: Closed Sundays LS.
■ ACTIVITIES: Sauna at hotel; horse-riding and
pleasure flights available nearby.
■ TARIFF: (1996) Single 2500–2700,
Double 3000–3300, Bk 500 (Euro/Access).
■ DISCOUNT: 5%

HÉVÍZ   23C

Danubius Thermal Hotel Aqua ★★★★
Kossuth L u 13-15, 8380 Hévíz.
Tel 83 340 947, Fax 83 340 970. English spoken.

Open all year. 229 bedrooms (all en suite).
Outdoor swimming pool, garage, parking. &

*Modern, comfortable hotel beside Europe's
largest warm water lake. Good facilities
including rooms for the disabled. Hévíz is just
north of the south-western tip of Lake Balaton.
(Prices in DM.)*

■ RESTAURANT: Restaurant and brasserie offering
international and Hungarian cuisine plus
special vegetarian and dietary menus.
■ ACTIVITIES: Indoor thermal pool, sauna, table
tennis. Horse-riding and tennis nearby.
■ TARIFF: Single 78–142, Double 128–204,
Set menu 15 (Amex, Euro/Access, Visa).

Danubius Thermal Hotel Hévíz ★★★★
Kossuth L u 9-11, 8380 Hévíz.
Tel 83 341 180, Fax 83 340 666. English spoken.

Open all year. 203 bedrooms (all en suite).
Indoor swimming pool, tennis, parking. &

*Modern and comfortable, hotel is set in
woodland by Europe's largest warm water
lake. Fully equipped accommodation; excellent
service. To the north of the south-western tip of
Lake Balaton. (Prices in DM.)*

■ RESTAURANT: Restaurant and brasserie;
international and Hungarian cuisine with
special diet menus also available.

■ ACTIVITIES: Spa centre offers special therapy utilising the world-renowned thermal water of Hévíz; open-air gymnastics, fitness centre, sauna, solarium and cycling; horse-riding nearby.
■ TARIFF: Single 78–142, Double 128–204, Set menu 15 (Amex, Euro/Access, Visa).

KESZTHELY 23C

Danubius Hotel Helikon ★★★
Balatonpart 5, 8360 Keszthely.
Tel 83 311 330, Fax 83 315 403. English spoken.

Open all year. 232 bedrooms (all en suite).
Indoor swimming pool, tennis, parking. &

Modern, lakeside hotel offering top quality facilities for both business and holiday guests alike. Keszthely is a small, historic town at the foot of hills sloping down to Lake Balaton. (Prices in DM.)

■ RESTAURANT: Enjoy Hungarian and international dishes accompanied by music.
■ ACTIVITIES: Private sports centre; cycling and horse-riding by arrangement; beer cellar with bowling alley.
■ TARIFF: Single 53–122, Double 84–160, Set menu 12 (Amex, Euro/Access, Visa).

SÁRVÁR 23A

Danubius Thermal Hotel Sárvár ★★★★
Rakoczi ut 1, 9600 Sárvár.
Tel 95 323 999, Fax 95 320 406. English spoken.
Open all year. 136 bedrooms (all en suite).
Indoor swimming pool, outdoor swimming pool, golf 25 km, parking.

Set in picturesque surroundings in the King's Garden, close to the medieval Nádasdy Castle. Modern, attractive hotel with excellent facilities. (Prices in DM.)

■ RESTAURANT: International and Hungarian cuisine with vegetarian and special diet menus also available.
■ ACTIVITIES: Hotel offers thermal bath, solarium, sauna and fitness room. Arrangments can be made for horse-riding, horse-drawn carriage driving and tennis nearby.
■ TARIFF: Single 136, Double 190 (Amex, Euro/Access, Visa).

SOPRON 23A

Solar Club Hotel ★★★
Panorama St 16, 9400 Sopron.
Tel 99 311 675, Fax 99 311 675. English spoken.
Open all year. 104 bedrooms (all en suite).
Outdoor swimming pool, tennis, parking.

Hotel consists of two- or four-bedded self-catering apartments, all with well-equipped kitchenette and dining area. Sopron is near the Austrian border and only about 70 km from Vienna.

■ ACTIVITIES: Sailing courses and horse-riding.
■ TARIFF: Single 4000–5000, Double 6000–8000 (Amex, Euro/Access, Visa).
■ DISCOUNT: 10%

Hungary

ITALY

Florence

Italy is a land of contrasts, not the least of which is the affluence of the north and the poverty of the south, but other strong cultural, as well as geographic, distinctions exist between its twenty regions – Italy did not achieve unified nation status until 1861.

From Piemonte region in the Alps to Calabria region in the south, the country can be loosely divided into three areas: the north with the Alps and the wonderful Italian lakes nestling at their southern edge; second, the valley of the River Po, whose broad plain cuts right across the country from west to east and embraces most of Italy's industrial heartland; third the long, boot-shaped part of the country – Tuscany, Umbria, Lazio, Marche, Abruzzi, Molisse, Puglia and Basilicata – with the Apennines running down the centre of the 'leg' and Calabria forming the toe of the boot.

It need hardly be said that the great magnets are Rome, Florence and Venice. But these can be crowded, hot and tiring in summer, and are much more enjoyable to visit out of season. Getting to know Italy on a motoring holiday is a delightful experience, from the rugged terrain and fierce independence of Abruzzi facing the Adriatic due east of Rome, to the mountains of the Dolomites; from Roman Pompeii to Renaissance Florence, from the smart streets of Milan to the quiet attraction of a small village in the Apennines. The Italian people combine with the Italian countryside to make this one of Europe's most vivacious holiday destinations.

Emergency numbers

Police 113, Fire Brigade 115, and Ambulance 118

Warning information

Warning triangle must be carried

Green Card recommended

Blood alcohol legal limit 80 mg

ABANO TERME 20C

Hotel Due Torri ★★★★
Via Pietro d'Abano 18, 35031 Abano Terme.
Tel 0498 669277, Fax 0498 669927. English spoken.
Open 15/03 to 31/12. 80 bedrooms
(all en suite). Indoor swimming pool, outdoor
swimming pool, tennis, golf 5 km, parking.

*In town centre, fully air conditioned and
surrounded by own park-like setting. 50 km
from Venezia. Ideal place for relaxation and
the 'cure'.*

■ RESTAURANT: Specialises in Italian cuisine and
serves a splendid lunchtime buffet.
■ ACTIVITIES: Own spa centre with 2 thermal
swimming pools; beauty parlour.
■ TARIFF: Single 100,000, Double 150,000,
Bk 15,000, Set menu 45,000–50,000
(Amex, Euro/Access, Visa).
■ DISCOUNT: 10% B&B only.

ALASSIO 20C

Diana Grand Hotel ★★★★
Via Garibaldi 110, 17021 Alassio.
Tel 0182 642701, Fax 0182 640304. English spoken.

Open 24/12 to 20/11. 51 bedrooms
(all en suite). Indoor swimming pool,
golf 15 km, garage, parking. ☎

*Modern hotel overlooking the sea and its own
private beach. Comfortable, air-conditioned
accommodation, including 9 suites. Situated
in Alassio off the S1 south of Savona.*

■ RESTAURANT: Air-conditioned terrace restaurant,
overlooking the sea. Creative regional and
international cuisine with seafood specialities.
■ ACTIVITIES: Fitness centre, including
hydromassage, with coaching available for
adults and children. Buffet/barbecue evenings
with music on the terrace. ● Special rates for
golfing weeks from February to May.
■ TARIFF: Single 95,000–240,000,
Double 160,000–330,000, Set menu 35,000–
65,000 (Amex, Euro/Access, Visa).

Hotel Majestic ★★★
Via Leonardo da Vinci 300, 17021 Alassio.
Tel 0182 642721, Fax 0182 643032. English spoken.
Open 10/04 to 30/09. 77 bedrooms
(all en suite). Garage, parking, restaurant.

*Family-run hotel on the west side of Alassio, at
the corner of the promenade. Air-conditioned
rooms. Private beach.*

■ TARIFF: Single 50,000–80,000,
Double 90,000–150,000, Bk 5,000,
Set menu 20,000–30,000 (Visa).

ASSISI 21A

Hotel San Francesco ★★★
Via San Francesco 48, 06080 Assisi.
Tel 0758 12281, Fax 0758 16237. English spoken.
Open all year. 44 bedrooms (all en suite).
Outdoor swimming pool, tennis, golf 1 km,
parking. ♿

*Recently modernised hotel, opposite St Francis'
Basilica. Rooms have all comforts and overlook
the church and the plain of Umbria. Roof garden.*

■ RESTAURANT: Carefully prepared cuisine with
local specialities.
■ TARIFF: Single 175,000, Double 230,000,
Set menu 40,000–70,000 (Amex,
Euro/Access, Visa).

BARI 21B

Hotel Ambasciatori ★★★★
Via Omodeo 51, 70125 Bari.
Tel 0805 010077, Fax 0805 021678.
English spoken.
Open all year. 177 bedrooms (all en suite).
Outdoor swimming pool, garage, parking.

*Modern hotel designed to offer maximum
comfort. Excellent business/technological
facilities including a congress centre.*

■ RESTAURANT: Panoramic dining room with
international cuisine and regional specialities.
■ TARIFF: (1996) Single 150,000–205,000,
Double 230,000–275,000, Set menu 40,000–
55,000 (Amex, Euro/Access, Visa).

Italy

DISCOUNTS

*This RAC Guide could save you
money. Many hotels offer discounts
to guests who can show that they
have used the directory to select
their hotel. Make sure you have the
book with you when you check in.*

BORDIGHERA 20C

Grand Hotel del Mare ★★★★
Via Portico Della Punta 34, 18012 Bordighera.
Tel 0184 262201, Fax 0184 262394.
English spoken.

Open all year. 114 bedrooms (all en suite).
Outdoor swimming pool, tennis, golf 8 km,
garage, parking. &

*Superior hotel with well-appointed rooms,
balconies with sea view, outdoor salt-water
pool and private beach. Meeting facilities for
up to 180 with fax available on request. 2 km*

from Bordighera, 55 km from Nice airport
(France).

SEE ADVERTISEMENT

■ RESTAURANT: Closed Mon.
■ ACTIVITIES: Fitness centre.
■ TARIFF: (1996) Single 130,000–160,000,
Double 200,000–320,000, Bk 22,000,
Set menu 60,000–75,000 (Amex,
Euro/Access, Visa).
■ DISCOUNT: 10%

BRIXEN 20A

Hotel Dominik ★★★★
Giardini Rapp, 39042 Brixen.
Tel 0472 830144, Fax 0472 836554.
English spoken.
Open 05/04 to 08/01. 29 bedrooms
(all en suite). Indoor swimming pool, garage.

*A member of the 'Relais & Châteaux', this fine
hotel has a superb location and offers
traditional hospitality. Ask for the 'Dolomite'
package.*

■ RESTAURANT: Closed Tues except Aug.
Excellent cuisine and cellar.
■ ACTIVITIES: Sauna; tours and excursions from
the hotel, car tours to the Dolomites.
■ TARIFF: (1996) Single 150,000–190,000,
Double 220,000–380,000 (Amex,
Euro/Access, Visa).

BRUNICO 20A

Hotel Post ★★★ Graben 9, 39031 Brunico.
Tel 0474 555127, Fax 0474 551603.
English spoken.
Open all year. 54 bedrooms (45 en suite).
Parking.

*Situated in the middle of town, the hotel has
been family run since 1850.*

■ RESTAURANT: Closed Mon.
■ TARIFF: Single 78,000–97,000, Double 138,000–
166,000, Set menu 23,000– 30,000
(Euro/Access, Visa).
■ DISCOUNT: 5%

CANNOBIO 20B

Hotel Pironi ★★★
Via Marconi 35, Cannobio, 28052 Novara.
Tel 0323 70624, Fax 0323 72398.
English spoken.
Open 01/03 to 31/10. 12 bedrooms
(all en suite). Parking.

*Recently restored 15th-century house with very
comfortable accommodation. In the historic
centre of Cannobio.*

Italy

■ ACTIVITIES: ● Private park with swimming pool nearby, free for guests of hotel.
■ TARIFF: (1996) Single 90,000–100,000, Double 145,000–160,000 (Amex, Euro/Access, Visa).

CASERTA 21B

Novotel Caserta Sud ★★★★
SS Sannitica 87, 81020 Capodrise.
Tel 0823 826553, Fax 0823 827238.
English spoken.
Open all year. 126 bedrooms (all en suite).
Outdoor swimming pool. ℓ &

Large and comfortable with air-conditioned rooms. 2 km from the motorway exit Caserta-Sud and the town centre. Free for children up to 16 sharing their parents' room.

■ RESTAURANT: The restaurant 'La Terrazza' serves regional and national cuisine. Grills are a speciality.
■ ACTIVITIES: Ideal base for day trips to Pompei, Napoli, Vesuvius and Capri.
■ TARIFF: Single 185,000–210,000, Double 230,000–260,000 (Amex, Euro/Access, Visa).
■ DISCOUNT: 10%

CASTELLAMMARE DI STABIA 21B

Hotel La Sirenetta ★★★ Via de Gasperi 153,
80053 Castellammare di Stabia.
Tel 0818 706600, Fax 0818 726280.
English spoken.
Open all year. 36 bedrooms (all en suite).
Outdoor swimming pool, garage, parking. ℓ

A comfortable, very friendly hotel beside the sea.

■ RESTAURANT: Overlooks the sea and offers typical Italian as well as international cuisine. Specialities include lasagne, fish soups and home-made rum baba.
■ ACTIVITIES: Ideally situated for touring and sightseeing. Napoli, Capri, Amalfi and Vesuvius are all within easy reach and day trips are available to these as well as many other destinations.
■ TARIFF: (1996) Single 65,000, Double 65,000–90,000, Bk 8,000, Set menu 20,000–25,000 (Amex, Visa).
■ DISCOUNT: 10%

CASTELLINA IN CHIANTI 20C

Romantik Hotel Tenuta di Ricavo ★★★★
Loc Ricavo, 53011 Castellina in Chianti.
Tel 0577 740221, Fax 0577 741014. English spoken.
Open 01/05 to 30/11. 23 bedrooms (all en suite). Outdoor swimming pool, parking. ℓ

Very quiet location in what was once an entire hamlet with villa, farm cottages, barns and church. Well-restored houses in local golden stone and brick, with terracotta and stone roofs and surrounded by flowered gardens. Rooms overlook the wooded hills and some of them have terrace or large balcony. Discounts for long stays.

■ RESTAURANT: Closed Tues & Wed. Evening meals only. The restaurant 'La Pecora Nera' serves regional and international cuisine. Advance booking essential.
■ ACTIVITIES: Table tennis, fitness room. Way-marked walks around the hotel; horse-riding nearby; Chianti wine route vineyard visits can be arranged as well as visits to private gardens in Tuscany.
■ TARIFF: Double 270,000–440,000 (Euro/Access, Visa).

COMO 20B

Albergo Terminus ★★★★
Lungo Lario Trieste 14, 22100 Como.
Tel 0313 29111, Fax 0313 02550.
English spoken.
Open all year. 38 bedrooms (all en suite).
Golf 5 km, garage. &

Turn-of-the-century building, completely renovated and located in the heart of Como near the lake. Terrace with panoramic view.

■ RESTAURANT: Closed Tues. 'Bar delle Terme' offers Italian cuisine and snacks served on the terrace.
■ ACTIVITIES: Sauna, gymnasium.
■ TARIFF: Single 160,000–200,000, Double 190,000–290,000, Bk 24,000 (Amex, Euro/Access, Visa).

Hotel Villa Flori ★★★★
Via per Cernobbio 12, 22019 Como.
Tel 0315 73105, Fax 0315 70379. English spoken.
Open all year. 45 bedrooms (all en suite).
Golf 10 km, garage. &

Set in a beautiful private park, yet only a short distance from the town centre with a splendid view of Lake Como. The original portion of this intimate hotel was constructed in 1860. Each of the distinctively decorated guest rooms boasts a lake-view terrace. Private mooring for sailing and motor boats.

■ RESTAURANT: Closed Mon. Very popular with good à la carte menu.
■ TARIFF: (1996) Single 160,000–130,000, Double 190,000–290,000, Bk 24,000, Set menu 50,000–75,000 (Amex, Euro/Access, Visa).

Italy

DIANO MARINA   20C

Hotel Torino ★★★
Via Milano 42, 18013 Diano Marina.
Tel 0183 495106, Fax 0183 404602.
English spoken.

Open 09/01 to 31/10. 80 bedrooms
(all en suite). Outdoor swimming pool, garage,
parking, restaurant.

*Quietly situated in the centre of Diano Marina,
with its own well-equipped private beach.*

■ TARIFF: (1996) Single 60,000–80,000,
Double 90,000–130,000, Bk 10,000,
Set menu 25,000–45,000 (Visa).

DOMODOSSOLA   20A

Hotel Eurossola ★★★
Piazza Matteotti 36, 28037 Domodossola.
Tel 0324 481326, Fax 0324 248748.
English spoken.
Open all year. 23 bedrooms (all en suite).
Outdoor swimming pool, tennis, garage,
parking.

*A first-class hotel of recent construction with
all modern facilities.*

■ RESTAURANT: Enjoys a good reputation with
specialities including gnocchi, seafood and
risotto ai funghi.
■ TARIFF: (1996) Single 80,000, Double 110,000,
Set menu 22,000–25,000 (Amex, Euro/Access,
Visa).

ELBA

PORTOFERRAIO   21A

Hotel Paradiso ★★★ Viticcio,
57037 Portoferraio, Elba.
Tel 0565 939034, Fax 0565 939041. English spoken.
Open 15/05 to 04/10. 38 bedrooms
(all en suite). Outdoor swimming pool, tennis,
golf 10 km, parking.

*About 5 km from town, the hotel is composed of
9 buildings, has an English owner and
occupies a quiet position overlooking the sea.
Modern facilities, informal, relaxing
atmosphere and lovely sunsets. The nearest
airport is Pisa (with connections to Elba); by
car, a 1-hour crossing from Piombino Port.*

■ RESTAURANT: Closed Thurs to non-residents.
Specialises in seafood and grills.
■ ACTIVITIES: Beach. ● Special prices for hotel
guests at nearby diving school.
■ TARIFF: Single 70,000–110,000,
Double 75,000–190,000, Bk 20,000,
Set menu 30,000–45,000 (No credit cards).
■ DISCOUNT: 10%

PROCCHIO   21A

Hotel Desiree ★★★★
Loc Spartaia, 57030 Procchio, Elba.
Tel 0565 907311, Fax 0565 907884.
English spoken.

Open 01/04 to 31/10. 69 bedrooms
(all en suite). Outdoor swimming pool, tennis,
golf 16 km, parking, restaurant. &

*Well-equipped seaside hotel with its own
private beach. Located in a green valley, 3 km
from the airport.*

■ ACTIVITIES: ● Special rate for green fees at
Acquabona Golf Club.
■ TARIFF: (1996) Single 90,000–180,000,
Double 120,000–240,000 (Amex,
Euro/Access, Visa).
■ DISCOUNT: 5%

END OF ELBA HOTELS

FERRARA   20C

Hotel Ripagrande ★★★★
Via Ripagrande 21, 44100 Ferrara.
Tel 0532 765250, Fax 0532 764377.
English spoken.

Open all year. 40 bedrooms (all en suite).
Garage, parking.

*Exceptional hotel, in one of the many
Renaissance palaces in town. Stylish entrance
hall made of the same brick used for most of
the famous monuments in Ferrara, with
marble columns reclaimed from Yugoslavian
ruins. Children under 9 free of charge. 30%
discount for newly-weds for minimum 3
nights' stay. Daytime playroom for children up
to the age of 6.*

■ RESTAURANT: Closed Aug & Mon all year. Local
cuisine served in original and quiet
atmosphere.
■ TARIFF: (1996) Single 190,000–230,000,
Double 250,000–300,000,
Set menu 35,000–55,000 (Amex,
Euro/Access, Visa).
■ DISCOUNT: 20% July & Aug only.

FIESOLE   20C

Albergo Villa Bonelli ★★★
Via Poeti 1, 50014 Fiesole.
Tel 0555 9513/98941, Fax 0555 98942.
English spoken.
Open 01/04 to 31/10. 20 bedrooms
(all en suite). Golf 7 km, garage.

*A family-run hotel in this old Etruscan village,
surrounded by a magnificent landscape and
with every modern convenience. Only
15 minutes from Firenze.*

■ RESTAURANT: Closed 01/11 to 30/03. Overlooks
the Florentine valley and offers typical Tuscan
cuisine.
■ TARIFF: Single 100,000–125,000,
Double 150,000–195,000,
Set menu 35,000–45,000 (Euro/Access, Visa).
■ DISCOUNT: 5%

FINALE LIGURE   20C

Hotel Punta Est ★★★★ Via Aurelia 1,
17024 Finale Ligure, Savona.
Tel 0196 00611, Fax 0196 00611.
English spoken.

Open 01/05 to 30/09. 40 bedrooms
(all en suite). Outdoor swimming pool, tennis,
golf 25 km, parking, restaurant.

*East of the historic town, hotel has been
converted from an 18th-century villa and
overlooks the sea. Cool, elegant interior; lovely
views from terraces and pool; American bar in
a natural cave.*

■ TARIFF: (1996) Single 240,000,
Double 300,000–400,000, Bk 20,000,
Set menu 50,000–75,000 (Amex,
Euro/Access, Visa).

FIRENZE (FLORENCE) 20C

Hotel Adriatico ★★★★
Via M Finiguerra 9, 50123 Firenze.
Tel 055 2381781, Fax 055 289661.
English spoken.
Open all year. 114 bedrooms (all en suite).
Parking. ✆

A modern hotel, centrally located and recently refurbished. Very comfortable accommodation with good facilities including its own private car park (free to hotel guests). Welcome drink on arrival for guests showing this guide.

■ RESTAURANT: 'La Vela' offers excellent value-for-money Italian cuisine with regional specialities.
■ ACTIVITIES: Ideally situated for sightseeing and shopping. ● Free use of nearby gymnasium for RAC guests staying at hotel.
■ TARIFF: Single 240,000–290,000, Double 320,000–370,000, Set menu 30,000–40,000 (Amex, Euro/Access, Visa).

Anglo American Hotel ★★★★
Via Garibaldi 9, 50123 Firenze.
Tel 0552 82114, Fax 0552 68513.
English spoken.
Open all year. 107 bedrooms (all en suite).
Golf 12 km. ✆

Quietly situated near the opera and just 5 minutes' walk from the historic centre and shopping area. Conference facilities.

■ RESTAURANT: 'Regina' offers Mediterranean and Italian specialities.
■ TARIFF: Single 310,000, Double 430,000, Set menu 55,000–80,000 (Amex, Euro/Access, Visa).
■ DISCOUNT: 10% on presentation of RAC membership card.

Albergo Croce di Malta ★★★★
Via della Scala 7, 50123 Firenze.
Tel 0552 18351, Fax 0555 287121. English spoken.

Open all year. 98 bedrooms (all en suite).
Outdoor swimming pool, golf 10 km. ♿

A fully restored, converted convent, hotel is in the historic and commercial centre of town.

■ RESTAURANT: Closed Sun & Mon lunch.
■ ACTIVITIES: ● Free entry to the nearby fitness centre and gymnasium.
■ TARIFF: Single 170,000–280,000, Double 240,000–390,000, Set menu 45,000– 75,000 (Amex, Euro/Access, Visa).
■ DISCOUNT: 10%

Hotel Nord Florence ★★★★
Via F Baracca 199A, 50127 Firenze.
Tel 0554 31151, Fax 0554 31202.
English spoken.
Open all year. 73 bedrooms (all en suite).
Parking. ♿

Conveniently situated close to the main road and Vespucci Airport but only 10 minutes' drive to the centre of Firenze. Fully equipped rooms.

■ RESTAURANT: Regional specialities.
■ ACTIVITIES: Sauna and fitness centre.
■ TARIFF: Single 150,000, Double 200,000, Set menu 30,000–45,000 (Amex, Euro/Access, Visa).
■ DISCOUNT: 10%

Hotel Plaza Lucchesi ★★★★ Lungarno della,
Zecca Vecchia 38, 50122 Firenze.
Tel 55 26236, Fax 55 2480921. English spoken.
Open all year. 97 bedrooms (all en suite).
Golf, garage.

In the city centre, close to the Church of Santa Croce and Ponte Vecchio, the hotel overlooks the Arno river. Some rooms have a balcony, some are duplex suites and all have air conditioning. American bar, piano bar.

■ RESTAURANT: Closed Sun.
■ ACTIVITIES: Hotel will make reservations for nearby horse-riding, tennis, health club, squash and swimming pool.
■ TARIFF: (1996) Single 310,000, Double 440,000 (Amex, Euro/Access, Visa).

Hotel Select ★★★
Via G Falliano 24, 50144 Firenze.
Tel 0553 30342, Fax 0553 51506.
English spoken.
Open all year. 38 bedrooms (all en suite).

A carefully renovated 19th-century villa near the main thoroughfares of Firenze. Bright, comfortable rooms with cherry-wood furniture, lots of antiques, frescoes, fine carpets and marble. Offers complimentary drinks and tit-bits at the bar.

Italy

■ ACTIVITIES: All that Firenze has to offer.
■ TARIFF: Single 110,000–170,000,
Double 150,000–250,000 (Amex,
Euro/Access, Visa).
■ DISCOUNT: 10% double room, HS rate.

Hotel Touring ★★★ Via Baccio da Montelupo,
Casellina, 50018 Firenze.
Tel 0557 53938, Fax 0557 55556.
English spoken.
Open all year. 28 bedrooms (all en suite).
Parking. &

*On the outskirts of the city, close to the
motorway (Firenze-Signa exit). All rooms have
modern facilities.*

■ RESTAURANT: Typical Tuscan cuisine.
■ ACTIVITIES: Guided tours of Chianti, Tuscany
and Firenze.
■ TARIFF: Single 100,000, Double 140,000,
Bk 10,000, Set menu 20,000–30,000
(Amex, Euro/Access, Visa).
■ DISCOUNT: 10%

Hotel Villa Le Rondini ★★★★ Via Bolognese
Vecchia 224, Trespiano, 50139 Firenze.
Tel 055 400081, Fax 055 268212.
English spoken.
Open all year. 43 bedrooms (all en suite).
Outdoor swimming pool, tennis, golf 15 km,
parking. & &

*Set in 22 ha of parkland, hotel comprises 4
fully-equipped luxury villas, all rooms with air
conditioning. Hotel has good conference/
banqueting facilities and its own helipad.
Trespiano is on route 65 approx 7 km north of
Firenze.*

■ RESTAURANT: Italian cuisine with regional
specialities.
■ ACTIVITIES: Good sports facilities including
sauna. Ideal base for sightseeing trips.
■ TARIFF: Single 145,000–240,000,
Double 220,000–270,000, Set menu 45,000–
90,000 (Amex, Euro/Access, Visa).
■ DISCOUNT: 15%

FORTE DEI MARMI   20C

Hotel Raffaelli Park ★★★★
Via Massini 37, 55042 Forte dei Marmi.
Tel 0584 787294, Fax 0584 787418.
English spoken.
Open all year. 28 bedrooms (all en suite).
Outdoor swimming pool, tennis, golf 1 km,
parking.

*A Best Western hotel, surrounded by a pretty
garden and with its own private beach. Very
comfortable accommodation. West of Lucca off
the A11/A12.*

■ RESTAURANT: Attractive restaurant offering
regional and international cuisine with seafood
specialities.
■ ACTIVITIES: Fitness room at hotel. Lots of sports
facilities nearby. Ideal location for sightseeing
and visits to Lucca, Pisa and Firenze.
● Discount at local golf course; free tennis LS
and discount given in HS.
■ TARIFF: (1996) Single 130,000–220,000,
Double 200,000–360,000,
Set menu 40,000– 60,000 (Amex,
Euro/Access, Visa).
■ DISCOUNT: 10% LS.

Hotel Raffaelli Villa Angela ★★★
Via Mazzini 64, 55042 Forte dei Marmi.
Tel 0584 787472, Fax 0584 787115.
English spoken.
Open 01/04 to 10/10. bedrooms. Outdoor
swimming pool, tennis, golf 1 km,
parking. &

*Old villa surrounded by a park, with very
comfortable rooms. West of Lucca off the
A11/A12.*

■ RESTAURANT: Regional and international
cuisine with seafood specialities.
■ ACTIVITIES: Fitness room; sailing, private
beach. Good location for sightseeing and visits
to Lucca, Pisa and Firenze. ● Discount at
local golf course; free tennis in LS and
discount in HS.
■ TARIFF: (1996) Single 90,000–150,000,
Double 160,000–260,000,
Set menu 40,000– 60,000 (Amex,
Euro/Access, Visa).
■ DISCOUNT: 10% LS.

GARDONE RIVIERA   20B

Grand Hotel ★★★★ Via Zanardelli 72,
25083 Gardone Riviera.
Tel 0365 20261, Fax 0365 22695.
English spoken.
Open 26/03 to 18/10. 180 bedrooms
(all en suite). Outdoor swimming pool,
golf 10 km, garage, parking, restaurant.

*Built at the end of the last century, hotel has
been completely modernised and offers
comfort and good amenities. North of
Desenzano on the lakeside.*

■ ACTIVITIES: Private lakeside promenade and
motor boat jetty; tennis 300 m.
■ TARIFF: Single 150,000–190,000,
Double 250,000–320,000,
Set menu 55,000–65,000 (Amex,
Euro/Access, Visa).

Italy

IMPERIA-PORTO MAURIZIO 20C

Hotel Miramare ★★★★ Viale Matteotti 24,
18100 Imperia Porto Maurizio.
Tel 0183 667120, Fax 0183 60635.
Open all year. 22 bedrooms (all en suite).
Indoor swimming pool, golf 20 km, garage,
parking. &

*Completely renovated 19th-century patrician
villa, surrounded by its own private park with
ancient trees. Centrally situated in a
residential district, 100 m from the sea and
with a marvellous view over the gulf. The air-
conditioned rooms are equipped with a small
kitchen area. Private beach.*

■ RESTAURANT: Ligurian specialities in the
panoramic restaurant.
■ TARIFF: Single 150,000–180,000,
Double 220,000–290,000, Bk 15,000
(Amex, Euro/Access, Visa).
■ DISCOUNT: 10%

Hotel Robinia ★★★
Via Pirinoli 14, 18100 Imperia.
Tel 0183 62720, Fax 0183 60635.
English spoken.
Open all year. 60 bedrooms (all en suite).
Outdoor swimming pool, golf 20 km, garage,
parking.

*Centrally situated, about 100 m from the
harbour and the sea. Fine views of the gulf.
Private beach.*

■ RESTAURANT: Closed 15/10 to 15/03. Light and
airy, restaurant offers a good choice of menus.
■ ACTIVITIES: Ideally located for exploring the
beautiful surrounding countryside. ● 20%
discount on sailing lessons with qualified
instructor for hotel guests.
■ TARIFF: (1996) Single 45,000–75,000,
Double 60,000–130,000, Bk 8,000,
Set menu 27,000–32,000 (Amex,
Euro/Access, Visa).
■ DISCOUNT: 10%

LIVORNO (LEGHORN) 20C

Grand Hotel Palazzo ★★★★
Via Italia 195, 57127 Livorno.
Tel 0586 805371, Fax 0586 803206.
English spoken.
Open all year. 105 bedrooms (all en suite).
Golf 12 km, parking. &

*Traditional 'grand' hotel overlooking the sea
and recently renovated. Close to the
commercial and historic centre of the town
with excellent facilities including air
conditioning. Free entry to beach with reserved
cabin opposite hotel.*

■ RESTAURANT: Regional and international
cuisine.
■ TARIFF: (1996) Single 170,000, Double 270,000
(Amex, Euro/Access, Visa).

LUCCA 20C

Hotel Peralta 55041 Lucca.
Tel 0584 951230, Fax 0584 951230.
English spoken.

Open 05/04 to 31/10. 10 bedrooms
(all en suite). Outdoor swimming pool, tennis,
golf 15 km, parking.

*Set in the hills in a small, private Tuscan
hamlet amidst olive groves and chestnut
woods. Sea views. From Genova to Livorno
motorway, exit Viareggio/Camaiore. From
Camaiore to Lucca road go towards Pieve and
hotel is 5 minutes.*

■ RESTAURANT: Home-made Tuscan dishes using
fresh produce with game in season. Meals can
also be taken on the terrace.
■ ACTIVITIES: Tennis 5 km; beautiful walks with
lots of wild flowers to discover; possibility of
painting/sculpture courses.

Italy

■ TARIFF: (1996) Single 70,000–100,000,
Double 120,000–150,000,
Set menu 25,000–40,000 (No credit cards).

MAIORI   21B

Hotel Il Pietra di Luna ★★★
Via G Capone 31, 84010 Maiori.
Tel 0898 77500, Fax 0898 77483.
English spoken.
Open 18/03 to 31/10. 96 bedrooms
(all en suite). Outdoor swimming pool, garage,
parking.

Modern building situated on Maiori beach.
Spacious rooms, good conference facilities.
Free parking and garage for the first night,
discount for long stays. Motorway exit Vietri
sul Mare.

■ RESTAURANT: Local and regional cuisine.
■ ACTIVITIES: Sauna and solarium.
■ TARIFF: Single 85,000–130,000,
Double 160,000–270,000,
Set menu 35,000–60,000 (Amex,
Euro/Access, Visa).
■ DISCOUNT: 5% except Aug.

MERANO   20A

Hotel Fragsburg ★★★★
Via Fragsburg 3, 39012 Merano/Meran.
Tel 0473 244071, Fax 0473 244493.
English spoken.

Open 10/04 to 03/11. 18 bedrooms
(all en suite). Outdoor swimming pool,
golf 15 km, garage, parking. ℂ ㋑

Once a hunting castle, this small hotel is
perched on a hilltop with stunning views over
valley and mountains, north of Bolzano. It
stands in a very peaceful park with tropical
trees and heated swimming pool.

■ RESTAURANT: Closed Mon. High quality
cuisine. Italian and Tyrolean specialities.
■ ACTIVITIES: Sauna, gymnasium, massage.

■ TARIFF: Single 100,000–140,000,
Double 180,000–250,000, Bk 25,000,
Set menu 35,000–70,000 (No credit cards).
■ DISCOUNT: 10% minimum 7-day stay.

Palace Hotel ★★★★★
Via Cavour 2-4, 39012 Merano/Meran.
Tel 0473 211300, Fax 0473 234181.
English spoken.

Open 01/02 to 15/11 & 20/12 to 10/01.
130 bedrooms (all en suite). Indoor swimming
pool, outdoor swimming pool, golf 15 km,
parking. ㋑
Modern comfort combined with tradition and
elegance in this luxury hotel.

■ RESTAURANT: Closed 20/06 to 20/07. Excellent
cuisine is served in the grill room.
■ ACTIVITIES: Spa, health, beauty and fitness
centre at the 'Espace Henri Chenot' offering
wide range of treatments.
■ TARIFF: Single 186,000–250,000,
Double 300,000–450,000, Set menu 70,000–
95,000 (Amex, Euro/Access, Visa).

MILANO (MILAN)   20C

Hotel Montini ★★★ Via G Di Vittorio 39,
20068 Peschiera Borromeo, Milano.
Tel 02 5475031, Fax 02 55300610.
English spoken.
Open 01/01 to 06/08 & 25/08 to 31/12.
51 bedrooms (all en suite). Golf 10 km,
parking. ℂ ㋑
Modern and comfortable with good facilities.
Just a few kilometres east of Milano and close
to Forlanini airport. ↘

■ RESTAURANT: Contemporary dining room with
international cuisine.
■ ACTIVITIES: Tennis and swimming pool 500 m
from hotel.
■ TARIFF: Single 157,000, Double 236,000
(Amex, Euro/Access, Visa).
■ DISCOUNT: 10% prior reservations only.

Italy

Novotel Milano Aeroporto ★★★★
Via Mecenate 121, 20138 Milano.
Tel 02 58011085, Fax 02 58011086.
English spoken.
Open all year. 206 bedrooms (all en suite).
Outdoor swimming pool, golf 8 km. ♨ ♿

*Large, modern hotel on 7 floors, with all the
facilities you would expect including
soundproofing, air conditioning and extensive
conference facilities. Large garden. Only 4 km
from Linate airport and close to Milano's east
ring road. Free shuttle bus to/from airport.
10% discount except during exhibition periods
and 30% discount in July and August on
double bedrooms.*

■ RESTAURANT: Offers traditional national and
international cuisine.
■ ACTIVITIES: Table tennis, piano bar;
jogging tracks.
■ TARIFF: (1996) Single 240,000–260,000,
Double 280,000–350,000,
Set menu 48,000–70,000 (Amex,
Euro/Access, Visa).

Novotel Nord Ca'Granda ★★★★
Viale Suzzani 13, 20162 Milano.
Tel 02 66101861, Fax 02 66101961.
English spoken.
Open all year. 172 bedrooms (all en suite).
Outdoor swimming pool, garage,
parking. ♨ ♿

*Large, modern hotel with soundproofing and
air conditioning. Excellent conference
facilities. 5 km from the town centre. Free
shuttle-bus to/from airport. Shuttle on request
to fairs.*

■ RESTAURANT: Traditional national and
international cuisine.
■ TARIFF: (1996) Single 215,000–260,000,
Double 260,000–300,000,
Set menu 43,000–65,000 (Amex,
Euro/Access, Visa).
■ DISCOUNT: 10% rising to 30% Jul/Aug except
during fairs/conventions.

Hotel Tiffany ★★★ Via L da Vinci 209,
20090 Trezzano San Naviglio.
Tel 02 48401178, Fax 02 4450944.
English spoken.
Open all year. 36 bedrooms (all en suite).
Parking.

Comfortable, modern hotel, 7 km from Milano.

■ RESTAURANT: Closed Aug. A la carte menu
specialising in French cuisine.
■ TARIFF: (1996) Single 95,000–100,000,
Double 120,000–130,000, Set menu 60,000
(Amex, Euro/Access, Visa).

MOLVENO   20A

Hotel du Lac ★★★
Via Nazionale 4, 38018 Molveno.
Tel 0461 586965. English spoken.
Open 01/06 to 30/09 & 20/12 to 06/01.
44 bedrooms (all en suite). Parking, restaurant.

*A family-run hotel set in matchless
surroundings of both lake and mountains.
Near the lakeside in Molveno, north of Trento
on the S421.*

■ TARIFF: (1996) Single 40,000–80,000,
Double 70,000–140,000, Set menu 20,000–
30,000 (Amex, Euro/Access, Visa).

MONTECATINI TERME   20C

Hotel Cappelli-Croce di Savoia ★★★
Viale Bicchieai 139, 51016 Montecatini Terme.
Tel 0572 71151, Fax 0527 71154.
English spoken.
Open 01/04 to 15/11. 73 bedrooms
(all en suite). Outdoor swimming pool,
golf 10 km, garage, parking.

*Conveniently located in the spa area, this
comfortable hotel has a lovely garden with
terrace and heated pool. Rooms are air
conditioned and tastefully furnished.*

■ RESTAURANT: Italian specialities and inventive
cuisine.
■ ACTIVITIES: Tennis nearby ● 40% discount at
Montecatini Golf Club.
■ TARIFF: (1996) Single 90,000–100,000,
Double 160,000–180,000, Set menu 30,000–
40,000 (Amex, Euro/Access, Visa).
■ DISCOUNT: 10%

Hotel Torretta II ★★★ Viale Bustichini 63,
51016 Montecatini Terme.
Tel 0572 70305, Fax 0572 70307.
English spoken.

Open 20/03 to 31/10. 63 bedrooms
(all en suite). Outdoor swimming pool, tennis,
golf 10 km, parking.

*Carefully managed, well-appointed,
comfortable hotel with modern facilities.*

■ RESTAURANT: Tuscan and Italian specialities.
Wide selection of wines.
■ ACTIVITIES: Tennis nearby. ● Guests at the
hotel enjoy a 30% discount at the Montecatini
Golf Club.
■ TARIFF: (1996) Single 90,000, Double 150,000,
Bk 15,000, Set menu 35,000 (Amex,
Euro/Access, Visa).

MONTEFALCO   21A

Villa Pambuffetti ★★★★
Via della Vittoria 20, 06036 Montefalco.
Tel 0742 378823, Fax 0742 379245.
English spoken.

Open all year. 15 bedrooms (all en suite).
Outdoor swimming pool, tennis, parking,
restaurant. &

*Elegant, secluded, quiet and friendly, in the
small hilltop town of Montefalco. South of
Foligno and Assisi on the S616.*

■ ACTIVITIES: Riding school 5 km.
■ TARIFF: (1996) Single 150,000,
Double 240,000–320,000, Set menu 50,000
(Amex, Euro/Access, Visa).
■ DISCOUNT: 15%

NAPOLI (NAPLES)   21B

Hotel Cavour ★★★
Piazza Garibaldi 32, 80142 Napoli.
Tel 0812 83122, Fax 0812 87488.
English spoken.
Open all year. 98 bedrooms (all en suite).
Golf 20 km, garage. ☎

*A comfortable, traditional hotel, elegantly
renovated. Situated close to the historic centre*

*of town and about 500 m from the new Napoli
'Directional Centre' which is directly linked to
the ring road, the central railway and the
Napoli/Vesuvius/Sorrento railway.*

■ RESTAURANT: 30s-style restaurant with good
atmosphere and fish and pasta specialities.
■ ACTIVITIES: Hotel can arrange excursions and
sightseeing tours. ● Free sightseeing tours to
Napoli.
■ TARIFF: (1996) Single 100,000–138,000,
Double 120,000–190,000,
Set menu 30,000–60,000
(Amex, Euro/Access, Visa).

ORTA SAN GIULIO   20B

Hotel San Rocco ★★★★
Via Gippini 11, 28016 Orta San Giulio.
Tel 0322 911977, Fax 0322 911964.
English spoken.

Open all year. 74 bedrooms (all en suite).
Outdoor swimming pool, tennis, golf 20 km,
garage, parking. &

*A former convent dating back to the 17th
century, now a stylish, well-equipped hotel.
Ideally and quietly situated in centre of town
and close to Lake Orta.*

■ RESTAURANT: Elegant dining rooms with view
of San Giulio island. Regional and international
cuisine offering fish and many other
specialities.
■ ACTIVITIES: Concerts on the terrace in summer;
water sports, diving and excursions.
■ TARIFF: (1996) Single 170,000–230,000,
Double 240,000–380,000,
Set menu 60,000–80,000
(Amex, Euro/Access, Visa).

Italy

ORVIETO 21A

La Casella ★★★ Antico Feudo di Campagna, 05016 Ficulle, Terni.
Tel 0763 86684/075, Fax 0763 86684.
English spoken.

Open 01/01 to 08/01 & 05/03 to 31/12.
32 bedrooms (all en suite). Outdoor swimming pool, tennis, parking. ☎

In a beautiful green valley, the hotel consists of a group of 4 comfortable houses, all rooms having en-suite facilities. Meals are served in the main house. Halfway between Roma and Firenze on the A1 motorway, take Fabro exit and go left towards Parrano. After 7 km turn right at sign for 'La Casella' and then travel along 6 km of country road. (Please contact hotel for detailed prices.)

■ RESTAURANT: Regional cuisine with creative specialities.
■ ACTIVITIES: Horse-riding for beginners and experts with qualified instructors (300 m from the main building, and run by the hotel), mountain-biking, table tennis, billiards.
■ TARIFF: (1996) Single 80,000–90,000, Double 120,000–140,000, Set menu 30,000–40,000 (Amex, Euro/Access, Visa).
■ DISCOUNT: 15%

PADOVA (PADUA) 20C

Hotel Le Calandre ★★★
Via Liguria 1, 35030 Sarmeola di Rubano.
Tel 0496 35200, Fax 0496 33026.
English spoken.
Open 06/01 to 24/12. 35 bedrooms (all en suite). Golf 5 km, garage, parking.

Modern hotel, 5 km from the centre of Padova.

■ TARIFF: Single 105,000, Double 142,000, Bk 13,000 (Amex, Euro/Access, Visa).

PAESTUM 21B

Hotel Calypso II ★★★ Via Molina Mare 63, 84063 Paestum.

Tel 0828 811031. English spoken.
Open all year. 30 bedrooms (all en suite).
Golf 5 km, garage, parking. ☎

Surrounded by a pine forest, the hotel has a family atmosphere and its own private beach.

■ RESTAURANT: Closed May. Traditional cuisine with Mediterranean specialities: spaghetti à la 'Calypso', fish soup and oven-cooked pasta.
■ ACTIVITIES: Water sports, sailing and windsurfing school nearby.
■ TARIFF: (1996) Single 50,000, Double 55,000–80,000, Set menu 25,000–30,000 (Visa).

PERUGIA 20C

Hotel La Rosetta ★★★★
Piazza Italia 19, 06121 Perugia.
Tel 0755 720841, Fax 0755 720841. English spoken.
Open all year. 96 bedrooms (all en suite).
Garage.

In the town centre, a hotel that believes in old-fashioned service and courtesy.

■ RESTAURANT: Famous restaurant offering both regional and international dishes. 15% discount on à la carte menu for RAC members.
■ ACTIVITIES: Within easy reach of monuments and museums.
■ TARIFF: Single 95,000–120,000, Double 195,000–240,000, Set menu 36,000–75,000 (Amex, Euro/Access, Visa).

Hotel Tiferno ★★★★
Piazza R Sanzio 13, 06012 Citta di Castello.
Tel 0758 550331, Fax 0758 521196. English spoken.
Open all year. 38 bedrooms (all en suite).
Garage, parking.

Former convent, sympathetically renovated with fully equipped accommodation. The combination of whitewashed walls, elegant but comfortable furniture and modern paintings by a local artist (Alberto Burri) create a stunning effect. About 25 minutes' drive north from Perugia and 90 minutes from Firenze or Siena.

■ RESTAURANT: Closed Mon. International and Umbrian cuisine.
■ TARIFF: Single 95,000–110,000, Double 150,000–180,000, Set menu 35,000–50,000 (Amex, Euro/Access, Visa).
■ DISCOUNT: 10%

PISA 20C

Hotel Granduca ★★★ Via Statale del Brennero 13, 56017 San Giuliano Terme.
Tel 050 814111, Fax 050 818811. English spoken.
Open all year. 176 bedrooms (all en suite).
Tennis, parking. ☎ ♿

Italy

On the east side of Pisa, 5 km from the Leaning Tower and 8 km from Lucca, the new 'pearl of Tuscany'. The air-conditioned, fully equipped rooms have facilities for the disabled and face the hills.

■ RESTAURANT: Tuscan specialities.
■ ACTIVITIES: Swimming pool nearby.
■ TARIFF: Single 90,000–110,000, Double 120,000–150,000, Set menu 30,000–40,000 (Amex, Euro/Access, Visa).

POSITANO   21B

Hotel Poseidon ★★★★
Via Pasitea, 84017 Positano.
Tel 0898 11111, Fax 0898 75833.
English spoken.
Open 25/03 to 30/11. 50 bedrooms (all en suite).
Outdoor swimming pool, garage, parking.

Originally a private villa, this charming hotel is surrounded by beautiful gardens and terraces. Centrally located, it's only a 10-minute walk to the beach, 1 hour's drive from Naples or a 90-minute drive from Salerno along the spectacular Amalfi coastline.

■ RESTAURANT: Indoor and outdoor restaurants, the latter attractively situated under a pergola of wisteria. Excellent local cuisine. Open to the public.
■ ACTIVITIES: Boat trips can be arranged.
● Special rates for hotel guests at the small health and fitness centre, consisting of gym, sauna, jacuzzi and qualified masseuse.
■ TARIFF: (1996) Single 230,000–310,000, Double 250,000–370,000, Set menu 60,000 (Amex, Euro/Access, Visa).

Hotel Tramonto d'Oro ★★★ Via G
Capriglione 119, 84010 Praiano.
Tel 089 874008, Fax 089 874670.
English spoken.
Open all year. 40 bedrooms (all en suite).
Outdoor swimming pool, parking.

Situated in a beautiful position overlooking the sea. Hotel has a lift and very good parking facilities.

■ RESTAURANT: Closed LS. Dining room has view over 'Faraglioni di Capri'. Mediterranean cuisine with typical regional dishes and fresh fish specialities.
■ ACTIVITIES: Sauna; free mini-bus transport to 'Praia' beach.
■ TARIFF: (1996) Single 60,000–130,000, Double 100,000–180,000, Set menu 30,000–50,000 (Amex, Euro/Access, Visa).
■ DISCOUNT: 10% except Aug.

RAPALLO   20C

Eurotel Rapallo 1 ★★★★
Via Aurelia Ponente 22, 16035 Rapallo.
Tel 0185 60981, Fax 0185 50635. English spoken.
Open all year. 64 bedrooms (all en suite).
Outdoor swimming pool, golf 1 km, garage, parking, restaurant. ✆

Overlooks the gulf, in a quiet area 500 m from the town centre. All rooms have balcony and sea view. 1 km from the Rapallo exit of A12.

■ ACTIVITIES: Boat trips; mini-golf, clay-pigeon shooting, scuba-diving lessons with instructors.
● Special discount on green fees.
■ TARIFF: (1996) Single 120,000–150,000, Double 190,000–230,000, Set menu 58,000 (Amex, Euro/Access, Visa).
■ DISCOUNT: 10%

RAVELLO   21B

Hotel Giordano & Villa Maria ★★★★
Via San Chiara 2, 84010 Ravello.
Tel 0898 57255, Fax 0898 57071. English spoken.

Open all year. 17 bedrooms (all en suite).
Outdoor swimming pool, parking.

Actually two separate, luxurious establishments, owned and run by the same family. Guests can enjoy all the amenities and services of both. Lovely gardens and panoramic views over the sea. Superb location.

■ RESTAURANT: Closed Mon. Well-known restaurant with gourmet cuisine. Specialities include spinach and cheese pancakes and fresh grilled fish with lemon.
■ ACTIVITIES: Solarium, hydro-massage, music room, dances.
■ TARIFF: (1996) Single 100,000–130,000, Double 170,000–210,000, Set menu 35,000– 50,000 (Amex, Euro/Access, Visa).

Italy

Hotel Santa Caterina ★★★★★
Via Nazionale 9 Amalfi.
Tel 089 871012, Fax 089 871351.
English spoken.
Open all year. 70 bedrooms (all en suite).
Outdoor swimming pool, garage, parking. ☎

*Built in the 1900s and family run since then.
Hotel is on the breathtaking Amalfi coastline
surrounded by terraces and gardens. Air
conditioning and lift to the private beach and
swimming pool. 6 km from Ravello.*

■ RESTAURANT: Two restaurants with panoramic
views. Regional cuisine and specialities
including grilled fish, lemon profiteroles,
chocolate and lemon soufflé.
■ TARIFF: Single 290,000–350,000,
Double 390,000–540,000, Set menu 70,000–
85,000 (Amex, Euro/Access, Visa).
■ DISCOUNT: 10%

RESIA (RESCHEN)   20A

Hotel Etschquelle ★★★
Val Venosta, 39027 Resia.
Tel 0473 633125, Fax 0473 633071.
English spoken.
Open 01/01 to 31/05 & 01/07 to 31/12.
23 bedrooms (all en suite). Golf 30 km,
parking. ☎

*Intimate and cordial atmosphere in a family-
run chalet-hotel. Set in the mountains with
both summer and winter activities.*

■ RESTAURANT: Choose from local Italian or
international cuisine in the restaurant, or enjoy
a pizza in the 'Liberty Pub'.
■ ACTIVITIES: Bowling, sauna, solarium,
mountain sports.
■ TARIFF: Single 44,000–70,000,
Double 68,000–110,000, Set menu 20,000
(Amex, Euro/Access, Visa).
■ DISCOUNT: 10%

RICCIONE   20C

Hotel Abner's ★★★★ Lungomare della
Repubblica, 47036 Riccione.
Tel 0541 600601, Fax 0541 605400.
English spoken.
Open all year. 60 bedrooms (all en suite).
Outdoor swimming pool, tennis, golf 14 km,
parking.

*Set on the promenade in the centre of town,
this luxury hotel is very much appreciated for
its superb location. It has every modern facility
including rooms with balcony and sea views.*

■ RESTAURANT: 'La Mer' restaurant offers
excellent cuisine with Italian fish specialities;

hot and cold buffet in the garden at lunchtimes.
■ TARIFF: Single 105,000–175,000,
Double 160,000–280,000, Bk 20,000,
Set menu 39,000–65,000
(Amex, Euro/Access, Visa).
■ DISCOUNT: 10% B&B basis.

Hotel Nevada ★★★
Via Milano 54, 47036 Riccione.
Tel 0541 601245, Fax 0541 606514.
English spoken.
Open 01/03 to 30/09. 48 bedrooms
(all en suite). Golf 1 km, parking, restaurant.

*Modern hotel, central position, near the sea.
South of Rimini on S16.*

■ TARIFF: (1996) Single 50,000–85,000,
Double 50,000–85,000,
Set menu 30,000–40,000 (No credit cards).

Hotel Vienna Touring ★★★★
Viale Milano 78C, 47036 Riccione.
Tel 0541 601700, Fax 0541 601762.
English spoken.
Open 01/05 to 30/09. 85 bedrooms
(all en suite). Outdoor swimming pool, tennis,
golf 14 km, parking.

*Hotel has very good facilities and is set in
private gardens, just 75 m from the beach.*

■ RESTAURANT: Italian and international cuisine,
with regional and seafood specialities. Kosher
dishes, prepared under the supervision of a
Rabbi, on request. If desired, lunch served
beside the swimming pool in fine weather.
■ ACTIVITIES: Sauna and fitness centre at hotel.
Comprehensive evening entertainment
programme throughout the summer season.
■ TARIFF: (1996) Single 100,000–140,000,
Double 150,000–250,000, Bk 20,000, Set
menu 35,000–60,000 (Amex, Euro/Access, Visa).
■ DISCOUNT: 10% B&B basis.

RIVA DEL GARDA   20B

Hotel Astoria ★★★
Viale Trento 9, 38066 Riva del Garda.
Tel 0464 552658, Fax 0464 521222.
English spoken.
Open 01/04 to 10/10. 94 bedrooms (all en
suite). Outdoor swimming pool, parking.

*Attractive hotel set in its own park-like
grounds.*

■ RESTAURANT: The pretty dining room has
lovely views of the garden. Specialities: pasta
with walnut sauce, home-made rabbit
casalinga, veal with mushrooms and cream.
■ ACTIVITIES: Adjacent tennis and sports
complex; sailing and water sports nearby.

■ TARIFF: Single 75,000–100,000, Double 126,000–170,000, Set menu 28,000–40,000 (Amex, Euro/Access, Visa).

Hotel Europa ★★★
Piazza Catena 9, 38066 Riva del Garda.
Tel 0464 555433, Fax 0464 521777.
English spoken.
Open 01/04 to 31/10. 63 bedrooms (all en suite). Restaurant. &

In the centre of the old town and facing the port, this comfortable hotel is carefully and lovingly managed by the owners. Pretty terrace/restaurant with spectacular view of the lake.

■ TARIFF: (1996) Single 95,000–115,000, Double 160,000–200,000, Set menu 30,000–40,000 (Amex, Euro/Access, Visa).

Hotel Mirage ★★★
Viale Rovereto 97-99, 38066 Riva del Garda.
Tel 0464 552671, Fax 0464 553211.
English spoken.

Open 27/03 to 25/10. 55 bedrooms (all en suite). Outdoor swimming pool, garage, parking.

Newly built hotel 30 m from the lake and the private moorings of Porto San Nicolo, and 90 m from the beach. Enchanting views of the northern part of Lake Garda. All rooms have balcony and are air conditioned in high season.

■ RESTAURANT: As well as the normal service, a candlelit dinner is usually arranged once a week from June to September.
■ ACTIVITIES: All water sports, horse-riding, rock climbing, archery and cycling available nearby.

■ TARIFF: Single 80,000–105,000, Double 130,000–180,000, Set menu 28,000 (Amex, Euro/Access).
■ DISCOUNT: 10%

ROMA (ROME) 21A

Hotel Celio ★★★
Via dei SS Quattro 35C, 00184 Roma.
Tel 06 70495333, Fax 06 7096377.
English spoken.
Open all year. 10 bedrooms (all en suite).
Golf 3 km, garage.

Small hotel, more like a private house, situated 100 m from the Colosseum and the Roman Forum in an elegant part of the city. Nearby garage facilities.

■ TARIFF: (1996) Single 180,000–220,000, Double 195,000–250,000 (Amex, Euro/Access, Visa).
■ DISCOUNT: 10%

Hotel Lord Byron ★★★★★
Via G de Notaris 5, 00197 Roma.
Tel 06 3220404, Fax 06 3220405.
English spoken.
Open all year. 37 bedrooms (all en suite).
Garage, parking. ☎

Close to the Borghese Gardens, the hotel is conveniently located near the Via Veneto and many of Roma's greatest cultural attractions. Well-decorated rooms with fine views.

■ RESTAURANT: Closed 3 weeks in Aug. The 'Relais le Jardin' is an award-winning gourmet restaurant; specialises in creative Italian cuisine based on fresh, seasonal products.
■ TARIFF: Single 310,000–380,000, Double 380,000–580,000, Set menu 100,000– 140,000 (Amex, Euro/Access, Visa).

Hotel Mondial ★★★★
Via Torino 127, 00184 Roma.
Tel 06 472861, Fax 06 4824822.
English spoken.
Open all year. 78 bedrooms (all en suite).
Garage.

Located just off Via Nazionale, opposite the Opera House. Hotel was completely renovated in 1994 and is within walking distance of Via Veneto, St Mary Majors and the Colosseum. Easy access to both bus and underground transport. Chargeable garaging available.

■ TARIFF: Single 160,000–260,000, Double 228,000–360,000 (Amex, Euro/Access, Visa).
■ DISCOUNT: 10% except Easter weekend.

Italy

Hotel Piazza di Spagna ★★★
Via Mario de' Fiori 61, 00187 Rome.
Tel 06 6796412, Fax 06 6790654.
English spoken.
Open all year. 16 bedrooms (all en suite).
Golf 10 km. ☏

Recently completely renovated, hotel dates from the early 1800s and offers classical Italian style together with modern-day comforts. Just one block from the descending side of the Spanish Steps and within easy reach of subway and train station.

■ ACTIVITIES: Ideally situated for sightseeing.
■ TARIFF: Single 170,000–210,000,
Double 200,000–290,000 (No credit cards).
■ DISCOUNT: 10%

Hotel Pincio ★★★
Via di Capo le Case 50, 00187 Roma.
Tel 06 790758, Fax 06 791233. English spoken.

Open all year. 20 bedrooms (all en suite).
Conveniently situated near the Spanish Steps, a B&B hotel with a roof garden and air-conditioned rooms.

■ TARIFF: (1996) Single 80,000–145,000,
Double 100,000–195,000 (Amex, Euro/Access, Visa).

Hotel Raphaël ★★★★
Large Febo 2, 00186 Roma.
Tel 06 682831, Fax 06 6878993. English spoken.
Open all year. 73 bedrooms (all en suite).
Parking.

Ivy-clad, comfortable hotel in the heart of Roma and close to the Piazza Navona. A collection of ceramics by Pablo Picasso, as well as antiques and paintings, are displayed in the lobby. The Bramante roof garden overlooks the ancient city. Some of the rooms have a private terrace.

■ RESTAURANT: Closed Sun. The restaurant 'Relais Picasso' serves international cuisine and offers Mediterranean specialities.

■ ACTIVITIES: Fitness centre, horse-drawn carriage rides; concerts and cultural events.
● Excellent variety of tours organised by the hotel.
■ TARIFF: Single 310,000–385,000,
Double 475,000–555,000, Bk 31,000, ☏
Set menu 47,000–84,000 (Amex, Euro/Access, Visa).

Hotel Villa del Parco ★★★
Via Nomentana 110, 00161 Roma.
Tel 06 44237773, Fax 06 44237572.
English spoken.

Open all year. 23 bedrooms (all en suite).
Parking. ☏

Charming 19th-century villa close to the historic sites. Recently renovated, rooms have all modern comforts. Personal and refined family management.

■ TARIFF: Single 165,000–180,000,
Double 215,000–230,000
(Amex, Euro/Access, Visa).
■ DISCOUNT: 10%

SAN GIMIGNANO   20C

Hotel Relais Santa Chiara ★★★★
Via Matteotti 15, 53037 San Gimignano.
Tel 0577 940701, Fax 0577 942096.
English spoken.
Open 01/03 to 31/12. 41 bedrooms
(all en suite). Outdoor swimming pool,
golf 15 km, parking. ☏ &

Between Firenze and Siena, and just 10 minutes' walk from the historic centre of San Gimignano. The hotel overlooks the Tuscan countryside towards Volterra and is set in its own elegant surroundings. Light meals are available beside the pool in summer and breakfast is a large buffet.

■ ACTIVITIES: Tennis nearby; itineraries available for trekking excursions that depart from the hotel and pass through the lovely Tuscan countryside around San Gimignano.
■ TARIFF: Single 120,000–180,000, Double 180,000–295,000 (Amex, Euro/Access, Visa).
■ DISCOUNT: 10% minimum 4 nights HS.

SAN MAMETE   20B

Hotel Stella d'Italia ★★★
Piazza Roma 1, 22010 San Mamete.
Tel 0344 68139, Fax 0344 68729.
English spoken.
Open 01/04 to 06/10. 35 bedrooms (all en suite). Outdoor swimming pool, golf 15 km, garage.

From Lugano follow Gandria/St Moritz signs. The hotel is situated directly on the shores of Lake Lugano.

■ RESTAURANT: Meals served in garden on lake shore. Specialities: fresh pasta and fish from lake.
■ ACTIVITIES: Private lido.
■ TARIFF: Single 85,000, Double 145,000–175,000, Set menu 35,000–50,000 (Amex, Euro/Access, Visa).

SAN REMO   20C

Hotel Beau Rivage ★★★
Lungomare Trieste 49, 18038 San Remo.
Tel 0184 505026, Fax 0184 505026.
English spoken.
Open 15/12 to 31/10. 29 bedrooms (all en suite). Golf 1 km, restaurant.

Town centre, beach-front hotel with garden and balconies.

■ TARIFF: (1996) Single 35,000–70,000, Double 55,000–110,000, Bk 6,000, Set menu 25,000–30,000 (Euro/Access, Visa).

Royal Hotel ★★★★★
Corso Imperatrice 80, 18038 San Remo.
Tel 0184 5391, Fax 0184 661445. English spoken.
Open 20/12 to 05/10. 146 bedrooms (all en suite). Outdoor swimming pool, tennis, golf 8 km, garage, parking.

A 5-star luxury resort hotel, uniquely located on the charming Italian Riviera of Flowers, with a fine view of San Remo Bay. Close to the centre of the town in a quiet and spacious subtropical garden. The hotel combines exclusive atmosphere with comfort and good service. Penthouse floor with large terraces. 3 km from San Remo West or 10 km from San Remo East motorway exits.

SEE ADVERTISEMENT

■ RESTAURANT: A wide variety of Italian cuisine in 'Fiori di Murano' restaurant, or try delicious seafood dishes in the garden or poolside restaurants (open from June to September).
■ ACTIVITIES: Heated sea-water pool, sauna (from April to September), gym, mini-golf; sail/power boat trips and water sports nearby.
● Discount at local golf course and riding stables.
■ TARIFF: Single 175,000–305,000, Double 312,000–500,000, Set menu 92,000 (Amex, Euro/Access, Visa).

Italy

Hotel Paradiso ★★★
Via Roccasterone 12, 18038 San Remo.
Tel 0184 571211, Fax 0184 578176.
English spoken.

Open all year. 41 bedrooms (all en suite).
Golf 3 km, garage, parking.

*Situated in a quiet, verdant area just 100 m
from the sea and close to the town centre. Most
attractive, light and airy accommodation and
very pretty gardens.*

■ RESTAURANT: Verandah restaurant overlooking
the garden. Regional and national dishes.
■ ACTIVITIES: ● Hotel arranges a number of
discounted excursions and theatre/concert
trips.
■ TARIFF: (1996) Single 90,000–120,000,
Double 150,000–210,000, Set menu 23,000–
46,000 (Amex, Euro/Access, Visa).
■ DISCOUNT: 10% except Aug.

SANTA MARGHERITA LIGURE   20C

Hotel Continental ★★★★ Via Pagana 8,
16038 Santa Margherita Ligure.
Tel 0185 286512, Fax 0185 284463.
English spoken.
Open all year. 76 bedrooms (all en suite).
Golf 4 km, garage, parking. &

*Centrally situated, family-run hotel which has
recently been completely refurbished. Pretty
gardens, terraces, and splendid sea views.
Private beach with snack bar.*

■ RESTAURANT: Very good food in this light and
airy restaurant with verandah and terrace.
Surrounded by a large palm garden with
stunning views over the Gulf.
■ ACTIVITIES: Lots to see and do, both day and
night. Nearby water sports, horse-riding, boat
trips, tennis and clay-pigeon shooting.
■ TARIFF: Single 125,000–255,000,
Double 212,000–297,000, Set menu 48,000–
65,000 (Amex, Euro/Access, Visa).

Hotel Grand Miramare I ★★★★ Lungomare
Milite Ignoto 30, 16038 Santa Margherita Ligure.
Tel 0185 287013, Fax 0185 284651.
English spoken.

Open all year. 84 bedrooms (all en suite).
Outdoor swimming pool, golf 4 km, garage,
parking. &

*The hotel boasts panoramic views of the Italian
Riviera and a restful environment. Offers
friendly service and has its own private beach.
On the road to Portofino (S1) from Genova.*

■ RESTAURANT: A choice of restaurants, with
panoramic views over the bay. Regional and
international cuisine with seafood specialities.
■ ACTIVITIES: Guided tours of surrounding area;
water-skiing tuition.
■ TARIFF: Single 230,000–290,000,
Double 370,000–450,000, Set menu 80,000
(Amex, Euro/Access, Visa).

Hotel Laurin ★★★★ Lungomare G Marconi 3,
16038 Santa Margherita Ligure.
Tel 0185 289971, Fax 0185 285709. English spoken.
Open all year. 43 bedrooms (all en suite).
Golf 4 km.

*A modern hotel centrally located in this tourist
port. Large terraces overlooking sea. Fine views.
Restaurant 'San Giacomo' in the same building.*

■ ACTIVITIES: Within easy reach of water sports,
boat trips, tennis, horse-riding and clay-pigeon
shooting.
■ TARIFF: Single 109,000–150,000, Double 174,000–
230,000 (Amex, Euro/Access, Visa).

Hotel Metropole ★★★★ Via Pagana 2,
16038 Santa Margherita Ligure.
Tel 0185 286134, Fax 0185 283495. English spoken.
Open all year. 50 bedrooms (all en suite).
Golf 4 km, garage, parking.

*Set in large, beautiful gardens with terraces,
private beach and snack bar, the hotel is
managed personally by the owner. Only 5 km
from Portofino and 35 km from Genova on A12.*

Italy

- RESTAURANT: Tempting local dishes; seafood specialities.
- ACTIVITIES: Water sports, horse-riding and tennis nearby. ● Discount at nearby golf course.
- TARIFF: (1996) Single 120,000–150,000, Double 200,000–260,000, Set menu 50,000–60,000 (Amex, Euro/Access, Visa).

Hotel Regina Elena ★★★★ Lungomare Milite Ignoto 44, 16038 Santa Margherita Ligure. Tel 0185 287003, Fax 0185 284473. English spoken. Open all year. 100 bedrooms (all en suite). Golf 4 km, parking, restaurant.

A modern hotel on the picturesque coast road towards Portofino. Garden, bar and private beach.

- ACTIVITIES: Jacuzzi, solarium; within easy reach of water sports, boating, horse-riding, tennis and clay-pigeon shooting.
- TARIFF: Single 130,000–162,000, Double 232,000–280,000, Set menu 50,000–65,000 (Amex, Euro/Access, Visa).

SARONNO 20B

Albergo della Rotonda ★★★★ Via Novara 53, 21047 Saronno. Tel 0296 703232, Fax 0296 702770. English spoken. Open 08/01 to 31/07 & 26/08 to 23/12. 92 bedrooms (all en suite). Tennis, golf 18 km, garage, parking. ☎ ⅙

Modern hotel furnished in country house style and only 20 minutes from the centre of Milano and the Monza motordrome. Ideal for business conferences. Near motorway Milano/Como/Lugano.

- RESTAURANT: Closed Sat.
- TARIFF: (1996) Single 280,000, Double 350,000, Set menu 48,000 (Amex, Euro/Access, Visa).
- DISCOUNT: 10%

SAVIGLIANO 20C

Hotel Granbaita ★★★ Via Cuneo 25, 12038 Savigliano. Tel 0172 711500, Fax 0172 711518. English spoken. Open all year. 79 bedrooms (all en suite). Outdoor swimming pool, tennis, golf 12 km, garage, parking. ☎ ⅙

Modern hotel with fully equipped, comfortable rooms. Set in quiet grounds in centre of Piedmont region, only half an hour from Torino.

- RESTAURANT: Closed Sun eve. Regional cuisine; meals are served in the garden in summer.
- ACTIVITIES: ● Free bicycle tours in the surrounding countryside.

- TARIFF: Single 105,000, Double 130,000, Bk 15,000, Set menu 32,000 (Amex, Euro/Access, Visa).
- DISCOUNT: 10%

SESTRI LEVANTE 20C

Grand Hotel Villa Balbi ★★★★ Viale Rimembranza 1, 16039 Sestri Levante. Tel 185 42941, Fax 185 482459. English spoken.

Open 25/03 to 25/10. 95 bedrooms (all en suite). Outdoor swimming pool, golf 25 km. ☎

17th-century villa transformed into an elegant, luxury hotel complete with antique furniture, marble, fine tapestries and paintings. On the sea-front, with a private beach and surrounded by a park with century-old trees.

- RESTAURANT: Large dining room and open-air restaurant offering Italian and international cuisine.
- ACTIVITIES: Water sports.
- TARIFF: Single 110,000–170,000, Double 250,000–300,000, Set menu 65,000–75,000 (Amex, Euro/Access, Visa).
- DISCOUNT: 10%

Italy

SICILIA (SICILY)

PALERMO   21D

Villa Igiea Grand Hotel ★★★★★
Salita Belmonte 43, 90100 Palermo, Sicilia.
Tel 0915 43744, Fax 0915 47654.
English spoken.

Open all year. 117 bedrooms (all en suite).
Outdoor swimming pool, tennis, parking,
restaurant. &

*2 km from the city centre, a comfortable hotel
with grounds running down to the beach.*

■ TARIFF: (1996) Single 210,000,
Double 330,000, Set menu 65,000 (Amex,
Euro/Access, Visa).

END SICILIA (SICILY) HOTELS

SIENA   20C

Hotel Duomo ★★★
Via Stalloreggi 38, 53100 Siena.
Tel 0577 289088, Fax 0577 43043.
English spoken.

Open all year. 23 bedrooms (all en suite).

*Comfortable air-conditioned hotel in the heart
of medieval Siena. A 5-minute walk from the
Duomo, within easy reach of the shopping
centre and with fine views of the hills
surrounding Siena. Chargeable parking
nearby. Prior booking advisable.*

■ TARIFF: (1996) Single 90,000–130,000,
Double 120,000–200,000 (Amex,
Euro/Access, Visa).

Hotel La Locanda del Ponte ★★★★
Ponte a Macereto, 53015 Monticiano, Siena.
Tel 0577 757108, Fax 0577 757110.
English spoken.

Open all year. 23 bedrooms (all en suite).
Outdoor swimming pool, parking.

*Tastefully modernised former staging post,
dating from 1600. Surrounded by extensive
gardens and ancient woods plus its own
private beach on the River Merse. Rooms have
all modern facilities including air
conditioning.*

■ RESTAURANT: Closed Wed. Rustic but elegant
restaurant specialising in Tuscan cuisine.
■ ACTIVITIES: Nearby: tennis, horse-riding,
thermal swimming pool.
■ TARIFF: Single 99,000–195,000,
Double 250,000–380,000, Set menu 45,000–
85,000 (Amex, Euro/Access, Visa).
■ DISCOUNT: 15%

Hotel Podere Terreno
Radda in Chianti, 53017 Siena.
Tel 0577 738312, Fax 0577 738312.
English spoken.
Open all year. 7 bedrooms (all en suite).
Parking, restaurant.

*16th-century stone inn, an oasis among the
hills in true Chianti country. Guests join in to
make one big family. Prettily furnished rooms
and delightful living room with huge open*

fireplace where meals are served at a long wooden table. Prices shown are for half-board.

■ ACTIVITIES: Table tennis, billiards, walking; tennis 5 km; fishing in the nearby lake.
■ TARIFF: (1996) Single 140,000, Double 240,000, Set menu 50,000 (Amex, Euro/Access, Visa).

Hotel Villa Scacciapensieri ★★★★
Via Scacciapensieri 10, 53100 Siena.
Tel 0577 41441, Fax 0577 270854.
English spoken.

Open 15/03 to 15/11. 32 bedrooms (all en suite). Outdoor swimming pool, tennis, garage, parking. ☎ ♿
Family-run hotel 1.5 km north of Siena overlooking the city walls. Beautiful gardens.

■ RESTAURANT: Closed Wed. In summer, meals are served on the terrace. Refined cuisine using produce from the hotel's own farm.
■ TARIFF: (1996) Single 100,000–200,000, Double 190,000–330,000, Set menu 55,000–65,000 (Amex, Euro/Access, Visa).

SORRENTO   21B

Hotel Bellevue Syrene ★★★★
Via Marina Grande 1, 80067 Sorrento.
Tel 0818 781024, Fax 0818 783963.
English spoken.
Open all year. 73 bedrooms (all en suite).
Overlooking the Golfo di Napoli and Vesuvius, hotel is ideally situated in a quiet position just 100 m from the historic town centre.

■ RESTAURANT: Restaurant overlooks the Golfo di Napoli. Regional and Italian cuisine.
■ ACTIVITIES: Private beach and water sports close by.
■ TARIFF: (1996) Single 200,000, Double 270,000, Set menu 40,000 (Amex, Euro/Access, Visa).

Grand Hotel Excelsior Vittoria ★★★★
Piazza Tasso 34, 80067 Sorrento.
Tel 0818 071044, Fax 0818 771206.
English spoken.
Open all year. 106 bedrooms (all en suite).
Outdoor swimming pool, parking.
Elegantly decorated hotel with excellent facilities, some stunning interior designs and equally stunning views. Built on a cliff overlooking the Golfo di Napoli, in a quiet position with private lift to the harbour. Within easy reach of Napoli.

■ RESTAURANT: A choice of a magnificent dining room or inviting, open-air panoramic terrace restaurant. Emphasis is on carefully prepared Italian cuisine. Tempting titbits and light meals can be enjoyed beside the pool.
■ ACTIVITIES: Sightseeing, touring, water sports.
■ TARIFF: Single 300,000, Double 536,000, Set menu 68,000 (Amex, Euro/Access, Visa).

SPOLETO   21A

Hotel dei Duchi ★★★★
Viale Giacomo Matteotti 4, 06049 Spoleto.
Tel 0743 44541, Fax 0743 44543.
English spoken.

Open all year. 49 bedrooms (all en suite).
Parking. ♿
In the centre of Spoleto, the hotel is surrounded by the Teatro Romano. Peaceful atmosphere.

■ RESTAURANT: Panoramic air-conditioned restaurant offering typical local specialities. Fish dishes for lunch or dinner should be ordered 24 hours in advance.
■ TARIFF: Single 120,000–150,000, Double 160,000–220,000, Set menu 40,000–60,000 (Amex, Euro/Access, Visa).
■ DISCOUNT: 10%

Italy

STRESA 20B

Hotel Astoria ★★★★
Corso Umberto I, 31, 28049 Stresa.
Tel 0323 32566, Fax 0323 933785. English spoken.
Open 01/04 to 31/10. 101 bedrooms
(all en suite). Outdoor swimming pool, tennis,
golf 4 km, parking.

*Modern, very comfortable lakeside hotel. Lovely
gardens and excellent views over the Borromeo
Gulf and the Alps.*

■ RESTAURANT: Good restaurant overlooking lake.
■ ACTIVITIES: Fitness room, Turkish bath,
solarium, jacuzzi, table tennis.
■ TARIFF: Single 160,000, Double 290,000,
Set menu 48,000 (Amex, Euro/Access, Visa).

Hotel Lido La Perla Nera ★★★
Viale Lido 15, 28049 Stresa.
Tel 0323 33611, Fax 0323 933785. English spoken.
Open 01/04 to 31/10. 36 bedrooms
(all en suite). Golf 4 km, parking, restaurant. &

*A few steps from the lake with wonderful views
of the Borromean gulf and its islands.
Tastefully decorated and very comfortable,
hotel is in a peaceful area not far from the
centre of the town.*

■ TARIFF: Single 120,000, Double 150,000,
Bk 15,000, Set menu 40,000 (Amex,
Euro/Access, Visa).

TODI 21A

Hotel Tuder ★★★
Via Maesta dei Lombardi 13, 06059 Todi.
Tel 075 894 2184, Fax 075 894 2184. English spoken.
Open all year. 40 bedrooms (all en suite).
Garage, parking. ℂ &

*Elegant, comfortable hotel offering a choice of
accommodation. Large, airy rooms with
balconies, air conditioning and lovely views.
Todi is an Etruscan town in the centre of
Umbria, convenient for exploring Assisi,
Perugia and Orvieto.*

■ RESTAURANT: Panoramic dining room.
Carefully prepared Umbrian dishes and
inventive home-made specialities.
■ ACTIVITIES: Solarium at hotel. Sightseeing and
touring the beautiful countryside.
■ TARIFF: Single 70,000–90,000,
Double 100,000–140,000, Set menu 25,000–
40,000 (Amex, Euro/Access, Visa).

TREMEZZO 20B

Hotel Rusall ★★★ Via S Martino 2, Frazione,
Rogaro, 22019 Tremezzo.
Tel 0344 40408, Fax 0344 40447. English spoken.

Open 18/03 to 31/12. 18 bedrooms
(all en suite). Tennis, golf 6 km, parking. ℂ

*Very quiet location with wonderful views over
the lake and private gardens. All rooms have a
balcony. 5 minutes from the centre of Tremezzo.*

■ RESTAURANT: Closed Wed. Panoramic views of
the lake. Specialities: local Italian dishes and
fresh fish.
■ ACTIVITIES: Trips to the mountains; tennis, beach,
sea and freshwater swimming pools all nearby.
■ TARIFF: (1996) Single 50,000–75,000,
Double 90,000–110,000, Bk 12,000, Set
menu 35,000–45,000 (Amex, Euro/Access, Visa).
■ DISCOUNT: 5%

TRENTO 20C

Hotel Montana ★★★
84 Vason di Monte Bondone, 38040 Trento.
Tel 0461 948200, Fax 0461 948177. English spoken.

Open 01/12 to 15/04 & 01/06 to 30/09.
52 bedrooms (all en suite). Tennis, garage,
parking. &

*A traditional family-run hotel with views of the
Dolomites. A panoramic mountain road
connects Trento Valley (20 km) and Riva del
Garda lake (38 km). Suites and apartments
are also available.*

■ RESTAURANT: Friendly atmosphere; regional specialities with good wines. Summer garden for barbecues and outside dining. Special menus for children.
■ ACTIVITIES: Stunning location for walking, trekking, skiing and skating; children's mini-club. ● Free tennis and use of mountain bikes in summer.
■ TARIFF: (1996) Single 75,000–90,000, Double 120,000–160,000, Set menu 25,000–40,000 (Amex, Euro/Access, Visa).
■ DISCOUNT: 10%

TRIESTE   20D

Grand Hotel Duchi d'Aosta ★★★★
Piazza Unità d'Italia 2, 34121 Trieste.
Tel 040 7600011, Fax 040 366092. English spoken.

Open all year. 52 bedrooms (all en suite). Garage. ℓ

Classic, traditional hotel offering excellent service and facilities. In the historic centre of Trieste, Piazza Unità d'Italia is a beautiful square which opens on to the waterfront.

■ RESTAURANT: Renowned in Trieste, 'Harry's Grill' offers regional and international cuisine.
■ ACTIVITIES: Ideally located for sightseeing and touring. All sporting facilities close by.
■ TARIFF: Single 150,000–265,000, Double 190,000–330,000, Set menu 45,000–100,000 (Amex, Euro/Access, Visa).
■ DISCOUNT: 10%

Hotel Riviera & Maximilian's ★★★
Strada Costiera 22, 34014 Trieste.
Tel 040 224551, Fax 040 224300. English spoken.
Open all year. 69 bedrooms (all en suite).
Tennis, golf 12 km, parking. ℓ &

Completely updated in 1996, hotel offers every comfort and a tranquil atmosphere in lovely surroundings. All rooms have a sea view and a lift provides convenient access to the beach.

■ RESTAURANT: Elegant dining room with fine

cuisine. Lunch is also served at the relaxing beach restaurant.
■ ACTIVITIES: Water sports from the beach.
■ TARIFF: Single 136,000–150,000, Double 160,000–210,000, Set menu 30,000–70,000 (Amex, Euro/Access, Visa).
■ DISCOUNT: 10%

UDINE   20D

Hotel Astoria ★★★★
Piazza XX Settembre 24, 33100 Udine.
Tel 0432 505091, Fax 0432 509070. English spoken.
Open all year. 75 bedrooms (all en suite).
Golf 10 km, garage.

Located in the heart of Udine's historic centre, the hotel has a warm atmosphere which has become the emblem of over a hundred years of tradition in service. Ideal meeting place for prestigious events and the perfect location for elegant entertaining.

■ RESTAURANT: Elegant dining room with very good regional and international cusine. Seafood specialities; excellent cellar.
■ TARIFF: Single 125,000–194,000, Double 175,000–260,000, Bk 19,000, Set menu 40,000–50,000 (Amex, Euro/Access, Visa).

VARESE   20B

Hotel Varese Lago ★★★
Via G Macchi 61, 21100 Varese.
Tel 0332 310022, Fax 0332 312697. English spoken.
Open all year. 45 bedrooms (all en suite).
Golf 10 km, parking. &

Set amongst the Lombardy lakes, a modern, most attractive ranch-style hotel offering relaxation and tranquillity. Ideal for the motorist, being only 4 minutes' drive from Varese town centre.

■ TARIFF: Single 100,000–135,000, Double 130,000–180,000 (Amex, Euro/Access, Visa).

Italy

VENEZIA (VENICE)　　　　20C

Hotel Metropole ★★★★
Riva Schiavoni 4149, 30122 Venezia.
Tel 0415 205044, Fax 0415 223679. English spoken.
Open all year. 74 bedrooms (all en suite).
Golf 5 km, restaurant.

*Only 3 minutes' stroll along the waterfront
from St Mark's Square, a very comfortable
hotel with a fine collection of antiques.*

■ TARIFF: Single 190,000–390,000,
Double 320,000–530,000, Set menu 42,000
(Amex, Euro/Access, Visa).

Hotel La Residenza ★★
Campo Bandiera e Moro 3608, 30122 Venezia.
Tel 041 5285315, Fax 041 5238859.
Open 01/02 to 30/11 & 01/12 to 31/12.
15 bedrooms (14 en suite, 1 bath/shower only).

*A friendly hotel with the atmosphere of an old
Venetian palace and just a few steps from St Mark's
Square, reached by boat from the Bacino
S'Marco. Arsenale station No 17, No 1 river bus.*

■ TARIFF: Single 145,000, Double 220,000
(Amex, Euro/Access, Visa).

Hotel Saturnia & International ★★★★
Calle Larga XXII Marzo,
San Marco 2398, 30124 Venezia.
Tel 041 5208377, Fax 041 5207131. English spoken.
Open all year. 95 bedrooms (all en suite).
Golf 12 km.

*A restored 14th-century palace just a few steps
from St Mark's Square. Family run since 1908,
the hotel offers every comfort, has a flower-
filled terrace and private entrance for
gondolas and water taxis. Hotel offers 40%
discount on car parking.*

■ RESTAURANT: Enjoy the fine cuisine in the
comfort of 'La Caravella' or outside on the
terrace in summer.
■ TARIFF: Single 230,000–360,000,
Double 320,000–525,000, Set menu 78,000
(Amex, Euro/Access, Visa).

Hotel Sofitel Venezia ★★★★
Santa Croce 245, 30135 Venezia.
Tel 0417 10400, Fax 0417 10394. English spoken.
Open all year. 100 bedrooms (all en suite).
Golf 12 km.

*With 18th-century-style décor, the hotel is in
the Papadopoli gardens, in the historic centre
of the city. Car parking 300 m; airport and
station within easy reach.*

■ RESTAURANT: Enjoy the winter garden
atmosphere of 'Papadopoli' restaurant.
Seafood and Italian specialities.

■ TARIFF: Single 460,000, Double 560,000, Set
menu 65,000–120,000 (Amex, Euro/Access, Visa).

VERBANIA　　　　20B

Hotel Cannero ★★★
Lungo Lago 2, 28051 Cannero Riviera.
Tel 0323 788046, Fax 0323 788048. English spoken.
Open 01/03 to 02/11. 40 bedrooms
(all en suite). Outdoor swimming pool, tennis,
golf 14 km, garage, parking. ᕗ

*Situated right on the shore, at the end of the
pedestrian promenade and in one of the
quietest resorts on the lake. (Hotel residents are
given a car pass.) The beautifully furnished
rooms are light and spacious with fine views of
the lake and mountains. Open-air pool is
heated. Cannero Riviera is north-east of
Verbania along the lake shore.*

■ RESTAURANT: Closed Mon from Mar to Oct. Has
a good reputation for its excellent local dishes
and fresh lake fish specialities; fine wines.
■ ACTIVITIES: Superb location for boat cruises,
mountain excursions, trekking, walking and
water sports.
■ TARIFF: Single 100,000–120,000,
Double 180,000–200,000, Set menu 45,000–
70,000 (Amex, Euro/Access, Visa).
■ DISCOUNT: 5%

Italy

VERONA   20C

Hotel Firenze ★★★★
Corso Porta Nuova 88, 37122 Verona.
Tel 0458 011510, Fax 0458 030374.
English spoken.
Open all year. 56 bedrooms (all en suite).
Modern and very comfortable with every possible facility in the rooms and suites, including air conditioning. Well-appointed conference rooms for up to 40 people. Close to Piazza Brà, the historic centre of Verona.
■ TARIFF: Single 140,000–200,000, Double 180,000–300,000 (Amex, Euro/Access, Visa).
■ DISCOUNT: 10%

Hotel Victoria ★★★★
Via Adua 8, 37121 Verona.
Tel 0455 90566, Fax 0455 90155. English spoken.

Open all year. 71 bedrooms (all en suite). Golf 25 km, garage, restaurant. &
Completely modernised hotel situated within the walls of the Palazzo Monga. Classically furnished and well equipped. Contains a small private museum of Roman antiquities. Apartments also available. Good conference facilities.
■ TARIFF: Single 280,000–350,000, Double 330,000–420,000 (Amex, Euro/Access, Visa).

VIAREGGIO   20C

Hotel Astor ★★★★
Viale Carducci 54, 55049 Viareggio.
Tel 0584 50301, Fax 0584 55181. English spoken.

Open all year. 68 bedrooms (all en suite). Indoor swimming pool, golf 5 km, garage, parking. ✆ &
Facing the Tyrrhenian Sea near the elegant shopping area and the famous Versilian pinewoods. Viareggio has a mild climate offering guests a pleasant stay all year round.
■ RESTAURANT: 'La Conchiglia' restaurant is fashionable and renowned for its fish specialities.
■ ACTIVITIES: Close to the beautiful artistic cities of Firenze, Pisa and Lucca.
■ TARIFF: Single 190,000–250,000, Double 270,000–370,000, Set menu 35,000 (Amex, Euro/Access, Visa).
■ DISCOUNT: 15%

Grand Hotel & Riviera ★★★★
Viale Pistelli 59, 55043 Lido di Camaiore.
Tel 0584 617571, Fax 0584 619533.
English spoken.
Open 06/04 to 12/10. 64 bedrooms (all en suite). Outdoor swimming pool, golf 12 km, garage.

Situated on the sea-front with rooms either overlooking the sea or mountains behind. Cool and very comfortable with all modern facilities, spacious lounges and friendly, helpful service. Lido di Camaiore is just north of Viareggio along the coast road.
■ RESTAURANT: Very comfortable dining room offering international and regional cuisine.
■ ACTIVITIES: Sauna and hydromassage at hotel.
■ TARIFF: Single 120,000–180,000, Double 180,000–260,000, Set menu 40,000–60,000 (Amex, Euro/Access, Visa).
■ DISCOUNT: 10%

VICENZA   20C

Hotel Continental ★★★
Viale Trissino 89, 36100 Vicenza.
Tel 0444 505476, Fax 0444 513319. English spoken.
Open all year. 60 bedrooms (all en suite). Golf 10 km, parking. &
Air-conditioned, modern hotel in quiet location near the historic town centre. Follow signs for 'Stadio'. Special weekend tariffs for individuals and groups.
■ RESTAURANT: Closed Aug. Regional and national specialities.
■ ACTIVITIES: ● 50% discount on guided tour of the town and the UNESCO monument (Saturdays only).
■ TARIFF: Single 60,000–130,000, Double 80,000–195,000, Bk 15,000, Set menu 25,000–50,000 (Amex, Euro/Access, Visa).
■ DISCOUNT: 10%

Italy

LUXEMBOURG

Esch-sur-Sûre

Sandwiched between Belgium, Germany and France, the Grand Duchy of Luxembourg may be one of Europe's smallest states – smaller than either Lancashire or Lincolnshire – yet it has its own royal family and its own language (French and German are also official languages). It also has its own currency, the Luxembourg franc, worth the same as, and completely interchangeable with, the Belgian franc.

Luxembourg City, the capital, sits spectacularly above the Rivers Petrusse and Alzette. In the old town, the black spire of Cathédrale Notre-Dame rises high above the two rivers, and the quickest way down to the valley is by lift from the town. Beyond the Alzette, to the north of the old town, is the Centre Européen, meeting place of the European Union's Council of Ministers.

To the north of Luxembourg City, the Ardennes landscape of deep-wooded valleys spills over from the Belgian border. At Vianden, close to the German border, an 11th-century castle can be reached by cable-car from the town. Or visit the Musée historique at Diekirch for an insight into the World War II Battle of the Bulge. While for nostalgic fans of Radio Luxembourg, the tall transmitter masts at Junglinster may rate as Luxembourg's most important monument!

Emergency numbers

Police 013, Fire Brigade and Ambulance 012

Warning information

Warning triangle must be carried

Blood alcohol legal limit 80 mg

BERDORF 7D

Hotel Bisdorff ★★★
39 rue de Heisbich, 6551 Berdorf.
Tel 790208, Fax 790629. English spoken.

Open 05/04 to 26/12. 27 bedrooms
(all en suite). Indoor swimming pool,
golf 10 km, parking. ☎ ⅙

Family-run hotel surrounded by gardens.
Quiet location in the forest, 2 km from Berdorf
going towards Consdorf.

■ RESTAURANT: Closed Mon & Tues, Jan to Mar.
French cuisine. Specialities include lobster, fish
and game.
■ ACTIVITIES: Walking in the forest, windsurfing
on Echternach lake; tennis nearby; guided
group tours to Echternach.
■ TARIFF: (1996) Single 1900, Double 3800,
Set menu 700–3000 (Amex, Euro/Access, Visa).
■ DISCOUNT: 2%

Hotel Parc ★★★★ 6500 Berdorf.
Tel 790195/790591, Fax 790223. English spoken.

Open 05/04 to 30/11. 19 bedrooms
(all en suite). Outdoor swimming pool,
golf 15 km, garage, parking.

On the fringe of the forest and a short distance
from the village, this traditional 'Silence' hotel
is surrounded by rare trees and shrubs.

■ RESTAURANT: Refined cuisine using fresh
local produce.
■ ACTIVITIES: Tennis, mini-golf and indoor
swimming pool close by.
■ TARIFF: (1996) Single 2000–3200,
Double 3000–4200, Set menu 800–1600
(Amex, Euro/Access, Visa).

CLERVAUX 7D

Golf-Hotel Le Claravallis ★★★★
3 rue de la Gare, 9708 Clervaux.
Tel 90134, Fax 929089. English spoken.

Open 01/01 to 15/02 & 15/03 to 31/12.
28 bedrooms (all en suite). Golf 3 km,
parking. ⅙

Very comfortable hotel, set in lovely gardens at
the edge of the forest. 400 m from the centre of
the picturesque town of Clervaux.

■ RESTAURANT: Closed 16/02 to 15/03. Pretty
dining room offering French and international
dishes prepared by the patron. Specialities are
seafood and game.
■ ACTIVITIES: Walking/hiking trails on the
doorstep. ● 15% discount on green fees.
■ TARIFF: (1996) Single 1400–1800,
Double 2200–2950, Set menu 490–1350
(Amex, Euro/Access, Visa).
■ DISCOUNT: 10%

ECHTERNACH 7D

Hotel Grand ★★★★
27 rte de Diekirch, 6430 Echternach.
Tel 729672, Fax 729062. English spoken.
Open 25/03 to 15/11. 26 bedrooms
(all en suite). Golf 20 km, garage, parking. ☎

Leave Echternach towards Diekirch and the
very comfortable, welcoming hotel is on the left
overlooking the Sûre river.

■ RESTAURANT: French cuisine using market-
fresh ingredients.
■ ACTIVITIES: ● Free use of bicycles for guests

using restaurant; lots of cycling tracks close by. In summer, tours of the Moselle, Trier and Luxembourg City are organised by bus, free of charge to hotel guests.
■ TARIFF: (1996) Single 1875–2650, Double 2700– 4600, Set menu 850–2500 (Amex, Euro/Access, Visa).

ETTELBRÜCK   7D

Hotel Dahm ★★★★
57 Porte des Ardennes, 9145 Erpeldange. Tel 8162551, Fax 816255210. English spoken.

Open all year. 25 bedrooms (all en suite). Golf 1 km, garage, parking. ☎ &

Traditional hotel in Erpeldange village centre. 1 km north of Ettelbrück.

■ RESTAURANT: Closed Mon & Tues eve. A la carte restaurant with game specialities in winter. Good wine cellar.
■ ACTIVITIES: Private trout fishing, mountain bikes, skittles; way-marked paths and tennis nearby.
■ TARIFF: Single 2000–2800, Double 3000–3350, Set menu 600–1800 (Amex, Euro/Access, Visa).

GRUNDHOF   7D

Hotel Brimer ★★★★ 6360 Grundhof.
Tel 86251, Fax 86212. English spoken.

Open 25/02 to 15/11. 23 bedrooms (all en suite). Golf 15 km, parking.

Country hotel in a lovely setting by the Sûre river on the German border. Cosy and comfortable with a family atmosphere. The village is 23 km east of Ettelbrück, south-east of Diekirch and 10 km from Echternach.

■ RESTAURANT: Has a very good reputation for its excellent cuisine and fine wines.
■ ACTIVITIES: Fitness centre, sauna and solarium at hotel. Ideal base for exploring the beautiful surroundings and nearby Parc Naturel Ardennes.
■ TARIFF: (1996) Single 2400–2700, Double 2850–3500, Set menu 900–1500 (Amex, Euro/Access, Visa).

LAROCHETTE   7D

Hotel du Château ★★★
1 rue de Medernach, 7616 Larochette. Tel 87009, Fax 879636. English spoken.

Open 15/02 to 31/12. 40 bedrooms (all en suite). Golf 4 km, parking.

Comfortable hotel in the main square of this picturesque little town. Conference facilities.

■ RESTAURANT: Good restaurant offering regional cuisine with fish and game specialities.
■ ACTIVITIES: Hang-gliding and ballooning nearby.
■ TARIFF: (1996) Single 2000–2300, Double 2600–2900, Set menu 800–1250 (Amex, Euro/Access, Visa).

LUXEMBOURG CITY   7D

Hotel Central Molitor ★★★★
28 av de la Liberté, 1930 Luxembourg City. Tel 489911, Fax 483382. English spoken. Open all year. 36 bedrooms (all en suite). Golf 6 km, parking.

Fine hotel with period façade. In a good location halfway between the financial centre and railway station and 3 blocks from the air terminal. (A charge is made for parking.)

- RESTAURANT: Closed eve & Sat.
- TARIFF: Single 3500, Double 4600,
Set menu 650–1400 (Amex, Euro/Access, Visa).

Hotel Delta ★★★ 74-78 rue Adolphe Fischer,
1521 Luxembourg City.
Tel 493096, Fax 404320. English spoken.
Open all year. 20 bedrooms (all en suite).
Garage, parking.

Fully renovated, the hotel is located in the heart of the city. Follow signs from La Place de Paris.

- RESTAURANT: Closed Sun. Gastronomic restaurant.
- TARIFF: Single 2500–3400, Double 2950–3800 (Amex, Euro/Access, Visa).

Hotel Grand Cravat ★★★★
29 bd Roosevelt, 2450 Luxembourg City.
Tel 221975, Fax 226711. English spoken.
Open all year. 60 bedrooms (all en suite).
Golf 8 km. ✆ &

Centrally located, elegant hotel in traditional style. Many of the rooms have lovely views.

- RESTAURANT: Choose either the restaurant or brasserie which offer regional and French cuisine.
- TARIFF: (1996) Single 5400–5900,
Double 6200–7200, Set menu 950–2000
(Amex, Euro/Access, Visa).

Hostellerie du Grunewald ★★★★
10-16 route d'Echternach, 1453 Dommeldange.
Tel 431882, Fax 420646.

Open all year. 23 bedrooms (all en suite).
Golf 3 km, garage, parking. ✆ &

Very comfortable hotel. Luxurious rooms with all modern facilities. Dommeldange is 4 km from Luxembourg City towards Echternach.

- RESTAURANT: Closed 01/01 to 23/01 & Sat lunch & Sun. Romantic gourmet restaurant. Specialities include game, fish and lobster.
- ACTIVITIES: Forest walks.
- TARIFF: (1996) Single 3900–4200,
Double 4700–5900 (Amex, Euro/Access, Visa).

Hotel Nobilis ★★★★
47 av de la Gare, 1930 Luxembourg City.
Tel 494971/72/73/74, Fax 403101. English spoken.
Open all year. 46 bedrooms (all en suite). ✆ &

Recently renovated, a comfortable hotel with all modern comforts. Only a few steps from the railway station in the town centre. (Chargeable car parking.)

- RESTAURANT: Traditional and French cuisine in the 'Taverne' and gourmet cuisine in the 'Calao'.
- ACTIVITIES: Cabaret evenings; sightseeing.
- TARIFF: (1996) Single 3000–3600,
Double 3600–4200, Bk 300, Set menu 295–785
(Amex, Euro/Access, Visa).
- DISCOUNT: 10%

Hotel Président ★★★★
place de la Gare, 1930 Luxembourg City.
Tel 486161, Fax 486180. English spoken.
Open all year. 40 bedrooms (all en suite).

200 m from the town centre, facing the station and air terminal.

- RESTAURANT: Attractively decorated Victorian-style restaurant. Original cuisine.
- ACTIVITIES: Whirlpool; walking, sightseeing.
- TARIFF: (1996) Single 5000, Double 6400
(Amex, Euro/Access, Visa).

Hotel Royal ★★★★★
12 bd Royal, 2449 Luxembourg City.
Tel 2416161, Fax 225948. English spoken.

Open all year. 210 bedrooms (all en suite).
Indoor swimming pool, golf 6 km, garage. &

Attractive, modern hotel located in city centre, convenient for sightseeing, business and the international airport.

- RESTAURANT: Choice of 2.
- ACTIVITIES: Superb indoor pool/fitness complex; variety of sports facilities and lovely walks nearby.
- TARIFF: (1996) Single 9200–13,500, Double 10,200–14,500 (Amex, Euro/Access, Visa).

Luxembourg

Sofitel ★★★★ European Centre,
2015 Luxembourg City.
Tel 437761, Fax 438658. English spoken.

Open all year. 364 bedrooms (all en suite).
Indoor swimming pool, golf 4 km, garage,
parking. &

*Large, modern hotel; close to the EU
institutions and motorway to city centre.*

■ RESTAURANT: Closed Sat lunch.
■ TARIFF: (1996) Single 6350–7900,
Double 7300–8900, Set menu 700–2000
(Amex, Euro/Access, Visa).

MONDORF-LES-BAINS   7D

Hotel du Grand Chef ★★★★
36 av des Bains, 5610 Mondorf-les-Bains.
Tel 668012/8122, Fax 661510. English spoken.

Open 23/03 to 30/11. 38 bedrooms
(all en suite). Golf 14 km, garage, parking. &

*A classically elegant 'Silence' hotel set in a
private park near the Moselle valley. Special
short-stay arrangements. 12 km from
motorway E411/A4 and 17 km from
Luxembourg City. Guide users are offered a
free 'welcome' apéritif.*

■ RESTAURANT: A variety of two and three-course
menus making the most of fresh produce.
French cuisine.
■ ACTIVITIES: Close to spa/thermal park and
sports facilities. ● Hotel organises visits to local
wine cellars. Ask about the special rates for
accommodation plus sessions at the Mondorf
Spa. Guests also receive free admission to the
local casino.
■ TARIFF: Single 2280–2550,
Double 3000–3600, Set menu 870–1550
(Amex, Euro/Access, Visa).

REMICH-SUR-MOSELLE   7D

Hotel Best Western St-Nicolas ★★★★
31 Esplanade, 5533 Remich-sur-Moselle.
Tel 698888, Fax 699069. English spoken.

Open all year. 43 bedrooms (all en suite).
Tennis, golf 10 km, parking. ☎

*Elegant hotel by the Moselle river amidst
famous wine area. Beautiful tourist resort
close to the capital. A bottle of wine is offered
per couple.*

■ RESTAURANT: French cuisine and superior
wines. Specialities include brochet au Riesling,
écrevisses à la Luxembourgeoise and
bouillabaisse.
■ ACTIVITIES: Fitness room with sauna and
solarium at hotel; mountain-biking and
swimming pool (in summer) nearby. Lovely
walks, ideal base for sightseeing.
■ TARIFF: (1996) Single 2400–2700,
Double 2900–3500, Set menu 790–1750
(Amex, Euro/Access, Visa).

NETHERLANDS

Flower auction, Aalsmeer

The Netherlands is one of the few countries in the world where you go *up* to the beach! About a quarter of its land mass lies *below* sea level and, over the centuries, the Dutch have worked hard on reclamation projects to create more space for an ever-growing population. To maintain the polders, as the reclaimed land is called, water is constantly pumped into the canals. Flooding has always been a danger, and the massive Oosterschelde barrier was built in the south of the country following the catastrophic floods of 1953.

One of the Dutch people's most ambitious projects was the changing of the Zuiderzee into the Ijsselmeer, separated from the Waddenzee inlet by a huge dam – the Afsluitdijk. Built across the north of the proposed lake between Den Dever and Harlingen, this impressive 30-km-long dyke carries a motorway and cycle track, with large locks at either end to allow ships to pass from the open sea into the Ijsselmeer.

If you plan to visit only one city while in the Netherlands then Amsterdam is likely to be high on the list, with its network of canals, cobbled streets and bridges, wonderful art galleries, coffee shops and busy, youthful atmosphere. But what about following the tourist board's designated route around Rotterdam, the world's largest port? – either by boat or car? Or Den Haag, or Delft, famous for its blue and white ceramic ware. Or visit Alkmaar's weekly cheese market, or the world's largest flower auction – every weekday morning, at Aalsmeer. Finally, if it's a spring holiday, don't forget the *Keukenhof* bulb gardens.

Emergency numbers

Police, Fire Brigade and Ambulance 0611

Warning information

Warning triangle must be carried

Blood Alcohol Legal Limit 50 mg

Netherlands

AMSTERDAM 13A

Hotel Ambassade ★★★
Herengracht 341, 1016 Amsterdam.
Tel 020 6262333, Fax 020 6245321. English spoken.
Open all year. 52 bedrooms (all en suite).
Golf 8 km. ☎

The hotel consists of ten 17th-century merchants' homes in the centre of Amsterdam, on one of the most beautiful canals. The personalised rooms have been decorated with the greatest of care and antiques, clocks and paintings are displayed in the public areas.

■ ACTIVITIES: Excursions and canal trips booked by hotel.
■ TARIFF: (1996) Single 240, Double 295 (Amex, Euro/Access, Visa).

Hotel Asterisk ★★
Den Texstraat 16, 1017 Amsterdam.
Tel 020 6241768, Fax 020 6382790. English spoken.
Open all year. 29 bedrooms (23 en suite, 1 bath/shower only). Golf 3 km.

A family-run hotel completely renovated and equipped with all modern conveniences. Tramline 16-24 or 25 from Central Station to the Weteringcircuit.

■ TARIFF: (1996) Single 65–125, Double 85–170, Bk 12.50 (Euro/Access, Visa).

Cok City Hotel ★★★ Nieuwezijds
Voorburgwal 50, 1012 SC Amsterdam.
Tel 020 4220011, Fax 020 4200357. English spoken.
Open all year. 106 bedrooms (all en suite). ☎ ♿

Modern, with original and exciting décor and furnishings. Convenient for all central city attractions. Full international buffet breakfast. (Chargeable garage parking available.)

■ TARIFF: Single 210, Double 250 (Amex, Euro/Access, Visa).
■ DISCOUNT: 10%

Cok Hotel (Tourist) ★★★
Koninginneweg 34-36, 1075 CZ Amsterdam.
Tel 020 6646111, Fax 020 6645304. English spoken.
Open all year. 70 bedrooms (all en suite). ☎

Modern hotel with well-equipped rooms and within easy reach of the city centre attractions. No restaurant as such but light meals are available in the bar area. Full international buffet breakfast.

■ TARIFF: Single 150–180, Double 210 (Amex, Euro/Access, Visa).
■ DISCOUNT: 10%

Hotel Estherea ★★★★
Singel 303, 1012 WJ Amsterdam.
Tel 020 6245146, Fax 020 6239001. English spoken.

Open all year. 75 bedrooms (all en suite). ☎

Ideally located on one of the most beautiful and quiet canals in the centre of the city, only 300 m from Dam Square and the Royal Palace. Behind the 17th-century façade is a comfortable hotel with renovated rooms.

■ ACTIVITIES: Canal trips; within easy walking distance of museums, theatres and top shopping streets.
■ TARIFF: (1996) Single 195–280, Double 220–375 (Amex, Euro/Access, Visa).

Hotel King ★ Leidsekade 85, 1017 Amsterdam.
Tel 020 6249603, Fax 020 6207277. English spoken.

Open all year. 25 bedrooms. Golf 2 km. ☎

A Royal Budget hotel, formerly a 17th-century canal house. Located in the heart of Amsterdam, overlooking the Grand Canal, next to the Leidseplein and near the museums. Close to rail and trams.

■ TARIFF: (1996) Single 55–75, Double 75–125 (No credit cards).

The Park Hotel ★★★★
Stadhouderskade 25, 1071 ZD Amsterdam.
Tel 020 6717474, Fax 020 6649455. English spoken.

Open all year. 187 bedrooms (all en suite). Garage. ✆ ♿

A classical, traditional hotel in the best city centre location of Amsterdam. All major attractions are within a stone's throw. Contact hotel's Reservations for details of leisure break packages.

■ RESTAURANT: Choose from 'Inn at the Park' with lovely canal views or 'De Stadhouder' restaurant.
■ ACTIVITIES: Trips on canal boats from opposite hotel; visit all the famous museums nearby.
■ TARIFF: Single 225, Double 325, Bk 25, Set menu 37.50 (Amex, Euro/Access, Visa).
■ DISCOUNT: 15% subject to prior booking/availability.

Hotel Wilhelmina ★★
Koninginneweg 167, 1075 Amsterdam.
Tel 020 6625467, Fax 020 6792296.
English spoken.

Open all year. 19 bedrooms (16 en suite). Golf 2 km, parking. ✆

Pleasant tourist hotel with large, comfortable rooms. Centrally located on tram route 2 and within walking distance of main museums, concert hall and Vondel Park. Excellent variety

of good restaurants in the neighbourhood.
■ ACTIVITIES: Arrangements made for sightseeing, bicycle hire and bicycle tours.
■ TARIFF: (1996) Single 55–145, Double 85–155 (No credit cards).

APELDOORN   13D

Hotel Bloemink ★★★★
Loolaan 556, 7315 AG Apeldoorn.
Tel 055 5214141, Fax 055 5219215.
English spoken.
Open all year. 76 bedrooms (all en suite). Indoor swimming pool, golf 5 km, parking. ✆

On the outskirts of the city, opposite the 'Het Loo' palace, and surrounded by forest and magnificent gardens.

■ RESTAURANT: Brasserie restaurant with French specialities.
■ ACTIVITIES: 6 bowling alleys, sauna and solarium at hotel; visit the national museums 'Paleis Het Loo' and 'Kröller Müller', the open-air museum and Apenheul nature park.
■ TARIFF: (1996) Single 105–160, Double 120–180, Set menu 29.50–49.50 (Amex, Euro/Access, Visa).

ARNHEM   13D

Golden Tulip Rijnhotel ★★★★
Onderlangs 10, 6812 AH Arnhem.
Tel 026 4434642, Fax 026 4454847. English spoken.

Open all year. 57 bedrooms (all en suite). Parking, restaurant. ✆

Standing on the banks of the Rhine, with well-equipped rooms and suites. By car, follow signs for Oosterbeek, or take bus from Arnhem railway station.

■ TARIFF: (1996) Single 205–300, Double 255–300, Set menu 39.50 (Amex, Euro/Access, Visa).
■ DISCOUNT: 10%

Netherlands

Postiljon Hotel Arnhem ★★★
Europaweg 25, 6816 SL Arnhem.
Tel 026 3573333, Fax 026 3573361. English spoken.
Open all year. 84 bedrooms (all en suite).
Golf on site, parking. ✆ ♿

Modern, comfortable hotel offering good facilities and a warm welcome. Arnhem is on the A12/A50 (exit 26/20).

■ RESTAURANT: Friendly atmosphere – good food.
■ ACTIVITIES: Hotel organises car and cycling holidays; lots of museums and other attractions within easy reach.
■ TARIFF: Single 115–141, Double 135–161, Bk 15.50, Set menu 32.50–37.50 (Amex, Euro/Access, Visa).

DELFT   13C

Hotel de Ark ★★★★
Koornmarkt 65, 2611 Delft.
Tel 015 157999, Fax 015 144997. English spoken.
Open 05/01 to 20/12. 24 bedrooms (all en suite). Golf 3 km, garage.

Near the canal in the centre of Delft, the hotel comprises 3 fully restored 17th-century houses. Five minutes' walk from the station.

■ TARIFF: (1996) Single 140–175, Double 175–235 (Amex, Euro/Access, Visa).
■ DISCOUNT: 10%

Hotel Leeuwenbrug ★★★
Koornmarkt 16, 2611 Delft.
Tel 015 2147741, Fax 015 2159759. English spoken.

Open all year. 38 bedrooms (all en suite). Golf 3 km, parking.

In the old part of town, ideal for sightseeing, shops and restaurants. Comfortably furnished and small enough to offer personal attention and service. For more information: Internet: http://www.luna.nl/leeuwenbrug or E-mail: Leeuwenbrug.luna.nl.

■ ACTIVITIES: Hotel will organise trips to museums, theatres, and different restaurants, for groups or individuals.

■ TARIFF: Single 95–148, Double 120–175 (Amex, Euro/Access, Visa).
■ DISCOUNT: 15% on weekends except Apr, May & June.

DEN HAAG (THE HAGUE)   13C

Bilderberg Europa Hotel Scheveningen
★★★★ Zwolsestraat 2, 2587 VJ Den Haag.
Tel 070 3512651, Fax 070 3506473. English spoken.
Open all year. 174 bedrooms (all en suite).
Indoor swimming pool, golf 15 km, garage. ✆ ♿

Part of the Queens Moat Houses group, a modern, comfortable first-class hotel, less than 100 m from the beach and 5 km from Den Haag shopping centre. Follow signs to Den Haag, Wassenaar/Scheveningen and Scheveningen Bad.

■ RESTAURANT: 'De Brasserie' has an inviting, warm atmosphere with good menus at reasonable prices.
■ ACTIVITIES: Free use of pool, Turkish bath and sauna; fitness facilities, massage, aerobics and solarium available at small charge. ● Discount at Sea Life Centre and free entry to Casino Scheveningen.
■ TARIFF: Single 230–310, Double 270–350, Bk 22.50, Set menu 39.50–52.50 (Amex, Euro/Access, Visa).
■ DISCOUNT: 20% prior booking/availability.

Parkhotel Den Haag ★★★★
53 Molenstraat, 2513 BJ Den Haag.
Tel 070 3624371, Fax 070 3614525. English spoken.
Open all year. 114 bedrooms (all en suite). Garage.

Traditional hotel in the city centre, on a picturesque street bordering the gardens of the Royal Palace. 2 km from the station.

■ TARIFF: Single 160–187, Double 250–285 (Amex, Euro/Access, Visa).

DEVENTER   13D

Postiljon Hotel Deventer ★★★
Deventerweg 121, 7418 DA Deventer.
Tel 057 0624022, Fax 057 0625346. English spoken.
Open all year. 99 bedrooms (all en suite). Parking. ✆ ♿

A modern hotel with friendly, helpful staff and good facilities. Deventer is on the A1, exit 23.

■ RESTAURANT: Good food at reasonable prices.
■ ACTIVITIES: Hotel organises car and cycling holidays; nearby are Slagharen Pony Park, Hellendoorn Adventure Park, the historic town of Deventer and various museums.
■ TARIFF: Single 126–141, Double 146–161, Bk 15.50, Set menu 32.50–37.50 (Amex, Euro/Access, Visa).

DORDRECHT   13C

Postiljon Hotel Dordrecht ★★★
Ryksstraatweg 30, 3316 EH Dordrecht.
Tel 078 6184444, Fax 078 6187940. English spoken.
Open all year. 96 bedrooms (all en suite).
Parking. ✆ ♿

Modern and friendly with good service and facilities. Take the A16 to Dordrecht and exit 20.

■ RESTAURANT: Good choice of menus at attractive prices.
■ ACTIVITIES: Hotel organises car and cycling holidays; visit nearby attractions including the National Glass Museum, windmills at Kinderdijk and two amusement parks.
■ TARIFF: Single 140–165, Double 160–185, Bk 15.50, Set menu 32.50–37.50 (Amex, Euro/Access, Visa).

EDAM   13A

Hotel de Fortuna ★★★
Spuistraat 1-7, 1135 AV Edam.
Tel 029 9371671, Fax 029 9371469. English spoken.
Open all year. 30 bedrooms (20 en suite).
Golf 5 km, parking. ✆ ♿

Just 18 km from Amsterdam, a pleasant, quiet hotel situated in the centre of historic Edam

and beside the canal. Consists of 5 beautifully restored houses dating back to the 17th century and a lovely garden.

SEE ADVERTISEMENT

■ RESTAURANT: A good choice of imaginative three-course menus. Meat, fish, poultry and game specialities using only the finest of fresh, seasonal produce.
■ TARIFF: (1996) Single 98–138, Double 122–172, Set menu 42.50–52.50 (Amex, Euro/Access, Visa).

Netherlands

GRONINGEN 13B

Hotel Mercure ★★★★
Expositielaan 7, 9727 Groningen.
Tel 050 5258400, Fax 050 5271828.
English spoken.
Open all year. 156 bedrooms (all en suite).
Indoor swimming pool, golf 5 km, parking. ⊂ &

*Recommended. A modern hotel on the ring
road around Groningen, next to the
Martinihal (Congress and Exhibition Centre),
City Park and Trade Centre. The city centre
itself is just a few minutes away.*

■ RESTAURANT: Closed Sat & Sun lunch. French-style restaurant with special daily and monthly menus, as well as à la carte.
■ ACTIVITIES: Day trips by boat to the Wadden Islands, visit the new Groningen museum; bicycle hire. ● Free entry to the 'Holland Casino' in Groningen.
■ TARIFF: (1996) Single 145–185, Double 165–245, Set menu 37.50 (Amex, Euro/Access, Visa).

Postiljon Hotel Haren-Groningen ★★★
Emmalaan 33, 9752 KS Haren-Groningen.
Tel 050 5347041, Fax 050 5340175.
English spoken.
Open all year. 97 bedrooms (all en suite).
Parking. ⊂ &

*Recommended. Modern hotel with a friendly
atmosphere, good service and facilities. Take
the A28 to Haren and exit 38.*

■ RESTAURANT: Good choice of menus at attractive prices.
■ ACTIVITIES: Hotel organises car and cycling holidays; nearby visit the seal sanctuary, botanical gardens, museums, Wadden Islands and the Martini Tower.
■ TARIFF: Single 120–145, Double 140–165, Bk 15.50, Set menu 32.50–37.50 (Amex, Euro/Access, Visa).

HARDERWIJK 13B

Hotel Marktzicht Klomp ★★★
Markt 6-9, 3841 CE Harderwijk.
Tel 034 1413032, Fax 034 1413230.
English spoken.
Open all year. 39 bedrooms (20 en suite, 7 bath/shower only). Golf 2 km, garage, parking, restaurant. ⊂

*Unusual hotel with historic links, situated in
the marketplace in the middle of the town.*

■ TARIFF: (1996) Single 42–118, Double 56–168, Bk 8.50, Set menu 18.50–35 (Amex, Euro/Access, Visa).

HEERENVEEN 13B

Postiljon Hotel Heerenveen ★★★
Schans 65, 8441 AC Heerenveen.
Tel 051 3618618, Fax 051 3629100.
English spoken.
Open all year. 55 bedrooms (all en suite).
Parking. ⊂ &

*Modern and comfortable with helpful, friendly
staff and good facilities. Heerenveen is on
the A7/A32.*

■ RESTAURANT: Good choice of reasonably priced menus.
■ ACTIVITIES: Hotel organises car and cycling holidays; lots to do and see nearby including visiting the Wadden Islands and Friesian lakes and towns.
■ TARIFF: Single 105–125, Double 125–145, Bk 15.50, Set menu 32.50–37.50 (Amex, Euro/Access, Visa).

'S-HERTOGENBOSCH 13D

Golden Tulip Central ★★★★
Burg Loeffplein 98, 5211 's-Hertogenbosch.
Tel 073 6125151, Fax 073 6145699.
English spoken.
Open all year. 124 bedrooms (all en suite).
Golf 10 km, garage. ⊂

*Located in the city centre, on the medieval
market square. 1 km from the central station.*

■ RESTAURANT: Housed in a cellar dating from the 14th century.
■ ACTIVITIES: Fitness centre with sauna 10 minutes from the hotel; cycling with bikes available from hotel.
■ TARIFF: (1996) Single 185, Double 235, Bk 20, Set menu 35.50–75.00 (Amex, Euro/Access, Visa).

NIJMEGEN 13D

Hotel Erica ★★★★ Molenbosweg 17, 6571 BA Berg en Dal, Nijmegen.
Tel 024 6843514, Fax 024 6843613.
English spoken.
Open all year. 59 bedrooms (all en suite).
Indoor swimming pool, tennis, golf 4 km, parking. ⊂ &

*Well-equipped hotel, on the edge of woodland
and only 3 km from the city of Nijmegen.*

■ RESTAURANT: Traditional Dutch cuisine.
■ ACTIVITIES: Good on-site recreational facilities including a pool complex with sauna and solarium; fishing.
■ TARIFF: (1996) Single 125–140, Double 170–210, Set menu 37.50 (Amex, Euro/Access, Visa).

Golden Tulip Val-Monte ★★★★
Oude Holleweg 5, 6572 Berg en Dal, Nijmegen.
Tel 024 6842000, Fax 024 6843353.
English spoken.
Open all year. 104 bedrooms (all en suite).
Indoor swimming pool, tennis, golf 4 km,
parking. &

Comfortable hotel with friendly staff. Set in an
area of outstanding natural beauty not far
from the German border and centre of Nijmegen.

■ RESTAURANT: Fish and beef specialities.
■ TARIFF: (1996) Single 149–200,
Double 205–245, Set menu 44
(Amex, Euro/Access, Visa).

NOORDWIJK   13C

Hotel de Witte Raaf ★★★★
Duinweg 119, 2204 Noordwijk.
Tel 025 2375984, Fax 025 2377578.
English spoken.

Open all year. 38 bedrooms (all en suite). Indoor
swimming pool, tennis, golf 1 km, parking.

Modern hotel near the beach, open countryside
and flower-growing area of Kenkenhof.
Member of the Relais du Silence.

■ RESTAURANT: Acclaimed for its good food,
restaurant overlooks the lovely gardens.
■ TARIFF: Single 85–135, Double 125–205, Set
menu 37.50–67.50 (Amex, Euro/Access, Visa).
■ DISCOUNT: 2%

PUTTEN   13D

Postiljon Hotel Nulde-Putten ★★★
Strandboulevard 3, 3882 RN Putten.
Tel 034 1856464, Fax 034 1858516. English spoken.
Open all year. 86 bedrooms (all en suite).
Parking. & &

Modern hotel with good facilities and helpful,
welcoming staff. Take the A28 for Putten and
exit 10.

■ RESTAURANT: Good choice of attractively
priced menus.
■ ACTIVITIES: Car and cycling holidays organised
by hotel; visit nearby dolphinarium,
amusement park, monkey sanctuary and
various museums.
■ TARIFF: Single 125–150, Double 145–170,
Bk 15.50, Set menu 32.50–37.50
(Amex, Euro/Access, Visa).

ROSMALEN   13D

Postiljon Hotel Rosmalen ★★★
Burg Burgerslaan 50, 5245 NH Rosmalen.
Tel 073 5219159, Fax 073 5216215. English spoken.
Open all year. 82 bedrooms (all en suite).
Parking. & &

Comfortable, modern hotel offering good
facilities and a warm welcome. Take the A2 to
Rosmalen and exit 20.

■ RESTAURANT: Good food at attractive prices.
■ ACTIVITIES: Hotel organises car and cycling
holidays; nearby visit Beekse Bergen Safari
Park, amusement parks and the Burgundian
city of 's-Hertogenbosch.
■ TARIFF: Single 115–140, Double 135–160,
Bk 15.50, Set menu 32.50–37.50
(Amex, Euro/Access, Visa).

ROTTERDAM   13C

Bilderberg Parkhotel ★★★★
Westersingel 70, 3015 Rotterdam.
Tel 010 4363611, Fax 010 4364212. English spoken.
Open all year. 189 bedrooms (all en suite).
Golf 3 km, parking. & &

Luxury hotel located in the heart of Rotterdam,
close to shopping facilities and all major
museums. An ideal base from which to
discover this bustling, international city.

■ RESTAURANT: Light French cuisine can be
enjoyed in the classic elegance of 'The
Empress'.
■ TARIFF: Single 265–365, Double 315–415,
Bk 29.50, Set menu 40 (Amex, Euro/Access, Visa).

Hotel Van Walsum ★★★
Mathenesserlaan 199, 3014 Rotterdam.
Tel 010 4363275, Fax 010 4364410. English spoken.
Open 02/01 to 24/12. 27 bedrooms
(all en suite). Parking, restaurant.

Traditional Dutch hotel, quietly situated in a
tree-lined avenue close to the city centre. Very
friendly and welcoming.

■ TARIFF: (1996) Single 100–145,
Double 135–200, Set menu 29.50 (Amex,
Euro/Access, Visa).

Netherlands

UTRECHT 13C

Hotel Malie ★★★★
Maliestraat 2-4, 3581 Utrecht.
Tel 030 2316424, Fax 030 2340661.
English spoken.
Open all year. 30 bedrooms (all en suite).
Golf 10 km, parking. ⓒ

Tastefully renovated, the hotel takes pride in being small enough to offer a warm welcome and personal attention. Half an hour from Schiphol Airport, close to Amsterdam, Rotterdam and Den Haag. Special weekend rates are available.

■ TARIFF: (1996) Single 145–175, Double 180–220 (Amex, Euro/Access, Visa).

Postiljon Hotel Utrecht-Bunnik ★★★
Kosterijland 8, 3981 AJ Bunnik.
Tel 030 6569222, Fax 030 6564074.
English spoken.
Open all year. 84 bedrooms (all en suite).
Golf on site, parking. ⓒ ♿

Modern hotel with a friendly atmosphere and good facilities. Take A12 to Utrecht and exit 19.

■ RESTAURANT: Good choice of menus at attractive prices.
■ ACTIVITIES: Hotel organises car and cycling holidays; various museums and castles as well as the zoological gardens to visit.
■ TARIFF: Single 139.50–159.50, Double 159.50–179.50, Bk 15.50, Set menu 32.50–37.50 (Amex, Euro/Access, Visa).

VALKENBURG 13D

Parkhotel Rooding ★★★★
Neerhem 68, 6301 CJ Valkenburg.
Tel 043 6013241, Fax 043 6013240.
English spoken.

Open 28/03 to 09/11. 92 bedrooms (all en suite). Indoor swimming pool, golf 7 km, garage, parking. ⓒ ♿

Run by the same family for 50 years, an attractive hotel in a unique garden setting, within a small forest. Up to date, with all modern facilities, a panoramic terrace and old-fashioned hospitality. Hotel is 10 km from Maastricht on the outskirts of Valkenburg, an area known for its healthy air and low crime rate.

■ RESTAURANT: Famous for its traditional Dutch-French cuisine. Specialities include tournedos 'Parkhotel' and asparagus in season. Fine choice of wines at reasonable prices and users of this guide are offered free house wine with dinner.
■ ACTIVITIES: Jogging track through the forest; 'Holland Casino' and many sports and recreational facilities including cycling, horse-riding and thermal spa within walking distance.
■ TARIFF: Single 90–150, Double 150–250, Set menu 35–65 (Amex, Euro/Access, Visa).

ZWOLLE 13B

Postiljon Hotel Zwolle ★★★
Hertsenbergweg 1, 8041 BA Zwolle.
Tel 038 4216031, Fax 038 4223069.
English spoken.
Open all year. 72 bedrooms (all en suite).
Parking. ⓒ ♿

Modern, friendly hotel with good service and facilities. Take A28 to Zwolle (exit 18).

■ RESTAURANT: Good choice of menus at reasonable prices.
■ ACTIVITIES: Hotel organises car and cycling holidays; lots of attractions nearby including De Weerribben nature reserve, Walibi amusement park, the pony park at Slagharen and various museums.
■ TARIFF: (1996) Single 125–146, Double 145–166, Bk 15.50, Set menu 32.50–37.50 (Amex, Euro/Access, Visa).

Netherlands

NORWAY

Sognefjord

Beyond the Arctic Circle, Norway offers seasonal extremes of either midnight sun or the winter's Northern Lights. The country has an excellent road network – covering even remotest Finnmark – and this means a Scandinavian round trip is a real possibility.

The capital, Oslo, is remarkably unmetropolitan: its houses straggle out into the forest or line the rocky coast and clear waters of the fjord. Two burial mounds south of Oslo yielded the greatest of all Viking relics, the Gokstad and Oseberg ships, now housed in a superb museum at Bydgoy, just outside the city, close to the latter-day Viking Thor Heyerdahl's *Kon Tiki* and *Ra II*. The Edvard Munch Museum betrays an angst-ridden undertone to apparently untroubled Oslo.

From Stavanger northwards, the coastline becomes a non-stop spectacle, mixing sheer-sided fjords with the more detailed world of the offshore islands. Bergen is the regular start for the Hurtigrute passenger ship, beginning an 11-day round-trip to and from Kirkenes, near the Russian frontier.

North of Trondheim, a long parade of mountains and fjords culminates in the jagged heights of the Lofoten Islands. From Narvik, north and eastwards, Norwegians overlap with indigenous Sami – or Lapps – many of whom, wearing their bright traditional costumes, still follow their reindeer herds in season. Hammerfest, in the open landscape of Finnmark, is considered the 'most northerly city in the world'. Beyond it lies the North Cape, the Pole... and, if you believe the brochures, Santa himself.

Emergency numbers

Police 112, Fire Brigade 110, Ambulance 113

Warning information

Carrying a warning triangle recommended

Blood Alcohol Legal Limit 50 mg

Norway

BALESTRAND   11A

Hotel Midtnes Pensjonat
5850 Balestrand.
Tel 57 69 11 33, Fax 57 69 15 84.
English spoken.
Open 01/02 to 20/12. 30 bedrooms
(all en suite). Parking, restaurant. ✆

In the centre of Balestrand, close to the English church. Own jetty with rowing boats. Five minutes' walk from bus stop and express boat quay.

■ TARIFF: Single 450–475, Double 610–690, Set menu 160 (Visa).
■ DISCOUNT: 10%

EVJE   11A

Grenaderen Motel 4660 Evje.
Tel 37 93 04 00, Fax 37 93 13 70.
English spoken.
Open all year. 30 bedrooms (all en suite).
Outdoor swimming pool, parking. ✆

Renovated in 1996, offering warm, comfortable accommodation.

■ RESTAURANT: Restaurant/cafeteria offering home-cooked Norwegian dishes as well as an international à la carte menu.
■ ACTIVITIES: Exploring the beautiful countryside.

KRISTIANSAND   11C

Hotel Christian Quart ★★★★
Markensgt 39, 4600 Kristiansand.
Tel 38 02 22 10, Fax 38 02 44 10.
English spoken.
Open all year. 111 bedrooms (all en suite).
Garage, restaurant. ✆ ♿

Town centre hotel close to the ferry terminal.

■ TARIFF: (1996) Single 590–995, Double 740–1095 (Amex, Euro/Access, Visa).

LOEN   11A

Hotel Alexandra Nordfjord, 6878 Loen.
Tel 57 87 76 60, Fax 57 87 77 70.
English spoken.
Open 12/01 to 31/12. 198 bedrooms
(all en suite). Indoor swimming pool, tennis, garage, parking, restaurant. ♿

Very comfortable; excellent facilities. In the midst of fjord country, surrounded by mountains and picturesque valleys.

■ ACTIVITIES: Close to Alexandra Park which is ideal for outdoor activities and also the departure point for trips to Briksdal, Geiranger and Lodal.

■ TARIFF: (1996) Single 855–2450, Double 1250–2450, Set menu 275–498 (Amex, Euro/Access, Visa).

SKEI I JØLSTER   11A

Hotel Skei 6850 Skei i Jølster.
Tel 57 72 81 01, Fax 57 72 84 23.
English spoken.

Open 25/01 to 15/12. 95 bedrooms
(all en suite). Indoor swimming pool, tennis, parking. ♿

Friendly, comfortable, family-run hotel with traditions dating back to 1889. Lots to do and see; excellent facilities. Situated in beautiful, natural surroundings at the northern end of Lake Jølster, about 195 km north of Bergen.

SEE ADVERTISEMENT

■ RESTAURANT: Traditional Norwegian-style restaurant offering a wide range of national and international dishes. Poached trout from Lake Jølster is a speciality.
■ ACTIVITIES: Tennis, badminton and putting green; health club offering sauna, jacuzzi

Norway

solarium and Turkish bath; bikes and rowing boats for hire; horse-riding, way-marked paths for hiking/mountain walks and fishing nearby.● The hotel organises ten different tours which cover all of the region's attractions, including flights over the glaciers and fjords.
■ TARIFF: Single 725–850, Double 990–1170, Set menu 245–395 (Amex, Euro/Access, Visa).
■ DISCOUNT: 10%

SOLVORN 11A

Hotel Walaker Sognefjord, 5815 Solvorn.
Tel 57 68 42 07, Fax 57 68 45 44.
English spoken.
Open 01/05 to 31/10. 24 bedrooms
(19 en suite). Parking.

Former inn and coaching station owned and run by different generations of the same family since 1690. Situated on the north bank of the Sognefjord, 3 km off route 55, 15 km east of Sogndal and 120 km west of Lom. Solvorn is a picturesque, well-preserved village.

■ RESTAURANT: Good Norwegian dishes are prepared by Mr Walaker, who is also the owner.

■ ACTIVITIES: Urnes stave church and the Jostedal glacier are within easy reach; art gallery showing Norwegian contemporary art is on hotel premises. ● Fjord cruises 3 days a week (6 hours' duration) with refreshments on board.
■ TARIFF: (1996) Single 380–680, Double 520–980, Set menu 90–260 (Visa).

Norway

POLAND

Much of Warsaw, the capital city, was destroyed during the Second World War and what you see today is largely reconstruction. To learn more about the history and people of this remarkable country, visit the National Museum which also includes archaeological exhibits and a display of medieval altarpieces; or, at the Castle Museum, muse upon the very Canaletto paintings that inspired the new city plan. At the Historical Museum a particularly poignant exhibition tells the story of the stalwart resistance of ordinary people during the last war. Warsaw boasts many palaces, mostly open to the public but if you can't decide between them take a trip instead to Wilano and the 'Polish Versailles'.

A northern tour from the city takes you to Poznan and the holy isle of Ostrow Tumski with its many museums. On then to Gdansk, formerly Danzig, and famed for its shipyards – the Maritime Museum is housed in the 15th-century Gdansk Crane.

Although hopefully you will never be banished to the salt mines, in Poland you can take a trip down one and see how well you would fare. Very well, judging by the mine at Wieliczka, where the atmosphere is supposedly rather good for you. So good, in fact, that there is a sanatorium sited 200m below ground. The Wieliczka salt mine is 15 km south of Krakow and open daily.

Emergency numbers

Police 997, Fire Brigade 998, Ambulance 999

Warning information

Warning triangle must be carried

Blood Alcohol Legal Limit 20 mg

Green card essential

KRAKOW (CRACOW) 22D

Hotel Forum ★★★★
ul Marii Konopnickiej 28, 30302 Krakow.
Tel 12 66 95 00, Fax 12 66 58 27.
English spoken.

Open all year. 277 bedrooms (all en suite). Indoor swimming pool. ☎ &

Modern hotel on the banks of the Vistula river; overlooks the royal castle and is 1 km from the old town. Direct access from motorways 7 and 4. 15 km from Balice airport. (Prices in DM.)

■ RESTAURANT: Closed 25 Dec. The main restaurant features Polish specialities and some international dishes. Menu for children and vegetarians also available. Special dinners with typical Polish food accompanied by folk music are arranged.
■ ACTIVITIES: Sightseeing tours of Krakow, Wieliczka Salt Mine and Auschwitz.
■ TARIFF: (1996) Single 150–215, Double 180–245, Set menu 30 (Amex, Euro/Access, Visa).

Hotel Pollera ★★
ul Szpitalna 30, 31024 Krakow.
Tel 12 22 10 44, Fax 12 22 13 89.
English spoken.
Open all year. 42 bedrooms (21 en suite, 12 bath/shower only). Parking. &

A family-run hotel with 150 years' tradition, offering large, light rooms. Near the station, a car park and theatre. (Prices in DM.)

■ RESTAURANT: Good selection of national and international dishes, including white borsch, roast pork with plums and pancakes flambée.

■ TARIFF: (1996) Single 45–77, Double 70–105, Set menu 8–13 (Amex, Euro/Access, Visa).
■ DISCOUNT: 10%

WARSZAWA (WARSAW) 22B

Hotel Orbis Grand ★★★
ul Krucza 28, 00522 Warszawa.
Tel 22 629 4051, Fax 22 621 9724.
English spoken.

Open all year. 317 bedrooms (all en suite).
Indoor swimming pool, tennis, golf 20 km. ✆

City centre hotel, close to main business and entertainment areas and a few minutes' walk from the famous old town. Facilities include non-smoking floor, meeting/conference rooms (some with modem) and a tourist service agency. (Prices in DM.)

■ RESTAURANT: Choice of restaurants offering a selection of Polish and international cuisine.
■ ACTIVITIES: Indoor pool complex with sauna, solarium and massage facilities; casino and 'Olimp' nightclub with live entertainment. Tennis 1 km. Museums and plenty of sights to see nearby.
■ TARIFF: Single 90–132, Double 110–162, Set menu 19–50 (Amex, Euro/Access, Visa).
■ DISCOUNT: 20%

Hotel Solec ★★★
ul Zagorna 1, 00441 Warszawa.
Tel 22 625 4400, Fax 22 621 6442.
English spoken.
Open all year. 140 bedrooms (all en suite).
Golf 25 km. ✆

In a quiet spot but conveniently situated near the intersection of two motorways, the hotel stands close to a large park and is just 4 km from Warszawa city centre and 10 km from the international airport. Good conference facilities. (Prices in DM.)

■ RESTAURANT: Renowned for its traditional Polish and regional cuisine.
■ ACTIVITIES: Good base for exploring Warszawa and the surrounding country.
■ TARIFF: Single 139, Double 158 (Amex, Euro/Access, Visa).
■ DISCOUNT: 10%

Poland

PORTUGAL

The Algarve: Oura Beach

To reach Portugal by car from Great Britain, the drive through France and Spain is not for the faint-hearted. A ferry to Santander in north-western Spain reduces the ordeal. Alternatively, fly to Lisbon or Faro and hire a car.

At half past nine in the morning of 1 November 1755 a great earthquake, strong enough to be recorded as far away as Scotland, hit Lisbon. Many rushed to the foreshore for safety, to be hit by a tidal wave. Forty thousand died and the city itself was all but destroyed.

From Lisbon, a trip out to Sintra will take you to the summer playground of the kings of Portugal and, earlier, of the Moors. Described by Byron in 1809 as 'having all the wildness of the Western Highlands with the verdure of the South of France'.

The Algarve is a popular beach holiday destination with a coast that is warm enough to be enjoyed out of season too.

Faro, halfway along the southern coast, has an international airport and is a popular fly-drive destination.

The countryside from Faro to Lisbon is an enormous cork plantation, cork being one crop that will survive the impoverished soil. Detour to Evora and you will find a city protected by UNESCO for the wealth and variety of its buildings, from a 2nd-century Roman temple to a collection of 16th-century palaces – with the lure of a wonderful market every Tuesday and Saturday and a lively festival at the end of June.

Emergency numbers

Police, Fire Brigade and Ambulance 115

Warning information

Warning triangle must be carried

Green Card recommended

Blood Alcohol Legal Limit 50 mg

ABRANTES 8C

Best Western Hotel de Turismo ★★★
Largo de St-Antonio, 2200 Abrantes.
Tel 41 21 261, Fax 41 25 218. English spoken.
Open all year. 41 bedrooms (all en suite).
Outdoor swimming pool, tennis, parking.
Quiet, comfortable hotel with all modern
facilities. Superb view over the Tagus river valley.
Close to Fatima and Lisboa to Spain motorway.
■ RESTAURANT: Panoramic views and regional
cuisine.
■ TARIFF: (1996) Single 9,500–10,500,
Double 11,400–13,000, Set menu 3,200
(Amex, Euro/Access, Visa).
■ DISCOUNT: 10%

AVEIRO 8A

Hotel Barra Av Fernandes Lavrador 18,
Praoa da Barra, 3830 Ilhavo.
Tel 34 36 91 56, Fax 34 36 00 07. English spoken.
Open all year. 64 bedrooms (all en suite).
Outdoor swimming pool, parking. ✆
Quiet, comfortable hotel with air conditioning.
Between the Atlantic and estuary of the Ria
river, 8 km south of Aveiro on N109.
■ RESTAURANT: On the 5th floor, panoramic
restaurant overlooking the sea.
■ ACTIVITIES: Disco, solarium, fishing and water
sports (water-skiing, rowing, sailing).
■ TARIFF: (1996) Single 9,980–14,700,
Double 11,000–16,250 (Amex, Euro/Access, Visa).
■ DISCOUNT: 10%

Hotel Imperial ★★★
Rua Dr Nascimento Leitao, 3800 Aveiro.
Tel 34 22 141, Fax 34 24 148. English spoken.
Open all year. 107 bedrooms (all en suite).
Restaurant. ♿
Comfortable, modern hotel in the city centre.
■ ACTIVITIES: Solarium with panoramic view of
Aveiro and the ocean.
■ TARIFF: Single 8,000–10,000, Double 10,500–
12,700 (Amex, Euro/Access, Visa).
■ DISCOUNT: 10%

BATALHA 8C

Hotel Dom Joao III ★★★
Av Dom Joao III, 2400 Leiria.
Tel 44 81 25 00, Fax 44 81 22 35. English spoken.
Open all year. 64 bedrooms (all en suite).
Garage, parking, restaurant. ♿
Situated in a quiet location near the town
centre. 20 km from Fatima and one hours'
drive from Lisboa airport.

■ TARIFF: (1996) Single 9,600, Double 11,800,
Set menu 2,500 (Amex, Euro/Access, Visa).

BRAGANÇA 8A

Hotel Bragança ★★★
Av Dr Francisco Sa Carneiro, 5300 Bragança.
Tel 73 331578/9, Fax 73 331242. English spoken.
Open all year. 42 bedrooms (all en suite).
Parking, restaurant. ✆
Town centre hotel.
■ TARIFF: (1996) Single 3,500–6,750,
Double 5,500–12,000, Set menu 1,750–3,000
(Amex, Euro/Access, Visa).

ERICEIRA 8C

Hotel Morais ★★
Rua Dr Miguel Bombarda 3, 2655 Ericeira.
Tel 61 86 42 00, Fax 61 86 43 08. English spoken.
Open 01/12 to 31/10. 40 bedrooms (all en
suite). Outdoor swimming pool, golf 25 km.
Small family hotel only 300 m from shops and
cafés and 8 minutes' walk to the beach.
■ TARIFF: (1996) Single 3,500–7,500,
Double 4,000–12,500 (Amex, Euro/Access, Visa).

ESTORIL 8C

Hotel Palacio ★★★★★
Rua do Parque, 2765 Estoril.
Tel 1 46 80 400, Fax 1 46 84 867. English spoken.

Open all year. 162 bedrooms (all en suite).
Outdoor swimming pool, tennis, golf 1 km,
parking, restaurant.
Large, traditional hotel in centre of Estoril,
elegantly decorated and furnished.
■ ACTIVITIES: Tennis nearby ● Special rates at
Palacio Golf Club.
■ TARIFF: Single 22,000–33,000, Double 24,000–
35,000, Set menu 4,750 (Amex, Euro/Access, Visa).
■ DISCOUNT: 10%

FATIMA 8C

Hotel Estalagem Dom Goncalo ★★★★
2495 Fatima.
Tel 49 53 30 62, Fax 49 53 20 88. English spoken.
Open all year. 42 bedrooms (all en suite).
Garage, parking. &

Quiet, very comfortable hotel, completely refurbished and updated in 1996. Surrounded by gardens yet only a minute away from the Lisboa-Porto highway. Run by a family who take pride in offering personalised service and a warm welcome. The shrine of Our Lady of Fatima is 2 minutes' walk from hotel.

■ RESTAURANT: Light, spacious dining room with excellent service. Traditional Portuguese specialities, seafood and fine wines.
■ ACTIVITIES: Visits to archaeological sites, historic monuments, caves; lovely beaches with water sports; religious festivals from 10th to 13th of months April to October.
■ TARIFF: (1996) Single 7,650–9,000, Double 9,350–11,000 (Amex, Visa).
■ DISCOUNT: 10% not 10th to 13th of months Apr to Oct.

LISBOA (LISBON) 8C

As Janelas Verdes Inn ★★★★
Rua das Janelas Verdes 47, 1200 Lisboa.
Tel 1 39 68 143, Fax 1 39 68 144. English spoken.

Open all year. 17 bedrooms (all en suite).
Golf 15 km, garage. ℂ

The inn, with a small but beautiful garden, is housed in a romantic aristocratic mansion dating from the late 18th century. Quiet location in the old part of the city, next to the National Museum of Ancient Art.

■ TARIFF: Single 17,500–27,500, Double 18,500–29,800 (Amex, Euro/Access, Visa).

Hotel Altis ★★★★★
Rua Castilho 11, 1200 Lisboa.

Tel 1 314 24 96, Fax 1 354 86 96. English spoken.
Open all year. 303 bedrooms (all en suite). Indoor swimming pool, golf 25 km, parking. ℂ &
Luxury hotel, well situated for exploring this beautiful old city.

■ RESTAURANT: Two restaurants: the 'Grill D Fernando' with a marvellous view over Lisboa centre and the Tagus river and the 'Girassol' with its magnificient buffet.
■ ACTIVITIES: Sauna, fitness room.
■ TARIFF: Single 22,000–28,000, Double 26,000–32,000 (Amex, Euro/Access, Visa).
■ DISCOUNT: 20% except during Formula 1 Grand Prix.

Best Western Eduardo VII ★★★
Av Fontes P de Melo 5, 1000 Lisboa.
Tel 1 35 30 141, Fax 1 35 33 879. English spoken.

Open all year. 121 bedrooms (all en suite).
Golf 15 km, garage. ℂ

Comfortable, air-conditioned hotel with panoramic view of Lisboa. Centrally located, close to Eduardo VII Park, shopping district and museums.

■ RESTAURANT: Panoramic rooftop restaurant with cocktail bar. Regional specialities.
■ TARIFF: Single 11,900–15,300, Double 14,000–17,500, Set menu 3,600 (Amex, Euro/Access, Visa).
■ DISCOUNT: 10%

Hotel Flamingo ★★★
Rua Castilho 41, 1200 Lisboa.
Tel 1 38 62 191, Fax 1 38 61 216. English spoken.
Open all year. 39 bedrooms (all en suite).
Golf 15 km, restaurant.

Situated near Praça Marquês de Pombal, with an ideal central location for exploring the city. Good facilities including air conditioning and very comfortable bar area.

■ TARIFF: (1996) Single 11,500–13,500, Double 13,500–16,500 (Amex, Euro/Access, Visa).

Hotel Britania ★★★
Rua Rodrigues Sampaio 17, 1150 Lisboa.
Tel 1 31 55 016, Fax 1 31 55 021. English spoken.

Open all year. 30 bedrooms (all en suite).
Golf 15 km, parking. ☏

*Located in the very heart of Lisboa, this hotel
combines a charming, warm atmosphere with
traditional and personal service.*

■ TARIFF: Single 14,200–22,200, Double 16,500–
23,500 (Amex, Euro/Access, Visa).

Hotel Lisboa Plaza ★★★★
Travessa do Salitre 7, 1250 Lisboa.
Tel 1 34 63 922, Fax 1 34 71 630. English spoken.

Open all year. 112 bedrooms (all en suite).
Golf 15 km, garage, parking. ☏

*Charming, family-owned and operated hotel
in the heart of the city, just off Av Liberdade,
Lisboa's main street. Warm and inviting, the
hotel was completely redecorated in 1991 by a
famous Portuguese interior designer.
'Paddock' bar and cocktail lounge 'Plaza
Club'. Accommodation and breakfast free for
children up to the age of 12 staying in their
parents' room.*

■ RESTAURANT: 'Quinta d'Avenida' restaurant

offers traditional Portuguese specialities. Buffet
and à la carte menu.
■ TARIFF: Single 18,500–25,500,
Double 19,500–28,000, Set menu 2,750–4,950
(Amex, Euro/Access, Visa).

MADEIRA

FUNCHAL

Reid's Hotel ★★★★★ Estrada Monumental 139,
9000 Funchal, Madeira.
Tel 91 700 71 71, Fax 91 700 71 77. English spoken.

Open all year. 168 bedrooms (all en suite).
Outdoor swimming pool, tennis, golf 10 km,
garage, parking. ☏ ♿

*Perched on the cliff top with panoramic views
over the bay of Funchal, this world-renowned
hotel is a haven of peace and luxury with
individually designed rooms and impeccable
service. With its own access to the sea, Reid's is
surrounded by a 4-hectare park with sub-
tropical trees. 3 km from downtown Funchal,
the harbour and the shopping area.*

■ RESTAURANT: Choose from the main restaurant
(closed Tue & Fri) specialising in classic
traditional cuisine; 'Les Faunes' (closed Sun)
which overlooks the bay, has a French chef
and is truly a gourmet's delight, or the Italian
'Trattoria Villa Cliff' which offers a superb
antipasta buffet including fresh fish and typical
pasta and meat dishes. Speciality Portuguese
and Italian buffets are held beside the pool on
Tuesdays and Fridays.
■ ACTIVITIES: The excellent choice of sporting
activities includes water-skiing, windsurfing,
sailing, scuba-diving, deep-sea fishing, boat
trips, jeep safaris, mountain-biking and trekking.
A children's club is open during July and August.
■ TARIFF: Single 27,000–57,200, Double 41,000–
76,400 (Amex, Euro/Access, Visa).

END OF MADEIRA HOTELS

Portugal

MONTE GORDO   8C

Hotel Vasco Da Gama ★★★ Avenida Infante
d'Henrique, 8900 Monte Gordo.
Tel 81 51 13 21, Fax 81 51 16 22.
English spoken.

Open all year. 167 bedrooms (all en suite).
Outdoor swimming pool, tennis, golf 10 km,
parking.

Set beside the beach, a comfortable hotel with
beautiful gardens. Faro international airport
is only 45 minutes' drive away.

■ RESTAURANT: Buffet service.
■ ACTIVITIES: Water sports/beach activities close
by. Ideal location for exploring the Algarve
region. ● Free one hour tennis session and 25%
discount at local golf course for bookings of 3
nights or more.
■ TARIFF: Single 5,600–16,300,
Double 7,500–21,700, Set menu 2,000 (Amex,
Euro/Access, Visa).
■ DISCOUNT: 20% except 15 Jul to 15 Sept.

PORTIMAO   8C

Hotel Algarve ★★★★★ 8500 Praia da Rocha.
Tel 82 41 50 01, Fax 82 41 59 99.
English spoken.

Open all year. 214 bedrooms (all en suite).
Outdoor swimming pool, tennis, golf 2.5 km,
parking. &

Luxury hotel/casino set on the cliffs directly
above the superb beach of Praia da Rocha. The
brand new casino, plus restaurant featuring
international floor shows, is adjacent to the
hotel. 2.5 km south of Portimao.

■ RESTAURANT: Good restaurant with
international and regional cuisine. Portuguese
specialities with lots of seafood dishes.
■ ACTIVITIES: Bridge and water sports at hotel;
● 5 golf courses within easy reach; 30% green
fee reduction for hotel guests.
■ TARIFF: (1996) Single 11,000–30,500,
Double 20,500–39,000, Set menu 3,900–5,500
(Amex, Euro/Access, Visa).
■ DISCOUNT: 15% except Jul, Aug & Sept.

Hotel Alvor ★★★★★
Praia dos Tres Irmaos Alvor.
Tel 82 45 89 00, Fax 82 45 89 99. English spoken.
Open all year. 198 bedrooms (all en suite).
Outdoor swimming pool, tennis, golf 2 km,
parking. &&

Elegant hotel ideally situated at one end of the
long Alvor beach, above the rock-encircled
cove of Praia dos Tres Irmaos. 2 km from Alvor
and 5 km from Portimao.

■ RESTAURANT: Portuguese and international
cuisine. Speciality is the chef's award-winning
fish soup. Panoramic sea views.
■ ACTIVITIES: Table tennis, billiards, mini-golf,
archery, volley ball.
■ TARIFF: Single 10,300–46,800, Double 13,800–
52,400 (Amex, Euro/Access, Visa).
■ DISCOUNT: 25%

Hotel Delfim ★★★★
Praia dos Tres Irmaos Alvor.
Tel 82 45 89 01, Fax 82 45 89 70.
English spoken.
Open all year. 312 bedrooms (all en suite).
Indoor swimming pool, outdoor swimming
pool, tennis, golf 2 km, parking. && &

Pleasant atmosphere and good service. 200 m
from the vast Alvor beach, 2 km from Alvor
town centre and 5 km from Portimao.

■ RESTAURANT: Portuguese and international
cuisine; good choice at the main restaurant
(buffet) or à la carte restaurant. View over the
pool.
■ ACTIVITIES: Table tennis, billiards, mini-golf,
archery.
■ TARIFF: (1996) Single 6,400–27,800,
Double 8,800–31,000 (Amex, Euro/Access, Visa).
■ DISCOUNT: 25%

Portugal

PORTO (OPORTO) 8A

Hotel Estalagem do Brasao ★★★★
Av D Joao Canavarro, 4480 Vila do Conde.
Tel 52 64 20 16, Fax 52 64 20 28.
English spoken.
Open all year. 30 bedrooms (all en suite).
Golf 2 km, parking, restaurant.

Renowned hotel, the property dating back to 1500. Now sympathetically restored, it still retains its old classic style whilst offering all modern comforts. Suites are also available. Situated in the centre of the old town within easy walking distance of the beach and nearby river. North of Porto on the E01.

■ ACTIVITIES: Perfect location for touring and sightseeing.
■ TARIFF: (1996) Single 5,900–9,400, Double 7,900–13,200 (Amex, Euro/Access, Visa).
■ DISCOUNT: 15% 15/06 to 31/08.

SERTA 8A

Estalagem Vale da Ursa ★★★★
Cernache Do Bonjardim, 6100 Serta.
Tel 74 90 981, Fax 74 90 982. English spoken.

Open all year. 17 bedrooms (all en suite). Outdoor swimming pool, tennis, garage, parking. &

Small, comfortable and very quiet family hotel with wonderful views over lake. 2 hours' drive from Lisboa in beautiful countryside. All rooms have terrace and air conditioning. Special winter rates. West of Serta, 17 km along N238.

■ RESTAURANT: Regional and vegetarian dishes with specialities including suckling pig and barbecued black bass.
■ ACTIVITIES: Fishing and water sports from hotel.
■ TARIFF: Single 7,500–12,500, Double 10,500–16,500, Set menu 2,500–3,000 (Euro/Access, Visa).
■ DISCOUNT: 15%

SESIMBRA 8C

Hotel do Mar ★★★★ Rua General Humberto Delgado, 10, 2970 Sesimbra.
Tel 1 22 33 326, Fax 1 22 33 888.
English spoken.

Open all year. 168 bedrooms (all en suite). Indoor swimming pool, outdoor swimming pool, tennis, parking.

Very comfortable hotel facing sandy beach. All rooms have air conditioning and sea view. Excellent conference and banqueting facilities. 30 km from Lisboa.

■ RESTAURANT: Panoramic views.
■ ACTIVITIES: ● Special rates for photographic expedition with guide to the Arrabiba nature park.
■ TARIFF: Single 9,200–17,300, Double 14,000–27,300, Set menu 3,700 (Amex, Euro/Access, Visa).
■ DISCOUNT: 15%

VIANA DO CASTELO 8A

Hotel do Parque ★★★★ Praca da Galiza, Costa Verde, 4900 Viana do Castelo.
Tel 58 82 86 05, Fax 58 82 86 12.
English spoken.
Open all year. 123 bedrooms (all en suite). Outdoor swimming pool, parking. &

A large, modern hotel with up-to-date amenities. Rooms are air conditioned and some have balcony overlooking the River Lima. Bar on the terrace. Winter garden.

■ RESTAURANT: Panoramic restaurant overlooking the Lima river. International cuisine and regional specialities.
■ ACTIVITIES: Good sports facilities, solarium and games room; bikes and tennis nearby.
■ TARIFF: (1996) Single 8,500–15,250, Double 9,500–18,750, Set menu 2,750–3,250 (Amex, Euro/Access, Visa).

Portugal

SPAIN

Tamarit

Browsing through the Spanish pages of a British holiday brochure, you might easily be forgiven for thinking that Spain's major, if not only attraction, is its beaches. Yet more than any other country in Europe, bar Switzerland, it is in fact a land of mountains.

The Cordillera Cantábrica mountains lie parallel to the north coast, along a line similar to that of the Pyrenees in the east. If your Spanish debut is made off the ferry at Santander, this is the mountain landscape that will shortly greet you. More mountains await those travelling to the country's epicentre at Madrid (rare among capitals for being so central); then further south lie the Sierra Morena mountains, with the Sierra Nevada lying between the old Moorish capital, Granada, and the Mediterranean.

Granada enjoys a breathtakingly beautiful situation at the foothills of the Sierra Nevada, as well as boasting one of Europe's most impressive collections of important buildings. One of these, the Alhambra Palace, recalls that Granada was for seven centuries a Moorish town (711–1491). By contrast, the cathedral at Santiago de Compostela is perhaps the most important monument to the spread of Christianity in the north.

The motorist exploring interior Spain will also happen upon the *pueblos blancos* hillside villages, close-knit communities where life goes on very much as it has done for centuries. Enjoy the hair-pin-bend exhilaration of a bus ride to market shared with the locals... and let the beaches of the Costa Brava waiting for another year.

Emergency numbers

For emergency numbers see the local directory

Warning information

Green card recommended

Bail bond recommended

Blood Alcohol Legal Limit 80 mg

Spain

ALGECIRAS 8D

Hotel Al-Mar ★★★
Avda de la Marina 2 & 3, 11201 Algeciras.
Tel 956 654661, Fax 956 654501. English spoken.
Open all year. 192 bedrooms (all en suite).
Garage. &

Modern hotel conveniently situated opposite the port. In the commercial district of Algeciras, on the main road from Cadiz to Malaga.

■ RESTAURANT: Modern dining room with wonderful sea views. National cuisine.
■ ACTIVITIES: Hotel will make reservations for excursions.
■ TARIFF: (1996) Single 4,800, Double 9,000, Set menu 1,600–3,000 (Amex, Euro/Access, Visa).

ALHAURIN EL GRANDE 8D

Hotel Finca La Mota ★★
Ctra Mijas, Alhaurin el Grande, 29120 Malaga.
Tel 952 594120, Fax 952 594120. English spoken.
Open all year. 13 bedrooms (9 en suite).
Outdoor swimming pool, tennis, golf 1 km, parking. ℂ

A charming country inn converted from a 16th-century farmhouse. Rustic, peaceful, cosy and comfortable with some rooms having four-poster beds. Surrounded by beautiful, mountainous countryside but only 15 km from beaches. Take the Mijas road from Alhaurin el Grande and follow hotel signs 2 km from village.

■ RESTAURANT: International cuisine with Indian specialities. Daily barbecued dishes include T-bone steaks and succulent leg of lamb with rosemary picked fresh from the mountains. Emphasis is on fresh, local produce, much of it home-grown.
■ ACTIVITIES: Mini-golf and horse-riding at the hotel. Wonderful base for walking and sightseeing.
■ TARIFF: (1996) Single 6,000, Double 8,000–10,000, Set menu 2,000 (Amex, Euro/Access, Visa).

ARANDA DE DUERO 8B

Hostal Aranda ★★ Calle San Francisco 51, Frente a la Plaza de Toros, 09400 Aranda de Duero.
Tel 947 501600, Fax 947 501604. English spoken.
Open all year. 44 bedrooms (all en suite).
Outdoor swimming pool, garage, parking. ℂ

Quiet location opposite the square in the city centre. From Burgos, take the Palencia/Aranda de Duero exit.

■ RESTAURANT: Specialities include boiled chorizo, fish and roast lamb served with black pudding and red peppers.
■ ACTIVITIES: Swimming pool nearby; tours to Santo Domingo de Silos, Covarrubias and Lerma.
■ TARIFF: (1996) Single 3,800, Double 6,300–7,600, Bk 500, Set menu 1,500 (Euro/Access, Visa).

Hotel Tres Condes ★★★
Avenida Castilla 66, 09400 Aranda de Duero.
Tel 947 502400, Fax 947 502404.
Open all year. 35 bedrooms (all en suite).
Golf 20 km, garage, parking. ℂ

In the centre of Aranda de Duero and not far from the monastery of Santo Domingo de Silos.

■ RESTAURANT: Closed Sun eve. Excellent cuisine. One of the specialities is lamb roasted in a wood oven.
■ ACTIVITIES: Night club at hotel; many historic sights to visit nearby.
■ TARIFF: Single 5600–6450, Double 7600–8100, Bk 550, Set menu 1700–2950 (Amex, Euro/Access, Visa).
■ DISCOUNT: 10%

BAILEN 8D

Hotel Yuma ★★ Ctra Madrid-Cadiz, Km 281, 23210 Guarroman.
Tel 953 615036, Fax 953 615256.
Open all year. 16 bedrooms (all en suite).
Parking. ℂ

Open 24 hours a day, providing an ideal stop-over location for weary travellers as well as the benefit of its own petrol station. Midway between La Carolina and Bailen on N4/E5 in beautiful surrounding countryside.

■ RESTAURANT: Typical regional dishes with home-made specialities.
■ TARIFF: (1996) Single 4,240, Double 6,100, Bk 500, Set menu 1,800–5,000 (Amex, Euro/Access, Visa).
■ DISCOUNT: 15%

Hotel Zodiaco ★★★ 23710 Bailen.
Tel 953 671058, Fax 953 671906. English spoken.
Open all year. 51 bedrooms (all en suite).
Garage, parking. ℂ &

Large hotel, spacious rooms, excellent facilities.

■ RESTAURANT: Award-winning restaurant offering local and international cuisine.
■ ACTIVITIES: Many cities to visit around Bailen as well as the Sierra Morena.
■ TARIFF: Single 4875–5220, Double 5955–6985, Bk 500, Set menu 1600–3000 (Amex, Euro/Access, Visa).
■ DISCOUNT: 8%

Spain

BARCELONA 9B

Hotel Fira Palace ★★★★
Avda Rius i Taulet 1-3, 08004 Barcelona.
Tel 934 262223, Fax 934 255047. English spoken.

Open all year. 276 bedrooms (all en suite).
Indoor swimming pool, golf 8 km, garage. ✆ ♿

Situated next to the Congress Hall and fair exhibition grounds and close to the Spanish village, Olympic area and Miro museum. Comfortable, modern hotel with a high standard of accommodation and facilities.

■ RESTAURANT: Catalan and barbecue specialities. The menu changes in accordance with the seasons.
■ ACTIVITIES: Fitness centre/gymnasium, squash court.
■ TARIFF: (1996) Single 18,400, Double 23,000, Bk 1,400, Set menu 2,800–3,200 (No credit cards).
■ DISCOUNT: 20% except public holidays.

Hotel Gran Via ★★★
Gran Via Corts Catalanes 642, 08000 Barcelona.
Tel 933 181900, Fax 933 189997.
English spoken.
Open all year. 53 bedrooms (all en suite).
Golf 5 km, garage. ✆ ♿

Elegant, grand hotel in centre of Barcelona. Close to the Plaza Cataluña in an ideal position for both business and pleasure.

■ TARIFF: (1996) Single 9,000, Double 9,000–11,500 (Amex, Euro/Access, Visa).

Hotel Princesa Sofia ★★★★
Plaza Pio XII 4, 08028 Barcelona.
Tel 933 307111, Fax 933 307621.
English spoken.
Open all year. 505 bedrooms (all en suite).
Indoor swimming pool, outdoor swimming pool, golf 15 km, garage, parking, restaurant.

Luxury hotel located in the exclusive Avda Diagonal in the new financial centre, and conveniently situated for all business and cultural points of interest. 20 minutes from airport and 10 minutes to station.

■ TARIFF: (1996) Single 17,000–20,000, Double 13,950–25,000, Bk 1,800 (Amex, Euro/Access, Visa).

BEGUR 9B

Hotel Aigua Blava ★★★★
Platja de Fornells, 17255 Begur.
Tel 972 622058, Fax 972 622112.
English spoken.
Open 20/02 to 14/11. 85 bedrooms (all en suite). Outdoor swimming pool, tennis, golf 12 km, garage, parking.

Very comfortable hotel in a superb location beside the sea and pine forests. Fornells is south-east of Begur.

SEE ADVERTISEMENT

■ RESTAURANT: Award-winning restaurant.
■ ACTIVITIES: Boating, water sports and horse-riding nearby; ● Special rates for hotel guests at nearby golf courses.
■ TARIFF: Single 8,000–10,400, Double 12,000–17,100, Bk 1,500, Set menu 3,500–5,000 (Amex, Euro/Access, Visa).

Spain

BEJAR 8B

Hotel Colon ★★★ Colon 42, 37700 Bejar.
Tel 923 400650, Fax 923 400450. English spoken.

Open all year. 54 bedrooms (all en suite). ☏
*Traditional and comfortable, hotel is
conveniently situated close to the centre of this
lovely old town. (A swimming pool is under
construction and should be ready for the 1997
summer season.) Bejar is on the N630 between
Salamanca and Plasencia.*

■ RESTAURANT: Modern restaurant offering
regional specialities.
■ ACTIVITIES: Mountain biking, hiking, climbing,
skiing in winter.
■ TARIFF: (1996) Single 4,600–6,000,
Double 7,400–8,500, Bk 600, Set menu 2,000
(Amex, Euro/Access, Visa).
■ DISCOUNT: 10%

BILBAO 8B

Hotel Carlton ★★★★
Pl F Moyua 2, 48009 Bilbao.
Tel 944 162200, Fax 944 164628. English spoken.

Open all year. 148 bedrooms (all en suite).
Golf 14 km, garage. ☏ ♿
*Centrally situated, a fine, elegant hotel that
was totally renovated in 1994. Has recently
been declared a monument of historic and
architectural interest.*

■ RESTAURANT: Restaurant 'Artagan' is renowned
for its excellent traditional and gastronomic
cuisine and has had the honour of
entertaining royalty.
■ TARIFF: (1996) Single 19,000, Double 24,000,
Bk 1,200, Set menu 4,000 (Amex,
Euro/Access, Visa).
■ DISCOUNT: 15% except national holidays.

BLANES 9B

Hotel Horitzo ★★★
Paseo Maritimo S'Abanell 11, 17300 Blanes.
Tel 972 330400, Fax 972 337863.
English spoken.

Open 01/04 to 31/10. 122 bedrooms
(all en suite). Golf 7 km, garage, parking.
*Family-run hotel with friendly atmosphere.
Faces the sea, some rooms with sea view and
all rooms with TV (satellite). Railway station
1.5 km. Nearest airport Gerona 40 km.*

■ RESTAURANT: Nice view of the beach.
Specialities: angler fish 'Groguillo', paella, veal
tenderloin 'Al Jabugo'.
■ ACTIVITIES: Many sports facilities nearby;
excursions including visit to the Botanical
Garden. ● Free entrance to the casino at Lloret
de Mar.
■ TARIFF: Single 3,900–6,325,
Double 6,250–11,050, Set menu 1,975 (Amex,
Euro/Access, Visa).

Spain

BOCEGUILLAS 8B

Hotel Tres Mermanos ★
Antigua Carretera, 40560 Boceguillas.
Tel 911 543040, Fax 911 543040.
Open all year. 30 bedrooms (all en suite).
Outdoor swimming pool, tennis, garage,
restaurant.

*Small comfortable hotel situated beside the
Madrid to Burgos road.*

■ TARIFF: (1996) Single 4,000, Double 6,000–
9,000, Set menu 1,400–3,800 (Visa).
■ DISCOUNT: 10%

BURGOS 8B

Hotel Rey Arturo Ctra Nacional 620,
Km 6.6, 09195 Villagonzalo Pedernales.
Tel 947 273399, Fax 947 273388. English spoken.
Open all year. 52 bedrooms (all en suite).
Garage, parking. ℓ &

*Modern hotel just off the highway. Ideal
for stop-over.*

■ RESTAURANT: Self-service restaurant offering
local and international cuisine.
■ ACTIVITIES: Visit the old city and the cathedral.
■ TARIFF: Single 4200–5250,
Double 6625–7900, Bk 950, Set menu 1100
(Amex, Euro/Access, Visa).
■ DISCOUNT: 15%

BURRIANA 9A

Hotel Aloha ★★
Avda Mediterraneo 74, 12530 Burriana.
Tel 964 585000, Fax 964 585000.
Open all year. 30 bedrooms (all en suite).
Outdoor swimming pool, golf 12 km, parking.

*Travellers in search of fine food, wines,
excellent bathing and a leisurely life will find
all they want at this hotel 200 m from the
beach on the Costa del Azahar (the Orange
Blossom Coast).*

■ RESTAURANT: Small restaurant serving excellent
regional specialities including paella de
langosta (lobster); set menus or à la carte; there
is also a larger dining room.
■ ACTIVITIES: Dancing, sailing and sailing school.
Perfect base for exploring the region.
■ TARIFF: (1996) Single 4,250–4,950,
Double 6,350–7,400, Bk 475, Set menu 2,000
(Euro/Access, Visa).

CACERES 8C

Parador Zurbaran ★★★★ Marques de la
Romana 10, Guadalupe, 10140 Caceres.
Tel 927 367075, Fax 927 367076. English spoken.

Open all year. 40 bedrooms (all en suite).
Outdoor swimming pool, tennis, garage. ℓ

*Former hospital of San Juan Bautista dating
from the 15th century. In the town centre
opposite the Monastery, the hotel has an
indoor garden.*

■ RESTAURANT: Typical regional cuisine.
Specialities include 'la calderata de cordero'
(lamb) 'la sopa de arroz cacereña' (rice soup)
and 'el pudding de casteñas' (chesnut
pudding).
■ ACTIVITIES: Horse-riding; tours to the
prehistoric sites and the Gothic church nearby.
■ TARIFF: Single 8,400–11,600, Double 10,500–
14,500, Bk 1,200, Set menu 2,500–3,200
(Amex, Euro/Access, Visa).
■ DISCOUNT: 10%

CADIZ 8C

Hotel Francia y Paris ★★★
Plaza S Francisco 6, 11004 Cadiz.
Tel 956 222348/9, Fax 956 222431. English spoken.
Open all year. 57 bedrooms (all en suite).
Golf 20 km. ℓ

*Dating from 1902, classical building in the
heart of the beautiful old city of Cadiz. Hotel
offers modern-day comforts, a café/bar and is
ideally situated for exploring the surrounding
area. Lots of restaurants, with varied cuisine,
close by.*

■ TARIFF: Single 6,634–7,490, Double 8,988–
9,951, Bk 749 (Amex, Euro/Access, Visa).
■ DISCOUNT: 10%

CALELLA 9B

Hotel Garbi ★★★
Av Costa Dorada 20, 17210 Calella.
Tel 972 614040, Fax 972 615803. English spoken.
Open 01/04 to 15/10. 30 bedrooms
(all en suite). Outdoor swimming pool,
golf 12 km, parking. &

Overlooking Calella de Palafrugell, the hotel is surrounded by gardens and pine trees.

■ RESTAURANT: Specialities include pasta with shellfish, grilled pork cutlet and grilled sausage.
■ ACTIVITIES: Water sports (sailing, diving), fishing, horse-riding, tennis.
■ TARIFF: (1996) Single 5,400–7,300, Double 8,900–12,700, Set menu 1,575–2,300 (Amex, Euro/Access, Visa).

CALPE   9C

Hotel Esmeralda ★★★
C/Poniente 1, 03710 Calpe.
Tel 965 836101, Fax 965 836004.

Open all year. 212 bedrooms (all en suite). Indoor swimming pool, outdoor swimming pool, golf 8 km. ✆ ↺

Facing Calpe beach, a modern air-conditioned hotel with excellent facilities. From the main road between Alicante and Valencia, take the Altea exit. Hotel is 7 km from there on the coast road, at the end of Levante beach.

■ RESTAURANT: Buffet and à la carte restaurant.
■ ACTIVITIES: Entertainment in high season, dancing, sauna, solarium, fitness and aerobic centre; excursions.
■ TARIFF: (1996) Single 5,155–7,200, Double 8,250–10,350, Set menu 2,000 (Amex, Euro/Access, Visa).

Hotel Galetamar ★★★
Playa de Levante, 03710 Calpe.
Tel 965 832311, Fax 965 832328. English spoken.
Open all year. 113 bedrooms (all en suite). Outdoor swimming pool, golf 15 km, parking.

Quiet, modern hotel 3 km from Calpe and just 50 m from the beach and promenade. Air-conditioned accommodation with a choice of double room or room with lounge; lovely gardens. Take Benisa or Altea exits (63 & 64) from A7 for Calpe.

■ RESTAURANT: Choose from the daily specialities or à la carte menu in 'La Caleta' which opens out on to the large, sunny terrace, swimming pool and gardens.
■ ACTIVITIES: Solarium and pool (heated in winter) at hotel. Activities arranged by hotel from time to time include Spanish lessons, dances and evening Flamenco shows. Fishing, diving, water sports and tennis close by. Wonderful base for sightseeing including the famous 'Peñon de Ifach'.
■ TARIFF: (1996) Single 6,000–9,900, Double 8,000–12,300, Set menu 1,500 (Amex, Euro/Access, Visa).
■ DISCOUNT: 20%

CHIPIONA   8C

Hotel Brasilia ★★★
Avda del Faro 12, 11550 Chipiona.
Tel 956 371054, Fax 956 371054. English spoken.

Open all year. 44 bedrooms (all en suite). Outdoor swimming pool, garage.

Elegant, classical-style hotel. Cool, clean and typically Spanish.

■ RESTAURANT: Closed 01/11 to 30/04.
■ TARIFF: (1996) Single 4,349–6,717, Double 5,880–8,965, Bk 675, Set menu 2,950 (Amex, Euro/Access, Visa).

CUENCA 8D

Hotel La Cueva del Fraile ★★★
Ctra Buenache, 16001 Cuenca.
Tel 969 211571, Fax 969 256047.
English spoken.
Open 28/02 to 10/01. 63 bedrooms
(all en suite). Outdoor swimming pool, tennis,
golf 7 km, parking. ℓ

This restored 16th-century building offers comfortable accommodation just outside the village of Cuenca.

■ RESTAURANT: Typical Castillian dishes served in 'La Hoz' restaurant as well as national and international cuisine.
■ ACTIVITIES: Mini-golf, soccer pitch, table tennis and billiards at hotel. Mountain-bike hire, horse-riding, parascending and hang-gliding courses available.
■ TARIFF: (1996) Single 5,000–7,500, Double 7,500–10,800, Bk 775, Set menu 2,400 (Amex, Euro/Access, Visa).

Posada de San Jose ★★
Calle Julian Romero 4, 16001 Cuenca.
Tel 969 211300, Fax 969 230365. English spoken.
Open all year. 30 bedrooms (21 en suite, 9 bath/shower only). Golf 16 km. ℓ

In the heart of the old quarter, this 17th-century building overlooks the Huecar river. Most rooms have magnificent views over the gorge. Terrace in summer. Comfortable bar area where light snack suppers are served.

■ TARIFF: (1996) Single 2,200–4,600, Double 3,800–8,900, Bk 450 (Amex, Euro/Access, Visa).
■ DISCOUNT: 5% advanced booking only.

DONOSTIA/SAN SEBASTIAN 9A

Hotel Lintzirin ★★ Oiartzun Gipuzkoa.
Tel 943 492000, Fax 943 492504.
English spoken.

Open all year. 130 bedrooms (all en suite).
Golf 9 km, garage, parking. ℓ

On the N1, the hotel is just a few minutes from San Sebastian, Hondarribia-Fuenterrabia and the sea.

■ RESTAURANT: Choice of restaurants, one with à la carte regional and international dishes, the other self-service.
■ TARIFF: (1996) Single 4,000–4,500, Double 6,500–7,500, Bk 600, Set menu 950 (Amex, Euro/Access, Visa).

Hotel Niza ★★★ Zubieta 56, 20000 San Sebastian.
Tel 943 426663, Fax 943 426663. English spoken.
Open all year. 41 bedrooms (all en suite).
Golf 4 km, garage.

Situated in central position overlooking La Concha bay. Comfortably and stylishly furnished.

■ RESTAURANT: Restaurant/pizzeria with lovely views. Offers home-made pasta and has a traditional wood-fired oven.
■ TARIFF: (1996) Single 5,950–6,950, Double 12,600–12,950, Bk 800 (Amex, Euro/Access, Visa).

ELCHE 9C

Hotel Huerto del Cura ★★★★
Porta de la Morena, 14, 03203 Elche.
Tel 965 458040, Fax 965 421910. English spoken.
Open all year. 80 bedrooms (all en suite).
Outdoor swimming pool, tennis, garage, parking. ℓ &

Set in a prodigious natural site, declared a National Artistic Garden by the government, the hotel is an oasis of peace and quiet. The air-conditioned bungalows are scattered throughout the palm tree-filled gardens. 10 km from the airport and 13 km from the beach.

■ RESTAURANT: Carefully prepared gourmet cuisine offering traditional Mediterranean specialities.
■ ACTIVITIES: Sauna.
■ TARIFF: (1996) Single 7,000–11,000, Double 10,000–15,000, Bk 1,250, Set menu 3,000 (Amex, Euro/Access, Visa).

ESTEPONA 8D

Hotel El Paraiso ★★★★
Ctra Cadiz-Malaga, 29680 Estepona.
Tel 952 883000/4317, Fax 952 882019.
English spoken.
Open all year. 200 bedrooms (all en suite).
Indoor swimming pool, outdoor swimming pool, tennis, golf on site, parking. &

First-class hotel with air-conditioned rooms and excellent facilities. 50 m from golf course and with panoramic views of mountains and towards the sea. 10 km from centre of Marbella and Estepona, 60 km from Malaga airport.

■ RESTAURANT: Luxurious surroundings and international cuisine.
■ ACTIVITIES: Spa clinic (alternative medicine) close by. ● Free green fees at El Paraiso golf course.
■ TARIFF: (1996) Single 11,475–15,750, Double 16,975–24,500, Bk 1,500, Set menu 3,750 (Amex, Euro/Access, Visa).
■ DISCOUNT: 15%

FIGUERES 9B

Hotel Ampurdan ★★★
Antigua Carretera a Francia, 17600 Figueres.
Tel 972 500566, Fax 972 509358. English spoken.
Open all year. 42 bedrooms (all en suite).
Golf 10 km, garage, parking. &

Just 1 km from the town centre, hotel is small and comfortable with air conditioning.

■ RESTAURANT: Renowned for its very good cuisine.
■ TARIFF: Single 6,000–7,600, Double 9,100–11,000, Bk 1,000, Set menu 6,000–4,500 (Amex, Euro/Access, Visa).

Hotel Duran ★★★
Calle Lasauca 5, 17600 Figueres.
Tel 972 501250, Fax 972 502609. English spoken.
Open all year. 63 bedrooms (all en suite).
Golf 6 km, garage, parking. &

A small hotel/restaurant with a friendly atmosphere. Built in 1842 and refurbished to provide comfortable, air-conditioned accommodation with all modern facilities. Situated in town centre and the nearest hotel to the Dali Museum.

■ RESTAURANT: Catalan atmosphere and noted for its high quality Mediterranean cuisine.

■ ACTIVITIES: Swimming pool and tennis courts nearby.
■ TARIFF: (1996) Single 4,800–5,900, Double 6,000–8,700, Bk 600, Set menu 1,600 (Amex, Euro/Access, Visa).

FUENGIROLA 8D

Hotel Florida ★★★
Paseo Maritimo, 29640 Fuengirola.
Tel 952 476100, Fax 952 581529. English spoken.
Open all year. 116 bedrooms (all en suite).
Outdoor swimming pool, golf 4 km, restaurant. &

Comfortable hotel on sea-front and opposite pleasure harbour. Sub-tropical garden and most rooms with sea view. 700 m from railway station.

■ TARIFF: (1996) Single 4,750–6,600, Double 7,250–10,000, Bk 650, Set menu 2,400 (Amex, Euro/Access, Visa).
■ DISCOUNT: 10%

GERONA 9B

Hotel Balneari Prats ★★★
Placa Sant Esteve 7, 17455 Caldes de Malavella.
Tel 972 470051, Fax 972 472233. English spoken.

Open all year. 78 bedrooms (all en suite).
Outdoor swimming pool, golf 13 km, garage, parking. ✆

In the centre of the town, the hotel has been created from an original old building and a modern spa. From the A7 (coming from Barcelona), take exit 9 (Lloret/St-Feliu) and then the N2 towards Girona.

■ RESTAURANT: Carefully prepared and inventive cuisine with traditional specialities.
■ ACTIVITIES: Bikes, boules, tennis at hotel; the hotel can reserve tennis, golf and helicopter flights for guests.
■ TARIFF: (1996) Single 3,300–12,300, Double 4,800–11,100, Bk 750, Set menu 2,200–2,500 (Amex, Euro/Access, Visa).

Spain

Hotel Fornells Park ★★★
Ctra Nacional 11, 17000 Gerona.
Tel 972 476125, Fax 972 476579.
English spoken.
Open all year. 53 bedrooms (all en suite).
Outdoor swimming pool, golf 5 km, parking,
restaurant.

*Very quiet hotel surrounded by woods and
gardens. 3 km from Girona town, 2 km from
exit 7 of motorway 17 (France to Barcelona).
30 km to the sea.*

■ ACTIVITIES: Tennis 3 km. ● Special rates for
hotel guests at nearby golf course.
■ TARIFF: Single 7,100–7,500,
Double 10,300–10,800, Bk 1,000,
Set menu 2,450 (Amex, Euro/Access, Visa).
■ DISCOUNT: 10%

GRANADA   8D

Motel Sierra Nevada ★★
Avda de Madrid 107, 18014 Granada.
Tel 958 150062, Fax 958 150954.
English spoken.
Open 01/03 to 01/11. 23 bedrooms
(all en suite). Outdoor swimming pool, tennis,
golf 15 km, parking. ℂ ♿

*A small motel with centrally heated double
rooms. On the north, Almanjayar side of
Granada (exit 126), 100 m from the central
bus station.*

■ RESTAURANT: Closed 01/11 to 01/03. Situated
beside the pool, restaurant specialises in local
and international cuisine.
■ ACTIVITIES: Fishing and skiing within easy
reach; ideal location for sightseeing.
■ TARIFF: (1996) Single 3,600,
Double 5,300, Bk 200, Set menu 950–1,200
(Amex, Euro/Access, Visa).

HARO   8B

Hotel Iturrimurri ★★★
Ctra Circunvalacion, 26200 Haro.
Tel 941 311213, Fax 941 311721.
English spoken.
Open all year. 47 bedrooms (all en suite).
Indoor swimming pool, outdoor swimming
pool, parking. ℂ ♿

*Excellent hotel located in a very quiet area of
the town. Very comfortable rooms and
good service.*

■ RESTAURANT: Gourmet restaurant specialising
in regional cuisine.
■ ACTIVITIES: Tours of the Rioja region, visits to
the famous 'Bodegas', wine tasting.

■ TARIFF: (1996) Single 6,000–7,500,
Double 8,900–10,500, Bk 975, Set menu 1,900–
3,500 (Amex, Euro/Access, Visa).

HUELVA   8C

Hotel Tartessos ★★★
Avda Martin Alonso Pinzon 13, 21003 Huelva.
Tel 955 282711, Fax 955 250617.
English spoken.

Open all year. 109 bedrooms (all en suite).
Golf 5 km. ℂ

*Completely updated in 1992, the hotel offers
comfortable, air-conditioned accommodation.
Situated on the main street in the town centre.
Piano bar.*

■ RESTAURANT: Closed Sun. 'El Estero' offers
good food and wines.
■ TARIFF: (1996) Single 8,000, Double 11,000,
Bk 650, Set menu 2,500 (Amex, Euro/Access,
Visa).

IRUN   9A

Apartments Jauregui ★★★ San Pedro 28,
20280 Fuenterrabia/Hondarribia.
Tel 943 641400, Fax 943 644404.
English spoken.

Open all year. 53 bedrooms (all en suite).
Garage. &

*Small hotel surrounded by restaurants. 2 km
from Irun, follow signs to Hondarribia.*

■ TARIFF: (1996) Single 7,800–10,000,
Double 10,900–13,250, Bk 850 (Amex,
Euro/Access, Visa).

LA ALBERCA   8B

Hotel Las Batuecas ★★
Ctra Las Batuecas, 37624 Salamanca.
Tel 923 415188/94, Fax 923 415055.
English spoken.
Open all year. 24 bedrooms (all en suite).
Garage, parking. ℓ

*Attractive stone building in a beautiful village;
the nearby mountains are covered in chestnut
and walnut trees. 75 km south-west of
Salamanca and 54 km from Bejar.*

■ RESTAURANT: Closed 10/01 to 10/02. Typical
regional dishes and a good choice of local wines.
■ TARIFF: (1996) Single 3,900–4,500,
Double 6,000–7,000, Bk 500,
Set menu 1,500–3,900 (Visa).

LA CORUÑA   8A

Hotel Finisterre ★★★★
Paseo del Parrote 2, 15001 La Coruña.
Tel 981 205400, Fax 981 208462. English spoken.
Open all year. 127 bedrooms (all en suite).
Outdoor swimming pool, tennis, parking.

*City centre location, in the historic and
cultural area. Superb view of the bay.
Attractive rooms with all facilities.*

■ RESTAURANT: Relaxed, comfortable restaurant
offering national and international cuisine.
■ ACTIVITIES: Excellent sports facilities at hotel as
well as gym, sauna and children's playground.
■ TARIFF: (1996) Single 11,340–13,650,
Double 14,490–17,325, Bk 1,200
(Amex, Euro/Access, Visa).

LA JUNQUERA   9B

Hotel Merce-Park ★★ 17700 La Junquera.
Tel 972 549038, Fax 972 549038. English spoken.
Open all year. 48 bedrooms (all en suite).
Golf 4 km, garage, parking. ℓ &

*A former spa, now completely renovated.
Picturesque setting beside the river, just south
of La Junquera and 5 km from Spanish/French
border.*

■ RESTAURANT: Typical cosy, Catalan-style dining
room with air conditioning.
■ ACTIVITIES: A wide variety of organised tours
will enable you to explore the surrounding
countryside. The area offers a multitude of flora
and fauna, historic sites, menhirs and dolmens.
■ TARIFF: (1996) Single 3,500–4,500,
Double 5,700–6,500, Bk 600, Set menu 1,600
(Amex, Euro/Access, Visa).
■ DISCOUNT: 5%

LA PLATJA D'ARO   9B

Hotel Xaloc ★★★ Cals Rovira La Platja d'Aro.
Tel 972 817300, Fax 972 816100.
English spoken.

Open 10/05 to 05/10. 47 bedrooms
(all en suite). Golf 6 km, parking. ℓ

*Totally renovated hotel occupying a privileged
position near the sea and just 300 m from the
Platja d'Aro shopping centre. Spacious
accommodation with most of the bedrooms
having balcony.*

■ RESTAURANT: Light and airy dining room;
shaded terrace.
■ ACTIVITIES: Dances held on the garden terrace.
■ TARIFF: (1996) Single 3900–6850, Double 5675–
11,500, Bk 700, Set menu 1,975 (Visa).

Spain

Hotel Columbus ★★★★ 17250 La Platja d'Aro.
Tel 972 817166, Fax 972 817503. English spoken.
Open all year. 110 bedrooms (all en suite).
Outdoor swimming pool, tennis, golf 2 km,
parking. ☎

*Comfortable, air-conditioned hotel, next to the
beach and with terraces overlooking the sea.*

■ RESTAURANT: Regional specialities.
■ TARIFF: (1996) Single 6,100–12,500,
Double 9,200–21,000, Set menu 2,750
(Amex, Euro/Access, Visa).
■ DISCOUNT: 10% except July & Aug.

LLAFRANC DE PALAFRUGELL   9B

Hotel Terramar ★★★ Paseo de Cypsele 1,
17211 Llafranc de Palafrugell.
Tel 972 300200, Fax 972 300626. English spoken.

Open 14/04 to 06/10. 56 bedrooms
(all en suite). Golf 9 km, garage. ☎ ㅤ

*A pleasant family atmosphere will be found at
this well-appointed hotel on the beach.
Panoramic views and a large terrace
overlooking the beach.*

■ RESTAURANT: Restaurant pizzeria offering a
variety of dishes.
■ ACTIVITIES: Tennis, horse-riding, squash, all
water sports as well as boat trips close by.
■ TARIFF: (1996) Single 6,500–9,000,
Double 9,000–12,000, Bk 900
(Amex, Euro/Access, Visa).
■ DISCOUNT: 10% except Aug.

LLANES   8B

Hotel Mirador de la Franca ★★★
33590 La Franca.
Tel 985 412145, Fax 985 412153. English spoken.
Open 31/03 to 15/10. 56 bedrooms
(all en suite). Tennis, golf 12 km, parking. ☎

*Very comfortable, inviting hotel overlooking a
safe, beautiful beach. On N634 east of Llanes,
Km 286.*

■ RESTAURANT: Panoramic restaurant with
national and international specialities.
■ ACTIVITIES: Good location for water sports, sea
and river fishing, exploring the countryside and
nearby towns. 4-wheel drive vehicles/tours
available on request. ● Reduction on green fees
for hotel guests.
■ TARIFF: (1996) Single 3,900–6,900,
Double 6,200–10,500, Bk 700, Set menu 1,850
(Amex, Euro/Access, Visa).

LLORET DE MAR   9B

Gran Hotel Monterrey ★★★★
Ctra de Tossa, 17310 Lloret de Mar.
Tel 972 364050, Fax 972 363512.
English spoken.

Open 01/03 to 05/11. 224 bedrooms
(all en suite). Indoor swimming pool, outdoor
swimming pool, tennis, golf 4 km, parking. ㅤ

*Large air-conditioned hotel situated in a quiet,
wooded area. 10 minutes from town centre
and beach, on road to Tossa de Mar. Children
very welcome.*

■ RESTAURANT: Very comfortable, buffet-service

Spain

restaurant. Breakfast and dinners are served on the terrace in summer. Catalan speciality meal once a week.

■ ACTIVITIES: Beauty/health centre with pool and jacuzzi; folk dancing shows in the romantic illuminated gardens in high season; table tennis, boules, volley ball; children's entertainments.

■ TARIFF: (1996) Single 6,000–8,000, Double 10,000–16,000 (Amex, Euro/Access, Visa).

Hotel Rigat Park ★★★★ Av Americas 1, Playa de Fenals, 17310 Lloret de Mar. Tel 972 365200, Fax 972 370411. English spoken.

Open 01/04 to 31/10. 105 bedrooms (all en suite). Outdoor swimming pool, tennis, golf 1.5 km, parking. &

Lovely gardens and terraces overlooking the sea. Hotel is on Fenals beach, 1 km from the town centre.

■ RESTAURANT: Indoor and outdoor gourmet restaurants. Member of the 'Chaine des Rotisseurs'. Specialities include fresh fish and seafood.

■ ACTIVITIES: Flume, water sports, diving, horse-riding, go-karting, table tennis, billiards; excursions.

■ TARIFF: Single 10,900–15,000, Double 15,000–23,000, Bk 1,500, Set menu 4,200–7,000 (Amex, Euro/Access, Visa).

■ DISCOUNT: 10%

LOJA 8D

Hostal El Mirador ★★★

Ctra Jerez-Cartagena, Km 485, 18300 Loja. Tel 958 323800, Fax 958 323804. English spoken. Open all year. 76 bedrooms (all en suite). Garage, parking. & &

The terrace of the hotel overlooks the Sierra de Loja. On the A92, 50 km from Granada, 75 km from Malaga and 2 km from Loja.

■ RESTAURANT: National and international cuisine.

■ ACTIVITIES: Disco; mountain bikes for hire, hiking, organised tours.

■ TARIFF: (1996) Single 5,000, Double 7,000 (Amex, Euro/Access, Visa).

MADRID 8B

Hotel Mindanao ★★★★

Pas San Francisco de Sales 15, 28003 Madrid. Tel 915 495500, Fax 915 445596. English spoken.

Open all year. 289 bedrooms (all en suite). Indoor swimming pool, outdoor swimming pool, garage. &

Luxury-class hotel in exclusive area of Madrid, a few minutes from the town centre. Fully air conditioned and high standard of comfort and service. Conference facilities.

■ RESTAURANT: Cocktail bar and coffee shop. Spanish and international cuisine with international specialities.

■ TARIFF: Single 24,000, Double 30,000, Bk 1,900 (Amex, Euro/Access, Visa).

■ DISCOUNT: 30%

Spain

Motel Los Olivos ★★★
Ctra de Andalucia Km 12,7, 28909 Getafe.
Tel 916 956700, Fax 916 818890. English spoken.

Open all year. 100 bedrooms (all en suite).
Outdoor swimming pool, golf 20 km, garage,
parking. ✆

*Just off the main road, Los Olivos is only
15 minutes south of the centre of Madrid.
Comfortable accommodation, large, park-like
gardens and an excellent view of the Cerro de
Los Angeles.*

■ RESTAURANT: Modern, functional restaurant
with national and international cuisine as well
as Castillian specialities. The café offers a
variety of dishes of the day.
■ TARIFF: (1996) Single 5,185, Double 6,850,
Bk 425, Set menu 1,250 (Amex,
Euro/Access, Visa).

MALLORCA (MAJORCA)

CALA RATJADA　　　　　　　　9D

Hotel Ses Rotges ★★★ Calle Rafael Blanes 21,
07590 Cala Ratjada, Mallorca.
Tel 971 563108, Fax 971 564345.
English spoken.

Open 01/03 to 30/11. 24 bedrooms
(all en suite). Tennis, golf 5 km.
*A converted old stone mansion of character in
this small fishing resort. The furnishings have
been chosen with care. Terrace garden.*

■ RESTAURANT: Pretty restaurant with excellent
cuisine and inventive specialities.
■ TARIFF: Single 8,200, Double 10,200, Bk 1,359,
Set menu 4,775 (Amex, Euro/Access, Visa).

VALLDEMOSSA　　　　　　　　9D

Vistamar de Valldemossa ★★★★
07170 Valldemossa, Mallorca.
Tel 971 612300, Fax 971 612583. English spoken.
Open 02/02 to 31/10. 18 bedrooms
(16 en suite). Outdoor swimming pool,
golf 18 km, parking.

*A truly lovely old house, beautifully restored
and furnished with genuine Mallorcan
antiques. Set amongst 100 hectares of pine,
evergreen oak and ancient olive trees, hotel
has an excellent reputation, lovely gardens
and wonderful views. 2 km from Valldemossa,
overlooking the sea.*

■ RESTAURANT: Closed Mon lunch. Traditional
Mallorcan and international cuisine using fresh
market produce. Paella and seafood specialities.
■ ACTIVITIES: Exploring the surrounding
countryside or enjoying a gentle stroll down to
the port of Valldemossa; excursions; water
sports and boat trips nearby. Piano concerts on
Saturday evenings.
■ TARIFF: (1996) Single 16,000–18,000,
Double 24,000–28,000 (Amex, Euro/Access, Visa).

END OF MALLORCA (MAJORCA) HOTELS

MALAGA　　　　　　　　　　8D

Hotel Las Vegas ★★★
Paseo de Sancha 22, 29016 Malaga.
Tel 952 217712, Fax 952 224889. English spoken.
Open all year. 106 bedrooms (all en suite).
Outdoor swimming pool, parking, restaurant. ✆

*Comfortable hotel with sea views and private
garden. Situated 2 km from town centre in a
residential area.*

■ TARIFF: (1996) Single 8,360–10,585,
Double 10,990–13,750, Set menu 2,300 (Amex,
Euro/Access, Visa).

MIRANDA DE EBRO　　　　　　8B

Hotel Tudanca ★★★ Ctra Madrid-Irun,
Km 318, 09200 Miranda de Ebro.
Tel 947 311843, Fax 947 311848. English spoken.

Open all year. 121 bedrooms (all en suite). Garage, parking. &

Modern hotel on outskirts of Miranda de Ebro. Easily accessible, close to the N1 on the Burgos side of town.

■ RESTAURANT: Two restaurants: self-service and à la carte. Regional menus.
■ TARIFF: Single 5,075–5,260, Double 7,415–7,750, Bk 575, Set menu 1,900–2,500 (Amex, Euro/Access, Visa).
■ DISCOUNT: 15%

MOJACAR 9C

Parador de Mojacar ★★★★
Playa de Mojacar, 04638 Mojacar.
Tel 950 478250, Fax 950 478183. English spoken.
Open all year. 98 bedrooms (all en suite). Outdoor swimming pool, tennis, golf 15 km, parking. &

On the beach of Mojacar and 2.5 km from town.

■ RESTAURANT: The dining room overlooks the sea. Regional cuisine. Specialities include 'Guajadera de pescado' (fish), 'sopa Dorada' (fish soup), 'gazpacho Almeriense' and 'pastel Mojaquero' (Mojacar tart).
■ ACTIVITIES: Fishing, horse-riding and water sports.
■ TARIFF: (1996) Single 9,200–10,800, Double 11,500–13,500, Bk 1,200, Set menu 3,500 (Amex, Euro/Access, Visa).
■ DISCOUNT: 10% LS.

MURCIA 9C

Hotel Conde de Floridablanca ★★★★
Calle Princesa 19, 30002 Murcia.
Tel 968 21 46 26, Fax 968 21 32 15. English spoken.
Open all year. 85 bedrooms (all en suite). Golf 8 km, garage. ℂ

Comfortable hotel with a family atmosphere next to the Floridablanca garden. Individually decorated rooms with baroque-style furniture.

■ RESTAURANT: Lobster, lamb and turkey specialities.
■ TARIFF: (1996) Single 5,500–8,800, Double 7,500–12,000, Bk 700, Set menu 2,000–4,000 (Amex, Euro/Access, Visa).
■ DISCOUNT: 10%

Hotel Rincon De Pepe ★★★★
Pl Apostoles 34, 30001 Murcia.
Tel 968 212239, Fax 968 221744. English spoken.
Open all year. 115 bedrooms (all en suite). Golf 10 km, garage. ℂ

Comfortable hotel with excellent facilities in the historic centre of town and next to cathedral.

■ RESTAURANT: Closed Sun eve and Aug.

Regional and national cusine served in an elegant dining room.
■ TARIFF: (1996) Double 14,000–16,000 (Amex, Euro/Access).

OROPESA 8B

Hotel Parador Nacional de Virrey Toledo
★★★★ Plaza del Palacio 1,
45560 Oropesa, Toledo.
Tel 925 430000, Fax 925 430777. English spoken.
Open all year. 48 bedrooms (all en suite). Outdoor swimming pool, parking. ℂ &

Former 16th-century palace, originally the ancestral seat of the Count and Countess of Oropesa. On N5 to Badajos and Lisboa, 149 km from Madrid.

■ RESTAURANT: Regional specialities.
■ TARIFF: Single 11,600, Double 14,500, Bk 1,200, Set menu 3,500 (Amex, Euro/Access, Visa).

OVIEDO 8B

Hotel Ramiro 1 ★★★★
Avda Calvo Sotelo 13, 33000 Oviedo.
Tel 985 232850, Fax 985 236329. English spoken.
Open all year. 83 bedrooms (all en suite). Parking.

Large, comfortable rooms with all modern facilities. Hotel has an excellent location close to the Parque de San Francisco and town centre. Easy access to the A66 Madrid road.

■ ACTIVITIES: Oviedo is on the pilgrim route to Santiago de Compostela and there are several important churches and monuments to be visited in the area. Coast is 28 km, mountains and ski resorts 50 km and renowned salmon rivers 40 km.
■ TARIFF: (1996) Double 9,600–13,800 (Amex, Euro/Access, Visa).

PALAMOS 9B

Hotel Rosamar ★★★ Paseo del Mar 33,
17252 San Antoni de Calonge.
Tel 972 650548, Fax 972 652161. English spoken.
Open 29/03 to 15/10. 52 bedrooms (all en suite). Golf 4 km, parking. &

Small, modern hotel, beside beach and with views over bay. Family atmosphere. Between Palamos and Platja d'Aro.

■ RESTAURANT: Closed 30/09 to 30/03. Regional and Mediterranean cuisine.
■ ACTIVITIES: ● Discounts arranged by hotel for various excursions and activities including mountain-biking and sailing.
■ TARIFF: (1996) Single 3,500–7,500, Double 6,000–13,500, Set menu 2,500–3,500 (Amex, Euro/Access, Visa).

Spain

PALENCIA 8B

Hotel Castillo de Monzon ★★★
34410 Monzon de Campos.
Tel 988 808075, Fax 988 808076. English spoken.
Open all year. 10 bedrooms
(all bath/shower only). Outdoor swimming
pool, tennis, garage, parking, restaurant.

*A 10th-century castle set on the side of a
mountain with wonderful views. 8 km north of
Palencia on N611. Very peaceful.*

■ TARIFF: (1996) Single 6,000–8,500,
Double 7,000–13,000, Bk 800, Set menu 2,500
(Amex, Euro/Access, Visa).

PANCORBO 8B

Hotel El Molino ★★★ 09280 Pancorbo.
Tel 947 354050, Fax 947 344420. English spoken.
Open all year. 48 bedrooms (all en suite).
Outdoor swimming pool, tennis, garage,
parking. ℓ

*A most attractive hotel with a mill. Set on a
small hill, the gardens lead to the nearby river.
3 km from Pancorbo heading towards Irun.*

■ RESTAURANT: Typical regional cuisine with
grilled meat and fish specialities.
■ ACTIVITIES: Lots to do nearby including fishing,
climbing and mountain-biking. Children's
playground.
■ TARIFF: (1996) Single 3500–4500,
Double 6000–8000, Bk 880, Set menu 1650–
4000 (Amex, Euro/Access, Visa).
■ DISCOUNT: 10% on meals in restaurant only.

PANES 8B

La Tahona de Besnes ★★ Penamellera Alta,
33578 Alles.
Tel 985 415749, Fax 985 415749.
English spoken.

Open all year. 20 bedrooms (all en suite).
Parking. ℓ

*Charming converted bakery set in woods in the
hamlet of Besnes, in the foothills of the Picos de
Europa, close to Panes and Arenas de Cabrales.
Corn mill in working order. From Panes head
towards Covadonga, then turn right after
10 km. Special offers from October to May.*

■ RESTAURANT: Small cosy restaurant in rustic
style. Specialities include goat, salmon, sirloin
of Besnes and onion paté.
■ ACTIVITIES: Horse-riding, fishing, mountain
walking, river canoeing, excursions by jeep.
■ TARIFF: Single 5,120–6,720,
Double 6,400–8,400, Bk 750, Set menu 1,850
(Amex, Euro/Access, Visa).
■ DISCOUNT: 10% LS only.

PENISCOLA 9C

Hosteria del Mar ★★★★
Avda Papa Luna 18, 12598 Peniscola.
Tel 964 480600, Fax 964 481363. English spoken.

Open all year. 86 bedrooms (all en suite).
Outdoor swimming pool, tennis, garage,
parking, restaurant.

*Decorated in Castillian style, this luxury hotel
is right by the beach on the promenade.*

■ TARIFF: (1996) Single 5,900–11,000,
Double 7,900–14,300, Bk 1,050,
Set menu 2,500 (Amex, Euro/Access, Visa).

PONTEVEDRA 8A

Hotel Parador de Turismo 'Casa del Baron'
★★★ Ctra Baron 19, 36002 Pontevedra.
Tel 986 855800, Fax 986 852195. English spoken.
Open all year. 47 bedrooms (all en suite).
Golf 25 km, parking. ℓ

*16th-century Renaissance palace, former
residence of the Counts of Maceda. Rising up
majestically in the centre of this historic town,
right in the heart of the Rias Bajas, the 'Casa
del Baron' is beautifully and elegantly decorated,
has some fine antiques and a lovely garden.*

■ RESTAURANT: Classical-style restaurant where one can savour the delicious and varied regional dishes. Specialities include octopus 'feria' style, seafood, 'filloas' (pancakes) and 'tarta de Santiago'. Good selection of fine wines. Meals can be taken outside on the terrace in summer.
■ ACTIVITIES: Horse-riding, 4x4 and raft excursions; sports/fitness centre with swimming pool and squash 1 km.
■ TARIFF: Single 8,400–11,600, Double 10,500–14,500, Bk 1,200, Set menu 2,300–3,200 (Amex, Euro/Access, Visa).

RONDA   8D

Hotel Polo ★★★
Mariano Soubiron 8, 29400 Ronda.
Tel 952 872447/48, Fax 952 874378.
English spoken.
Open all year. 33 bedrooms (all en suite). Garage. ☏ ♿

Small comfortable hotel with a friendly atmosphere. Central position and convenient for the Plaza de Toros.

■ RESTAURANT: Rustic-style restaurant. Specialities: paella, cordero, pollo al asillo.
■ ACTIVITIES: Horse-riding, trekking, hot-air balloon trips.
■ TARIFF: (1996) Single 4,700–6,000, Double 6,500–8,500, Bk 475, Set menu 1,100–2,000 (Amex, Euro/Access, Visa).

ROSES   9B

Hotel Goya ★★★ Apartado 2, 17480 Roses.
Tel 972 256123, Fax 972 151461. English spoken.
Open 01/04 to 31/10. 75 bedrooms (all en suite). Outdoor swimming pool, golf 20 km, garage, parking. ☏

Hotel with family atmosphere in quiet spot 150 m from beach. Completely renovated in 1996. Rooms have balconies. Outdoor café, bar, gardens.

■ RESTAURANT: Closed from 01/04 to 15/06 & 15/09 to 31/10. Air-conditioned dining room.
■ ACTIVITIES: Children's playground. Sea and mountain excursions.
■ TARIFF: Single 3,225–5,225, Double 4,600–9,300, Bk 800, Set menu 1,500 (Amex, Euro/Access, Visa).
■ DISCOUNT: 5% payment by cash.

Hotel Monterrey ★★★
Sta Margarita, 17480 Roses.
Tel 972 257650, Fax 972 253869.
English spoken.

Open 01/04 to 30/11. 135 bedrooms (all en suite). Outdoor swimming pool, golf 15 km, garage, parking.

Family-run hotel, on the beach and with garden. All rooms have private terrace and satellite TV can be hired. 2 km from Roses, 18 km from Figueres.

■ RESTAURANT: Good traditional food.
■ ACTIVITIES: Fitness room at hotel. Diving, windsurfing, boat hire, horse-riding, parascending and tennis within easy reach. 5 golf courses within less than an hour's drive.
■ TARIFF: Single 6,045–8,720, Double 8,400–13,321, Set menu 1,700 (Amex, Euro/Access, Visa).

Spain

Hotel Almadraba Park ★★★★

Playa de la Almadraba, 17480 Roses.
Tel 972 256550, Fax 972 256750. English spoken.
Open 25/04 to 14/10. 66 bedrooms
(all en suite). Outdoor swimming pool, tennis,
golf 14 km, garage, parking. ᵹ

A comfortable, modern hotel with air conditioning and a delightful view across the bay. 5 km from Roses town centre.

■ RESTAURANT: Offers regional cuisine.
■ TARIFF: (1996) Single 6,700–9,300,
Double 12,000–16,000, Bk 1,200, Set menu 4,100–
6,000 (Amex, Euro/Access, Visa).

S'AGARO   9B

Hotel Caleta Park ★★★★

Platja de Sant Pol, 17248 S'Agaro.
Tel 972 320012, Fax 972 324096. English spoken.
Open 01/04 to 07/04 & 15/05 to 02/10.
95 bedrooms (all en suite). Outdoor swimming
pool, tennis, golf 3 km, garage, parking.

Standing on a hill with wonderful views across the bay, hotel has direct access to the beach. Each week a magnificent Catalan dinner is offered to guests staying on half-board basis at no extra cost. Just north of Sant Feliu de Guixols along the coast road.

■ RESTAURANT: Very attractive restaurant with a good reputation. Gastronomic cuisine with Catalan specialities.
■ ACTIVITIES: Water sports; ● Free use of tennis court for 3 hours per week.
■ TARIFF: (1996) Single 4,500–7,500,
Double 7,800–15,800, Set menu 2,400–2,500
(Amex, Euro/Access, Visa).

SAN PEDRO DE ALCANTARA   8D

Linda Vista Bungalows ★★★

29670 San Pedro de Alcantara.
Tel 952 781492, Fax 952 781492. English spoken.
Open all year. 56 bedrooms (all en suite).
Outdoor swimming pool, tennis, golf 1 km,
parking, restaurant. ᵹ

1- and 2-bedroom bungalows with own parking and garden. Situated 1 km south of town by the sea.

■ TARIFF: (1996) Double 6,000–8,500, Bk 500
(Amex, Euro/Access, Visa).

SANTANDER   8B

Hostel Liebana ★★

Nicolas Salmeron 9, 39009 Santander.
Tel 942 223250, Fax 942 229910. English spoken.
Open all year. 30 bedrooms (all en suite).
Golf 4 km, garage.

Comfortable, family-run hostelry. Family rooms available. Bar. Reductions for groups of 4 or more. Follow signs to 'zona maritime' via Marquel de la Hermida street and then take the last turning left into Nicolas Salmeron.

■ ACTIVITIES: Biking, excursions around the bay, water sports.
■ TARIFF: (1996) Single 2,801–4,873,
Double 3,530–6,108 (Amex, Euro/Access, Visa).

SANTILLANA DEL MAR   8B

Hotel Altamira ★★★ Canton No 1,

39330 Santillana del Mar, Cantabria.
Tel 942 818025, Fax 942 840136. English spoken.
Open all year. 32 bedrooms (all en suite).
Parking. ℓ

Former 17th-century palace decorated in regional mountain style. Small and comfortable. 100 m from the famous church of La Colegiata.

■ RESTAURANT: Has a good reputation. Game and roast meat specialities.
■ ACTIVITIES: Horse-riding, 4X4, excursions available.
■ TARIFF: (1996) Single 4,200–5,000,
Double 5,700–10,000, Bk 500, Set menu 1,500–
2,500 (Amex, Euro/Access, Visa).

SEGOVIA   8B

Hotel Los Linajes ★★★

Dr Velasco 9, 40003 Segovia.
Tel 921 460475, Fax 921 460479.
English spoken.
Open all year. 55 bedrooms (all en suite).
Garage, parking, restaurant. ℓ ᵹ

Small hotel located in old part of Segovia. 16th-century palace façade and terrace with views over the city's monuments.

■ TARIFF: Single 6,300–7,200, Double 8,700–
10,500, Bk 775 (Amex, Euro/Access, Visa).
■ DISCOUNT: 15%

SEVILLA (SEVILLE)   8C

Hotel Becquer ★★★

Reyes Catolicos 4, 41001 Sevilla.
Tel 954 222172, Fax 954 214400.
English spoken.
Open all year. 120 bedrooms (all en suite).
Golf 6 km, garage.

Elegant, air-conditioned hotel offering excellent service. Centrally positioned and easy to find. Convenient for shopping and sightseeing. Special weekend prices.

■ DISCOUNT: 10% by prior arrangement.

Spain

Hotel Inglaterra ★★★★
Plaza Nueva 7, 41001 Sevilla.
Tel 954 224970, Fax 954 561336. English spoken.

Open all year. 113 bedrooms (all en suite).
Golf 5 km, garage, restaurant. &

In town centre, with terrace overlooking Plaza Nueva. Air-conditioned rooms and lounges.

■ TARIFF: (1996) Single 13,600–16,500,
Double 17,000–21,000, Bk 1,200,
Set menu 3,000 (Amex, Euro/Access, Visa).
■ DISCOUNT: 10% April.

Hotel Oromana ★★★ Pinares de Oromana,
41500 Alcala de Guardaira.
Tel 956 86400, Fax 956 86400. English spoken.

Open all year. 30 bedrooms (all en suite).
Outdoor swimming pool, golf 15 km, garage,
parking. ☎

15 km south of Sevilla on the top of a hill, a farmhouse-style hotel built in 1929 and surrounded by pine trees.

■ RESTAURANT: Regional and international
cuisine with Andalusian and Arabic specialities.
■ ACTIVITIES: Biking, horse-riding; tennis nearby.
■ TARIFF: (1996) Single 7,700, Double 10,200–
14,200, Set menu 2,000 (Amex, Euro/Access, Visa).
■ DISCOUNT: 10% LS.

SITGES   9B

Hotel Terramar ★★★★
Paseo Maritimo 30, 08870 Sitges.
Tel 938 940050, Fax 938 945604. English spoken.

Open 01/05 to 31/10. 209 bedrooms
(all en suite). Outdoor swimming pool, tennis,
golf on site, parking.

On the sea-front, all rooms having modern facilities plus private terrace. 7 halls for meetings and conferences; bar.

■ RESTAURANT: Restaurant and snack bar.
■ ACTIVITIES: Table tennis at hotel. Casino and
harbour (700 moorings) 3 km. ● 50% reduction
for hotel guests on green fees at adjacent golf
course.
■ TARIFF: Single 7,315–10,315, Double 12,500–
16,550, Set menu 2,200 (Amex, Euro/Access, Visa).
■ DISCOUNT: 10%

SORIA   9A

Hotel Santa Maria de Huerta ★★★ Soria.
Tel 975 327011, Fax 975 327011.
English spoken.
Open all year. 40 bedrooms (all en suite).
Outdoor swimming pool, golf on site, garage,
parking. ☎

Family 'parador' hotel (luxury state-owned hotel, often housed in historic buildings) with fully equipped rooms. Exit 178 from Zaragoza to Madrid motorway.

■ RESTAURANT: Award-winning international
restaurant. Specialities include roast lamb, wild
rice and salted cod.
■ ACTIVITIES: Health treatment (beauty, weight,
stress, etc). Many historic places of interest to
visit nearby.
■ TARIFF: (1996) Single 7,700, Double 12,100,
Set menu 2,900 (Euro/Access, Visa).
■ DISCOUNT: 10%

Spain

TARRAGONA 9A

Hotel Astari ★★★
Via Augusta 97, 43003 Tarragona.
Tel 977 236900, Fax 977 236911. English spoken.
Open all year. 83 bedrooms (all en suite).
Indoor swimming pool, outdoor swimming
pool, golf 4 km, garage, restaurant.

*Renovated in March 1996, the hotel is in a
residential area, 300 m from Rambla Nova
(shopping centre), 6 km from Port Aventura,
0.5 km from the beach and 800 m from the
sports marina.*

■ ACTIVITIES: ● Special rates at Costa Dorada golf.
■ TARIFF: Single 7,200, Double 8,900, Bk 850
(Amex, Euro/Access, Visa).
■ DISCOUNT: 15% except July & Aug.

Hotel Lauria ★★★
Rambla Nova 20, 43004 Tarragona.
Tel 977 236712, Fax 977 236700. English spoken.
Open all year. 72 bedrooms (all en suite).
Outdoor swimming pool, golf 5 km, garage. ᕒ

*Modern, comfortable hotel in town centre and
close to sea-front. Air-conditioned rooms and
good facilities.*

■ TARIFF: (1996) Single 7,000, Double 9,500,
Bk 700 (Amex, Euro/Access, Visa).
■ DISCOUNT: 15%

Hotel Termes Montbrió ★★★★
Ctra 38 bis, 43340 Montbrió del Camp.
Tel 977 82 64 13, Fax 977 82 62 51. English spoken.

Open all year. 150 bedrooms (all en suite).
Indoor swimming pool, outdoor swimming
pool, tennis, golf 5 km, parking. ᕒ ᕒ

*6 km from the coast, a luxury resort hotel
complex set in 3 ha of exquisite landscaped
gardens. Excellent facilities for meetings, shows
and weddings. From motorway A7 exit 37.*

■ RESTAURANT: Hotel has two restaurants, 'La
Sequoia' and L'Horta Florida' offering a wide
range of international cuisine.

■ ACTIVITIES: Health, relaxation and toning
programmes are available at the hotel's superb
thermal centre, carefully monitored by a team
of professionals. Facilities include thermal
pool, giant and alga mud jacuzzi's as well as
panoramic gymnasium. Sailing, horse-riding,
pleasure flying and Port Aventura theme park
within easy reach.
■ TARIFF: Single 9,200–14,950, Double 10,350–
19,550, Set menu 3,700 (Amex, Euro/Access, Visa).

TOSSA DE MAR 9B

Hotel Mar Menuda ★★★
Playa de Mar Menuda, 17320 Tossa de Mar.
Tel 972 341000, Fax 972 340087. English spoken.
Open 01/03 to 07/01. 50 bedrooms
(all en suite). Outdoor swimming pool, tennis,
golf 12 km, garage, parking. ᕒ

*Quiet hotel, surrounded by pine trees and
facing the beach. Comfortable, air-conditioned
accommodation with some suites available.*

■ RESTAURANT: Closed 30/09 to 03/04. Terrace
restaurant facing the sea. International dishes
as well as specialities including seafood, simi-
tomba, paella and regional salads.
■ ACTIVITIES: Organised bridge tournaments;
arrangements made for golf; own diving school
centre.
■ TARIFF: (1996) Single 5,200–10,500,
Double 8,800–18,600, Set menu 2,700
(Amex, Euro/Access, Visa).

VALENCIA 9C

Hotel Casino Monte Picayo ★★★★★
46530 Puzol.
Tel 961 420100, Fax 961 422168. English spoken.

Open all year. 82 bedrooms (all en suite).
Indoor swimming pool, outdoor swimming
pool, tennis, golf 10 km, garage, parking.

*Luxurious, peaceful hotel facing the sea with
views over orange groves. Some rooms have a*

private jacuzzi. 18 km north of Valencia and convenient for the airport and international trade fair.

■ RESTAURANT: Typical Valencian cuisine with shellfish and paella specialities.
■ TARIFF: (1996) Single 17,500, Double 21,950, Bk 1,300, Set menu 3,100 (Amex, Visa).

VALLADOLID 8B

Hotel El Montico ★★★ Carretera Burgos-Salamanca, 47100 Tordesillas.
Tel 983 795000, Fax 983 795008. English spoken.
Open all year. 55 bedrooms (all en suite).
Outdoor swimming pool, tennis, golf 15 km, garage, parking.

Modern hotel set amongst pine trees with comfortably furnished rooms. On the N620 between Tordesillas (4 km) and Valladolid (22 km).

■ RESTAURANT: Award-winning restaurant offering international and regional cuisine. Speciality: roast lamb.
■ ACTIVITIES: Two squash courts, indoor driving range; gymnasium; sauna.
■ TARIFF: Single 6,000–7,500, Double 8,500–11,000, Bk 900, Set menu 2,750 (Amex, Euro/Access, Visa).
■ DISCOUNT: 20%

VIELLA 9A

Hotel Aran ★★ Avda Castiero 5, 25530 Viella.
Tel 973 640050, Fax 973 640053. English spoken.
Open all year. 48 bedrooms (all en suite).
Parking, restaurant.

Small and comfortable, in the centre of town. Only a few minutes from the ski resort of La Tuca.

■ ACTIVITIES: Sauna and jacuzzi at hotel; riding school nearby, ski slopes 12 km; adventure sports including trekking, rafting, descending ravines, paragliding and archery.
■ TARIFF: (1996) Single 2,750–5,050, Double 4,500–9,100, Bk 450, Set menu 1,450–1,950 (Amex, Euro/Access, Visa).

Hotel Tuca ★★★★ Ctra Baqueira, 25539 Betren.
Tel 973 640700, Fax 973 640754. English spoken.
Open 20/12 to 15/10. 118 bedrooms (all en suite). Outdoor swimming pool, garage, parking, restaurant. &

A very comfortable, modern hotel in heart of the Valle de Aran. 10 minutes by car to ski resorts of Baqueira. From Viella, go east towards La Tuca.

■ ACTIVITIES: Fishing, skiing.
■ TARIFF: (1996) Single 5,100–7,800, Double 8,700–14,000, Set menu 2,350 (Amex, Euro/Access, Visa).

VILLAJOYOSA 9C

Hotel Eurotennis ★★★
Partida Montiboli 33, 03570 Villajoyosa.
Tel 965 891250, Fax 965 891194. English spoken.
Open 28/06 to 31/10. 98 bedrooms (all en suite). Outdoor swimming pool, tennis, golf 18 km, parking. ☎

Award-winning hotel offering much more than its 3-star rating would suggest. Set in lovely grounds with its own beach, about 3.5 km from the picturesque fishing town of Villajoyosa.

■ RESTAURANT: Air-conditioned dining room with daily à la carte menus. Speciality is paella Valenciana. Barbecues are held on the beach and there is also a café.
■ ACTIVITIES: Fitness centre, mountain bikes, tennis lessons, archery, water sports. ● Free tennis on one of the 17 courts for guests staying a minimum of 7 days.
■ TARIFF: Single 5,500–9,500, Double 7,500–13,000, Set menu 1,500 (Amex, Euro/Access, Visa).
■ DISCOUNT: 10%

VINAROZ 9A

Hotel Roca ★★ N340 Km1049, 12500 Vinaroz.
Tel 964 401312, Fax 964 400816. English spoken.
Open all year. 36 bedrooms (all en suite).
Tennis, golf 15 km, garage, parking.

Comfortable hotel with family atmosphere. Beautiful gardens and only five minutes' walk to the beach.

■ RESTAURANT: International and regional cuisine with seafood specialities.
■ TARIFF: (1996) Single 3,100–3,500, Double 4,300–5,000, Bk 450, Set menu 1,200 (Euro/Access, Visa).

ZAMORA 8B

Hotel Il Infantas ★★★
Cortinas de San Miguel 3, 49002 Zamora.
Tel 980 532875, Fax 980 533548.
Open all year. 68 bedrooms (all en suite). Garage.

Small hotel with all modern facilities including air conditioning. In the main commercial centre of Zamora.

■ TARIFF: Single 6,500–7,000, Double 9,250–10,250, Bk 575 (Amex, Euro/Access, Visa).
■ DISCOUNT: 10%

Spain

SWEDEN

Topographic treat for canoeists

The largest of the Scandinavian countries, sparsely populated Sweden is still half-covered in forest. It is said that God forgot to properly divide the land from the water here: off its long indented eastern coastline are some 20 000 islands, while the country as a whole boasts 100 000 lakes. Northern Sweden stretches up into the Arctic Circle, but its southern tip is on the same line of latitude as Newcastle.

Leaving England from Newcastle or Harwich, you arrive at Gothenburg, where the Göta Canal begins its journey to the Baltic. Avoid the temptation to ignore Gothenburg: a wander on foot or by boat around its old canals – as well as out to the island fortress of Nya Älvsborg – will make an excellent introduction to your Swedish holiday.

After Gothenburg, Stockholm, via a variety of alternative routes: the most direct one roughly follows the line of the 600-km-long Göta Canal; a longer, more northerly route passes through the province of Dalarna, described as the 'true heart of Sweden'.

Stockholm is known as the 'Venice of the North', and with so much to see, the Stockholm Card is recommended: available for 1, 2 or 3 days, this gives entry to 50 places of interest, bus tours, boat trips and public transport pass.

Emergency numbers

Police, Fire Brigade and Ambulance 112

Warning information

Carrying a warning triangle recommended

Blood Alcohol Legal Limit 20 mg

Although you are unlikely to win a Nobel prize yourself, in Stockholm you can enjoy a Nobel prize-winner's dinner – without all the hassle of a lifetime's dedication. Given a few days' notice, the chefs at the City Hall's cellar restaurant will oblige with a choice of past Nobel menus!

Sweden

ARLANDASTAD   11B

Eurostop Hotel ★★★
Cederströms Slinga, 19586 Arlandastad.
Tel 08 595 11100, Fax 08 595 10110.
English spoken.
Open all year. 228 bedrooms (all en suite).
Golf 2 km, garage, parking. ℭ ⅙
*High standard budget hotel, 4 km from
Arlanda International Airport. Shuttle to
airport. Shopping mall and car rental on site.*
■ RESTAURANT: Two restaurants: the 'Snabba
Krogen' for light meals and the 'Bistro' for à la
carte.
■ ACTIVITIES: New floodlit 9- and 18-hole golf
course 2 km. Visit Sigtuna, an historic town
(10 km).
■ TARIFF: (1996) Single 795–1260,
Double 880–1260 (Amex, Euro/Access, Visa).
■ DISCOUNT: 10%

ESKILSTUNA   11A

Hotel Statt ★★★★
Hamngatan 9-11, 63220 Eskilstuna.
Tel 016 137 225, Fax 016 127 588. English spoken.
Open all year. 220 bedrooms (all en suite).
Indoor swimming pool, golf 13 km, garage. ℭ
*Beautifully situated in the heart of Eskilstuna,
close to the park and the River Eskilstuna.*
■ RESTAURANT: Comfortable restaurant with
dancing several times a week.
■ ACTIVITIES: Sauna, jacuzzi, indoor driving range.
■ TARIFF: (1996) Single 465–1200,
Double 610–1350 (Amex, Euro/Access, Visa).

FILIPSTAD   11A

Hotel Hennickehammars Herrgård
68222 Filipstad.
Tel 590 125 65, Fax 590 717 17. English spoken.

Open all year. 54 bedrooms (all en suite).
Tennis, golf 15 km, parking. ℭ

*18th-century manor house beautifully situated
in its own park by Lake Hemtjärn. Individually
decorated rooms. 4 km from Filipstad in the
heart of Värmland.*
■ RESTAURANT: Lovely dining rooms. The
'Smörgåsbord', served at weekends, is one of
the specialities.
■ ACTIVITIES: Jacuzzi, sauna and fully equipped
fitness room; bicycles, rowing boats, canoes
available at hotel; fishing, walking and jogging
trails.
■ TARIFF: Single 395–755, Double 590–1070,
Set menu 315–365 (Amex, Euro/Access, Visa).
■ DISCOUNT: 10%

GÖTEBORG   11C

Mornington Hotel ★★★★
Kungsportsavenyn 6, 41136 Göteborg.
Tel 031 176 540, Fax 031 711 3439. English spoken.
Open all year. 91 bedrooms (all en suite).
Golf 10 km, garage. ℭ
*A modern, town centre hotel with nightclub;
easy access to shopping, sightseeing, museums,
etc. Follow the signs for 'Centrum' and the
hotel is situated on the main street.*
■ RESTAURANT: Closed Sun LS. French
specialities; 2 bars.
■ ACTIVITIES: Nightclub.
■ TARIFF: Single 965–1295, Double 1495–1800
(Amex, Euro/Access, Visa).
■ DISCOUNT: 33% 20/06 to 17/08 only.

Reso Hotel Rubinen
Kungsportsavenyn 24, 40014 Göteborg.
Tel 031 810 800, Fax 031 167 586. English spoken.
Open all year. 190 bedrooms (all en suite).
Golf 5 km. ℭ
*Excellent location in the middle of the main
avenue in the town centre.*
■ RESTAURANT: International cuisine prepared by
a renowned chef.
■ ACTIVITIES: Many places of interest in the town.
■ TARIFF: (1996) Single 1055–1345,
Double 1345–1745, Set menu 195–495
(Amex, Euro/Access, Visa).

Spar Hotel ★★★
Karl Johansgatan 66-70, 41455 Göteborg.
Tel 031 420020, Fax 031 426383. English spoken.
Open all year. 150 bedrooms (all en suite).
Golf 6 km, garage, parking. ℭ
*Close to the town centre, the hotel has cosy
rooms and a warm, friendly atmosphere.*
■ TARIFF: Single 495–545, Double 645–745
(Amex, Euro/Access, Visa).
■ DISCOUNT: 10% on presentation of this guide.

Sweden

GRÄNNA 11C

Hotel Örensbaden Örserum, 56391 Gränna.
Tel 390 30170, Fax 390 30397. English spoken.
Open all year. 53 bedrooms (50 en suite).
Golf 10 km, parking, restaurant. ℄

Modern hotel beautifully situated on the shore of Lake Ören. 10 km east of Gränna on route 133.

■ ACTIVITIES: Sauna, mini-golf; rowing boats available free of charge for hotel guests.
■ TARIFF: (1996) Single 400–485, Double 500–770, Set menu 110 (Euro/Access, Visa).

KIRUNA 10B

Hotel Vinterpalatset
Järnvägsgatan 18, 98121 Kiruna.
Tel 980 83170, Fax 980. English spoken.
Open all year. 20 bedrooms (all en suite).
Golf 6 km, parking. ℄

In the town centre, an old, recently renovated hotel. Individually decorated rooms. Good conference facilities.

■ RESTAURANT: International cuisine and Swedish and Lappish specialities.
■ ACTIVITIES: Sauna and jacuzzi. Rafting, fishing, hunting, hiking, dog-sleigh tours, snow-mobile safaris, various cultural and historic events and tours.
■ TARIFF: (1996) Single 375–990, Double 495–1250 (Amex, Euro/Access, Visa).

KRAMFORS 11A

Frånö Hotel Riksvägen 25, 87243 Kramfors.
Tel 0612 30520, Fax 0612 30585.
English spoken.

Open all year. 12 bedrooms (10 en suite).
Parking. ℄

Family-run hotel in a mansion dating from 1880. Situated in a quiet location 3 km south of Kramfors centre and close to the national

highway 90. Right on the river, Kramfors is a splendid location for exploring the region.

■ RESTAURANT: Restaurant has a good reputation for its regional cuisine.
■ ACTIVITIES: Hotel will organise boat trips and visits to the construction site of the new High Coast Suspension Bridge over the River Ångerman (3rd longest in the world).
● Discount on green fees.
■ TARIFF: (1996) Single 390–590, Double 490–690, Set menu 55–210 (Amex, Euro/Access, Visa).
■ DISCOUNT: 15%

MALMÖ 11C

Prize Hotel Carlsgatan 10c, 21120 Malmö.
Tel 040 611 2511, Fax 040 611 2310.
English spoken.
Open all year. 109 bedrooms (all en suite). ℄ ⅋

Modern town centre hotel with well-equipped comfortable rooms. Car park adjacent. Hot and cold bar snacks available.

■ TARIFF: Single 395–595, Double 495–745, Bk 55 (Amex, Euro/Access, Visa).

NORRKÖPING 11A

Hotel Sodra
Sodra Promenaden 142, 60231 Norrköping.
Tel 011 189 990, Fax 011 124 696. English spoken.
Open all year. 23 bedrooms (21 en suite).
Parking.

In town centre, just a few minutes from the airport. Many restaurants nearby.

■ DISCOUNT: 10%

PITEÅ 10D

Piteå Stadshotell ★★★★
Olof Palmesgata 1, 94121 Piteå.
Tel 0911 19700, Fax 0911 12292. English spoken.
Open all year. 103 bedrooms (all en suite).
Golf 3 km, parking. ℄ ⅋

Lovely old building, recently renovated to offer all modern conveniences whilst still retaining its original character. In the town centre.

■ RESTAURANT: Choice of two highly recommended restaurants as well as a tavern. International and regional cuisine.
■ ACTIVITIES: Hotel offers dances, live music and conference facilities. Happy to assist in organising and booking various cultural and recreational activities.
■ TARIFF: (1996) Single 530–995, Double 730–1195, Set menu 75 (Amex, Euro/Access, Visa).

Sweden

STOCKHOLM 11B

Hotel Diplomat ★★★★
Strandvagen 7c, 10440 Stockholm.
Tel 08 663 5800, Fax 08 783 6634. English spoken.
Open all year. 130 bedrooms (all en suite).
Golf 2 km, garage.
Very comfortable hotel with personal atmosphere. In city centre, overlooking the harbour and convenient for shopping and cultural interests.
■ RESTAURANT: Closed Christmas.
■ TARIFF: Single 1495–1995, Double 2095–2295, Set menu 195 (Amex, Euro/Access, Visa).

Frälsningsarméns Gästhem
Djurgårdsvägen 7, 13246 Saltsjö-Boo.
Tel 08 715 1158, Fax 08 747 1176.
English spoken.
Open all year. 29 bedrooms (20 en suite).
Parking, restaurant. (&
Wonderful position near the sea and just 15 minutes from the centre. From Stockholm on route 222 towards Nacka/Gustausberg, take Lännerster exit.
■ ACTIVITIES: Boat trips.
■ TARIFF: (1996) Single 330–380, Double 450–600 (No credit cards).

Hotel Lady Hamilton
Storkyrkobrinken 5 Stockholm.
Tel 08 234680, Fax 08 111148. English spoken.
Open all year. 34 bedrooms (all en suite).
Golf 22 km, garage.
Beautiful hotel with Swedish folk-art décor, in the centre of the old town. 50 m from the Royal Palace and close to all points of interest.
■ TARIFF: Single 1380–1770, Double 1600–2140 (Amex, Euro/Access, Visa).

Hotel Lord Nelson
Vasterlanggatan 22, 10000 Stockholm.
Tel 08 232390, Fax 08 101089. English spoken.
Open all year. 31 bedrooms (all en suite).
Golf 22 km, garage. (
Beautifully located on the old city island of Stockholm. Near the Royal Palace and all points of interest.
■ TARIFF: Single 1100–1460, Double 1370–1850 (Amex, Euro/Access, Visa).

Hotel Malardrottningen ★★★
Riddarholmen, 11128 Stockholm.
Tel 08 243 600, Fax 08 243 676. English spoken.
Open 01/01 to 23/12 & 29/12 to 31/12.
59 bedrooms (all en suite). Tennis, golf 10 km. (
Unique hotel converted from a luxury yacht permanently berthed on the waterfront, a few blocks from the old town. 800 m from the station. Compact air-conditioned cabins with modern comforts.
■ RESTAURANT: Well-known Swedish restaurant.
■ DISCOUNT: 10%

Prize Hotel Stockholm
Kungsbron 1, 11122 Stockholm.
Tel 08 149 450, Fax 08 149 848. English spoken.
Open all year. 158 bedrooms (all en suite).
Garage. (&
Recently built, hotel is centrally situated near the air terminal and central station.
■ RESTAURANT: Scandinavian and international dishes.
■ ACTIVITIES: Shopping area and amusement centres within walking distance; reservations made for guided tours.
■ TARIFF: (1996) Single 520–880, Double 620–1030, Bk 55 (Amex, Euro/Access, Visa).

TÄLLBERG 11A

Hotel Siljansgården Gasthem
Sjögattu 36, 79370 Tällberg.
Tel 0247 50040, Fax 0247 50013. English spoken.
Open all year. 27 bedrooms (15 en suite).
Tennis, golf 8 km, parking. (
A traditional old-style hotel with the personal touch, situated on the shore of Lake Siljan. Centrally located for the area's many attractions. Also has self-catering cottages. Hotel is signposted from the town.
■ RESTAURANT: Good, home-made dishes at reasonable prices.
■ ACTIVITIES: Hotel is happy to advise and book activities, tours, etc.
■ TARIFF: Single 250–395, Double 395–750, Set menu 55–175 (Euro/Access, Visa).

YSTAD 11C

Sekelgården Hotel
Stora Västergatan 9, 27123 Ystad.
Tel 041 173 900, Fax 041 118 997. English spoken.
Open all year. 16 bedrooms (all en suite).
Golf 6 km, parking.
A former merchant's residence, dating back to 1793. Lots of wood and warm, welcoming rooms with a personal touch. Well-situated near the marketplace and church in the centre of Ystad.
■ ACTIVITIES: Good sports facilities in town;
● 30% discount on green fees at nearby golf courses.
■ TARIFF: (1996) Single 450–595, Double 550–695 (Amex, Euro/Access, Visa).

Sweden

SWITZERLAND

Off-piste at Adelboden

The history of Switzerland as a nation began in 1291 when representatives from the regions of Uri, Schwyz and Unterwalden met in a meadow on the edge of Lake Uri to pledge mutual assistance against the common enemy, the Austrian Emperors. Today, this confederation of cantons, the *Cantons helvétiques,* numbers 23.

Switzerland is known for its mountains, its banks, its engineering and its efficiency – this in spite of using four languages (French, German, Italian and Romansch). It is also punctuated by some very beautiful lakes.

Lake Lucerne lies at the heart of Switzerland, and the drive through the Alps from Lucerne to Lake Locarno on the Italian border is one of Switzerland's many scenic treats.

South west of Lucerne, Switzerland shares Lac Léman (often called Lake Geneva) with France. This is western Europe's largest lake, with ferry links between Geneva, Lausanne and Montreux.

To the north of Lac Léman, Lac Neuchâtel lies just below the French border parallel to the Jura mountains. Then north again and France, Germany and Switzerland meet on the Rhine at Basle, whose fine medieval city deserves a place on any itinerary.

As the Swiss and French share Lac Léman, so do the Swiss and Germans share the Bodensee, or Lake Constance, lying on the north-eastern Swiss border. The peaks here are lower but still afford mountain-railway and cable-car trips and wonderful walking.

Switzerland offers tremendous variety and makes an ideal holiday destination, no matter what the season.

Emergency numbers

For emergency numbers see the local directory

Warning information

Warning triangle must be carried

Blood alcohol legal limit 80 mg

Switzerland

AIROLO   18D

Hotel Forni ★★★ Via Stazione, 6780 Airolo.
Tel 091 869 1270, Fax 091 869 1523.
English spoken.
Open 08/12 to 06/11. 19 bedrooms
(all en suite). Garage, parking. ℭ ♿

*Comfortable and elegant, a traditional hotel in
a mountain village in the Gotthard region.
Pleasant gardens. 5 minutes' walk from
station, or take exit for Airolo.*

■ RESTAURANT: Elegant dining room; classic
regional specialities.
■ ACTIVITIES: Winter sports. ● Special rates for
cycling trips in summer.
■ TARIFF: (1996) Single 75–100, Double 130–
160, Set menu 15–37 (Amex, Euro/Access, Visa).

ALTDORF   18B

Hotel Goldener Schlussel ★★★
Schutzengasse 9, 6460 Altdorf.
Tel 044 210 02, Fax 044 211 67.
English spoken.
Open all year. 50 bedrooms (20 en suite).
Garage, parking.

*Located in the centre of Altdorf, next to the
theatre. Private parking is available behind the
hotel. Take exit Altdorf-Flüelen. All rooms are
equipped with modern comforts.*

■ RESTAURANT: Closed Sun and Jan. Excellent
food in the cosy restaurant.
■ ACTIVITIES: ● A sightseeing tour is offered
by hotel.
■ TARIFF: (1996) Single 85–130,
Double 130–210 (Euro/Access, Visa).
■ DISCOUNT: 10%

ARBON   18B

Hotel Rotes Kreuz ★★
Hatenstr 3, 9320 Arbon.
Tel 071 461 914, Fax 071 462 485.
English spoken.
Open all year. 28 bedrooms (15 en suite).
Golf 20 km, parking.

*Highly recommended. Traditional,
comfortable hotel with a typical Swiss air about
it. Set in an idyllic location on the edge of Lake
Bodensee within easy walking distance of all
amenities. North of St-Gallen and north-east of
Zürich.*

■ RESTAURANT: Closed Thur. Fish specialities.
■ ACTIVITIES: Exploring the beautiful
countryside surrounding the lake.
■ TARIFF: (1996) Single 55–60, Double 110–130,
Set menu 17.50 (Euro/Access, Visa).

BASEL (BASLE)   18A

Hotel Admiral ★★★
Rosentalstrasse 5/Messeplatz, 4021 Basel.
Tel 061 691 7777, Fax 061 691 7789.
English spoken.
Open all year. 130 bedrooms (all en suite).
Outdoor swimming pool, garage, parking,
restaurant.

*Modern, comfortable hotel situated in central
location near the Trade Fair and Conference
Centre. Conference rooms and bar. 8 km from
Basel airport.*

■ ACTIVITIES: Rooftop heated swimming pool,
open from April to October.
■ TARIFF: Single 145–200, Double 180–295
(Amex, Euro/Access, Visa).

Basel Hilton ★★★★★
Aeschengraben 31, 4002 Basel.
Tel 061 271 6622, Fax 061 271 5220.
English spoken.

Open all year. 214 bedrooms (all en suite).
Indoor swimming pool, garage. ℭ ♿

*With the typical excellent comforts and
facilities of a Hilton, the hotel is centrally
situated within walking distance of the airport
terminal, railway station and main
shopping/museum area. Less than an hour
from the Black Forest in Germany, the Alsace
in France and the Alps.*

■ RESTAURANT: The 'Wettstein Restaurant' offers
French and international gourmet cusine and
'Café de la Marine Suisse' a choice of dishes
with Swiss specialities.
■ ACTIVITIES: Tours to Luzern, Bern, Zürich, the
Black Forest, Alsace and '3-Ländereck' (the
point where 3 countries meet); visit the
museums and zoo and enjoy a river trip
on the Rhein.
■ TARIFF: (1996) Single 245–295,
Double 320–495, Bk 24, Set menu 11.50
(Amex, Euro/Access, Visa).

Switzerland

Hotel Europe ★★★★
Clarastrasse 43, 4005 Basel.
Tel 061 690 8080, Fax 061 690 8880.
English spoken.
Open all year. 166 bedrooms (all en suite).
Garage.

Completely renovated first-class hotel, with non-smoking rooms available on request. Underground garage with 130 parking spaces. Motorway connections (exit 3, Basel Ost/Wettstein) for Berne/Lucerne/Zürich. Germany and France only 450 m away.

■ RESTAURANT: Closed Sun. Award-winning gourmet restaurant 'Les Quatre Saisons' and 'Bistro Bajazzo', which stays open on Sundays.
■ ACTIVITIES: Sightseeing and cultural excursions.
■ TARIFF: Single 175–290, Double 235–390, Set menu 35–150 (Amex, Euro/Access, Visa).

Hotel Krafft am Rhein ★★★
Rheingasse 12, 4058 Basel.
Tel 061 691 8877, Fax 061 691 0907.
English spoken.
Open all year. 52 bedrooms (45 en suite).
Garage, parking.

Classical-style hotel, sympathetically renovated and situated right on the banks of the Rhein. Family managed; pretty terrace.

■ RESTAURANT: Hotel has 2 restaurants.
■ TARIFF: (1996) Single 125–180, Double 200–340, Set menu 14.50–21 (Amex, Euro/Access, Visa).

Hotel Muenchnerhof ★★★
Riehenring 75, 4058 Basel.
Tel 061 691 7780, Fax 061 691 1490.
English spoken.
Open all year. 45 bedrooms (35 en suite, 3 bath/shower only). Garage, parking. ℂ ♿

Central position, close to the Swiss Trade Fair and motorway exit for Mulhouse, Karlsruhe and Luzern. Follow signs to Messe Basle.

■ RESTAURANT: French and Italian specialities.
■ TARIFF: (1996) Single 75–235, Double 140–345, Set menu 15–55 (Amex, Euro/Access, Visa).

BELLINZONA   18D

Hotel Internazionale ★★★
Piazza Stazione 35, 6500 Bellinzona.
Tel 091 825 43 33, Fax 091 826 13 59.
English spoken.
Open all year. 20 bedrooms (all en suite).
Golf 1 km, parking. ℂ ♿

Situated in the centre of Bellinzona, opposite the station.

■ RESTAURANT: Pizza and ice cream specialities.
■ ACTIVITIES: ● Free entry to museum and 3 historic buildings.
■ TARIFF: (1996) Single 100–130, Double 130–180 (Amex, Euro/Access, Visa).
■ DISCOUNT: 10%

Mövenpick Hotel ★★★
Area Servizio, Bellinzona Sud,
6513 Monte Carasso.
Tel 092 27 01 71, Fax 092 27 76 35.
English spoken.
Open all year. 55 bedrooms (all en suite).
Parking. ℂ ♿

Close to the motorway, the hotel has quiet rooms with view over the mountains. Good restaurant 50 m from hotel.

■ TARIFF: Single 98, Double 150, Bk 14 (Amex, Euro/Access, Visa).
■ DISCOUNT: 10%

BERN   18A

Hotel Ambassador ★★★★
Seftigenstr 99, 3007 Bern.
Tel 031 370 9999, Fax 031 371 4117.
English spoken.
Open all year. 97 bedrooms (all en suite).
Indoor swimming pool, golf 1 km, garage, parking. ℂ

Completely renovated, hotel is opposite the station, near the famous arcades of Berne. From the motorway, exit 'Köniz' then follow Belp (airport) signs for approx 3.5 km.

■ RESTAURANT: Closed (Japanese): 4 weeks in summer. Attractive choice from the buffet and good à l carte service; Japanese restaurant.
■ ACTIVITIES: Sauna, hiking and cycling.
■ TARIFF: Single 130–165, Double 170–190, Bk 16, Set menu 15.50–23.00 (Amex, Euro/Access, Visa).
■ DISCOUNT: 20% Friday to Sunday only.

Hotel City am Bahnhof ★★★
Bahnhofplatz, 3011 Bern.
Tel 031 311 5377, Fax 031 311 0636.
English spoken.
Open all year. 57 bedrooms (all en suite).

This modern hotel opened in 1994 after total renovation. Centrally located near the railway station, restaurants, shopping and parking.

■ ACTIVITIES: Museums and sightseeing. Mountain and lake region excursions including the Eiger and Jungfrau, Neuchâtel and Fribourg.
■ TARIFF: (1996) Single 105–145, Double 135–175, Bk 16 (Amex, Euro/Access, Visa).
■ DISCOUNT: 20% Fri to Sun only.

Switzerland

BIASCA 18D

Hotel al Giardinetto ★★★
Via Aleardo Pini, 6710 Biasca.
Tel 091 862 1771, Fax 091 862 2359.
English spoken.
Open all year. 33 bedrooms (25 en suite,
8 bath/shower only). Garage, parking. &
*Recently renovated hotel, centrally situated not
far from N2. Large terrace. From N2 take
Biasca exit and follow signs for Biasca Centro.*
■ RESTAURANT: Toscan specialities.
■ ACTIVITIES: Guided tours of the surrounding
countryside in high season; possibility of
mountain excursions.
■ TARIFF: (1996) Single 80–100, Double 85–150,
Set menu 21–38 (Amex, Euro/Access, Visa).

BIEL/BIENNE 18A

Hotel Elite ★★★★
14 rue de la Gare, 2501 Biel/Bienne.
Tel 032 225 441, Fax 032 221 383.
English spoken.
Open all year. 68 bedrooms (all en suite).
Garage.
*Between rolling hills and the lake, a
comfortable hotel that is only 3 minutes' walk
from the main station.*
■ RESTAURANT: Closed 19/07 to 08/08. Good
food, traditional hospitality.
■ TARIFF: (1996) Single 140–170,
Double 180–260 (Amex, Euro/Access, Visa).

BULLE 18C

Hotel du Tonnelier ★★
Grand Rue 31, 1630 Bulle.
Tel 026 9127745, Fax 026 9123986.
English spoken.
Open all year. 21 bedrooms (16 en suite,
5 bath/shower only). Golf 6 km, parking. ☎
*Small hotel in the town centre, 2 km from
motorway M12. Ideally situated in the heart of
Gruyère, 30 minutes' drive from Bern and
1 hour from Genève.*
■ RESTAURANT: Italian specialities.
■ ACTIVITIES: Sightseeing tours can be arranged
by the hotel.
■ TARIFF: (1996) Single 40–60, Double 85–95,
(Amex, Euro/Access, Visa).

Hotel du Vignier ★★★
1644 Avry-Devant-Pont.
Tel 026 915 21 95, Fax 026 915 20 61.
English spoken.
Open 01/02 to 07/01. 7 bedrooms (all en suite).
Golf 7 km, garage, parking. ☎

*Charming hotel in a small village on the banks
of Lake Gruyère. Avry-Devant-Pont is north of
Bulle on the tourist route.*
■ RESTAURANT: Inventive cuisine using fresh,
local produce.
■ ACTIVITIES: Windsurfing, hiking, skiing, cross-
country skiing.
■ TARIFF: (1996) Single 80–120,
Double 120–170, Set menu 32–95
(Amex, Euro/Access, Visa).

BUOCHS 18B

Hotel Rigiblick am See ★★★★
am Seeplatz 3, 6374 Buochs.
Tel 041 620 4864, Fax 041 620 6874.
English spoken.

Open 01/03 to 31/01. 16 bedrooms
(all en suite). Golf 10 km, parking. ☎
*Right beside the lake, a lovely, traditional
building dating from 1910. The interior has
been stylishly decorated and modernised to
offer a peaceful, relaxing atmosphere, all
comforts and some spectacular views. South-
east of Luzern on the N2, take Buochs/
Beckenried Nord exit and hotel is just
2 minutes ahead.*
■ RESTAURANT: Closed Tues LS. Dining room is
light and airy with panoramic views. Has
earned an excellent reputation for its refined à
la carte cuisine and hearty local dishes. Good
selection of wines and malt whiskies.
■ ACTIVITIES: Hotel offers a games room and
mountain bikes year-round. In summer,
pedalos and outdoor games including table
tennis, pool and chess. All mountain and lake
activities are reachable within half an hour.
■ TARIFF: Single 147–177, Double 234–274,
Set menu 16.50–53 (Euro/Access, Visa).
■ DISCOUNT: 10%

Switzerland

CHEXBRES-LAVAUX 18C

Hotel du Signal ★★★★ 1604 Puidoux-Chexbres.
Tel 021 946 0505, Fax 021 946 0515.
English spoken.
Open 30/03 to 01/11. 78 bedrooms
(all en suite). Indoor swimming pool, tennis,
golf 18 km, garage, parking. &

*Set in 20 hectares overlooking Lac Léman.
Excellent facilities and superb views. A few
minutes from Vevey and Lausanne and 1 km
from highway, exit Chexbres.*

■ RESTAURANT: French cuisine in a picturesque
setting.
■ TARIFF: Single 105–160, Double 178–272,
Set menu 32–70 (Euro/Access, Visa).

DAVOS 18B

Hotel Schweizerhof ★★★★
Promenade 50, 7270 Davos.
Tel 081 413 2626, Fax 081 413 4966.
English spoken.

Open 30/11 to 13/04 & 29/06 to 30/09.
90 bedrooms (all en suite). Indoor swimming
pool, golf 1 km, garage, parking. &

*Modern, first-class hotel with a friendly
atmosphere and offering personal attention.
Centrally situated near ski lifts. Several
lounges, bar with pianist mid June to mid
September and winter season. Sun terrace and
garden with children's playground.*

■ RESTAURANT: Elegant dining room.
■ ACTIVITIES: Special guided walking weeks.
■ TARIFF: (1996) Single 111–151,
Double 192–240, Set menu 48–58 (Amex,
Euro/Access, Visa).

EGERKINGEN 18A

Mövenpick Hotel ★★★★
Höhenstrasse 666, 4622 Egerkingen.
Tel 062 398 0707, Fax 062 398 2282. English spoken.

Open all year. 140 bedrooms (all en suite).
Parking. ℓ &

*Ideally situated at the intersection of the main
motorways N1 and N2 and within 40 minutes
of Basel, Zürich, Bern and Luzern. Modern,
attractive hotel with excellent facilities and an
emphasis on friendliness and efficiency.
Fully equipped accommodation with rooms
and suites attractively furnished in light-
coloured wood; multi-functional
seminar/conference centre.*

■ RESTAURANT: With a choice of four, something
for all tastes. Ranges from the gourmet 'La
Huetta', 'Mövenpick', offering a wide range of
international specialities, its own winter garden
and panoramic views, to the 'Boulevard Café'
and 'Feldschlössen Pub'. There is also a
summer terrace where meals can be taken in
fine weather.
■ ACTIVITIES: Facilities offered by the hotel
include a jogging track, extensive hiking and
cycling routes (bicycles available from hotel
free of charge) and a children's playground.
Nearby are tennis, squash, horse-riding and a
fitness centre. Excursions and sightseeing tours
can be arranged on request.
■ TARIFF: Double 160–280, Bk 20.50,
Set menu 12.50–39.50 (Amex, Euro/Access, Visa).
■ DISCOUNT: 10% except fair/convention periods.

GENEVE (GENEVA) 18C

Hotel Cornavin ★★★★
Place de la gare, 1208 Genève.
Tel 022 732 2100, Fax 022 732 8843.
English spoken.
Open all year. 125 bedrooms (all en suite). ℓ

*Follow signs to 'Gare Cornavin' (main station)
and hotel is just to the right of it.*

■ TARIFF: Single 150–215, Double 215–265,
Bk 8 (Amex, Euro/Access, Visa).
■ DISCOUNT: 20% Friday to Sunday only.

Switzerland

Hotel Cristal ★★★ 4 rue Pradier, 1201 Genève.
Tel 022 731 3400, Fax 022 731 7078.
English spoken.
Open all year. 79 bedrooms (all en suite). &

*Modern hotel in a quiet location but in easy
reach of parking, airport, station and shopping
street. Air conditioned, cable TV. Easy to find,
just 100 m from the railway station.*

■ TARIFF: (1996) Single 144–175, Double 202–
234, Bk 8 (Amex, Euro/Access, Visa).
■ DISCOUNT: 20% Friday to Sunday only.

Hotel Grand Pré ★★★★
35 rue Grand Pré, 1202 Genève.
Tel 022 918 1111, Fax 022 734 7691.
English spoken.
Open all year. 89 bedrooms (39 en suite).
Golf 18 km, garage, parking.

*Located in a quiet neighbourhood, convenient
for all international organisations, the railway
station, airport and Conference Centre.
Transport from railway station and airport by
hotel car available. Good choice of
international restaurants nearby.*

■ ACTIVITIES: All that the picturesque and
exciting lakeside town of Genève has to offer.
Ski slopes are within 30 minutes.
■ TARIFF: Single 210–225, Double 280–300
(Amex, Euro/Access, Visa).

Hotel Pax ★★
68 rue du 31 décembre, 1207 Genève.
Tel 022 787 5070, Fax 022 787 5080.
English spoken.

Open all year. 32 bedrooms (12 en suite,
12 bath/shower only). Golf 3 km, parking.
*Family hotel in the centre of town on the left
bank of the lake; parking nearby. Comfortable
rooms with all modern facilities.*

■ TARIFF: Single 78–113, Double 91–131
(Amex, Euro/Access, Visa).
■ DISCOUNT: 10%

Hotel Métropole ★★★★★ 34 quai Gén
Guisan, Rive gauche, 1204 Genève.
Tel 022 318 3200, Fax 022 318 3300.
English spoken.
Open all year. 127 bedrooms (104 en suite,
23 bath/shower only).

*Elegant, luxurious hotel dating from the 1850s
and now completely renovated. Town centre
position, facing the lake and the Jardin
Anglais. (Chargeable car park nearby.)*

■ RESTAURANT: Extensive menus in this
showpiece.
■ TARIFF: Single 290–350, Double 380–455
(Amex, Euro/Access, Visa).

GISWIL 18A

Hotel Landhaus ★★★★
Brunigstrasse, 6074 Giswil.
Tel 041 675 1313, Fax 041 675 2252.
English spoken.

Open all year. 46 bedrooms (all en suite).
Indoor swimming pool, outdoor swimming
pool, parking. & &
*Extremely comfortable hotel in a lovely setting.
The terrace of the hotel has panoramic views of
Lake Sarnen. 30 minutes by car from Luzern.*

■ RESTAURANT: Choice of 3 restaurants offering a
wide range of national and international
cuisine.
■ ACTIVITIES: Sauna, solarium, billiard room at
hotel; walking/hiking, water sports, skiing.
■ TARIFF: (1996) Single 80–100,
Double 150–180 (Amex, Euro/Access, Visa).

Switzerland

GLARUS 18B

Minotel Tödiblick 8784 Braunwald.
Tel 055 643 1236, Fax 055 643 1129.
English spoken.

Open all year. 15 bedrooms (10 en suite).
Indoor swimming pool, golf 1 km. ☎

Picturesque and cosy chalet-hotel, ideal for family holidays in beautiful, quiet surroundings with breathtaking views. As Braunwald is car free, cars should be left at Linthal. Take the funicular railway up to Braunwald where guests are met by the hotel porter with a pony cart.

■ RESTAURANT: Renowned restaurant with local specialities such as raclette; vegetarian dishes also available.
■ ACTIVITIES: In summer, walking, trekking and climbing in park-like surroundings; winter skiing, cross-country skiing and sledging on perfectly prepared slopes; round-trips with ponycart. ● Free entry to village's indoor swimming pool.
■ TARIFF: (1996) Single 75–130, Double 150–260, Set menu 20–40 (Amex, Euro/Access, Visa).
■ DISCOUNT: 10%

GOTTHARD 18D

Romantik Hotel Stern & Post ★★★
6474 Amsteg am Gotthard.
Tel 041 883 1440, Fax 041 883 0261.
English spoken.
Open all year. 32 bedrooms (20 en suite).
Garage, parking.

This inn is the last coaching house along the St-Gotthard road; long established in the wonderful alpine landscape of the Maderaner valley. Traditional welcome.

■ RESTAURANT: Excellent local cuisine.
■ ACTIVITIES: Hiking, jogging, mountaineering, trout fishing, cycling, mountain-biking, rafting,

swimming; trip to the heart of Switzerland and over passes in the central Alps.
■ TARIFF: (1996) Single 65–120, Double 120–240, Set menu 45–70 (Amex, Euro/Access, Visa).

GRINDELWALD 18C

Chalet Hotel Gletschergarten ★★★
3818 Grindelwald.
Tel 036 531 721, Fax 036 532 957. English spoken.

Open 20/12 to 31/03 & 31/05 to 01/10.
26 bedrooms (all en suite). Golf 20 km, parking.

Delightful chalet-hotel built in 1899, in the heart of the Bernese Oberland. Very comfortable, attention having been paid to even the smallest detail. 1 km from station.

■ RESTAURANT: Closed Mon. Lots of atmosphere and good food in this cosy room.
■ ACTIVITIES: Sauna, solarium and steam bath at the hotel. Every kind of mountain sport almost on the doorstep.
■ TARIFF: (1996) Single 85–140, Double 170–250, Set menu 35–40 (Visa).

Romantik Hotel Schweizerhof ★★★★
3818 Grindelwald.
Tel 033 853 2202, Fax 033 853 2004. English spoken.

Open 21/12 to 08/04 & 01/06 to 05/10.
50 bedrooms (all en suite). Indoor swimming
pool, golf 18 km, parking, restaurant. ℃

*In the centre of picturesque Grindelwald and
two minutes' walk from the station. (Prices
quoted are for half-board.)*

■ ACTIVITIES: Sauna and fitness room at hotel;
mountain-biking, paragliding, climbing, skiing,
hiking, ice-skating; train trip to Jungfrau-Joch
and boat trips available nearby.
■ TARIFF: (1996) Single 172–227,
Double 314–554, Set menu 35–85 (Amex,
Euro/Access, Visa).

GSTAAD   18C

Hotel Ermitage ★★★
Le Petit Pré, 1837 Château-d'Oex.
Tel 026 924 6003, Fax 026 924 5076.
English spoken.

Open 12/11 to 27/10. 21 bedrooms
(all en suite). Golf 12 km, parking. ℃

*A member of 'Welcome Swiss Hotels', this
chalet-style hotel stands in magnificent
surroundings, with family flats available all
year. 10 minutes from Gstaad.*

■ RESTAURANT: French and regional cuisine is
prepared under the direction of a renowned,
award-winning chef.
■ ACTIVITIES: Ballooning, horse-riding, mini-
golf, tennis and heated swimming pool close
by. Winter sports.
■ TARIFF: Single 80–100, Double 120–160,
Set menu 12–45 (Amex, Euro/Access, Visa).
■ DISCOUNT: 10%

IMMENSEE   18B

Seehotel Rigi-Royal ★★★ 6405 Immensee.
Tel 041 850 3131, Fax 041 850 3137. English spoken.
Open 24/01 to 24/12. 44 bedrooms (42 en suite,
1 bath/shower only). Outdoor swimming pool,
golf 1.5 km, garage, parking. ℃ ㄴ

*Enchanting lakeside hotel with private beach
and boathouse. Rooms have spectacular views
of the surrounding countryside and pretty
gardens. Immensee is south of Zug on the west
side of the lake.*

■ RESTAURANT: Award-winning restaurant
specialising in fish and regional delicacies.
■ ACTIVITIES: Chess and table tennis at hotel;
cycling, hiking; tennis nearby.
■ TARIFF: (1996) Single 90–105, Double 150–190,
Set menu 14.50–30 (Amex, Euro/Access, Visa).
■ DISCOUNT: 8%

INTERLAKEN   18C

Hotel du Lac ★★★★
Höheweg 225, 3800 Interlaken.
Tel 033 822 29 22, Fax 033 822 29 15. English spoken.
Open 15/02 to 15/01. 40 bedrooms
(all en suite). Golf 3 km, parking. ℃ ㄴ

*With a stunning position on the River Aare,
hotel is warm and comfortable and an ideal
starting point for lake and mountain
excursions in the Jungfrau region. Skiing,
sporting and 'discovery' packages available.
Write to hotel for details.*

■ RESTAURANT: Closed 15/01 to 15/02.
Waterfront restaurant offering fish dishes from
Brienzersee, gourmet and standard menus.
■ ACTIVITIES: Jogging, biking and hiking trails
from the hotel; water sports, bungee jumping,
ice-skating, swimming pool and skiing all
within easy reach.
■ TARIFF: Single 90–150, Double 160–280,
Set menu 15–35 (Amex, Euro/Access, Visa).
■ DISCOUNT: 10% half-board only.

Hotel Splendid ★★★
Höheweg 33, 3800 Interlaken.
Tel 036 227 612, Fax 036 227 679. English spoken.
Open 25/12 to 31/10. 35 bedrooms
(all en suite). Golf 3 km, parking, restaurant. ℃

*Conveniently situated in the town centre, this
traditional Swiss hotel has a warm, family
atmosphere.*

■ ACTIVITIES: Lots to do and see nearby
including winter sports, tennis, sailing and
mountain activities.
■ TARIFF: (1996) Single 95–125, Double 145–
190, Set menu 15–30 (Amex, Euro/Access, Visa).
■ DISCOUNT: 15% not valid for special offers.

Hotel Seiler au Lac ★★★★
Bonigen, 3806 Interlaken.
Tel 033 822 3021, Fax 033 822 3001.
English spoken.
Open 10/02 to 30/10 & 20/12 to 10/01.
45 bedrooms (all en suite). Golf 5 km, garage,
parking. ♿

*Completely refurbished family hotel in an
idyllic, peaceful location overlooking Lake
Brienz. Very friendly atmosphere. 2 km from
Interlaken. Bus/boat landing in front of hotel.
(Special family rates.)*

■ RESTAURANT: French-style restaurant serving
excellent seasonal specialities (closed on
Mondays). Also 'La Bohème' pizzeria, open
evenings, Sundays and public holidays (closed
on Tuesdays). Gala dinners with pianist
(alternate Mondays), summer buffets.
■ ACTIVITIES: Massage available at hotel. ● Free
entry to nearby heated swimming pool in
summer.
■ TARIFF: Single 120–175, Double 190–320,
Set menu 25–55 (Amex, Euro/Access, Visa).

KANDERSTEG   18C

Hotel Adler ★★★ 3718 Kandersteg.
Tel 033 751 121, Fax 033 751 961.
English spoken.
Open all year. 24 bedrooms (all en suite).
Garage, parking. ♿

*Charming family-run chalet-hotel with
mountain views and good facilities. Most
rooms have balcony and some have jacuzzi
and fireplace.*

■ RESTAURANT: Cosy and informal village
restaurant; grill room with specialities including
saddle of lamb, fresh local trout and venison.
■ ACTIVITIES: Free sauna; weekly apéritif party
for guests.
■ TARIFF: Single 95–115, Double 160–190,
Set menu 18–80 (Amex, Euro/Access, Visa).

Hotel Schweizerhof ★★★★ 3718 Kandersteg.
Tel 033 675 1919, Fax 033 675 1927.
English spoken.
Open 20/12 to 31/10. 31 bedrooms
(all en suite). Tennis, garage, parking. ☎

*In the centre of the village, very comfortable
hotel and pleasant atmosphere. Viennese café.*

■ RESTAURANT: Closed Thur & Fri LS. Regional
specialities.
■ ACTIVITIES: Sauna at hotel; hiking, paragliding,
skiing and cross-country skiing.
■ TARIFF: Single 95–130, Double 160–210,
Set menu 25–45 (Amex, Euro/Access, Visa).
■ DISCOUNT: 10%

KÜSSNACHT AM RIGI   18B

Hotel Hirschen ★★★ 6403 Küssnacht am Rigi.
Tel 041 81 10 27, Fax 041 81 68 80.
English spoken.

Open all year. 27 bedrooms (all en suite).
Tennis, golf 3 km, parking, restaurant. ☎ ♿
*Family run for 8 generations, hotel is in the
town centre and offers all modern comforts.*

SEE ADVERTISEMENT

■ ACTIVITIES: Good area for walking; water
sports, tennis, horse-riding and mini-golf
nearby. Various excursions available.

Switzerland

■ TARIFF: Single 80–90, Double 140–170, Set menu 15.50–40 (Amex, Euro/Access, Visa).
■ DISCOUNT: 10%

LAUSANNE 18C

Hotel Agora ★★★★
av du Rond-Point 9, 1003 Lausanne.
Tel 021 617 1211, Fax 021 616 2605.
English spoken.
Open all year. 83 bedrooms (all en suite).
Golf 15 km, garage, parking. ᕱ

Modern, air-conditioned hotel in a quiet, convenient position. Easy access to lakeside activities and only 5 minutes' walk from the railway station. Suites with kitchenettes also available.

■ RESTAURANT: Closed Sat & Sun. Fine dining and impeccable service. French and nouvelle cuisine specialities.
■ ACTIVITIES: Visit nearby museums; walks in the mountains and boat trips on the lake.
■ TARIFF: Single 140–160, Double 180–200, Bk 8, Set menu 23–64 (Amex, Euro/Access, Visa).
■ DISCOUNT: 20% Fri to Sun only.

Hotel Alpha ★★★★
rue du Petit-Chêne 34, 1003 Lausanne.
Tel 021 323 0131, Fax 021 323 0145.
English spoken.
Open all year. 133 bedrooms (all en suite).
Golf 15 km, garage, parking. ☎

Modern hotel, within easy reach of all amenities. Individually air-conditioned rooms. Quiet position between the station and the centre of St-Francois.

■ RESTAURANT: Enjoy seasonal dishes in 'Calèche' or Swiss specialities in the 'Carnotzet'.
■ ACTIVITIES: Ideal base for sightseeing; museum visits; excursions in the mountains or on the lake.
■ TARIFF: Single 140–160, Double 180–200, Bk 8, Set menu 23 (Amex, Euro/Access, Visa).
■ DISCOUNT: 20% Fri to Sun only.

Hotel City ★★★
rue Caroline 5, 1007 Lausanne.
Tel 021 320 2141, Fax 021 320 2149.
English spoken.
Open all year. 51 bedrooms (all en suite).
Golf 15 km.

Totally renovated in 1992, the hotel is in the heart of the old city and faces the cathedral. All modern amenities, quiet and very comfortable.

■ ACTIVITIES: Walking in the mountains, boat trips on the lake and museums to visit.

■ TARIFF: Single 105–140, Double 150–180, Bk 8 (Amex, Euro/Access, Visa).
■ DISCOUNT: 20% Fri to Sun only.

Hotel Victoria ★★★★
46 av de la Gare, 1003 Lausanne.
Tel 021 320 5771, Fax 021 320 5774.
English spoken.
Open all year. 60 bedrooms (all en suite).
Golf 5 km, parking.

Comfortable, quiet hotel near the station in town centre. Conference facilities for up to 40 people.

■ TARIFF: (1996) Single 145–195, Double 190–265 (Amex, Euro/Access, Visa).

LENK 18C

Parkhotel Bellevue ★★★★
3775 Lenk-im-Simmenthal.
Tel 033 733 1761, Fax 033 733 3761.
English spoken.

Open 26/12 to 16/03 & 01/06 to 05/10.
40 bedrooms (all en suite). Outdoor swimming pool, golf 20 km, parking.

Hotel is set in beautiful parkland with some spectacular views. Next to a spa, cable and ski lifts. Managed by the same family for three generations, it offers every comfort and a friendly, personal atmosphere.

■ RESTAURANT: 'Flösch-Stube' is a rustic à la carte restaurant specialising in fresh, seasonal dishes. Grill restaurant beside the pool. Special diet menu on request with no extra charge.
■ ACTIVITIES: Garden chess, children's playground, guided walks. ● Free use of mountain bikes; tobogganing parties in winter; direct access to cross-country ski tracks from hotel grounds.
■ TARIFF: Single 97–162, Double 194–314, Set menu 34–52 (Amex, Euro/Access, Visa).
■ DISCOUNT: 10%

Switzerland

LIECHTENSTEIN

VADUZ   18A

Park Hotel Sonnenhof ★★★★
Mareestrasse 29, 9490 Vaduz, Liechenstein.
Tel 075 232 1192, Fax 075 232 0053.
English spoken.
Open 15/02 to 22/12. 29 bedrooms
(all en suite). Indoor swimming pool,
golf 15 km, garage, parking. ☎

Family-managed hotel, surrounded by a well-
kept park in the quiet residential district above
Vaduz, 10 minutes' walk from the town centre.
Magnificent panoramic views across this tiny
principality and the Swiss Alps.

■ RESTAURANT: Restaurant is for hotel guests and
friends only. French and Italian cuisine with
seasonal specialities.
■ ACTIVITIES: Excellent hiking/walking country;
tennis close by.
■ TARIFF: Single 200–270, Double 290–430
(Amex, Euro/Access, Visa).

END OF LIECHTENSTEIN HOTELS

LOCARNO   18D

Hotel Belvedere ★★★★
44 Via ai Monti, 6601 Locarno.
Tel 091 751 0363, Fax 091 751 5239.
English spoken.

Open all year. 64 bedrooms (all en suite).
Outdoor swimming pool, golf 3 km, garage. ☎ ♿

Lovely hotel with gardens and sports centre.
5 minutes' walk from town centre, served by
funicular railway. All rooms face south to the
lake. Excellent rates for longer stays; details
from hotel on request.

■ RESTAURANT: Choice of two sunny terrace
restaurants with fine Swiss and north Italian
dishes.
■ ACTIVITIES: ● Weekly activity programme
includes guided walks, swimming and exercise
lessons, picnics and breakfast parties.
■ TARIFF: Single 145–205, Double 210–300,
Set menu 35–60 (Amex, Euro/Access, Visa).
■ DISCOUNT: 15% minimum stay 3 nights.

LUGANO   18D

Hotel Bellevue au Lac ★★★★
Riva Caccia 10, 6902 Lugano.
Tel 091 994 3333, Fax 091 994 1273.
English spoken.

Open 01/04 to 31/10. 70 bedrooms (all en suite).
Outdoor swimming pool, golf 10 km.

On lakeside with beautiful views over the lake
and the mountains. A 10-minute walk into
centre of Lugano. One hour's drive to Milano.

■ RESTAURANT: Large covered terrace and indoor
restaurant offering various Italian, Swiss and
French specialities.
■ TARIFF: Single 140–200, Double 240–350,
Set menu 35–70 (Amex, Euro/Access, Visa).

Hotel Splendide Royal ★★★★★
Riva A Caccia 7, 6900 Lugano.
Tel 091 985 7711, Fax 091 994 8931. English spoken.

Open all year. 100 bedrooms (all en suite). Indoor swimming pool, golf 12 km, garage, parking.

One of the most fashionable hotels in Lugano. 5 minutes from city centre, 1.5 km from railway station and 8 km from local airport Agno/Lugano. Member of 'Swiss Leading Hotels' and 'Leading Hotels of the World'. From highway, take Lugano Sud exit to lake, turn left and the hotel is immediately on the left.

■ RESTAURANT: 'La Veranda' classic restaurant with French, regional, Italian and flambée specialities.

■ ACTIVITIES: Sauna and solarium. Art and culture programme during July and August at special rates. Special Christmas and Easter programmes can be arranged. Details available on request.

■ TARIFF: Single 250–380, Double 380–580, Set menu 38–68 (Amex, Euro/Access, Visa).

■ DISCOUNT: 15%

Hotel Campione ★★★
Via Campione 62, 6816 Bissone.
Tel 091 649 9622, Fax 091 649 6821.
English spoken.
Open all year. 37 bedrooms (all en suite).
Outdoor swimming pool, golf 15 km, garage, parking. ℓ ⅃

SEE ADVERTISEMENT

Comfortable rooms and apartments with all modern facilities. 7 km from Lugano exit Bissone/Campione d'Italia motorway at entrance to Campione enclave. Hotel has a private bus service. (Special rates for weekends and stays of 7 days or more available from hotel on request.)

■ RESTAURANT: Classic and regional cuisine; new panoramic restaurant opened in 1995.
■ ACTIVITIES: Fitness room at hotel.
■ TARIFF: Single 110–160, Double 150–230, Set menu 22–50 (Amex, Euro/Access, Visa).
■ DISCOUNT: 10%

Switzerland

Hotel Continental-Beauregard ★★★
Via Basilea 28, 6903 Lugano.
Tel 091 966 1112, Fax 091 966 1213.
English spoken.
Open 15/02 to 15/11. 100 bedrooms
(all en suite). Parking.

Central position near town centre, in large attractive park with views over the lake and mountains. Follow signs to 'Stazione'.

■ RESTAURANT: Panoramic restaurant with Swiss, Italian and French specialities.
■ TARIFF: Single 75–115, Double 130–180, Set menu 20–30 (Amex, Euro/Access, Visa).

Hotel International au Lac ★★★
Via Nassa 68, 6901 Lugano.
Tel 091 922 7541, Fax 091 922 7544.
English spoken.
Open 30/03 to 28/10. 80 bedrooms
(all en suite). Outdoor swimming pool, golf 8 km, garage, parking, restaurant. &

In the centre of Lugano, the only hotel on the lake promenade to have its own garden, private parking and swimming pool.

■ TARIFF: (1996) Single 120–170, Double 180–280, Set menu 28–38 (Amex, Euro/Access, Visa).

Motel Vezia ★★★
Via San Gottardo 32, 6943 Vezia.
Tel 091 966 3631, Fax 091 966 7022. English spoken.

Open 01/02 to 30/11. 50 bedrooms
(all en suite). Outdoor swimming pool, golf 6 km, garage, parking. ☎ &

Only 3 km from the centre of Lugano with buses every 12 minutes. Modern soundproofed and air-conditioned hotel. Gardens and secure parking. Motorway exit Lugano-Nord, follow signs 'Televisione'.

■ RESTAURANT: Specialises in Mediterranean cuisine.
■ ACTIVITIES: Table tennis, chess, bike rental.

■ TARIFF: Single 88–126, Double 118–168, Bk 11, Set menu 19–29 (Amex, Euro/Access, Visa).
■ DISCOUNT: 10%

LUZERN (LUCERNE)   18B

Hotel Seeburg ★★★★
Seeburgstrasse 51/61, 6006 Luzern.
Tel 041 370 1922, Fax 041 370 1925.
English spoken.
Open all year. 89 bedrooms (87 en suite).
Golf 1 km, garage, parking, restaurant.

Set in extensive grounds bordering Lake Luzern with beautiful mountain views. 2.5 km from the town centre and close to the Transport Museum and steamer pier.

■ TARIFF: (1996) Single 107–141, Double 180–246, Set menu 39–69 (Amex, Euro/Access, Visa).

Hotel Wilden Mann ★★★★
Bahnhofstrasse 30, 6000 Luzern 7.
Tel 041 210 1666, Fax 041 210 1629.
English spoken.

Open all year. 43 bedrooms (all en suite).
Golf 2 km.

Swiss hospitality at its best in an historic setting. Tastefully appointed bedrooms and lounges. On the left bank of the River Reuss, near the Kesselturm car park, close to the Jesuite church and the chapel bridge.

■ RESTAURANT: Two restaurants: 'Burgerstube' for Swiss specialities and the 'Wilden Mann Stube' for fine French cuisine.
■ TARIFF: (1996) Single 150–190, Double 220–390, Set menu 16–59 (Amex, Euro/Access, Visa).

MARTIGNY 18C

Hotel Le Catogne ★★
La Douay, 1937 Orsières.
Tel 027 783 1230, Fax 027 783 2235.
English spoken.

Open 01/12 to 31/10. 25 bedrooms
(all en suite). Parking. ♿

*Comfortable chalet-hotel. Extra beds available.
15 km from Martigny on road to the Grand-St-
Bernard tunnel.*

■ RESTAURANT: A good restaurant built in typical
rustic style.
■ ACTIVITIES: Summertime mountain activities,
winter sports.
■ TARIFF: (1996) Single 40–60,
Double 60–80 (Euro/Access, Visa).

Hotel du Rhône ★★★
av du Gd-St-Bernard 11, 1920 Martigny.
Tel 027 722 1717, Fax 027 722 4300.
English spoken.
Open 20/12 to 10/11. 55 bedrooms
(all en suite). Golf 20 km, garage, parking. ☎ ♿

*Elegant hotel in the centre of Martigny. Rooms
are soundproofed and have all modern
facilities.*

■ RESTAURANT: French restaurant with excellent
cuisine; bistro for quick, but delicious meals.
■ ACTIVITIES: Skiing, tennis; excursions.
■ TARIFF: Single 86–108, Double 125–150,
Set menu 15–40 (Amex, Euro/Access, Visa).

MORGES 18C

Hotel du Mont-Blanc au Lac ★★★
quai du Mont-Blanc, 1110 Morges.
Tel 021 802 3072, Fax 021 801 5122. English spoken.

Open all year. 46 bedrooms (all en suite).
Golf 10 km. ☎

*Situated on the lake promenade, next to the
charming old port of Morges and facing the
Alps and Mont-Blanc. A few minutes' walk
from shopping centre.*

■ RESTAURANT: Terrace restaurant offering
French and regional specialities.
■ ACTIVITIES: ● Offers 'Tourist passport'
including 10 discount coupons for minimum
of 2 nights' stay.
■ TARIFF: (1996) Single 112–157,
Double 150–220, Set menu 22–85 (Amex,
Euro/Access, Visa).

NEUCHATEL 18A

Novotel Neuchâtel Thielle ★★★
Verger 1, 2075 Thielle.
Tel 038 357 575, Fax 038 357 557.
English spoken.
Open all year. 60 bedrooms (all en suite).
Outdoor swimming pool, golf 5 km, parking. ☎

*8 km from Neuchâtel. From Neuchâtel go
straight on to St-Blaise and follow signs to
Thielle-Berne.*

■ RESTAURANT: Comfortable, attractive
restaurant, completely renovated and
overlooking a flowered terrace. Speciality:
filets de perche.
■ ACTIVITIES: Boating, mountain-biking;
good walks nearby.
■ TARIFF: (1996) Single 125, Double 156, Bk 16,
Set menu 15 (Amex, Euro/Access, Visa).
■ DISCOUNT: 5% subject to availability & by
prior reservation.

ROUGEMONT 18C

Hotel Valrose ★★ 1838 Rougemont.
Tel 026 925 81 46, Fax 026 925 88 54.
English spoken.
Open 01/12 to 31/10. 16 bedrooms
(12 en suite, 4 bath/shower only). Tennis,
golf 15 km, garage, parking. ☎

*Family owned for four generations, this small
hotel in a pretty village offers comfort and a
warm, friendly atmosphere.*

■ RESTAURANT: Closed Nov and Tues. Bistro
restaurant with local and traditional cuisine;
cheese specialities.
■ ACTIVITIES: Mini-golf 7 km; 40 different sports,
from skiing in winter to tennis in summer,
within 8 km.
■ TARIFF: Single 58–80,
Double 110–145, Set menu 21–75
(Amex, Euro/Access, Visa).

Switzerland

ST-LUC 18C

Hotel Bella Tola et St Luc ★★★
Valais, 3961 St-Luc.
Tel 027 65 1444, Fax 027 65 2998.
English spoken.

Open 20/12 to 15/04 & 20/06 to 15/10.
33 bedrooms (all en suite). Golf 20 km,
parking. ℓ

*Dating back to 1859, a traditional hotel that
has retained its original façade and open
fireplaces. Elegant but cosy accommodation,
some lovely antiques and parquet flooring.
Panoramic views of the spectacular
surrounding countryside.*

■ RESTAURANT: Typical mountain restaurant with
Swiss cheese specialities, or enjoy French
cuisine in the winter garden restaurant 'La
Limonaia'.
■ ACTIVITIES: Hiking, bridge, skiing; special
week/short break packages available for
various activities including skiing, jazz and
flower arranging.
■ TARIFF: Single 95–130, Double 140–210,
Set menu 16–42 (Amex, Euro/Access, Visa).
■ DISCOUNT: 10%

STANSSTAD 18B

Hotel Winkelried ★★★★ 6362 Stansstad.
Tel 041 610 9901, Fax 041 610 9631.
English spoken.
Open all year. 29 bedrooms (all en suite).
Golf 25 km, garage. ℓ &

*Built in 1992, hotel offers excellent facilities
and has a superb situation right on the edge of
Lake Luzern. Very comfortable, with some
wonderful views.*

■ RESTAURANT: Choice of three comfortable
restaurants offering panoramic views; enjoy à
la carte cuisine in 'Seeblick', typical Swiss
dishes in 'Winkelried' and Italian specialities in
the 'Hafenrestaurant'.

■ ACTIVITIES: Short distance to Engelberg-Titlis
ski resort. Sailing, water sports, tennis,
mountain-biking and paragliding nearby;
wonderful area for walking/hiking and touring.
■ TARIFF: Single 130–170, Double 190–330,
Set menu 16.50–28.50 (Amex, Euro/Access, Visa).

THUN 18C

Hotel Hirschen am See ★★★★
Staatsstrasse, 3654 Gunten.
Tel 0332 512 244, Fax 0332 513 884.
English spoken.
Open 22/03 to 02/11. 68 bedrooms
(all en suite). Outdoor swimming pool,
golf 10 km, garage, parking. &

*Take the Thun-Sud exit from N6 and follow
signs for Gunten. The hotel is in the middle of
the village on the eastern shore of the lake,
10 km from Thun.*

■ RESTAURANT: 2 restaurants; good menus with
fish specialities.
■ ACTIVITIES: Hiking, fishing, windsurfing,
horse-riding, sailing and water-skiing.
■ TARIFF: Single 74–155, Double 150–280
(Amex, Euro/Access, Visa).

Hotel Holiday Gwattstrasse 1, 3600 Thun.
Tel 033 365 757, Fax 033 365 704.
English spoken.
Open all year. 57 bedrooms (all en suite).
Garage, parking. &

*Ideally positioned directly beside the lake,
yacht harbour and beach, with marvellous
mountain views. Approx 1 km from Thun.*

■ RESTAURANT: Coffee shop plus gourmet
restaurant with seasonal specialities.
■ ACTIVITIES: Heated swimming pool, tennis,
sailing, rowing, walking and surfing close by.
Casino-Kursaal in Thun and Interlaken.
■ TARIFF: (1996) Single 90–130,
Double 145–200, Set menu 12–40 (Amex,
Euro/Access, Visa).

VEVEY 18C

Hotel du Lac ★★★★ rue d'Italie 1, 1800 Vevey.
Tel 021 921 1041, Fax 021 921 7508.
English spoken.
Open all year. 56 bedrooms (all en suite). Outdoor
swimming pool, golf 20 km, garage, parking.

*Spacious, elegant hotel with 19th-century
charm and 20th-century comfort. Lovely views
of the lake and mountains. Was the setting for
Anita Brookner's book, which won the Booker
Prize in 1984. Immediate access to Lac Léman
and its promenades. One hour from Genève
airport and easy access via modern highways.*

Switzerland

■ RESTAURANT: French cuisine as well as fresh lake fish specialities.
■ TARIFF: (1996) Single 170–250, Double 250–340, Set menu 40–60 (Amex, Euro/Access, Visa).
■ DISCOUNT: 20% weekends.

Hotel Les Trois Couronnes ★★★★★
49 rue d'Italie, 1800 Vevey.
Tel 021 921 3005, Fax 021 922 7280.
English spoken.
Open all year. 63 bedrooms (all en suite).
Parking. &

Built in 1842, a small, luxury hotel standing on the shores of Lac Léman, near the old town and shopping area. Beautiful terrace with views over the lakes and Alps. From the railway station (Gare CFF Vevey), follow the brown hotel signs via rue Simplon to rue d'Italie.

■ RESTAURANT: French gourmet cuisine, seasonal menus and à la carte service in beautiful Louis XIV-style surroundings. Coffee shop serving light dishes and snacks.
■ ACTIVITIES: Steam boat cruises on the lake; mountain-bike hire.
■ TARIFF: Single 190–270, Double 300–450 (Amex, Euro/Access, Visa).

VILLARS-SUR-OLLON   18C

Grand Hotel du Parc ★★★★★
route du Col de la Croix, 1884 Villars.
Tel 024 495 2121, Fax 024 495 3363.
English spoken.
Open 19/12 to 17/04 & 01/06 to 30/10.
65 bedrooms (all en suite). Indoor swimming pool, tennis, golf 7 km, parking.

Luxurious hotel set in parkland and right on the ski slopes.

■ RESTAURANT: 'La Taverne' offers Swiss specialities including raclette and fondue and 'Le Mazarin' specialises in classic French cuisine; in summertime, enjoy a buffet or barbecue outside in the garden.
■ ACTIVITIES: Skiing (two private ski lifts in the grounds), horse-riding, 3 summer tennis courts, swimming with an instructor, massage/fitness facilities.
■ TARIFF: Single 155–285, Double 290–570, Set menu 45 (Amex, Euro/Access, Visa).
■ DISCOUNT: 8% except New Year.

WEGGIS   18B

Hotel Beau-Rivage ★★★★
Lac Luzern, 6353 Weggis.
Tel 041 390 1422, Fax 041 390 1981.
English spoken.

Open 01/04 to 31/10. 41 bedrooms (all en suite). Outdoor swimming pool, golf 8 km, garage, parking, restaurant. &

Situated right on the lake, just 3 minutes' walk from the boat jetty.

■ TARIFF: (1996) Single 115–170, Double 190–310, Set menu 50–60 (Amex, Euro/Access, Visa).

WENGEN   18C

Hotel Eiger ★★★ 3823 Wengen.
Tel 033 855 1131, Fax 033 855 1030.
English spoken.
Open 12/06 to 31/10 & 01/12 to 15/04.
33 bedrooms (all en suite). Outdoor swimming pool, golf 13 km.

Centrally positioned, modern, friendly hotel in car-free Wengen. Within sight of Jungfrau; children welcome.

■ RESTAURANT: Local and international specialities; pub.
■ ACTIVITIES: In summer, weekly walks, sightseeing tours, outdoor grill parties and cocktail parties. In winter, once-a-week ski-days with guide and members of the owner's family.
■ TARIFF: Single 90–140, Double 180–310, Set menu 35–50 (Amex, Euro/Access, Visa).

Switzerland

WILDERSWIL   18C

Hotel Alpenblick ★★★ 3812 Wilderswil.
Tel 036 220 707, Fax 036 228 007.
English spoken.
Open all year. 35 bedrooms (31 en suite).
Golf 5 km, parking. ✆

*In the centre of the small village, an extremely
comfortable chalet-style hotel offering a
friendly, relaxed atmosphere. Set in beautiful
countryside, close to Interlaken and
Grindelwald.*

■ RESTAURANT: Closed Mon & Tues. Renowned
restaurant offering excellent cuisine using
fresh, local produce. Meals can be served on
the terrace.
■ ACTIVITIES: Skiing, hiking; arrangements can
be made for golf and cookery lessons.
● Special ski-safari packages.
■ TARIFF: (1996) Single 73–97, Double 126–218
(Amex, Euro/Access, Visa).

WILDHAUS   18B

Hotel Acker 9658 Wildhaus.
Tel 071 9999111, Fax 071 9992011.
English spoken.
Open all year. 100 bedrooms (all en suite).
Indoor swimming pool, tennis, golf 20 km,
garage, parking. ✆ ＆

*Quiet hotel with view over the mountains. All
rooms have a balcony.*

■ RESTAURANT: Panoramic restaurant offering
French cuisine and international specialities.
Special diet and children's menu. Large
selection of wines.
■ ACTIVITIES: Sauna, solarium, fitness room,
table tennis, mini-golf; hiking trails, mountain
climbing, fishing, horse-riding, skiing, cross-
country skiing, ice-skating nearby.
■ TARIFF: Single 92–160, Double 150–230,
Set menu 25–52 (Amex, Euro/Access, Visa).
■ DISCOUNT: 10%

ZUG   18B

Hotel Guggital ★★★ Zugerbergstrasse, 6300 Zug.
Tel 041 711 28 21, Fax 041 710 14 43.
English spoken.
Open all year. 32 bedrooms (all en suite).
Golf 10 km, garage, parking. ✆

*Above the town, the hotel overlooks the lake
and the mountains.*

■ RESTAURANT: Good choice of local and
international dishes with seasonal specialities.
■ ACTIVITIES: Water sports; boat trips on Lake
Zug; sightseeing.

■ TARIFF: (1996) Single 130–152,
Double 187–215, Set menu 17–33
(Amex, Euro/Access, Visa).

ZÜRICH   18B

Hotel Dolder Grand ★★★★★
Kurhausstrasse 65, 8032 Zürich.
Tel 012 516 231, Fax 012 518 829.
English spoken.
Open all year. 18 bedrooms (all en suite).
Outdoor swimming pool, tennis, golf 1 km,
garage. ✆ ＆
■ TARIFF: (1996) Single 370–390,
Double 490–650
(Amex, Euro/Access, Visa).

Mövenpick Hotel ★★★★
Walter-Mittelholzerstrasse 8, 8152 Glattbrugg.
Tel 018 088 888, Fax 018 088 877.
English spoken.
Open all year. 335 bedrooms (all en suite).
Golf 10 km. ✆ ＆

*Very comfortable hotel offering typical Swiss
service and efficiency. Take Glattbrugg exit
from N11 (heading towards Zürich-Kloten
airport) and then follow brown signs to hotel.*

■ RESTAURANT: Choice of three restaurants
offering international, Chinese or Swiss and
French dishes.
■ ACTIVITIES: Boat trips, shopping and
sightseeing.
■ TARIFF: Single 240–295,
Double 290–345, Bk 23, Set menu 25–30
(Amex, Euro/Access, Visa).

Hotel Savoy Baur en Ville ★★★★★
Paradeplatz, 8022 Zürich.
Tel 01 215 25 25, Fax 01 215 25 00.
English spoken.

Open all year. 112 bedrooms (all en suite).
Golf 4 km, garage. ✆ ♿
*In the heart of Zürich with elegant and
spacious rooms.*
■ RESTAURANT: French and Italian cuisine.
■ TARIFF: (1996) Single 400, Double 630,
Set menu 49–95 (Amex, Euro/Access, Visa).

Hotel Tiefenau Zürich ★★★★
Steinwiesstrasse 8-10, 8032 Zürich.
Tel 012 512 409, Fax 012 512476.
English spoken.
Open 06/01 to 20/12. 70 bedrooms
(all en suite). Golf 2 km, parking.

*Right in the city centre near the Museum of
Fine Art, Conservatory, Playhouse and Opera.
Built in 1835, the hotel is furnished in Louis
XV style but has every modern comfort with
well-equipped rooms, including modem
connections. Private parking; sun terrace,
flowered garden and bar.*

■ RESTAURANT: The only restaurant in town
specialising in local Zürich specialities. Shady
garden for outside dining in summer.
■ ACTIVITIES: Day trips to many places including
Basel, Luzern, Bern; horse-riding, tennis and
water sports nearby.
■ TARIFF: (1996) Single 200–300,
Double 300–400, Set menu 20.50–28.80
(Amex, Euro/Access, Visa).

Switzerland

GLOSSARY

Glossary of French food terms to help you round the tempting menus shown in this guide and in other restaurants you may visit.

agneau, *lamb*

agneau de pré-salé, *lamb pastured in salt meadows (particularly on Atlantic coast, giving it a special flavour)*

aigrette, *fritter, usually savoury*

ail, *garlic*

aïoli, *garlic flavoured mayonnaise*

aligot, *fresh uncured cheese (Auvergne, Rouergue)*

amande, *almond*

amer, amère, *bitter*

andouille, *type of pork sausage usually sliced and served cold*

andouillette, *type of pork sausage usually grilled and served with strong mustard*

anguille, *eel*

anis, *aniseed flavoured aperitif*

AOC, appellation (d'origine) contrôlée, *system of quality control applied to wine and cheese*

Armagnac, *brandy*

artichaut, *artichoke*

assiette du pêcheur, *mixed fish platter*

autruche, *ostrich*

baie, *berry*

ballotine, *meat/poultry loaf*

Banyuls, *strong sweet red wines from the Grenace grape*

bar, *sea bass*

barbue, *brill*

basilic, *basil*

baudroie, *monkfish*

betterave, *beetroot*

beurre, *butter*

beurre blanc, *reduction of shallots in wine or vinegar + butter*

blanc de *-, *white meat*

blanquette de *-, *something cooked in white sauce*

blini, *small thick Russian pancake*

boeuf, *beef*

bouillabaisse, *fish soup*

bourride, *fish stew*

braisé, *braised*

brandade (à la), *served with salt, olive oil and cream sauce*

brochet, *pike*

brochette, *kebab, food cooked on a skewer*

brouillade aux truffes, *scrambled eggs with truffles*

Cabécou, *soft round cheese*

caille, *quail*

calamar/calmar/calmaret, *squid, inkfish*

Calvados, *apple brandy from Normandy*

canard, *duck*

caneton, *duckling*

canette, *female duckling*

carré d'agneau, *rack of lamb*

carte menu, *fixed price meal*

carte/menu gastronomique, *gourmet's menu*

cassis, *blackcurrant*

cassolette, (or cassette) *small portion of food for hors d'oeuvre or dessert*

cassoulet, *haricot beans and meats stew*

cèpes, *boletus (type of mushroom)*

cervelles, *brains, usually calf's)*

champignons, *mushrooms*

chanterelle, *variety of mushroom*

chaource, *soft creamy cheese with fruity flavour from Champagne*

charcuterie, *cooked pork products*

Chardonnay, *variety of white grape used for wine*

Charolais, *excellent beef of pale-coated cattle; dry goat's milk cheese*

charolais, à la, *garnish of puréed turnips and cauliflower*

chaud, *hot*

chaudrée, *conger eel and white fish stew*

chausson, *puff pastry turnover with savoury or sweet filling*

(en) chemise, *in pastry/pancake or similar*

(aux) cheveux d'Ange, *layered*

chèvre, *goat, goat's milk cheese*

chevreuil, *roe deer, venison*

chicorée, *endive (salad green)*

chiffonade, *thin ribbons of green vegetables added to soup*

chipirons (Basque), *squid*

chou, *cabbage*
chou de mer, chou marin, *sea kale*
chou vert, *green cabbage*
choucroute, *pickled white cabble (Sauerkraut)*
cidre, *cider*
citron, *lemon*
citron vert, *lime*
civet de, *rich stew of (hare, venison)*
clafoutis, *batter pudding with (traditionally) black cherries*
cochon (de lait), *(suckling) pig*
colin, *hake*
colvert, *type of wild duck*
compote, *stewed fruit; or pigeon stew*
confit, *meat cooked and preserved in stone pot; also for fruits*
confit de canard, *conserve of duck*
confit de poule, *conserve of chicken*
coq, *chicken*
coquillages, *shellfish*
coquilles Saint-Jacques, *scallops*
côte, *rib*
coulis, *strong clear broth/sauce*
court bouillon, *broth for poaching fish, made from vegetables, herbs and white wine*
crème, *cream*
un crème, a white coffee
crêpe, *pancake*
croustillant, *crisp, crunchy*
croûte (en), *cooked in patry*
cru (classé), *vineyard of special quality*
cuisse, *thigh, drumstick*
cuit sur l'arête, *whole fish cooked on the bone*
daube, *braised meat, poultry, game, fish, served with vegetables*
diable, *hot wine and vinegar sauce*
diot de Savoie, *vegetable and pork sausage cooked in wine*
eau douce, *fresh water*
écrevisse, *crayfish, freshwater prawn*
émincé, *thinly sliced cooked meat/poultry reheated in sauce*
encornet, *squid*
encre, *ink (of squid, octopus)*
épices, *spices*
épicé, *spicy*
épinard, *spinach*
escalope, *thin slick of meat/fish*
escargot, *snail*
estragon, *tarragon*
étuvé, *stewed, braised, steamed*

farci, *stuffed*
fenouil, *fenne*
féra, *highly prized Savoy lake salmonl*
fermier, *farm-made/reared*
à la fermière, *meat or fish cooked with mixed vegetables*
feuillantine, *small light pastry*
feuilleté, *made of flaky pastry*
ficelle normande/picarde, *pancake stuffed with cream/ cheese and ham/mushrooms*
figue, *fig*
filet de boeuf, *filet of beef*
flamber, *to flame with spirit or fortified wine*
flamiche, *type of tart*
foie, *liver*
foie gras, *liver of force-fed goose or duck*
fondu, *melted*
(au) four, *baked*
frais, fraîche, *fresh, cool*
fraise, *strawberry*
framboise, *raspberry*
frangipane, *custard with crushed macaroons; almond paste*
fricassé, *sautéed fish or meat finished in a cream sauce*
froid, *cold*
fromage, *cheese*
fruits de mer, *seafood*
fruits rouges, *soft fruit*
fumé, *smoked*
gamba, *large prawn*
à la gardiane, *marinated then stewed in herbs, wine and tomatoes*
gazpacho, *Andalusian cold soup made from tomatoes, peppers, onion,cucumber, garlic, olive oil*
gelée, *aspic*
genièvre, *juniper berry; liqueur made from same*
gésier, *gizzard (of poultry)*
gibier, *game*
gigot d'agneau, *leg of lamb*
gingembre, *ginger*
girolle, *type of mushroom*
glace, *ice-cream*
glacé, *frozen; iced; glazed*
gougère, *cheese-flavoured choux pastry ring*
granité, *water-ice sprinkled with sugar*
gratin, *dish browned under grill with breadcrumbs/cheese*
grenouille, *frog*
grillade, *grilled meat or fish*

griottes, *bitter, bright red cherry*
herbes, *herbs*
hollandaise sauce, *butter, egg, yolks, lemon juice and white wine*
homard, *lobster*
huître, *oyster*
jambon, *ham*
jambonette, *dried salted meat in shape of a ham*
joue, *cheek*
jus, *juice*
lapin, *rabbit*
langouste, *crayfish*
langoustine, *Dublin Bay prawn, scampi*
lapereau, *young rabbit*
lard, *pork fat, bacon*
légumes, *vegetables*
lotte, *monkfish, burbot*
lotte de mer, *monkfish*
loup (de mer), *bar, sea bass*
magret de canard, *breast of fattened duck served rare*
maison, *of the establishment, home-made*
manoul, *lamb's tripe with white wine and tomatoes*
marcassin, *young wild boar*
marron, *chestnut*
matelote, *stew of freshwater fish in wine*
menthe, *mint*
merlu/merluche merluzza, *hake*
meurette, *red wine sauce with onions, mushrooms, carrots and bacon*
miel, *honey*
mignon (filet mignon), *small fillet steak*
mijoté, *simmered*
mille-feuille, *thin layers of flaky pastry with sweet or savoury filling*
mirabelle, *small gold plum from Alsace; liqueur of same*
mode, à la mode de, *in the manner of*
mont-blanc, *chestnut cream dessert*
morille, *morel, type of mushroom*
moule, *mussels*
mousseline, *purée*
mousseron, *highly estemmed St-George mushroom*
Munster, *cheese from Alsace with strong smell and spicy flavour*
Muscat, *wine made from muscat grape*
(à la) normande, *with cream and Calvados/cider/apples*
noix, *topside (of veal); walnut*

oeuf, *egg*
oeufs brouillés, *scrambled eggs*
oie, *goose*
oseille, *sorrel*
oursin, *sea urchin*
palombe, *wild pigeon*
panaché, *mixed (un panaché = a shandy)*
panaché de la mer, *mixed seafood*
papillotte, *meat/fish baked in foil/greaseproof*
parfait, *rich mousse/cream, flavoured with chocolate, coffee etc*
parmentier, *with potatoes*
pavé, *thick slice of beef steak*
pavot, *poppy seeds*
du pays, *local*
paysanne (à la -), *with vegetable*
pêche, *peach*
perche, *perche*
persil, *parsley*
persillade, *chopped parsley with shallots or garlic*
pétoncle, *queen scallop*
pied de cochon, *pig's trotter*
pigeonneau, *young pigeon*
Pinot Noir, *black grape from which great Burgundy wines are made*
pintadeau, *young guinea fowl*
pipérade, *omelette/scrambled eggs with tomatoes, peppers, onions*
pissaladière, *flat, open pizza-like tart from Provence*
pistache, *pistachio nut*
pistou, *basil (pesto sauce)*
poireau, *leek*
plateau, *platter, tray*
pleurote, *highly prized mushroom*
poêlé, *pot-roasted on bed of vegetables*
poêlon de, *cooked in (earthenware) casserole*
poire, *pear*
poireau, *leek*
poisson, *fish*
poisson bleu, *fresh-caught fish plunged in boiling vinegar bouillon resulting in bluish hue*
poitrine, *breast*
poivre, *pepper*
poivron, *sweet pepper, red or green*
polenta, *maize meal porridge with butter and cheese*
pomme, *apple*
pomme de terre, *potato*
porcelet, *suckling pig*
potage, *soup*

potée, *thick meat and vegetable soup*

poularde, *fattened hen; roasting chicken*

poulet, *chicken*

pounti, *hash of bacon and Swiss chard*

praliné, *praline/almond-flavoured*

produits de mer, *sea food*

(à la) provençale, *cooked with tomatoes, garlic, onions, olives, anchovies, aubergines etc*

quenelle, *type of light mousse-cum-dumpling, served lightly poached*

queue (de boeuf), *oxtail*

raclette, *Alpine potato and melted cheese speciality prepared at table, usually served with salamis etc*

ragoût, *light stew*

raie, *ray, skate*

raisin, *grape*

ratafia, *liqueur made by infusing fruits or nuts in brandy*

ratatouille, *aubergine, peppers, courgette, onion and garlic stew*

réglisse, *liquorice*

réserve, *term indicating age of Armagnac, Calvados, Cognac etc.*

rillauds, *pork pieces cooked and presented in jars*

ris, *sweetbreads*

rognon, *kidney*

romarin, *rosemary*

Roquefort, *strong sheep's milk blue cheese*

rôti, *roasted*

rouget, *red mullet*

rouennaise (sauce), *with red wine, duck liver and shallots*

rouille, *spicy mayonnaise with red pepper and garlic*

safrané, *flavoured or coloured with saffran*

Saint-Jacques, *short for coquille Saint-Jacques, scallop*

Saint-Pierre, *John Dory fish whose dark spots on either side of the back are said to be the thumb marks of Saint Pierre*

en saison, *in season*

salers, *large, cylindrical Auvergne cheese*

salmis, *game or poultry dish part-roasted then finished in wine sauce*

Sancerre, *wine-growing region*

sandre, *pike-perch*

saucisse, *sausage for grilling or frying*

saucisson, *usually ready cooked and eaten cold*

saumon, *salmon*

saupiquet, *piquant wine and vinegar sauce*

sauvage, *wild*

savayon/zabaglione, *warm egg yolk and Marsala wine dessert*

selle, *saddle (of lamb)*

soja, *soya bean*

sole, *sole*

sorbet, *water ice*

supion, suppion, sépiole, *cuttlefish*

suprême, *(breast and wing) filet*

table d'hôte, *meal of several courses at fixed price*

tartiflette, *potatoes and onion cooked in wine and cheese, served with charcuterie and salad*

terrine, (pâté) *baked in covered earthenware dish*

terroir, *country, rural*

thym, *thyme*

tiède, *luke warm, tepid*

torchon, *cloth, napkin*

tournedos, *small round filet steak*

tournedos Rossini, *small round filet steak with truffles*

tourte, *pie*

tripes à la mode de Caen, *ox tripe and trotters cooked in cider*

tripoux, *heavily seasoned stuffed veal or lamb tripe*

truffade, *potato cake with Cantal cheese*

truffe, *prized underground fungus; chocolate sweet*

truffé, *garnished/studded/stuffed with truffles*

truite, *trout*

tuile, *small almond biscuit*

vacherin, *Alpine Cheese/ cream gâteau*

veau, *veal*

viande, *meat*

vin, *wine*

vin jaune, *yellow wine made in France-Comté region from Savagnin grape*

vinaigre, *vinegar*

volaille, *poultry, chicken*

à volonté, *as much as you like*

à la vosgienne, *in the style of Vosges (mountain region of Lorraine and Alsace)*

INDEX

The index covers the Hotel Directory. Places shown in **bold type** are headings used in the Hotel Directory under which towns are grouped

INDEX

KEY TO MAPS

LEGEND

• Tonnerre	town with one campsite
• Alençon	town with more than one campsite
▬▬▬	motorway
▬▬▬	main road
▪▪▪▪▪▪▪▪	international border
....	regional border

Cartography by RAC Publishing

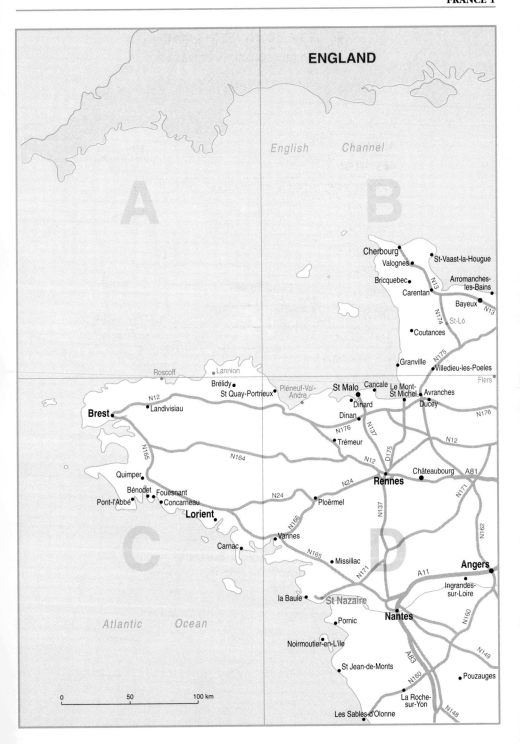

ENGLAND

English Channel

A

B

Cherbourg
Valognes • • St-Vaast-la-Hougue
Bricquebec • Arromanches-les-Bains
Carentan N13
Bayeux N13
N174 St-Lô
Coutances
Granville Villedieu-les-Poeles
N175 Flers
Roscoff Lannion
Brélidy • St Malo Cancale Le Mont-
St Quay-Portrieux • Pléneuf-Val- St Michel • Avranches
Andre Dinard Ducey
N12 St Malo
Brest • Landivisiau Dinan N176
N176 N137
N165 N164 Trémeur
N12
Quimper Châteaubourg A81
Bénodet Fouesnant N24 Rennes N171
Pont-l'Abbé • Concarneau Ploërmel
Lorient N137 N162
N166
Vannes
Carnac Missillac
N165 Angers
N171 A11 Ingrandes-
sur-Loire
la Baule • St Nazaire Nantes N160
Atlantic Ocean Pornic
Noirmoutier-en-L'ile A83 N149
St Jean-de-Monts Pouzauges
N160
0 50 100 km La Roche-
sur-Yon N148
Les Sables-d'Olonne

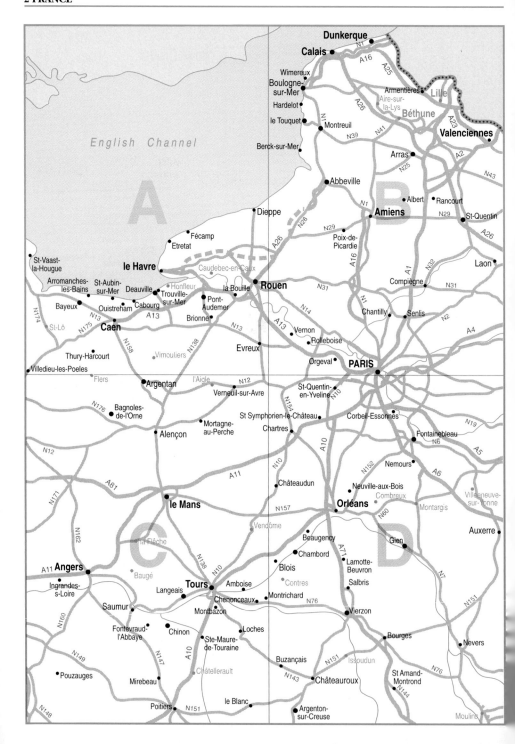

Dunkerque
Calais
Wimereux
Boulogne-sur-Mer
Hardelot
le Touquet
Montreuil
Berck-sur-Mer
Armentières
Aire-sur-la-Lys
Lille
Béthune
Valenciennes
Arras
Abbeville
Albert
Rancourt
Amiens
St-Quentin
Dieppe
Poix-de-Picardie
Laon
Fécamp
Etretat
Caudebec-en-Caux
Compiègne
St-Vaast-la-Hougue
le Havre
Honfleur
la Bouille
Rouen
Chantilly
Senlis
Arromanches-les-Bains
St-Aubin-sur-Mer
Deauville
Trouville-sur-Mer
Pont-Audemer
Bayeux
Ouistreham
Cabourg
Brionne
Vernon
Rolleboise
St-Lô
Caen
Evreux
Orgeval
PARIS
Thury-Harcourt
Vimoutiers
Villedieu-les-Poeles
Flers
Argentan
l'Aigle
Verneuil-sur-Avre
St-Quentin-en-Yvelines
Corbeil-Essonnes
Bagnoles-de-l'Orne
Mortagne-au-Perche
St Symphorien-le-Château
Chartres
Fontainebleau
Alençon
Nemours
Châteaudun
Neuville-aux-Bois
Combreux
Villeneuve-sur-Yonne
le Mans
Orléans
Montargis
Vendôme
Beaugency
Gien
Auxerre
Chambord
la Flèche
Angers
Baugé
Blois
Lamotte-Beuvron
Salbris
Ingrandes-s-Loire
Langeais
Tours
Amboise
Contres
Montrichard
Vierzon
Saumur
Chenonceaux
Montbazon
Bourges
Nevers
Fontevraud-l'Abbaye
Chinon
Loches
Ste-Maure-de-Touraine
Pouzauges
Mirebeau
Châtellerault
Buzançais
Issoudun
St Amand-Montrond
Poitiers
le Blanc
Châteauroux
Moulins
Argenton-sur-Creuse

English Channel

A
B
C
D

A16
A25
N1
A26
N41
N39
A23
N25
A2
N43
N1
N29
N29
A26
A1
N32
A16
N31
N31
N2
N14
A13
N13
N13
A13
N1
A4
N174
N13
N175
N158
N138
N12
N176
A10
A5
A6
N19
N12
A81
N10
A11
N152
N6
N171
N157
N60
N162
A71
N138
N10
N7
A11
N160
N151
N147
A10
N149
N143
N151
N76
N144
N148
N151

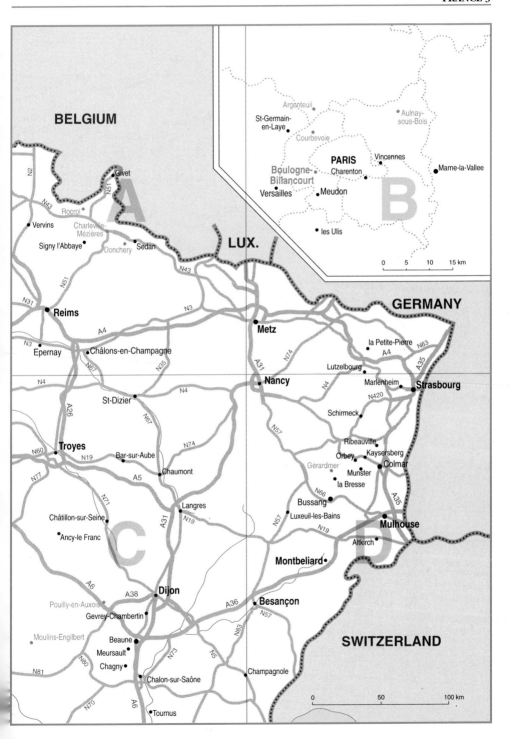

BELGIUM

N2

Givet

N51

N43

Rocroi

Vervins

Charleville-
Mézières

Signy l'Abbaye

Donchery

Sedan

N43

LUX.

N31

N51

Reims

N3

GERMANY

A4

N3

Epernay

Châlons-en-Champagne

Metz

la Petite-Pierre

N63

A4

N67

N35

N74

A31

Lutzelbourg

A35

N4

Nancy

N4

Marlenheim

Strasbourg

St-Dizier

N4

N420

A26

N67

Schirmeck

Troyes

N74

N57

Ribeauville

Orbey

Kaysersberg

N60

N19

Bar-sur-Aube

Gérardmer

Colmar

Chaumont

Munster

A5

la Bresse

N77

N71

N66

N57

A35

Langres

Bussang

Châtillon-sur-Seine

A31

N19

Luxeuil-les-Bains

Mulhouse

Ancy-le Franc

N19

Altkirch

Montbeliard

A6

A38

Dijon

A36

Besançon

Pouilly-en-Auxois

N57

Gevrey-Chambertin

N83

Moulins-Engilbert

Beaune

SWITZERLAND

N80

Meursault

N73

N5

N81

Chagny

Chalon-sur-Saône

Champagnole

N70

A6

Tournus

0   50   100 km

St-Germain-
en-Laye

Argenteuil

Aulnay-
sous-Bois

Courbevoie

PARIS

Vincennes

Marne-la-Vallee

Boulogne-
Billancourt

Charenton

Versailles

Meudon

les Ulis

0   5   10   15 km

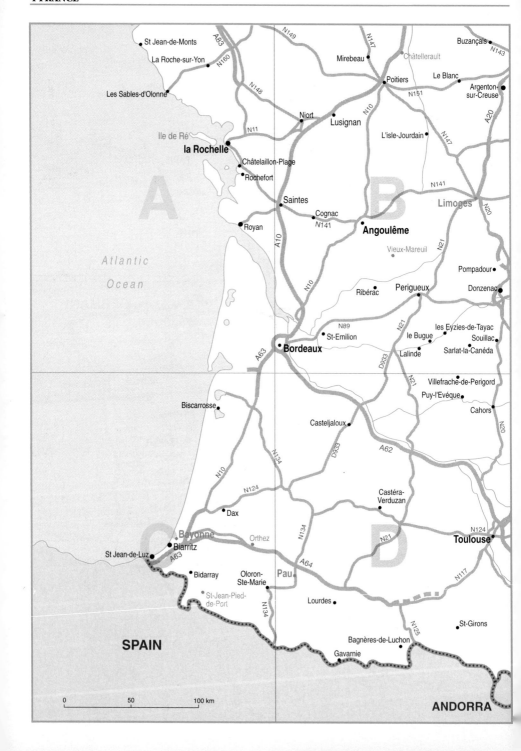

St Jean-de-Monts

La Roche-sur-Yon

Les Sables-d'Olonne

Île de Ré

la Rochelle

Châtelaillon-Plage

Rochefort

Saintes

Cognac

Royan

Atlantic

Ocean

Niort

Lusignan

Mirebeau

Châtellerault

Poitiers

Le Blanc

Buzançais

Argenton-sur-Creuse

L'isle-Jourdain

Limoges

Angoulême

Vieux-Mareuil

Pompadour

Ribérac

Perigueux

Donzenac

St-Emilion

le Bugue

les Eyzies-de-Tayac

Souillac

Lalinde

Sarlat-la-Canéda

Bordeaux

Villefrache-de-Perigord

Puy-l'Evéque

Cahors

Biscarrosse

Casteljaloux

Castéra-Verduzan

Dax

Bayonne

Biarritz

Orthez

Toulouse

St Jean-de-Luz

Bidarray

Oloron-Ste-Marie

Pau

St-Jean-Pied-de-Port

Lourdes

Bagnères-de-Luchon

St-Girons

SPAIN

Gavarnie

0   50   100 km

ANDORRA

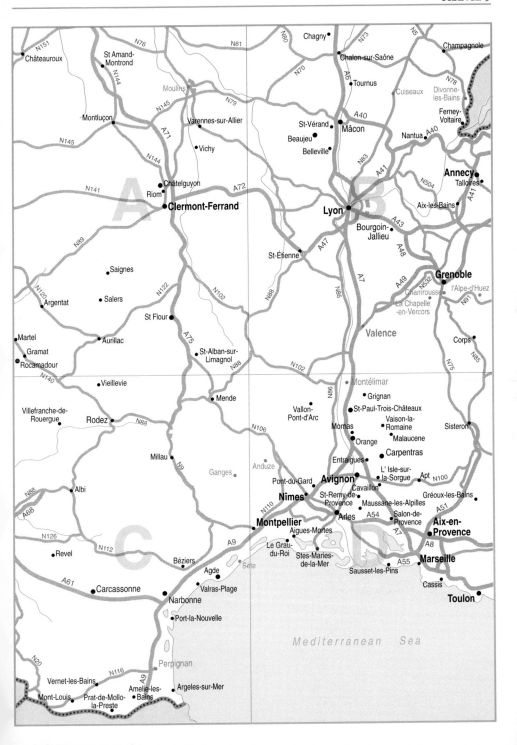

Châteauroux
N151
St Amand-Montrond
N76
Moulins
N81
N144
N145
Montluçon
N144
N145
N79
Varennes-sur-Allier
A71
Vichy
Chagny
N80
N70
Chalon-sur-Saône
A6
Tournus
N73
Cuiseaux
N5
Champagnole
N78
Divonne-les-Bains
Ferney-Voltaire
A40
St-Vérand
Mâcon
Beaujeu
Belleville
Nantua
A40
N83
A41
Annecy
N504
Talloires
Aix-les-Bains
A41

N141
Chätelguyon
Riom
A72
Clermont-Ferrand
N89
Lyon
Bourgoin-Jallieu
A43
A47
A48

N120
Argentat
Saignes
Salers
N122
St Flour
N102
St-Étienne
N88
A7
A49
N52
Grenoble
Chamrousse
l'Alpe-d'Huez
N91
La Chapelle-en-Vercors

Martel
Gramat
Rocamadour
N140
Aurillac
A75
St-Alban-sur-Limagnol
N88
N102
N86
Valence
Corps
N75
N85

Vieillevie
Mende
Montélimar
Grignan

Villefranche-de-Rouergue
Rodez
N88
N106
Vallon-Pont-d'Arc
St-Paul-Trois-Châteaux
Mornas
Vaison-la-Romaine
Malaucene
Orange
Sisteron
Carpentras

Millau
N9
Ganges
Anduze
Entraigues
L'Isle-sur-la-Sorgue
Apt
N100
N88
Albi
A68
Pont-du-Gard
Avignon
Cavaillon
St-Remy-de-Provence
Gréoux-les-Bains
Nîmes
Maussane-les-Alpilles
A51
N126
N110
Montpellier
Arles
A54
Salon-de-Provence
A7
Aix-en-Provence
A8
Revel
N112
Aigues-Mortes
A9
Béziers
Agde
Sète
Le Grau-du-Roi
Stes-Maries-de-la-Mer
A55
Marseille
A61
Carcassonne
Valras-Plage
Sausset-les-Pins
Cassis
Narbonne
Toulon
Port-la-Nouvelle

Mediterranean Sea

N20
Vernet-les-Bains
N116
A9
Mont-Louis
Amelie-les-Bains
Prat-de-Mollo-la-Preste
Argeles-sur-Mer
Perpignan

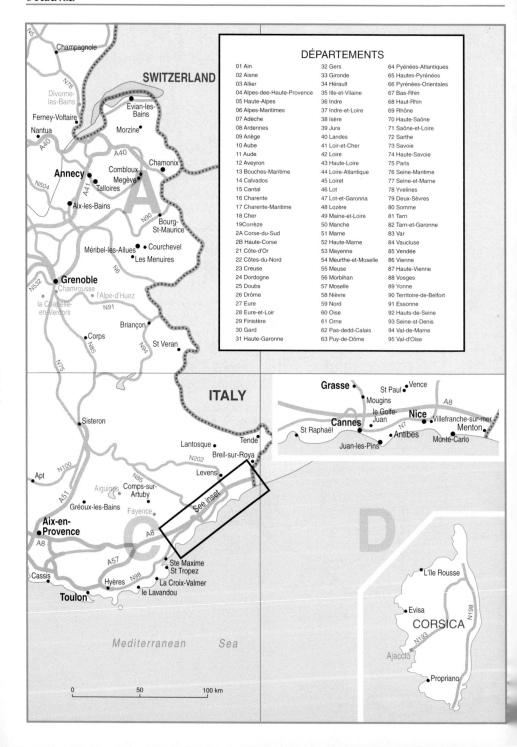

DÉPARTEMENTS

01 Ain	32 Gers	64 Pyénées-Atlantiques
02 Aisne	33 Gironde	65 Hautes-Pyrénées
03 Allier	34 Hérault	66 Pyrénées-Orientales
04 Alpes-dee-Haute-Provence	35 Ille-et-Vilaine	67 Bas-Rhin
05 Haute-Alpes	36 Indre	68 Haut-Rhin
06 Alpes-Maritimes	37 Indre-et-Loire	69 Rhône
07 Adèche	38 Isère	70 Haute-Saône
08 Ardennes	39 Jura	71 Saône-et-Loire
09 Ariège	40 Landes	72 Sarthe
10 Aube	41 Loir-et-Cher	73 Savoie
11 Aude	42 Loire	74 Haute-Savoie
12 Aveyron	43 Haute-Loire	75 Paris
13 Bouches-Maritime	44 Loire-Atlantique	76 Seine-Maritime
14 Calvados	45 Loiret	77 Seine-et-Marne
15 Cantal	46 Lot	78 Yvelines
16 Charente	47 Lot-et-Garonna	79 Deux-Sèvres
17 Charente-Maritime	48 Lozère	80 Somme
18 Cher	49 Maine-et-Loire	81 Tarn
19Corrèze	50 Manche	82 Tarn-et-Garonne
2A Corse-du-Sud	51 Marne	83 Var
2B Haute-Corse	52 Haute-Marne	84 Vaucluse
21 Côte-d'Or	53 Mayenne	85 Vendée
22 Côtes-du-Nord	54 Meurthe-et-Moselle	86 Vienne
23 Creuse	55 Meuse	87 Haute-Vienne
24 Dordogne	56 Morbihan	88 Vosges
25 Doubs	57 Moselle	89 Yonne
26 Drôme	58 Nièvre	90 Territoire-de-Belfort
27 Eure	59 Nord	91 Essonne
28 Eure-et-Loir	60 Oise	92 Hauts-de-Seine
29 Finistère	61 Orne	93 Seine-st-Denis
30 Gard	62 Pas-dedd-Calais	94 Val-de-Marne
31 Haute-Garonne	63 Puy-de-Dôme	95 Val-d'Oise

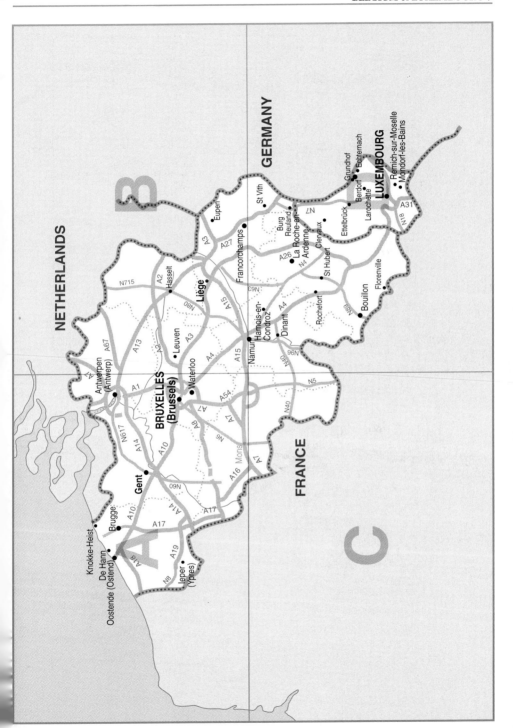

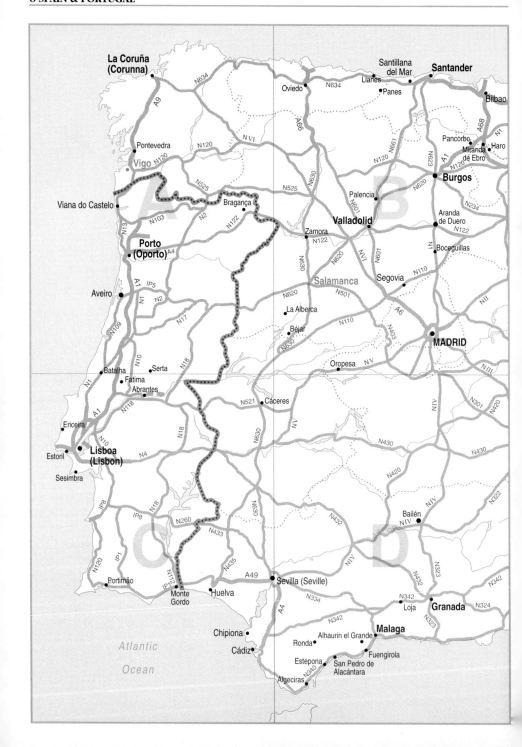

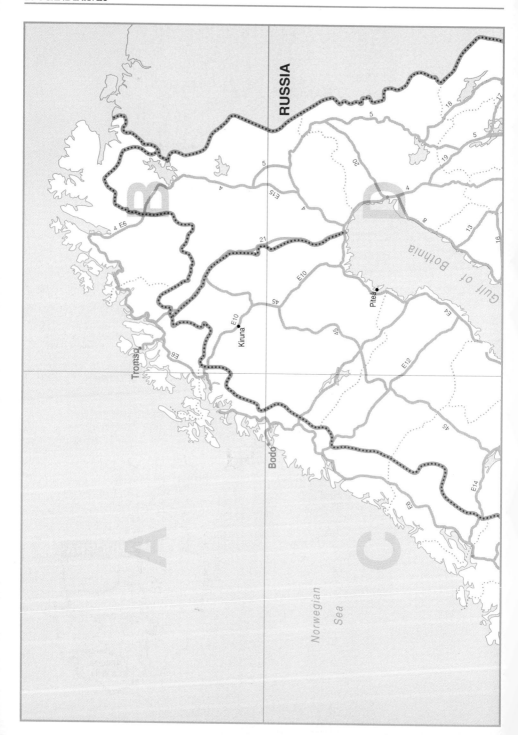

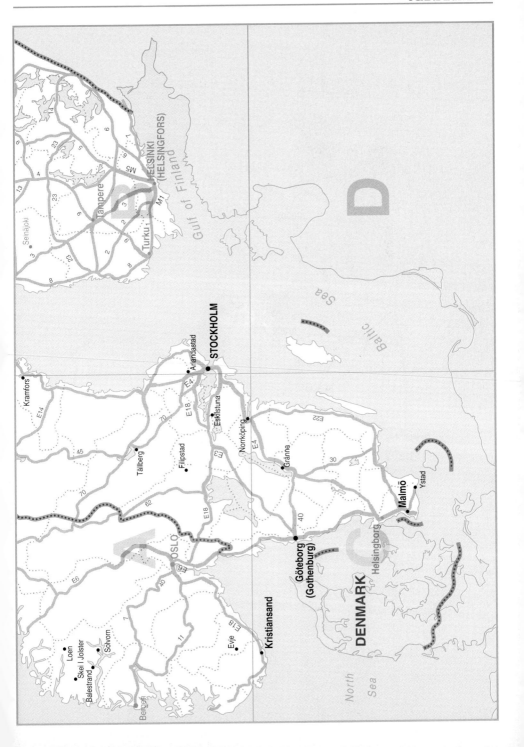

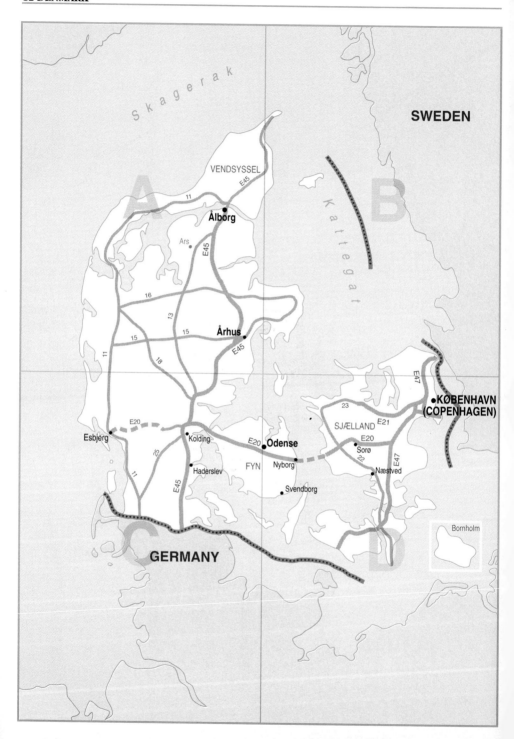

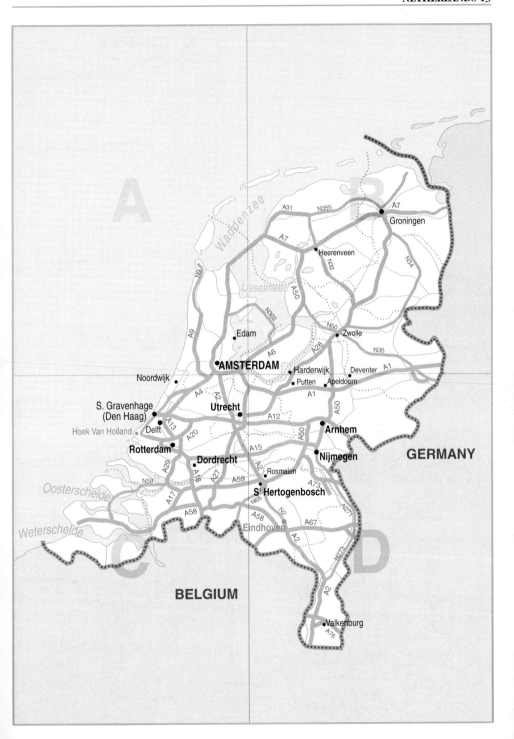

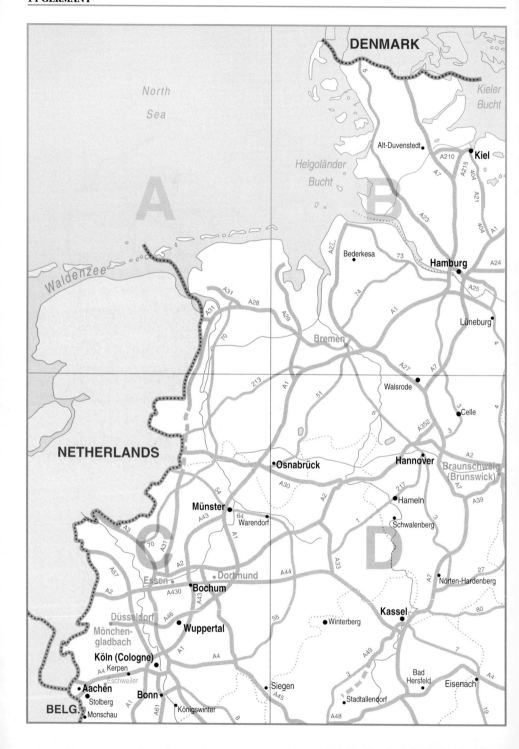

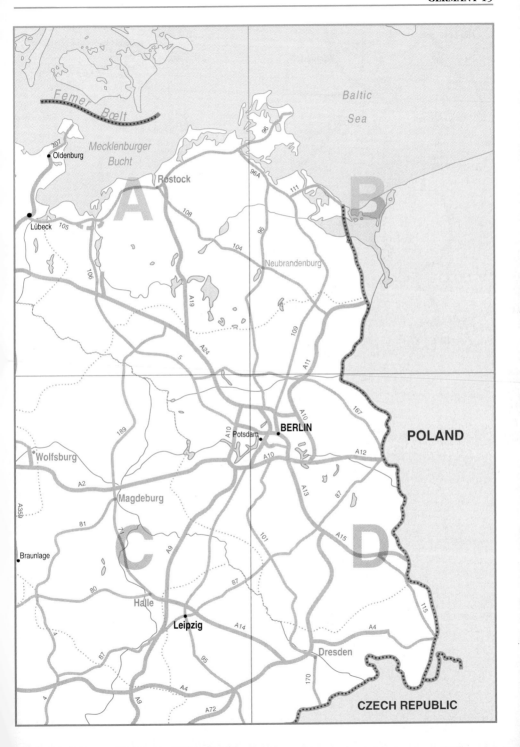

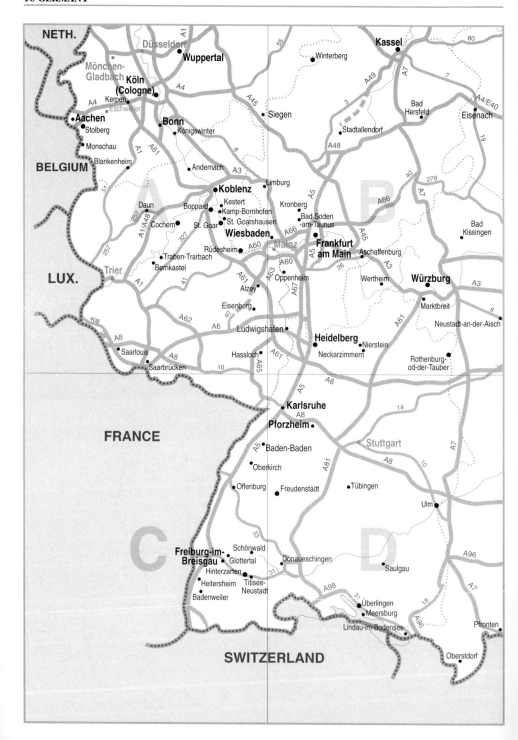

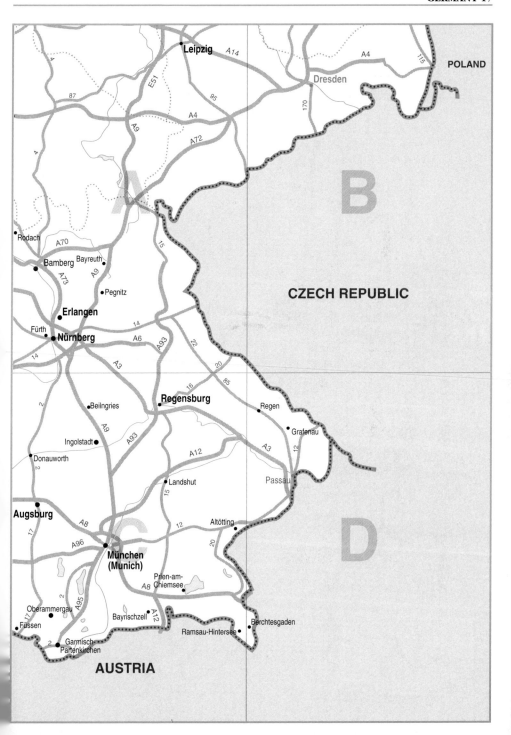

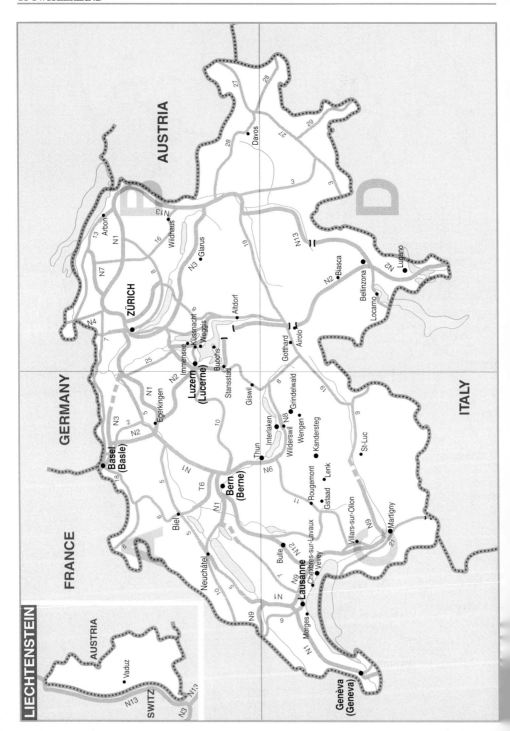

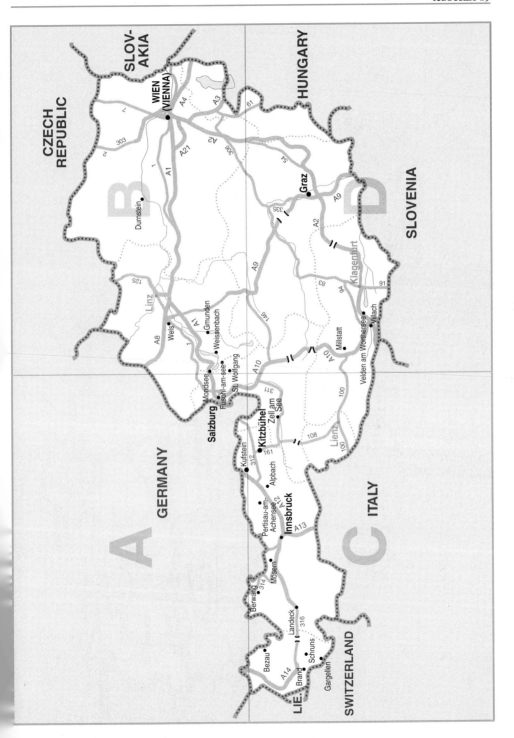

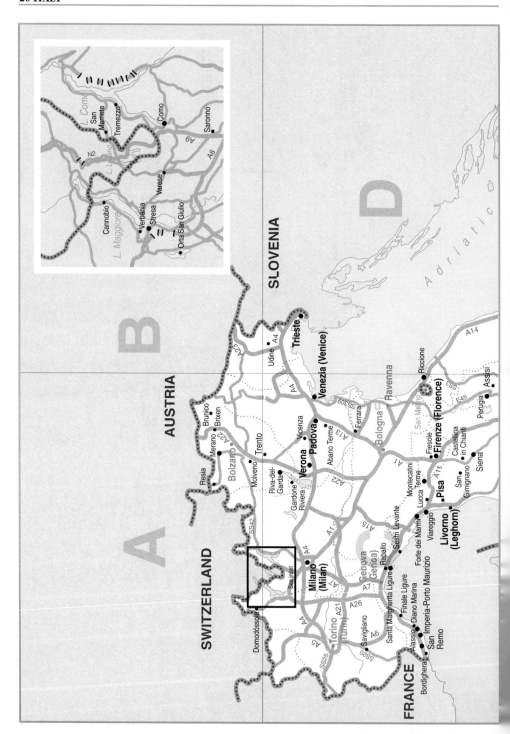

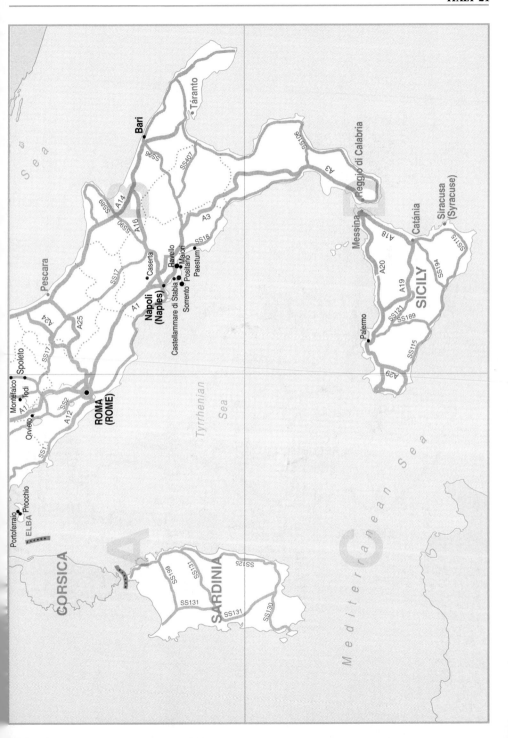

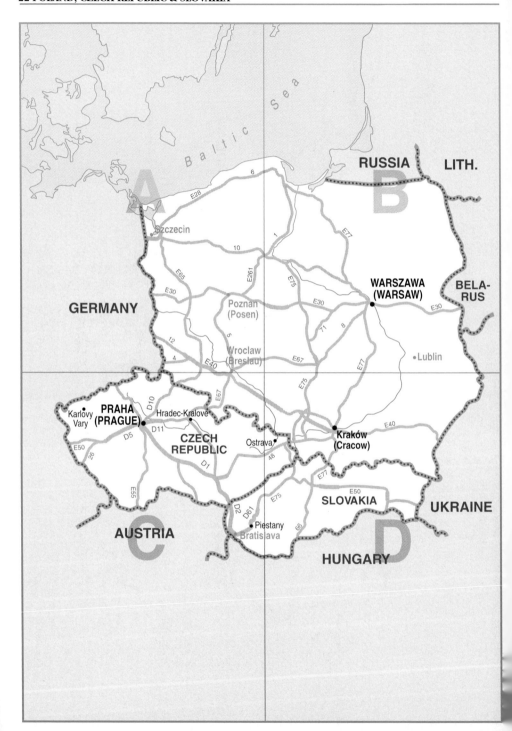

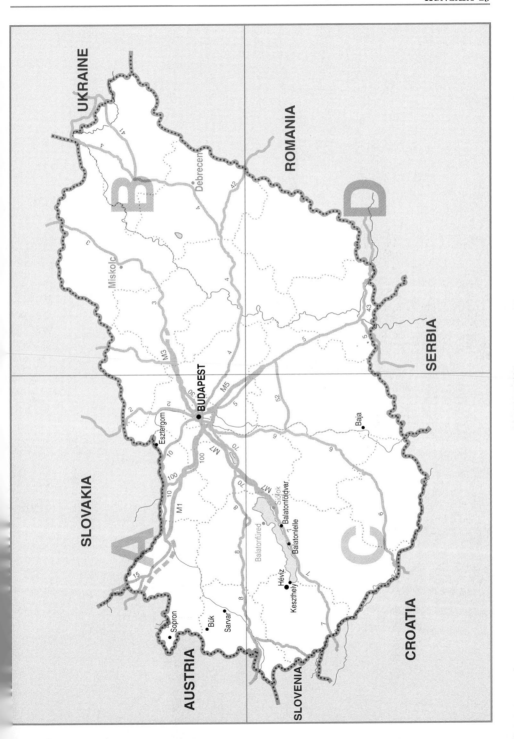

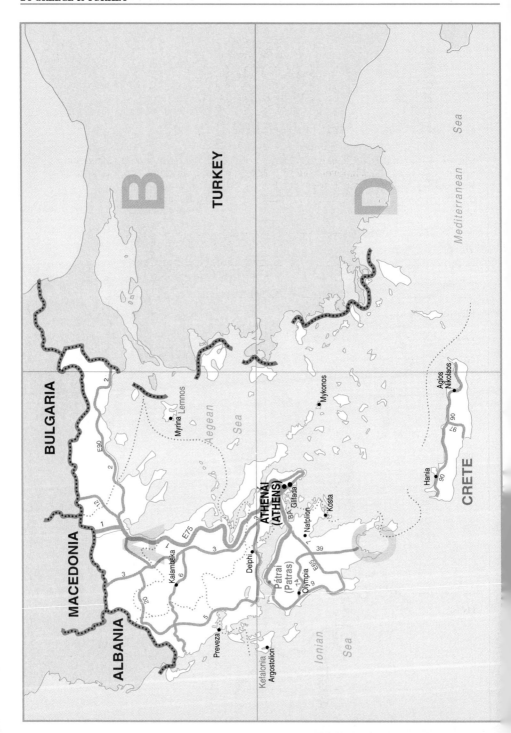

RAC
HOTELS
IN EUROPE
HOTEL REPORT 1997

The publisher of this guide welcomes your comments about any hotels visited that appear in this guide. Whatever your experience, good, indifferent or poor, do write to RAC Publishing, PO Box 8, Harleston, Norfolk IP20 0EZ expressing your views.

Hotel name

Town

Dates of stay

Please tick the appropriate box	Yes	No
Did any of the hotel staff speak English?	☐	☐
Were the staff helpful?	☐	☐
Did the hotel have a restaurant?	☐	☐
Was the hotel quiet?	☐	☐
Were the parking facilities adequate?	☐	☐
Was the service *good?*	☐	
adequate	☐	
poor	☐	
Was the food *good*	☐	
average	☐	
poor	☐	

Hotel report

continued

Hotel report *continued*

_____

_____

_____

_____

_____

_____

_____

_____

_____

_____

_____

_____

_____

_____

_____

_____

_____

_____

_____

_____

_____

Name

Address

RAC
HOTELS
IN EUROPE

HOTEL REPORT 1997

The publisher of this guide welcomes your comments about any hotels visited that appear in this guide. Whatever your experience, good, indifferent or poor, do write to RAC Publishing, PO Box 8, Harleston, Norfolk IP20 0EZ expressing your views.

Hotel name

Town

Dates of stay

Please tick the appropriate box		Yes	No
Did any of the hotel staff speak English?		☐	☐
Were the staff helpful?		☐	☐
Did the hotel have a restaurant?		☐	☐
Was the hotel quiet?		☐	☐
Were the parking facilities adequate?		☐	☐
Was the service	*good?*	☐	
	adequate	☐	
	poor	☐	
Was the food	*good*	☐	
	average	☐	
	poor	☐	

Hotel report

continued

Hotel report *continued*

_____

_____

_____

_____

_____

_____

_____

_____

_____

_____

_____

_____

_____

_____

_____

_____

_____

_____

_____

Name

Address

HOTELS
IN EUROPE

HOTEL RECOMMENDATION 1997

The publisher of this guide welcomes your suggestions for hotels which might be included in future editions of this guide. Please write to RAC Publishing, PO Box 8, Harleston, Norfolk IP20 0EZ expressing your views.

Hotel name

Address

Telephone   *Fax*

Dates of your stay

Reason for suggestion

HOTELS
IN EUROPE

HOTEL RECOMMENDATION 1997

The publisher of this guide welcomes your suggestions for hotels which might be included in future editions of this guide. Please write to RAC Publishing, PO Box 8, Harleston, Norfolk IP20 0EZ expressing your views.

Hotel name

Address

Telephone   *Fax*

Dates of your stay

Reason for suggestion